W9-DCJ-881

THE ARCHITECTURE
OF ANCIENT ISRAEL

Published with the assistance of
the Dorot Foundation, New York

THE ARCHITECTURE
OF ANCIENT ISRAEL

FROM THE PREHISTORIC TO THE PERSIAN PERIODS

In Memory of
Immanuel (Munya) Dunayevsky

Editors
Aharon Kempinski, Ronny Reich,

Consulting Editor
Hannah Katzenstein

Editorial Director
Joseph Aviram

The United Library
Garrett-Evangelical/Seabury-Western Seminaries
2121 Sheridan Road
Evanston, IL 60201

NA
240
.A72
1992
sec b

Israel Exploration Society
Jerusalem 1992

Editors of the Hebrew Edition
Hanna Katzenstein (coordinator)
E. Netzer, A. Kempinski and R. Reich

Photo Acknowledgments
The Oriental Institute, University of Chicago
The Hebrew University of Jerusalem
Israel Antiquities Authority
Israel Exploration Society
Pierre de Miroschedji — CNRS
Tel Aviv University

Plans and Illustrations
Leen Ritmeyer, Ronny Reich, Judith Dekel

Style Editing
Ann Horowitz, Shelley Sadeh

Layout and Cover
Avraham Pladot

© *Copyright*
Israel Exploration Society and Authors

ISBN 965–221–013–7

Plates
Old City Press Ltd.

Printed in Israel, at Ahva Press, Jerusalem 1992

Contents

IMMANUEL (MUNYA) DUNAYEVSKY (1906–1968):
THE MAN AND HIS WORK

Immanuel Dunayevsky, 'Munya' to those who knew him, belonged to the generation of giants in Israeli archaeology. His work in the field extended over a period of some thirty years. During the last decade of his life he reached the peak of his professional skills, earning recognition as Israel's foremost authority on stratigraphy and architecture in archaeology.

Munya was born in Odessa in 1906. He completed his studies in structural engineering at the Prague Polytechnic in 1934 and two years later emigrated to Palestine, where he settled in Haifa and worked as an engineer for the Mandatory Government's Public Works Department. Before long Munya was also participating in Benjamin Mazar's (Maisler) excavations at Bet Shearim. A deep and fruitful friendship developed between the two men that was to last over thirty years. Fate had it that the last excavations in which Munya took part were those conducted by Mazar next to the walls of the Temple Mount in Jerusalem.

In 1939 Munya moved to Jerusalem. During World War II he enlisted in the British Engineering Corps. In the mid-1940s he joined an archaeological expedition to Bet Yeraḥ, where he worked with Benjamin Mazar, Moshe Stekelis, and Michael Avi-Yonah. From 1949 to 1951 he participated in Mazar's excavations at Tell Qasile, and in 1953–1954 worked with Moshe Dothan at Ḥorvat Beter, a Chalcolithic site near Beersheba, and at Nahariyya, at the site of a Canaanite shrine. In Jerusalem during that same period, he established, together with a group of colleagues, an architectural and engineering company called Ha-Mehandes ('the engineer'). Those were years of intense inner conflict as he struggled to decide whether to continue in engineering or to make archaeology his life's work.

In 1955 Munya joined Yigael Yadin's expedition to Hazor as staff architect. It was during his years at Hazor that Munya crystallized his scientific approach to fieldwork and his techniques for preparing site plans. It was at Hazor, too, that Munya encountered and enthralled his first students, young architects and archaeologists; it was by example that he led them to appreciate the architectural aspects of archaeology. When he was not at Hazor, Munya was at Ha-Mehandes in Jerusalem, but his growing involvement in the site, along with his participation in other excavations during those years (such as the 1955–1956 survey expedition to Masada), weighted the scales decisively in favour of archaeology. Munya decided to leave engineering and joined the Hebrew University of Jerusalem as the architect for the Institute of Archaeology and as an instructor in the archaeology department. His decision left him free to do research and to act as consultant for excavations all over the country. Between 1958 and 1968 there was hardly an excavation in Israel that did not avail itself of Munya's expertise. At times he took part in the day-to-day tasks of surveying and preparation of plans. He participated in the excavations at Tel Mor (1960), Makhmish (Tel Mikhal) (1960), 'En Gedi (1961), 'En Gev (1961), the Ḥammat Tiberias synagogue (1961) and in the soundings at Megiddo (1961, 1966, and 1967). Yadin's extensive excavations at Masada presented Munya with a formidable challenge, not just because of the archaeological and national significance of the site, but because Munya had just suffered a mild heart attack. Munya was not one to run from a challenge, and now, joined by Ehud Netzer, became the expedition's architect. Munya left many plans of Masada, each one evidence of his conscientious involvement in that project.

Munya's greatness lay in his tireless striving for the most comprehensive picture possible of a site or structure and his uncompromising attention to deciphering every bit of evidence. When Munya arrived at a site, he would at once begin scratching away, with his celebrated *patishon* (little pick), at some detail that had aroused his interest, even before the field archaeologist had finished explaining the nature of the work at hand. Munya persisted in the effort to understand each and every detail excavated — even those that at first glance seemed to be inexplicable and out of context. It was only after exhaustively studying every shred of evidence that he would accept, or reject, archaeologists' conclusions. In some instances, it was the analysis of those apparently trivial details that enabled the excavators to grasp the breadth of meaning of their site in technical terms.

In the field, in every excavated area, Munya immediately sought the interrelationship among the various elements: floors, walls, and other parts of the building, foundation and robber trenches, pits (floors 'running to', 'cut by', 'running-over,' or 'running-under', and walls 'hanging in the air,' as he termed them). He would tirelessly review the local stratigraphy, from the most recent to the most ancient, consistently preoccupied with fitting each piece into its proper place in the puzzle — pit after pit, locus after locus, area after area.

Soon after visiting a site, Munya would have its excavation plan ready, with each stratum and phase marked with its own symbol or colour. These drawings usually contained numerous signs of broken lines, and Munya often added handwritten comments. Although the final picture was often at variance with the initial drawings, these first attempts gave Munya both a means of attacking the stratigraphic puzzle and the opportunity to use each piece of evidence as it was discovered or deciphered in completing the overall picture.

Munya's strong will, his patience, his tenacity, his perspicacity, his powers of analysis and synthesis, and his objectivity were the qualities that helped him substantiate his working hypotheses and attain his impressive achievements. His patience and tenacity in particular were limitless. When a problem in the field preoccupied him he would devote long hours of enormous mental and physical effort to solving it, disregarding any discomfort caused either by the weather or his physical needs. During the afternoon, when everyone else was either resting or sorting sherds, Munya would climb the mound with the drawing board and *patishon* that were his constant companions. Although the 'mess' his scratchings left would sometimes anger the field archaeologists, there was no contradiction here with

Munya's demand for a systematic excavation and careful and frequent photographs. For Munya, a 'clean' dig was as mandatory as a field photograph or drawing. If the excavation was not supported by a clear understanding of the problem and correct reading of the fieldnotes, the research was useless and wasted.

It is almost impossible to separate Munya the man from Munya the scholar. He was blessed with a rare love of humanity. Munya sometimes seemed distant from events around him, but that was deceptive. A cerebral man, he was simply, by his nature, beyond participating in some of the vagaries of human behavior. The range of his interests was vast. Even his casual remarks showed his mastery of things around him, on personal and professional levels. A quietly modest man, Munya made no pretension of expertise in history, chronology, or ceramics; he would always ask for a clarification of the historical events relevant to an excavation and of the site's ceramics. For Munya, all these elements ultimately would be a part of the solution: a stratigraphic solution inconsistent with the historical, chronological, or ceramic data was equivocal in his eyes. Intrinsic to his very being were the elucidations, the joint weighing of alternatives, with each of the excavators or students. These conversations, sometimes hours long, would help Munya clarify for himself still-unsolved problems. His mathematical mind would repeatedly build, discard, and rebuild the various stratigraphic alternatives, testing each logical possibility, in an unremitting search for the most comprehensive solution.

Munya's method has been criticized on the ground that he failed to include 'objective' cross-sections in his plans. His method was essentially 'nongeological', unlike the method practiced by Kathleen Kenyon and later adapted by the American archaeologists following G.E. Wright. Basically it was a method in which the mound was seen as a layering of architectonic complexes, one on top of another, with each layer containing floors, accumulations, fills and the like. Munya first encountered the 5 × 5 m. excavation square and cross-section approach at the Ḥazor excavations, where Jean Perrot introduced it. Subsequently it became an essential element in Israeli archaeological excavations.

Munya, however, did not unduly rely on every earth line or nuance of colour in the cross-section's various accumulations. His approach to the cross-section was pragmatic: it was a prime instrument in critically studying levels — their relationship to walls and to each other — and for locating pits, disturbances, foundation trenches and robber trenches, and fills. When he was examining the Early Bronze Age shrines at Megiddo with his students, Munya often commented, 'Having no cross-section is like having no eyes.' The remark illustrates his approach to excavation. He drew detailed cross-sections not as an end in themselves, but as the means to provide the information to clarify, emphasize, or illuminate stratigraphic conditions. He saw the *plan*, however, as the way to recapture the period during which a structure had been built and functioned, revealing the connections between the structure and its surroundings, and between the building and the activities that took place in it.

We have already mentioned the first plans Munya used in his fieldwork. His next step was the precise measuring of stone after stone (usually on a scale of 1:50). But before he sketched the final plans according to strata and phases, Munya would prepare a series of key plans (a separate plan for each stratum), on a scale of 1:100. At this stage he would study the site's stratigraphy with its excavators, examining each piece of evidence in the field that was out of

context in a stratum. It was also at this stage that Munya would attempt to visualize a structure three dimensionally and to reconstruct its upper storeys, insofar as possible. In the final stage, Munya prepared the plans for publication, generally on a scale of 1:50. This stage included discussions with the excavators which were reflected later in the final excavation report. Munya's influence on the four volumes of the Hazor report, for example, is apparent.

During his last years, before he was stricken with cancer, Munya prepared the Hazor and Masada excavation plans for final publication and taught at the University, where he analysed stratigraphic problems of various sites — Megiddo, Ashdod, Arad, and 'Ai. He was also an advisor to various excavations, including those at Dan and Ashdod. The excavations south of the Western Wall in Jerusalem and the fifth season at Hazor (1968) were the last in which Munya took part before he succumbed to his illness.

Munya was in a class with a long line of great architect-archaeologists, men like Dorpfeld, Andrae, Kohl, and Butler. His name is engraved in the history of Israeli archaeology.

Ehud Netzer and Aharon Kempinski

PREFACE

Buildings are a direct expression of mankind's needs, both the individual's and the society's. Architectural elements are among the principal remains of the work of man's hands unearthed in the course of archaeological excavations in Israel from the Neolithic period onward. In every age they must be viewed in the context of man's intellectual level, his technological competence, his traditions and culture, and his relations with other peoples and cultures, both near and far. Although occasionally man's artistic inclinations find expression in his building enterprises, it must be acknowledged that not every construction bears the stamp of an architect-artist. Not all buildings from the periods discussed in this book can be studied in terms of such architectural concepts as use of space, geometric proportion, ornamentation, and style. Nevertheless, there are buildings in Israel whose underlying logic and artistic-geometric conception can be traced. The student of ancient architecture must deal with its components as a cultural phenomenon, in order to discover, describe, and explain its characteristic manifestations, and its changes through the ages. It is also his or her duty to trace its irregular features, and to provide an explanation.

In contrast to other finds discovered in archaeological excavations — flint and stone artifacts, pottery and metal vessels — building remains are 'immovable property' and, from a stratigraphic point of view, this is their advantage over the others, whose location at the time of their discovery is not necessarily evidence of their place of origin. It is to the subject of ancient building and architectural remains in Israel that this book is devoted.

Archaeological research in Israel has been going on for approximately 150 years. As a result, information about ancient architecture here is substantial and increases with every new archaeological excavation.

Indeed, although much research on the subject has been published, the continual flow of new data and detailed studies and, in their wake, up-dated conclusions, is so great that it is justifiable to review them from time to time. It is to this purpose that the present volume is dedicated, even while its editors are aware that the material in it will need to be updated in time.

In the past, the subject of architecture in antiquity has generally been discussed within the framework of broad surveys dealing with the material culture of Palestine, rather than in separate monographs. Among the first of these extensive surveys was the work of Carl Watzinger.[1] A substantial part of his book was devoted to building remains, from the beginnings of architecture to the end of the Byzantine period. The book was a landmark in the research of ancient architecture. From its publication to the present time, chapters dealing with building remains have appeared in the surveys of A.-G. Barrois,[2] W.F. Albright,[3] K. Galling,[4] K.M. Kenyon,[5] Y. Aharoni,[6] and R. Naumann.[7] Each of these scholars emphasized some particular principle or period, according to his or her inclination and opinions. M. Avi-Yonah and S. Yeivin's treatment[8] is perhaps the only survey that

1. C. Watzinger: *Denkmäler Palästinas*, I-II, Leipzig, 1933–1935.
2. A.-G. Barrois: *Manuel d'archéologie biblique*, I-II, Paris, 1939–1953.
3. W.F. Albright: *The Archaeology of Palestine*, Harmondsworth, 1960.
4. K. Galling: *Biblisches Reallexicon* (2nd ed.), Tübingen, 1977.
5. K.M. Kenyon: *Archaeology in the Holy Land* (3rd rev. ed.), London, 1970.
6. Y. Aharoni: *The Archaeology of the Land of Israel*, Jerusalem, 1982.
7. R. Naumann: *Architectur Kleinasiens* (2nd ed.), Tübingen, 1971.
8. M. Avi-Yonah and S. Yeivin: *The Antiquities of Israel*, Tel-Aviv, 1955.

deals solely with the ancient architectural remains of Israel.[9]

The first attempt to review the architecture of different periods in Palestine was undertaken in the form of a collection of articles, published in *Eretz-Israel* Volume 11 and dedicated to the memory of Immanuel Dunayevsky.[10] The volume includes a list of the plans prepared by Munya (as he was called by his friends) of the various sites excavated here.[11]

The present book differs from preceding ones, in that each of its chapters is written by a scholar who specializes in a particular period or phenomenon and who is well suited to discuss its architecture. The objectives the editors of the present book have set before themselves are twofold: (a) to present the reader with (as far as possible) an up-to-date survey of the ancient architecture of Palestine, from its beginnings to the end of the Persian period; and (b) to make available to students of archaeology in Israel a clear guide to the data, opinions, and conclusions of a variety of scholars that are dispersed throughout the scientific literature.

The reader will therefore find in this book a summary of the architecture of Palestine from its beginnings to the Persian period and the specification of its principles, as well as bibliographic references to appropriate excavation reports and to specific research for each topic.

In this research on ancient architecture, as in research on every other archaeological phenomenon, there is a great divergence of opinion over the interpretation of particular finds, such as their date and the exact cultural framework to which they belong. Naturally, each writer here will express his or her opinion and interpretation of this or that find. In many cases, this is the majority opinion. The writer will also present opinions that may be contrary to his or her own, or will at least draw the reader's attention to their existence.

The editors accept the principle that one building plan is equal to many words and therefore have endeavoured to include as many illustrations in this volume as possible. Nevertheless, we have only been able to bring the reader a small but reliable selection. Included are examples of plans of characteristic buildings and plans of unique design. In order to enable the reader to make exact comparisons of architectural components from various sites and periods, great pains have been taken to present the graphic data in an accurate and uniform manner.

The initiative for the publishing of this book came principally from the circle of Munya's students and close colleagues, men and women who wished to honour his memory by collaborating on the volume. It was the original intention of the editors to involve as great a number of contributors as possible from among those engaged in the historical periods under discussion, each according to his or her particular area of specialization. However, in the end, as some scholars could not fulfill their obligations to the volume, the editors assigned themselves the task of completing it.

Throughout the book three terms for the geopolitical entity of ancient Palestine are used: Palestine, the Land of Israel and Israel. Palestine, like the terms Anatolia and Mesopotamia, is the classical name of the country and is used for pre-Biblical times, especially for the prehistoric periods and the Bronze Age. The Land of Israel is used for the Iron Age, when the term first came into being in the Biblical traditions. Israel is the name of the modern political entity as defined since 1948.

The editors express their thanks to all those who helped in implementing this project: to Ahuvah Dunayevsky, Munya's widow, who followed our progress; to Joseph Aviram, who assisted us in organizing the project; to Leen Ritmeyer and Judith Dekel who drew many of the plans; to Dr. Ann Horowitz and Shelley Sadeh who style edited the English version; and to Karen Greenberg who typed the manuscripts.

This book could not have been published without the generous financial assistance of our friend Nataliah (Natasha) Delougaz - we extend to her our heartfelt thanks.

The first steps toward creating this book were made possible by the generous gift of Elisheva Levine, of Blessed Memory, who contributed a considerable sum of money to the memory of Munya and consented to our suggestion that it be used for this purpose. That noble lady had accompanied Munya to many excavations. The following remarks are attributed to her: 'Before Munya arrived at an excavation, there were scattered stones and fragments of walls, but after he left, houses, streets, walls, and gates would have emerged.'

The Editors

---

9. See also. G.R.H. Wright: *Ancient Building in South Syria and Palestine*, Leiden-Köln, 1985 (appeared while the Hebrew version of this book was in press).

10. *Eretz Israel*, 11, Jerusalem, 1973.

11. E. Netzer: A List of Selected Plans Drawn by I. Dunayevsky, (above, n. 10), pp. XIII–XXIV (Hebrew).

List of Contributors

Dan Bahat — Jerusalem

Ofer Bar-Yosef — Harvard University, Boston

Jacob Baumgarten — Archaeological Survey of Israel

Itzhaq Beit-Arieh — Tel Aviv University

Meir Ben-Dov — Jerusalem

Amnon Ben-Tor — The Hebrew University of Jerusalem

Rudolf Cohen — Israel Antiquities Authority, Jerusalem

Rivka Gonen — Israel Museum, Jerusalem

Zeev Herzog — Tel Aviv University

Aharon Kempinski — Tel Aviv University

Amihai Mazar — The Hebrew University of Jerusalem

Zeev Meshel — Tel Aviv University

Ehud Netzer — The Hebrew University of Jerusalem

Eliezer Oren — Ben-Gurion University, Beer Sheva

Yosef Porath — Israel Antiquities Authority, Jerusalem

Ronny Reich — Israel Antiquities Authority, Jerusalem

Yigal Shiloh — The Hebrew University of Jerusalem
  (passed away in 1987)

Ephraim Stern — The Hebrew University of Jerusalem

Chronological Table

All dates in this table are approximate. In the earlier periods, shifts of up to *c.* 100 years are possible, in the later periods (starting with the Late Bronze Age), up to *c.* 50 years.

Pre-Pottery Neolithic Period	8000–6000 BC
Pottery Neolithic Period	6000–4500 BC
Chalcolithic Period	4500–3300 BC
Early Bronze Age I (a–b)	3300–2900 BC
Early Bronze Age II	2900–2700 BC
Early Bronze Age IIIa*	2700–2400 BC
Early Bronze Age IIIb (IV)	2400–2200 BC
Intermediate Early Bronze-Middle Bronze Age (Middle Bronze Age I)	2200–2000 BC
Middle Bronze Age IIa	2000–1750 BC
Middle Bronze Age IIb	1750–1600 BC
Late Bronze Age I	1600–1450 BC
Late Bronze Age IIa	1450–1300 BC
Late Bronze Age IIb	1300–1200 BC
Iron Age I	1200–1000 BC
Iron Age II	1000– 586 BC
Babylonian and Persian Periods	586– 332 BC

* Dates of the later part of the third millenium and the early second millennium B.C. are based on the Mesopotamian 'Middle Chronology'.

MATERIALS AND FASHIONS OF CONSTRUCTIONS

BUILDING MATERIALS AND ARCHITECTURAL ELEMENTS IN ANCIENT ISRAEL

Ronny Reich

Introduction

Ancient Israel can be divided roughly into two regions as far as the use of building materials — stone and sun-dried mud brick — is concerned. This division is the result, in general, of the country's geomorphological division into mountainous regions, valleys and wadi beds. Of course, stones can also be found in wadi beds, in the *kurkar* formations along the coast, and elsewhere beyond the mountainous areas, and mud for bricks can be collected in the wadis of the mountainous areas as well. In addition, the building material most readily available in a certain area is not necessarily the one best suited for cutting and dressing or for constructing all parts of a house. For this reason, a combination of materials is used in residential buildings, with a preference for stone or mud brick for the walls according to the region.

A survey of the materials used to build dwellings in various regions of the country throughout the ages shows that preference generally went to local resources, as people chose the most available and cheapest supplies. This tendency is especially noticeable in residential buildings, where construction is directly related to the owner's economic resources and technical and organizational ability. The situation changes to some degree where public buildings, or buildings erected mainly with public funds, are concerned, and when buildings required special materials not found in the vicinity.

The following discussion will centre on descriptions of the various building materials used in Palestine during the periods treated in this book. It will include both commonly and infrequently used materials and techniques. This will be followed by a survey of architectural elements designed to solve the construction problems that arose as building methods developed and improved.

Stone as a Building Material

In studying in detail the parts of buildings constructed of stone, two components should be examined: (1) the kind of stone used or the materials substituted, and (2) the methods of dressing the stone and utilizing it.

Much of Israel consists of mountains in which different kinds of stone are exposed. The most common is a variety of limestone, but extensive areas in the north are covered with basalt. Smaller quantities of *kurkar*, beachrock, flint, sandstone, and some igneous rocks are also found.

Limestone. — Most of the rock exposed in Israel is limestone. Since it was formed in the geological past under a variety of conditions, it is found in varying degrees of hardness, colour, texture, and composition. The hard limestone group comprises the *mizzi yahudi, mizzi ḥilu* and *meleke. Mizzi yahudi* is a very hard stone, not easily quarried or dressed and not generally used for ashlars. However, it has been found used for door sockets and thresholds due to its hardness and resistance to wear. Although the other two kinds are close-grained limestones that can be dressed to produce stones of excellent quality, quarrying and dressing them are expensive. This kind of stone was exploited extensively for columns, capitals, and bases from the Hellenistic period onwards. The most famous example of the use of *meleke* limestone is the Herodian enclosure walls of the Temple Mount in Jerusalem.

Among the soft limestones are chalk and *nari*. Chalk is very soft and becomes even softer when it comes into contact with water. It was, therefore, almost never quarried for building stones in antiquity. However, the same properties made it suitable for hewing out burial caves, subterranean spaces, and water installations. *Nari*, on the other hand, is a friable, chalky rock that resulted from the disintegration of chalk in a

1

RONNY REICH

process still insufficiently understood. *Nari* is more easily quarried and dressed, although the surface of the dressed stone is never quite smooth, as in *meleke* and *mizzi hilu*. This stone is also suitable for carving details of architectural ornamentation. Y. Shiloh and A. Horowitz have shown that, in the Iron Age, *nari* was the main raw material for producing ashlars and proto-Aeolic capitals for monumental buildings.[1]

Basalt. — Extensive areas in the north of the country — Galilee, Golan, and Bashan — are covered with basalt rock. The stone is distinguished by its hardness and porosity, as well as by its black colour and its resistance to heat, weathering, and water. It has unique properties absent from other building stones and was also carved into implements used for grinding and crushing. In areas where the basalt rock is exposed, most buildings and their component parts were of basalt — either fieldstones collected on the surface or dressed ashlars. Due to the stone's properties, it was also in demand elsewhere, not as the exclusively-used building stone, but for door sockets and door pivots (Fig. 1). Such basalt elements are found in public buildings — palaces, city-gates, and temples — which had large, heavy doors and in whose construction financial considerations did not play a part. Some good examples of this use of basalt come from Hazor. Its hardness and resistance to wear also made basalt a good choice for steps and thresholds (Fig. 2), of which the existing examples also come from public buildings, which had countless pedestrians and heavy chariot traffic.

1. Basalt door socket and pivot, Hazor. **Hazor** III–IV, Pl. CXXVI:3.

Due to its black colour, which shows up well against white limestone, its relative hardness, and perhaps also its porosity, basalt was the preferred material for orthostats (Fig. 2), steles, and movable

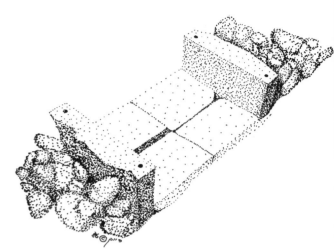

2. Entrance with threshold paved with basalt blocks, and two fixed basalt orthostats, Hazor. **Hazor** III–IV, Pl. X:1.

cultic furniture. The use of basalt for the Hazor orthostats[2] indicates almost certainly that the choice follows a tradition that developed outside the region (in northern Syria) and was brought to Hazor with the plan of the building, the deity, and its cult.[3]

The resistance of basalt to erosion by water action made it suitable for drain pipes and segments of drainage channels (Fig. 3), especially when the channels had to pass through the walls of buildings or city-walls.[4]

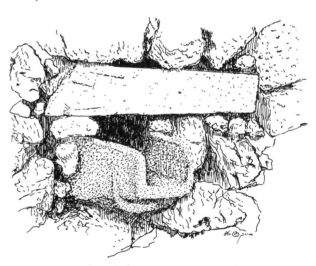

3. Basalt drainage channel through a wall of fieldstones, Hazor. **Hazor** III–IV, Pl. XCIV:1.

1. Y. Shiloh and A. Horowitz: Ashlar Quarries of the Iron Age in Palestine in the Hill Country of Israel, *BASOR* 217 (1975), pp. 37–48.

2. *Hazor* III–IV, Pls. CI–CIII, CIV:1; *Hazor*, pp. 75–96; *Megiddo* II, Fig. 46.

3. R. Nauman: *Architektur Kleinasiens*,[2] Tubingen, 1971, pp. 75–86.

4. *Hazor* III–IV, Pl. XCIV:1.

2

Masonry Methods

Masonry methods develop from the properties of the particular stone and the requirements and purpose of the structure to be built.

Fieldstone. — Fieldstones are loose surface rocks and rubble that are collected in the fields. No particular kind of stone was selected, and as a result there are fieldstone walls of limestone, basalt, sandstone, etc. As no further work was to be expended on shaping the stones, attention was given to size and shape when they were being collected in the field so that they would fulfill the requirements of the planned construction.

4. Construction of fieldstones.

5. Construction of polygonal stones.

Fieldstone can be used for more than one kind of masonry: for stones placed randomly or laid in courses (Fig. 4), and for polygonal building (Fig. 5), in which many-sided stones are fitted so that as few small stones as possible are needed to fill the interstices. The polygonal building method was sometimes used for fortifications, such as the city-wall at Shechem[5] (Tell Balata, Wall A) and the supporting wall of the ramp leading to the city-gate in Area K at Hazor.[6]

5. W.G. Dever: Shechem (Balata), *IEJ* 22 (1972), pp. 156–157, Pl. 25.
6. *Hazor* III-IV, Pl. CXXXII:1, 2.

Ashlars. — Ashlars are square-hewn stones that represent the optimal use of stone as a building material. Their sides are chisel-dressed to achieve a straight, smooth surface where they adjoin other ashlars. Usually, the following process for producing ashlars was used: after locating an exposed area of rock, a block of stone of the required size was quarried. In antiquity, two methods of quarrying were practised, both of which were used until recently in the traditional Arab quarry[7] (before the introduction of mechanical equipment):

1. Long, narrow grooves (5–10 cm. wide and on average 30–60 cm. deep) were hewn into the rock. Then the block was separated from the mother rock with lateral pressure produced by inserting wooden or iron rods into the grooves. This method was suitable for providing relatively small building blocks.

2. Rows of deep holes were drilled into the rock and pieces of wood inserted. Then the wood was wet, producing inner stresses that split the rock along the rows of holes, detaching it from the mother rock.

What remains of ancient quarries are the stepped rock faces created by the extraction of blocks of stone. Sometimes blocks that were not completely separated from the mother rock are visible.

Rough-hewn Stones. — Rough-hewn stones represent an intermediate degree of dressing, between fieldstones and well-finished ashlars (Fig. 6). They are fieldstones that have been roughly shaped with a simple mallet but without a chisel. A few hammer blows by a skilled stone cutter gives the amorphous fieldstone a roughly rectangular shape. This shaping facilitated the laying of the courses. It reduced the number and size of the interstices between the stones and reinforced the corners of the building. Rough-hewn stones should

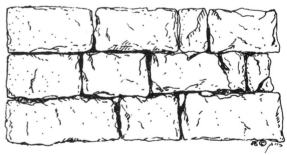

6. Construction of rough-hewn stones.

7. Shiloh and Horowitz (above, n. 1); see also nn. 18–22 for traditional Arab building methods.

not necessarily be considered a primitive forerunner of ashlars. Both were used in the Iron Age, ashlars particularly. Examples are the city-wall of the First Temple period in the Upper City of Jerusalem[8] and the podium wall of the Israelite palace at Lachish.[9] Hewing the stones into shape was not necessary in areas where the limestone beds were thin or where there was tabular flint in quantities, because the natural shape of the blocks did not require further work. A case in point is the Early Bronze Age palace, or Temple A at 'Ai, which is built of tabular limestone,[10] and the Ha-Ro'ah fort in the Negev, which is built mainly of tabular flint.[11]

Very large blocks of stone quarried and dressed to varying degrees appear in the east gate of Tell Balata (Shechem) and as square monoliths and long proto-Aeolic capitals in Iron Age II.[12] The heaviest of these huge blocks must have weighed up to two tons before dressing. A stone of this size could be transported and set in place without particular difficulties by a small group of workers and a cart harnessed to draught animals. Much larger stones, such as obelisks, weighing dozens of tons, were quarried in neighbouring countries (Egypt, Assyria, and Babylonia). Transporting them from the quarry to the building site required extraordinary efforts and, in several cases, the operation was commemorated on reliefs.[13] In Israel such huge stones were used from the Herodian period (first century B.C.) onward. As already mentioned, transporting the stones and setting them up at the building site required technical skill, organizational ability, and enormous financial resources.

Stone Dressing. — Information about the tools used by stone cutters and masons in antiquity appears in a variety of sources, but the tools are rarely found in archaeological excavations. Something can be learned about their use and shape from the written sources

that mention building activities. Several tools are mentioned in the Bible: the axe (*grzn*) in 1 Kings 6:7 (and in the Siloam Tunnel inscription); the hammer, or mallet (*mqbt*) in 1 Kings 6:7 and in Judges 4:21; the saw (*mswr*) in Isaiah 10:15; another kind of saw (*mgrh*) in 2 Samuel 12:31, 1 Kings 7:9, and 1 Chronicles 20:3; and the hammer (*ptiš*) in Jeremiah 23:29.[14] However, it is not always possible to determine the exact function of each. Building tools are also mentioned in Egyptian and Mesopotamian written records, but their appearance in reliefs showing building activities is especially instructive.[15]

Another way of learning about stone-dressing tools is to study the tool marks left on the finished stone. For instance, traces left by the stone-cutting saw are visible on the stone bases of Palace A at 'Ai, dated to the Early Bronze Age.[16] Marks from the drill used to bore holes in the top of the basalt orthostats at Hazor in the Late Bronze Age are also visible.[17]

However, the tools most commonly used to dress stone were the chisel and hammer. Straight lines were drawn with a ruler and right angles were marked with a sharp instrument. This method of dressing stone (for various requirements and items) came into use in the EB II, at the beginning of the period of urbanization, when fortifications and planned houses began to be built in Palestine, and it has been used without any significant change up to the present day. Therefore, examining traditional Arab building methods in this country has contributed to our understanding of the tools and methods of stone work in antiquity. (See the studies by C. Schick,[18] F.J. Dickie,[19] T. Canaan,[20] G. Dalman[21] and others[22]).

The use of ashlars (Fig. 7) requires that at least the face of the stone block be perfectly rectangular,

8. N. Avigad: *Discovering Jerusalem*, Nashville, 1983, Figs. 29, 31.
9. Especially at the corners of the buildings; *Lachish* III, Pls. 17:4, 19:1; and D. Ussishkin: Excavations at Tel Lachish — 1973-1977, Preliminary Report, *Tel Aviv* 5 (1978), Pls. 11:1-2, 12:1.
10. *'Ay*, Pls. IV:1-2, IX:1-2.
11. R. Cohen: Atar Haro'a, *'Atiqot* (Hebrew Series) 6 (1970), p. 8, Pl. IV:1-2 (Hebrew, English Summary, pp. 1-3*); and below, Chap. 26, p. 294.
12. Y. Shiloh: *The Proto-Aeolic Capital and Israelite Ashlar Masonry* [*Qedem* 11], Jerusalem, 1979, p. 15, nos. 144, 145; *Shechem*, pp. 71-79, Figs. 24, 27-29.
13. R. Reich: Dur-Sharukin (Khorsabad), *Qadmoniot* 12 (1979), p. 11 (bottom) (Hebrew); Nauman (above, n. 3), Figs. 15-17.

14. See also *Ens. Miqr.*, s.v כלי מלאכה, מלאכה (Hebrew).
15. Above, n. 13.
16. Above, n. 10, Pl. IX:1.
17. *Hazor* III-IV, Pls. X:1, 2, CII:2.
18. C. Schick: Arabic Building Terms, *PEFQSt* (1893), pp. 194-203.
19. A. C. Dickie: Stone Dressing of Jerusalem, Past and Present, *PEFQSt* (1897), pp. 61-67.
20. T. Canaan: *The Palestinian Arab House — Its Architecture and Folklore*, Jerusalem, 1933.
21. G. Dalman: *Arbeit und Sitte in Palastina*, VII, *Das Haus*, Gutersloh, 1942.
22. J. Pinkerfeld: *Arab Building* [Studies of the Institute for Building and Technical Research 1], Tel Aviv, 1953, pp. 125-57 (Hebrew); and Hirschfeld: The Rural Dwelling House in the Hebron Region, a Case Study of the Traditional Type of Building in Eretz-Israel, *Cathedra* 24 (1982), pp. 79-114 (Hebrew).

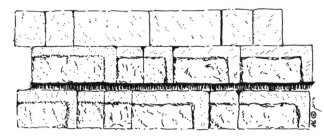

7. Construction of ashlar stones, with and without drafted margins (note gap which contained wooden beam).

with four right angles. The edges abutting adjacent stones must also be straight and smooth to ensure proper bonding. Any additional work on the face of the stone was structurally unnecessary and was done only for aesthetic reasons. Thus, the face of the stone block was dressed to achieve either a smooth surface[23] or drafted margins along one or more of its sides, leaving a prominent rough boss in the centre. The drafted margins, which were sometimes very wide, are characteristic of royal buildings in the Israelite period (for example, at Megiddo, Hazor, Samaria, and Ramat Rahel).[24]

Sometimes smoothing the face of the stone obliterated the tool marks. This was done with the stone cutter's tools or by polishing one stone with another. The basalt orthostats characteristic of neo-Hittite architecture and the orthostats uncovered at Hazor and Megiddo, appear to have been polished this way. Smoothing the face of the stone with a toothed (comb-like) chisel probably began in the Hellenistic period.[25]

As ashlars were easy to handle in construction work, and as the financial investment and effort to produce them were high, they are found reused from ruined buildings, which were sometimes dismantled down to the original rock-cut foundation trench, as at Samaria[26] and Ramat Rahel.[27]

23. Shiloh (above, n. 12), pp. 61–63, Pls. 24:2, 27.
24. *Ibid.*, pp. 61–63, Pls. 22:1, 26:1, 28:2, 31:3.
25. When the toothed (comb-like) chisel began to be used is controversial. In Y. Aharoni's view, based on his finds in the Israelite fortress at Arad, it was the Iron Age. However, it now appears, according to Y. Yadin and C. Nylander, that its use began in the Hellenistic period. See Y. Aharoni and R. Amiran: Excavations at Tel Arad, 1962, *IEJ* 14 (1964), p. 135, Pl. 32B; Y. Yadin: A Note on the Stratigraphy of Arad, *IEJ* 15 (1965), p. 180; and C. Nylander: A Note on the Stonecutting and Masonry of Tel Arad, *IEJ* 17 (1967), pp. 56–59.
26. *Samaria Sebaste* I, Pls. XIX, XXII:2, XXVII:2.
27. Y. Aharoni: Excavations at Ramat Rahel, 1954, Preliminary Report, *IEJ* 6 (1956), p. 140, Fig. 9; *Ramat Rahel* II, Fig. 6

Sun-Dried Mud Brick

Undoubtedly, sun-dried mud bricks were the most widely used building material in the Ancient Near East. Their use was especially widespread in areas where stone was not available, such as Mesopotamia throughout the millennia ('And they had brick for stone...,' Genesis 11:3).[28] In Palestine buildings were constructed of mud brick in the coastal plain, in the valleys, and in wadi beds, where suitable clay was available in quantity, but it was also in demand in the hill country. The mud-brick house on fieldstone foundations and roofed with a few wooden beams covered by reeds and rushes has been the most characteristic dwelling in Palestine, from the Early Neolithic period until modern times.

Since brick making does not require special tools or skills, it did not develop as a craft in antiquity to the degree achieved by workers in wood and stone.

Clay, in its pure state in the wadi bed, is not easy to handle. It is 'oily' and is apt to crack when drying. Therefore other substances had to be added to it when it was kneaded (with the feet, see Nahum 3:14 and Isaiah 41:25, 'as the potter treads clay'). Bricks were made from a mixture of clay and sand, straw (Exodus 5:7), sherds, stone grits, and organic material taken from refuse dumps (Job 4:19). If the wet earth contained sufficient clay, it too was used to make bricks.

At first, mud bricks were made by hand and were shaped like buns (Fig. 8). The bricks were laid one next to the other in courses and the spaces between them were filled with mud of a similar composition.

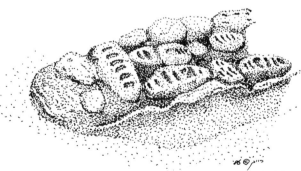

8. Construction of hand-made bricks with fingerprints, Jericho. *Jericho* III (Plates), Pl. 116a.

28. A. Salonen: *Die Ziegeleien im Alten Mesopotamien*, Helsinki, 1972. Although the book deals mainly with the philological aspect, a great deal of information concerning our subject is collected there. See also Nauman (above, n. 3), pp. 41–53, and A.J. Spencer: *Brick Architecture in Ancient Egypt*, Westminster, 1979.

Handmade mud bricks were used in Palestine from the beginning of the Neolithic period until the beginning of the EB I, when moulds began to be used.

At Jericho (Area M, dating from the Pre-Pottery Neolithic A or a little before) rounded lumps of mud resembling fieldstones are the earliest attempts at brick making that have come to light.[29] Later, various other kinds of handmade mud bricks were produced there — some plano-convex and others with deep impressions made by the hand on the back of the brick, which provided a keying for the mud between the bricks. These kinds of bricks were subsequently found on sites from the Chalcolithic period and the EB I, such as Teleilat el-Ghassul,[30] Afula,[31] and Tel Kittan.[32]

It was only from the end of the EB I or the beginning of the EB II onward that the rectangular mould-made mud brick came into use. This mould (*mlb*n, Nahum 3:14) was a frame made of four small wooden boards. Egyptian reliefs (Fig. 9) depict in detail the manufacture of bricks in moulds: in fact, in modern Egypt the same process continues to be used. The prepared clay was pressed into the moulds to obtain bricks of uniform shape and size. The clay 'bricks' were removed from the moulds and set out in rows in a field to dry in the sun. Use of the mould speeded up the process and produced much greater quantities than before. The uniform size and the greater quantities accelerated the scale of urbanization and fortification at many EB II-III sites in Israel.

Sun-dried mud bricks, although they are inexpensive and easy to produce, have several disadvantages. The chief one is that they deteriorate rapidly when they come into contact with water, either rainwater or the runoff water that flowed down alleyways alongside the outer faces of walls of houses. To protect against this danger, walls were plastered every year (Ezekiel 13:10–12).

Public buildings built of mud brick faced the additional risk of damage to the walls at shoulder

9. Brick-making and wall-plastering, Tomb of Rekmira, Egypt. *ANEP*, Fig. 115.

29. A distinction should be made between handmade plano-convex bricks like those from Jericho and the bricks called by the same name in Mesopotamia in the pre-Sargonid period. There the bricks were made in moulds and only the excess clay, which was not removed from the mould, gave the brick its convex back.

30. *Ghassul* I, pp. 34–36, Pl. 14; *Ghassul* II, p. 11.

31. E.L. Sukenik: *Archaeological Excavations at 'Affula*, Jerusalem, 1948, pp. 7–8, Pls. XXII: 1–2, XXIII:1–2.

32. The method of laying plano-convex bricks characteristic c Mesopotamia in the pre-Sargonid period is very rarely found in Palestine. Only at Tel Kittan have walls built of such bricks been discovered, dating from the EB I. The bricks were laid on their narrow sides and slightly inclined, each course in a different direction, in a herringbone pattern (before the wall was plastered). See P. Delougaz: *Plano-Convex Bricks and the Method of their Employment* [The Oriental Institute of the University of Chicago, Studies in Ancient Oriental Civilization 7], 1933, pp. 1–38.

height where friction was created by crowds (at temples, city-gates, and throne rooms). To counter this damage, walls were sometimes faced to shoulder height with stone orthostats or wooden boards. In both private houses and public buildings, stone was used for architectural elements that could not be constructed of mud brick, such as door thresholds and sockets, gutters, and column bases. Wood was used for roof beams, jambs and lintels, doors and windows.

33. *Ens. Miqr.*, s.v בנייה, Fig. 3 (after N. de G. Davies: *The Tomb of Rekh-Mi-Re' at Thebes*, New York, 1943, Pls. LVIII–LX; *ANEP*, Fig. 115).

34. *Ens. Miqr.*, s.v בנייה, Fig. 4; *EAEHL* III, p. 714, s.v. Kheleifeh, Tell el-.

Sun-dried mud brick has been almost completely neglected as a subject for research in architecture. Only Flinders Petrie, the first excavator in Palestine, took the trouble to record systematically the measurements of the mud bricks unearthed in his excavations.[35] He hoped to establish a chronological series of brick sizes, but it has never been proven that changes in brick size can be related to different periods.

Because sun-dried mud brick deteriorates fairly rapidly, brick walls preserved to some height are rarely found. When they are, they are usually thick, massive city-walls or gates, such as the EB city-gates at Tell el-Far'ah (North)[36] and Hazor,[37] and the city-wall and gate at Lachish (Strata IV–III).[38] Far less preserved are remains of arches and vaults built of mud brick. Only two examples are known in the country, the recently uncovered MB city-gate at Tel Dan, which is preserved with its vaulted roof intact,[39] and the vaults of the Assyrian residency excavated at Tell Jemmeh.

Kiln-fired Bricks

No buildings of kiln-fired bricks dated earlier than the Early Roman period have been found in Israel.[40] They were used in Mesopotamia, because of their hardness and resistance to water, to pave areas or reface mud brick walls, especially in throne rooms, temple shrines, and bathing installations. So far the only example of kiln-baked bricks in this country is the pavement of the Assyrian temple in northern Sinai (Chap. 22, p. 221).

In the Early Roman period (first century B.C.) kiln-baked bricks were used for the hypocaust system in bathhouses.

35. See, for instance, *Gerar*, p. 6, Pl. LXXII (right); *Beth Pelet* I, Pl. LXIII (bottom).
36. R. de Vaux: Les fouilles de Tell el-Far'ah, *RB* 69 (1962), Pls. XVII–XVIII, XXIV, XXVI.
37. *Hazor* III–IV, Pl. XXIX:1.
38. Ussishkin (above, n. 9), Pl. 17:2.
39. A. Biran: The Discovery of the Middle Bronze Age Gate at Dan, *BA* 44 (1981), pp. 139–144; idem, The Triple-Arched Gate of Laish at Tel Dan, *IEJ* 34 (1984), pp. 1–10 and G.W. Van Beek, Arches and Vaults in the Ancient Near East, *Scientific American* (July 1987), pp. 78–85, 98.
40. The excavators of Megiddo claimed that the buildings in Stratum VIA were built of 'partially-burnt' bricks. These were certainly sun-dried mud bricks that had been burned when the city was destroyed by fire.

Wood

Various kinds of wood were used as building materials in the houses of the Ancient Near East. The Bible and other literary sources mention several kinds. Graphic representations — especially Egyptian and Assyrian reliefs — furnish details of wood working,[41] of how the raw material was transported,[42] and of where and how the wood was used. Archaeological evidence completes the picture: directly, when fragments of wood, usually charred, are found at a site; and indirectly, when finds, such as stone column bases, indicate that wooden elements, in this case columns that were positioned on the bases, had been used.

Timber, either as unhewn logs or as sawn planks, was a popular roofing material for rooms and halls — as it is today. The wooden beams used in the construction of private houses were taken from local trees, such as the tamarisk in the Negev and the sycamore in the Shephelah.

Most biblical references to the use of wood are to public buildings, such as temples, palaces, patrician houses, and fortifications. These accounts mention difficulties in obtaining and working a particular wood. The Bible describes in considerable detail the public buildings King Solomon was responsible for in Jerusalem, including the Temple, the royal palace, the 'house of the forest of Lebanon', and the house of Pharaoh's daughter. These descriptions record, in addition to the measurements of various parts of the buildings, technical details and terms, some of which occur only in those passages and remain obscure (*blwlim, spt, 'ab*).

Producing timber for building purposes required skill in felling the trees (1 Kings 5:6), transporting them (1 Kings 5:9), sawing and preparing the wood for use, and fixing the finished piece in its designated place. The descriptions of Solomon's building activities also mention the various kinds of wood used. Most were imported from Lebanon and other countries: the cedar (*'erz*), a tree (*brwš*), usually translated in the Bible as 'cypress' (but see below), the 'oil tree' (*'eṣ šmn*), and the *almogim*, or *algumim* tree (*'algwmym*), sometimes identified as sandalwood. Many technical terms connected with wood working — carpentry, joinery, and decorating the finished building (*krwtwt, ṣl'wt, qwrwt, šqwfym*) — are also mentioned. The

41. *ANEP*, Figs. 122, 123.
42. P.E. Botta: *Monuments de Ninive*, I, Paris, 1849, Pl. 34; ANEP, Pl. 107; cf. also M. Elat: *Economic Relations in the Lands of the Bible*, Jerusalem, 1977, especially the chapter 'Wood and Wood Products', pp. 58–68 (Hebrew).

cedar of Lebanon (*Cedrus libani*) was used both as a structural material — for columns, 'beams' (?) *krwtwt* on the columns, and *şl'wt* — and as panelling for the walls: "and covered the house with beams and boards" *gbim wsdrwt*, of cedar;[43] 'all was cedar, there was no stone seen' (1 Kings 6:9, 18). The other timber mentioned in these verses, translated as 'cypress' in the Bible, does not refer to the tree called cypress today (*Cupressus sempervirens*); it is generally accepted that it refers to a tree of the juniper family (see below). The oil tree ('*eş šmn*) probably provided timber more suitable for furniture and perhaps for carving. It was used for doors and the carved cherubim.

Today palaeobotanists can identify by microscopic examination the species of tree to which the wood found in excavations belongs. As wood was also used in antiquity for making furniture, handles and parts of tools as well as for firewood, it is impossible to relate all the information obtained in these investigations to the subject discussed here. One of the first published studies on wood is from the excavations at Tel Beersheba. In one experiment, the samples of wood (especially of Strata III-II of the ninth-eighth centuries B.C.) were plotted on the town plan in order to study their distribution — which samples came from public buildings and which from residential buildings.[44] This mapping showed, among other things, that the amount of timber used in public and private buildings was more or less equal. The timber most commonly used came from the tamarisk (*Tamarix aphylla*) and acacia trees, whose natural habitat is the Beersheba basin. Many remains of white broom (*Retema roetam*) were also found, mainly in domestic courtyards and near ovens — indicating that it was used for firewood rather than as a building material. Among the imported timber found was cedar of Lebanon, but not earlier than Strata III–II. This evidence indicates the existence of trade in cedar wood at that time. Another study shows that there was no cypress wood (*Cupressus sempervirens*) in any Iron Age strata in Israel.[45] This wood first appears in the Hellenistic period (second century B.C.), when it was used for beams; it was widely used in the

Herodian period (first century B.C.) and later.[46] These studies are significant for identifying the tree species called *brwš* in the Bible, usually translated as 'cypress', but that should be identified as a kind of juniper (*Juniperus*).

In Iron Age ashlar buildings at Hazor, Samaria, and Megiddo, long, narrow (6–10 cm.) gaps are visible between the masonry courses.[47] A comparison with the building method in Anatolia, in which wooden beams and ashlar masonry are combined, suggests that sawn wooden beams were inserted between the masonry courses to stabilize the masonry, leaving gaps when they decayed.[48]

Earth and Loose Stones

The cities in Palestine in the biblical period were built, destroyed, and rebuilt repeatedly, thus creating, over centuries, the tells that dot the land. In the process of building a city on top of the ruins of an earlier one, a large-scale preliminary levelling operation was usually undertaken. Varying quantities of earth and stones were transferred in bulk from place to place inside the city limits and were sometimes even brought from a distance. During a city's lifespan, earth was also repeatedly spread and stamped down on floors, courtyards and alleys, creating higher and higher surfaces.

Earth fills are themselves a building material used to avoid empty spaces or raise floor levels. Sometimes the fills remained in the city area by default, because the inhabitants could not or would not remove them. For the archaeologist, the earth fills, which contain loose stones, potsherds, and other small objects, are of great chronological value: the fill was put down and stamped before the new floor was laid over it, so that the potsherds randomly scattered within it are earlier than the floor and the building to which it belongs (or, at most, contemporaneous with it).

Sometimes the quantities of earth used in public structures were very large. For example the earthen ramparts that were the main fortifications in the Middle Bronze Age required huge masses of earth (Chap. 16, p. 129). In order to raise public buildings, such as palaces and temples, a few metres above their surroundings, retaining walls were erected around

43. G. Barkay has suggested that the design of the walls in the large Iron Age tombs north of Jerusalem imitates in stone the timber construction of 'beams and boards', — *gbim wsdrwt*.

44. M. Homsky and S. Moskovitz: The Distribution of Different Wood Species in the Iron Age II at Tel Beer-Sheba, *Tel Aviv* 3 (1976), pp. 42–48.

45. M. Homsky and S. Moskovitz: Cypress Wood in Excavations in Eretz-Israel, *Tel Aviv* 4 (1977), pp. 71–78.

46. A. Fahn: A Burned Wood Specimen from an Archaeological Excavation in Jerusalem, *IAWA Bulletin* (1972/2), pp. 23–24.

47. Shiloh (above, n. 12), p. 61, Pls. 21:2, 22:2, 26:1, 28:2; but also in an LB gate, *Megiddo* II, Fig. 45.

48. Nauman (above, n. 3), pp. 85–108.

them that were then filled with earth and stones and packed to create a platform. This method was especially common in Mesopotamia, where it was called *tamlu*. Together with its name, it was transferred to Palestine (the *millo* (in 1 Kings 9:15), where it was used for the palace at Lachish (Strata V-III), Palaces 1052 and 1369 at Megiddo (Stratum III) (Chap. 22, p. 218), and at the Assyrian fortress at Sheikh Zuweyd (see below, p. 221).

Earth was also used in erecting siege ramps, which required the expert skills of an architect or builder. The technique of the siege ramp was developed by the Assyrians, who built one at Lachish.[49] The siege ramp at Masada[50] is from a later period, as is probably the one at Kh. el-Hammam (Narbata ?).[51]

Lime Mortar and Plaster

Burning limestone to produce caustic lime
$$CaCO_3 \rightarrow CaO + CO_2$$
and combining it with water to make slaked lime
$$CaO + H_2O \rightarrow Ca(OH)_2$$
which is a strong cement, or mortar, was known in the First Temple period (Deuteronomy 27:2, Isaiah 33:12, Amos 2:1).

The subject has not yet been studied adequately to determine when the method first came into use, the variable composition of the mixtures (the proportions of lime and other ingredients), and the material's different uses. The widespread use of lime for mortar, plaster for interiors, and hydraulic plaster for cisterns and other water installations began in Palestine in the Hellenistic period, which places the subject beyond the scope of this book.

Architectural Elements

The construction of the main components of a private dwelling — its foundations, walls, and roofings — are discussed in Chap. 2. In addition to these main structural components a series of architectural elements were incorporated: doors, columns, stairs, etc., that were architectural solutions to problems that arose in building a house, that improved its functioning and, thus, the quality of life in it. The most common architectural elements are described here briefly.

Columns and Pilasters. — In antiquity the simplest way to support a roof was to make a column out of a rough tree trunk. The column held up several roof beams whose ends rested on the tops of adjacent walls. The column had to be of sufficient diameter to carry the weight placed on it. The drawback to this kind of a column was that it would sink into the ground from its own weight and the weight it supported. Moreover, it was difficult to attach several beams to its narrow end.

Column Bases. — To keep wooden columns from sinking, they were set on flat stone slabs, either of fieldstone or of hewn stone. This reduced or minimized the pressure (the weight per unit of surface) and the danger of sinking. Sometimes the base of the column was inserted into a hollow space in the ground that was subsequently filled in around the column with rubble and earth. The flat, sometimes slightly sunken, stones on floors and the traces of rubble-filled hollows that are excavated, are what have survived of these architectural solutions.

Stone bases were either a small slab of fieldstone or a large block of stone. The two column bases in the Canaanite temple on the summit of Lachish are 1.2 m. in diameter;[52] they suited the size of the columns, the size and character of the building, and the weight they had to bear. Sometimes, the stone base was roughly hewn into a rounded shape (as the column bases in the orthostat temple at Hazor,[53] and the bases in the Megiddo temples [Fig. 10][54]), into rectangular blocks

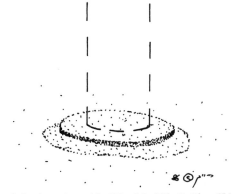

10. Rounded column base, Megiddo. *Megiddo* II, Figs. 174, 185.

49. D. Ussishkin: Excavations at Lachish 1973-1977, Preliminary Report, *Tel Aviv* 5 (1978), pp. 67-74; idem, Excavations at Tel Lachish 1978-1983, Second Preliminary Report, *Tel Aviv* 10 (1983), pp. 137-146.
50. Y. Yadin: *Masada, Herod's Fortress and the Zealots' Last Stand*, London, 1966, pp. 226-231.
51. A. Zertal: The Roman Siege System at Khirbet el-Hammam (Narbata) in Samaria, *Qadmoniot* 14 (1981), pp. 112-118 (Hebrew).

52. Ussishkin, 1978 (above, n. 49), Fig. 3, Pl. 4:2.
53. *Hazor* III-IV, Pls. CIII:1-2, CVII:4, CIX:1-3, CXI:1, CXV:1-2, CXXVIII:1-2, etc.
54. *Megiddo* II, Figs. 174, 180-181, 182-185.

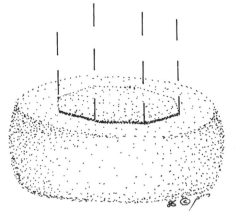

11. Base of polygonal column, Lachish. *Qadmoniot* 9 (36) (1976), P. 114.

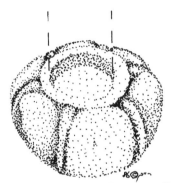

12. Round, carved base, Tel Dan. *Qadmoniot* 4 (13) (1971), p. 8.

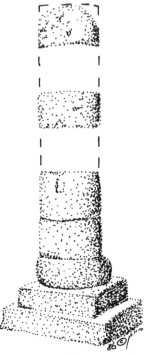

13. Stone column constructed of hewn base and round stone drums, Lachish. *Tel Aviv* 10 (1983), Pl. 43:3.

(as the bases in Palace A at 'Ai), or even carved ornamentally.[55] As examples of the latter type of base, which is rare, one should mention bases for polygonal columns (Fig. 11) that show an Egyptian influence;[56] the round stone bases at Tel Dan that were influenced by the art of northern Syria (Fig. 12);[57] and those at Lachish (Fig. 13) influenced by the Persians.[58]

In small spaces, where the width or length did not exceed *ca.* 5 m., one column placed in the centre was sufficient to support a roof. Larger spaces required more columns, usually arranged in a central row or in several rows, according to the size and character of the building. Columns were also placed in wide doorways. In addition to supporting the lintel, columns of this type enhanced the aesthetic appearance of the doorway and endowed it with symbolic and cultic significance. Such columns have been preserved and reconstructed at the entrance to the fortress temple at Shechem[59] and in the Assyrian palaces at Megiddo.[60]

Column bases are also found located near walls rather than in the centre of the room. These had an ornamental and cultic function rather than a structural one, like the columns of the 'Jachin and Boaz' type (1 Kings 7:21) that stood on both sides of a doorway at Hazor[61] and the column bases along the walls of Palace A at 'Ai.[62]

Capitals. — Initially, the problem of the tapering tree trunk was probably solved by making the fork-like branches part of the column and attaching the roof beams to them (Fig. 14). By analogy with examples from modern rural buildings in the Middle East, it can be assumed that, from the time boards were sawn and connected by metal nails, a short wooden board was nailed to the head of the column to broaden it, which acted as a simple capital.[63] When stone columns were introduced (below, p. 11), stone capitals replaced the wooden ones. It is also possible that large stone slabs, which could carry the roof beams that rested on the column, were used. In the course of time,

55. Above, n. 10.
56. Ussishkin (above, n. 9), Fig. 3, nos. I–III, Pls. 4:2, 5:2.
57. A. Biran: Tel Dan, *BA* 37 (1974), pp. 45–47, Figs. 19–20.
58. *Lachish* III, Pl. 22:3, 4, 6, 7; Ussishkin, 1983 (above, n. 49), p. 165, Pl. 43:3.
59. *Shechem*, Figs. 41–43, 47.
60. See the columns south of the room in building 1369 in *Megiddo* I, Fig. 89.
61. *Hazor* III–IV, Pls. CI (the base at the bottom of photo), CXI:1, CXV:2, and *Hazor*, pp. 87–89, Fig. 20; *Ens. Miqr.*, s.v. ובועז יכין.
62. Above, n. 10.
63. Shiloh (above, n. 12), pp. 43–44, Fig. 66, Pl. 20: 1–3.

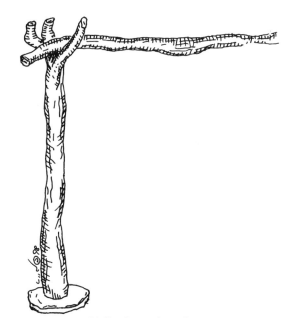

14. Simple wooden column.

Phoenician Hathor-head capitals (Chap. 27, Fig. 4) and the Iron Age proto-Aeolic capitals (Chap. 22, Figs. 9, 10).

Stone Columns. — Trees suitable for timber for building purposes were not available in many parts of the country. For private buildings local materials were generally used, and where suitable timber was not available, substitute materials were found. Although stone columns and piers often replaced wooden ones, wooden roof beams continued to be used because there were almost no alternatives.

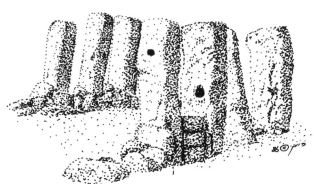

16. Monolithic columns in private dwelling, Megiddo. **Megiddo Cult**, Pl. IX.

Stone columns can be made out of one long block (monolith) (Fig. 16) or by stacking smaller blocks on top of each other. The first method produces a strong and very stable column, but it is technically more difficult and presupposes the availability of rock suitable for quarrying long blocks.[65] By contrast, a column made of flat fieldstones placed one on top of the other (Fig. 17) — a kind of precursor to a later column built of dressed stone drums — is inexpensive and easy to construct but much less stable (Chap. 2, p. 17).[66]

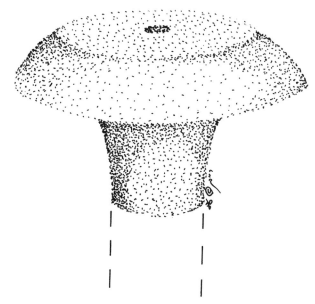

15. Egyptian capital, Bet Shean. **Beth Shan** II, Pl. XXVI:20.

17. Columns made of fieldstone blocks, Tell en-Nasbeh. **Tell Nasbeh**, Pl. 77:2.

this particular architectural element was ornamented. Only a few capitals from the period discussed here are known in this country: the Egyptian palmette or papyrus-shaped capitals (Fig. 15);[64] the Egypto-

64. Ussishkin (above, n. 9), pp. 22–24, Pl. 9:1; *Beth Shan* II, pp. 8, 16, Pls. XXVI:20, LIIA:4; and A. Siegelmann: A Capital in the Form of a Papyrus Flower from Megiddo, *Tel Aviv* 3 (1976), p. 141.

65. See Chaps. 21 and 23 in this book. Cf. also *Lachish* III, p. 77, Pl. 19:7 and Ussishkin (above, n. 9), pp. 14–15, Pl. 5:3.

66. For instance, Cohen (above, n. 11), pp. 10–11, Fig. 6, Pls. II:2, III:2, IV:1-2 (Hebrew).

Tel Masos. Row of columns in an Iron Age I private dwelling.

The stacked-fieldstone column achieved its final stage of development only in the Persian period. The Persian phase of the residency at Lachish (Fig. 13) is the earliest evidence in this country of columns made of drums dressed to provide an exact fit.[67] These columns achieved the stability of the monolith and retained the advantage of easy construction. The method also made it possible to erect higher columns.

Because these columns had to carry a heavy load, they could not sit on the floor or on a stone slab; they required a subterranean foundation (stylobate) — an underground masonry block that would absorb and diffuse the weight and thus prevent the columns from subsiding. The foundations under the column bases in the palace in the Persian phase at Lachish served just such a purpose.[68]

Entrances and Doors. — Architecturally, an opening in a wall is not a particular problem.[69] However, a stone or wooden beam had to be found for a lintel

that would be strong enough and long enough to bear the pressure of the wall above the opening up to the roof level.

Any opening in one of the walls created a weak point in the structure and deprived it of one of its most important features: the provision of a safe refuge. This was particularly true when the opening in question was a gate in the city-wall. Making a door for a large gate was difficult technically. The usual building materials — stone and mud brick — were not suitable, so wood, either beams or boards, was used almost exclusively. The first solution was probably an unattached door that was kept in place with diagonal wooden poles or heavy stones. This, however, would have been an awkward solution. There is evidence as early as the beginning of the Bronze Age of doors that turned on an axis.[70] The first wooden door post

67. *Tel Masos* I, pp. 22–26, 28–29, Fig. 4; II, Pls. 21–24. Cf. also n. 58 above.

68. Ussishkin, 1983 (above, n. 49), p. 165; *Lachish* III, Pl. 43:3.

69. Sometimes spaces, or rooms, are uncovered that have no openings in the walls. They were probably accessible through an opening in the ceiling or roof by means of a ladder. It can be

assumed that such spaces and rooms served purposes for which an ordinary doorway would have been a disadvantage (for example, a grain silo). However, when only the foundations of a room have survived, the location of the doorway(s) cannot be determined, because the lines of the foundation continued under the door sill and would not have been interrupted by the doorway.

70. Door sockets have been found in EB houses at Arad, for instance, *Arad*, p. 14, Pls. 143:3, 163:1, 3.

was probably stuck into the ground and propped up by three or four stones to prevent shifting. However, very shortly the bottom of the door post was placed in a hollow stone, the door socket,[71] and the other end into a prepared hollow in the lintel.

Hard stones, such as basalt and *mizzi yahudi* limestone were selected so that the door socket would not wear out quickly. In large, heavy doors (of city-gates and temples), the axis was sometimes reinforced with a pin of hard stone — as in the basalt axis of the Hazor temple (Fig. 1)[72] — or by metal sheathing — as on the axis of the Jaffa city-gate (Fig. 18).[73]

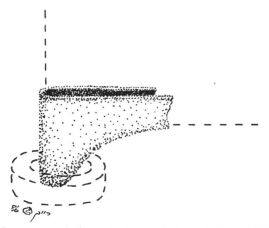

18. Bronze sheathing on axis of city-gate door, Jaffa. **Enc. Miqr.** vol. III, col. 739.

There is no archaeological evidence in this country for the fastening of doors in the period discussed here, but several biblical passages refer to it: Judges 3:23-25 ('and shut the doors of the roof chamber and locked them'); 1 Kings 4:13 ('bronze bars'); Isaiah 22:33 ('key'); Isaiah 45:2 and Psalms 107:16 ('doors of bronze and bars of iron'); Nehemiah 3:3 ('doors, locks, and bars,'); and Chronicles 9:27 ('and they had charge of the key').

In order to prevent the wooden doors of city-gates from burning, metal sheets were nailed on their outer face. The bronze plaques that covered the city-gate doors of the Assyrian cities of the ninth century B.C.

are well known,[74] but fragments of sheathing and of fittings have also been found at Lachish.[75] (See also 2 Chronicles 12:4, 9 and Psalms 107:16.) Iron, which is difficult to flatten by hammering but is easily worked in the forge, was used mainly to make bolts and nails. (See Isaiah 45:2, Psalms 107:16, and 1 Chronicles 22:3.)

Windows. — There is almost no direct evidence for the existence of windows in the periods under discussion because only the lower parts of buildings have been preserved. On the basis of scanty indirect evidence, it can be assumed that there were windows in public rather than private buildings. House models that have been preserved also furnish some information about the absence or presence of windows. The house model from Arad from the Early Bronze Age (Fig. 19),[76] and that from Iron Age Tell el-Far'ah (North)[77] (Chap. 27, Fig. 3) have no windows. The openings in Chalcolithic ossuaries[78] and in the temple model from Bet Shean (Fig. 20) are interpreted by some scholars as imitations of windows in contemporary houses.[79] Moreover, the stone balustrades found in Iron Age

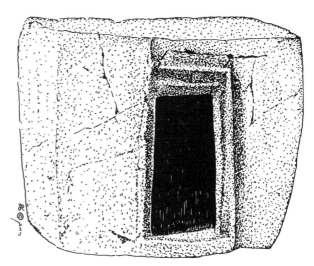

19. Model of an early house, Arad. *Arad*, Pl. 115:1.

71. Many examples of this architectural element have been found, for instance, *Hazor* III-IV, Pls. CVI:1, 3, CXXVI: 1–3; and *Megiddo* I, Fig. 84.
72. *Hazor* III-IV, Pl. CXXVI: 1–3.
73. *Ens. Miqr.* s.v יפו, photo on p. 202, bottom (Hebrew); and Y. Kaplan: *The Archaeology and History of Tel Aviv–Jaffa*, Ramat Gan, 1959, Fig. on p. 61, photo facing p. 60 (Hebrew).
74. L.W. King: *The Bronze Reliefs from the Gates of Shalmaneser, King of Assyria*, London, 1915.
75. Ussishkin (above, n. 49, 1983), pp. 123–124.
76. *Arad*, Pls. 66, 115.
77. R. de Vaux: Les fouilles de Tell el-Far'ah, RB 62 (1955), Pl. XIII; and S. S. Weinberg: A Moabite Shrine Group, *Muse* 12 (1978), pp. 30–46.
78. J. Perrot: Une tombe a ossuaires du IVe millenaire a Azor pres de Tel Aviv, 'Atiqot 3 (English Series) (1961), Figs. 7, 15, 25, 26, 29, Pl. V: 1, 3.
79. *Beth Shan* II, Pls. LVIA, LVIIA: 1, 2.

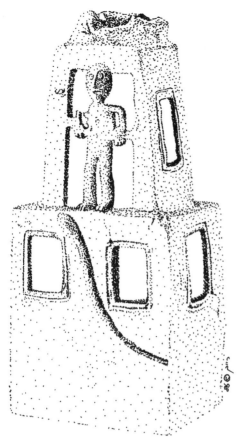

20. Model of a multi-storied temple, Bet Shean. **Beth Shan** II, Pl. LVIA.

palaces (as at Ramat Rahel, Chap. 27, Fig. 6) are considered to have been part of the windows, based on their similarity to balustrades on ivory carvings of windows (Chap. 27, Fig. 5).[80] In any case, buildings seem rarely to have been provided with windows, and then only when the entrance opening did not give sufficient air and light. Some windows were undoubtedly only narrow slits at the top of walls, to prevent people, animals, and strong winds from entering. Large windows were almost certainly closed by means of boards, like the wooden doors.

Stairs. — Stairs were needed in buildings with several storeys, particularly fortifications, as well as in cisterns and underground silos. However, a difference in height which is to be overcome by means of a staircase might possess religious or ritualistic values (like a *bammah*) or be the result of prestige manifestation, as in the case of a raised dais for a throne. Both cases are in need of a staircase in which emphasis is given not only to the practical but also to cultic and aesthetic qualities.

The need for stairs is as old as the need for buildings. The earliest steps were probably no more than flat fieldstones placed next to a terrace wall so that people could go from terrace to terrace without climbing on their hands and knees. Steps were also used in stone-lined pit dwellings to facilitate descent. There is no evidence of a gradual development for this architectural element, as a skillfully built flight of steps appears early in this country, in the round Neolithic 'tower' at Jericho (Chap. 3, Fig. 4).[81]

Throughout history the domestic dwelling has usually had a single storey (see other chapters in this book). The roof was used for many activities (storage, sleeping, crafts), and it can be assumed that access was by a wooden ladder. In a few Iron Age houses a flight of steps was built to give access to the upper storey. These 'stairways' were a thick wall built against one of the walls of a house, with steps either of fieldstones or of hewn stones laid on their sloping tops, as at Hazor[82] and Beersheba.[83] In the Israelite palace at Lachish, there is an exterior flight of steps built in this same manner.[84]

Sometimes stairs were placed in a special room, the stairwell. If the flight of steps was straight, the room had to be long and narrow (its length depended on the number of steps and their rise). Such a stairway was safe, but gave access to only one floor.[85] It was difficult to fit a long, narrow room into a building, because a single wall was not long enough for the entire flight of steps, which then had to be continued along one or more of the room's walls, creating stairs with right-angled turns. These stairs were only protected on one side by the wall, and the handrail necessary for safety on the other side was unknown in antiquity. Moreover, this kind of construction would have been weak since the stairs were attached to the wall only on one side. Very soon such drawbacks must have led to the construction of a staircase whose steps were built around a square or rectangular pilaster and anchored both in the walls and in the central pilaster.

80. *Ramat Rahel* II, pp. 56–58, Pls. 44:2, 45-48; cf. also below, Chap. 22, p. 207.

81. *Jericho* III, Pls. 9-11, 244.
82. *Hazor* III-IV, Pl. LXXXII:1.
83. Y. Yadin: Beer-Sheba: The High Place Destroyed by King Josiah, *BASOR* 222 (1976), Figs. 2–5. However, the stairs here are in a private house and not in a *bammah*, as Yadin thought.
84. *Lachish* III, Pl. 18:2, 3, 6.
85. This is the meaning of the narrow passages on both sides of some MB gates. See below, Chap. 16, pp. 134–136.

Aphek. Staircase in the Late Bronze Age Palace.

Presumably, the steps of such a staircase could have been built on a base of earth and rubble or mud brick around four sides of the pilaster, although so massive a base was unnecessary. The steps, either wooden boards or stone slabs, could be anchored in the walls of the room and in the central pilaster. This technique created a useful space under the steps and made it possible to continue them upward beyond the first four turns in buildings of several storeys or unusual height. Sometimes steps were of both wood and of stone, as, for instance, in the LB Canaanite palace at Aphek (Fig. 21).

An interesting feature of passageways through Bronze Age city-gates is the steps found at Tell el-Far'ah (North) from the Early Bronze Age;[87] at Megiddo, Stratum XIII, from the Middle Bronze Age;[88] and in the East Gate at Tell Balata (Shechem),

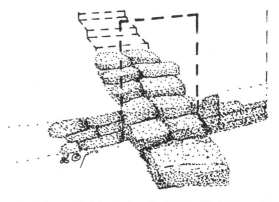

21. Staircase, Aphek. *Qadmoniot* 10 (38–39) (1977), p. 65.

from the Middle-Late Bronze Ages.[89] These steps made the ascent to the city-gate easier for pedestrians but hindered the passage of chariots and carts. (Of course, these cities may have had another gate for vehicles.) The possibility cannot be excluded that these are not really steps but a stepped subterranean

86. M. Kochavi: The History and Archaeology of Aphek-Antipatris, BA 44 (1981), Figs. p. 78.
87. R. de Vaux: Les Fouilles de Tell el-Far'ah, *RB* (1962), pp. 221–236, Pls. XVIII, XXVII:b, XXIX, XXXI.
88. *Megiddo* II, pp. 6–8, Figs. 7–8.

89. *Shechem*, pp. 73–74

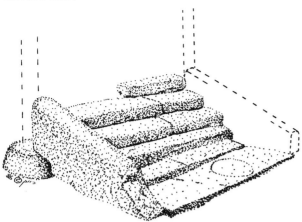

22. Limestone staircase and railing, Lachish. *Tel Aviv* 5 (1978), Pl. 5:1.

reinforcement originally built to stabilize a layer of beaten earth for a ramp.

Flights of steps ascending to a *bammah*, or altar, are often found in temples. Sometimes it seems doubtful that such steps, especially when made of mud brick, were meant to be ascended, but were perhaps places on which offerings were set, as in the temples at Lachish[90] and Tell Qasile.[91] In other cases, the steps were definitely for the ceremonial ascent to the *bammah*. They were usually made of a hard material, either stone, as in the temples at Lachish[92] (Fig. 22) and Bet Shean,[93] or kiln-dried bricks, as in the Assyrian temple at Sheikh Zuweyd.[94]

Floors and Pavements. — Throughout the millennia, domestic buildings in Palestine had earthen floors (stamped by foot or with a stone roller), without any additional flooring.[95] The alleyways between the houses also were usually beaten earth.

Earthen floors can only be distinguished in a careful archaeological excavation, usually from traces left by the occupants — organic remains from kitchens and courtyards, vessels and remains of installations. Floors in houses were probably covered with straw mats and carpets, but such remains are very rarely found. Of special interest are the mat impressions on the floors of houses in Jericho.[96]

Pavements out of hard materials — pebbles,[97] shells, field-stone slabs,[98] or layers of hard lime plaster[99] — were laid in addition to simple earthen floors. They had several advantages: they dried quickly, if the water was drained by channels or the floor sloped, unlike the beaten-earth floors which turned to mud. The hardness of the stone, especially when used in the form of slabs or flags, made it ideal for paving entrances, gate passages,[100] and streets that were used by carts and chariots.

Drainage Channels. — In densely built-up urban areas and especially in walled cities, excess rainfall was a problem. While some rainwater was directed into cisterns and some seeped into the earth in the courtyards, after a heavy rainfall puddles formed inside the city area, endangering the bases of house walls (Chap. 2, p. 17), and had to be drained off beyond the city limits. It was collected into shallow drainage channels that ran down the middle of the streets. This feature is especially characteristic of Iron Age cities. The channels were usually lined with fieldstones and covered with flat fieldstone slabs. They were connected to a large drain that passed through the city-wall or under the city-gate, which was usually situated at one of the lowest points in the fortification line (see Lachish, Strata IV-III;[101] Megiddo;[102] and Gezer[103]). A main drainage channel through the city-wall required planning, as it had to be built with the city-wall (Fig. 3) and had to take into account the street levels inside the city. There was a major problem when the city-wall was of mud brick, and a stone channel of good workmanship had to be built to prevent the seepage of water into the wall and the eventual disintegration of its foundations. The channel had to be large enough so that it would not become clogged, but the outer opening could not be so large that it would be a security risk — it could not be large enough to permit a stranger to enter the city during a siege (perhaps the 'way into the city', in Judges 1:24). A stone closing device was attached to the opening that prevented entrance but allowed the water to flow out, as can be seen at Lachish[104] and Gezer.[105]

90. *Lachish* II, Pls. VI:4–6, LXVIII, LXX, LXXI.
91. A. Mazar: *Excavations at Tell Qasile, Part 1* [*Qedem* 12], Jerusalem, 1980, Figs. 9-11, Pls. 11:1, 3, 4.
92. Ussishkin (above, n. 9), pp. 15–16, Fig. 3, Pls. 4:2, 5:1.
93. *Beth Shan* II, Pls. VI, VII, VIII, IX, XLIIIA:1, LA:1.
94. See below, p. 221. Fig. 17.
95. Avigad (above, n. 8), Figs. 118, 119.
96. *Jericho* III, Pls. 41:a, b, 49:a, b, 147:1, 150:a, b, 158:a, b, 159:a, b, 161:a.
97. *Hazor* III-IV, Pls. CVIII:2, CXIV. For a shell pavement see, for instance, *Ancient Gaza* V, Pl. XXXIX:29; *Megiddo* II, Figs. 50–52.

98. *Hazor* III-IV, Pls. XX:1, CXI, CXII; and Megiddo II, Fig. 154.
99. *Hazor* III-IV, Pl. LV:1–3.
100. *Ibid.*, Pl. CXXXVI:1–3; *Megiddo* I, Fig. 89, L. 500.
101. Ussishkin (above, n. 9), Figs. 15, 16, Pls. 18:1–2, 19:3; idem, 1983 (above, n. 49), Figs. 11, 17.
102. *Megiddo* I, Figs. 89, 82, 92, 93.
103. *EAEHL* II, p. 436.
104. Ussishkin (above, n. 9), p. 62, Pl. 19:3; idem, 1983 (above, n. 49), p. 131, Pl. 32:2.
105. *Gezer* I, Fig. 109, p. 223.

2 MASSIVE STRUCTURES: PROCESSES IN CONSTRUCTION AND DETERIORATION

Ehud Netzer

Introduction

Construction in Palestine, from the Neolithic period to modern times, has been characterized by the use of massive walls and flat roofs laid on wooden beams. Flat roofs on wooden beams remained the most common method of roofing even after domes and arches were incorporated in buildings at the end of the Hellenistic period.

In this article, the processes of both construction and deterioration of massive structures in Israel will be discussed. Comprehension of these processes is vital to the understanding of various phenomena and the solving of many stratigraphic problems often encountered in archaeological excavations. It may also help us to understand how tells were formed. Only principles of construction will be reviewed here, without going into calculations, engineering handbook details, etc. There will also be no reference to the period during which one method or another was used, as the principles remain the same throughout the periods discussed in this book.

The function of a building is to protect its inhabitants, man and livestock alike, from the elements, maintain a comfortable temperature and offer physical protection against wild animals, thieves, etc. Sometimes it also offers the dwellers privacy.

In this regard massive structures are excellent and are usually far superior to other structures used by man, such as caves, tents and huts. Massive structures enjoy great flexibility in design, number of storeys and locations suitable for construction. However, they also have disadvantages, such as poor resistance to prolonged humidity and to fire (when containing wooden roof beams), as well as wasted space due to thick walls, and difficulty in spanning the roof. Each part of the building, foundations, walls and roof, will be discussed separately.

Foundations

The foundation of a massive structure is the link between it and the ground. Its role is to prevent the sinking of the building in whole or in part. In other words, the foundation transmits the load of the building to the ground in such a way that the building remains firmly in its place. The load of the building includes, first of all, the weight of its components (walls, ceilings, etc.), and in multi-storey buildings, its contents (people, furniture, etc.) as well. It also includes, of course, the weight of the foundations themselves.

Unlike modern sophisticated foundation techniques, based mostly on reinforced concrete, the technique used almost exclusively in ancient Palestine was that of the 'continuous foundation', that is, foundations following the walls throughout their length. Even when preparing foundations for rows of columns and pillars, the builders often preferred laying a continuous course rather than a separate foundation for each pillar. When arches became more common, the builders occasionally omitted the continuous foundation where the ground was unstable, and constructed the wall upon an arch which needed a foundation only at two points.

The width and depth of the foundation, and at times even the method used in its construction, are a function of the type and quality of the soil on which the different parts of the building stand, in accordance with the changing ground conditions (see below). The builder's aim was to base the structure on a foundation as firm as possible, preferably on bedrock wherever it was exposed or close to the ground. When the bedrock was too deep beneath the surface, the builders did their best to base the structure on the layer of earth which appeared firm enough to carry the load.

The depth of the foundation could vary from one

1. Cross section along length of wall: foundations of varying depth.

2. Cross section of wall: foundations are the same width as the wall.

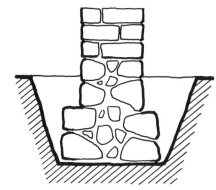

3. Cross section of wall: foundations are wider than the wall.

4. Cross section of wall: foundations widen with depth.

section to another according to the condition of the ground (Fig. 1). When sinking foundations in tells or other multi-layer sites, the builders often stopped as soon as they reached an old wall, yet continued to dig on either side until they reached soil which appeared firm. In other cases, the builders did not trust the old walls, cut them, and continued to dig until they reached bedrock or suitable soil. When they hit an old pit or cistern filled with soft material, they dug through to the bottom of the pit, while laying the foundations higher outside it.

The ability of soil to carry a load without sinking changes in some types of soil when wet. While a structure may, in dry conditions, be well supported by a certain kind of soil, it may be in danger of sinking in the rainy season. This change in the soil's stability can be very sudden. *Terra rossa*, for example, is such a soil. With sand, on the other hand, there is hardly any difference in load-carrying capacity between dry and wet conditions.

The foundation's width is determined both by the load it is supposed to carry, and by the type of soil in which it is laid. Where the bedrock is close to the surface, or where the soil is firm enough when damp, there is no need for the foundation to be any wider than the wall resting on it (Fig. 2). On the other hand, where the soil is not firm enough, the foundation must be wider than the wall in order to spread the load on a wider surface. This lowers the pressure on the soil, and avoids the danger of sinking. The lower the soil's capacity, under the worst conditions, the wider the foundation should be. Today it is possible to test any type of soil and calculate the maximum load-carrying capacity in standard units. Evidently, in ancient times this was done empirically rather than by calculations, and the builders relied on their experience.

Widening the foundations downward was usually done in stages. When the foundation was to be made twice as wide as the wall, a step was usually added on each side (Fig. 3). To widen the foundation further, more steps were added (Fig. 4). Similarly, when a change was made in the foundation's depth, it too was made in steps, and not on a slant.

How were the foundations built? There was often no difference between the way foundations were built and the method by which walls in the same building, or in the vicinity, were constructed. The similarity is sometimes so great, that when no clear indication of the adjacent floor levels is found in an excavation, it is impossible to discern between walls and foundations. For that reason, the techniques of foundation construction will not be discussed separately, but only as part of a general discussion on wall construction. Only the cases in which foundation construction is different from that of walls will be discussed here.

Before a foundation can be laid, a 'foundation trench' must be dug. The foundation trench is usually as deep in the ground as the foundation itself. In a few cases, in order to prevent humidity from collecting at the base of the foundation, the bottom of the trench was padded with sand before the foundation was built. In these cases the trench was deeper than the foundation. The minimum width of the foundation trench depends on the maximum width of the foundation. The wider the foundation is at the bottom, as dictated by need, the wider the trench.

The foundation trench was often wider at the top than at the bottom (Fig. 5). The need to have sloping sides in the trench resulted both from the tendency of the soil to cave in, and from the work habits and convenience of the builder.

The three most common methods of foundation construction are:

1. The foundation trench is wider than the foundation wall. The builder constructs the wall while standing above the trench, as is usually done with walls (see below). When the foundation wall is finished, the spaces between the sides of the trench and the foundation wall are filled with earth and small stones. During archaeological excavations, the foundation trench can be observed in the cross-section. It is usually easily noticed.

2. The trench is as wide as the foundation. Here, the builder works standing inside the trench and without seeing the sides of the foundation wall. The stones are laid against the sides of the trench. This system can only be applied where the sides of the trench are upright and there is no danger of their caving in during construction. The side of a foundation wall thus laid is similar to that of the one constructed using the former method, but it cannot be made as precisely.

3. The foundation is cast into the trench. The builder stands alongside the top of the trench and pours stones and mortar alternately. Here too, the width of the trench is the same as the foundation's (Fig. 6). It is easy to recognize this type of foundation when excavated as its surfaces are rough and stones are laid in it without any order and tend to fall out easily when exposed.

Building Materials Used in Foundations

The effect of humidity on different kinds of soil has already been discussed. Water or humidity, in penetrating the soil, can also affect the strength and

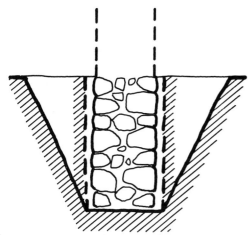

5. Gross section: narrow foundation trench in comparison with foundation trench which widens towards the top.

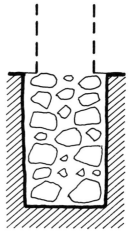

6. Cross section: foundation built without courses by pouring mortar and stones into trench.

stability of the foundation itself, and not just the soil carrying it. It usually affects the mortar between the stones of the foundation as well as the bricks in mud-brick foundations (see below). For that reason the builders preferred using stones in the foundations. Only where stone was rare, especially in the south of the coastal plain, were the foundations occasionally made of mud brick. It should be remembered, however, that the soil in the coastal plain often contains much sand which prevents the water from concentrating at the side of the foundation wall.

In order to ensure that bricks in mud-brick foundations remained stable in damp conditions, the builders sometimes used sand-based mortar when building the foundation wall, or poured a layer of sand underneath the foundation in order to prevent water from gathering at its side and help drain the water to the surrounding soil.

It has already been mentioned above that foundations were often built in the same way as walls. However, a difference between foundations and walls is found, in many cases, in the use of many different materials — fieldstones in contrast to dressed stone, or stones in contrast to mud bricks. The choice was made according to economic considerations as well as topographic conditions. It is important to note that the foundations were almost always continuous, for reasons of stability as well as convenience in construction. Therefore, in those cases where the building is destroyed below floor levels, it would be impossible to determine from the foundations alone where the doorways were. On the other hand, total lack of openings in a wall suggest it is part of the foundation.

Walls

The main components of massive walls were stones or mud bricks. In both cases mortar was used to connect the building blocks. An exception to this is the 'dry construction' method which does not contain mortar at all and was mostly used in building fences and retaining walls (e.g. agricultural terraces).

The structural importance of the mortar is that it makes the wall into one unified mass. It transfers the compressive forces taking place in the wall (i.e. the weight) from one building unit to the next. Thus, each stone or brick participates completely and

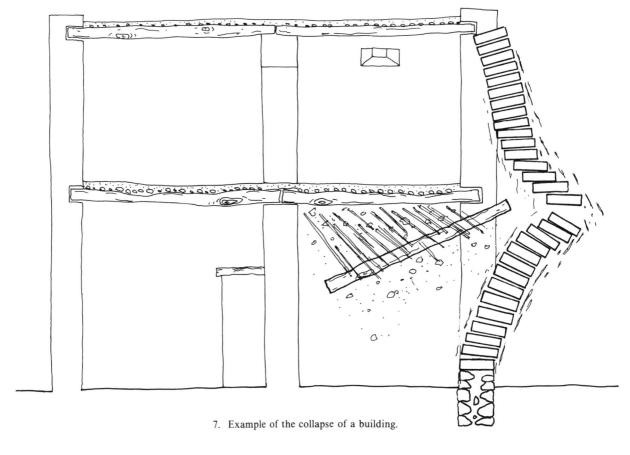

7. Example of the collapse of a building.

uniformly in transferring the pressure. In stone walls built without mortar (especially fieldstones), contact between stones is limited to a few points. The transfer of pressure is then limited to only a few parts of each stone. Stone or mud-brick walls built with mortar, on the other hand, act structurally as single, uniform units, which generally increases their stability and pressure-carrying capacity.

Before dealing with the different methods of construction, the factors which determine the wall's thickness have to be discussed. Only walls whose thickness is not dictated by special needs, such as defence, will be discussed here. The wall's thickness is determined by the following factors:

1. Building materials (stones, clay, bricks) of which the wall is made, their size, shape and stability.

2. Type, quality and strength of the mortar used.

3. The load on the wall. This includes the wall's own weight as well as that of everything laid on it (ceiling, upper storey, etc.).

4. Building techniques and precision of the wall construction.

5. External horizontal forces, chiefly winds.

6. The wall's geometric form, its height, length and position in the structure: corners, angles, **interlevel** ceilings, roofs connected to the wall, etc.

The thickness of a wall is particularly significant in high walls and in buildings which have more than one storey. Every wall of a given thickness and subject to the considerations mentioned above could collapse if built over a certain height. When this happens, the middle of the wall moves sideward and the whole wall collapses (Fig. 7). The danger of collapse can be prevented by reinforcing the wall with buttresses or other means. In multi-storey buildings the interlevel ceilings actually serve as such a reinforcement Fig. 8). It is therefore possible to build multi-storey buildings with thinner walls than might be expected considering their height alone. A wall built with fieldstones and limeless mortar, and whose width is 0.5–0.6 m., for example, would remain stable up to a height of 3–4 m. Beyond this height it would be in danger of collapsing. However, the same wall could be safely built as high as 6–8 m. if reinforced in the middle. A two-storey house thus built will remain firm as long as its interlevel ceiling supports the walls. Should, however, the ceiling be destroyed by a fire or by some other cause, the walls would suddenly become, in effect, unsupported walls 6–8 m. high, and the building would be likely to collapse. A similar danger exists in multi-storey buildings during earthquakes (see below).

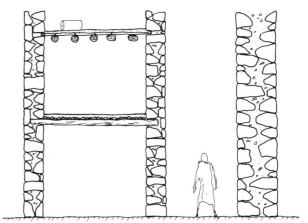

8. Thickness of walls: freestanding wall compared to walls of multi-storied building.

Wall Construction Methods

The preparatory actions required before beginning the construction itself are:

1. Supply of building materials.

2. Preparing the means and appliances with which to mark the course of the wall and with which to control the precision of its construction.

3. Preparing means for lifting building materials to the required height and providing the builder with easy access to all the points at which construction is carried out.

Easy access to the working place and convenient means of lifting building materials were generally taken care of by erecting a system of scaffoldings and ladders. The scaffoldings were needed because construction was always conducted from without (that is, the builder stood outside the wall's boundaries, facing the wall) and also because upon completion of the wall, it would be necessary to seal the gaps between the stones (in stone walls), or to plaster the whole wall (in brick walls and in some stone walls).

The scaffoldings and the means for marking the wall outlines (builder's line, level and plumb-bob) did not usually leave any traces. The builder's line was necessary for the building of every straight wall, and it most likely served also for marking the exact location of the building, its foundation and walls on the ground, before construction commenced. Pegs too must have been used for that purpose. It is reasonable to assume, however, that most of the detailed design in ancient days was carried out not at the drawing board, but rather during the stages of outlining the building on the ground.

When building a wall the builder generally used two

strings (one on each side of the wall), which marked the width of the wall. These strings did not have to be level, but in walls built with courses of stones (either dressed or rough), care was usually taken to level the line in order to make sure that the courses were indeed level. The wall was kept exactly vertical with the aid of a plumb-bob (a string with a pointed weight at its end).

The fact that walls were built with the aid of strings is affirmed by the manner in which dressed stones (from several different periods) were planed on some or all of the four sides, while the face of the stone was left rough, or only partially cut. Some dressed stones from the Iron Age are particularly interesting, as only two of their edges are planed, one for adjusting the stone to the horizontal line which the builder put up for marking the course, and the other for adjusting to the plumb-bob.

Construction of Massive Stone Walls

Two categories of stone walls were common in Palestine: those built with fieldstones, and those built with cut, or dressed, stones. The wall is made of a core and two surfaces (inner and outer ones on an external wall, or two inner surfaces on an inner wall). Some walls are made with only one row of stones and no core (Fig. 9). Other walls (usually thicker) are made of two rows of stones and a filling between them, often of smaller stones than those of the wall surface (Fig. 10).

Walls were often built with the same kind of stone on both surfaces, but some walls have one side made of dressed stones (usually the outer side), and the other side made of fieldstones (Fig. 11). It should be noted here, that in thick walls the core is often the main mass of the wall and the surfaces are only an outer shell. In such walls, surface stones have often fallen out or been stolen, while the core has remained standing.

The string, as mentioned above, was the builder's most important accessory. In order to ensure a straight line, the surface stones of the wall were laid along the string. Once stone and mortar were laid to a height of 25–50 cm., the builder would raise the string to the next layer. Before that, however, he would have built the edges of the wall, that is, the corners of the building. Here, precision is always important, therefore the cornerstones are big and smoothed, and thus firm enough to hold the string in place. When the wall was long, it was necessary to fix the string in place at a few more points. For that purpose bigger,

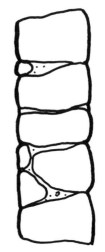

9. Cross section: wall with no core.

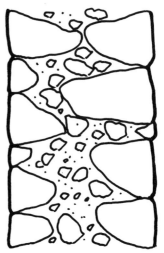

10. Cross section: wall with a core.

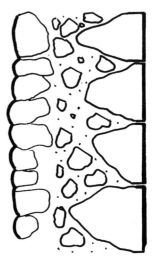

11. Cross section: wall constructed on one side of fieldstones, on the other side of dressed stones.

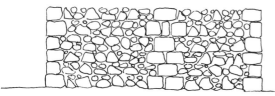

12. Wall constructed of a combination of fieldstones and dressed stones.

rectangular and sometimes even dressed stones were laid at these points. Thus, a "column" of stones is sometimes created in the wall, with stones protruding intermittently from both sides (Fig. 12).

In a wall built of courses of fieldstones, relatively big stones were generally laid first, and the course was then levelled with smaller ones, in order to prepare a flat base for the next course. Exact levelling of the courses was especially important in the transition level between stone and mud brick. Such transition is found mostly where foundations become walls, and occasionally between first and second storeys. Familiarity with this phenomenon of precise levelling of courses is essential for the archaeologist; in cases where floors are not found, the shift from stone to mud brick may aid in determining where the floor was. The transition from stone foundation to brick wall is generally 5–10 cm. above the adjacent floor.

Construction of Massive Brick Walls
(unbaked bricks known also as mud bricks)

Knowledge of construction techniques in handmade brick in Palestine, before the use of mud bricks cast in moulds, is scant. However, from the moment the use of moulds became common, wall construction meant laying course upon course of uniform bricks. The bricks, unlike dressed stones, are uniform as long as they are made from one mould. Even when more than one mould is used during construction, uniformity may be adhered to at least partially.

When the bricks are uniform, the width of a mud-brick wall depends on the size of the bricks. Bricks can be laid in different ways, or bonds: they can be laid so that the wall's thickness is the bricks' width, or length; they can be laid in double courses, crosswise and in many other ways. In any case, brick-laying in Palestine did not adhere to any particular tradition of brick-laying patterns as it did, for example, in Egypt.

In the construction of mud-brick walls the builders used a mortar with a similar composition to that of the bricks themselves. The mortar which filled the horizontal spaces between the bricks was 1–3 cm.

thick, occasionally more. In the vertical spaces it was generally thinner.

Weatherproofing the Wall

An external wall is exposed to rainwater which either hits it directly or runs down from the roof. When strong winds blow, the effect of the rain is particularly damaging, as the wind drives the water into the wall with great force. The most vulnerable part of the wall is the mortar between the stones (especially clay- or soil-based mortar). The stones themselves are not usually affected by humidity.

In a stone wall, weatherproofing, is usually accomlished through the use of a superior quality plaster, either covering the whole wall or covering the gaps between the stones. In the latter case the edges of the stones were covered as well as the small stones laid between the larger ones. Obviously, using prime mortar between the stones (especially lime-based mortar), helps prevent dampness from penetrating the wall.

In a mud-brick wall the outer surface has to be completely plastered. The external plaster demands permanent maintanance in order to avoid penetration of water through cracks, holes, etc. Covering the inner side of brick walls with plaster is a matter of convenience, cleanliness and aesthetics, and makes painting the room possible.

Roofing Massive Structures

In many cases roofing was, in the past as it is today, the main problem the builder or engineer had to face. The wall itself usually has to support only the load, and internal forces (stresses) which are not vertical, in general do not operate in the wall. In the horizontal roof, on the other hand, tensile forces also exist. These stresses are caused mainly by the weight of the roof itself, and they increase with the distance between the walls (in a squared ratio and see below). They increase even more when the roof carries external weight, such as snow or human activity. As a result of its own weight, and of the weight it carries, the ceiling sags, especially in the middle. When it sags the bottom part of the roof streches and the top part is compressed. Tensile stresses are created in the lower side, while compressive stresses develop in the upper part. A different kind of stress, circular, is sometimes created at the edges of the ceiling if it is inserted into the wall on which it rests, but circular stresses are irrelevant to the discussion here.

The building materials used in walls (stones, mud bricks, mortar) are resistant to pressure, but not to the tensile stresses created on the lower side of the ceiling when it sags. Mortar and mud brick are particularly non-resistant to tensile forces, but even stone, which can stand great pressure, has only limited resistance to stretching, beyond which it cracks or breaks. Obviously the quality, the size, and the shape of the stone affect its durability, but even the hardest stone (not to mention the soft limestone used in Israel) cracks when subject to tensile forces. For that reason stone was not commonly used in the past as roofing material, at any rate, not for areas greater than about one metre, in spite of stone's high resistance to moisture. A more common use of stone in roofing was as girders (between pillars), but here too, as the stone is prone to crack, big and hard stones were required and not easily found.

Wood, on the other hand, is much more resistant to stretching due to its fibrous composition. The natural structure of a tree trunk keeps it firm even in strong winds and enables it to bend.

The structural solutions to roofing problems in the past can be divided into three groups:

1. Roofs and ceilings, constructed of wood, resistant to tensile forces.

2. Roofs and ceilings, constructed of stone and mortar (e.g. domes and arches), resistant to compressive forces.

3. Roofs and ceilings, built of stone and wood, in which both principles were utilized.

The first group will be fully discussed here, while the second and third ones will only be reviewed in brief, as the first one was by far the predominant method before the Hellenistic period.

Roofs and Ceilings Based on the Principle of Tension. — Wood was widely used as a building material even before man learned how to build massive buildings. By the time massive structures started appearing, at the end of the Neolithic period, wood had already become a major component in roofs. It seems reasonable to assume that the method of building flat roofs laid on wooden beams has remained basically unchanged from Neolithic times to this day. Wooden beams were laid parallel to each other and at fixed intervals (usually 40–80 cm.). Above the beams, and at a right angle to them, branches, canes (single or in bunches), palm fronds or straw mats were laid (Fig. 8). The top layer of the roof was made of mortar, marl or clay. This layer was made as waterproof as possible (and see below).

In a ceiling built this way, the wooden beams carry the whole load of the roof. The ability of the beams to withstand tensile stress ensures the stability of the ceiling. In such ceilings, it makes no difference whether they are flat or slightly sloping, but it may be assumed they were usually flat. The top level of the mortar, marl or clay, as pointed out above, prevents rainwater from getting into the building. The roof was also used to sleep on (in the summer), for storage or drying fruit, and served as a floor when there were more storeys above it.

In order to prevent penetration of rainwater through the upper layer, the builders incorporated minimal slopes in the roofs which deterred water from collecting, occasionally used sealants, such a. marl (*Hawar*) and clay, and packed the marl with a stone roller. The last act had to be redone every year before the winter. The roof gradients had to be properly drained so that the water would not run down the walls. For that purpose gutters were built, which drained the water from the roof. Penetration of moisture into the buildig due to a leaky roof not only endangers the contents of the building, but may also cause the wooden roof beams to rot, and the whole roof may then cave in. Although the roof, like the walls, could be protected by a layer of high grade mortar (such as lime-based mortar), mortar would be likely to crack here due to the vibrations caused by the elasticity of the wooden beams and branches. These vibrations increase whenever heavy objects are placed on the roof and when people walk on it, therefore such a coating was therefore not commonly applied to roofs of the kind discussed here. However, on interlevel ceilings (in multi-storey buildings), there was no need for waterproofing, but rather for a surface suitable for walking on, without slopes.

The thickness of the wooden beams depends on the size of the roofed area. For roofing a room 2–2.5 m., wide wooden beams 8–12 cm. in diameter are needed (depending, of course, on the type of the wood, its quality, etc.). Wood of that diameter and length is easy to find and transport. It should be born in mind, though, that the beam must be 30–50 cm. longer than the width of the actual aperture, as it must rest on solid surfaces on both sides. Such beams were probably easy for anybody to obtain. Their availability varies, of course, from one place to another, but transporting them, as mentioned before, is not difficult.

The problem becomes more serious when a bigger room or hall is to be roofed. The stresses operating within the beams increase in a squared proportion to the width of the aperture. In a ceiling 4 m. wide, the stresses are four times (and not twice) as great as the stresses in a ceiling 2 m. wide, and in a ceiling which is 6 m. wide, they will be nine times as great as those in a ceiling 2 m. wide (3^2). Therefore, while for a 2 m. aperture beams 8–10 cm. thick would suffice, a ceiling with an aperture of 4 m. requires beams 15–18 cm. thick, and for a ceiling 8 m. wide (in which the stresses are 16 times as great as those in a 2 m. ceiling), one needs beams 25–30 cm. thick. Beams of this thickness, and 4.5–8.0 m. long (and of course, straight), are much more difficult to obtain and transport and their cost is naturally much higher.

Structurally, the important measure in roof beams is their height (i.e. the height of the beam in its cross-section). The higher the cross-section, the better the ability of the beam to withstand the various stresses and the wider the aperture it can cover. Wooden beams behave in that respect exactly like stone beams. In order to get a wooden beam whose height measurement is greater than its width, the wood must be either planed down or sawn into a few beams. The standard practice, however, was to use the natural, round profile of the wood.

In order to overcome the need for very thick and long beams, ceiling support pillars were used. While the beams between one pillar to the next still had to be thick, those between the main beams and the walls (the secondary beams), could be much thinner, since the apertures were now much smaller. For example, in order to roof a room of 5 x 8 m., a pillar is erected in the middle of the room and a beam, which rests on it, is laid across the room (either one beam, 8.5 m. long, or two beams, 4.2–4.5 m. each). Thus, the room is divided into two spaces, each 8 m. long and 2.5 m. wide, which can be roofed using beams 2.8 m. long and 8–12 cm. thick. Had a central pillar not been used, one would have had to use beams 5.5 m. long and 20 cm. thick, which would have rendered the building much more complicated and expensive.

Wooden beams, branches, cane and straw are exposed to two dangers:

1. Rotting, caused by prolonged contact with moisture. Rotting weakens the beams and they may gradually collapse under the pressure of the roof.

2. Fire. In this case, unlike the former one, the collapse of the ceiling may be immediate.

Roofs and ceilings based on wooden beams were the classic solution to the roofing problem in Palestine before the arrival of iron beams and reinforced concrete. Wood was available in most parts of the country and even where there were no trees,

wood could be transported with relative ease. The construction of roofs using wooden beams is fast, easy and economical in space (in comparison with arches and domes).

In the Roman and Byzantine periods a new type of roof, also based on wood but more complex, appeared: a gable or a truss carrying a covering of fired clay roof tiles (in other parts of the world straw or slate were used occasionally for the same purpose). This method of roofing was used, of course, only for external roofs and not for interlevel ceilings. The advantage of this kind of roof is not only that it offers better protection against rain, but that it makes better use of wood, which enables larger apertures to be covered. That was of particular importance in the construction of large buildings, such as synagogues and churches.

Massive Roofs Based on the Pressure Principle. — Roofs based on the pressure principle were used mostly during later periods (beginning at the end of the Hellenistic period) and shall therefore only be discussed briefly. The basic principle of these ceilings is the utilization of the properties of the arch, in which the stresses are compressive rather than tensile. The earliest ceilings based on this principle were barrel-vaulted ceilings (actually half barrel). This type of arch was known in Mesopotamia as early as the third millennium B.C. and in Egypt from the second millennium B.C. In Palestine such arches are found, among other places, at Tel Dan (in the city-gate), and Tell Jemmeh (in the Assyrian buildings). But on the whole, the use of arches in the earlier periods was, as mentioned above, rare and exceptional. Arches can be built with stone, baked clay bricks or mud bricks. The few early arches found were all made of bricks, but all the arches built in Israel from the Persian-Hellenistic period onward, as well as the domes from the Roman period and later (such as the bathhouse in Herodium, the mausoleum in 'Askar, the Hulda Gates at the Temple Mount in Jerusalem, and the Persian Residency at Lachish), were built of stone cut for the purpose. Some domes and arches built of undressed stone and mortar were also found.

Arches and domes were incorporated in buildings in two ways:

1. The arch or dome projects from the upper surface of the roof. The roof cannot then be used for other purposes. However, its weight is relatively low, and the pressure on the walls is therefore reduced.

2. The arch or dome is incorporated and hidden within the roof. A flat upper surface is therefore created, which can be used as storage space or as a

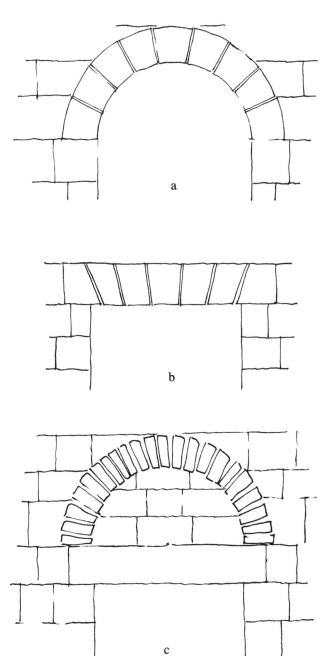

13. Types of arches: a) true arch; b) flat arch; c) relieving (light) arch.

floor for a second storey. The disadvantage of this system is that the volume of the roof is much larger and the pressure on the walls is consequently greatly increased (which makes the building of additional storeys more difficult). As these roofs are based on the pressure principle, no wood need be incorporated in them, but wood is nevertheless needed for scaffolding during construction itself. Scaffolding is needed not only for lifting building materials to the roof, but also, or rather mostly, to support the ceiling until its construction has been completed and the mortar dried and hardened. Preparation of scaffolding suitable for that purpose requires professional know-how which is not needed for building the flat roofs described earlier.

3. Roofs incorporating both principles. Using this method, arches are built over the room or hall at fixed distances, and stone slabs are laid over them (as was done in the Negev in the Nabataean and Byzantine periods and in the Hauran during various periods). On other occasions, wooden beams and branches are used instead of stone slabs (as in the Galilee and Judea until recent days).

Lintels over Openings, Doors and Windows

Covering openings in a wall is generally simpler than roofing, but the technical problems are similar. As in ceilings, the wider the opening is, the more difficult it is to cover. To cover doors, windows and similar openings, a big stone was used, but this method has a serious drawback: the stone may crack as a result of the pressure of the wall on it. Here again wood has excellent properties and indeed was commonly used when the openings were wider than 0.5–0.6 m.

In the Herodian period, combinations of wood and stone lintels can be found: the outer side of the opening was covered with a stone slab, while the inner side was covered with a wooden beam. This ensures that the wall remains stable even if the stone cracks.

Wooden beams were also used when there was a need to build a wall in an upper storey over a space in the storey below. Relatively thick beams were then used, which could support the load of the wall built over them. Sometimes those walls were also supported by pillars built in rows on the ground floor. That was done, for example, in the four-room houses (see Chap. 21, p. 193), in stables and storehouses. Here, use was sometimes made of stone beams (e.g. at Tel Masos and Ha-Ro'ah) and occasionally of wooden beams too, when the distance between the pillars was more than one metre.

From the moment arches came into use, they were utilized for covering openings in the wall as well. Three types of arches are particularly worthy of mention (Fig. 13): a true arch, a flat arch and a relieving arch. The latter is integrated in the wall (usually above openings), and lightens the load on the stone lintel or the flat arch.

Destruction Processes

Processes of destruction in massive structures can be divided into two types: sudden, or spontaneous destruction, and gradual decay. In most cases the two processes are combined: a sudden destruction ruins a part of the structure, which then continues to deteriorate gradually; or the opposite situation, the gradual decay of the structure is speeded up by a sudden collapse.

The three main reasons for sudden destruction are:

1. An earthquake.

2. Destruction due to a fire either as a result of an accidental incident, or as part of an intended destruction, such as the burning down of a city after it has been captured.

3. Intentional destruction which is not due to fire. This is done with the intention of rendering certain structures unusable (e.g. destruction of fortifications by someone who is interested in their removal, or pulling down structures.

The extent of damage caused by an earthquake depends on its intensity, the geological structure of the area, the direction of the vibrations, the quality of construction of the building and other factors. The damage caused to multi-storey buildings (with flat roofs laid on wooden beams) is particularly noteworthy. In such buildings the connections between the roof beams and the walls are loosened, if only for a few seconds, and the danger of collapse is thus created. The greater the number of quakes, the greater the chances that the ceiling will cave in and the walls collapse. A fire may have a similar effect when it consumes the wooden beams in the ceiling.

Every building, from the moment it is abandoned by its inhabitants, is exposed to gradual decay, due to neglect, the effects of weather, and plundering of the building materials. In this process the external layers which prevent penetration of moisture into the building, such as the overall plaster or the plaster which covers the gaps between the stones and the compressed mortar (or marl or clay) on the roof, are the first to be affected. Rain penetrating the ceiling, in flat roofs, causes rotting to take place in the wooden beams; in arched or domed roofs, water seeping into the walls gradually breaks up the unifying mortar, and subsequently, the mud bricks also. The deterioration is accelerated even more by plundering of building materials, such as wooden beams, from the ceilings (or from door lintels) and stones from different parts of the building. In the process of gradual decay, two opposing trends may be noticed. As time passes, the decaying process, which usually affects the upper parts of the building first, is accelerated, and as the upper part crumbles, the bottom part becomes covered with the debris. This actually stops the decaying process in the bottom part and prevents complete destruction. However, this is not the case when building materials are robbed. Stone robbers often dig below the surface in their search for walls and foundations from which to extract stones for reuse.

Summary

This article describes basic principles and methods of construction which are based on building materials and climatic conditions in Israel. These methods prevailed at most sites during the periods covered in this book and, in some cases, remained prevalent till the beginning of this century. Identical conditions and continuing traditions resulted in almost identical construction methods being employed during different periods. Therefore, in most cases one cannot use building techniques as a means for dating a structure. On the other hand, understanding the processes of both construction and deterioration can aid the archaeologist in analysing and understanding structures as well as strata, and in solving certain stratigraphic problems.

THE GENESIS OF ARCHITECTURE

BUILDING ACTIVITIES IN THE PREHISTORIC PERIODS UNTIL THE END OF THE NEOLITHIC PERIOD

Ofer Bar-Yosef

Introduction

Erecting shelters against rain, wind, and sun, and creating storage facilities were among mankind's earliest activities. The existence of structures built mainly of perishable materials is known in Africa, Asia and Europe from the Middle Palaeolithic. Hut dwellings with their lower parts dug into the loess have been discovered in Eastern and Central Europe and dated to the Late Palaeolithic. Post holes indicate some form of roofing, and underground pits the storing of food. Similar structures from the end of the Upper Pleistocene are also known in Palestine. The clearest archaeological evidence seems to be the remains of Kebaran and Geometric Kebaran huts at the sites near 'En Gev.

At 'En Gev I, a number of strata accumulated in an oval structure dug into the sandy soil.[1] The structure, which has a diameter of 5–7 m., is dug into the sand on the east and is closed off by a low undressed stone wall (up to 0.4 m.) on the west. A hearth was uncovered in the hut, with a small wall next to it that protected the fire from the northwesterly wind. In a second hut attributed to the Geometric Kebaran culture ('En Gev III), several heaps of stones apparently supported wooden poles. At its edge, a circular installation (about one metre in diameter) was built of one course of slabs. Its function is as yet

unknown. The excavation of the hut has not been completed.[2]

The remains found in the rock-shelter of 'Iraq ez-Zigan in Haifa have also been attributed to the Geometric Kebaran. They consisted of two parallel rows of undressed stones, with a hearth between them. A stone platform next to the rear rock-shelter face was built by filling the space between the two rows with rubble. The nature of this structure has not yet been clarified.[3]

The most impressive prehistoric structures in Palestine were erected by the bearers of the Natufian and Harifian cultures and their descendants, known in the literature as the Sultanian (Pre-Pottery Neolithic A) and Tahunian (Pre-Pottery Neolithic B) cultures. For the Pottery Neolithic period that followed, building remains are few and fragmentary. The dating of the structures discussed here is based on radiocarbon dates.[4]

Natufian and Harifian Structures

Natufian structures. — The remains of Natufian structures have been discovered at the following sites:

1. Most of the plans and selected photographs appear in the monumental work of O. Aurenche: *La Maison Orientale*, Lyon, 1981; cf. also M. Stekelis and O. Bar-Yosef: Un habitat du Paleolithique Superieur a Ein Guev (Israel), *L'Anthropologie* 69 (1965), pp. 176–183; B. Arensburg and O. Bar-Yosef: Human Remains from Ein Gev I, Jordan Valley, Israel, *Paleorient* 1 (1973), pp. 201–206.

2. G. Martin and O. Bar-Yosef: Ein Gev III, Israel, 1978, *Paleorient* 5 (1979), pp. 219–220.

3. E. Wreschner: Iraq ez-Zigan, (Notes and News), I*EJ* 25 (1975), pp. 160-161, 254–255.

4. For a short summary of the Epipalaeolithic and Neolithic periods, their phases and cultures, as well as a list of radiocarbon dates updated to 1986, see O. Bar-Yosef: The Epi-Palaeolithic Complexes in the Southern Levant, in J. Cauvin and P. Sanlaville (eds.): *Prehistoire du Levant*, Paris, 1981, pp. 389–408; and Bar-Yosef, The Pre-Pottery Neolithic Period in the Southern Levant, in *op. cit.*, pp. 551–570.

Yiftaḥ'el Neolithic buildings (rectilinear), and Early Bronze Age buildings (oval).

'Eynan (Fig. 1),[5] Hayonim Cave[6] and Hayonim Terrace,[7] Naḥal Oren Terrace (Figs. 2, 3),[8] El-Wad Terrace,[9] Rosh Zin,[10] Rosh Ḥorsha,[11] and Wadi

5. J. Perrot: Le gisement natoufien de Mallaha (Eynan), Israel, *L'Anthropologie* 70 (1966), pp. 437–484; F. Valla: Les etablissements natoufiens dans le nord d'Israel, in Cauvin and Sanlaville (eds.) (above, n. 4), pp. 409–420.
6. O. Bar-Yosef and N. Goren: Natufian Remains in Hayonim Cave, *Paleorient* 1 (1973), pp. 49–68.
7. D. O. Henry, A. Leroi-Gourhan, and S. Davis: The Excavations of Hayonim Terrace: An Examination of Terminal Pleistocene Climatic and Adaptive Changes, *Journal of Archaeological Science* 8 (1981), pp. 33–58.
8. M. Stekelis and T. Yizraeli: Excavations at Nahal Oren, Preliminary Report, *IEJ* 13 (1963), pp. 1–12.
9. D. A. E. Garrod and D. M. A. Bate: *The Stone Age of Mount Carmel*, I, Oxford, 1937.
10. D. O. Henry: Rosh Zin, A Natufian Settlement Near Ein Avdat, in A. E. Marks (ed.): *Prehistory and Palaeoenvironments in the Central Negev, Israel*, I: *The Avdat/Aqev Area*, Dallas, 1976, pp. 317–348.
11. A. E. Marks and P. A. Larson: Test Excavations at the Natufian Site of Rosh Horesha, in A. E. Marks (ed.): *Prehistory and Palaeoenvironments in the Central Negev, Israel*, II: *The Avdat/Aqev Area and the Har Harif*, Dallas, 1977, pp. 191–232.

Hammeh 2. The clearest remains are the dwellings excavated at 'Eynan. However, although these may be considered representative of the Natufian culture, the remains of the winding terrace walls of Nahal Oren and el-Wad may indicate a different kind of structure.

The Natufian rooms and houses are circular or oval and range in diameter from 2–3 m. in Hayonim Cave, through 4 m. in the upper strata of 'Eynan (Ib), to 9 m. in the Stratum III structure at the same site. Few freestanding walls have been found in the excavated buildings. Most of the walls are terrace walls that were built against the excavated side of the slope. At 'Eynan these walls are about one metre high and slightly slanting towards the interior of the house. In Hayonim Cave, where the rooms are joined, the walls also slant inward.

The largest structure at 'Eynan, No. 131 in Stratum III, is semicircular and about 9 m. in diameter. The seven post holes in its floor are 0.3 to 0.4 m. deep, have a diameter of about 0.2 m. and are lined with undressed stones. Their location indicates that the front of the structure must have been rectilinear. The entrance was also in the front.

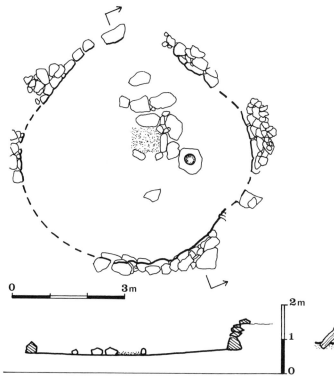

1. Dwelling, plan and cross section, Eynan Building 26. *IEJ* 10 (1960), p. 16, Fig. 1; p. 18, Fig. 4.

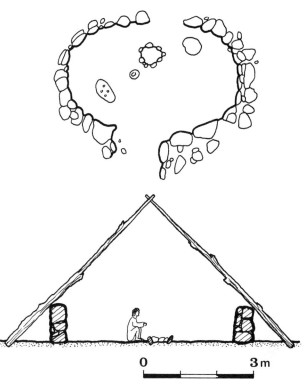

3. Dwelling, plan and cross section, Nahal Oren (detail). *IEJ* 13 (1963), Fig. 4.

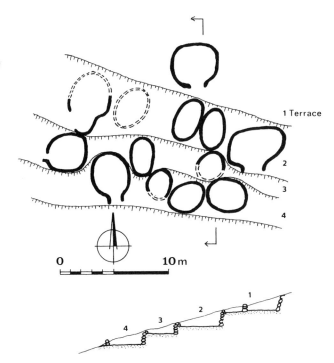

2. Buildings on terraces, plan and cross section, Nahal Oren. IEJ 13 (1963), Fig. 3.

In Natufian structures all the walls were constructed of undressed stones, and sometimes included mortars in secondary use. There is evidence at Hayonim Terrace and at 'Eynan of the use of plaster, apparently made from a mixture of mud (clayey soil) and crushed burnt limestone. At Hayonim Cave a kiln was uncovered, as well as pestles with traces of crushed lime. The most conspicuous use of this plaster is found at 'Eynan in Structure 1. The upper edges of a shallow pit, about 5 m. in diameter, and the low wall that lined the structure, were coated with smoothed plaster. There are traces of red pigment on this plaster, indicating that it was painted.

The terrace walls uncovered on the el-Wad Terrace and at Nahal Oren were 8 m. or more in length. Huts or tents made of organic materials were probably erected in front of the terrace walls, which were built of undressed stones. The method of construction was similar to that used at 'Eynan.

No complete structure has been excavated at Rosh Horsha, and the exact contours of the structures at Rosh Zin are not clear. At Rosh Zin a circular-oval structure about 4 m. long was exposed that had been paved with small limestone slabs. Fragments

33

of decorated ostrich eggshells were found on this pavement. A limestone monolith about one metre high stood at the narrow end of the structure. At the foot of the monolith, a hoard of flint cores and a pair of whetstones were uncovered. The function of the structure and the monolith remains obscure.

Harifian Structures. — The Harifian is a desert culture whose remains have been recorded in the Negev highlands, in the western Negev, and in northern Sinai. This culture represents the adaptation of late Natufian groups to a semiarid environment. Dwelling structures have been uncovered at two sites in the Har Harif region, at Abu Salem and Ramat Harif (G8).[12] They were dug into the loess and had a diameter of about 3 m. The walls were lined with undressed cobbles and limestone slabs. Large limestone slabs with shallow cup marks, assumed to have been produced by some vegetal substance having been pounded or crushed on the slabs, were found in each structure. A few mortars, stone bowls, rubbing stones and pestles were also present.

The continuation of the Natufian-Harifian tradition can be found at the site of Abu Madi I in southern Sinai. There an oval house (3 x 4 m.) was uncovered in a depression at the foot of a large granite boulder. The walls, which are built of local stones, lined the sides of the natural pit. A hearth was built in the centre of the floor, which was made of sorted, packed, yellowish sand. A bell-shaped silo lined with stone slabs adjoined the structure.

Pre-Pottery Neolithic A

Building remains dating from the Sultanian culture (Pre-Pottery Neolithic A) have been discovered in Palestine at four sites: Jericho,[13] Gilgal,[14] Netiv Hagedud,[15] and Nahal Oren.[16] At Nahal Oren an area of about 250 sq. m. has been excavated. This site, like 'Eynan and el-Khiam, is located on a sloping terrace at the foot of a cliff. As at 'Eynan, the houses were built on four terraces dug by the inhabitants. The fifteen exposed structures are either circular or

oval, with a diameter of 2–5 m. Their rear walls, of fieldstones, are built against the face of the terrace wall. Freestanding walls, up to one metre in height, exist only near the entrances. The upper parts of those walls seem to have been made of mud, branches, and other organic materials. Some entrances have been preserved. In a few of the structures a hearth was built in the beaten-earth floor. Next to it stone slabs, usually with four cup marks each, were uncovered.

Houses were also uncovered at Gilgal I and Netiv Hagedud. At Gilgal I shallow pits were dug into the soil and lined with one course of stone slabs. Nothing is yet known about the middle and upper parts of the walls of these structures. Numerous grinding tools and stone slabs with cup marks were found on the floors of the structures.

At the nearby site of Netiv Hagedud, the buildings were oval, with diameters of 4–9 m. The lower parts of the walls are built with cobbles grouted with a yellowish clay. Some of the structures had double

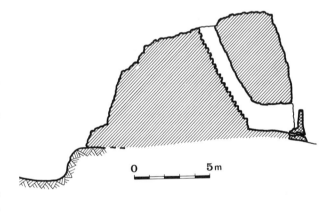

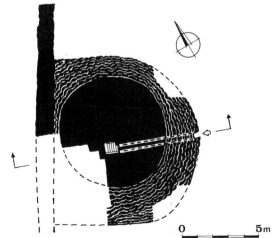

4. Wall and round tower, plan and cross section, Jericho. *Jericho* III (Plates), Pls. 203, 244.

12. T. R. Scott: The Harifian of the Central Negev, in A. E. Marks (ed.) (above, n. 11), pp. 271–322.
13. Jericho III.
14. T. Noy, J. Schuldenrein, and R. Tchernov: Gilgal, A Pre-Pottery Neolithic Site in the Lower Jordan Valley, *IEJ* 30 (1980), pp. 63–82.
15. O. Bar-Yosef, A. Gopher, and A. N. Goring-Morris: Netiv Hagedud: A Sultanian Mound in the Lower Jordan Valley, *Paleorient* 6 (1980), pp. 201–206.
16. Stekelis and Yizraeli (above, n. 8).

walls — two courses of fieldstones with a space between them — that may well have been supports for a superstructure of reeds, rushes, or branches. The largest building excavated at Netiv Hagedud is oval and was originally about 9 m. long. Part of the floor is stamped, smoothed mud; the rest is paved with fine gravel and flat fieldstones. The lowest courses of the wall, built of stone slabs, have been preserved. The upper parts were built of mud bricks. Another circular building, with a diameter of 3.5 m., was constructed of plano-convex (hog-backed) bricks known from Jericho; about half of the building has been excavated, revealing plastered walls and floors.

Many installations were interspersed between the buildings, including small silos built of limestone slabs, roughly as deep (0.3–0.4 m.) as their diameters. Stone slabs with one, two, or four cup marks were found set into the floors. Hearths were oval, cobble-paved, installations.

At Jericho in this period houses were built of mud brick; their lower part was dug into the soil or into earlier occupation strata. The floors were clay and sometimes covered by a round mat. Two or three steps (some of wood) led down into the dwellings. Door sockets next to the steps indicate that there were wooden doors.

The earliest evidence of public buildings is the walls and tower of Jericho, which were uncovered in Trench I in the western part of Tell es-Sultan (Jericho) (Fig. 4).[17] The first wall, which is fronted by a rock-cut ditch, is 3 m. wide at its base and has been preserved to a maximum height of 3.9 m. It has been exposed over a length of about 9 m. Other remains, which probably belong to the same wall, were uncovered at the north end of the tell, where only the lowest course was preserved, and at the south end, where the width of the wall was 1.6 m., and its height reached 2.05 m.

A great tower built of cobbles, still standing 8.5 m. high with a diameter of 10 m. at its base, was erected inside the wall. A flight of twenty-two steps led from the entrance to the top. Because alluvial soil rapidly accumulated in front of the wall, additional walls were built on top of the original one, ultimately reinforcing the tower with an additional wall one metre thick. This wall was erected after an intermediate phase in which plastered brick structures were built against the tower.

These were used as silos or installations for storing water. The occupation debris which accumulated on the eastern side blocked the entrance to the tower during PPNA times.

The presence of a wall and a tower led their excavator, Kenyon, to suggest that they were part of the defense system of an urban settlement. Perrot's alternative hypothesis, that the walls were sections of a walled settlement and resembled sheep pens, was rejected. Recently, it was suggested that the wall was intended to protect the settlement against flash floods and alluviation. The rapid accumulation of fill against the front wall, the destruction of the northern section by water flowing in the wadi, the rapidly deposited alluvial fill in the Neolithic period, and the existence of a similar wall at Beidha support this conjecture.

Pre-Pottery Neolithic B

Sites are attributed to the Pre-Pottery Neolithic B period based on radiocarbon dating and typological analysis of the lithic industries. Because the sites are scattered all over Israel, Jordan, and Sinai, a wide range of habitation forms is represented.

The sites vary greatly in size, ranging from 30,000 sq. m. to 100 sq. m. There are also differences in architectural planning and in the form of the installations. At sites like Jericho and Nahal Oren, the transition from the characteristic rounded structures of the Sultanian culture to the rectangular buildings of Pre-Pottery Neolithic B in the Mediterranean region is particularly evident. The stratigraphic sequence of Beidha, in Edom, the southernmost Mediterranean region in the Levant, reveals the gradual transition from rounded, through polygonal, to rectangular buildings.

The rectangular buildings vary in length (4–6 m.) and width (2–4 m.). The location of the entrances may be in the short side (long-room), or the long side (broad-room). The foundations were usually built of undressed stones (Beisamun [Fig. 5], Tel 'Eli, Yiftah'el (Fig. 8), Nahal Oren, Abu Gosh, and Beidha),[18] but examples exist of one row of

17. Jericho III, pp. 6–10, 19–21, 26, 29–31; P. Dorrell: The Uniqueness of Jericho, in R. Moorey and P. Parr (eds.): *Archaeology in the Levant, Essays for Kathleen M. Kenyon*, Warminster, 1978, pp. 11–18.

18. M. Lechevallier: Les débuts de l'architecture domestique en Palestine, *EI* 13 (1977), pp. 252–259; idem, *Abou Gosh et Beisamoun, deux gisements du VIIe millénaire avant l'ere chretienne en Israel* [Memoires et Travaux du Centre de Recherches Prehistoriques Francais de Jerusalem 2], 1978; D. Kirkbride: Five Seasons at the Pre Pottery Neolithic Village of Beidha in Jordan, *PEQ* 98 (1966), pp. 8–72; idem, Beidha 1967, *PEQ* 100 (1968), pp. 90–96; Stekelis and Yizraeli (above, n. 8); M. W. Prausnitz: *From Hunter to Farmer and Trader*, Jerusalem, 1970, pp. 96–106.

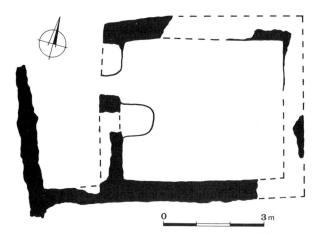

5. Dwelling, Beisamun. M. Lechevallier: *Abou Gosh et Beisamoun*, Paris, 1978, p. 135, Fig. 47.

fieldstones on the outer face and bricks on the inner face (Munhata)[19] or only of mud bricks (Jericho).[20]

Although not all the excavated houses had plastered floors, these floors have become the hallmark both of the rectangular buildings and of the entire period. The floors were covered with a mixture of ashes, sand, and lime. The lime was produced by burning limestone, crushing it, at times even sifting it.[21] Sometimes basins (rectangular hearths) were set into the plastered floor, which was burnished and often painted red. At Jericho the plaster also covered some of the walls, steps, and door jambs.

The corridor houses excavated at Beidha in Stratum II (Fig. 6)[22] belong to a distinct type of rectangular building. They have two interior buttresses that probably helped to carry the roof (and perhaps also an upper storey). The suggestion that these houses were used solely as workshops can only be substantiated with the publication of the full report on the excavations of these buildings.

Round, oval and polygonal structures contemporaneous with the rectangular buildings (and similar to Strata IV and V at Beidha) were erected at sites in the arid regions. The sites in southern Sinai (Wadi Jibba I, 'Ujrat el-Mehed, Wadi Tbeiq)[23] and in the southern

19. J. Perrot: La troisieme campagne de fouilles a Munhata, Syria 43 (1966), pp. 49–63.
20. *Jericho* III, pp. 270–271, 289–308.
21. H. Balfet et al.: Une invention neolithique sans lendemain, *Bulletin de la Societe Prehistorique Francaise* 66 (1969), pp. 188–192; H. Balfet: Examen d'echantillons de sols enduits provenant des sites d'Abou Gosh et Beisamoun, in Lechevallier: *Abu Gosh et Beisamoun* (above, n. 18), pp. 273–277.
22. Kirkbride, (above n. 18, 1966), pp. 11–18.
23. O. Bar-Yosef: Pre-Pottery Neolithic Sites in Southern Sinai, *BA* 45 (1982), pp. 9–12.

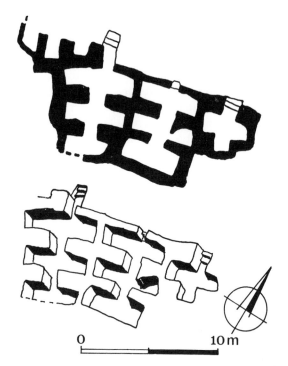

6. Dwellings with three spaces, plan and reconstruction, Beidha (Transjordan). *PEQ* 98 (1966), p. 10, Fig. 1; p. 12, Fig. 2.

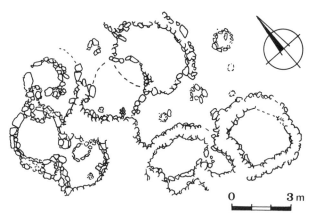

7. Dwelling, Nahal Issaron. *IEJ* 33 (1983), p. 154, Fig. 3.

Negev (Nahal Issaron) (Fig. 7)[24] that were completely excavated have shed light on the habitations of desert dwellers. Rounded rooms built-up of undressed stone or natural slabs have a diameter of 2.5–3.5 m. In a few sites, entrances with a threshold and sometimes one or two steps that led to the floor level were exposed. Constructed hearths were found in some of

24. A. N. Goring-Morris and A. Gopher: Nahal Issaron, a Neolithic Settlement from the Southern Negev, Israel, *IEJ* 33 (1983), pp. 149–162.

the buildings. At 'Ujrat el-Mehed, near St. Catherine's monastery in Sinai, the 'buildings' consisted of stone slabs set around the edges of a shallow pit that had been dug to a depth of 0.2–0.4 m. below surface level. The contour of the buildings resembles a figure eight; possibly only a portion of each structure was roofed with organic materials. These flimsy dwellings are considered to have been summer huts.

There is evidence that wooden posts were used in the polygonal buildings at Beidha, where they formed part of the framework of the house and constituted the inner face of the walls.

Direct archaeological evidence for cultic activities during this period have accumulated rapidly in recent years. The caches of human plaster statues and busts, uncovered at 'Ain Ghazal (Jordan), are among the most outstanding discoveries. Fragments of similar statues were found by Garstang in Jericho. The plastered skulls found at Ramad (Syria), Beisamun, Jericho and 'Ain Ghazal are considered to represent an ancestor cult. The cache from Nahal Hemar cave, including asphalt modelled skulls, stone masks and figurines, indicates the presence of sacred locales outside the sedentary villages. However, the direct architectural evidence for existence of cultic activities is rather ephemeral.

Several buildings appear to have been built for a special purpose. The 'shrine' at Jericho[25] contained a basalt monolith 0.45 m. high in a niche in the wall.

The sanctuary area uncovered at the edge of the site at Beidha[26] consisted of the remains of three circular structures. In one of them a massive stone slab was found on its side, and a shallow basin (0.25 x 2.65 x 3.80 m.) was found outside. Its floor was paved with small cobbles surrounded with upright stone slabs. It is difficult to interpret this installation, as the excavation has not been completed. Also at Beidha, a square building enclosed on two sides by a corridor has been reconstructed by its excavator as an animal pen.[27]

At Munhata, a circular building in Stratum III has been excavated that looks like a central courtyard surrounded by rooms.[28]

Finally, the wall of Jericho from the Pre-Pottery Neolithic B period should be mentioned. It is a sloping terrace wall that was built against the occupation strata of the preceding period.[29] It resembles the retaining wall uncovered at Beidha, over a length of some tens of metres, which had a staircase on its outer face.[30] These features suggest that an important factor in building these walls was either to protect against floods or, alternatively, to create terraces at whose top or foot houses could be built.

In the excavated sites, installations such as hearths and ovens and bell-shaped silos dug into the ground were found.

Pottery Neolithic

Most scholars suggest that the beginning of the Pottery Neolithic period is marked by a climatic change, namely, the transition from humid and somewhat cooler conditions to a period of higher mean annual temperatures followed by an increase in annual precipitation (known in Europe as the Atlantic period). Changes in settlement patterns in the southern Levant are attested to by pit dwellings and mud-brick huts, the remains of which were uncovered at Sha'ar Ha-Golan, Tel 'Eli, Munhata, 'En Soda, Jericho, Lod, Teluliyot Batashi, Herzliya, Giv'at Haparsa, Nizzanim, Ziqim, and elsewhere.[31]

The pits and structures can be classifed by way of generalization as follows:
— Small, shallow pits used as hearths or ovens.
— Narrow, deep pits that may have been used as storage pits (silos?).
— Shallow pits with a diameter of 1–1.5 m. that may

25. *Jericho* III, pp. 306–307, Fig. 15:1, Pls. 308c, 172a, b.
26. Kirkbride, (above, n.18, 1968).
27. Kirkbride, (above, n.18, 1966), p. 14.
28. J. Perrot: Les deux premiere campagnes de fouilles a Munhata (1962–1963), *Syria* 41 (1964), pp. 323–345.

29. J. Mellaart: *The Neolithic of the Near East*, London, 1975, p. 59.
30. Kirkbride, (above, n. 18, 1968), pp. 92–93.
31. M. Stekelis: *The Yarmukian Culture of the Neolithic Period*, Jerusalem, 1972; Prausnitz (above, n. 18); Perrot (above, n. 19); *Jericho* III, pp. 116–117, 136–145, 222–223, 254–257; E. Yeivin and Y. Olami: Nizzanim, A Neolithic Site in Nahal Evtah: Excavations of 1968–1970, *Tel Aviv* 6 (1979), pp. 99–135; Y. Kaplan: Hamadiya, *Hadashot Arkheologiyot* 13 (1965), pp. 16–17 (Hebrew); idem, Neolithic and Chalcolithic Remains at Lod, *EI* 13 (1977), pp. 57–75 (Hebrew, English summary, p. 291*); idem, Teluliot Batashi, *EI* 5 (1958), pp. 9–24 (Hebrew, English summary, p. 83*); T. Noy: Neolithic Sites in the Western Coastal Plain, *EI* 13 (1977), pp. 13–18 (Hebrew, English summary, p. 290*); Y. Olami, F. Burian, and E. Friedman: Excavations in Giv'at Haparsa — A Neolithic Site in the Coastal Region, *EI* 13 (1977), pp. 34–47 (Hebrew, English summary, p. 29*); M. Pausnitz, F. Burian, E. Friedman, and E. Wreschner: Excavations in the Neolithic Site of Herzlia, *Mitekufat Ha'even* 10 (1970), pp. 11–16 (Hebrew, English summary, p. 16*).

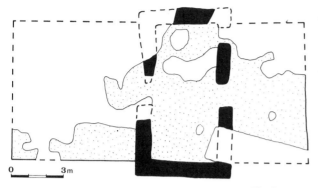

8. Dwelling, Iphtahel. *IEJ* 35 (1985), p. 60, Fig. 1.

have been quarried for clay. These pits gradually filled up with ashes and refuse.

— Shallow pits (up to one metre deep) with a diameter of 2–3 m. that apparently were dwellings. At Munhata a brick bench was found in one of these pits and at Jericho a clay oven.

To these should be added remains of huts whose floor levels were almost equal with the surrounding surfaces, such as have been excavated at Sha'ar Ha-Golan and Nizzanim. The latter had a floor of stamped *kurkar*. Fragmentary pebble- or cobble-paved floors and built hearths have been found at these sites. Ovens constructed of stone slabs and silos lined with stone slabs have been excavated at Kadesh Barnea.[32]

Many of these fragmentary structural remains are reminiscent of tents and booths, similar to abandoned Beduin tent encampments recorded in surveys, or excavated at Tepe Tula'i in Iran.[33]

32. O. Bar-Yosef: Neolithic Sites in Sinai, *EI* 15 (1981), pp. 1–6 (Hebrew, English summary, p. 78*).
33. F. Hole: Tepe Tula'i: An Early Campsite in Khuzistan, Iran, *Paleorient* 2 (1974), pp. 219–242.

Table of Prehistoric Periods and Cultures

Period	Culture	Date (based on C14)
		5,000 BC
Pottery Neolithic	Yarmukian etc.	
		5,800/6,000 BC
	Tahunian	
Pre-Pottery Neolithic		7,300/7,500 BC
	Sultanian	
		8,300 BC
	Harifian/Khiamian	
		8,500/8,800 BC
Epi-Palaeolithic	Natufian/Negev Kebaran	
		10,500 BC
	Geometric Kebaran/Mushabian	
		17,000 BC
Upper Palaeolithic		
		40/42,000 BP*
	Mousterian	
Middle Palaeolithic		90/100,000 BP
	Magharian tradition	
		130/140,000 BP
	Acheulian	
Lower Palaeolithic		
	Oldovian	
		2/2,300,000 BP

* Before Present

Discussion

In recent years ethnoarchaeological research has shown that the archaeological evidence from the late Pleistocene and the early Holocene can be interpreted in terms of changing social structures. It is more difficult to interpret the architectural evidence as reflecting seasonal activity or permanent settlement. In the Kebaran and Geometric Kebaran cultures, the remains of circular structures indicate the existence of flimsy huts or tents, and small sites generally represent single families. The large Natufian base camps reflect the agglomeration of several families into communities whose houses were close to each other. Structures continue to be circular and to be built of undressed stones and organic substances. Clay and plaster are first used in the Natufian period.

The circular shape of the buildings, the spaces between them, and the groupings into small and large villages are characteristic features of the Pre-Pottery Neolithic A period (the Sultanian culture). Cobbles and slabs continue to be exploited and unbaked plano-convex mud bricks are used extensively. The plaster found in many of the structures is made of a mixture of lime and clay. Jericho is an example of a large community which accommodated a number of clans that subsisted on agriculture, hunting, gathering and trade.

During the Pre-Pottery Neolithic B period, social changes are represented by the transition to square or rectangular (orthogonal) houses. The construction materials are cobblestones and mud bricks, used together or separately, with plaster for paving the floors. Basin-shaped hearths are set into the floors.

In this period we find buildings that were probably used as shrines or other cultic practices (Jericho, Beidha).

The transition to pit dwellings and flimsy huts in the Pottery Neolithic period is explained by the change in the social system — the shift from sedentary village life to an existence based on seasonal migrations and reliance on agriculture, hunting, and herding flocks. Sites from this period are scattered all over Israel, including the Negev. This change is considered to have been the result of an economic crisis caused by a severe change of climate at the beginning of the Atlantic period (the early sixth millennium B.C.).

DOMESTIC ARCHITECTURE OF THE CHALCOLITHIC PERIOD[1]

Yosef Porath

Introduction

In the Chalcolithic period a variety of installations were used as dwellings, all of them in conformity with environmental conditions and cultural patterns. Natural shelters (caves and rock shelters) in many cases were improved by their inhabitants by quarrying or by constructing walls and partitions. Temporary structures (huts, tents, and pens), were made of perishable materials, and subterranean dwellings (caves or deep pits) were dug out.[2] But the most common dwellings were houses made of stone, bricks or a combination of the two, built above the ground.

Only scattered and unclear remains have survived of the temporary structures, owing to the perishable nature of their building materials. Nature provided the natural shelters and determined their form, and few traces of construction by their inhabitants, who tried to improve these shelters, have been preserved.[3]

1. The term Chalcolithic used throughout this paper refers to the Ghassulian-Beersheba phase of the Chalcolithic period.
2. These were uncovered mainly in the loess soil zones of the northern Negev (cf. *EAEHL* I, pp. 152–159) where soil and climate enabled such constructions. For a criticism of Perrot's ideas cf. the recent article by I. Gilead (below, n. 4). The present writer shares Gilead's ideas. J. Kaplan claims that some of the Chalcolithic caves cut in the *kurkar* sandstone at Tel Aviv, which he excavated, were used for dwellings (J. Kaplan: The Chalcolithic and Neolithic Settlements at Tel Aviv and its Surroundings, Unpublished Ph.D. dissertation, Hebrew University, Jerusalem (Hebrew). It is not clear from this preliminary publication whether these caves were used primarily for dwellings or if this was a secondary use of burial caves for storage and/or dwellings. Dwellings in caves dug into *kurkar* sandstone are uncommon in the coastal plain of Israel, in contrast to the many burial caves, as at Palmahim, Azor, Tel Aviv, Benei Beraq, Giv'atayim, Ma'abarot, Hadera, etc.).
3. Y. Govrin: Horvat Hor, a Dwelling Cave from the Chalcolithic Period in the Northern Negev, *Mitekufat Haeven* 20 (1987), pp. 119*–127*.

The subterranean dwellings were confined to the northern Negev, where the combination of climatic conditions and soil type enabled the settlers to excavate pits and live in them.[4] The most satisfactory form of dwelling, and the most suitable for the way of life led by the permanent settlers in the Chalcolithic period, was the stone and brick house. The materials for its construction were readily obtainable, it could be erected quickly and easily, and its plan adapted to the needs, customs and way of life of the owners. This solid structure could provide a comfortable shelter from the region's climatic conditions.

Numerous sites settled during the Chalcolithic period have been discovered in archaeological excavations and surveys throughout the country. At several sites the remains of houses, some with a complete, clear plans, were discovered. Despite different local conditions (climate, soil, rock formation, and vegetation), their basic plan was similar: a large, usually rectangular or trapezoidal structure that contained a courtyard with one or more rooms attached. All the rooms are broad-rooms in design, i.e. the entrance was in the middle of a long wall.

Houses Recovered in Excavations

Teleilat el-Ghassul. — In the complicated architectural plan of the settlement excavated at Teleilat el-

4. On the use of the subterranean structures and dugouts in the loess soil of the northern Negev for storage and/or as pits for domestic use, see: I. Gilead: A New Look at Chalcolithic Beer-Sheba, *BA* 50 (1987), pp. 110–117; *idem*, The Economic Basis of Chalcolithic Settlements in the Northern Negev, *Michmanim* 3 (1987), pp. 17–30 (Hebrew). For the uncomfortable winter conditions prevailing in the Beersheba subterranean dugouts at Newe-Noy (Bir es-Safadi), see: Y. Baumgarten and I. Eldar: Newe-Noy, A Chalcolithic Site near Beer-Sheva, *Qadmoniot* 16 (1984), pp. 51–56 (Hebrew).

Ghassul,[5] several architectural units of similar plan can be distinguished. They consist of a large rectangular or trapezoidal structure subdivided into unequal parts by a wall running parallel to one of the short outer walls, at a distance of 2–4 m. The overall length of these units was 12–15 m.; the width was 5–8 m. or more. The first excavators at Ghassul defined these units as two-room houses: one large room (5–8 x 8–12 m.) and a small one (2–4 x 5–8 m.). It would have been impossible to roof the large space, according to the excavators, with the wooden beams that were available to the Ghassulian settlers in the Chalcolithic period. Pillars would have been required to support such a roof, but no pillars have been discovered in the excavations. On the other hand, the narrow side space, measuring only 2–4 m., could have been roofed without any additional support. It is therefore suggested that these units were houses in which the larger space served as a courtyard and the smaller one as a broad-room. Examples of such units are represented by Nos. 2, 15 and 16 (Fig. 1:1), 25 and 26 (Fig. 1:2), 29 Fig. 1:3), 38 and 39, and several others excavated in Stratum IV at Teleilat 1,[6] or Units 15, 32, 113 and 114 and others in Stratum IVA at Teleilat 3.[7] No complete house plan was distinguished in the later excavations conducted by R. North and J. B. Hennessy,[8] although the building remains appear to correspond with the reconstruction proposed here.[9]

The location of the installations inside the houses at Ghassul was uniform. The hearths were always in the courtyard (probably because of the smoke), as were most of the silos. There were hardly any

installations in the rooms, except simple ones such as shelves, storage jars, paved areas, etc.[10]

The entrance to the rooms was in the centre of the long wall.[11] The openings were closed by doors that turned on a post. The door sockets — wherever they have been preserved — were sunk into the floor on the inside of the right-hand door jamb, as in Rooms 32 and 42.[12]

Meser. — Stratum III at Meser, which was assigned to the Chalcolithic period (Ghassulian stage), contained a rectangular building whose outer dimensions were approximately 6 x 13 m. The excavator described it as a two-room house, with a large room (B13) occupying most of the area and a smaller room (B15) attached at its western end.[13] The building should be seen as a typical Chalcolithic 'house', with a courtyard (B13) and a broad-room (B15) at its western end (Fig. 1:4). No traces of doors or household installations were uncovered.

Beersheba. — The uppermost strata at Chalcolithic sites in the Beersheba region revealed foundations of oblong structures. As they were badly damaged by erosion, no complete plan could be established in detail.

Rectangular structures were excavated by Dothan in Stratum I at Horvat Beter,[14] by Perrot in Stratum IV at Tell Abu Matar[15] and in Stratum IV at Bir es-Safadi.[16] Two building phases could be distinguished in the upper stratum at each of these sites.[17] Most of the rectangular structures at the Beersheba sites are quite small, with average dimensions of only 3 x 7 m., although some reach a length of 15 m.[18] The longer structures are divided into a courtyard and an adjoining room at its narrow end, similar to

5. *Ghassul* I, Fig. 12; *Ghassul* II, Plans I, II
6. *Ghassul* I, Fig. 12.
7. *Ghassul* II, Plans I, II
8. J.B. Hennessy: Preliminary Report on a First Season of Excavations at Teleilat Ghassul, *Levant* I (1969), pp. 1–24; R. North: *Ghassul 1960, Excavation Report* [Analecta Biblica 14], Rome, 1960.
9. North (above n. 8), pp. 23–25, n. 104, wondered how the roofing of spaces 5 m. long, or greater, was carried out. He suggested that the rows of stone-lined pits, uncovered along the long wall in the larger space of such structures and called by him 'orthostat bins', should be considered as column bases despite their position. The explanation of these installations simply as bins or silos along the wall of the courtyard (larger space) of the typical Chalcolithic house at Ghassul is preferred. Hennessy (above, n. 8), p. 5 points out that in some buildings there was evidence of a row of columns along the central long axis, but he does not give a plan. The writer suggests that in the few cases where the larger spaces had column bases (if these are indeed column bases) they supported the pillars of a partly roofed courtyard.
10. For a list of installations see *Ghassul* I, pp. 44–47; *Ghassul* II, pp. 27–33

11. *Ghassul* I, Fig. 12; *Ghassul* II, Plans I, II.
12. The entrance to Room 32 (*Ghassul* II, Plan II) is located in the eastern part of the room, and not in the centre. But in this particular room, the entrance is in the centre of the freestanding wall, as it is observed from outside the building.
13. M. Dothan: Excavations at Meser 1957, *IEJ* 9 (1959), p. 14, Fig. 2.
14. M. Dothan: Excavations at Horvat Beter (Beersheba), *'Atiqot* (English Series) 2 (1959), pp. 3–5, Fig. 3.
15. J. Perrot: Excavations at Tell Abu Matar, Near Beersheba, *IEJ* 5 (1955), p. 74, Pl. 10:A; *idem*, Structures d'habitat, mode de vie et environment: les villages souterrains des pasteurs de Beersheva, dans le sud d'Israel, au IVe millénaire avant l'ere chretienne, *Paleorient* 10 (1984), pp. 75–96.
16. J. Perrot: Beersheba: Bir es-Safadi (Notes and News), *IEJ* 6 (1956), p. 126; *idem* (above, n. 2), p. 153, Photo p. 155; *idem* (above, n. 13, 1984).
17. Dothan (above, n. 14); Perrot (above, n. 15, 1984), Fig. 6; *idem* (above, n. 16).
18. Perrot (above, n. 2); *idem* (above, n. 13, 1984), Figs. 6, 11, Pl. IV.

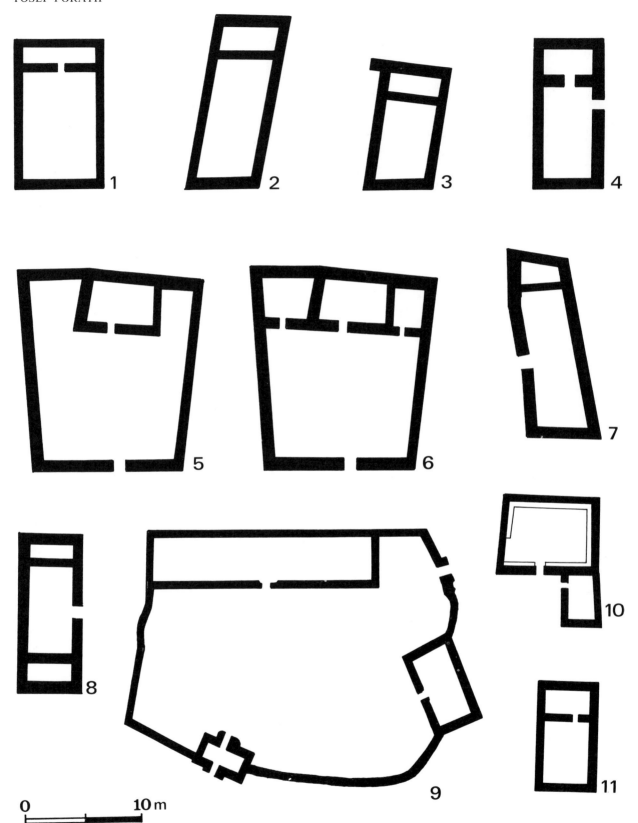

1. Chalcolithic Buildings: 1-3) Teleilat el-Ghassul (Transjordan); 4) Meser; 5-6) Fasa'el; 7-8) Golan Heights; 9) 'En Gedi (Temple); 10) Arad; 11) Beisamun. *Atiqot* 17 (1985), p. 15, Fig. 7.

the Chalcolithic 'houses' at Ghassul and Meser.[19] The smaller structures are apparently single rooms without an attached courtyard.

The limited number of well-preserved buildings and the preliminary nature of the publications do not enable a detailed reconstruction of the plans of these buildings.[20] Only one or two stone courses of the walls have survived, which may have served as foundations for a brick superstructure. This evidence may explain why doorways were found in only a few structures. A doorway with a socket for the door pivot was uncovered at Tell Abu Matar. The socket was found inside the right-hand door jamb. At the foot of the left-hand door jamb was another stone with a hole, which was probably intended to receive a vertical door bolt.[21] The floor of this room was lower than the floor level outside, and the threshold served as a step.

Shiqmim. — Several rectangular buildings, measuring 3–4 x 6–8 m., were excavated at Shiqmim (*ca.* 18 km. west of the Beersheba sites on the north bank of Nahal Beersheba.[22] It seems that most of these buildings were houses composed of only one room without a walled courtyard, similar to those uncovered at nearby Beersheba.

Fasa'el. — The well-preserved building excavated at Fasa'el is a typical example of the Chalcolithic house.[23] In its earliest stage, it consisted of a large courtyard and one broad-room that occupied part of its western side (Fig. 1:5). Later the space on either side of the room was enclosed and the building was turned into a three-room house (Fig. 1:6). The rooms were broad-rooms.[24] Their floor level was lower than that of the courtyard, which was again lower than the living surface outside, as the building had been erected in a purposely-excavated shallow pit. This is clearly attested in the outer walls; the foundation course of the outer face is higher than the corresponding course of the inner face. The walls of the house were built to their full height with limestone cemented with mud. The entrances to the rooms and the courtyard were uniformly arranged in the middle of the long walls; the thresholds also served as steps leading down into the room, and a socket for the door pivot was on the inner side of the right-hand jamb. At Fasa'el, as at Ghassul, a silo and a hearth are located in the courtyard. Most of the stone bowls and grinding stones were unearthed in the rooms, but a few were found near the walls of the courtyard.

Golan. — The largest number of private houses with complete ground plans, were explored and excavated by C. Epstein on the Golan.[25] More than twenty settlements are known to have existed there in the Chalcolithic period, mostly on the basalt plateau of central Golan. The houses were built according to a unified architectural concept and have similar plans. They all are rectangular, measuring on the average 5 x 15 m., and usually subdivided into a large courtyard and a broad-room on its narrow or longitudinal side (Fig. 1:7).[26] In some cases there were two broad-rooms arranged around the courtyard in any combination (two on each narrow side, one on the narrow side and another on the long side, two on the same narrow side, etc., Fig. 1:8).[27] No fences or other courtyards,

19. Like the building in the right lower corner of the photograph of Stratum IV at Tell Abu Matar, Perrot (above, n. 15), Pl. 10:A. The poorly preserved foundations of the large building uncovered at Bir es-Safadi also point to its subdivision into a larger courtyard and a smaller room on its side (the poor remains of the partition wall are observed in the lower picture of this building, Perrot (above, n. 15), Pl. IV:1.
20. Dothan (above, n. 14, pp. 3–5, Fig. 3) describes the building at H. Beter Stratum I as one architectural unit composed of Rooms 3, 4, 5, 9. Examination of the width of the stone foundations of these rooms and their bottom levels indicates that they belong to two different building phases in a poor state of preservation. Dothan mentioned the existence of two building phases in Stratum I (above, n. 14, p. 3). The same is true of other Chalcolithic sites at Beersheba (above, n. 17).
21. The excavator assumed that this hole served as a socket for the second door in the entrance (Perrot, above, n. 15, 1955, p. 74, Pl. 11:A). This assumption is unfounded. In the photograph, the difference can easily be observed between the round door socket on the right side of the opening with abrasion resulting from use, and the almost vertical hole, without any abrasion, on the left side of the opening. We suggest that this vertical hole was used for the vertical door bolt. As seen in the photograph which lacks a scale, the distance between the two stones with holes (door socket and bolt hole, as suggested) is less than twice the width of the wall, which is usually about 80 cm. For such an opening there is no need for a two-leaved door, compare: Y. Porath: A Chalcolithic Building at Fasa'el, *'Atiqot* (English Series) 17 (1985), p. 4, Fig. 2.
22. T.E. Levy (ed.): *Shiqmim I* [B.A.R. International Series 356], Oxford, 1987.
23. Y. Porath (above, n. 21), pp. 1–19.
24. One of the rooms (L. 214, i.e. the right one in Fig. 6) is in fact a long-room according to its dimensions, but these dimensions were created as a result of closing in the space between the original room and the courtyard.
25. C. Epstein: The Chalcolithic Culture of the Golan, *BA* 40 (1977), pp. 57–62; *idem,* A New Aspect of Chalcolithic Culture of the Golan, *EI* 15 (1981), pp. 15–19 (Hebrew); *idem,* Chalcolithic Settlements Patterns and House Plans in the Golan, *Michmanim* 3 (1987), pp. 5–16 (Hebrew, English summary pp. 34–35).
26. Epstein (above, n. 25, 1987), Figs. 5, 6, 10:1, 2.
27. Epstein (above, n. 25, 1977), Fig. 2; *idem* (above, n. 25, 1987), Figs. 5, 6, 10:3.

aside from those incorporated in the houses, were found in any of these settlements. At several sites the houses were built one next to the other, touching on the narrow side, thus forming rows of four to six houses.[28] The numerous pottery jars, stone bowls and grinding stones discovered in the buildings attest that most domestic chores were done in the courtyard. A widespread feature in the Chalcolithic houses on the Golan, not encountered in houses elsewhere, was a stone shelf built along the long wall of the courtyard.[29]

'En Gedi. — The Chalcolithic enclosure discovered at 'En Gedi followed the same architectural principles that can be observed in the private houses. It was a polygonal building, composed of a large courtyard, a large broad-room (the shrine) on the western side, a broad-room on the northern side, and an entrance hall (architecturally a broad-room with two opposite doorways) on the eastern side (Fig. 1:9).[30] The doorways were constructed in an identical manner: they were located in the centre of the long wall, the stone-paved threshold was stepped, leading down into the rooms, (as the floor level of the rooms was lower than that of the courtyard), and the socket to hold the doorpost was located on the inner side of the right-hand doorjamb.

Fragmentary remains of rectangular structures from the Chalcolithic period, probably houses with a courtyard and a broad-room, have also been excavated at Wadi Rabah,[31] Teleilat Batashi,[32] Jamosin,[33] Gilat,[34] and elsewhere.

Architectural Details

The walls of the Chalcolithic houses were constructed of local material. In many cases the lower part of the wall was built of stone and the superstructure of mud brick (Ghassul, Beersheba, Gilat, 'En Gedi, Meser). In some houses, the walls were built entirely of brick without a stone foundation (Ghassul) or entirely of stone (Fasa'el and the Golan). The sun-dried mud bricks were made of local soil and box-shaped. They were made by hand, not shaped in a mould, as testified by the craftsman's fingerprints, so they are not uniform in size or shape. Some of the bricks are plano-convex in shape.[35]

The stones used for building were always local, and were apparently collected, not quarried. On the Golan large blocks of natural rock were used, either incorporated into the building at their original spot or brought from nearby. With the exception of the sockets for the doorposts, no dressed architectural elements have yet been discovered. The lack of proper stone-cutting and hewing tools may account for this.

Stone walls were usually built in two rows and the space between them was filled with pebbles and mud mortar. The walls were usually from 0.5–0.7 m. wide, so it is probable that they were no higher than 2–3 m. and carried only one storey.

The walls were coated on both faces with mud plaster. Several houses at Ghassul displayed a polychrome plastered wall decoration.[36] The dry climatic conditions at Ghassul were apparently responsible for the better preservation of polychrome mud plaster than at other sites. That climate was the major factor in preservation is also supported by a fragment of painted plaster discovered at 'En Gedi.[37] Wall plaster was renewed from time to time (yearly?) and repainted. In the small plaster fragment discovered at 'En Gedi three layers of decorated plaster could be distinguished. Several plaster layers also were noted at Ghassul, where both the plaster and the paintings had been renewed frequently. One fragment contained more than twenty layers of painting.[38]

The floors of the houses were generally made of *terre pisé*, without any special preparation (directly on the natural surface at one-stratum sites or on the occupational debris at multi-strata sites). Stone pavings were often laid in special areas, such as next to doorways, and in working or cooking areas. Some

28. C. Epstein: Golan 1977 (Notes and News), *IEJ* 28 (1978), p. 116, Fig. 1; *idem* (above, n. 25, 1987), Figs. 5–6.
29. C. Epstein: Golan (Notes and News), *IEJ* 23 (1973), Pl. 64:B; *idem*, Golan (Notes and News), *IEJ* 25 (1975), Pl. 21:D; *idem* (above, n. 25, 1978), Fig. 2: A.
30. D. Ussishkin: The Ghassulian Shrine at En-Gedi, *Tel Aviv* 7 (1980), pp. 1–44.
31. J. Kaplan: Excavations at Wadi Rabah, *IEJ* 8 (1958), p. 153, Figs. 2, 3.
32. J. Kaplan: Excavations at Teluliot Batashi in the Vale of Sorek, *EI* 5 (1958), p. 12, Fig. 4 (Hebrew).
33. J. Kaplan: The Archaeology and History of Tel Aviv–Jaffa, Tel-Aviv 1959, p. 32 (Hebrew).
34. D. Alon: A Chalcolithic Temple at Gilat, *BA* 40 (1977), pp. 63–65.

35. *Ghassul* I, Pls. 55–57, 66–72. Such bricks were also uncovered in a Chalcolithic rectangular structure at Tel Kittan (E. Eisenberg, personal communication).
36. *Ghassul* I, pp. 129–143; *Ghassul* II, pp. 32–37, Pls. II, V; Hennessy (above, n. 8), p. 7. The structures in which polychrome plaster was uncovered display the common architectural plan and assemblage, and do not bear any sign of special use (i.e. ritual or other).
37. The painted plaster possibly coated some installation and not the wall, Ussishkin (above, n. 30), p. 12, Fig. 6, Pl. 3:10.
38. Hennessy (above, n. 8), p. 7.

houses had finer-quality floors, where the top layer was a different material, such as beaten lime ('En Gedi)[39] or mud brick (Gilat).[40] The Golan houses have larger paved sections compared with other sites. This is not surprising as there are many exposed basalt surfaces in the Golan, and it is difficult to dig the foundation pit for the house.[41]

Typically, floors of Chalcolithic houses, regardless of their building material, were covered with a thick accumulation of occupational debris containing a large amount of ashes, decomposed organic material, potsherds, discarded stone implements, bones and other food remains. It seems as if refuse was not removed from the houses in the Chalcolithic period, so that the occupation level rose continuously during use.

There is little information concerning the roofs of Chalcolithic houses and their form is a subject of disagreement among scholars. Remains at Ghassul[42] and 'En Gedi[43] indicate that the roofs were composed of a layer of mud laid over a substructure of branches and reeds and supported by wooden posts. These remains, however, provide no indication of the roof's shape — whether it was flat, inclined, gabled or rounded.

Nevertheless, it is reasonable to assume that the roof was flat or slightly inclined. The archaeological evidence does not support the conjecture that it was gabled or rounded, like the pottery ossuaries of the period. The width of the dwelling rooms in Chalcolithic houses was only 2–4 m.; a short enough span that wooden beams could be laid from wall to wall, with a horizontal or inclined layer of branches and reeds over them. No traces have been found of pillars to support roofs, and it is doubtful that the technology existed in the Chalcolithic period to construct a frame of wooden beams strong enough to bear the weight of a mud-brick gabled or rounded roof without pillars for support. Considerable use of the saw and the means to securely fasten the material (nails) would have been required. There is corroboration of the proposal that the roof of the Chalcolithic house was flat in the model of a flat-roofed house found at Arad (from the Early Bronze Age).[44]

The Functional Arrangement of the Chalcolithic House

As was already noted, the Chalcolithic house was composed of an open courtyard and one or more rooms on its narrow side. Was this division purely architectural or did it also reflect functional purposes? The objects and installations discovered in the various parts of the house can help to answer this question.[45] Apparently the courtyard was utilized as a kitchen, dining room, pantry, storeroom and balcony. The occupants apparently spent the day there and used the room mainly as the sleeping quarter.

From the size of the Chalcolithic house, it can be assumed that it was the home of a single nuclear family, and that the extended family occupied a group of similar houses arranged around a central courtyard[47] or built in a row.[47]

The Origin and Heritage of the Chalcolithic House

Houses with broad-rooms have a long tradition in Palestine, and the Chalcolithic house does not appear to be the earliest example of the broad-room. Rectangular houses have been discovered at sites bearing pre-Ghassulian ceramic cultures, such as Tel 'Eli[48] and Wadi Rabah,[49] as well as Pre-Pottery Neolithic sites: Beisamun (Fig.1:11),[50] Munhata,[51] Jericho,[52] and Nahal Oren.[53] Very little

39. Ussishkin (above, n. 30), p. 14.
40. Alon (above, n. 34).
41. Epstein 1981, Fig. 2 (above, n. 25).
42. North (above, n. 8), p. 5; Hennessy (above, n. 8), p. 21.
43. Ussishkin (above, n. 30), p. 13.
44. *Arad*, Pls. 66, 115.

45. See the list of installations at Ghassul (*Ghassul* I, pp. 44–47; *Ghassul* II, pp. 27–33), Golan (above, n. 25) and Fasa'el (above, n. 21).
46. *Ghassul* I, Fig. 12, 'Rooms' Nos. 1, 12–28.
47. Epstein (above, n. 28), p. 116, Fig. 1.
48. M.W. Prausnitz: Tel 'Eli (Kh. esh-Sheikh 'Ali) (Notes and News), *IEJ* 10 (1960), p. 120.
49. Kaplan (above, n. 31).
50. At Beisamun a rectangular building was uncovered, measuring *ca.* 4 x 8 m., divided into a larger (4 x 5 m.) and a smaller part (2.2 x 4 m.), J. Perrot: Beisamoun in the Hula Valley, *Qadmoniot* 8 (1975), p. 115, Plan p. 115, Photo p. 116 (Hebrew). We suggest that the larger part was the courtyard. The hearth found there indicates that it was not roofed, that is, it was not a room, as suggested by the excavators. The smaller part is a typical broad-room and not a corridor. The floor of this small broad-room is lower than that of the courtyard. The building uncovered at Beisamun should probably be considered an early prototype of the house comprising a courtyard and a broad-room, typical of the Chalcolithic and Early Bronze periods.
51. J. Perrot: La troisieme campagne de fouilles a Munhata (1964), *Syria* 43 (1966), pp. 50–52, Fig. 2, Pl. ? .
52. J. Garstang and J.B.E. Garstang: *The Story of Jericho*, 1940, pp. 47–49, Fig. 5.
53. Tamar Noy, A.J. Legge and E.S. Higgs: Recent Excavations at Nahal Oren, Israel, *PPS* 39 (1973), pp. 78–79, Fig. 3.

information, however, is available at present on the architecture of houses of the pre-Ghassulian periods, so that no conclusions can be reached. It should, nevertheless, be stressed that houses with broad-rooms are typical of the architectural tradition of Palestine in the Chalcolithic period and are not encountered in neighbouring lands.[54]

Early Bronze Age houses are well-known as examples of broad-room architecture (Fig.1:10).[55] Chalcolithic and EB houses have a number of architectural features in common:

1. The rooms are broad-rooms.
2. The floor level of the rooms is lower than that of the surrounding level.
3. The doorways have stepped thresholds that lead down into the room.
4. The doorways are closed by doors that open inward.

Side by side with these common elements are differences in floor plans:

1. Compared to the spacious courtyards of the Chalcolithic period, the Early Bronze Age courts are small and in many cases are absent altogether. At early Arad, for example, several houses shared one courtyard.[56] It seems that the smallness of the courtyard was due to EB settlements having been encircled by a city-wall.
2. The rooms are larger in EB houses. Thus it was necessary to support the roof with pillars, whose bases have been discovered in excavations.
3. EB houses are equipped with benches built along the walls, which are lacking in most of the Chalcolithic houses.
4. In Chalcolithic houses the sockets of the door pivots are located on the right-hand side of the door, while in EB houses they appear on the left-hand side.[57]

The similarities between the houses of the Chalcolithic period and those of the Early Bronze Age are much greater than the differences, so that the houses can be considered to share the same architectural tradition. The differences noted here are of secondary importance and derive mainly from the social and technological evolution that accompanied the transition from an open settlement to a fortified one.

Ossuaries and the Form of the Chalcolithic House

The discussion of the architecture of the Chalcolithic period would be incomplete without dealing with ossuaries, as some scholars consider that certain ossuary types reflect the form of houses in that period.

One burial method in the Chalcolithic period was secondary interment in caves.[58] In the first stage, the body of the deceased was set aside until its flesh decayed. The bones were then collected in receptacles known as ossuaries, and placed in burial caves. Caves of this type have been examined mainly on the coastal plain and in the Shephelah.[59] A variety of materials was used for producing ossuaries. Most ossuaries were made of pottery (Fig. 2), a small number of stone. Excavations at undisturbed burial caves revealed secondary burials without any ossuary, that look like heaps of bones, especially in the upper phases of the caves.[60] It is possible that organic material (straw, cloth, woven branches, animal skins), was used to prepare an ossuary which later totally decomposed. Stone ossuaries are uniform in shape: a chest with

54. A. Kempinski: The Sin Temple at Khafaje and the En-Gedi Temple, *IEJ* 22 (1972), pp. 14–15; V. Muller: Types of Mesopotamian Houses: Studies in Oriental Archaeology III, *JAOS* 60 (1940), pp. 151–180; *idem*, Development of the 'Megaron' in Prehistoric Greece, *AJA* 48 (1944), pp. 342–348.

55. A. Ben-Tor, (Chap. 7, pp. 60–67).

56. *Arad*, pp. 10–11, Fig. 1.

57. This is true not only for houses uncovered in Palestine but also in Sinai, see I. Beit-Arieh, (Chap. 9, pp. 81–84).; *idem*, An Early Bronze Age II Site at Nabi Saleh in Southern Sinai, *Tel-Aviv* 1 (1974), p. 149, Pl. 26:2.

58. Other methods used in Palestine include the articulated burials of mostly young and premature infants under house floors, as at Ghassul (*Ghassul* I, pp. 48–49, Pls. 24–25; *Ghassul* II, pp. 15, 36, pls. 17, 22, 24, 29) and Beersheba (J. Perrot: The Excavations at Tell Abu Matar, near Beersheba, *IEJ* 5 (1955), pp. 26, 76, 173–174; articulated burials in cists excavated at Adeimah (M. Stekelis: *Les monuments chalcolithiques de Palestine*, Paris, 1935); or secondary burials (mostly collections of bones, but some in ossuaries) in the necropolis of Shiqmim (T.E. Levy and D. Alon: *The Chalcolithic Mortuary Site near Mezad Aluf* [BASOR Supplement Series 23], Cambridge, Mass., 1985, pp. 121–135, or summarizing data, see C. Elliot: The Religious Beliefs of the Ghassulians, *PEQ* 109 (1977), pp. 20–23.

59. Some scholars suggest that these cemeteries served for deceased persons brought from a long distance (i.e. shepherds migrating seasonally from the Beersheba region to the coastal plain (see J. Perrot: Une tombe a ossuaires du IVe millenaire a Azor pres de Tel-Aviv, *'Atiqot* (English Series) 3 (1961), p. 27); this theory is rejected by others, including the present writer. The discovery of the Shiqmim necropolis (above, n. 58) disproves the theory that skeletons were transported from the Negev to be buried in the coastal plain.

60. Such burials were uncovered at Azor (above, n. 59), Haderah (E.L. Sukenik: A Chalcolithic Necropolis at Haderah, *JPOS* 17 (1937); and Ma'abarot (Y. Porath et al.: *Qadmoniot Emek Hepher*, Tel Aviv, 1985, pp. 185–192, (Hebrew).

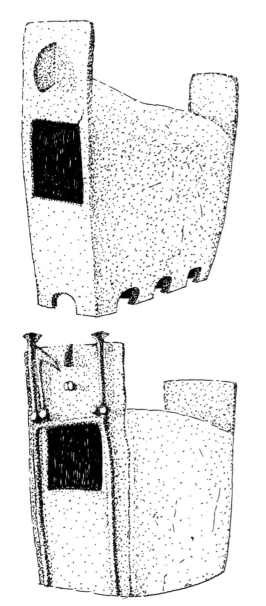

2. Chalcolithic ossuaries from Azor and Ben Shemen (drawing R. Reich)

modified for the purpose of burial — jars whose upper part has a special opening for inserting the bones, modified during the pottery-making process, before firing;[63] 3. rectangular chests open at the top;[64] and 4. rectangular chests with a top shaped like a rounded or gabled roof with an opening in the short side, generally named 'house-shaped' ossuaries.[65]

Despite their different shapes, all ossuary types share certain features: All have an opening wide enough to insert a skull and are long enough to hold the longest human bone, the thigh bone. Since their discovery by E. L. Sukenik, most scholarly interest has been concentrated on the house-shaped ossuaries because of their unique shape. Statistical study shows that less than one-fourth of the total number of the dead buried in the caves were interred in house-shaped ossuaries.[66] Sukenik, and others, suggested that the house-shaped ossuary was a small-scale model of the typical house of the Chalcolithic period.[67] Still other scholars claim that the ossuaries, because they are of unusual shapes, have no connection with the typical Chalcolithic house.[68] Some support for the latter view can perhaps be provided by the mud silos, used in rural areas of India[69] and Egypt,[70] that are similar in shape to ossuaries.

Sukenik's proposal was apparently based on the assumption that the oblong building discovered at

63. Like those uncovered at Azor (above, n. 59), Fig. 35; Benei Beraq (J. Kaplan: Excavations at Benei-Beraq, 1951, *IEJ* 13 [1963], Fig. 4:10); Ben-Shemen (above, n. 61), Pl. XII:2, 13; Giv'atayim (above, n. 61), Fig. 4:4.
64. Such as the ones from Haderah (above, n. 60), pp. 19–20, Fig. 35, Pl. II:1–2; Ma'abarot (above, n. 60), Fig. 78.
65. Ossuaries of this shape were uncovered at Haderah (above, n. 60), pp. 20–21, Figs. 4–5, Pls. II:3–4; III; Benei-Beraq (above n. 61, Ory) Figs. 4–5, and (above, n. 63), Fig. 3; Giv'atayim (above, n. 61), Fig. 4:5–6; Azor (above, n. 59), pp. 9–13, Figs. 7–9, 21–26; Palmahim (R. Gophna and S. Lifshitz: A Chalcolithic Burial Cave at Palmahim, *'Atiqot* [English Series] 14 [1980]), Fig. 3:2–3).
66. This number does not include burials without any stone or pottery ossuaries ('organic ossuaries', p. 46 above).
67. Sukenik (above, n. 60); Perrot (above, n. 54), pp. 28–32, Fig. 18.
68. B.A. Martin: Chalcolithic Ossuaries and 'Houses for the Dead', *PEQ* 97 (1965), pp. 153–160.
69. R. Singh: Granaries from Clay and Dung, *National Geographic* 151 (1977), pp. 238–239. I wish to thank E. Ayalon for drawing my attention to this reference.
70. In Egyptian villages, many silos and other installations made of clay and dung are of similar shape to 'box-shaped' and 'house-shaped' ossuaries (personal observation). It seems that this phenomenon is popular in primitive cultures of the great river valleys.

an opening at the top through which the bones were inserted.[61] Pottery ossuaries appear in a variety of forms: 1. large kraters and jars identical to everyday vessels found in the settlements;[62] 2. everyday vessels,

61. Like stone ossuaries from Benei Beraq (J. Ory: A Chalcolithic Necropolis at Benei Beraq, *QDAP* 12 [1946], Fig. 5); Azor (above, n. 59), Fig. 16:42); Ben-Shemen (J. Perrot: Les ossuaires de Ben Shemen, *EI* 8 [1967], pp. 46*–49*, Pl. XII:1); Giv'atayim (V. Sussman and S. Ben-Aryeh: A Necropolis at Giv'atayim, *'Atiqot* (Hebrew Series) 3 [1967], Fig. 5 [Hebrew]).
62. Like the ones found at Haderah (above, n. 60), Ma'abarot (above, n. 60), Figs. 74–75, Giv'atayim (above, n. 61), Pl. 4:1.

Ghassul were 'long-houses' composed of two rooms. As has been explained above, however, the evidence from Ghassul and other sites subsequently excavated, proves that this theory is erroneous. The Chalcolithic house is of the broad-room type while the house-shaped ossuaries resemble the long-room house type. The details of the ornamentation on the fronts of the ossuaries are of cultic and symbolic significance and are not only structural elements.[71] Thus, at present,

there is neither direct nor indirect evidence to support the theory that the house-shaped ossuary is a model of the Chalcolithic house.[72]

Summary

Chalcolithic houses excavated in Palestine have a long architectural tradition and a distinctive form. In shape — a broad-room with a courtyard — and function, they conform with the way of life and social needs of the period. Despite regional differences in the material culture of the Chalcolithic period in Palestine, the basic plan of the Chalcolithic house is uniform throughout the country. Any resemblance between the Chalcolithic house and the house-shaped pottery ossuaries, or any of their decorative details, is apparently mere chance and for the time being is not demonstrated by the archaeological record.

71. The schematic reconstruction of a Chalcolithic house made by Perrot (above, n. 59), pp. 30–32, Fig. 18, does not share details with most of the house-shaped ossuaries, and certainly not with the houses uncovered by archaeological excavations. The ornaments on ossuary frontons resemble these on the crowns and standards found in the 'Cave of the Treasure' in the Judean Desert (P. Bar-Adon: *The Cave of the Treasure*, Jerusalem, 1972, items Nos. 7, 23, 25, 33, 34, 41, 48, 98, 99 and others) and the basalt pillar figures from the Golan (C. Epstein: Aspects of Symbolism in Chalcolithic Palestine, in R. Moorey and P. Parr (eds.): *Archaeology in the Levant, Essays for Kathleen Kenyon*, Warminster, 1978, pp. 22–35). Similar knobs, seen by Perrot to symbolize wooden logs, also decorate many aspects of Chalcolithic culture, J. Perrot: *BASOR* 229 (1978), Figs. 2:c,e, 5:a).

72. In his lecture at the Ninth Archaeological Congress in Israel (21st April, 1982), Perrot reconsidered his original theory that the house-shaped ossuary reflects the shape of the Chalcolithic house.

THE EARLY AND INTERMIDIATE
BRONZE AGE

INTRODUCTION: THE EARLY BRONZE AGE

Amnon Ben-Tor

The Early Bronze Age I, one of the most significant and critical eras in the history of Palestine, is the subject of sharp disagreement as it is shrouded in mystery. Scholarly debate centres on the definition of the character of the period: Was it a continuation of the Chalcolithic Age, or did it mark the inception of the Bronze Age? Or should the Early Bronze Age I be subdivided into periods and distributed between the Chalcolithic and the Early Bronze Ages? As a result of the disagreement among scholars, a variety of names and chronological limits have been assigned to the period. Without addressing these major differences of opinion, it is possible to maintain that during the Early Bronze Age I a process was set in motion whose results affected the political organization of Palestine for the following 2,000 years — from the beginning of the EB II until the beginning of the first millennium B.C.

The culture of the Chalcolithic period was primarily one of villagers, nomads, and seminomads who inhabited the semiarid areas of Palestine and subsisted mainly on pasturage. By contrast, in the EB II there were permanent settlements on the coastal plain, in the valleys, and in the central mountainous region, and the livelihood of the inhabitants was based on a Mediterranean economy. The basic social unit was the city and its satellites. Although a consideration of the nature and history of the urbanization of Palestine is beyond this discussion, apparently its origins lie in the EB I. The period was marked by infiltration into new areas and by the adoption of a Mediterranean economy; its key settlements were to become the principal 'future' settlements in Palestine: Jericho, Bet Shean, Megiddo, Bet Yerah, Tell el-Far'ah (North), Hazor, 'Ai, Gezer, and others.

The identification of the initiators of this shift in settlement and economic patterns is the subject of sharp scholarly debate: Was the change in lifestyle initiated by the influx of new populations into Palestine — and if so, from where, or was it the result of internal developments? Regardless of the answer, the archaeological evidence clearly demonstrates that during this period Palestine maintained close ties with its neighbours: in the north with Syria, and via Syria with northern Mesopotamia, and in the south, increasingly, with Egypt — ties that persisted in the EB II.

It is here that the question of whether those foreign ties influenced the contemporary architecture of dwellings in Palestine arises. Apparently, the answer is negative, unless foreign origins can be found in the future for the apsidal building plan that appeared at several sites during the period. On the other hand, clear evidence for the continuity of local building traditions exists in the architectural type known as the Arad House, the single-room broadhouse. The broadhouse is known from several Chalcolithic sites (Ghassul, Meser, and sites on the Golan Heights), and continues into the EB II-III strata. The intermediate link is the EB I double temple at Megiddo, constructed according to the same architectural principle, and closely related to the Chalcolithic temple at 'En Gedi. The broadhouse principle of construction, known from both temples and houses, is unmistakably local in origin. Its consolidation began during the Chalcolithic Age, when it became the dominant but not single, principle of construction in Palestine, lasting until the end of the Early Bronze Age.

The consolidation of urban culture in Palestine reached its peak in the EB II-III. Whereas the EB I had been a tumultuous period, this relatively long time span of approximately 700-800 years was characterized by stability and conservatism, demonstrated in its architecture, pottery, and other aspects of its material culture. However, it is not possible to conclude from this that the period was peaceful; in fact, the archaeological remains include impressive fortifications, and more than a few sites show evidence of conflagration and destruction. Cities rose and fell, and some destroyed during the period remained abandoned for centuries. Although the cultural and political history of Palestine during this era largely remains a mystery, there is no indication of foreign invasion as the causative factor of the destruction. It is more likely that the unrest resulted from internal jockeying for supremacy among the cities of the land.

At the inception of the EB II, close ties, apparently commercial in nature, were still maintained between Canaan and Egypt. For reasons unknown to us, the ties were subsequently cut and not renewed for centuries. The focus of Egyptian commerce shifted to Syria, excluding Palestine. During the second half of the EB III (the Fifth—Sixth Dynasties in Egypt), several Egyptian forays for plunder into Palestine inflicted damage on several southern sites. Concurrently, perhaps as a result of the break in ties with Egypt, closer relations developed between Palestine and the areas bordering it on the north. These relations reached their peak in the EB III. Ties clearly existed with Syria, with Anatolia via Syria, and perhaps with the Aegean sphere even farther to the west. However, it is doubtful that ties with Mesopotamia extended beyond sporadic indirect relations. The connection between immigration from the north and the appearance of Bet Yerah ware (i.e. 'Khirbet Kerak Ware') in Palestine remains a moot point: it could have resulted from commercial exchanges. Nevertheless, even if this ceramic family accompanied immigration, its appearance was not widespread and it had a very limited influence on the pottery of the indigenous population of Palestine.

Recently, the view that no clear-cut cultural break occurred in Palestine between the end of the EB IIIB and the Intermediate EB/MB has gained acceptance. It is now held that aspects of EB culture continue to be found in the following period.

Cultural conventions established in the Early Bronze Age governing pottery, burial, and — to a certain degree — village architecture continued to apply. However, a notable change occurred both in population distribution and socioeconomic cultural indicators; the urban lifestyle that characterised the Early Bronze Age gave way to a seminomadic and village culture. The seminomadic population, which apparently originated on the fringes of the urban society of Palestine and Transjordan in EB IIIB, was augmented by an influx of population that had ethnic and cultural ties with central Syria. This group brought with it 'Syrian' ceramic forms, as well as other Syrian items, and may have introduced northern architectural models as well. The chronological frame of this period is *ca.* 2250-2000 B.C. The synchronistic elements enabling the establishment of an absolute chronology are found in Syria (Tell Mardikh, Hama) and on the Lebanese coast (Byblos).

CHALCOLITHIC AND EARLY BRONZE AGE TEMPLES

Aharon Kempinski

Although in the Neolithic period deities were worshipped in closed buildings in Palestine, it is only from the Chalcolithic period onward that the plans of temples are clearly discernible.

The relationship between the congregation of worshippers and the place where the divine statue — or the cult object — was set up was an important architectural principle in the planning of these early temples. Indeed, in the first examples of cultic architecture two approaches are evident. In one, the divine statue stood on a pedestal or on the back section of the altar opposite the entrance, so that

worshippers and those officiating in the cult could see the holy image from the temple courtyard. In the other, which is not characteristic of the Syro-Palestinian region, the divine statue was so placed that those coming to worship or offer sacrifices had to make a ninety-degree turn in order to see the image. Temples with a direct, or straight-axis, entrance were the most common in the Early Bronze Age; those with an indirect, or bent-axis, entrance were rare and are found only toward the end of the period, apparently the result of Mesopotamian influence.

Some of the temples erected at the end of the

Tel Yarmut. Early Bronze Age II temple.

Megiddo. Early Bronze Age III temple.

Chalcolithic period and in the EB IA and IB resemble private dwellings, making their identification difficult where finds do not indicate cultic use. However, some temples were more impressive and are therefore more easily identifiable. This resemblance between the house of the god and the houses of men underwent a gradual change during the EB II and III, when temples in Palestine were built either according to a plan borrowed from foreign sources or in a more monumental style.[1]

In Palestine, temples attributed to the Early Bronze Age are always of the broadhouse type. Even when the plan of the building was not of local character, the temple was built according to broadhouse proportions.[2] All the temples discussed

here are of the direct-entrance type, with the exception of the latest in the series of city-wall temples at 'Ai (Temple A).

The earliest temples uncovered in this country (Figs. 1, 2) are of the fenced enclosure type of which the 'En Gedi temple (Figs. 1, 13) is the most characteristic. The distinctive feature of this temple is its enclosed courtyard, which was entered through a well-built gateway. The worshipper approaching the gate from the southeast had to ascend a steep slope for the last twenty metres. The gateway led into a spacious, enclosed courtyard that had a sacred circular installation in the centre. The shrine's facade, which was apparently adorned with wall paintings,[3] was opposite the gateway. To the right of the shrine was a small structure whose function is unclear but may have served to house the priest or the temple equipment.

The shrine itself comprises a single cult chamber of the broadhouse type. Opposite the entrance stood a semi-circular altar, on which were placed the

1. For the problem of temple identification, see S. Yeivin: Temples that Were Not, *EI* 11 (1973), pp. 163–172 (Hebrew, English summary, p. 28*).

2. On this point see A. Ben-Tor: Plans of Dwellings and Temples in Early Bronze Age Palestine, *EI* 11 (1973), pp. 97–98 (Hebrew, (English summary, p. 25*); also Z. Herzog: Broadroom and Longroom House Type, *Tel Aviv* 7 (1980), pp. 86–88. As Herzog suggests, architectural tradition, rather than the angle at which the cult object was visible, seems to have been of considerable importance in determining the proportions of length and width of the sacred structure.

3. D. Ussishkin: The Ghassulian Shrine at 'En-Gedi, *Tel Aviv* 7 (1980), pp. 1–44.

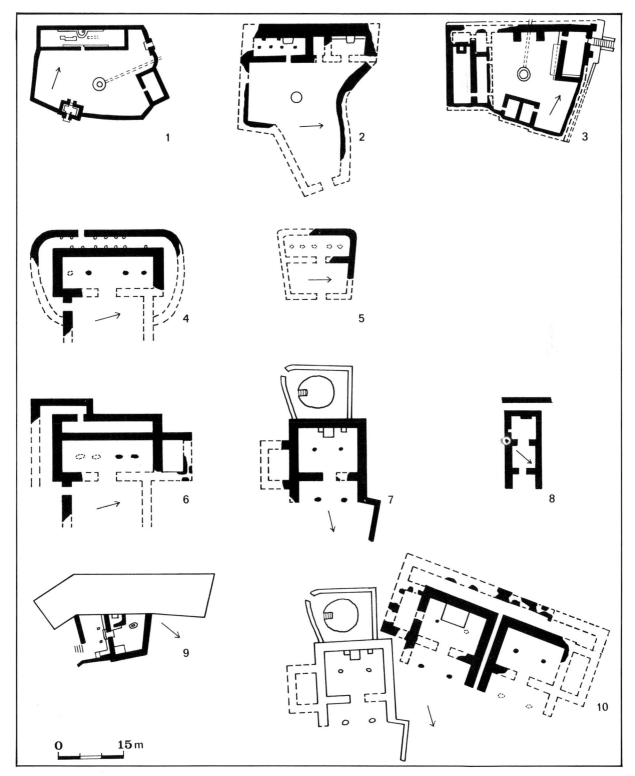

1. 'En Gedi. *IEJ* 22 (1972), p. 11, Fig. 1:A.   2. Megiddo Stratum XIX. *IEJ* 22 (1972), p. 11, Fig. 1:C.   3. Khafaje, Mesopotamia. *IEJ* 22 (1972), p. 11, Fig. 1:B.   4. 'Ai. *'Ay*, Pl. XCII.   5. Megiddo Stratum XVIII. *Megiddo* II, Fig. 391.   6. 'Ai. *'Ay*, Pl. XCII; *BASOR* 178 (1965), p. 32, Fig. 12.   7. Megiddo Stratum XVI. *Megiddo* II, Figs. 393, 394.   8. Tell Huwara, Syria. A. Moortgat: *Tell Chuera 1960*, Koln, 1962, Plan III.   9. 'Ai. *'Ay*, Pl. XCVIII.   10. Megiddo, Twin Temples, Stratum XV. *Megiddo* II, Fig. 394.

cultic utensils and objects.[4] The installation in the centre of the courtyard was also an important focus of worship, probably connected with the libation of water. A drain was uncovered in the northern wall of the sacred enclosure which had been connected to the enclosure by a channel. The channel was destroyed when the temple was abandoned. Low shelves lined the walls of the central cult chamber; additional shelf-like benches stood in the centre of the the chamber. At both ends of the chamber were pits, or *favissae*, in which the remains of the sacrifices and the offerings presented to the deity on the altar were deposited. A small postern gate in the northern corner of the enclosure led from the courtyard to the spring of 'En Shulamit.

Some resemblance can be traced between the 'En Gedi temple and that of Stratum XIX at Megiddo: they were contemporaneous, although the Megiddo temple continued to exist until the end of the EB IB;[5] the approach to both was from the east, with a moderately steep slope, at Megiddo leading up from the spring of 'Ein el-Qubi to the hilltop on which the temple's main chambers were built; and both were enclosed by a temenos wall. The gateway to the temenos at Megiddo, which is situated at the end of the enclosure, has not been preserved and may have been destroyed by the builders of Stratum XVIII. To the right of the approaching worshipper was an altar, or a *bamma*, for offerings (Locus 4008), where flat stones incised with scenes connected with the magic rituals practised there were found. The earlier finds on the *bamma* (a Neolithic figurine) indicate that its construction preceded that of the sacred enclosure and that it also was a focal point of worship during the development of the shrines on the eastern slope of the Megiddo mound. A roughly circular installation, in which a ceremonial javelin head was found, stood in the centre of the paved courtyard.

4. Ussishkin's suggestion (*ibid.*, pp. 38–41) that the Chalcolithic hoard from Nahal Mishmar originated in the 'En Gedi temple is very convincing. The objects were probably mounted on wooden staffs and placed in the centre of the circular altar so they were also visible to the worshippers in the courtyard. Other pieces of cult equipment were stored in the auxiliary room northeast of the enclosure. They would have been taken from there during ceremonies to the installation in the centre of the courtyard and to the temple itself.

5. I. Dunayevsky and A. Kempinski: The Megiddo Temples, *ZDPV* 89 (1983), pp. 161–186; Ben-Tor (above, n. 2), p. 94; C. Epstein: The Sacred Area at Megiddo in Stratum XIX, *EI* 11 (1973), pp. 54–57 (Hebrew). Much additional evidence has accumulated concerning the cultural overlap between the end of the Chalcolithic culture in the south of the country and the EB IA culture in the north.

The temple was planned as a rectangular block containing three units. The broad-room units at either end had a rectangular altar opposite the entrance and were used for cult purposes. In the southern unit, which was better preserved than the northern one, a central row of columns supported the roof. Ornamental pilasters were built along the western wall. A small compartment, probably a temple storeroom, was built between the two cult chambers.

Architectural analogies to these two temples are found at 'Ai, as well as outside Palestine. There is, for example, a strong similarity between them and the earliest in the series of temples at Byblos and the temple of Sin at Khafaje, in the Diyala region of Mesopotamia[6] (Fig. 3). The origin of the EB I temple type described here should be sought in the Syro-Palestinian region at the end of the Chalcolithic period, when it took form under the influence of the domestic enclosures of the village culture. This architectural type reached Mesopotamia from Syria in the wake of the Semitic tribes that migrated to the Diyala region. The existence of such architectural elements as the gateway and the enclosing fence (at 'En Gedi, Khafaje, and Byblos) shows that the builders of the temple wished to separate and isolate it from its surroundings, as well as to protect the temple treasures by keeping an eye on the worshippers. These needs are evident also in later periods, but their origin should be sought at the end of the Chalcolithic period, when wealth accumulated and rank and status were acquired, creating new societal needs.

Another characteristic architectural feature that first appears in the early group and continues to be found in the EB II, is the location of the entrance to the main cult chamber in the east, where the rays of the rising sun illuminated the statue of the god or sacred object.[7] Shrines and cult rooms from the Chalcolithic period have been found at Tuleilat Ghassul and at Gilat. The room used for cult purposes at Ghassul has a broad-room plan, making it similar to other houses on the site, but it had remains of a wall painting

6. A. Kempinski: The Sin Temple at Khafaje and the En-Gedi Temple, *IEJ* 22 (1972), 99. 10–15; also Ben-Tor (above, n. 2), p. 95. It should be noted that the comparison of the temples of Palestine, those on the Lebanese coast, and those of Mesopotamia, deals only with similarities in their general plan and architectural elements. Differences exist, mainly between the bent-axis entrance to the cult chamber, which is traditional in Mesopotamia, and the straight-axis entrance usual in Syria and Palestine.

7. This feature was already identified by Ben-Tor (above, n. 2), p. 98. The awakening of the god and the accompanying rituals are known in all the cults of the ancient East.

representing a cult scene on its walls. At Gilat cult objects were found in a broad-room, but the nature of the architectural complex to which it belongs is not sufficiently clear.[8]

In the Early Bronze Age, Palestine underwent a rapid and intensive urbanization process, and the temple and its vicinity became an integral part of the town (see also Chap. 8). Little has survived of the temple at Megiddo on the ruins of the Stratum XIX shrine. The temple of Stratum XVIIIb (Fig. 5), built on a broadhouse plan with massive walls 1.75 m. wide, was erected after the fenced enclosure was destroyed. The wall remains of the Stratum XVIIIb temple are sufficient to reconstruct it on a plan that reveals some similarity to the acropolis temple at 'Ai.[9]

According to R. Amiran, who excavated the twin temples and the sacred precinct at Arad, they belong to the same period — the beginning of the EB IIA.[10] The twin temples are similar to the twin temples at Megiddo, except that at Arad the finds neither differentiated it from a prosperous private house nor marked it as a temple or cult place. Moreover, the published ceramic assemblage from the building is identical — except for an Egyptian jar — to the assemblages found in Arad's private houses.[11]

The oblong structure with benches and something resembling a *bamma* at Tell el-Far'ah (North) was tentatively identified by R. de Vaux as a temple, an identification that should be treated with a measure of scepticism. It may, however, have served as a cult room for the inhabitants of the quarter in which it was discovered. The evidence for the 'Babylonian' shrine excavated by J. Garstang at Jericho also is insubstantial. The 'shrine' looks more like a room in a residential building.

A monumental building on the acropolis at 'Ai, which was at first described as a palace, has been identified with certainty as a temple first built in the EB II. The building (Fig. 4) is massive and sturdily constructed; its walls of stone blocks, cut to the size of bricks and laid in courses of headers and stretchers,

are about 2 m. Some scholars have suggested that the origin of the building method should be sought in Egypt at the beginning of the Third Dynasty, but the theory has not proved to be convincing.[12] The temple plan is of the broad-room type; in its first and second phases, the cult chamber measured 6 × 17.5 m. on the inside and had a row of columns down the centre. A square courtyard, of which only a few wall fragments have survived, extended in front of the temple.[13] The acropolis temple at 'Ai is the largest cult building from the Early Bronze Age as yet uncovered in Israel. In its earliest phase it was enclosed by a curvilinear temenos wall. Ornamental pilasters were erected in the space between the temenos wall and the temple. Undoubtedly, this wall was erected to protect the temple from contact with unclean elements and to guard it from defilement. Apparently, it was considered especially necessary to protect the western wall of the temple, where the altar was placed.

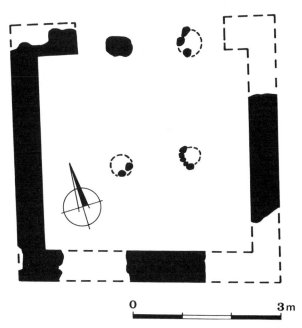

0   3 m

8. D. Alon: The Chalcolithic Temple at Gilat, *Qadmoniot* 9 (1976), pp. 102–105 (Hebrew).

9. See Ben-Tor's interpretation of it as an early antae temple, (above, n. 2), p. 96; for its stratigraphic position, see *Megiddo* II, Fig. 147.

10. For a recent discussion, see R. Amiran: Some Observations on Chalcolithic and Early Bronze Age Sanctuaries and Religion, in A. Biran (ed.): *Temples and High Places in Biblical Times*, Jerusalem, 1981, pp. 47–53.

11. *Arad*, Pl. 154, facing Pl. 166. In this difference of opinion concerning the nature of Assemblage 1876–2102 from Arad, this writer agrees with Yeivin (above, n. 1), pp. 165–166.

11. Temple, Bet Yerah. Plan located in archives of Antiquities Authority, excavations of P. Bar-Adon.

12. S. Yeivin: The Masonry of the Early Bronze People, *PEFQSt* (1934), pp. 189–191.

13. A temple similar in plan, and with a well-preserved courtyard, was recently uncovered at Tel Yarmut, and see photograph p. 53. Another temple with a similar plan, although the details are still unclear, has been excavated at Bab edh-Dhra'; see W. Rast, Jr. and T. Schaub: The 1979 Expedition to the Dead Sea Plain, *BASOR* 240 (1980), pp. 30–31.

In the later stage of the building, in the EB III, the cult room remained unchanged, but the earlier column bases were replaced with rectangular stone column bases sawn by a method used in Egypt.[14] Instead of the curving temenos wall, a complex of walls was erected that closed off the back of the temple (Fig. 6). A rectangular room was added to the north of the central cult room, apparently as a storeroom or a treasury for the sacred implements. The same changes occur at Megiddo (see below).

In Stratum XVI at Megiddo a type of temple appears that is an innovation in the temple architecture of Palestine, the megaron, or antae, type of temple, according to B. Hrouda's terminology.[15] This building has a long tradition in its country of origin, Anatolia, as well as in the northern Syro-Mesopotamian region. An impressive example of this style has been uncovered at Tell Huwara in the Upper Khabur region (Fig. 8). This temple, which in its first phase was a longhouse building with a single chamber, became in its second phase a temple comprising two spaces: a hall and the inner sanctuary, or *hekhal*. This type of temple reached the north of Palestine along with migratory waves of people entering the country in the EB III, and took root there; at the same time the broad-room proportions traditional in local architecture were adopted.[16] Unlike the Tell Huwara temple in the second phase, the Megiddo temple (Fig. 7) had only one closed space; the front space however, which was open toward the courtyard, was covered by a roof (on the evidence of the two solid column bases uncovered in its front part). From that area the statue of the god in the cult chamber was visible. The roof of the cult chamber was also supported by two columns and had an altar at its southern end. In its early phase this temple had a temenos wall that enclosed its back wall and the large circular altar in its back courtyard, which had been built before the temple had been erected. In contrast to the temples in the EB II, its entrance faced north instead of east.

A temple uncovered at Bet Yerah (Fig. 11) has some of the features of the Stratum XVI temple at Megiddo. The temple at Bet Yerah is small, with

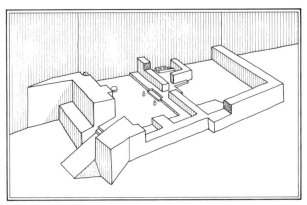

12. 'Ai, reconstruction of the Citadel Temple. *EI* 11 (1973), p. 169, Fig. 4.

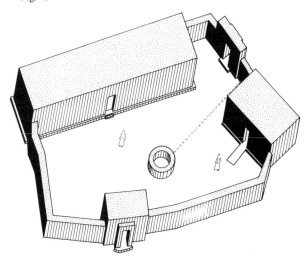

13. 'En Gedi, reconstruction of temple (I. Dunayevsky). *Tel Aviv* 7 (1980), p. 6, Fig. 4.

dimensions similar to the contemporaneous cult cells with antae at Byblos.[17]

Two identical antae temple-type structures were built in Stratum XV at Megiddo (Fig. 10) at the end of the EB IIIB. Like the Stratum XVI temple and the acropolis temple at 'Ai, they were enclosed by a temenos wall, whose remains were traced south of their back wall.[18]

---

14. See J. A. Callaway: The 1964 'Ai (et-Tell) Excavations, *BASOR* 178 (1965), pp. 31–39 for a discussion of the phases; A. Ben-Tor and E. Netzer: The Principal Architectural Remains of the Early Bronze Age at 'Ai, *EI* 11 (1973), pp. 2–3 (Hebrew), for their citing of Dunayevsky's interpretation.

15. B. Hrouda: Die 'Megaron' Bauten in Vorderasien, *Anadolu* 14 (1972), pp. 1–14.

16. Ben-Tor (above, n. 2), p. 97.

17. According to the excavator, stands of the Bet Yerah (Kh. Kerak) pottery tradition were found in the temple, dating it to the beginning of the EB IIIA. The Megiddo temple is therefore later than the one at Bet Yerah. For the cult cells at Byblos, see M. Dunand: *Fouilles de Byblos*, II, Paris, 1958, p. 895, Fig. 1007.

18. See also the suggested reconstruction, (Fig. 10). Remains of an enclosure, or temenos, wall were also found in the Stratum XVI temple, but they had been pretty much destroyed by the Stratum XV temples. See Dunayevsky and Kempinski (above, n. 5), pp. 162–167, Fig. 1 (Wall A).

'En Gedi. Chalcolithic temple.

Exceptional in plan is Temple A at 'Ai, which adjoins the city-wall (Figs. 9 and 12).[19] In its late phase this temple consisted of two spaces, but it already contained the elements subsequently found in MB and LB temples: the hall (*ulam*), the sanctuary (*hekhal*), and the holy-of-holies (*debir*). The worshipper entering Temple A at 'Ai (Fig. 12) ascended steps or a ramp to a hall, whose walls were lined with benches and shelves for offerings. From there he entered a doorway that was flanked by

19. 'Ay, pp. 17–20.

incense burners, and then moved into the sanctuary, which contained basins and other equipment built along its walls. Here he had to make a ninety-degree turn to the holy-of-holies, an altar enclosed by a low fence. The distinctive character of this structure, which already features the division into various components of the cult and the right-angle turn towards the sacred object, seems to reflect strong outside influences—perhaps the Syro-Mesopotamian elements that reached the major cities of Palestine during the later part of the EB III.

EARLY BRONZE AGE DWELLINGS AND INSTALLATIONS
Amnon Ben-Tor

Types of Buildings

The factors that determined the plans of private dwellings differed significantly from those that influenced the plans of sanctuaries, palaces, and fortifications. The latter, because they were public buildings, display a greater degree of uniformity, which was determined either by tradition (in the case of temples) or by tactical considerations (fortifications). By contrast, the private domicile was neither restricted by such considerations, nor subject, as we are today, to the authority of a central planning board. It is likely that the planning and construction of a house were entirely at the discretion of its intended residents. A family's needs, its economic status, and skill of the planner and builder influenced the structure's form. The result was that we find greater variety in private dwellings than in public buildings.

We can, nevertheless, identify several 'types' of buildings represented at EB sites. Although there are common elements in their plans, there are not enough to suggest a central planning authority during the period. The similarities most likely resulted from climatic conditions, whatever was the current 'fashion' in construction, and from social, cultural, ethnic, and other ties. The buildings within each group differed enough in the quality of their construction to indicate that they were initiated and built by private individuals.

Curvilinear Buildings. — Until less than ten years ago, available information concerning types of dwellings in the Early Bronze Age I was extremely limited, coming mainly from the sites of Megiddo, Bet Shean, Jericho, Meser, 'Ai and Tell el-Far'ah (N). The archaeological reports, including the plans of the buildings under discussion, were in most cases incomplete, if not entirely unavailable. The result was that the type

of building known as the 'apsidal house' was taken by scholars to represent the main, and even only, important type of dwelling in that period.[1]

A great amount of relevant information was added as a result of work carried out in recent years: many more sites with EBI strata were excavated, and synthetic studies were published.[2] We now know that the view that the apsidal house was the main type of dwelling in the EBI is oversimplified, and that we need 'a reappraisal of the architectural traditions...to exclude the apsidal house from any place of importance, and substitute it with a truly and wholly curvilinear style of domestic architecture.'[3] It appears that alongside a limited number of rectilinear structures, the main type of dwelling during that period was curvilinear — round, oval, and 'sausage-shaped'. These curvilinear plans are clearly in contrast to the rectilinear house plans typical of the preceeding Chalcolithic period, as well as those of the later phases of the Early Bronze Age. The unique nature of EBI plans has a bearing on our understanding of that phase in general, but that discussion is beyond the scope of the present study.

The best known apsidal building in this country is the one unearthed at Megiddo[4] (Fig. 1). A close examination of this building shows clearly that it

1. J.B. Hennessy: *The Foreign Relations of Palestine during the Early Bronze Age*, London, 1967, pp. 44–45; P. de Miroschedji: *L'epoque pre-urbaine en Palestine*, Paris, 1971, pp. 41–44; Y. Aharoni: *The Archaeology of the Land of Israel*, Philadelphia, 1982, p. 51.
2. E. Braun: The Problem of the Apsidal House: New Aspects of Early Bronze Age I Domestic Architecture in Israel, Jordan and Lebanon, *PEQ* (1989) pp. 1–25.
3. *Ibid*, p. 1.
4. R.M. Engberg, G.M. Shipton: *Notes on the Chalcolithic and Early Bronze Age Pottery of Megiddo*, Chicago, 1934, p. 5, Fig. 2.

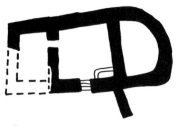

1. Dwelling, Megiddo Stage IV. R. Engberg and G.M. Shipton: *Notes on the Chalcolithic and Early Bronze Age Pottery of Megiddo*, Chicago, 1934, Fig. 2.

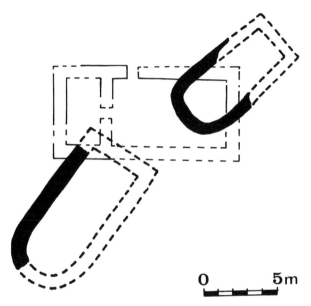

2. Dwelling, Meser. *IEJ* 9 (1959), p. 15, Fig. 2.

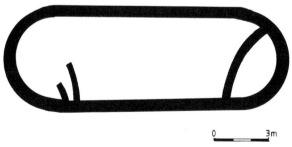

3. Dwelling Yiftah'el.

consists of more than one building phase. The lack of any detailed plans makes the study of each of these phases impossible; however, in one of these phases it seems to have had an apsidal plan, i.e. a building with two right angles opposite a semicircular end.

Several buildings excavated by Kenyon at Jericho, and dated to her Proto-Urban phase, also seem to

merit that definition.[5] Remains of other structures described as apsidal, at such sites as Meser (Fig. 2) and Bet Shean,[6] are too fragmentary, and may be reconstructed as having been of oval plan.

The earliest known apsidal building, dating to the fifth millennium B.C., has been uncovered at Byblos.[7] At present, it is unique, without direct precursors or descendants. Another apsidal building unearthed at this site,[8] is dated to the same period as the apsidal buildings in Palestine. As at Megiddo, this apsidal building had several stages, only one of which can be termed 'apsidal'.

Recent studies thus demonstrate clearly that the apsidal type of building is only of marginal importance in this country.

Oval buildings are clearly the most common type in the EBI. Clear examples were unearthed at Yiftah'el (Fig. 3), Tel Teo, 'En Shadud, Palmahim and Kfar Ata,[9] that is, mainly in the northern regions of Israel. One oval structure in the Sinai and another one unearthed in Jordan, are, however, noteworthy.[10] Fragmentary curvilinear walls unearthed at such sites as Bet Ha-Emeq, Rosh Ha-Niqra, Bet Yerah and others are too fragmentry to allow definite classification.

The EBI village consisting of oval dwellings unearthed at Yiftah'el finds a very close, parallel at Sidon-Dakerman on the Lebanese coast, dated to the same period.[11] Similar buildings, also dating to the

5. K. Kenyon: *Excavations at Jericho*, vol. III, London, 1981, Pls. 313b–314a-b.

6. M. Dothan: Excavations at Meser 1957, *IEJ* 9 (1959) pp. 13–29, Figs. 2,4; G.M. Fitzgerald: Excavations at Beth Shean in 1933, *PEQ* (1934) pp. 126–127, Pl. 3, Fig. 1.

7. M. Dunand: Fouilles de Byblos, Vol. V, Paris, 1973, pp. 24–25, Fig. 9.

8. *Ibid.*, pp. 222–223, Figs. 139, 146.

9. E. Braun: The Transition from the Chalcolithic to the Early Bronze Age in Northern Israel and Jordan: Is There a Missing Link? in P. de Miroschedji (ed.): *L'urbanisation de la Palestine a l'age du Bronze ancien; Bilan et perspectives des recherches actuelles* (BAR International Series 527), 1989, Oxford, p. 16, Fig. 4; E. Eisenberg: in: *ibid*, p. 31, Fig. 2; E. Braun: *En Shadud: Salvage Excavations at a Farming Community in the Jezreel Valley, Israel* (BAR International Series 249), Oxford, 1985, Fig. 28b; As for the as yet unpublished buildings from Palmahim and Kfar Ata — oral communication by E. Braun.

10. I. Beit-Arieh: A Chalcolithic Site Near Serabit el Khadim, *Tel Aviv* 7 (1980), p. 48, Fig. 4; .E. Hanbury-Tenison: *The Late Chalcolithic to Early Bronze I Transition in Palestine and Transjordan* (BAR International Series 311) Oxford, 1986, Fig. 18 (lower register).

11. R. Saidah: Fouilles de Sidon Dakerman: l'agglomeration chalcolithique, *Berytus* 27 (1979) p. 32, Fig. 2.

Yiftaḥʾel. Oval building.

EBI, were noted at Byblos.[12] The Lebanese coast, between Sidon-Dakerman and Byblos, most probably was the source of influence for this type of building in Palestine.

That same region most probably was the source of another type of building appearing in Palestine in the EBI — the rounded-corners building, thus called because its corners are rounded on the outside and angled 90⁰ on the inside. Clear examples of such houses were unearthed at Megiddo, ʾAi (Fig. 4), Tel Kittan and Tel Qashish.[13] All these buildings are dated to the EBI, as are several such buildings unearthed at Byblos.

The Single-Room Broadhouse. — The largest group of broadhouse buildings in Palestine has been uncovered at Arad.[14] Because the type is so prevalent there, it

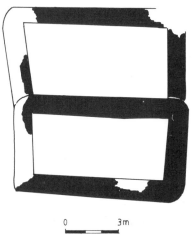

0   3m

4.   Dwelling, Ai, Callaway, 1980, Fig. 49.

has been designated the Arad house. Its construction followed certain principles:

1. The building was a broadhouse.

2. The building was essentially comprised of a single room (Fig. 5). In most cases, a small secondary room was attached to the living quarters.

3. There were benches along at least two of the walls of the main room.

12. M. Dunand (above n. 7), Figs. 116, 117, 141, 142.
13. R.M. Engberg, G.M. Shipton (above n. 4), Fig. 2; J.A. Callaway: *The Early Bronze Age Citadel and Lower City at Ai: (et Tell)*, Cambridge, 1980, Fig. 49 (building MK215, 238); H. Bernik, R. Greenberg: Excavations at Tel Qashish 1987, *Hadashot Arkheologiyot* 90 (1987), p. 23, Fig. 25; Tel Kittan, oral communication by E. Eisenberg.
14. *Arad*, pp. 14–17.

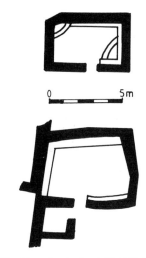

5. Dwelling, Arad. *Arad*, Pl. 178, No. 1076.

4. The door opened inward, with the door socket on the left.

5. The floor of the main room was below street level, and two to three steps led down into the room. A stone slab set in the floor often served as a base for the roof support.

A clay model of a house was found in one of the buildings at Arad (Chap. 1, Fig. 19). Assuming that this model faithfully depicts the broadhouse, the following principles of construction also can be assumed:

6. The roof was flat with raised edges — apparently to catch rainwater.

7. The ceiling slightly exceeded the height of a person, and the height of the doorway was the same as the ceiling (but note that the floor was lower than the threshold).

8. The house was windowless; light and air entered only through the doorway. Even in the many walls preserved to a height of 1.70 m. no signs of windows were found.

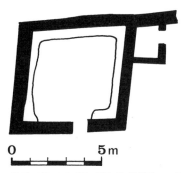

6. Dwelling, Tell el-Far'ah (N). *RB* 64 (1957), p. 558, Fig. 2, No. 543.

Buildings similar in many particulars to those uncovered at Arad — single or double rooms, sunken floors, benches along the walls, etc. — are known from Tell el-Far'ah (Fig. 6), Jericho, and, most recently, from many examples uncovered at Nabi Salah in southern Sinai.[15] The buildings uncovered in Sinai are similar to those at Arad and can be seen as the southernmost extension of one of the EB Canaanite building traditions (see Chap. 9, p. 81).

Broadhouse buildings date from the EB II. Nonetheless, the limitations of the current archaeological data must be noted, especially since most of the published material relates to the EB II and only a small amount to the EB III. Remains of EB III buildings displaying the typical features of the Arad house, found at Bet Yerah, Ta'anakh, Tell Nagilah, and Hazor indicate the continuation of this type of construction.[16] Additional evidence is provided by the EB III graves at Bab edh-Dhra', which were constructed according to the same broadhouse principle,[17] apparently in imitation of contemporary dwellings at the site.

The broadhouse plan is almost certainly indigenous to Palestine. Despite the appearance of individual features of the overall plan at several sites in Syria and Asia Minor,[18] its most typical examples are known in the greatest numbers only within the borders of Palestine. Its formulation probably began during the Chalcolithic period. The most common plan for dwellings at Ghassul, Stratum IV, consists of one

15. R. de Vaux and A.M. Steve: La premiere campagne de fouilles a Tell el-Far'ah, près Naplouse, *RB* 54 (1947), Pl. XI; R. de Vaux: Les fouilles de Tell el-Far'ah, près Naplouse, sixieme campagne, *RB* 64 (1957), p. 558, Fig. 2; and *idem*, Les fouilles de Tell el-Far'ah, rapport preliminaire sur les 7e, 8e, 9e campagnes, 1958–1960, *RB* 68 (1961), Pl. XXXIV. See also E. Sellin and C. Watzinger: *Jericho*, Leipzig, 1913, Pl. II; R. Amiran, Y. Beit-Arieh, and J. Glass: The Interrelationship Between Arad and Sites in Southern Sinai in the Early Bronze Age II, Preliminary Report, *IEJ* 23 (1973), pp. 193–197; and Y. Beit-Arieh: Chap. 9.

16. R. Amiran and A. Eitan: A Canaanite — Hyksos City at Tell Nagila, *Archaeology* 18 (1965), p. 115; and P. W. Lapp: The 1966 Excavations at Tell Ta'annek, *BASOR* 185 (1967), p. 12, Fig. 7. As well as buildings from unpublished reports of various excavations, including structures from Stratum XI of P. Bar-Adon's excavation at Bet Yerah and from Area L at Hazor.

17. P. W. Lapp: The Cemetery at Bab edh-Dhra', Jordan, *Archaeology* 19 (1966), pp. 106–108.

18. R. J. and L. S. Braidwood: *Excavations in the Plain of Antioch*, I, Chicago, 1969, p. 347, Fig. 263, Pl. 9: C-D; and H. Goldman: Excavations at Gözlü-Kule, *Tarsus*, II: *From the Neolithic through the Bronze Age*, Princeton, 1956, pp. 15–20, Figs. 57–58, Plans 5–14.

Arad. Early Bronze Age II private dwelling.

main room, to which a second room and a courtyard are attached. Unfortunately, the placement of the doorways in these buildings cannot be determined. A contemporaneous building with a similar plan at Meser (Fig. 7) is clearly a broadhouse.[19]

Clear parallels existed in the Early Bronze Age between the construction plan for private dwellings and those used for sanctuaries — note for example, the EB I paired sanctuaries at Megiddo Stratum XIX and the Jericho Stratum VII sanctuary, the EB II Arad sanctuary and the Megiddo Strata XV-XVI sanctuaries, and the acropolis temple at 'Ai from the end of the EB II period.[20]

The widespread distribution of the broadhouse plan for dwellings, sanctuaries, and even the burial monuments at Bab edh-Dhra' during the period, supports the view that this architectural plan originated in Palestine.

The Forecourt Building. — These structures were typically composed of two or three rooms (but usually two), arranged in a row: the main room and the vestibule; hence the source of the name.

19. M. Dothan (above, n. 6), p. 15, Fig. 2; and *Ghassul* I, Fig. 12. The Chalcolithic dwellings uncovered and investigated by C. Epstein on the Golan Heights must be added to the group above. A large number of these structures were single-room broadhouses with benches. See, for example, C. Epstein: A New Aspect of Chalcolithic Culture, *BASOR* 229 (1978), p. 27, Fig. 1:A-B; and *idem*, More on the Chalcolithic Culture of the Golan, *EI* 15 (1981), pp. 15–20 (Hebrew).

20. For a discussion of ground-plans and bibliography, see A. Ben-Tor: Plans of Dwellings and Temples in Early Bronze Age Palestine, *EI* 11 (1973), pp. 92–98 (Hebrew, English Summary p. 25); and R. Amiran: Some Observations on Chalcolithic and Early Bronze Age Sanctuaries and Religion, in A. Biran (ed.): *Temples and High Places in Biblical Times*, Jerusalem, 1981, p. 48, Fig. 1.

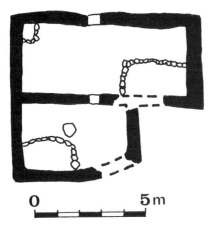

7. Dwelling, Meser. *IEJ* 9 (1959), p. 16, Fig. 3.

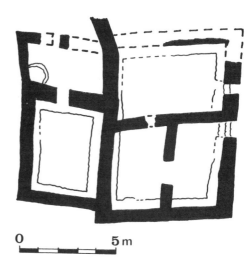

8. Dwelling, Arad. *Arad*, Pl. 183, No. 2318a.

Building B2-B8 from Stratum I at Meser (Fig. 7) is one of the earliest buildings of this type.[21] It is a broadhouse entered through the forecourt, B8, which apparently served as the courtyard. Like the Arad house, the door opened inward, with the door socket on the left. Another door leads from B8 to the main room, B2; the doors are opposite each other.

Buildings of this type are known from other sites in Israel, including Arad (Fig. 8), Tell el-Far'ah (North) (Fig. 9), and Tel Qashish.[22] Most of these are broadhouses, but exceptions exist. Although the placement of the door is not fixed, it usually is in the centre or close to the centre of the wall; occasionally it is set in a corner.

Three other buildings (at Arad, Bet Shean, and 'Ai), each composed of three rooms, should probably be included in the group under discussion (Fig. 10).[23] Unfortunately the data available on the function of the three rooms in each building are incomplete. It is likely that the anterior space served as a courtyard, while the posterior spaces were roofed living quarters. The presence of installations (a silo?, an oven?) in the anterior space (the courtyard) in the buildings at Arad and Bet Shean and of bases for columns in the rear rooms at 'Ai, supports this hypothesis.

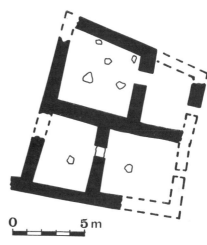

9. Dwelling, Tell el-Far'ah (N). *RB* 68 (1961), Pl. XXXIV, No. 638.

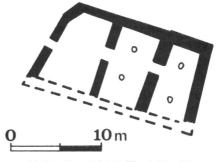

10. Dwelling, 'Ai. *'Ai*, Fig. 6, No. 195.

21. M. Dothan (above, n. 6), p. 16, Fig. 3.
22. *Arad*, Pl. 183, Buildings 1162a–1163a; R. de Vaux RB 68 (1961), Pl. XXXIV, Building 609, 623, 638; and A. Ben-Tor, Y. Portugali, and M. Avissar: The First Two Seasons of Excavations at Tell Qashish, Preliminary Report, *IEJ* 31 (1981), p. 164, Figs. 12, 14.
23. Fitzgerald *PEQ* (1934), Pl. IV, Fig. 1; R. Amiran: Tel Arad (Notes and News), *IEJ* 24 (1974), p. 258, Fig. 1 (the southern corner of the palace complex); *'Ay*, Pl. C, Loc. 198, 195, 215; N. E. Wagner: Early Bronze Age Houses at 'Ai (et-Tell), *PEQ* 104 (1972), pp. 9–11.

The doorways in each of the three rooms in these buildings are in the long walls, which creates three successive broad-rooms. The three-room structures at Arad and Bet Shean almost certainly were dwellings, whereas the exceptional size of the three-room building at 'Ai may suggest some public function (see Chap. 8, p. 78).

Buildings of the forecourt type, including the three-room houses mentioned here, were common in Palestine throughout the entire Early Bronze Age, from the EB I at Meser, the EB II at Arad and Tell el-Far'ah (North), until the EB III at Tel Qashish. The argument in favour of an indigenous origin for this architectural plan, with its broad-rooms, is supported by its widespread geographical and temporal distribution during the Early Bronze Age.

Other Structures. — The main thrust of this discussion has concentrated on three typical categories of EB buildings that have features in common. It must be stressed, however, that not every EB building belonged to one of the three categories. A significant group of EB buildings that vary in size and number of interstices (courtyards and rooms) is known, each of which must be judged as an individual, unparalleled phenomenon. These variations are a direct result of the needs, talents, and means available to the builder. Such buildings have been uncovered at all stages at every EB site.

In order to complete this description, caves, another type of dwelling, must be mentioned. The use of natural caves for dwellings, although marginal statistically, coexisted with urban and village settlements in Palestine in all periods. There is archaeological evidence of caves used as dwellings concurrent with the use of man-made dwellings in the EB I (Gezer, Lachish, and Arad), the EB II (Lachish and Arad), and the EB III (Lachish).

Installations

Installations preserved because they were constructed of durable materials include benches, platforms, cooking and heating units, and storage facilities — both pits and clay vessels.

Benches and Platforms. — Furniture in the Early Bronze Age was probably not only scant but constructed of perishable materials like wood, leather, and straw. The only furniture found are benches and platforms.[24] Although only a few benches from the EB I have survived (mostly at Tell el-Far'ah [North]), they are very common in EB II buildings, and to a lesser extent in EB III buildings. Benches were generally made of stone; their excellent state of preservation

at several sites enables us to discern their mud and plaster coating (Hazor, Tell el-Far'ah [North], Bet Yerah). The average depth of a bench was 0.50 m. They were probably used as seats or shelves.

Platforms are rarer. At present, examples are known from Meser, Arad, Nabi Salah, and Tell el-Far'ah (North). The platform at the latter site was constructed of bricks; elsewhere they are of stone. The average depth of a platform was *ca.* 1.50 m., suggesting that it served as a bed.

Cooking Installations. — While benches and platforms are generally found in the living quarters, cooking and storage facilities are generally located in the unroofed portion of the house, the courtyard. In fact, the location of cooking facilities is a major criterion for defining a particular space as the courtyard. Installations in the living quarters that show signs of combustion were used for heating rather than cooking.

There are distinctions between an open cooking installation (hearth) and a closed one (oven). The hearth was generally constructed from one or more flat stone slabs surrounded by small, unhewn stones. This type of hearth is found at various sites throughout the entire Early Bronze Age, including Tell el-Far'ah (North), 'Ai, and Ta'anakh. At Arad the hearth was paved with a layer of flint stones and was usually located in the service rooms attached to the buildings. At Ta'anakh the hearth had a base of broken basalt. The hearth was not uniformly located in the courtyard; some were adjacent to the wall while others were freestanding.

Relatively few ovens are known from EB sites, in comparison with later periods. This may either reflect a greater use of open installations or indicate that the ovens, constructed largely of clay, were not preserved. EB I ovens are known from Bet Yerah, and Ha-Zorea;[25] EB II-III ovens are known from Tel Qashish, Ta'anakh, and Bet Yerah. The best examples of ovens have been uncovered at Bet Yerah, in the late phase of a public building identified as a granary. Ovens were generally constructed of clay and had round contours. At Ta'anakh, the ovens were placed on a stone base and constructed largely of pottery sherds.[26]

Storage Facilities. — Storage facilities were generally located in the courtyard of buildings; only a few have been found in living quarters. Storage facilities fall

---

24. Both benches and platforms abutted the wall of the structure, but the benches were narrower.

25. E. Anati *et al.*: *Hazorea*, I, Brescia, 1973, p. 71, Fig. 41.
26. P. W. Lapp: The 1968 Excavations at Tell Ta'annek, *BASOR* 195 (1969), p. 16.

into three categories: dug silos, built silos, and pottery vessels.

The simplest dug silos had no constructed walls, but in many cases were lined with mud, small stones, or stone slabs. Excellent examples of the latter type are found at 'Ai, Lachish, and Jericho.[27]

Built silos were generally located in corners. They were rectangular or a quarter-circle in shape and built of stone or brick. Examples of built silos not adjacent to walls are also known. Three such silos, round ones made of clay, have been uncovered in the "apsidal" building at Bet Shean. A similar brick installation was found in the courtyard of the forecourt building at the same site, as well as in the courtyards of EB III structures at Jericho.[28] Circular stone installations, slightly raised above floor level, have been discovered in EB II strata at Arad and Nabi Salah and identified as silos by their excavators.[29] A different type of installation, at Kh. el-Mahruq, was identified as a granary by its excavator because it contained large amounts of charred grain.[30]

Large pottery vessels, particularly pithoi and jars, also were used for storage. They sat on the floors of rooms and courtyards or were partially sunk into the floor — sometimes up to their necks. This practice continued throughout the entire Early Bronze Age.[31]

Summary

As far as can be determined, no drastic changes in the composition of the population of Palestine occurred during the Early Bronze Age. The ties between Palestine and its neighbours, whether friendly or antagonistic, had only a limited influence in the realm of material culture. No foreign influences are apparent in the construction of private dwellings; insofar as architectural types can be defined, their plans are of local origin.

27. 'Ay, Pl. XXXIV:1, Fig. 1; *Lachish* IV, pp. 266–68. At Jericho the silos were generally built of brick, *Jericho* III, pp. 334–35, Pls. 180b, 181a.
28. K. M. Kenyon: Excavations at Jericho, 1955, *PEQ* 87 (1955), p. 114; *idem*, Excavations at Jericho, 1956, *PEQ* 88 (1956), p. 77.
29. *Arad*, p. 17; Y. Beit-Arieh: An Early Bronze Age II Site at Nabi Saleh in Southern Sinai, *Tel Aviv* 1 (1974), p. 147, Fig. 4.
30. Z. Yeivin: Khirbet el-Mahruq (Notes and News), *IEJ* 24 (1974), p. 260.
31. See, for example, R. de Vaux and A.M. Steve: La seconde campagne de fouilles a Tell el-Far'ah, près Naplouse, *RB* 55 (1948), p. 555; Kenyon (above, 1955, n. 28); and *Jericho* III, p. 334, Pl. 180a.

FORTIFICATIONS, PUBLIC BUILDINGS, AND TOWN PLANNING IN THE EARLY BRONZE AGE

Aharon Kempinski

Fortifications

The fortification of settlements was a new phenomenon in the architecture of Palestine in the Early Bronze Age. There is no evidence of its existence in the Pottery Neolithic and Chalcolithic periods.[1] (On the existence of fortifications at Jericho in the Pre-Pottery Neolithic period see Chap. 3, p. 34). The concept of fortification is inevitably associated with permanent settlement, when, with the consolidation of agriculture, a population becomes attached to a specific region and feels that its land must be defended. Fortifications were intended to protect the settlement nucleus, which in the majority of cases was already urban, from the attacks of nomads and seminomads and even from neighbouring urban units attempting to enlarge their domain.

The following phases in the development of fortifications can be distinguished: The first city-walls were narrow — only 1.5 m. to 3 m. thick. They were built at the end of the EB IB or at the beginning of the EB II (*ca.* 3000–2800 B.C.), and in most cases were fortified with semicircular towers. Evidence of the planned gatehouse is still rare in Palestine even though it is found in the Neolithic and Chalcolithic periods in neighbouring lands. The gatehouse at the entrance to the sacred precinct at 'En Gedi was carefully planned, indicating that this structure was also known in Palestine in the Late Chalcolithic period. Its rarity in EB IB and IIA fortifications may thus be pure chance (Fig. 1).

During the EB IIB the use of rectangular rather than semicircular towers became more widespread;

the thickness of city-walls reached 5 to 7 m. In the EB IIIA and IIIB (*ca.* 2650–2200 B.C.), the thickness of city-walls reached 8 to 10 m.; only square towers were used; the glacis, which first appeared in the EB II, came into widespread use; the gatehouse was improved; and a new type of gatehouse appeared.

City-walls, Towers and the Glacis. — The date of the earliest city-walls in Palestine has been determined on the basis of ceramic data from Jericho, Aphek, Tell el-Far'ah (North), and 'Ai. However, it is only from Tel Arad and Tel Erani that we now possess clear chronological data for the absolute chronology of the period. At Tel Erani, in Area N, a part of a city-wall was uncovered that its excavators ascribe to Stratum VI. It is earlier than Stratum V, in which a grafitto with the name of the first pharaoh, Narmer (*ca.* 3000 B.C.), was found. Thus, the city-wall of Stratum VI must be one of the earliest city-walls in Palestine.

Unlike other early city-walls (those built toward the end of the EB IB or the beginning of the EB IIA), which have semicircular towers, the towers in

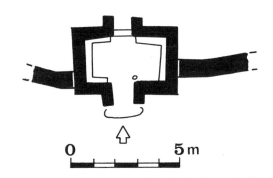

1. Gate house in the temenos of the 'En Gedi temple. *Tel Aviv* 7 (1980).

1. While writing this chapter, the following studies were most useful: A. Ben-Tor: Problems in the Early Bronze Age II-III in Palestine, Jerusalem, 1968; and Z. Herzog: *Das Stadttor im Israel und in den Nachbarländern*, Mainz, 1986.

the city-wall at Tel Erani are rectangular, about 5.5 m. long and about 4 m. wide. The city-wall is about 4.5 m. thick, made of bricks without a stone foundation. A glacis abutted both the city-wall and the towers, which were attached to the wall at a later stage.[2] City-walls with rectangular towers are known during this period from Mersin (Stratum XIV, the Late Chalcolithic period) and Habuba Kabira on the Upper Euphrates in Syria (see below, note 41). From depictions on Protodynastic ceremonial palettes from Egypt of fortifications that belong to the opponents of Narmer and other kings of the First Dynasty, it is apparent that these opponents had cities or fortifications with rectangular towers.[3] Such a city is depicted on the Narmer palette. The city is in the process of being destroyed by the pharaoh, who appears in the shape of Apis the bull (Fig. 2). It is reasonable to assume, therefore, that the fortifications of Tel Erani, which were influenced by northern sources, are part of the system of fortifications in the Delta and in the south of Palestine that Narmer and his successors conquered.[4]

At Jericho K. Kenyon noted that the thickness of the first wall that surrounded the site was 1.10 m. It was made of mud bricks on a stone foundation. It is to this wall that the semicircular tower discovered by J. Garstang belongs, as do the line of Canaanite

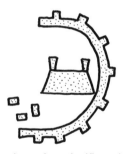

2. Schematic drawing of a fortified city, Narmer Palette (detail). *ANEP*, Fig. 279.

2. See S. Yeivin: Early Contacts Between Canaan and Egypt, *IEJ* 10 (1960), pp. 201–202; for a different view see B. Brandl: Observations on the Early Bronze Age Strata on Tel Erani, in P. Miroschedji (ed.): *L'urbanisation de la Palestine a l'âge du Bronze Ancien*, BAR Inter. Ser. 527, 1989, pp. 379–383.
3. See W.B. Emery: *Archaic Egypt*, Pelican Books, 1961, pp. 116–118.
4. Some scholars tried to connect the Tel 'Erani fortifications with the Narmer palette. The intensive connections between Dynasty 0 and Palestine are now emphasized by the discovery of 400(!) vessels imported from southern Palestine found in Cemetery U at Abydos (G. Dreyer: New Discovery at Abydos, in E. van den Brink (ed.): *The Nile Delta in Transition*, forthcoming).

city-walls and remains of towers that E. Sellin and C. Watzinger discovered. The city-wall was built in sections, with slight recesses between them. This technique is characteristic of the Early Bronze Age and can be distinguished at other sites as well.

The narrow primary wall that Kenyon dated to a later stage of the EB I was soon broadened by a parallel wall abutting it inside the city. In the course of the Early Bronze Age, the wall was strengthened several times until it was 5 m. thick. Kenyon succeeded in distinguishing 17 phases of construction and additions.[5]

From the same period (EB IB, *ca.* 3000 B.C.) at Tel Aphek, a wall was uncovered to a length of 12 m. It was preserved to a width of about one metre but had been destroyed on its inner face by erosion and modern construction at the edges of the mound. So far no towers have been found in the city-wall.[6]

At Arad the primary wall was preserved without any significant changes all through the EB II (Fig. 9). The city was surrounded by a wall in Stratum III, and here, as at Tel Erani, the chronology is based on a Narmer grafitto, in this case found in the previous stratum (IV). Presumably, then, the wall was constructed in the beginning of the EB IIA.[7] The thickness of the city-wall, of which only the stone socle has been preserved, is 2–2.5 m. The socle was preserved to a height of 1.6 m. The towers were not joined to the city-wall but abutted it (Fig. 3). The distance between the towers is 25–40 m. The towers had entrances inside the city that are from 0.6 to 0.7 m. wide. No staircases were preserved inside the towers, so the second storey, if there was one, must have been reached by steps or ladders set against the wall's inner face. At a later phase of the city-wall (Stratum II or I) a large rectangular tower was built onto its southern side. The wall was destroyed along with the city at the end of the EB IIB (± 2560 B.C.).

The fortifications of the early phase at Tell el-Far'ah (North) (Fig. 12) are very similar to those at Arad. The city-wall at Tell el-Far'ah (North) is about 2.5 m. thick. It is built of brick on a stone socle and it abuts on the early city-gate. The excavator dates the construction of the wall to the end of the EB IB. A later stone wall was built during the second

5. K. Kenyon: *Archaeology of the Holy Land*, 4th ed., 1979, pp. 91–92; also Ben-Tor (above, n. 1), pp. 39–40.
6. M. Kochavi: Excavations at Aphek-Antipatris, *Tel Aviv* 2 (1975), p. 13, Fig. 10.
7. As for the date of the wall see *Arad*, pp. 11–13; the chronology was dealt with by Amiran in *IEJ* 24 (1974), pp. 4–12.

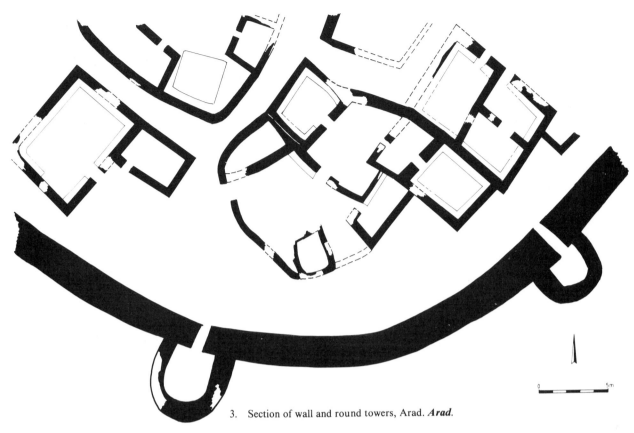

3. Section of wall and round towers, Arad. *Arad*.

Arad. Early Bronze Age II city-wall and tower.

phase of settlement, at some distance from the early brick wall.[8] The space between them was subsequently filled in. The later stone wall, which was about 4 m. thick, increased the overall depth of the fortifications to 7.5 m. The towers joined to the city-wall are in ruins, making it impossible to know whether they were rectangular, like the tower near the gate.

The glacis, of alternating layers of black and red beaten earth, characterized the last phase of fortification. The depth of the fortifications in this phase reached about 15 m. Tell el-Far'ah (North), like Arad, was destroyed and abandoned at the end of the EB IIB.

At Tel Yarmut[9] the line of the first fortification wall was identified, dating to the late EB IB or the initial phase of the EB II. To this wall a glacis was later abutted. A gate of the indirect-entrance type was already constructed in this phase.

At Kh. Mahruq, a site that was unquestionably the main city in the central Jordan Valley in the EB IIA-B, a city-wall was discovered whose thickness and construction technique were identical to the wall at Tell el-Far'ah (North). It was 2.5 m. wide, made of brick on a stone foundation. The proximity of this site to Tell el-Far'ah (North) and its size (250 dunams) suggest that the builders of the wall at Tell el-Far'ah (North) came from the main site at Kh. Mahruq. The first phase of the wall was built at the beginning of the EB IIA. A glacis was already a feature in this phase; its lower part was composed of mud mixed with mud-brick fragments, and its upper part of gravel quarried from the ditch around the city-wall. In the wall's second phase (EB IIB), as at Tell el-Far'ah (North), a brick wall was added in one area and a stone wall in another. The fortifications in this phase were more than 4 m. wide. A glacis also abutted the last phase of the wall.[10]

'Ai witnessed a development similar to that at Tell el-Far'ah (North): the early city-wall (Phase C) was built at the end of the EB IB (or the EB IC according to the excavator's terminology).[11] The thickness of the wall reaches 5.5–6 m. This wall has several posterns and a tower that is identical in plan and construction

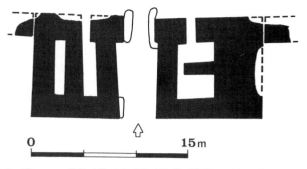

4. City-gate, Tell el-Far'ah (N). *RB* 69 (1962), p. 223, Fig. 1, Pl. XIX-XXI.

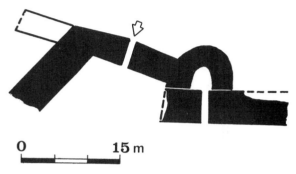

5. Section of wall and round tower, 'Ai. *'Ay*, Pl. XLV.

technique (built onto rather than into the city-wall) to the semicircular towers at Arad (Fig. 5). The wall is made of large fieldstones; there is no sign of bricks. In the second phase of the fortified settlement (still within the EB IIA, according to its excavator, J. Callaway), another encircling wall, Wall B, was built. It is about 5 m. thick. The excavator called this the middle wall, but as Dunayevsky showed, in the area of the semicircular tower and the gate it becomes the outer wall. The wall already had rectangular projecting towers. When the new wall was built, several parts of Wall C were already in disuse and houses had been built on top of them.

At Megiddo the citadel was first enclosed by a wall in Stratum XVIII (the beginning of the EB IIA). It is about 4 m. thick and was preserved to a height of nearly 3.5 m. The wall was built as a raised stone foundation with rectangular towers; like the walls at Tell el-Far'ah (North) and Jericho, it was built in sections.[12]

City-walls with semicircular towers are found during this period also in Greece and the Cyclades, and

8. For the various stages of the fortification see A. Ben-Tor (above n. 1), pp. 40–41.
9. P. de Miroschedji: *Yarmuth 1*, Paris, 1988, pp. 45–68.
10. See *Hadashot Arkheologiyot* 51–52 (1974), pp. 18–21.
11. See J.A. Callaway: *The Early Bronze Age Sanctuary at Ai (et-Tell)*, London, 1972, pp. 28–30, 99–105, 146–150. For Dunayevsky's analysis of the fortification system see A. Ben-Tor and E. Netzer: *EI* 11 (Dunayevsky vol.) (1973), pp. 1–2, Fig. 1 (Hebrew).

12. See *Megiddo* II, p. 66, Figs. 152–153. As for the date of the city-wall see I. Dunayevsky and A. Kempinski: The Megiddo Temples, *ZDPV* 89 (1973), pp. 168, 172–174.

at sites in the western Mediterranean basin as far west as Spain.[13] Square and rectangular towers are widespread in Mesopotamia — exceptions being the city-wall at Erekh (Uruk-Warka) and the fortification wall at Tell Agrab.[14] In Egypt, where rectangular or square towers were similarly widespread, enemy forts and cities from the early dynasties were sometimes depicted with semicircular towers.[15] The wall relief from Dashasheh is especially curious. It shows the siege of a city or fort whose inhabitants, to judge from their dress, are Canaanites from Syria or Palestine. The fort has a wall with semicircular towers. The relief can be dated with certainty to the Sixth Dynasty, when the semicircular tower had already gone out of use in Palestine. It is reasonable to assume then that this representation of fortifications in Syria and Palestine is anachronistic and that the artist rendered a fortress whose form had crystallized during the First and Second Dynasties.[16]

The origin of this type of fortification, despite its wide distribution in the Palestinian, Aegean (and its offshoots to the west), and Mesopotamian geographical-cultural spheres, cannot yet be determined because there is no consensus on an absolute chronological synchronization for these areas. However the affinity between the semicircular towers and the apsidal structures of the EB IB-IIA and their links with the Anatolian-Aegean West may point to their origins.

The absence of the semicircular tower in the EB IIB, despite the period's economical use of building materials and the notable structural military effectiveness of the semicircular tower (total coverage of the 'dead' areas around it), indicates that there was a gradual takeover by a new style of fortification. The rediscovery and use of the semicircular tower in the Hellenistic and Roman periods through to the Middle Ages speaks for its superiority in many respects over the rectangular tower.

The EB III is characterized by a continuity in trends in the architecture of fortifications that began in the EB II. In those cities in which settlement continued, there was a trend towards an increase in the depth of the system of fortifications, or the widening of the glacis abutting the city-walls — as at 'Ai, Jericho,

Tel Yarmut, Megiddo, and Ta'anakh. At 'Ai the system of fortifications was deepened again by the addition of Wall A, bringing the overall thickness to about 17 m. At Megiddo Strata XVI-XVII (Fig. 11), part of the early fortifications became a terrace with public buildings leaning against it. The city-wall was made deeper and a glacis added. The overall depth of the fortifications reached about 9 m., not including the glacis.[17] At Tell Ta'anakh, near Megiddo, a glacis similarly constructed to the one at Megiddo, but with a clearer building technique (alternating layers of earth and crushed limestone), was discovered.[18]

Recent excavations at Tell el-Hesi revealed part of a city-wall with an elongated rectangular tower built into it; a glacis abuts both the wall and the tower. The glacis is built of alternating layers of beaten *kurkar* and *hamra* in the so-called sandwich technique. The technique is identical in every respect to that used in the glacis of the Middle Bronze Age (Chap. 16, p. 129). The thickness of the glacis at Tell el-Hesi reached 12 m.[19]

At Tell Furan, a large EB III site (about 120 dunams) north of Ashkelon, a thick brick wall was discoverd with an abutting brick and *kurkar* glacis. However, because both elements were in continuous use during the MB period, the boundary between the EB and MB glacis cannot be clearly defined.[20]

In the EB III the semicircular tower disappeared entirely and the rectangular tower became the established form. The first appearance of the bastion before the Middle Bronze Age should be pointed out (Chap. 16, p. 133). At Jericho a bastion of the EB type was uncovered (Fig. 6). It is about 16 m. long and 7 m. thick and had a central room against which a monumental staircase with a central pier was built.[21] W.F. Petrie and F. Bliss excavated a similar bastion at Tell el-Hesi that measures about 9 × 18 m. It has two rooms of equal size and is joined on one side to a double wall. In the course of more recent excavations at Tell el-Hesi, another bastion was discovered, longer than the one found by Petrie and Bliss, measuring

13. See O. Hockmann: Die Kykladen und das westliche Mittelmeer, in J. Thimme (ed.), *Kunst und Kultur der Kykladeninseln*, Karlsruhe, 1976, pp. 168–177.

14. See *Arad*, p. 13.

15. See Ben-Tor (above, n. 1), pp. 47–50, Fig. 5.

16. The same relief also represents boats, which may indicate a naval expedition to the Lebanese or Syrian coast.

17. *Megiddo* II, p. 7, Fig. 158; and see also A. Kempinski: *Megiddo, A City-state and Royal Centre in North Israel,* Munchen, 1989 (AVA Materialien Bd. 40), p. 108.

18. P. Lapp, *BASOR* 185 (1967), pp. 7–12.

19. J.F. Ross: Early Bronze Age Structure at Tell Hesi, *BASOR* 236 (1979), pp. 9–15.

20. See R. Gophna: Fortified Settlements from the Early Bronze and Middle Bronze II at Tel Furan, *EI* 13 (1977), pp. 87–90 (Hebrew).

21. See J.B. Garstang: *The Story of Jericho*, London, 1948, pp. 85–86, Fig. 4.

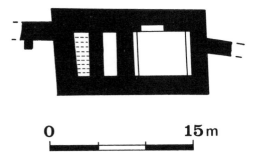

0   15 m

6. Bastion in the city wall, Jericho. J. Garstang: *The Story of Jericho*, London 1948, Fig. 4.

approximately 10 m. wide and 20–25 m. long.[22] In plan it resembles somewhat Petrie and Bliss' bastion. The glacis already mentioned here was heaped against these fortifications.

The square tower uncovered in the latest phase of EB fortifications at Ta'anakh should perhaps be attributed to this group of bastions. The tower's dimensions are approximately 10 × 10 m. Its excavator surmises that this may have been the eastern wing of a gate that is still buried in the debris west of it. Naturally only further excavation can settle the issue.

The enhancement of fortifications, the improvement of the glacis, and the appearance of bastions are hallmarks of the EB III period, which, throughout the ancient Middle East, can be characterized as militant.[23] It was an age in which military campaigns and conquests had an ever-increasing impact on daily life; the civilian population constantly had to improve and strengthen its fortifications. It is worth noting that all the architectural elements mentioned here were in use from the end of the third millennium to the beginning of the second millennium and were basic to the art of fortification, which crystallized towards the close of the Early Bronze Age and continued into the Middle Bronze Age.

City-gates. — The earliest gatehouse uncovered thus far in Palestine is at 'En Gedi (Fig. 1). It is small and its purpose seems to have been more ornamental-ceremonial than defensive. The entrance is about one metre wide, and flanked by a pier on either side. On the basis of the socket inside the gate, the door must have opened inward, toward the gate chamber. There were built-in benches inside the chamber that

were probably used by the temple guards. The door at the exit of the temple courtyard stood between two ornamental pillars. The appearance of a gate in the temple precincts at 'En Gedi, from the end of the Chalcolithic or beginning of the EB IA, is evidence of powerful foreign influences in Palestine at that time, for the fortified temple precinct did not originate here. The gate and the plan of the temple undoubtedly came from northern Syria or perhaps even Mesopotamia.[24]

Recently, gates were discovered at Jawa in Jordan. Due to problems dating them to the third millennium, they will not be discussed here.[25]

The city-gate at Tell el-Far'ah (North) was built at the beginning of the EB IB and subsequently became a unique example of an EB IB-II city-gate (*ca.* 3000–2650 B.C.). In its early phase it was a gate with an opening about 2 m. wide. The discovery of two sockets *in situ* near the door jambs of the opening tells us that a door with two wings locked it. Two square towers guarded the entry; they projected about 7 m. from the face of the wall. In this first stage the gate chamber lacked steps; they were only added in the second phase (Fig. 4). The roof was reached by wooden ladders. In its original phase the gate was about 4 m. high. In its second phase, rectangular stairwells were built in it, and the passageway was elevated by means of wooden beams that served as a base for a steep ramp. In the third phase the gate was blocked off with a stone wall, but it was reopened later, and the level of the passageway was raised again, this time by about 2 m.[26]

The first phase of the city-gate at Tel Yarmut[27] also dates from the EB II. It was a simple indirect-entry type which was rebuilt and enlarged during the EB III (and see below).

The city-gate at Tell el-Far'ah (North) — particularly in its earliest phase — resembles the one in Stratum XVI at Mersin in southern Anatolia. This resemblance indicates the direction from which ideas in military architecture came at the end of the Chalcolithic and the beginning of the Early Bronze Age — namely, southern Anatolia and northern Syria-Mesopotamia, which had undergone urbanization

22. F.J. Bliss: *A Mound of Many Cities*, London, 1894, p. 26; for the new excavations see Ross (above, n. 19), pp. 9–21, Fig. 2.

23. See C.L. Redman: *The Rise of Civilization*, San Francisco, 1978, pp. 320–321; A. Kempinski: *The Rise of an Urban Culture*, Jerusalem, 1978, pp. 33–34.

24. As for the south Anatolian origins of the gate at Tell el-Far'ah, see the following. On the Syro-Mesopotamian elements at 'En Gedi see A. Kempinski: The Sin Temple at Khafaje and the En-Gedi Temple, *IEJ* 22 (1972), pp. 10–15.

25. See S.W. Helms: *Jawa*, London, 1981, Chap. 12: The Gates of Jawa, pp. 102–115; for a review of the dates see A. Kempinski: Review of Jawa, *IEJ* 36 (1986), pp. 280–281.

26. For detailed treatment see Herzog (above, n. 1), pp. 26–30.

27. See E. Nodet in Miroschedji (above, n. 9), pp. 61–68.

Tel Yarmut. Early Bronze Age II-III city-gate.

before Palestine. They continued to influence military architecture into the EB II-III.

One characteristic building element in the EB II was the existence of numerous posterns in city walls. These narrow openings, whose widths do not exceed one metre, were found in many excavations of the period. In some cases they were protected by a tower, as at 'Ai (Fig. 5). Their narrowness made it easy to block them at the approach of an enemy. Their function is unclear because we know so little about EB urban defense methods. Perhaps, like the LB Hittite posterns, they were exits used by the city's defenders for surprise attacks on the besiegers. It is also possible, as Z. Herzog has suggested, that the posterns were for civilian use, enabling easy egress to the fields and surrounding areas.[28]

In the EB III there is somewhat more evidence for city-gates. At Bet Yerah a gate was uncovered whose passageway was about 3 m. wide. Inside the gate steps led down to the city. The gate had two guard-rooms and its door jambs were faced with basalt. At Rosh Ha-Niqra an indirect-entry gate was uncovered, but the published data do not enable complete reconstruction.[29] An indirect-entry gate of this period was discovered recently at Tel Yarmut which has two piers in its upper part and a type of fore-gate construction in its lower part; the masonry is very massive and unusual for the EB period.

The eastern gate at Megiddo, Stratum XV is a characteristic EB gate. It projected about 8 m. from the proposed line of the city-wall and abutted it on the eastern slope (Fig. 7). The city-wall itself is a casemate in this area that was subsequently filled. The wall was about 5.5 m. thick. The gate was designed so that two flights of stairs, guarded by rectangular towers, led up to a piazza that extended from the

28. See Herzog (above, n. 1), p. 30.

29. For the publication of Bet Yerah (Khirbet Kerak), see Ephrat and S. Yeivin: The Fortifications in Eretz Israel in Antiquity, in I. Eph'al (ed.): *The Military History of Eretz Israel during the Biblical Period*, Jerusalem, 1964, pp. 365–366 (Hebrew); Rosh Ha-Niqra was published by M. Tadmor and M. Prausnitz in *Atiqot* II (1959), pp. 72–88, but unfortunately without any elevations, sections or heights of the various walls and floors of the gate.

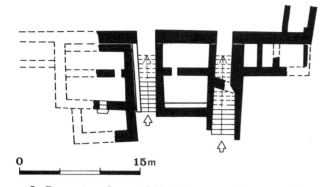

7. Eastern gate, Stratum XV, Megiddo. *Megiddo* II, Fig. 394.

gate to the revetment of the temple area. The doors of the gate must have stood at the upper end of the stairs. There the width of the opening was about 2 m. This difference in height of about 3.5 m. enables us to reconstruct the angle of the stairs. The northern staircase is longer than the southern and resembles Gate FN at Troy, Stratum II. Its builders may have been influenced, as they were in other contemporary structures, by Anatolian architectural elements.[30]

Public Buildings

Public buildings, including temples (to which Chap. 6 is devoted), are of great importance in understanding the Early Bronze Age in Palestine because they are a significant indicator of the level of civilization and urbanization that the settlements had achieved.[31]

One of the earliest public buildings discovered to date is the 'administrative centre' at Tel Erani (Fig. 8), which has been partially excavated.[32] The structure is built entirely of bricks without a stone foundation; its walls are up to 1.5 m. thick. The brick courses are joined to each other inside the wall, a common feature in monumental architecture in Mesopotamia

30. *Megiddo* II, Figs. 187 and 394; for Gate FN at Troy, see R. Naumann, *Architektur Kleinasiens*,[2] Tübingen, 1971, p. 270, Fig. 347.
31. The relationship between public buildings and the level of civilization was profoundly treated by G. Childe: The Urban Revolution, *Town Planning Review* 21 (1950), pp. 3–17; see also Redman (above, n. 23), pp. 254–259.
32. The building was published by Antonia Ciasca: Tel Gat, *Oriens Antiquus* I (1962), pp. 27–29; for a reevaluation of the material see now Brandl (above, n. 2), pp. 360–378. In order to check the stratigraphy and the urban development at Tel 'Erani, three short seasons of soundings were executed by the author together with I. Gilead of Ben Gurion University of the Negev. For a summary of the second season see A. Kempinski and I. Gilead: Tel Erani 1987, *IEJ* 38 (1988), pp. 88–90.

and Egypt during that period. Owing to their sound construction, the walls were preserved to a height of 2.5–3 m.

Through an opening 1.8 m. wide on the eastern face of the structure a broad hall was entered in which seven pillars support the upper structure (Fig. 8). A group of rooms was discovered south of this hall. The structure was first built in Stratum VIII, at the very beginning of the EB I, and continued in use, with minor changes, until Stratum VI.

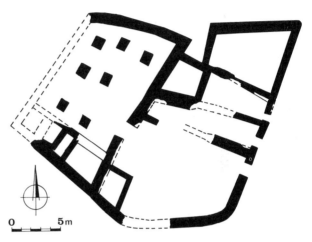

8. Building 7102, Tel Erani. *Or. Antiq* I (1962), Fig. 1.

At Arad, a building called the Water Fortress was uncovered adjacent to the settlement's central reservoir (Fig. 9). It measures about 8 × 18 m. and its walls are about 1.5 m. thick. Its socle is of very large stones. This type of construction is not typical at Arad. According to its plan it was a rectangular building with five broad-room spaces. It closely resembles Building 195 at 'Ai (Chap. 7). Its excavator, R. Amiran, called it a public building because of its plan. Its character, construction technique, and location near the settlement's central water source all indicate its purpose, as well as the function of the administrator who resided there (he was probably in charge of rationing water during dry seasons).[33]

The paucity of architectural evidence from the EB I-II is especially striking in contrast to the relative abundance for public structures in the EB III. At Bet Yerah a public granary (Fig. 10) was discovered that was built at the beginning of the EB III. The structure, a stone podium measuring 30 × 40 m., had nine round brick silos erected on it. The silos, whose diameters

33. See *Arad*, p. 3.

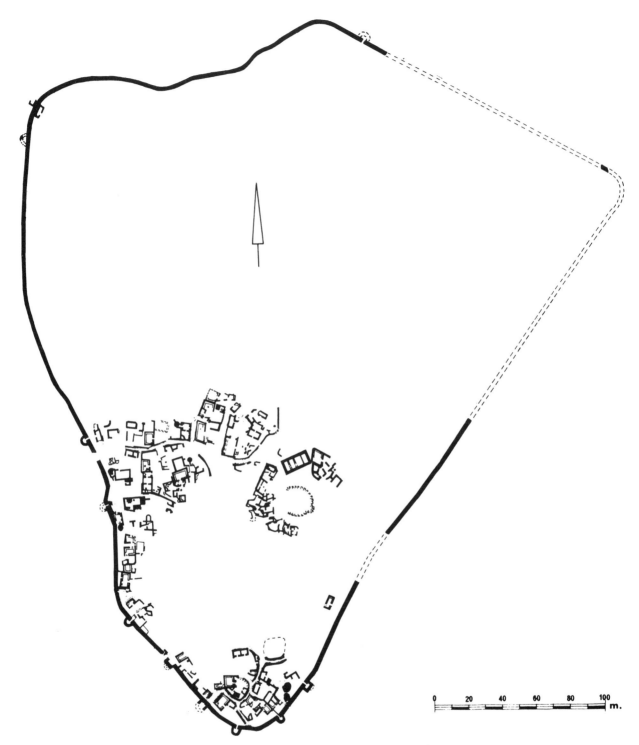

9. Arad, city plan. **Qadmoniot** 13 (49–50) (1980), p. 5.

varied from 7 to 9 m., were not preserved. Each one was divided into quarters by means of partitions that supported columns for the silo's domed roof. There was a court in the centre of the structure, and a room with a transverse entrance at the end of the court that probably was used for administrative purposes connected with the granary.

The public granary at Bet Yerah has several

Bet Yerah. Early Bronze Age III storehouse.

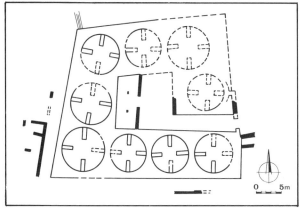

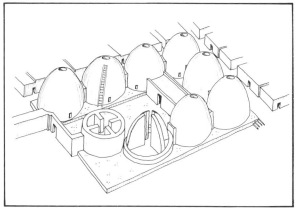

10. Storerooms, plan and reconstruction, Bet Yerah. *IEJ* 2 (1952), p. 224.

parallels. The silo units have an almost exact parallel in a central silo unit discovered at Yanik Tepe in eastern Anatolia. This connection with Bet Yerah in the EB III is entirely likely in light of the cultural ties between Palestine and eastern Anatolia at that time.[34] An identical architectural plan was discovered in an ancient model of a public granary from the island of Melos in the Cyclades. Other examples have since been found at other sites.[35] The links between the Cyclades and Palestine in the EB II-III show that the parallel is

34. See Ruth Amiran: Yenik Tepe, Shengavit and Khirbet Kerak Ware, *An. St.* 15 (1965), pp. 165–167.

35. The first analogy was brought by Yeivin in M. Avi-Yonah and S. Yeivin: *The Antiquities of Israel*, Tel Aviv, 1955, p. 107 (Hebrew), but for more examples see P. Getz in *Kunst und Kultur der Kykladen* (above n. 13), pp. 108–109, Figs. 360–363.

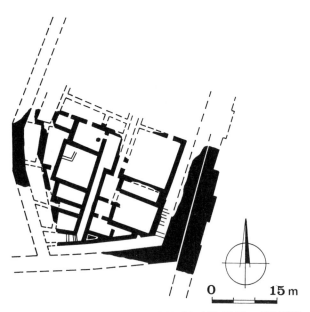

11. Palace, Megiddo Strata XVII-XVI. *Megiddo* II, Figs. 393, 3977.

a relevant one. The silos depicted in the wall drawings of the mastabas of the Fifth and Sixth Dynasties in Egypt indicate a similar pattern — namely, units of conical structures on brick platforms.

In Megiddo Strata XVII–XVI extensive remains of a palace were uncovered in the eastern part of Trench B-B. This structure, which was well preserved in Stratum XVI, was planned as a complex of inner courtyards, dwellings, and ceremonial rooms (Fig. 11). The distinction between the courtyards and dwellings and ceremonial rooms is clear: the courtyards were paved with pebbles, whereas the floors of the rooms were plastered with mud.

The palace had two separate wings. The eastern wing was next to the road that ran along the city-wall in a late phase. This wing had a central courtyard (No. 6). There is an area that is devoid of pebbles at its southern end which measures 1 × 2 m. The absence of pebbles suggests that a podium had been erected there (probably of wood).[36] In the eastern section of the palace a shaft (No. 9) admitted light into the rooms around it. Room 8 is unusually large (about 6 × 9 m.) and probably was this section's central room (the throne room?). The western wing of the palace is across the corridor, which was partly open (No. 2). There is a large court at the northern

end that has not yet been excavated. In this wing, Room 1 served as a light shaft. Room 5 contained a carved column base like the ones in the temples on the upper terrace (Chap. 6, p. 54) — evidence that in several rooms the ceiling was supported by columns. In the corridor of the western wing, a staircase led up to the temple area; this staircase, as well as another hypothetical flight of stairs built to the north of the palace that has not yet been uncovered, connected the palace with the sacred area above it.

The structure's many outstanding architectural features suggest that it is a palace: its size, its walls, the thick plaster on the walls and floors of the rooms, the clear distinction between the open spaces (which are paved) and the enclosed spaces, the light shafts, and the subterranean drainage system.[37]

There is no parallel contemporary structure from the Syro-Palestinian region. The palace at Tell Mardikh (Ebla) has an entirely different plan, with Mesopotamian influence in its large central courtyard, a colonnaded porch surrounded by rooms, and a central stairwell in the corner of one room that led to the upper storeys.[38] Although the number of inner courts and light shafts constructed in the palace at Megiddo suggests a link with the Anatolian-Aegean region, the meagreness of the finds from that region prevents any clear comparisons.

M. Krause excavated remains of an EB III monumental structure at 'Ai whose walls were about 2 m. thick. It may have been the palace of the ruler of 'Ai during that period. Two units can be distinguished: a southern one, in which there was a complex of rooms surrounding a central open court, and a northern one, connected to it, that is too fragmentary to reveal a plan.[39]

The fact that only five units from over a period of some one thousand years can be identified as public buildings (excluding temples) indicates how few remains from this period in Palestine have been uncovered. It is also clear, despite the small sample, that the EB urban culture in Palestine was poor compared to neighbouring lands.

The Town Plan

The paucity of architectural finds from the Early Bronze Age, by contrast with those from later

36. See *Megiddo* II, Figs. 393, 168–175. A podium built of mud bricks was found in the court of the Palace at Ebla, see P. Matthiae: *Ebla*, London, 1980, pp. 69–77.

37. Wrongly attributed by the excavators to Stratum XVII only, it was most probably also used in the palace of Stratum XVI.

38. For the comparisons with Ebla see Matthiae (n. 36), pp. 74–79.

39. See J. Marquet-Krause: *Les fouilles de Ay, 1933*, Paris, 1949, Fig. C; and Kempinski: (above, n. 23), p. 28, Fig. 19.

periods in Palestine, makes it difficult to discuss the plan of EB cities. Unlike its neighbours — Syria, Mesopotamia, Egypt, and even Anatolia, where town plans were already evident in the third millennium B.C. — Palestine, except for Arad, displays only partial town planning. However, it should be possible by assembling the available fragments, to draw a reliable picture of a third-millennium city in Palestine.

The city in the Early Bronze Age was entirely surrounded by an external belt of fortifications. The design of the peripheral encircling road (Figs. 9, 12) proves that the houses inside the fortified area were constructed after the city-wall had been built, and that the road along the city-wall was planned both for convenience and to aid the defenders in time of siege. Originally the road was clear of structures, but with time various installations were erected on it, blocking parts of it. A parallel is to be found in a later period (the EB III) at Megiddo, Strata XVII–XVI, as well as at Tell el-Far'ah (North) in Period 3.[40] In these two cases the city-wall existed before the encircling road and the structures beyond it.

The network of roads was designed, as in later periods, to serve as arteries within the city and to connect with the posterns and gates. At Arad such an arterial road (Fig. 9) clearly connects one of the exits with an open space in the wealthy residential area. At Arad two residential quarters are apparent: a poor quarter with small units including a board-room and an adjacent service unit in the southern part of the site, and more complex units arranged around central courtyards in the northern part, on both sides of the road leading to the city-gate. In the latter quarter Amiran identified some of the homes of the wealthy as 'temples' (p. 57), but this is still very hypothetical. In the two quarters which were excavated up to now, neither a plan nor a prototype of a city plan is apparent.

A comparison of Arad, a provincial city on the fringes of urban culture in Palestine, with the remains of other cities in the Syro-Palestinian sphere emphasizes their advanced design. Habuba Kabira, an almost completely excavated city on the Upper Euphrates in northern Syria, is almost exactly contemporary with Arad.[41] The finds indicate an extremely high level of urban planning: the city had a double system of fortifications, broad parallel streets branching off into alleys and large courtyard houses

with a uniform plan that were almost exactly the same size.

The plan of the EB II citadel is not yet clear, but there are indications that it was located on the highest part of the mound, commanding the entire site. At 'Ai, the earliest temple was also built on the highest part of the site, and the governor's, or local prince's, palace may also be buried below this area. In Trench B-B at Megiddo, which was originally the highest part of the mound, an early row of temples was discovered (Chap. 6, p. 57), to which the palace was added in the EB III. The citadel at Megiddo affords the opportunity of studying the plan of that area in the EB III. The citadel was divided in two by a retaining wall. On its upper terrace the temple faced a large court; on its lower terrace a palace was built against Retaining Wall 4045 (Fig. 9). The citadel was separated from the northern part of the city by City-wall 4045A. A path along the eastern and southern walls of the palace led to the upper terrace. A parallel lane with private

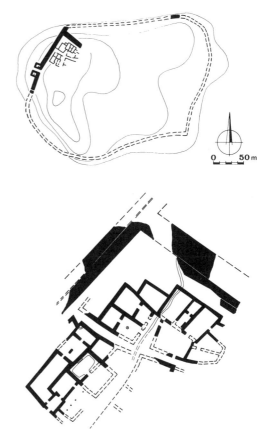

12. City plan, Tell el-Far'ah (N), and detail of the excavated area.
A. Kempinski: *The Rise of an Urban Culture in the Early Bronze Age*, Jerusalem, 1978, Figs. 11, 14.

40. Kempinski, *ibid.*, Figs. 5 and 14.
41. See E. Stromminger: Habuba Kabira am syrischen Euphrat, *Antike Welt* 8 (1977), pp. 11–20, Fig. 6.

houses along it on both sides ran behind the temple there. It is worth noting that the citadel at Megiddo was built on the eastern edge of the settlement and not at its centre because the edge had been the nucleus of the sacred area since the end of the Chalcolithic period. During the Middle Bronze Age, the citadel was moved closer to the centre of the mound (Chap. 15, p. 121).

In reconstructing the plan of an EB city in Palestine the following elements have emerged: a belt of fortifications completely surrounded the city; a road encircled the city inside the city-walls; blocks of houses were sometimes divided by streets intersecting at right angles (an indication of this is found at Tell el-Far'ah (North) (Fig. 12); there were streets between the residential quarters or in front of public structures (as at Arad and Megiddo); and the citadel area was determined by the location of an important structure (at Megiddo it was the temple and at Arad it was most probably the water system).

In comparing EB cities in Palestine with those in the contemporary Syro-Mesopotamian region, a couple of notable parallels appear: there were temples in the area of the citadel on the highest part of the mound, and there were fortifications from the very beginning of the city's existence, as at Habuba Kabira and most probably at Tell Mardikh. In Palestine, however, the cities are smaller and the quality of construction is inferior and less sophisticated than in their Syro-Mesopotamian counterparts.

BUILDINGS AND SETTLEMENT PATTERNS AT EARLY BRONZE AGE II SITES IN SOUTHERN ISRAEL AND SOUTHERN SINAI

Itzhaq Beit-Arieh

Archaeological excavations and surveys carried out between 1971 and 1980 in the deserts of southern Israel and southern Sinai provided evidence of widespread settlement in those areas during the first half of the third millennium B.C. (Early Bronze Age II). Of particular interest are the buildings and settlement patterns found to be unique to the period at sites in southern Sinai such as Nabi Salah, Sheikh Muhsein, the opening of Wadi ʿUmm Tumur, the entrance to the Watiyeh pass, Sheikh ʿAwad (Fig. 1), the eastern approach to the Feiran Oasis, and in the Negev at Kadesh Barnea, Ramat Matred, and Biqʿat ʿUvda[1].

The architectural remains and limited material finds (mainly pottery vessels) reveal a close relationship between these sites and complementary strata at ancient Arad.[2] The architectural characteristics of the Arad single-room house have already been discussed (Chap. 7).[3] This type of house, with minor variations, served as the main component of the dwelling units in settlements in southern Sinai and southern Israel. It essentially has four characteristics:

1. The dwelling chambers are either rectangular or trapezoidal, *ca.* 3 × 5 m., with rounded corners and

1. Dwelling units, Sheikh ʿAwad, Southern Sinai. *Tel Aviv* 8 (1981), p. 103, Fig. 6.

an opening in one of the long walls (a broadhouse). The walls are either straight or slightly curved (Figs. 1, 2).

2. The width of the opening is between 0.55 and 0.6 m. It is flanked by two monoliths, *ca.* 0.7 m. high, that enclose a stone threshold. At Nabi Salah and Sheikh Muhsein door sockets were found to the left of the entrance, evidence that the doors turned on hinges similar to those at Arad.

3. The beaten-earth floor is 0.2–0.5 m. lower than the threshold and the ground level outside. (In several

1. I. Beit-Arieh: An Early Bronze Age II Site at Nabi Salah in Southern Sinai, *Tel Aviv* 1 (1974), pp. 144–156; I. Beit-Arieh and R. Gophna: Early Bronze Age II Sites in Wadi el-Qudeirat (Kadesh Barnea), *Tel Aviv* 3 (1976), pp. 142–150; I. Beit-Arieh: *Sinai in the Early Bronze Age*, Ph.D. Dissertation, Tel Aviv University, 1977; *idem, Hadashot Arkheologiyot* 72 (1979), pp. 1–6; 74–75 (1980), pp. 35–49 (Hebrew); *idem*, An Early Bronze Age II Site near Sheikh ʿAwad in Southern Sinai, *Tel Aviv* 8 (1981), pp. 95–127; *idem*, An Early Bronze Age II Site near the Feiran Oasis in Southern Sinai, *Tel Aviv* 9 (1982), pp. 146–156.
2. Ruth Amiran, I. Beit-Arieh and J. Glass: The Interrelations Between Arad and Sites in Southern Sinai in the Early Bronze Age II, *IEJ* 23 (1973), pp. 193–197; I. Beit-Arieh (above, n. 1, 1974, 1977).
3. See also Chap. 8.

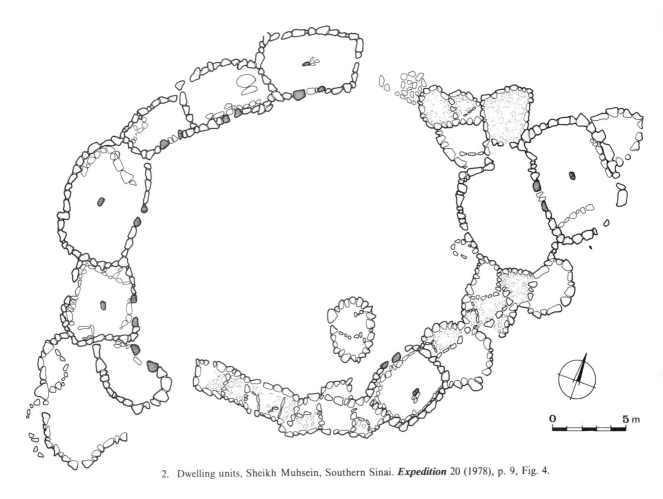

2. Dwelling units, Sheikh Muhsein, Southern Sinai. *Expedition* 20 (1978), p. 9, Fig. 4.

instances the floor level is even lower.) From one to six steps descend to the interior (Fig. 1).

4. Stone benches abut the walls of most of the dwellings, and there are sometimes small compartments in the corners. In some cases stone slabs, bases for the wooden pillars that supported the roof, were found in the centres of the rooms, opposite the entrances, while in other cases stone segments (the remains of pillars) and monoliths preserved in their entirety were found *in situ*.

These 'sunken' rooms were constructed by first clearing the earth from the building area to create a shallow pit. The pit was lined with large, closely placed foundation stones, sunk about 0.10 m. into the ground and tilted slightly towards the sides of the pit (Fig. 3). Especially large stones (measuring *ca.* 0.6 × 0.7 m.) were used at the corners.

The basic similarity between the buildings uncovered at Arad and in southern Sinai indicates a common building tradition. The minor architectural variations between them may be attributed to the external factors that shaped the unique type of construction in the southern Sinai settlements, the most significant being climatic conditions, the function of the settlements, and the building materials.

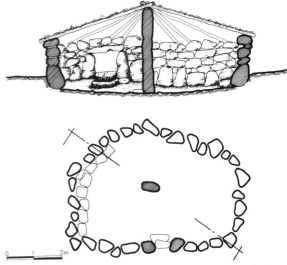

3. Typical dwelling, plan and section, Southern Sinai.

Sheikh 'Awad, Sinai. Early Bronze Age II private dwelling.

Southern Sinai has an extreme desert climate with an average annual precipitation of only 60 mm. The data from excavations indicate that the Sinai settlements were scattered and of a seasonal, or temporary, nature. Undressed granite with round contours, readily available in the igneous regions of southern Sinai, was the primary building material.

In contrast, Arad's climate is more temperate, and yearly precipitation reaches an average of 150 mm. Ancient Arad was a large, permanent urban settlement, fortified and well planned. Care was exercised both in the planning and execution of construction. The local building material was sissile chalk, which is easily dressed.

A subject worthy of consideration in its own right is the widespread distribution of the broad-room house during this period. The preference for the broad-room rather than the long-room house in southern Sinai, and perhaps at other sites as well, may be attributable to the ease with which it can be divided into two activity zones. A survey of the broad-rooms in the sites under discussion reveals that the left side of the room was used for cooking, storage, and related tasks, while the right side served as living space. In all the rooms the hearths were found to the left of the entrance. The small compartments found nearby apparently were used for storage. The interior was free of such installations, leaving more space for sleeping and other activities. The low partitions found in several instances clearly divided the rooms into two distinct functional areas.

The broad-room was certainly suited for such a division. Placement of the single entrance in the long wall facilitated access into the room without interfering with the on-going activities on either side. Placing the door in the short wall would have been a disadvantage (Fig. 3) in arranging the living space.[4]

A second typical component of these dwelling units is subsidiary structures. These rooms differ radically from the living quarters in size, shape, building techniques, and area (1.5–10 sq. m.). They are circular in shape and paved with stone slabs. Many such rooms were divided into small compartments by laying stone

4. See for example: K.V. Flannery: The Origins of the Village as a Settlement Type in Mesoamerica and the Near East: A Comparative Study, in P.J. Ucko et al.: *Man, Settlement and Urbanization*, London, 1972, p. 33.

slabs vertically. The floor level is the same as the courtyard, or higher — never lower, as in the living quarters. No doors, roof supports, or benches were uncovered. The very small amount of rubble found in and adjacent to these structures attests to the fact that they had low walls — one or two courses high — enclosing and supporting the stone floor.

The dwelling units uncovered in the Sinai, as well as many of those found in the Negev Highlands, belong to a single type: they and adjoining subsidiary structures are arranged in a belt around a large oval or rectangular courtyard (Figs. 1,2). The type is unique to EB II desert settlements, differing from models common during other periods. The average courtyard measures *ca.* 12 × 15 m., but examples measuring 20 or more metres are known. One or two entrances provide access to the central courtyard. The dwelling chambers in the large units are generally located along one side of the courtyard, with shared walls; the subsidiary structures are located on the remaining sides. The openings in the living spaces face the central courtyard, and ingress is always through the yard. The size of the dwelling units varies: the largest units have several dwelling chambers (six to nine rooms per site) and a larger number of subsidiary structures (ten to fourteen per site), whereas the smallest ones have one room and an enclosed courtyard. Intermediate units contain one or two rooms plus subsidiary structures surrounding, sometimes incompletely, a circular courtyard. This arrangement of the settlement and the dwelling units undoubtedly served as a comprehensive peripheral defense system against the elements and wild animals. This plan is eminently suited to small unfortified desert settlements.

The size and number of components in each unit is undoubtedly directly related to the size of the family dwelling in it. The various sites contain several dwelling units, sometimes extending over large areas (Nabi Salah, 75 dunams; Sheikh 'Awad, 20 dunams; and Sheikh Muhsein, 10 dunams).

The proposed reconstruction of the original plan is based on the remains of buildings *in situ*, both those preserved in their entirety and those found in ruins nearby. The preserved height of the walls ranges from one course to 1.6 m. Monoliths extending from 1.8 to 2.2 m. in height were found in the centres of the structures; they served as roof supports. Monoliths flanking the openings were 0.75 m. high, which was also the original height of the entrance. This conclusion is based on the uniform height at the different sites and on the availability of taller monoliths. Thus, the entrances were deliberately low, perhaps to make blocking them off easier, if necessary. Note that similar low entrances were found in Bedouin structures of the last century. A low doorway is advantageous in buildings designed to provide protection from the elements and wild animals. The doorways were roofed with flat stone lintels, which were found nearby.

The height of the walls was calculated according to the amount of rubble found at the site. On this basis, the central pillar both at Nabi Salah and Sheikh Muhsein was slightly higher than the walls, and the roof pitched steeply (Fig. 3). At Sheikh 'Awad the central pillar and the walls were the same height, which means that the roofs were flat. The roofing material was probably organic — branches (Pistacia Khinjuk Stock) or goatskins.

The small amount of rubble found around the subsidiary structures leads to the conclusion that they were enclosed only by low partitions (0.3–0.5 m.). They lacked doorways and roofs, and functioned as work and storage areas. Daily life centred around the courtyard, which could be closed off in the evening to serve as an animal pen.

ARCHITECTURE IN THE INTERMEDIATE EARLY BRONZE/MIDDLE BRONZE PERIOD

Rudolph Cohen

Introduction

In the Intermediate EB/MB period, which follows the first period of urbanization in Palestine (EB II-III), the way of life reverted in certain respects to a pattern that had prevailed earlier. Unfortified settlements were inhabited by seminomads or, more accurately, by people whose subsistence was based on crop cycles, so that part of the population had to follow the pasturage, wandering within a definite territory that was their living space.

Only scant architectural remains have come to light in the Intermediate EB/MB settlements hitherto excavated in the northern and central parts of the country. Above the ruins of the fortified EB II-III cities, remains of occupations of a transient nature have been found, such as those described by K. Kenyon on the tell of Jericho.[1] Sometimes, as on the tells of Megiddo[2] and Hazor,[3] the only evidence of occupation is pottery with no associated structures. Tombs of the period, on the other hand, are numerous, and many rock-cut tombs at these sites contained a wealth of pottery and copper weapons.

The situation is entirely different in the Negev Highlands, where dozens of Intermediate EB/MB settlements have been recorded in surveys carried out by E. Anati, N. Glueck, Y. Aharoni, B. Rothenberg,[4] M. Kochavi, and R. Cohen. During the Emergency

Survey begun in the Negev in 1979, even more sites were surveyed.[5] In addition, in recent years settlements from this period have been excavated at Har Yeruham,[6] H. Ahdir, Atar Nahal Boqer, Har Harif,[7] H. Be'er Resisim,[8] Ramat Matred, and Biq'at 'Uvda.[9]

Building remains were dated correctly to the Intermediate EB/MB period for the first time by W.F. Albright at Tell Beit Mirsim, Stratum H, where the period was represented by a small, unwalled settlement that also made use of natural caves for habitation. Albright conjectured that the settlement

1. *Jericho* I, II; K. M. Kenyon: *Digging Up Jericho*, London, 1957, p. 191, Pl. 42A.
2. *Megiddo* II. The Intermediate EB/MB material on the tell is found in Loci 2149, S. 3154, 4009, 4040, 5139, 5184, 5273, and 5612, attributed to Strata XVI–XIII.
3. *Hazor*, pp. 120–121.
4. N. Glueck: *Rivers in the Desert*, New York, 1960, pp. 60–84; *idem*, Further Explorations in the Negeb, *BASOR* 137 (1955), pp. 10–22; *idem*, The Third Season of Exploration in the Negeb, *BASOR* 138 (1955), pp. 7–29; *idem*, The Fifth Season of Exploration in the Negeb, *BASOR* 145 (1957), pp. 11–25; *idem*,

The Sixth Season of Archaeological Exploration in the Negeb, *BASOR* 149 (1958), pp. 8–17; *idem*, The Seventh Season of Archaeological Exploration in the Negeb, *BASOR* 152 (1958), pp. 18–38; B. Rothenberg: *Negev, Archaeology in the Negev and the Arabah*, Ramat Gan, 1967, pp. 79–86 (Hebrew); Y. Aharoni: Appendix II: Finds of the Middle Bronze Age, in M. Evenari *et al.*: The Ancient Desert Agriculture of the Negev, *IEJ* 8 (1958), pp. 247–250.
5. R. Cohen: The Negev Archaeological Emergency Project (Notes and News), *IEJ* 29 (1979), pp. 250–251.
6. M. Kochavi: The Excavations at Har Yeruham (Preliminary Report), *Bulletin of the Israel Exploration Society* (*Yediot ha-Hevrah*) 27 (1963), pp. 284–292 (Hebrew); *idem*, *The Settlement of the Negev in the Middle Bronze (Canaanite) I Age*, Ph.D. Dissertation, Hebrew University, Jerusalem, 1967 (Hebrew); R. Cohen: Har Yeruham (Notes and News), *IEJ* 24 (1974), pp. 133–34.
7. R. Cohen: Rescue Excavations in the Negev (Notes and News), *IEJ* 29 (1979), pp. 253–254.
8. R. Cohen and W. G. Dever: Preliminary Report of the Pilot Season of the 'Central Negev Highlands Project', *BASOR* 232 (1979), pp. 29–45; *idem*, Preliminary Report of the Second Season of the 'Central Negev Highlands Project', *BASOR* 236 (1980), pp. 41–60; *idem*, Preliminary Report of the Third and Final Season of the 'Central Negev Highlands Project', *BASOR* 243 (1981), pp. 57–77.
9. R. Cohen: Notes on a Particular Technique of Architectural Decoration, *IEJ* 30 (1980), 231–234; *idem*, The Negev Emergency Project — Biq'at 'Uvda, *Hadashot Arkheologiyot* 74–75 (1980), pp. 35–49 (Hebrew).

had been surrounded by a city-wall destroyed by the builders of Stratum G.[10]

In fact, Intermediate EB/MB building remains had already been discovered at Jericho by E. Sellin and C. Watzinger,[11] but they had erroneously attributed them to the Late Bronze Age. A hoard of copper weapons was found there in a series of thin-walled brick buildings. The hoard contained a fenestrated axe that dates the finds to the Intermediate EB/MB period. The existence of structures from that period at Jericho was confirmed in Kenyon's excavations.[12]

Intermediate EB/MB settlements with architectural remains are known in Israel also at Lachish (a wall fragment on the tell and perhaps a building on a hill northwest of the tell)[13] at Tell el-'Ajjul,[14] Tel Bira[15] and Tel 'Ashir.[16]

Rectangular structures with stone doorsills and door sockets were uncovered at Bet Yerah,[17] on both sides of a 'street' paved with pebbles and gravel. Recently, a fairly extensive settlement near Sha'ar Hagolan[18] was excavated at which three concentrations of structures were traced, at a distance of 60 m. from each other. About twenty adjoining rooms were exposed over an area of 300 sq. m., built of mud brick on top of one or two courses of large cobbles, and paved with packed earth.

In the Negev Highlands, the desert region of southern Israel, the Intermediate EB/MB is one of the periods in which settlements flourished. Remains of these settlements are usually on hilltops and are visible on the surface, unlike the large mounds, or tells, elsewhere in Israel, in which early remains are covered by the ruins of later occupations.

Settlement Categories

M. Kochavi has proposed dividing Intermediate EB/MB settlements in the Negev into three categories, according to size:[19]

10. *Tell Beit Mirsim* II, pp. 14–16.
11. E. Sellin and C. Watzinger: *Jericho, Die Ergebnisse der Ausgrabungen*, Leipzig, 1913, Pl. III.
12. Above, n. 1; *Jericho* III, pp. 105–108, 166–67, 213–15.
13. *Lachish* IV, pp. 29–45, 137–39, 156–75, 275–79.
14. *Ancient Gaza* II, p. 2, sect. 9, Pl. XXXVI.
15. M. Prausnitz: Tell Bira — 1978, *Hadashot Arkheologiyot* 69–71 (1979), pp. 33–34 (Hebrew).
16. R. Gophna and E. Ayalon: Tel 'Ashir — 1981/1982, *ESI* 1 (1982), p. 6.
17. P. Bar-Adon: *Excavation at Bet Yerah* (unpublished).
18. E. Eisenberg: Sha'ar Hagolan, *Hadashot Arkheologiyot* 73 (1980), p. 12 (Hebrew).
19. Above, n. 6.

Central settlements. Central settlements extended over a large area and were usually situated near a source of fresh water. The following sites belong to

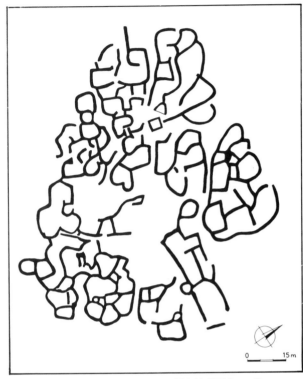

1. Site of Nahal Nissana. *HA* 83 (1984), p. 62.

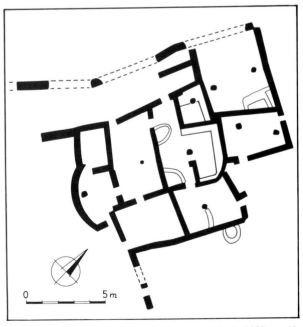

2. Site of Har Yeruham (partial). *Qadmoniot* 2 (6) (1979), p. 41.

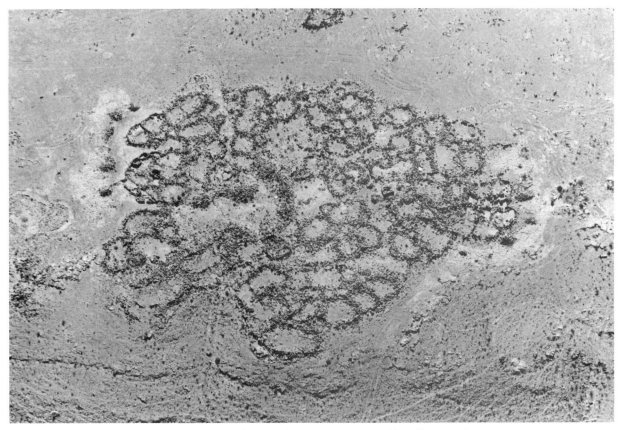

Nahal Nizzana site. Aerial photo. Intermediate Bronze Age.

this category: H. 'En Ziq,[20] Mashabbe Sade,[21] Nahal Nissana[22] (Fig. 1), Be'er Resisim (Fig. 3), Har Yeruyam (Fig. 2), and H. Har-Sayyad.[23]

Large settlements. Large settlements comprised between ten to fifteen large units. Unlike in central settlements, however, the structures were not crowded together; their various units were scattered, sometimes at a distance of 10–40 m. from each other. The following sites belong to this category: H. Nahal Zalzal,[24], H. Nahal Boqer, Har Harif, H. Avnon,[25] (Fig. 4), Ro'i (site 2),[26] and H. Talma.[27]

20. R. Cohen: Negev Emergency Project (Notes and News), *IEJ* 35 (1985), pp. 203–204.
21. *Ibid.*, pp. 202–203.
22. R. Cohen, Negev Emergency Project (Notes and News), *IEJ* 34 (1984), p. 203.
23. R. Cohen: Horvat Har Sayyad, *ESI* 4 (1986), pp. 44–45.
24. R. Cohen: *Archaeological Survey of Israel, Map of Sede Boqer West (167), 13-02*, Jerusalem, 1985, Site No. 3.
25. R. Cohen (above, n. 20), p. 202.
26. Y. Baumgarten: Ro'i 2, *ESI* 1 (1982), p. 103.
27. Surveys in the Dimona Region, *Hadashot Arkheologiyot* 53 (1975), p. 32.

Small settlements. Small settlements consisted of isolated houses and sheep pens. This type of settlement was very common; hundreds have been recorded in the Negev Highlands.[28]

Plans of Intermediate EB/MB Structures

Type 1. — Most of the settlements in the Negev Highlands follow a uniform plan, comprised of round or rectangular dwelling units, with a central pillar that supported the roof. In the large settlements, the rooms were clustered around a spacious courtyard (6–12 m. in diameter) and various installations adjoined them (Fig. 2). In the central settlements most of the courtyards were smaller (*ca.* 2 × 3 m.). The Intermediate EB/MB settlements in the Negev Highlands are generally considered to have been seasonally inhabited by seminomads, who derived their livelihood from pasturage, hunting, and sporadic agriculture. This assumption is correct for the small

28. R. Cohen: *Archaeological Survey of Israel, Map of Sede Boqer West (168), 13-03*, Jerusalem, 1981, p. X.

settlements, but the central and large ones appear to have been permanent foci for the small, transient villages.

Intermediate EB/MB structures in the Negev Highlands are apparently similar in plan to the EB II structures in southern Sinai,[29] some of which have also been discovered recently in the Negev Highlands.[30] It may well be that the similarity between them should be explained by the geographical conditions prevailing in these regions of marginal settlement. However, the possibility cannot be excluded that the people in the Intermediate EB/MB period were influenced by the layout of the EB II structures, which, because they were on the surface, would have been visible.

Type 2. — The second most common settlement consisted of small, round structures (2–6 m. in diameter) built a few metres apart. They were scattered over an area of one to five dunams, as at the site opposite Giv'at Mesora near Nahal Ha-Besor, and the many small sites in the Negev Highlands (Figs. 3, 4).

Type 3. — A third type of settlement consisted mainly of round rooms arranged in a circle, such as Structure C at the site of Har Harif, which has thirteen rooms ranging in diameter from 1.5 to 4 m. A similar structure is situated on the ridge southeast of Tel Kadesh Barnea.

The 'Frontal-space' House. — Structures consisting of two or three square rooms arranged in a row are characteristic of Area B at Har Yeruham (Fig. 2). They were in widespread use throughout the country in the EB II (above, p. 21). The first room was an entrance space, or courtyard, in front of the living quarters, which consisted of one or two rooms. The appearance of such structures at Arad[31] is especially significant.

Long, Rectangular Structures. — Long, rectangular structures have been found both in many settlements or on nearby hilltops in the Negev Highlands. Their attribution to the Intermediate EB/MB period is uncertain since none yielded sherds — as for example, those excavated at Horvat Be'er Resisim in the Sede Boqer area, or at Har Yeruham, or surveyed sites such as H. Nahal Zalzal. These structures are between 5 to 8 m. wide and 7 to 25 m. long; tumuli are sometimes found at the edges of these structures. The structures

29. I. Beit-Arieh: Central Southern Sinai in the Early Bronze Age II and its Relationship with Palestine, *Levant* 35 (1983), pp. 39–48; R. Cohen: The Mysterious MB I People, *BAR* 9 (1983), pp. 16–29.

30. M. Haiman: Har Horsha, *Hadashot Arkheologiyot* 77 (1981), pp. 39–40, (Hebrew), *ibid.*, Har Sagi, pp. 43–44.

31. *Arad*, pp. 14–17.

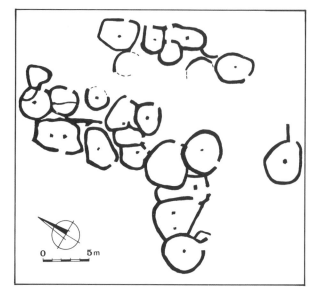

3. Site of Be'er Resisim. *BASOR* 236 (1980), p. 47, Fig. 6.

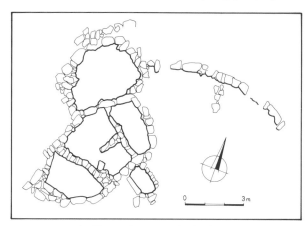

4. Horvat Avnon, author's plan.

are generally preserved to a height of four or five stone courses, while in other parts of the building only the foundations have survived.

Animal Pens. — Round and square structures that probably served as pens for the flocks are found in settlements and on neighbouring hilltops in the Negev Highlands. The considerable number of these pens indicates that sheep and goat herds were the economic mainstay of the population. The round pens had a diameter of 12–25 m.

Furnishings, Cooking and Storage Installations

Benches. — Benches are a characteristic feature of EB II houses in the Negev Highlands and Sinai (for instance at Arad, Strata II-III). In the Intermediate

Horvat Be'er Resisim. Intermediate Bronze Age dwellings.

EB/MB period, on the other hand, they are extremely rare. The only examples that can be attributed with certainty to the period were found at Har Yeruham (especially in Area B, Loci 2 and 9). These are stone benches 0.5 m. wide and about 0.3 m. high, used as shelves.

Cooking installations. — Cooking installations have been found both in the dwellings and in the courtyards: generally circular stone hearths from 0.5 to 0.7 m. in diameter that contained a layer of ashes from 0.2 to 0.3 m. deep. In some instances, only ash deposits were found.

Storage installations. — Rounded or rectangular silos built of small stones were uncovered in considerable numbers both in the dwellings and the courtyards, generally located in the corners. At H. Be'er Resisim and at Har Yeruham, many storage facilities were found inside the rooms, whereas at H. Nahal Zalzal numerous installations were attached to the outside of the courtyard wall. Eleven flint hammers and stone pounding and grinding tools were found in Installation 16 at Har Yeruham. Compartments built of small, narrow, elongated stones were attached to

rounded rooms in Structures 62 and 63 at H. Nahal Zalzal. Their function has not yet been determined.

Materials and Building Methods

The dwellings in the Negev Highlands are built in a uniform fashion, apparently because only stone was available as building material, and the needs of their occupants were similar.

Walls. — Wall foundations at sites in the Negev Highlands were a single row of large, upright stones. The superstructure was constructed of relatively small stones. In northern Israel, on the other hand, foundations for brick walls were constructed of two rows of fieldstones (at Sha'ar Hagolan). The wall remains uncovered at Jericho were also brick. In the Negev Highlands the width of the walls corresponds to the width of the foundations, from 0.3 to 0.6 m., whereas at Jericho the walls were 0.3 m. wide and at Sha'ar Hagolan they were 0.5 m. wide.

Floors. — The floors in the majority of Intermediate EB/MB buildings are of beaten earth. At Har Yeruham, H. Be'er Resisim, H. 'En Ziq and Mashabbe

Sade, as well as at numerous other Negev sites, however, floors were the natural rock surface that had been levelled and smoothed and whose fissures and hollows had been filled with small flat stones.

Roofing. — Intermediate EB/MB houses in Palestine were single-storey buildings. In most cases, no evidence of roofing was found, but it is reasonable to assume that they had been roofed with wooden beams covered with organic materials. At some sites, such as H. Be'er Resisim, Har Yeruham, H. 'En Ziq, Mashabbe Sade, H. Har Sayyad and Ro'i (Site 2), there is evidence of roofing with flat, thin limestone slabs (Fig. 5). At H. Be'er Resisim, wooden beams

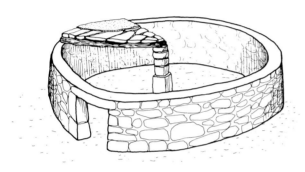

5. Be'er Resisim, reconstruction of a building. *Qadmoniot* 16 (62–63) (1984), p. 55.

were found *in situ* in a building at the southern end of the site. The roofs of the houses were flat and seem to have been covered with mud, and the ceilings were supported by a stone pillar — sometimes by two and in a few cases by three pillars. At H. Be'er Resisim, Mashabbe Sade, and H. 'En Ziq there were two kinds of pillars: a monolith generally preserved to a height of 1.5 m., but which may have originally been higher, and a pillar constructed of seven to nine drums. At Har Yeruham only pillars of roughly rounded stone drums were found.

Doorways. — At H. Be'er Resisim, Mashabbe Sade, and H. 'En Ziq a number of doorways have been preserved. They are uniformly constructed of monolithic door jambs carrying a monolithic lintel. The entrances are from 0.5 to 0.6 m. wide and from 0.55 to 0.65 m. high, so anyone entering the house had to stoop.

Tombs: Tumuli

The tombs in the Negev differ from those in other parts of the country in that they are built on the surface rather than hewn into the rock. Tumuli, which are visible from afar, rise in the vicinity of every village, on many hilltops, and sometimes even inside settlements (at Har Yeruham and at H. 'En Ziq). Two main types of tumuli can be distinguished. The most common type is a circle of large, upright stones 6–7 m. in diameter, that is filled with stones to a height of from 0.5 to 0.6 m. A rectangular cist in the centre of the circle is built of large stones and covered with flat stone slabs. The deceased was placed in the centre of the cist. A second type is a cairn 3–5 m. in diameter that is built of medium-sized stones laid in courses to a height of one metre (Har Yeruham).

It may well be that the close resemblance between the tumuli and the rounded houses so common on Intermediate EB/MB sites in the Negev Highlands indicates a desire to provide the dead with a dwelling similar in appearance and sometimes even in size to the houses of the living.

DOLMENS IN PALESTINE

Dan Bahat

Dolmens, the largest subgroup within the class of megalithic structures,[1] were constructed in Palestine during two distinct periods: the Late Chalcolithic–Early Bronze Age I, and the Intermediate EB/MB Period. This division is based on finds associated with the dolmens as well as structural differences.

Dolmens belong to a world-wide phenomenon of Megalithic structures which are distributed throughout the Mediterranean basin, North Africa, western Europe and even the Far East. It should be noted that the dolmens in these areas date mainly to the third millennium B.C., while their earliest appearance in Palestine is fixed to the late fourth–early third millennium B.C. The similarity of the Palestinian dolmens to those of western Europe, and their early date, have stimulated many theories and explanations for the Near Eastern origin of the Megalithic culture of Europe.[2]

A dolmen is a rectangular chamber constructed of large stone slabs placed vertically and capped by another large stone slab. The dolmens of the earlier period (Chalcolithic–EB I) were created by the parallel placement of two long stones (2.5–3 m. long) with smaller stones laid in between; the structure's interior chamber measured 1.5 × 2 m. The floor was paved with small stones, either limestone (in the southern Jordan Valley) or basalt (in the later group in the

Golan Heights and in the northern Jordan Valley). In the earlier group, a square opening (0.6 × 0.6 m.) was hewn in one of the narrow partitions, 0.2–0.3 m. above ground level, with grooves for a sealing stone.[3] Several dolmens at the 'Ala-Safat field[4] had two-storeyed chambers. Other examples with two storeys are known from the Intermediate EB/MB dolmen field at Biq'at Bteiha.[5] The dolmen was usually covered with a circular or elliptical pile of stones (tumulus) measuring up to ca. 7 × 8 m. in height.

In the later period (EB III and Intermediate EB/MB) the rectangular chamber of the dolmen was constructed of large stones supporting a very large capstone (at times weighing up to 30 tons). An additional smaller stone was set above the entrance to the chamber, as a lintel, and a threshold was also found. From the entrance an 'approach corridor', the same width as that of the chamber, extended outward to the perimeter of the tumulus covering the chamber. The height of the chamber generally exceeded that of

1. This group of structures includes: the menhir — a freestanding single-stone monument, stone circles, and one-centred stone circles like that of Rujm el-Hiri (Rogem Hiri) on the Golan Heights. See M. Kochavi (ed.): *Judaea Samaria and the Golan*, Jerusalem, 1972, p. 277, Site 115, as well as M. Zohar: Rogem Hiri: A Megalithic Monument in the Golan, *IEJ* 39 (1989), pp. 18–31, with extensive bibliography in note 16.
2. The best treatment of the subject is still G.E. Daniel: *The Megalith Builders of Western Europe*, London, 1958.
3. The shape of this opening is reminiscent of the openings of Chalcolithic ossuaries. See E. C. Broome: The Dolmens of Palestine and Trans-Jordania, *JBL* 59 (1940), p. 491; M. Stekelis: *Les monuments mégalithiques de Palestine*, Paris, 1935, Figs. 29–39, Pls. I–XI; Stekelis noted that all dolmens were originally believed to date from the Chalcolithic period.
4. Stekelis thought, with some reason, that these fields were the model for the later groups of dolmens as well. See his latest treatment: M. Stekelis: La Necropolis de 'Ala-Safat, Transjordania, *Ampurias* 22–23 (1960–61), pp. 49–115. An Intermediate EB/MB group of tumuli in the Negev may be seen as a link between the early and late group of dolmens; they are associated with third-millennium B.C. events in Transjordan. See D. Bahat: The Date of the Dolmens near Kibbutz Shamir, *IEJ* 22 (1972), pp. 44–46.
5. Because of their peculiar shape, these dolmens are referred to as 'Tanks'. See C. Epstein: Dolmens in the Golan, *Atiqot* XVII (1985) (English series), pp. 20–58, especially Type 6 in Fig. 1; and Stekelis (above, n. 2), p. 58.

Ala-Safat, Intermediate Bronze Age dolmen.

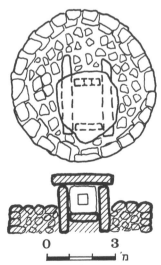

1. Dolmen, 'Ala-Safat, Transjordan. M. Stekelis: la Necropolis megalitica de Ala Safat Transjordania, *Ampurias* 22–23 (1960-1961), Fig. 29:9.

the corridor, so that if the corridor were covered, its roof would have been lower than that of the chamber.[6]

The floor of the dolmen was paved with close-fitting stones, 0.15–0.20 m. thick, laid on a level bed of smaller stones, or occasionally on levelled bedrock.

The dolmens of both periods were covered by stone tumuli. The tumuli of the old type were never larger than 3 m. in diameter, while later examples were approximately 12 m. in diameter. A single example of a tumulus filled with earth is known from Wadi Tarafa. In locations where a dolmen was erected on a slope, circular supporting walls, three to four courses high, were built to stabilize the tumulus. At the excavations near Shamir, a wall one course high,

6. Bahat (above, n. 2), p. 58; Broome (above, n. 2), p. 482, calls this type the *allee couverte* type. See also A. Druks and S. Moshkowitz: Survey of Megalithic Remains in the Meiron Area, *Mitekufat Haeven* 9 (1969), pp. 9–13 (Hebrew).

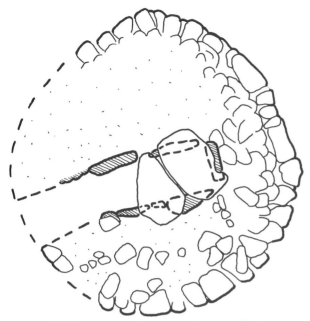

2. Dolmen, Shamir. *EI* 11 (1973), p. 59, Fig. 1.

sunk in the ground, was found in the heart of the tumulus. Its significance is not known (Fig. 2).

Dolmens in Palestine are found concentrated in the Jordan Valley (particularly on the eastern side of the river) as well as on the Golan Heights, the Hauran plateau, and in the eastern part of the Orontes Valley in upper Syria. They are also found in the hills of Upper Galilee. The earlier group of dolmens is located mainly in the hilly region of Transjordan in close proximity to water sources. The dolmen fields at el-Adeimah near Teleilat Ghassul, and 'Ala-Safat near the ed-Damiyah Bridge have been intensively studied. At the latter site, several dolmens cut into bedrock were discovered (Fig. 1).

The distribution of dolmens in predominantly basaltic areas leads to the hypothesis that this type of burial was chosen in areas where graves could not be easily dug. The fact that no dolmens have been found on the coastal plain or in southern Israel supports this view and provides insight into the means by which dolmens were erected. The accepted view now is that dolmens were used for burial during both periods, and that they were constructed by nomadic pastoralists.

The dolmen was most probably intended as a burial chamber for a chief of a clan or other member of the pastoralist elite.[7] If we pursue Stekelis' original idea that the architectural roots of the dolmen should be sought in the Late Chalcolithic–EB I period, its origin in the sedentarian house-form was adapted into the culture of the nomadic pastoralists of the Bronze Age.

7. See the summary of this problem in D. Gilead: Burial Customs and the Dolmen Problem, *PEQ* 100 (1968), pp. 22–24; as well as M. Zohar (above, n. 1), pp. 29–31.

THE MIDDLE AND LATE BRONZE AGES

12 THE MIDDLE AND LATE BRONZE AGES: INTRODUCTION

Aharon Kempinski

The end of the twenty-first century B.C. marked a turning point in the cultural history of Palestine: political and cultural developments in northern and central Syria and Egypt brought about changes in settlement patterns; the domination of Palestine by seminomadic tribes and rural communities that had characterized the Intermediate Early Bronze/Middle Bronze Age ended, and an era characterized by renewed urbanization and the formation of Canaanite city-states began. The chronology employed in this article divides this era into two sub-periods: the MB IIA[1] and the MB IIB. However, the major cultural indicators which define this division are no longer clear-cut; we find, rather, that in architecture, ceramics, and small finds, there was a cultural continuum that extended into the Late Bronze Age (post-1600 B.C.).

During the period from 2050 to 1800 B.C., which largely corresponds to the MB IIA, the second-millennium culture took shape. It was characterized in Palestine by the founding and renewal of urban settlements. These comprised the local core of the Canaanite city-states, distributed throughout Palestine and Syria, which maintained their existence until the founding of the national kingdoms of Israel and Judah, and the kingdoms of Transjordan.

The reestablishing of urban centres in Palestine was influenced from two opposing directions: primarily from the north, via two main paths of migration — the coast and the Great Rift Valley — and secondly from the south, by the Egyptian Middle Kingdom (the Twelfth Dynasty), whose political and economic influence increased during the twentieth century B.C., extending along the coastal plain to the Lebanese coast. Lack of historical documentation leaves us in the dark regarding the means by which this process of renewed urbanization occurred, although references are found later in the Mari tablets. The earlier Egyptian records, dated to the twentieth century B.C., list cities established along the Syro-Palestinian coast; the later records, from the eighteenth century B.C., indicate the extensive urbanization of Palestine and southern Syria. Archaeological remains provide insight into the form and direction this new development took. Apparently, the village and seminomadic settlements of the prior period (the Intermediate EB/MB) were swallowed by the new wave of immigrants who densely settled the coastal plain. However, seminomadic village settlements continued to exist in the hilly regions and in the valleys. The survival in many settlements, especially nonurban ones, of earlier architectural and ceramic forms[2] alongside newer forms, provides evidence for this pattern of settlement.

Features originating in northern and central Syria characterized the new era: the use of brick walls on stone foundations, earthen ramps, gates, and the well-planned house with a courtyard. The architecture of cult buildings preserved the traditional temple (as the divinity's dwelling) which had originated during the Early Bronze Age (as at Nahariyah, for example), and continued into the Intermediate EB/MB (Megiddo). At the same time a new cultic phenomenon appeared in Palestine — bammot, or 'high places' (Megiddo, Nahariyah, and Gezer).

---

1. Although the term MB I has been replaced by Intermediate Early Bronze/Middle Bronze Age, MB IIA has been retained for the sake of convenience.

2. For example, the use of columns built of stone drums, as found at Giv'at Sharett near Bet Shemesh. See D. Bahat: Excavations at Giv'at Sharett near Beth-Shemesh, Qadmoniot 8 (1975), pp. 64–67 (Hebrew), and the preservation of the typical cooking pot in use during the Intermediate EB/MB.

The cultural orientation of the MB IIA was directed mainly towards its source: the Lebanese coast and northern and central Syria. The influence of this area is also reflected in ceramic wares and small finds. Egypt, on the other hand, despite the great political influence and commercial ties it exercised from the beginning of the Twelfth Dynasty, had only a loose political domination over Palestine. No convincing evidence of Egyptian influence on the architecture of the MB IIA exists. Egyptian cultural influence on Palestine peaked during the Second Intermediate Period in Egypt (the MB IIB of Palestine).

Two processes — the weakening of Egyptian influence on Palestine and the Lebanese coast during the late Twelfth Dynasty, and the death of Hammurabi of Babylon, with its resultant lifting of expansionist pressure on northern Syria — establish *ca.* 1750 B.C. as the beginning of the Middle Bronze Age. The next 150 years (1750–1600 B.C.) saw the rise and evolution of the Canaanite city-state to its classic form: a strongly fortified city with large earthen ramps, defensive towers, and gates — major architectural features that originated in Syria. Further evidence of Syrian influence is found in a number of urban cult centres built on the model of the Syrian temple. Even the few examples of palaces uncovered thus far show signs of northern and Syro-Mesopotamian influence in their planning. Egyptian cultural influences are represented by the appearance of the octagonal column, and apparently by the use of colonnades. Towards the end of the period, Egyptian influence became more marked, as a result of the domination of southern, and perhaps central sections of Palestine by the Fifteenth, 'Hyksos', Dynasty.

Around 1570 B.C., Palestine, along with parts of Syria and the Lebanese coast, came under Egyptian rule (the Eighteenth Dynasty); however, it did not become an Egyptian province until the end of the campaigns of Tuthmose III (1480 B.C.). Egyptian architectural influences increasingly penetrated into Palestine during the fourteenth, thirteenth, and early twelfth centuries. They existed alongside the local Canaanite traditions that continued to develop the forms that had originated in the Middle Bronze Age. The Near East of the Late Bronze Age was characterized by imperialistic expansion, and Palestine and Syria were within the spheres of influence of two empires, Egyptian and Hittite. Architectural forms and motifs from both empires were adopted. Canaanite culture adopted the temple facade, with its monumental lions (Hazor), from the Hittites, and the temple plan and decorative features from the Egyptians.

Northern Syria continued to exert an important influence on the Lebanese coast and Palestine. Middle Bronze Syrian techniques of dressing ashlars and smoothing orthostats spread to Palestine mainly during the Late Bronze Age, and their use continued into the Iron Age as well.

Palestine was affected by profound cultural and political changes towards the end of the thirteenth century and the beginning of the twelfth. Egyptian rule receded; by the mid-twelfth century, it extended only over the southern coastal plain and the cities on the main highways. Egypt was the main support of the Canaanite city-states, who from mid-century onward were subjected to dual pressures — from the Israelite tribes pushing outward from the central hills toward the fertile valleys, and from the Philistines who had settled on the southern coast. While the entry of these new ethnic groups wrought political and cultural changes in Palestine, many of the architectural features of Canaanite culture were preserved. Those traditions were transmitted to the people who ruled Palestine at the beginning of the next period, the Iron Age.

13 MIDDLE AND LATE BRONZE AGE DWELLINGS

Meir Ben-Dov

Despite years of study and the extensive finds from the Middle and Late Bronze Ages (twentieth–twelfth centuries B.C.) excavated in Israel, knowledge of the private structures of these periods is limited. This is due to the fact that the Bronze Age areas accessible to excavation at stratified sites are small, and information is sometimes based on narrow cross sections only. Furthermore, archaeologists tend to prefer excavating public buildings (fortifications, palaces, and temples), the locations of which can often be surmised prior to digging. Posing appropriate questions during the excavation, and analysing the data subsequently, are vital in studying these structures; providing plans alone, as accurate as they may be, is insufficient.

MB and LB settlements can be divided into two types: walled urban settlements and unfortified settlements. Although both subsisted on agriculture, a minor difference existed. The walled cities sustained themselves mainly on crops, and the unfortified settlements concentrated on animal husbandry within the confines of the settlement. Apparently the residents of fortified cities who raised animals kept their flocks in caves and pens outside the city limits, whereas the farmers kept their work animals in small courtyards attached to their houses. In comparison to the walled cities, which required centralization, the unfortified settlements (and their sheep pens) were spread over a relatively large area. Examples of concentrations of buildings exist, nonetheless, constructed either to save on materials for walls or to provide peripheral protection from robbers. The very existence of unfortified settlements is evidence of the sense of security felt by the inhabitants, particularly during the Middle Bronze Age. As a result of historical events, these open settlements disappeared almost entirely during the Late Bronze Age.

Although no examples of walls of dwellings preserved to full height are known from the Middle and Late Bronze Ages, it is likely that roofs and ceilings were constructed of wooden beams covered with a beaten-earth fill. The thickness of the walls, 0.6-0.7 m., indicates that most dwellings had a second storey, reached by a ladder from the courtyard, or by steps adjoining one of the walls. Building contiguous walls in densely built areas, especially in walled cities, economized on building material and space, and indicates a well-regulated way of life, perhaps even the existence of building ordinances.

Village Construction

This survey opens with the plans of houses from unfortified settlements because the beginning of the MB IIA marks the founding of permanent villages and unfortified settlements that later developed into cities.[1] The Jordan Valley sites uncovered by R. Gophna (Fig 1) and E. Eisenberg are good examples of unfortified settlements. Three-room units can be discerned: two large side rooms (*ca.* 5 × 8 m.) served as enclosed courtyards, quartering both animals and people (the climate in the Jordan Valley is comfortable all year). The interstice between the two courtyards served as a living quarter; it generally measured between 3 × 4 m. and 4 × 4 m. The division of the courtyards into discrete units (by analogy to the Bedouin life-style

---

1. This article deals only with small dwellings. Larger dwellings, called palaces by some, are treated separately in Chap. 14 pp. 105–120. Also, at present, only initial reports from a small number of excavations of MB unfortified settlements have been published.

The drawings in this article were adapted by the author from published excavation plans. The sketches of cross-sections and perspectives are also the author's. Martha Reitmeyer executed the final drawings.

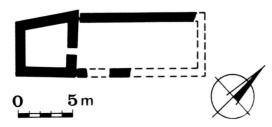

1. Dwelling, site in the Jordan Valley. *Qadmoniot* 10 (37) (1977), p. 22.

in modern Israel) was intended to separate the flock of sheep and the household work area, from the pack animals. In addition, many walls of double thickness were found in these settlements.[2]

D. Bahat uncovered a different type of dwelling in the unfortified settlement at Giv'at Sharett near Bet Shemesh (Fig. 2). Its ground plan is based on one or more rooms attached to an enclosed courtyard of much larger dimensions. There are examples of such a building with a forecourt (*ca.* 2.5 × 4 m.) and a rear courtyard connected by a passageway. The rear courtyard, which probably was partially covered (in its centre is a base for a pillar), is surrounded on three sides by small narrow rooms. The greater thickness of the walls of several of these rooms shows that some had two storeys. In this case the second storey was used for living quarters, and the

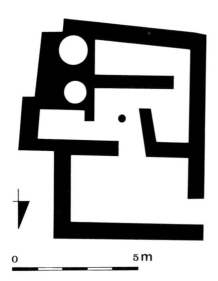

2. Dwelling, Giv'at Sharett near Bet Shemesh. *Qadmoniot* 8 (30-31) (1975), p. 65 (above).

2. R. Gophna and E. Eisenberg: Remains of a Middle Bronze Age Village in the Jordan Valley, *Qadmoniot* 10 (1977), pp. 22–24.

lower storey for storage and animal pens. At any rate, small rooms surrounding an enclosed courtyard characterize the structures at Bet Shemesh, which were constructed of sun-baked bricks laid on rough-hewn stone foundations resting on bedrock. The buildings were built in close proximity to form a security ring.[3]

Urban Construction

A high degree of organization characterizes the urban dwellings excavated in walled cities. The simplest type of buildings, those most similar to village construction, were uncovered by R. Amiran at Tell Nagilah (Fig. 3).[4] This settlement subsisted on crop cultivation

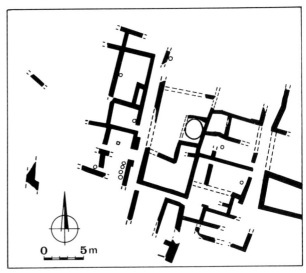

3. Dwelling, Tell Nagilah. *Archaeology* 18 (1966), p. 114, Fig. 3.

and cattle raising. Because of low precipitation and prolonged drought, cattle raising may have been the more important activity, a fact apparently reflected in the ground plans of the houses. The streets in Tell Nagilah were well laid out — usually parallel to each other — with houses placed in double rows between them. Note that the houses were built with shared walls. All the houses are of the courtyard-house type, containing a relatively large courtyard with adjoining rooms, although individual buildings differ. For example, one structure had an enclosed courtyard (3 × 4.5 m.) near the street and a living room (1.5 × 3 m.) on the opposite side. A second building had a 2 × 3 m. courtyard with three small

3. D. Bahat: The Excavations of Giveat-Sharet near Beth-Shemesh, *Qadmoniot* 8 (1975), pp. 64–68.
4. Tel nagila, *EAEHL* III, pp. 592–589.

adjoining rooms. A third measured 5 × 8 m., half of which was an enclosed courtyard; the other half was divided into two unequal rooms. The walls were built of sun-baked bricks on a foundation of small, undressed stones and smooth stones gathered from nearby wadis.

Megiddo exemplifies the crystallization of the courtyard-house type that accompanied the inception of urbanization in the MB II. The earliest examples of the courtyard-house type are found in Area B-B, near the cultic centre (beginning in Stratum XIIIA). Especially noteworthy are two adjoining units, each with a row of rooms that open onto an enclosed courtyard.[5] Stratum XII contains houses surprisingly similar to the courtyard houses at Tell Nagilah: their plan consists of three to four rooms that surround a courtyard entered directly from the street (Figs. 4, 5). Strata XI, X, and IX at Megiddo, dating to the MB IIB and the early Late Bronze Age, contain the courtyard house in its fully developed classic form: a house with a central enclosed courtyard surrounded

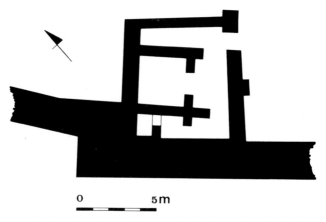

6. Dwelling, Bet Shemesh Stratum V. *Ain Shems* V, p. 28, Fig. 2.

by rooms on all four sides, with one room serving as a sort of gatehouse.[6]

Outstandingly well-planned MB buildings were uncovered in Area A-A, Strata XII–XI, at Megiddo; they continued to be occupied, with alterations, until the Late Bronze Age.[7] In the initial stage, adjoining courtyard houses of the broadhouse type, entered through the courtyard, were uncovered. The courtyard contained various installations — ovens, storage facilities, and chicken coops — and was adjoined by a row of contiguous rooms along its length, two to three rooms per house. It is likely that these buildings had a second storey. The largest of these houses reached dimensions of 8 × 10 m., with the courtyard encompassing approximately half the area.

A typical courtyard house uncovered at Bet Shemesh was assigned by its excavators to the Middle Bronze Age (Fig. 6).[8] The approximately square house, 7 × 7.5 m., is located near the city-wall. It was entered through an enclosed courtyard that was surrounded by rooms on three sides; the side rooms are long and narrow. The plan is very similar to the four-room house known from the Iron Age (Chap. 21, p. 123). Apparently the building had a second storey, as well.

At Tell Beit Mirsim, an especially spacious MB dwelling, identified by W.F. Albright as a patrician house, heralds a significant change in the ground plans of houses (Fig. 7).[9] However, it could only be considered a patrician house if it had been occupied by a single family — and this is not certain. The structure, which measures 8 × 11 m., was divided

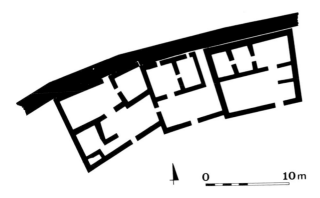

4. Dwellings, Megiddo Stratum XII. *Megiddo* II, Fig. 378.

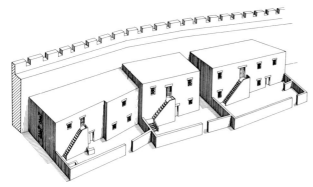

5. Dwellings, Megiddo Stratum XII, reconstruction.

5. *Megiddo* II, Fig. 397.

6. *Ibid.*, Figs. 399–401.
7. *Ibid.*, Figs. 378–379.
8. *'Ain Shems* IV, V, Fig. 2.
9. W.F. Albright: Tell Beit Mirsim, *EAEHL* Vol. I, p. 569.

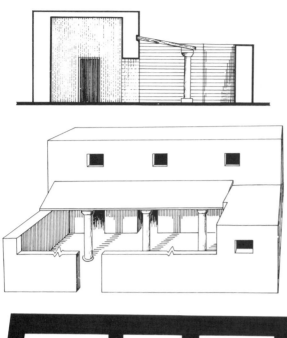

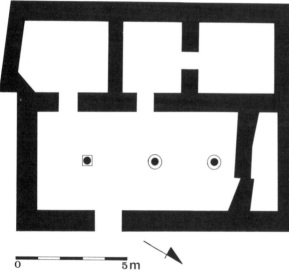

7. Dwelling, plan, section and reconstruction, Tell Beit Mirsim. *Tell Beit Mirsim* II, Pl. 56:G.

into a courtyard and a row of rooms. The courtyard was roofed and divided by a row of pillars. The courtyard may have functioned as a living quarter, while a narrow room attached to the courtyard served either as a kitchen, storage facility, or for domestic animals. Two of the dwelling chambers were attached to each other. This may mean that the building was occupied by different families (similar to the present-day practice among Israeli Arabs). The building may have had a second storey.

At Hazor, Y. Yadin uncovered another well-planned housing unit. The excavations in Area G in the lower

city revealed a residential quarter that enabled a study of dwellings from the Middle Bronze Age to the end of the Late Bronze Age.[10] The buildings exhibit typical MB features: entry from the street into an enclosed forecourt, with rooms on the far side.

LB Houses in Walled Cities

Although LB dwellings show continuity with the previous period, they are characterized by great advances in the quality of building plans and techniques. The buildings belong mainly to the courtyard-house type. Examples are limited to three sites — Megiddo, Tel Batash, and Tell Abu Hawam — for which reasonably complete information is available, thus facilitating analysis of the structures.

Megiddo. — Area B-B at Megiddo, a cultic area illustrates the development of courtyard houses, which had undergone very little change during the Late Bronze Age. The location of the various housing units remained fixed, and the network of streets was not altered. The houses apparently belonged to wealthy families connected for generations with the city's ritual and economic activities. The plan of House 3002 is typical. Built during the Middle Bronze Age, it developed into a courtyard house with a unique

8. Dwelling, Tel Batash. Biblical Archaeology Today (Proceedings of the Intl. Congress on Biblical Archaeology, Jerusalem, April 1984), Jerusalem, 1985, p. 67 (upper figure).

10. *Hazor* II, p. 72, Pls. XXX–XXXVII, CCVII, CCVIII.

Tel Batash (Timnah). Late Bronze Age dwelling.

ground plan in Strata IX and VIII. It continued to stand until the end of the Late Bronze Age, with only minor changes. The building (12 × 12.5 m.) had an entrance hall that led into a central enclosed courtyard (4 × 5 m.) containing a granary. The courtyard was the focal point of household tasks: it provided access to all of the surrounding rooms and served as a source of light and air. The northern end of the house contained two small rooms used as storage facilities or silos.

Tel Batash. — At Tel Batash, a large, well-preserved LB building was uncovered (Fig. 8).[11] The street entrance led to an enclosed courtyard that was joined by a roofed 'passage' to several storerooms, cattle and sheep pens. A second storey, one-half to two-thirds the area of the ground storey, served as the main living area. This building also bears some resemblance to the Iron Age four-room house.

Tell Abu Hawam. — Large sections of an LB residential area have been preserved in Strata V and IV at Tell Abu Hawam near the mouth of the Kishon River.[12] The buildings in both strata have similar ground plans: they are nearly square (10 × 10 m.) and have an enclosed courtyard adjoined by two rooms whose total area equals the area of the courtyard. Some of the buildings deviated from this plan because of physical conditions and the proximity of neighbouring buildings. Some buildings had an extra room at the edge of the courtyard. The rough-hewn stone walls (0.7–0.8 m. thick), resting on foundations of similar rough-hewn stones,, were

11. A. Mazar and G. Kelm: Canaanites, Philistines and Israelites in Tell Batash, *Qadmoniot* 13 (1980), pp. 89–97.

12. R. W. Hamilton: Excavations at Tell Abu-Hawam, *QDAP* 4 (1934), pp. 8–13. This discussion includes eleventh-century B.C. houses, which, at Abu Hawam, belong to the LB culture. A significant number of Canaanite cities maintained their independence (having escaped capture during the Israelite conquest) in politics and building traditions until their subjugation by David in the late eleventh and early tenth centuries B.C.

preserved to a height of about 0.8 m. Stratum V buildings had large, partially dressed cornerstones that endowed greater strength to the walls. Thus, the walls at Tell Abu Hawam could have easily supported a second storey.

The inhabitants of Tell Abu Hawam made their living from the sea (as fishermen, sailors, and traders) and from agriculture; nevertheless, there is no significant difference between their houses and houses at other sites. Note that this settlement reflects both town planning and uniformity in the size and layout of the buildings.

Hazor. — The LB buildings in Area G at Hazor are of special interest because there is evidence of preplanning for the streets, plaza, alleys, and dwellings. The buildings do not conform to a single plan; rather, they harmonize with the nearby public areas and adjacent streets. The buildings vary in size from small — a courtyard with one or two adjoining rooms, to large — a spacious courtyard surrounded by many rooms and containing installations — ovens, silos, and chicken coops (similar to the yards in modern Arab villages). Stone benches abutting the walls were found in some rooms; these were used as seating or for storing household utensils. Most houses had beaten-earth floors; only in a few instances were the floors paved with stones. These rooms may have housed horses and other domestic animals. The walls, some of which are preserved to a height of 0.5 m., were built of small, unhewn stones but may have been topped with sun-baked bricks. The thickness of the walls (0.5–0.7 m.) indicates that some buildings had two storeys. Stone rollers found in nearby rubble are indirect evidence that mud roofing had been spread over wooden beams or branches.[13]

Conclusions

It is essential to note the architectural innovations made in private dwellings in the Middle and Late Bronze Ages. Although the houses are an intrinsic development and refinement of EB buildings, nonetheless the era marks the crystallization of the courtyard-house type in Palestine, the typical house type in the entire Near East until a fairly late date. The source of this type in Palestine is unclear. The local-origin thesis has basis, but the possibility of its having been imported in the MB IIA waves of immigration from central Syria and Mesopotamia cannot be ruled out.

The quality of life in the private dwellings improved significantly during the Middle and Late Bronze Ages in comparison to the Chalcolithic and Early Bronze Ages. The central courtyard became the place where daily household tasks and cooking were performed, rooms on the ground floor served as storage or cattle pens, and the actual living quarters were transferred to the upper storey. This improvement was accompanied by the introduction of advanced building techniques. The Middle and Late Bronze Ages mark the final development of the art of private construction as it was known until the conclusion of the Iron Age.

13. The stone rollers were uncovered at various MB and LB sites, among them, Hazor. See *Hazor* II, Pl. XX. These specimens date to the Iron Age; identical Bronze Age rollers were found but not reported.

PALACES AND PATRICIAN HOUSES IN THE MIDDLE AND LATE BRONZE AGES

Eliezer D. Oren

Introduction

It is difficult to identify palaces, patrician houses and governors' residencies at sites in Israel for a variety of reasons — among them the lack of written sources and, above all, the fragmentary nature of the building remains. It is evident, however, that major contributions to the formation of a 'Canaanite' architectural concept in Palestine were made by the neighbouring cultures of Egypt, and especially Syria, Anatolia, and Mesopotamia. The dominant influence on both private and public architecture was the traditional 'Oriental' house, which was built around a central, unroofed courtyard. This tradition characterized the eastern Mediterranean basin, and continued without significant change up to the classical period. Building remains of palaces in Israel exhibit an unbroken continuity from the Middle to the Late Bronze Age. Thus it is possible to speak of an architectural concept for buildings designed for the ruling classes of Middle and Late Bronze Age Canaanite cities. Identification of these buildings and their classification is based on their location in the city (near the gate or the temple, in the elite zones), as well as by the quality of the building materials and certain construction techniques. The fragmentary nature of the building remains also makes it difficult to elucidate the function of the various units - offices, storerooms, living quarters, servants' and service rooms. Nor can it always be established with certainty whether the buildings had a second storey. Construction details of roofing, windows, doorways, stairways, water supply and drainage systems, washing facilities, and lighting arrangements also cannot be reconstructed with any certainty.

Courtyard Palaces

The basic plan of a palace consists of a spacious, rectangular-shaped courtyard with rooms surrounding it on all sides or flanking it on two sides. The walls were relatively thick and constructed of mud brick on stone foundations. A characteristic feature of the palaces is a ratio of 1:1, or even 2:3, between the area of the courtyard and that of the rooms. Well-designed courtyard palaces appear for the first time in MB IIA occupation strata, and became the typical public building in Syria and Palestine from that time through the Late Bronze Age. The palaces occupied a considerable part of the urban area allocated for public buildings, and were usually situated near the temple; later, at the end of the MB IIC, they were erected near the city-gate. Since palaces extended over large areas and were located on sites that were continuously rebuilt, only a small number have been completely excavated (mainly in Syria). The high quality building materials used in their construction — hewn stones, orthostats, dressed stones — were in great demand by later generations of builders, thus the palaces were greatly destroyed by plundering. For these reasons reconstructions of the plans of these palaces often exceed the material evidence.

Megiddo is an excellent example of a prosperous Canaanite city with advanced civic architecture. It is possible to trace in detail the development of the palace plan in the Middle and Late Bronze Ages and to study its integration within the general layout of the city. Remains of palaces were uncovered in three areas: AA, BB, and DD; of these the most complete picture was revealed in Area AA.

In Area BB, west of the sacred precinct, fragmentary

Kabri. Middle Bronze Age II Palace

remains of monumental buildings, apparently palaces, were unearthed in Strata XII–X. In this period (MB IIA–B), the palace and the temple formed a single architectural unit separate from the rest of the city. Towards the end of the Middle Bronze Age (Stratum X), a new architectural concept can be distinguished: the palace was moved from the temple area and henceforth became an integral part of the city-gate area.

In Stratum XII (MB IIA), the city plan was reorganized and the palace was established in the vicinity of the sacred area (Fig. 1).[1] The evidence from the excavations of G. Schumacher and G. Loud can help in reconstructing the western part of the monumental courtyard palace assigned to this

stratum.[2] The outer wall, which was 2 m. thick, was preserved in this section, with small halls and rooms built along it. The palace extended over an area of at least 1,000 sq. m. In Stratum XI (MB IIB) it was rebuilt (Building 5059) on foundations of field stones and the floors of the rooms were coated with thick plaster. It is possible to discern a basic plan consisting of a large courtyard with a beaten lime floor flanked by small rooms.[3] In Strata X–IX the palace continued in use in its original plan, with only minor changes.[4]

In Area AA the palace (4031) of Stratum X (MB IIC) was erected in the vicinity of the city-gate, and served as the nucleus of the monumental buildings of the successive strata. It should be noted that in

1. The shift in location of the palace from the sacred precinct to the area of the gate has also been noted at other sites as, for example, Alalakh, Strata VII–V.

2. See *Megiddo II*, Fig. 415.
3. See *Megiddo II*, Fig. 399; I. Dunayevsky and A. Kempinski: Megiddo Temples, *EI* 11, Jerusalem, 1973, p. 22, Fig. 15.
4. See *Megiddo II*, Figs. 400–401; Dunayevsky and Kempinski (above note 3), p. 24, Fig. 16.

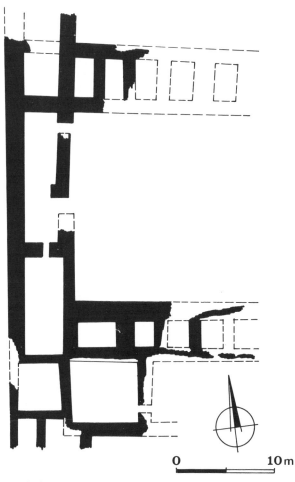

1. Palace, Megiddo Stratum XII. *Megiddo* II, Fig. 415.

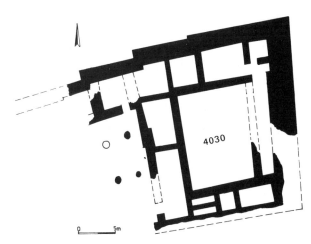

2. Palace, Megiddo Stratum IX. *Megiddo* II, Fig. 381.

these strata very few changes were made in the city-gate area. Palace 4031 continued in use in Stratum IX, with only the raising of floors and slight repairs. The plan of Building 2134 of Stratum IX is thus an exact replica of the original plan of the palace of Stratum X (Fig. 2).[5] Buildings 4031 and 2134 are typical examples of MB Canaanite courtyard palaces, very similar in plan to the palaces at Tell el-'Ajjul, Aphek, and Tel Sera'. The dimensions of the later building are 22 × 25 m. and of the central courtyard, 9 × 12 m.; the latter comprising approximately one-fifth of the total area of the palace. A drainage system was found in the courtyard and a staircase leading to a second storey was found in the southwestern corner. The walls of the building on the west (and south?) were 1.2 m. thick, while on the north and

east they were as thick as 4 m! The massive walls on the north side, near the gateway and on the edge of the mound, indicate that the palace was also meant to serve as a fortress.

Following changes in the city plan in Stratum IX, the houses west of the palace were razed and the palace complex expanded into this area. The destruction of Stratum IX, attributed by the excavators to the campaign of Thutmose III, was apparently not complete in Area AA. Although the new palace erected here (Stratum VIII, Building 2041) (Fig. 3) was based on a different plan from that of the Stratum IX palace (Building 2134), the two shared walls on the northern and eastern sides and the floors were very close together.[6] Building 2041 extended over an area

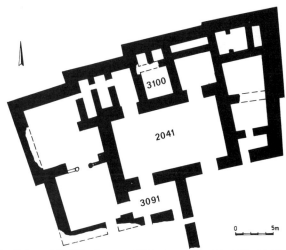

3. Palace, Megiddo Stratum VIII, Area A-A. *Megiddo* II, Fig. 383.

5. See *Megiddo II*, Figs. 380–381; A. Kempinski: *Syrien and Palastina (Kanaan) in der latzten Phase der Mittelbronze IIB Zeit (1650–1570 V. Chr.)*, Wiesbaden, 1983, pp. 93–94, 169–172 and Plan 1.

6. See *Megiddo II*, Fig. 382.

of 1,500 sq.m. (30 × 50 m.); the walls were from 2–4 m. thick, and the rooms had lime floors and sophisticated drainage systems. The central courtyard (2041) was entered through a wide opening. An inner courtyard (3091), with a shell pavement and a basin, seems to have had a series of doors that communicated directly with the important rooms of the palace. A group of rooms and courtyards on the eastern side were entered through a separate doorway in the south. The most luxurious wing was on the west side. It contained a forecourt in whose northern wall was a monumental entrance with basalt columns and piers. The entrance led to a group of rooms, one of which was presumably the throne room (*cf.* Ugarit, Fig. 10). An Egyptian lotus-shaped capital found in the eastern courtyard may have belonged to one of these columns.[7] Beneath the floor of one of the small rooms (3100) on the northern side of the building, a hoard of gold vessels, ivory plaques, jewelry and ornamental objects was found.

The thick northern wall was destroyed and replaced by a narrower one, with buttresses built directly on top of the glacis of Stratum VIII. The principal change in Stratum VIIB occurred in the west wing. The courtyards and monumental entrance were replaced by a row of small rooms, with their doorways aligned along a central axis (3186) which led to a corner room (3103). Here were found a small raised platform and steps, which the excavators identified as a household shrine.

In Stratum VIIA, which came to an end at the beginning of the Iron Age, a special annex was built here consisting of three subterranean rooms (3073) 1.4 m. deep. The absence of any finish or plaster on the exterior surface of the building supports the assumption that these rooms were constructed within a foundation trench.[9] In the rooms was found a collection of unique ivory objects whose date of concealment was established by an ivory pen box bearing the cartouche of Rameses III. The courtyards of the Stratum VIIA palace were paved with very large stones coated with plaster. The quantities of painted plaster fragments found indicate that the walls of the palace originally had painted decorations. The palace of Stratum VIIA was destroyed in a great conflagration, probably in the middle of the twelfth century B.C.

Remains of additional palaces were uncovered in Area DD (Fig. 5). Stratum VIII contained a

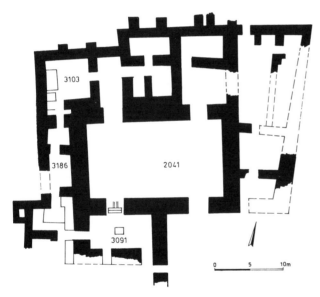

4. Palace, Megiddo Stratum VIIB. *Megiddo* II, Fig. 382.

The palace of Stratum VIII continued in its original plan, including the forecourt (3091) and central courtyard (2041) and a well-built threshold between them, in the succeeding Strata VIIB–VIIA (Fig. 4).[8] It should be stressed that there was only a slight change in the floor levels between Strata VIII–VIIB.

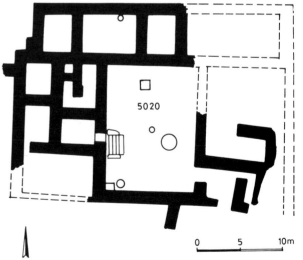

5. Palace, Megiddo Stratum VIII, Area D-D. *Megiddo* II, Fig. 411.

7. See A. Siegelmann: A Capital in the Form of a Papyrus Flower from Megiddo, *Tel Aviv* 3 (1976), p. 141.

8. See *Megiddo II*, Figs. 383–384.

9. T. Dothan: *The Philistines and Their Material Culture,* Jerusalem, 1982, pp. 70–76.

Megiddo. Late Bronze Age Palace (Strata VIII-VII).

magnificent courtyard palace (Building 5020) that was similar in size and plan to Palace 2134 of Stratum IX in Area AA.[10] The building included a central courtyard (11 × 15 m.) with a beaten lime floor on a gravel base, a table (for offerings, an altar?), and stone storage installations. The palace apparently continued in use without change in Stratum VIIB from the thirteenth century B.C.

One of the finest examples of a courtyard palace was uncovered by W.M.F. Petrie in his excavations at Tell el-ʿAjjul.[11] In a raised area in the northwestern corner of the mound were discovered a group of buildings that he identified as palaces. W.F. Albright, however, has shown that only Palace I should be

considered a palace. Palace II was apparently a patrician house (see below, p. 115), and Palaces III-V served as fortresses.[12] Palace I (Fig. 6) was built on a foundation of large, well-dressed stone slabs, shaped like orthostats, approximately 0.7 m. high and 0.2 m. thick. The slabs were placed into wide foundation trenches with stone fills and surmounted by brick walls about 2 m. thick. According to Petrie, the slabs lining the foundations were quarried from the city's fosse, thus providing the chronological link between the city's fortifications and the palace. The fragmentary remains of the southern half of the palace do not permit the reconstruction of the building. Petrie initially reconstructed the plan as consisting

10. Megiddo II, Fig. 411.
11. See W.M.F. Petrie: *Ancient Gaza, II*, London, 1932, pp. 2–5, Pl. XLV.

12. See W.F. Albright: The Chronology of a South Palestinian City, Tell el Ajjul, *AJSL* 55 (1938), pp. 337–359.

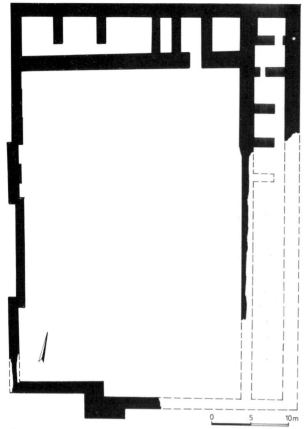

6. Palace I, Tell el-'Ajjul. A. Kempinski: *Syrien und Palastina in der letzten Phase der Mittel Bronze IIB Zeit*, Wiesbaden, 1983, Plan 6.

of a square courtyard surrounded by rooms. It later became evident that the palace, measuring 35 × 50 m., contained a rectangular courtyard (25 × 40 m.) bounded by a row of rooms on the northern and eastern sides. The archaeological evidence indicated that the building was never completed, that there had

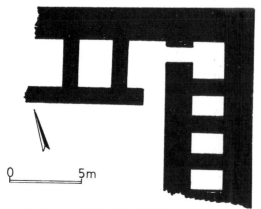

7. Palace, Tel Sera' (detail). Plan by author.

been two phases of construction and that the floors had been raised. The main entrance of the palace cannot be located with certainty. The drainage system in the southeastern corner and the adjoining massive construction (a tower?) indicate that the entrance gate was in the southern wall. With a single exception (in Room OG), no doorways were found connecting the courtyard and the rooms. One of the rooms (MK) which had a plastered floor was a washroom.

The palace has been dated by scholars to the MB II, and its destruction, by fire, to the end of that period, during the expulsion of the Hyksos (Albright) or even earlier.[13] In the opinion of this writer, the construction of the palace should be attributed to the end of the Middle Bronze Age and its destruction to the beginning of the Late Bronze Age.

In the southeastern corner of Tel Sera', in the area in which the public buildings stood in the Late Bronze Age, impressive remains of a monumental building were uncovered on bedrock. The building, only one corner of which has been exposed so far, belongs to Stratum XII (Fig. 7).[14] Its foundations were built on an artificial platform, about one metre high, constructed of large fieldstones with a fill of pebbles and earth containing sherds dating from the Chalcolithic period to the Intermediate EB/MB. The walls, which were about 2 m. thick and preserved to a height of 2.5 m., were built of alternating courses of brown and white bricks thickly coated with plaster. The remains excavated so far include part of a courtyard with a row of small rooms on its eastern side. The rooms have door jambs and piers in the entrances and thick lime-plastered floors. The original structure is similar in plan to Palace I at Tell el-Ajjul. Four building phases, with changes including the raising of floors, were distinguished. The earliest palace has been attributed to the end of the Middle Bronze Age. The palace remained in use during the first phase of the Late Bronze Age.

On the acropolis at Lachish sections of a massive structure were uncovered in Stratum VIII. Most of it is still buried beneath the foundations of the fortified palace of Stratum V.[15] Its walls, which are about 2 m. thick, were constructed on stone foundations and

13. See O. Tufnell: Tell el Ajjul, *EAEHL* I, Jerusalem, 1978, p. 57; A. Kempinski: Tell el Ajjul, Beth Aglayim or Sharuhen?, *IEJ* 24 (1974), pp. 145–152.
14. See E.D. Oren: Ziglag — A Biblical City on the Edge of the Negev, *BA* 45 (1982), pp. 164–165.
15. See D. Ussishkin: Excavations at Tel Lachish 1973–1977, Preliminary Report, *Tel Aviv* 5 (1978), pp. 6–10, Fig. 2.

coated with thick plaster, as were the floors. Despite the very fragmentary state of the remains at Lachish, the thick walls, the use of piers, and other features can be compared to the palaces of Tell el-'Ajjul and Tel Sera'. The various phases of the Lachish palace belong to the MB IIB-C; it was destroyed at the end of that period or at the beginning of the Late Bronze Age.

In the northwestern corner of Aphek (Area A) the remains of a huge building were discovered, of which only the central courtyard was exposed. The building extended over an area of more than 750 sq. m. Three building phases of the MB IIA could be distinguished.[16] On the basis of the published data, the building can be classified as a typical courtyard palace, a large part of which was occupied by its central courtyard. The construction was of excellent quality: the walls were thick and laid on stone foundations, and extensive use was made of columns. The earliest palace (Phase c) contained a large courtyard with a row of column bases in the centre (to support the roof?). The latest palace (Phase a) contained two rectangular courtyards with thick lime-plaster floors and drainage channels. After this palace was abandoned, a new and larger one was built on the acropolis. It contained a central courtyard with two column bases more than one metre in diameter and was surrounded by a series of small dwelling and service rooms.[17] This palace was attributed to the MB IIB (Fig. 8).

In Area IV at Shechem, east of the fortress temple, the Drew-McCormick expedition uncovered a large MB IIB-C building that G.E. Wright initially interpreted as a palace then later as a courtyard temple with casemate rooms (Fig. 9).[18] In the absence of detailed excavation reports, it is difficult to discern the exact plan of each of the four phases of the structure (Temene 2-5) and their stratigraphical relationship. Nevertheless, the identification of the building as a temple on the basis of its similarity to Anatolian temples is untenable, and the original suggestion to consider it a palace seems more reasonable.[19] The palace was bounded on the east and west by massive walls (Wall 900 and Wall D) that created an enclosed trapezoid-shaped area. It is possible, as was suggested by the excavators, that Wall D separated the palace

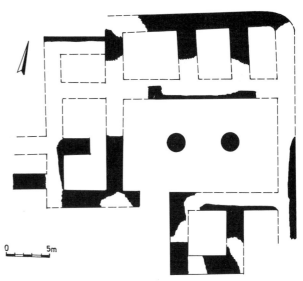

8. Palace, Tel Aphek. plan by M. Kochavi, Aphek excavations.

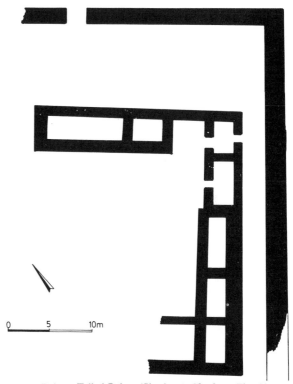

9. Palace, Tell el-Balata (Shechem). *Shechem*, Fig. 64.

from the area of the city and even served as an enclosure wall.[20] An examination of the building phases, especially Phases 2-4, suggests that the palace included an extensive courtyard (about 15 × 20 m.)

16. M. Kochavi: The First Two Seasons of Excavations at Aphek-Antipatris, *Tel Aviv* 2 (1975), pp. 17 f., Figs. 3, 6.
17. M. Kochavi: *Aphek-Antipatris: Five Thousand Years of History*, Tel Aviv, 1989 (Hebrew).
18. See *Shechem*, pp. 103 f., Figs. 64-70.
19. See G.E. Wright: *BASOR* 161 (1961), pp. 33-39.
20. For a reconstruction see G.E. Wright: Shechem, *EAEHL* IV, p. 1084.

Aphek. Late Bronze Age Palace.

flanked by a row of rooms on the north and east. Here, too, the courtyard occupied more than half of the building's area.

At Hazor, in Strata XVII-XVI of Area A, from the MB IIB-C, beneath the Israelite pillared building of Stratum VIII, the corner of a huge structure (Building 387) was uncovered that was, without doubt, a royal palace.[21] The building's deep foundations and massive walls (more than 2 m. wide) indicate that it probably had an upper storey.

The function of the public building in Area F in the lower city of Hazor is still a subject of dispute. The building was originally identified as a palace, but its excavator, the late Y. Yadin, subsequently reconstructed it as a double temple.[22]

Recent excavations at Tel Kabri uncovered a section of an extensive and well-planned palace in Area D, dating to the MB IIB (17th century B.C.).[23] Its plan, however incomplete, seems to have resembled that of the palace at Alalakh, and included a central courtyard flanked on the north, and probably on the south, by halls and subsidiary rooms (photo, p. 106). The ceremonial hall (611) to the north of the courtyard, adjacent to a large staircase, measured 10 × 10 m. and had a sunken jar in the centre. It appears that the walls were originally lined with orthostats above floor level, all of which have been robbed. The plastered floor of Hall 611 is frescoed with a rich

21. See *Hazor III-IV*, Plates V–VII; Y. Yadin: *Hazor*, pp. 124–125.
22. See Dunayevsky and Kempinski (above note 3), p. 21, Fig. 14, contra Yadin: *Hazor*, pp. 96–98.

23. A. Kempinski: Four Seasons of Excavations at Tel Kabri, *Qadmoniot* XXIII (1990), pp. 37–38; A. Kempinski and W.D. Niemeier (eds.): *Excavations at Kabri, Preliminary Report of 1989 Season, No. 4*, Tel Aviv, 1990, pp. 43–46, XVI–XXVI.

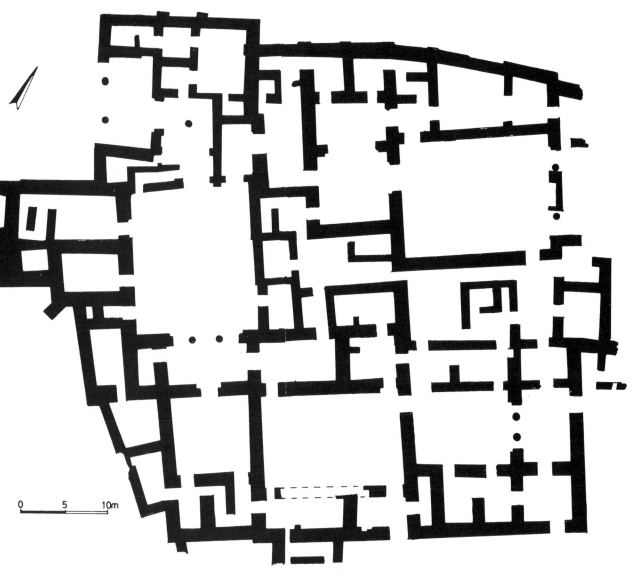

10. Palace, Ugarit (Syria). C.F.A. Schaeffer: *Ugaritica* IV, Paris, p. 1462, Fig. 21.

repertoire of geometric, floral and figurative motifs. Frescos are known from 18th century B.C. palaces at Mari and Alalakh. However, this unique fresco is best paralleled, stylistically and iconographically, by the contemporary Cretan-Theran Late Minoan IA wall painting tradition.

In the Middle and Late Bronze Ages, the cultures of Mesopotamia and northern Syria had a far-reaching influence on the development of the urban architectural tradition of Palestine. Although this survey cannot include a detailed comparative study, several examples — the palaces at Ebla, Mari, Alalakh and Ugarit — should suffice to reveal the

sources of inspiration for the architecture of Syria and Palestine.[24]

In the lower city of Tell Mardikh (Ebla) in northern Syria, part of a great palace (Royal Palace E) was uncovered in Stratum IIIA-B (MB IIA-B). The palace was built above an earlier public building in Stratum IIB2, dating from the end of the

24. See H. Frankfort: *The Art and Architecture of the Ancient Orient* (4th ed.), London, 1970, pp. 75–76; R. Naumann: *Architektur Kleinasiens* (2nd ed.), Tubingen, 1971, pp. 389 f.

third millennium B.C.[25] The palace had an extensive rectangular courtyard (8 × 15 m.) bounded on the north and east by rooms and halls, and on the west by a very thick wall (retaining wall? fortification?). The courtyard and the rooms had stone pavements set in clay, and thick plaster covered the stones. The rooms on the northern and eastern sides were panelled with orthostats, and the lintels and thresholds were built of smooth stones. Access to the central court was through a corridor paved with stone slabs and from there through two wide entrances. In the opinion of the excavators, the group of rooms south of the corridor forms the boundary of the southern quarter of the palace. The different building technique and absence of orthostats in the southern wing, however, cast doubt on the suggestion.

The monumental palace complex of the kings of Mari in the nineteenth-eighteenth centuries B.C. provides a detailed picture of the varied functions carried out in palaces in that era. The palace occupied an area of about 25 dunams (120 × 200 m.) and contained some 300 rooms, halls, and courtyards — including kitchens, bathrooms, a throne room, cult rooms, schoolrooms, workshops, storerooms, offices for clerks, and diplomatic, religious, and administrative archives. This was a well-designed plan: in Mesopotamian architecture the courtyard was not merely an open space, but a central, enclosed element in the palace complex in which a great variety of activities and functions were concentrated.[26]

Strata VII–VI at Alalakh provide us with valuable comparative data on public architecture from the Middle and Late Bronze Ages in Syria. The MB IIB 'Yarim-Lim' palace complex of Stratum VII contains all the characteristic components of the courtyard palaces, i.e. spacious courtyards surrounded by various rooms, thick walls, extensive use of buttresses, orthostat facing, etc.[27] At Alalakh, as at other MB centres, the palace was adjacent to the temple and the two actually formed one architectural unit. The Alalakh palace comprised a ceremonial wing in the northwest, and residential and storage units in the southwest. The former, with its orthostat-lined walls, included a spacious courtyard, 9 × 21 m., that was surrounded by storerooms and other subsidiary chambers as well as a staircase leading to the second storey. The royal wing contained a large throne room

and reception halls, the walls of which were richly decorated with fresco paintings.

The royal palace at Ugarit is one of the largest buildings of its kind from the Late Bronze Age in the Near East. It extends over an area of about 10 dunams and so far more than 100 rooms and halls arranged around ten inner courtyards, and a number of stairways leading to a second storey, have been uncovered (Fig. 10). The plan of the palace reveals that it was constructed in several building stages during the fifteenth-thirteenth centuries B.C. Some sections of the walls were built of well-dressed ashlar blocks with drafted margins and raised bosses. Wide grooves in the stone walls held horizontal wooden beams that gave the walls some flexibility, important during earthquakes. These last two features are also found at LB sites on Cyprus (Enkomi, Kition) and are especially typical of ashlar building in Iron Age Israel. The excavation of the palace disclosed sophisticated drainage systems and fine flagstone pavements in the courtyards. The spacious courtyard inside the gate to the palace contained a deep well. The elaborate courtyard on the southeastern side contained an ornamental pool to which water was conveyed through a network of stone channels installed beneath the palace floor. Important archives were found in the rooms of the palace, and one of the courtyards contained a kiln for firing cuneiform clay tablets.

A distinctive feature of Ugaritic palace architecture is the incorporation of a portico into the building units — elaborate entranceways, some of them stepped, with a pair of columns between stone piers. Buildings with this type of facade from the Iron Age are termed *bit hilani* in the literature, although the term was used primarily to designate the portico itself in the facade or in one of the wings of the building.[28] At Alalakh Stratum IV (15th century B.C.) was found an excellent example of a courtyard palace which was entered through a monumental portico unit. The building, known as Niqme-pa's palace, has a composite plan extending over an area of more than 5000 sq.m., comprising ceremonial, residential and storage units. Its complex ground plan, monumental portico entrance, the use of orthostats, as well as the royal archives, all point to its role as the central palace complex of LB Alalakh.

Courtyard palaces from sites of Palestine and Syria exhibit a number of common architectural features:

25. See P. Matthiae: Die Furstengraber des Palastes Q in Ebla, *Antike Welt* 13 (1982), Figs. 1, 7.
26. See A. Parrot: *Mission Archeologique de Mari: Le Palais*, Paris, 1958–1959.

27. L. Woolley: *Alalakh*, London, 1955, pp. 91–131.
28. See Naumann (above note 24), pp. 408–411; Frankfort (above note 24), pp. 151–152; 253, 276.

thick walls, massive foundations, sometimes even a platform on which the entire building was constructed, paved courtyards, etc. The outstanding feature of the structure is without doubt the extensive courtyard, which occupied a major part of the total area of the palace. The palaces in the north and centre of Palestine are apparently earlier than those in the south, appearing in fully-developed form already in the first stage of the MB II. The resemblance of palace plans of Palestine and northern Syria attests to the adoption of Mesopotamian architectural concepts as a result of the extension of Mesopotamian culture into Syria and Palestine in the Mari period via cultural and commercial ties. This phenomenon is crucial to understanding the structure and social stratification of the urban population of Palestine in the Middle Bronze Age.

It should also be emphasized that, in comparison with the palaces of Palestine, those in Mesopotamia and northern Syria were extremely complex in plan. The courtyard served as an important element of the building, but the palace complex also contained numerous rooms and halls that served a variety of functions: throne room, reception halls, offices, storerooms, lavatories, etc. Palaces in Palestine were simpler in plan and it is difficult to determine the exact use of the rooms that surrounded the courtyards. The limited number of rooms which have been found around courtyards, and their modest dimensions (see the palaces at Tell el-'Ajjul, Megiddo, and Aphek), leave open the possibility that these remains may represent only part of the complex, or its nucleus. The term 'palace', as applied to the unparalleled examples found in Mesopotamia and northern Syria, is more appropriate for the complex of courtyards, halls and rooms of Building 2041 at Megiddo (Stratum VIII) than for the series of small rooms flanking the central courtyard of Building 4031 in Stratum X there.[29]

Patrician Houses

The multiplicity of terms found in the literature to designate the dwellings of the wealthy classes — patrician houses, palaces, governors' residencies — results primarily from the lack of exact criteria for defining the functions of the various quarters (bedrooms, living quarters, service rooms, lavatories, servants and domestic quarters, storerooms, etc.).

In this survey we will use a definition approaching that of R. Naumann, according to which a patrician house was more luxurious than an ordinary house and a palace was the largest and most magnificent building in a city.[30] Patrician houses will be identified by their location in the general city plan; their proximity to the gate, palace, or temple; their dimensions and symmetry; whether their walls were thick enough to support a second storey; whether the plan included service rooms, living quarters, storerooms; the existence of a drainage system; the quality of the floors; and whether the choicest building materials were used. In contrast to the plans of temples and palaces, no uniform plan for patrician houses can be distinguished, even at the same site. Three buildings were erected in close proximity at Megiddo (3066, 3046, 3050) in the same period (Stratum X), but each exhibits a different plan.[31] Accordingly, this survey presents only a sample and not a typology of patrician houses or a description of all such buildings so far discovered in excavations.

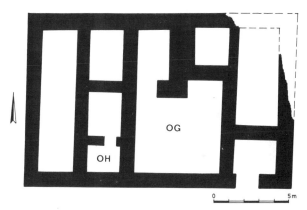

11. "Palace II", Tell el-'Ajjul. *Ancient Gaza* II, Pl. XLVI.

Palace II at Tell el-'Ajjul is in fact a patrician house that was built directly above the northern wing of Palace I.[32] Because the thin brick walls (approximately one metre wide) of Palace II were built in the Egyptian style — namely, without stone foundations — Albright suggested that it had been the residence of the local Egyptian governor at the beginning of the Eighteenth Dynasty (Fig. 11). The building has an inner courtyard (OG) with steps leading to a second storey. There were a number of small rooms alongside the courtyard, including a bathroom (OH) with a plastered floor and

29. See *Megiddo II*, Fig. 380; if this suggestion is correct, the fragmentary remains of rooms found to the west of Building 4031 are an integral part of the palace complex.

30. See Naumann (above note 24), p. 389.
31. See *Megiddo II*, Fig. 400.
32. See Petrie (above note 11), Plate XLVI.

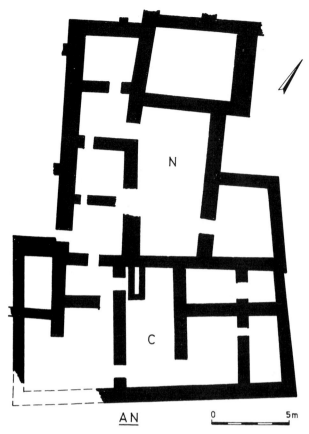

12. Building AM, Tell el-'Ajjul. *Ancient Gaza* II, Pl. LIV.

a drainage system. The remains of another building (PW), built on the southwestern corner of Palace I, also belong to this phase. The plan of the building, and the arrangement and size of the rooms, suggest that it was a luxurious residence. Palace II was attributed by Petrie to the Twelfth Dynasty; this was later corrected to the end of the Middle Bronze Age, at the beginning of the sixteenth century B.C.[33] In the opinion of this writer, the stratigraphic and ceramic evidence corroborates Albright's proposal to assign the construction of the 'palace' to a later date — the beginning of the Late Bronze Age.[34] In the southern quarter of 'City II', which dates to the beginning of the Late Bronze Age, a number of buildings have survived that, on the basis of their plans and the thickness of the walls, can be classified as courtyard patrician houses (Fig. 12). Building AM, for example, is constructed on brick foundations and has walls that are from 1.0 to 1.5 m. thick. It

has two courtyards (C, N) that are surrounded by halls and rooms. Building EAD has a rectangular courtyard flanked by groups of rooms, as apparently does Building TCT, which also has very thick walls set on stone foundations.[35]

In excavations at Ashdod a spacious building (12 × 16 m.), the residence of a wealthy family, was uncovered in Strata 16–15 from the fourteenth century B.C. (Fig. 13). The building included a rectangular courtyard flanked by storerooms and service rooms. It cannot be determined from the thickness of the walls whether there was a second storey.[36]

At Tell Beit Mirsim, in Stratum D, dating from the end of the Middle Bronze Age, Albright excavated a structure he identified as a palace or patrician house.[37] The plan of the building is incomplete, and underwent changes and repairs. A large rectangular courtyard attached to the house served as a forecourt for a group of rooms on the west side (Fig. 14). The courtyard contained a plastered basin about 2 m. in diameter. The rooms on the south side (1, 4) yielded numerous fragments of storage jars and were apparently storerooms. The rooms on the north, in the excavator's opinion, were stables for horses and service rooms. No traces of stairways were found, but the walls were sufficiently thick (1.3 m.) to support a second storey for living quarters. Plastered benches, or shelves, ran along the walls. Numerous precious objects were found in the rooms, such as ivory inlays and a fragment of a 'serpent' stele. The house was destroyed in a conflagration at the end of the Middle Bronze Age, perhaps during one of the campaigns against the Hyksos.

At the top of the western glacis at Ta'anakh, E. Sellin excavated a square building (18 × 20 m.) that he called a fortified palace or fortress (Fig. 15). At Ta'anakh, as at Tell Beit Mirsim, the rooms were arranged along two sides of the courtyard rather than surrounding it. The courtyard contained a well 8 m. deep, and its floor was made of *terre pisee*. The building had carefully constructed stone foundations that were preserved to an average height of one metre. A guard-room (?) occupied the southwestern corner, and there was a row of four small rooms, or compartments (average 2 × 2 m.) on the northeastern side of the courtyard.

33. See Tufnell (above note 13), Kempinski (above note 13).
34. See Albright (above note 12), p. 33 f.

35. See W.M.F. Petrie: *Ancient Gaza*, I, London, 1931, Pl. LIV; *idem*, *Ancient Gaza*, IV, London, 1934, Pls. LXII–LXIII; Kempinski (above note 5), pp. 105–107.
36. M. Dothan: Ashdod — Seven Seasons of Excavation, *Qadmoniot* 5 (1972), pp. 4–5.
37. See *Tell Beit Mirsim* II, pp. 35–39, Pl. 55.

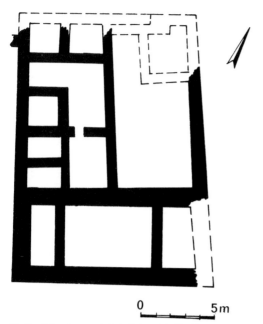

0   5m

13. Patrician house, Ashdod Area B. *EAEHL*, p. 108.

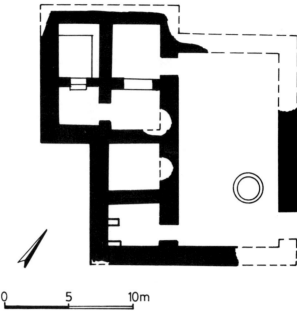

0   5   10m

14. Patrician house, Tell Beit Mirsim. *Tell Beit Mirsim* II, Pl. 55.

The rooms were separated from the courtyard by a long, narrow corridor. It is not known how the rooms were entered because almost no doorways were found, nor is it known whether there was a second storey for living quarters. A considerable accumulation of bricks was found on the stone foundations, which Sellin attributed to a later stratum, although it is possible that the collapsed bricks belonged to this building. The excavators assigned the building to the end of the Middle Bronze Age; however, according to S. Yeivin it was a fort of the Late Bronze Age.[38]

Egyptian-Type Governors' Residencies

Petrie was the first to apply the term 'residency' to define one of the buildings at Tell el-Far'ah (South).[39] Buildings that were influenced by Egyptian architecture of the New Kingdom period are here included in this category (Fig. 16). These buildings apparently served as residencies for the local (Egyptian?) governors or rulers. The buildings were square, with thick brick walls usually built on brick foundations, following the Egyptian tradition. Access was through a corner doorway. An inner central area

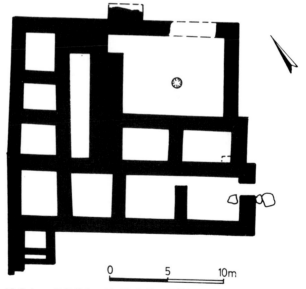

0   5   10m

15. Palace, Tell Ta'anakh. E. Sellin: *Tell Ta'annek*, Wien, 1904, p. 43, Plan III.

(a courtyard or hall) was surrounded by small rooms, with a stairway in the corner. Structures similar in plan and size, although more complex, are characteristic of private buildings at such Egyptian sites as el-Amarna, Gurob, and Deir el-Medineh.[40]

38. M. Avi-Yonah and S. Yeivin: *Kadmoniot Arzeinu*, Tel Aviv, 1955, p. 89; E. Sellin: *Ta'annek*, Vienna, 1904, p. 43; A.E. Glock: Taanach, *EAEHL* IV, p. 1143.
39. See *Beth Pelet*, I, pp. 15f.

40. See W.M.F. Petrie: *Tell el-Amarna*, London, 1894, pp. 20–22, Pls. XXXVIII–XXXIV; L. Borchardt & H. Ricke: *Die Wohnhauser in Tell el-Amarna*, Berlin, 1980, *passim*.

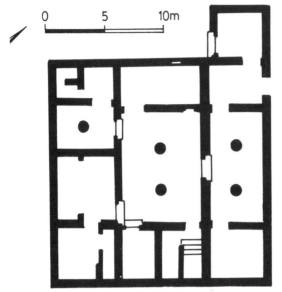

16. Private dwelling from Tell el-Amarna, the New Kingdom, Egypt. L. Borchardt and H. Ricke: *Die Wohnhauser in Tell el-Amarna*, Berlin, 1980, Plan 87.

In Stratum VI at Bet Shean (the end of the Late Bronze Age to the beginning of the Iron Age), two imposing buildings (1500 and 1700) were excavated that displayed Egyptian architectural details — carved door jambs and T-shaped doorsills. According to Egyptian inscriptions, Building 1500 was the residence of the Egyptian governor Rameses-Wesr-Khapesh during the reign of Rameses III (Fig. 16).[41] The building was square (21 × 22 m.), its walls were about 2 m. thick, and its foundations were about 2 m. deep. An entrance room led to an inner courtyard or hall that contained two column bases in the centre. Small rooms and long corridors surrounded the courtyard. Scholars have suggested that the columns in the innermost area supported the ceiling, which was higher than the other parts of the building, and admitted light into the hall through a clerestory window beneath the roof. Contrary to the accepted practice in Egyptian buildings, in which the entrance was usually situated in one of the corners, the entrance here was set in the middle of one of the walls.

At Tel Sera' (Tell esh-Shari'a) in the western Negev, three phases of repairs and additions were distinguished in a massive structure (Building 906) in Stratum IX (Fig. 17).[42] Its northwestern wing was found beneath the four-room house of Stratum VII but has not yet been excavated. The original building, which was square (25 × 25 m.), had brick walls about 2 m. wide built on a brick foundation set into a trench layered with *kurkar*. The building included a narrow courtyard or hall, with three column bases in its centre. Small rooms and corridors (basements?) flanked it. A paved area was found in the north wing. The roof beams were of cedar. The building was destroyed by fire in the middle of the twelfth century B.C. A rich collection of Egyptian objects was found in the rooms, including a group of bowls with hieratic inscriptions, one of which mentions 'Year 20+X', apparently referring to a regnal year of Rameses III. Building 906 was built on the foundations of a structure with a similar plan from the thirteenth century B.C. (Stratum X). The transition from Stratum X to Stratum IX was peaceful.

The remains of a massive structure at Tell Jemmeh (Building JF) can also be reconstructed as a governor's residency (Fig. 21).[43] The plan is square (17 × 17 m.), with brick walls 1.5 to 2.0 m. thick. It has a central courtyard and is flanked by small rooms (basements?) on two sides. An indirect(?) entrance was located on the south side. Petrie assigned the building to the Eighteenth Dynasty, although the pottery points to a date at the end of the Late Bronze Age or the beginning of the Iron Age.

In the excavations at Tell Hesi, near the wall of 'City IV', F.J. Bliss uncovered a similar building that measured 18 × 18 m. and had walls about 1.5 m. thick (Fig. 20). The walls were laid on brick foundations set in trenches with a thick *kurkar* fill. The building contained a rectangular courtyard with small rooms alongside it and long corridors in the east wing.[44] As no doorways were found, it is impossible to ascertain whether these were subterranean rooms, or the thresholds of the doorways were higher than the floor level. The building was destroyed by fire at the end of the Late Bronze Age.

At Tel Masos a building in the Egyptian style (Building 480) was found in Stratum II, from the twelfth-eleventh centuries B.C. It measured 15 × 15 m. and its walls were about one metre wide. The building included a forecourt (489), an inner space (480) with a row of column bases, and narrow rooms and corridors on three sides. The excavators maintained that the

41. See F.W. James: *The Iron Age at Beth Shan*, Philadelphia, 1966, pp. 8f.
42. Oren (above note 14), pp. 164–166.
43. See W.M.F. Petrie: *Gerar*, London, 1928, pp. 5–6, Pl. VI.
44. See F.S. Bliss: *A Mound of Many Cities*, London, 1894, p. 72; also the erroneous reconstruction as a fortress in Ruth Amiran: Tel Hesi, *EAEHL* II, p. 518.

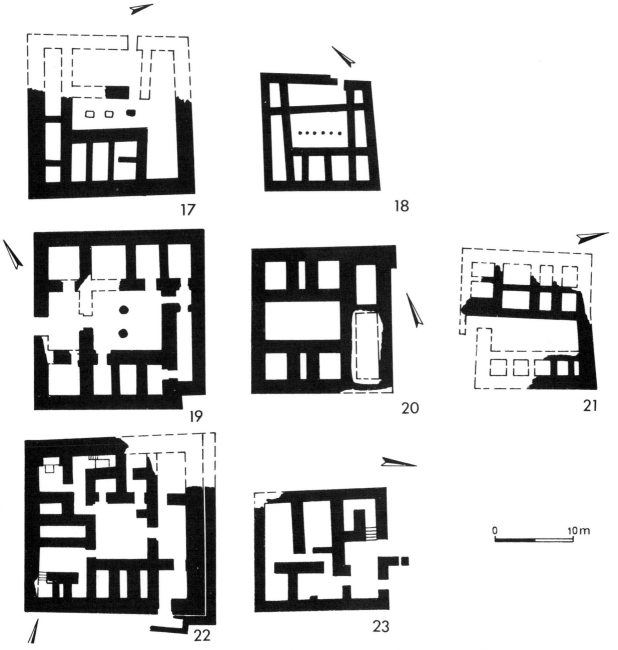

17. Tel Sera'. *EI* 18 (1985), p. 184, No. 1.   18. Tel Masos. *Tel Masos* III, Plan 18.   19. Bet Shean, Building 1500. F. James: *The Iron Age at Beth Shan*, Philadelphia, 1966, p. 9.   20. Tell Hesi. F. Bliss: *Mound of Many Cities*, London, 1898, p. 72.   21. Tell Jemmeh. *Gerar*, Pl. VI.   22. Tell el-Far'ah (S). *Beth Pelet* I, Pls. LI-LIV.   23. Tel Aphek. *BA* 44 (1981), p. 78.

building had been erected earlier, in Stratum IIIA, at the beginning of the twelfth century B.C.[45] (Fig. 18).

At Tell el-Far'ah (South), Petrie excavated an elaborate structure of the governor's residency type whose plan and architectural details closely resemble those of Egyptian private houses of the period (Fig. 22).[46] The building is 550 sq.m. in area (22 × 25 m.) and the walls are 1.5–2.0 m. thick and set on brick foundations. The roof was made of cedar beams. The building included an inner area surrounded by

45. A. Kempinski et al.: Excavations at Tel Masos — Summary of Three Seasons of Excavation (1972, 1974, 1975), *EI* 16 (Aharoni Book), Jerusalem, 1981, pp. 161, 163, Fig. 6.

46. See *Beth Pelet*, I, p. 15, Pls. LII, LIV; *Beth Pelet*, II, pp. 28–29, Pl. LXIX.

rooms and a bathroom in which steps were found. There was also an external flight of stairs. In Petrie's opinion, the inner area was not an open courtyard but a hall which rose above the rest of the building, and was lit by windows set high in the walls. As in the Egyptian courtyard houses, here too the roof was supported by a central wooden column. According to Petrie, this central area served as the executive office of the Egyptian governor and as a reception hall. In one of the rooms 45 storage jars with clay stoppers were found, and in the court, a fragment of a vessel with cartouches of Seti II. Two building phases were distinguished (ZR and YR) from the time of the Nineteenth-Twentieth Dynasties. The building was destroyed by fire at the end of the twelfth century B.C.

Another elaborate building that seems to have been indirectly influenced by the Egyptian architectural tradition — although its identity as an Egyptian-type governor's residency is doubtful — was discovered on the acropolis at Aphek in Stratum X-12 (Building 1104). The excavators identified it as the local governor's palace.[47] This monumental building was square (18 × 18 m.) and the stone foundations of its walls were 1.5 m. wide in places (Fig. 23). There was a flagstone entrance hall with a built-in bench, long hallways, small rooms, and a splendid staircase. The destruction levels of the building yielded cuneiform tablets and a faience plaque bearing the cartouche of Rameses II. As already noted, the plan of the building and the stone construction indicate it is not an Egyptian-style building; there is no doubt,

47. See M. Kochavi: Aphek-Antipatris, *BA* (1981), pp. 75–86.

however, that it was used by the local (Egyptian?) administration.[48]

The remains of palatial buildings that served as (Egyptian?) governors' residencies in the Late Bronze Age have been discovered at Canaanite sites which testify to the adoption of Egyptian building methods, and the influence of the Egyptian private house plan on Canaanite architecture. Their geographical distribution indicates that they were found at sites that exhibit ties with Egypt as well as at sites known as centres of Egyptian rule and administration in Canaan. This type of construction is found in occupation levels from the thirteenth–twelfth centuries B.C. — the time of the Nineteenth–Twentieth Dynasties in Egypt. This evidence is of great value for reconstructing the history of Egyptian rule in Canaan and for understanding the reciprocal contacts between Egypt and Canaan at the end of the New Kingdom period.

48. Y. Aharoni proposed that the square structures on Mt. Gerizim and at the Aman Airport, which are generally interpreted as temples, were probably Egyptian-type residencies. Because of architectural, chronological and other considerations, this proposal cannot be accepted. See Y. Aharoni: *The Archaeology of the Land of Israel*, Jerusalem, 1982, pp. 133–134, and A. Mazar in the present volume, pp. 182–183. Recently two more structures were identified as Egyptian residencies, i.e. the buildings excavated by Macalister in Trenches IIIa 27–28 and IV 14–16 at Gezer. Stratigraphical and architectural considerations make these hypotheses highly speculative. See I. Singer: A Governor's Residency at Gezer?, *Tel Aviv* 31 (1986), pp. 26–31; A.M. Maeir: Remarks on a Supposed Egyptian Residency at Gezer, *Tel Aviv* 15-16 (1988–1989), pp. 65–67; S. Bunimovitz: An Egyptian Governor's Residency at Gezer? — Another Suggestion, *Tel Aviv* 15-16 (1988–1989), pp. 68–76.

URBANIZATION AND TOWN PLANS IN THE MIDDLE BRONZE AGE II

Aharon Kempinski

The resurgence of urban culture in Palestine in the Middle Bronze Age II, the early twentieth century B.C., introduced new planning concepts, different from those that had been current in the Early Bronze Age. The source of these concepts should be sought in central and northern Syria and on the Phoenician coast. A decisive change from the Early Bronze Age was the sudden foundation of towns that were built rapidly, uniformly, and according to a master plan. However, as in the Early Bronze Age, some cities also followed the pattern of slow and progressive growth around an early nucleus of the site. An example of this pattern begins the survey presented here.

Megiddo

The town plan of Megiddo Strata XIIIB–X represents an example of a city which evolved gradually from the remains of an early urban nucleus around a sacred precinct. The development of the town plan can be traced in three areas excavated by the Oriental Institute of the University of Chicago[1]: Area A-A (the gate area), Area B-B (the temples), and Area C-C (the living quarter).

In Area B-B urban growth began around the sacred precinct, which at that time was an open-air altar enclosed by a fence (Stratum XIIIB); it was only in the next stratum (XIIIA) that the first residential insulae were built in the area, together with the early phase of the city-wall. A paved peripheral street ran parallel to the city wall. It was used as a service road and gave rapid access to the top of the wall in case

of attack. Houses were built between this and the second peripheral street. In Stratum XII the area was reorganized: between the sacred area and the city-wall, which was doubled in width in this stratum, residential quarters were built and the peripheral street along the city-wall was abolished. Apparently in time of need the wall and the towers could be manned from the roofs of the houses abutting the city-wall. The sacred area was surrounded by an open space entered through a gate with an indirect entrance. West of the sacred area, insulae of private houses were erected, as well as a spacious palace (25 × 60 m.).

Elements of Stratum XIIIA have been preserved in the gate area (A-A), but — according to Dunayevsky's interpretation of the data — the city-gate itself, with indirect access, was only built in Stratum XII.[2] A small open space led into the city and from it the first peripheral street branched off to the east and west. In Stratum XII private houses were built between this road and the city-wall (Fig. 1). The continuation of this peripheral road was exposed in Area B-B. The construction of the insulae against the city-wall, and the abolition of the peripheral road along it, are significant, and may indicate some military use. Erecting the houses of soldiers or guards (?) against the city-wall continued until the Iron Age and appears also in Beersheba Stratum II (see Chap. 24, pp. 258).

At the end of the Middle Bronze Age, in Stratum X, the town plan of Megiddo was reorganized (Fig. 2). Area B-B was then divided into three main parts:

---

1. *Megiddo* II, *passim*. For an analysis of the stratigraphy, see I. Dunayevsky and A. Kempinski: The Megiddo Temples, *ZDPV* 89 (1973), pp. 175–181, as well as A. Kempinski: *Megiddo — a City State and Royal Center*, Bonn (1987), pp. 4–64; 149–156.

2. The main points of Dunayevsky's proposal appear in Fig. 1 a summary of his interpretation appears in his handwriting in the margins of the plans (see his interpretation of the gate sequence [unpublished plans kept at the archive of the Institute of Archaeology, the Hebrew University, Jerusalem]. Dunayevsky labelled (in the gate area) the excavators' Stratum XII as XIB and Stratum XI as XIA.

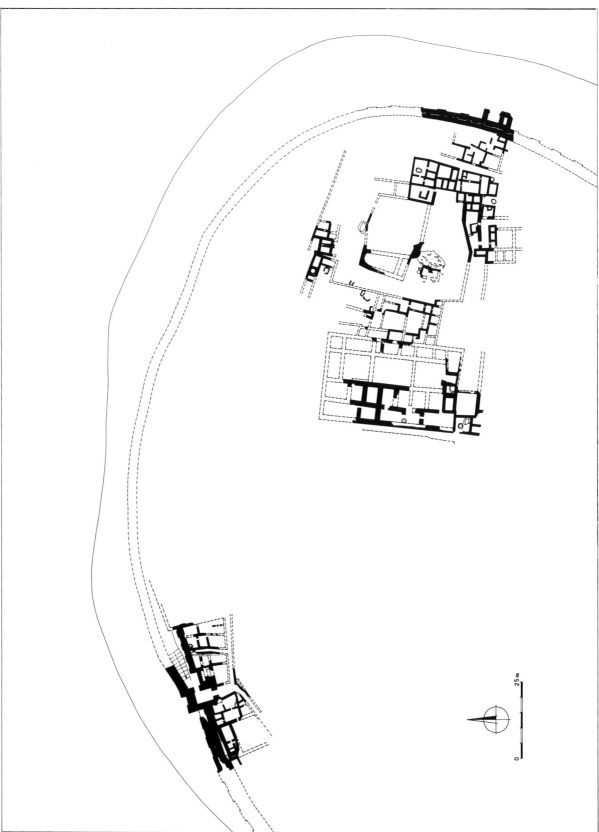

1. City plan, Megiddo Stratum XII. *Megiddo* II, Figs. 378, 398, 415.

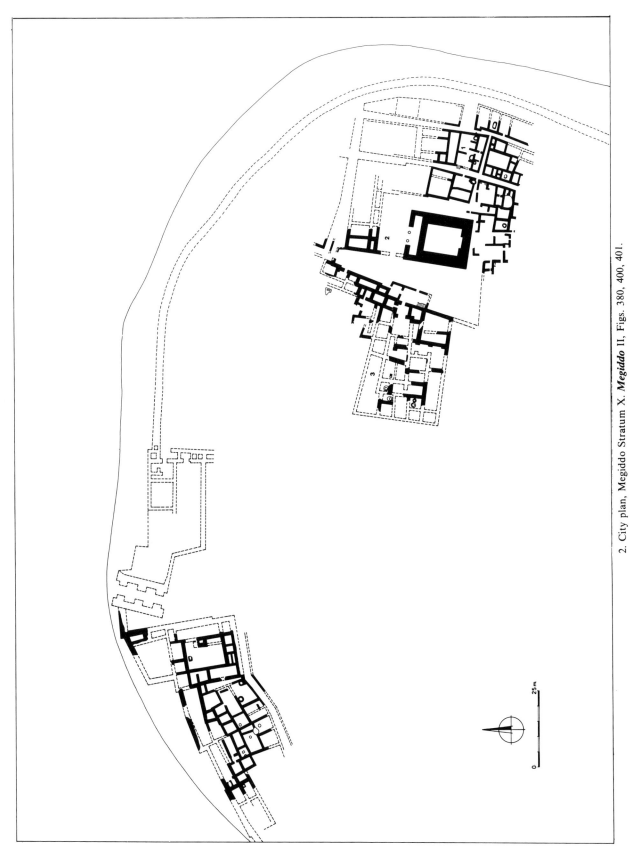

2. City plan, Megiddo Stratum X. *Megiddo* II, Figs. 380, 400, 401.

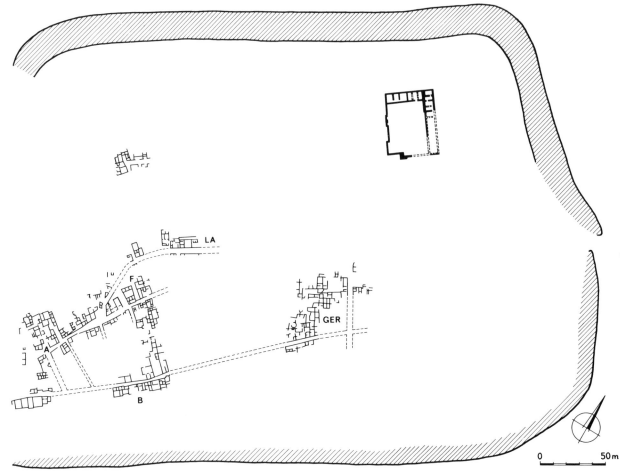

3. City plan, Tell el-'Ajjul Stratum II. *Ancient Gaza* I, Pl. LIV; *AG* III, Pls. XLV-XLVII; *AG* IV, Pls. LXI-LXIII; *AG* V, Pl. XXXII.

1. Residential insulae for the middle or upper classes in the east and in the direction of the fortifications (there are remains of a rampart and an inner wall with offsets that is eroded); 2. The temple area with its service buildings and a large open space west of it; and 3. The palace complex.

Shechem

At Shechem the data, although less clear, also indicate the slow growth of the city.[3] Only part of the public space in the sacred area (Field VI), several private houses in Fields VII, VIII, and XIII, and a considerable part of the fortifications have been excavated. The size of the city area on the south was

never established and therefore no data are available concerning the relationship between the citadel and the lower city, which extended below the Balata Quarter of modern Nablus.[4]

In the first stage (the MB IIA), when the city began to take shape in Temenos 2, a number of buildings were erected that G.R.H. Wright interpreted as an early phase of the 'temple' and that later, in Temenos 4 (see Chap. 19), evolved into a courtyard building with a public character, perhaps part of a palace.[5] East of this building is an insula of private houses and beyond them a main street that led to the city-gate. A marked change in planning occurred in Temenos 6,

3. G. R. H. Wright: Survey of Shechem over Sixty Years, *ZDPV* 89 (1973), pp. 188–194, and its comprehensive bibliography.

4. The German expedition dug a trial pit in the southeastern area, but the pit is not located far enough to the west to make possible the determination of the city's southern boundary, *ibid.*, III, p. 191, Fig. 2.
5. This is contrary to E. Wright: *Shechem*, New York (1965), pp. 106–120, where he describes the building as a 'Hittite temple'.

when the Fortress-Temple was built and the area in front of it became an open space. This space was extended eastward by several service structures built against Wall 943. East of this wall, and facing the inner city, another open space or street led to the northeastern gate. The construction of the southern gate should also be attributed to this phase, and a central street seems to have traversed the royal citadel and connected the two gates.

Hazor

In contrast to Megiddo and Shechem, where an inner development of the town plan can be discerned, at Hazor there is an interesting combination of a slowly developing nucleus in the upper city and a new city area, rapidly planned and constructed simultaneously. The following picture can be outlined from the few published data: the nucleus of the re-established city was situated on the high tell, where the early MB IIA city was built on the ruins of the EB IIIB city. Remains of the palace (and the attached temple?) in Area A, and the wall of an enclosure or inner citadel in Area B, were probably constructed in the early MB IIA city. However, it remains unclear to which phase during the time span of the MB IIA each of these structures should be attributed. In this early phase the eastern spur was added to the initial nucleus, thus establishing the first lower city.[6]

In the early eighteenth century B.C., when Hazor became one of the most important trading cities in southern Syria and northern Palestine, a rectangular enclosure (Chap. 16, Fig. 4) was built in the area of the lower city (650 × 900 m.), north of the tell and the eastern spur.[7] Little is known of its layout, mainly because excavation areas were opened only where surface remains hinted at the existence of public buildings or temples. Thus, no residential quarters or areas connected with public buildings were excavated in the enclosure. A small area (Area 210) in which private houses appeared, was excavated in the geometric centre of the lower city. The

fragmentary structures exposed may indicate the orientation (north–south) of the long walls and thus of the streets. Two gateways uncovered in the east, in Areas K and P, suggest that two main roads issued from them, running toward the centre of town. The drainage system exposed in several areas shows that the builders were aware of the problem of sewage disposal from the lower and upper cities.

This description of Hazor indicates that the governor's palace and the attached temple, and perhaps also other administrative buildings, remained in the upper city (support for this interpretation is given by the fragments of two cuneiform documents found there). The lower city served mainly residential purposes, but cult buildings connected with the various quarters, like the temple in Area H, were also built there.

Tell el-ʿAjjul

Tell el-ʿAjjul, situated at the mouth of the Wadi Ghazzeh, seems to have been a city that was planned during a short span of time. It was one of the important cities in southern Palestine during the MB II.[8] The total destruction of Stratum II in the wake of Ahmose's campaign (in *ca.* 1570 B.C.), preserved many buildings, especially in the excavated southern areas (Areas A–F). For this reason it is possible to reconstruct today many details of the town plan. In areas where the stratigraphy was checked, it was evident that the town plan of Stratum III (the foundation stratum of the city) continued to exist, in general, in Stratum II. Chronologically, the transition between the two strata should be dated to the mid-seventeenth century B.C.

When the city was founded, towards the end of the nineteenth century B.C., it was planned as a rectangle measuring 325 × 480 m. The city was fortified by means of a rampart and a fosse dug deep into the *kurkar* rock (see Chap. 16, p. 140). A palace (Chap. 14, p. 110) was built at the northern corner of the raised area; Quarter L extended southwest of it. The city-gate was erected on the narrow side of the rectangle, facing east. The

---

6. *Hazor*, pp. 28–32, 42–44, 48–49, 67–105.

7. The symmetry is disturbed because of the area joining the eastern spur and the northern enclosure. It is connected with the construction of the gate in Area P. Similar planning can be seen in the MB city of Qatna in central Syria and at Tel Batash. See A. Mazar and G. Kelm: Canaanites, Philistines and Israelites at Timna/Tel Batash, *Qadmoniot* 13 (1980), p. 89 (Hebrew), and the aerial view on the cover. Apparently the architects of the Middle Bronze Age like to use a rectangular or square shape for the outer frame of the city.

8. The excavation reports were concisely written by W. F. Petrie and his students, *Ancient Gaza* I-V. For a summary of the stratigraphy and the finds, see O. Tufnell: Teil el-ʿAjjul, *EAEHL* I, pp. 52–61. For a possible identification with Sharuhen as well as its stratigraphy and chronology see A. Kempinski: Tell el-ʿAjjul, Beit Aglayim or Sharuhen?, *IEJ* 24 (1974), pp.145–153.

location of the gate also determined the east–west direction of the main traffic arteries: the northern one led from Area LA toward Area A; the central one — north of Area GER — also led to Area A, where the two merged into one road; the southern one — south of Area GER — led to Area B. These main roads were intersected by streets running south–north; at the road junction in Area A there was a small open space. It is possible to reconstruct the street network of Tell el-ʿAjjul only in the central and southern areas; there is no way of knowing how it was organized in the unexcavated northwestern and northern areas.

In addition to the palace, there was another public building in Area GER, a structure with thick brick walls, a central courtyard dug into the *kurkar*, and numerous, relatively small rooms. The building was partly excavated and its function is not clear. Next to it there are a few poor structures that probably belonged to the serfs who worked for the inhabitants of Area GER. Building F, in Quarter A, seems to have been a temple that served the inhabitants of the quarter.

On the southwest the city is bounded by Wadi Ghazzeh. There, where the wadi is especially wide and water flows most of the year, lay the anchorage. House AM is situated at the centre of Area A, fairly near the anchorage; it seems to have been a patrician house and may have had some administrative function. Next to it are houses whose plans and narrow walls indicate that they belonged to the poorer classes. Small rooms or compartments were built facing the main street of Area A and may have been shops or stalls. This part of the street going down to the anchorage may have been a market.

Conclusions

The data presented here, which have been compiled from four sites, enable the identification of several elements that are characteristic of urbanization and town plans in the MB II. The origins of urbanization are connected with the revival of civilization in Palestine at the beginning of the MB IIA. An effective architectural approach can be discerned in the town plan, which attempted — after the fortifications were planned in the rectangular or square form — to provide the town with a reasonably efficient network of roads and streets. The location of the palace in a central, or elevated, area is characteristic of the architecture of that time, but was also true of other periods in the ancient Near East. Evidently, great care was taken in planning the drainage system; the gradient of the sewers and the layout of the system indicate a high standard of planning and execution. The residential quarters were built for a mixed population (except at Megiddo Area B-B), so that none of the quarters were destined for a single class of people. The wealthy lived side by side with the poor and the slaves. At Hazor and Tell el-ʿAjjul there is some evidence of local temples in the quarters, whereas Megiddo and Shechem have central temples.[9] This appears to reflect the difference between the plan of a royal citadel and that of a residential quarter in the lower city.

9. It seems, though, that the temple in Area H at Hazor is at least a central temple for a large part of the population of the lower city.

MIDDLE AND LATE BRONZE AGE FORTIFICATIONS

Aharon Kempinski

The Middle Bronze Age

The first settlements in Palestine to have their fortifications rebuilt appear in the Middle Bronze Age IIA in connection with the revival of urbanism. Fortified settlements were located along the coastal plain and in the valleys; it is only at a later stage that there is evidence of their existence in the highlands and hinterlands.

The earliest clear evidence is from Megiddo, Aphek, Akko, and Tel Kabri. From the earliest phase of resettlement, at the beginning of the MB IIA, earthen ramparts, in addition to a wall, are an important element of the fortifications; both seem to have been in use simultanously in that period.

City-Walls. — At Megiddo, Aphek, Gezer, Tell Beit Mirsim, and perhaps also at Tel Zeror,[1] the first circumferential fortification wall was an offset-inset wall or wall with towers. The city-walls were built of mud bricks on stone foundations. This type of fortification has several variations, but each embodies the same defense idea — the creation of a fortified zone that entirely surrounded the settlement. The towers set into the city-wall were intended to protect areas not visible to defenders on the wall. The distance between the towers at Tell Beit Mirsim is about 20 m. (Fig. 1); at Aphek *ca.* 3.5 m.; at Gezer 20–30 m. At Megiddo the distance between each offset (Stratum XIIIA) is about 3 m. However, at a later stage of the same wall (Stratum XII), the distance increases to 5 m. (Fig. 2). This indicates that at Megiddo and Aphek the function of the offsets was purely structural. In the MB IIA the fortification walls were not very thick.

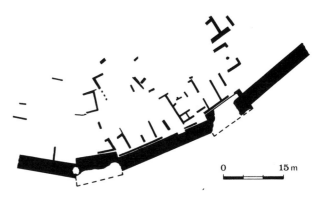

1. A section of the city-wall, Tell Beit Mirsim Stratum G. *Tell Beit Mirsim* II, Pl. 49.

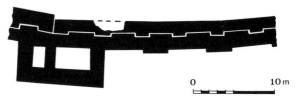

2. A section of the city-wall, Megiddo Stratum XII. *Megiddo* II, Fig. 398.

At Megiddo in the first phase, the thickness of the fortifications reaches 2 m., whereas in the late phase, towards the end of the MB IIA (Stratum XII), it reaches 4 m. (Fig. 2). At Tell Beit Mirsim, as well as at Gezer, the thickness of the fortifications is *ca.* 2 m. and the width of the towers is 4 m. At Megiddo a glacis abutting the city-wall of Stratum XIIIA was uncovered. At a later phase (Stratum XII) a thick wall abutted the glacis next to the gate; the glacis on the eastern part of the mound continued in use in the latest phase. Another type of fortification, closest to that just described, is the city-wall with bastions. Walls of this type are found at Tel Poleg, Tel Zeror,

1. *Megiddo* II, pp. 84–85; M. Kochavi, P. Beck and R. Gophna: Aphek-Antipatris, Tel-Poleg, Tel-Zeror and Tel-Burga: Four Fortified Sites of the MB Age in the Sharon Plain, *ZDPV* 95 (1979), pp. 126–155.

Megiddo. Middle Bronze Age fortifications (Stratum XII).

and Gezer.[2] At Tel Poleg, as at Megiddo, a glacis abuts the city-wall.

These facts indicate that at the beginning of the MB IIA, no great effort was made to fortify settlements and that, hence, the process of settlement in Palestine was generally peaceful. At a later stage of the MB IIA, and particularly in the MB IIB, the beaten-earth rampart plays a greater part in fortifications, and the city-wall becomes part of a more complex defense unit. Thus at Megiddo (Stratum XI),[3] a city-wall was built with inner projections that resemble teeth (Fig. 3). Their purpose was to anchor the wall within the earthen rampart. At Tell el-Far'ah (North)[4] there is a city-wall that is practically identical to that at Megiddo. This form of construction, in which internal piers were created in order to strengthen the wall and set it into the ramp, may have originated in

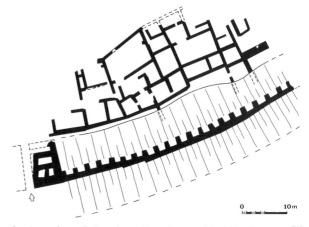

3. A section of the city-wall and gate, Megiddo Stratum XI. *Megiddo* II, Fig. 379.

the northern coastal region, where, at Byblos, the French expedition uncovered an identical city-wall, presumably dating to the MB IIA.[5]

2. Kochavi, Beck and Gophna (above, n.1), pp. 151–155; J. Seger: The MB II Fortifications at Shechem and Gezer, *EI* 12 (1975), pp. 39–42.

3. *Megiddo* II, p. 15, Fig. 379.

4. R. De Vaux: la troisieme campagne de fouilles a Tell el-Far'ah, *RB* 58 (1951), pp. 421–422; J. Mallet: *Tell el-Far'ah* II, 2 plan 4 and pp. 43–50.

5. M. Dunand: Les Fouilles de Byblos, *Bulletin de Musee de Beiruth* 19 (1966), pp. 95–101.

Ramparts. — As a form of fortification, the beaten-earth rampart originated in Mesopotamia and northern Syria. It generally surrounds a city's wall from below. The purpose of any earthwork rampart is to raise the protected area above its surroundings, thereby creating an artificially raised wall protected by a glacis, as for example at Tell Mardikh (Ebla). In Palestine this type of fortification first appeared in the MB IIA.[6] The rampart has a number of variants (Figs. 5–10), but the two basic components are the glacis and the rampart.

The Glacis (Figs. 5, 6). A glacis serves a double purpose: as a sloping, external retaining wall, it protects the base of the city-wall by keeping besiegers away; it is also an element in strengthening the foundations of the city-wall. This form of glacis was a feature of the art of fortification from the Early Bronze Age (at Megiddo, Ta'anakh, and Tel Dothan) to the eithteenth century C.E.

The Rampart. A rampart is a mass of earth with a slope on one or both sides; its width varies from 25 to 40 m., and its height from 10 to 15 m. It surrounds an entire settlement area like a belt (Figs. 7–9). A rampart usually has an internal core that anchors its layers of earth. Its outer slope is covered with a protective coating or with stone and serves as a glacis for the city-wall at its upper part. At the foot of the rampart there is sometimes a fosse, or ditch. The ramparts that can be dated with certainty to the MB IIA are those at Tel Kabri, Akko (early phase), Tel Dan (Fig. 7), and Yavneh-Yam (Fig. 8). The eastern rampart at Hazor (Area A-A) (Fig. 9) and the early rampart at Shechem (Wall C) (Fig. 10) are not part of this discussion of the earliest period because their dating is uncertain. They will be discussed in the survey of MB IIB ramparts.

The Ramparts at Tel Dan and Akko. Ramparts were found in two phases at Tel Dan and Akko: the early one began in the MB IIA, and the later one was added in the MB IIB. At both sites gates connected with the early phase of the rampart were found which had been covered by the later phase of construction.[7]

The early rampart at Akko differs from the later one in that it was built of beaten layers of earth and sand. Parts of the later rampart, which covers

6. J. Kaplan: *The Fortifications of Palestine in the MB II Period* (Publications of Jaffa Museum 4), Jaffa, 1972; for Tell Mardikh, see A. Kempinski: Tell Mardikh-Ebla, *Qadmoniot* 12 (1979), pp. 108–109.

7. M. Dothan and A. Rabban: The Sea Gate of Akko, *IEJ* 34 (1984), pp. 189–191; A. Biran: Two Discoveries at Tel Dan, *IEJ* 30 (1980), pp. 89–91.

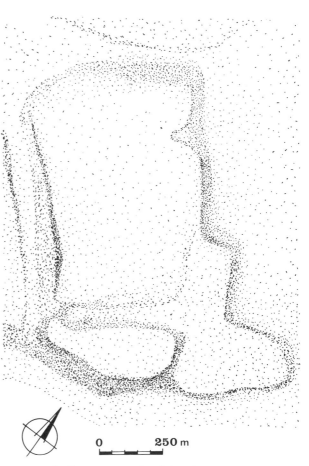

4. Hazor, topography of the tell. *Hazor*, Fig. 3.

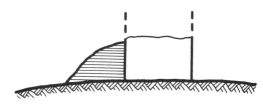

5. Rampart, schematic cross section, Tel Poleg. *ZDPV* 91 (1975), p. 5, No. 1.

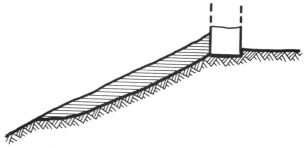

6. Rampart, schematic cross section, Tel Gerisa (Jerisha). *ZDPV* 91 (1975), p. 5, No. 2.

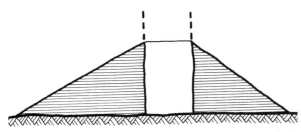

7. Rampart, schematic cross section, Tel Dan. **ZDPV** 91 (1975), p. 8, No. 7.

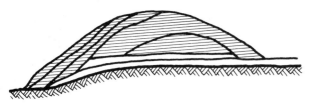

8. Rampart, schematic cross section, Tel Yavneh-Yam. **ZDPV** 91 (1975), p. 8, No. 5.

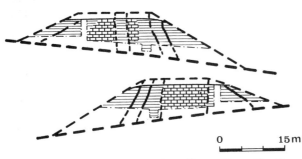

9. Rampart, schematic cross sections, Hazor. **Hazor**, Fig. 11.

10. Rampart, schematic cross section, Tell Balata (Shechem). **Shechem**, Fig. 22.

it, were constructed of layers of various materials. The MB IIA rampart was dated with the aid of a tomb from that period which had been dug into it, and by the ceramic finds at the level of the early gate (see the section on city-gates, p. 134). At Tel Dan the picture is more complex. On the western side of the tell, the early rampart abutted the central stone core, which resembled a stone city-wall (Fig. 7); a stone core of another kind, resembling the steep slope of a hill, was excavated elsewhere on

the tell. On the eastern side of the tell there is no core at all. Inside the stone core, which is constructed like a steeply sloped hillside, some MB IIA graves were discovered. In a later phase of the gate which was connected to the early rampart the pottery finds were also dated to the MB IIA.

Yavneh-Yam. An enormous compound was discovered at Yavneh-Yam; the length of its eastern face is approximately 800 m.; its width was about the same before it was partially eroded by the sea on the west. The compound was founded in the MB IIA, but most of it was not settled[8] apart from several houses along the rampart and in the nucleus of the settlement at Minat Rubin. The Yavneh-Yam rampart is a classic example of piling up layers of earth on top of a core (Fig. 8) and then covering the sloping areas with cement.

Hazor. The ramparts encircling the lower city and part of the upper city at Hazor (Fig. 9) are well preserved. The ramparts at Hazor were built by various methods, in keeping with topographic conditions and the requirements of each area.[9] The western rampart is the most impressive. It is preserved to a height of some 15 m., and it is approximately 60 m. wide. On the outer side a fosse was dug from which most of the fill was taken. At present the depth of the fosse is *ca.* 15 m. As the excavators did not excavate a trench in this rampart, there are no details regarding its method of construction.

In Area H, in the northern part of the compound, a low rampart made of layers of earth was piled on a slope. The rampart did not have to be high because of the deep wadi north of the lower city that served as a natural moat. The width of the rampart in this area was *ca.* 30 m.

In Area A-A a cut was made to the core of the rampart that clearly revealed the methods used to construct it.[10] The use of the inner core to strengthen the rampart created a kind of *Kastenmauer* whose internal spaces were filled with pebbles and earth. The inner face of the *Kastenmauer* had toothlike structures to which the piled-up material of the rampart adhered. The rampart was built up in three stages: each stage

8. Kaplan (above, n. 6).
9. *Hazor*, pp. 51–57.
10. I. Dunayevsky and A. Kempinski: The Eastern Rampart of Hazor, *Atiqot* 10 (Hebrew series), pp. 23–28, 13*.
11. A. Kempinski and E. Miron: Kabri, 1986–1987, *IEJ* 37 (1987), pp. 176–177; E. Miron: Area C2; Stratigraphy, Architecture and Ceramic Assemblage, in A. Kempinski (ed.): *Kabri, Preliminary Report of 1987 Season*, Tel Aviv, 1988, pp. IV–VI, 15–29..

Tel Dan. Middle Bronze Age city-gate.

was covered with chalk and reinforced with matting, which kept the rampart from collapsing during the construction. At present it is not known how the earth was piled on the core wall, although here, too, two stages could be distinguished.

The level of the earliest floor discerned inside the city — which cut through the inner slope of the rampart — contained MB IIA pottery. However, because of the method of excavation and the meagreness of the ceramic finds, there is no conclusive proof of the date of the rampart's construction. There is, however, a striking resemblance between its construction technique and that used at Tel Dan, suggesting the same builders.

In Area B-B, approximately 150 m. west of Area A-A, this building technique was not discerned, so it is probable that a solid core, like the *Kastenmauer* in Area A-A, was only used where special reinforcement was needed.

The Rampart at Tel Kabri. At Tel Kabri the rampart encircled an area of some 320 dunams. It was approximately 40 m. wide. Two areas were excavated: at the eastern end (in 1961), in a test trench with the aid of a bulldozer; and at the northern end, in a controlled excavation carried out by the Department of Antiquities and Museums and Tel Aviv University.[12]

The rampart has three main elements:

1. The core, which is a hill-like mass at the centre of the rampart.

2. Sandwich-like slopes on both faces of the core. As in other ramparts, these slopes were made of various kinds of earth, namely chalk and mud containing pebbles. Some of the slopes are covered with chalk or clay.

12. A. Kempinski: Kabri, *Preliminary Report of 1987 Season*, Tel Aviv, 1988, pp. 30–31.

3. A sloping outer retaining wall that also served as an outer revetment and as the foot, or base, of the rampart.

The city-wall, which was built from the rampart inward, served as the city's fortification. The rampart dates to the later phase of the MB IIA.

Shechem. A very complex two-phase system of fortifications was found at Shechem, comprising Rampart Wall C and City-Wall A.[13] Rampart Wall C (called a retaining wall by the excavators) is a northern wall whose stone outer face made it a sloping retaining wall. The northern part of this rampart was levelled when the 'temple-tower' (see p. 124) was built on it. The rampart was excavated by Walter and Wright in several narrow trenches only (Fig. 10). In the one published trench, the rampart seems to have been 30 m. wide. On the inner side, facing the city, it was bounded by Wall D, which Wright dated to the MB IIA, which may well have been the earliest phase of the rampart.[14]

At a later phase of the MB II, the rampart was raised and Wall A was built as an outer revetment. Wall A — an enormous wall of cyclopean masonry that was preserved to a height of about 10 m. — is one of the most impressive examples of the art of fortification in the MB IIB. It is connected with the construction of a new city gate.

The fortifications of Shechem represent a new type of rampart: they preserved the traditional principles of building while adding a new element — the chalk-covered glacis was replaced by an outer revetment of stone that strengthened and enlarged the retaining wall, or foot, of the rampart.

Jericho. The rampart at Jericho is a special case. Against the slopes of the ancient mound the builders erected a series of ramparts that reinforced the edges of the mound (Fig. 11).[15] Characteristic of this series of ramparts is the fact that, in its last phase, the ramparts were abutted by a stone glacis. The glacis was built at an acute angle and closely resembled Wall A at Shechem in construction (although not in size). The last two phases of the glacis at Jericho are

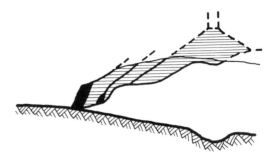

11. Rampart, schematic cross section, Jericho. *ZDPV* 91 (1975), p. 8, No. 6.

separated by a burnt layer, so they cannot be seen as construction phases.[16] In the last building phase, there are cyclopean stones at the base of the retaining wall. Apparently its builders were influenced by the construction of Wall A at Shechem, and may even have been the same builders. The evolution of the strong retaining wall — which begins at Shechem with Wall C and ends with Wall A and the cyclopean retaining wall of the latest glacis at Jericho — seems to have been an internal development in the MB II in Palestine.

Towers and Bastions. — In the MB II towers were either inserted into the city-wall or abutted it, as at Megiddo, Tel Zeror (Fig. 12), and Tell el-Far'ah (South).[17] Their dimensions vary from 5 × 10 m. for the small units (Tell Beit Mirsim), to 7 × 13 m. for the large units (Tel Zeror). In towers whose plans have been preserved, and not merely sections of their foundations, two rooms are discernible: a spacious rectangular room and, adjoining it, a small stairwell leading to the upper storey.

Only one bastion has been found, at Gezer, Tower 5017. The dimensions of the conjectured structure are 26 × 26 m. (Fig. 13). The structure was built with a massive foundation of unhewn stones that had been worked on their outer faces. Its mud-brick walls were

13. G.E. Wright: *Shechem*, New York, 1965, pp. 62–71; see also my remarks on the fortification system: A. Kempinski: *Syrien und Palastina (Kanaan) in der letzten Phase der Mittelbronze II B Zeit (1650–1570 v. Chr)*, Wiesbaden, 1983, 3.5.2.

14. J. Seger: The MB II Fortifications at Shechem and Gezer, *EI* 12 (1975), pp. 36*–45*, especially Seger's note about Wall D, p. 35*.

15. K. Kenyon: *Digging up Jericho*, London, 1957, pp. 214–216; but see recently D. Ussishkin: *EI* 22 (1992), in print (Hebrew).

16. Y. Yadin, *Hazor*, p. 56, following an idea of Dunayevsky, tried to see in all stages of the rampart constructive elements which actually belong to one building phase. But in contrast to Hazor, the stone revetments in Jericho are separated by a layer of ashes, testifing to two different building phases (personal observation of the southern section during a 1975 tour of the site). For a different explanation see now D. Ussishkin: Fortifications of MB II Jericho and Shechem, *BASOR* 276 (1989), p. 40.

17. *Megiddo* II, p. 87; Kochavi, Beck and Gophna (above n. 1), pp. 133–155; R. de Vaux (above n. 4), p. 396–430 and Pl. VI; A. Rowe: The 1934 Excavations at Gezer, *PEQST* 67 (1935), pp. 19–33.

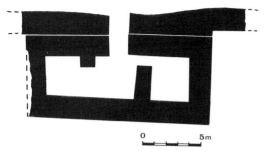

12. Tower, Tel Zeror. *EI* 15 (1981), p. 51, Fig. 14.

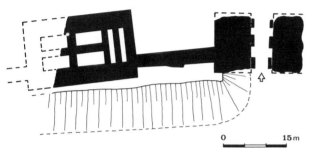

13. A section of the city fortifications, Tel Gezer. *EI* 12 (1975), p. 41.

built on this foundation. The structure consisted of four rectangular rooms and had a staircase at its eastern end. Bastion 5017 had several phases: the earliest, before the gate to the east was built, may have been a wing of a gate extending to the west. In its last phase it protected the entrance to the city-gate and abutted it as a new wall. In a late phase a

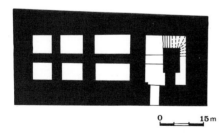

14. A bastion, Ebla (Tell Mardikh, Syria). *Qadmoniot* 12 (1979), p. 109.

glacis consisting mostly of ground chalk, abutted the bastion, the city-wall, and the gate.[18] The bastion at Gezer is very similar to Building M at the beginning of the rampart at Tell Mardikh (Ebla) in northern Syria

18. Above n. 13, pp. 39–42.

(Fig. 14). The structure at Tell Mardikh is from the MB IIA, as is probably the one at Gezer. At Gezer, however, excavators of the tower attributed it to the MB IIB or even IIC.[19]

City-Gates. — The direct-entrance gateway with two or three piers on either side comes into use in Palestine in the MB II. The gate was in common use in Syria, and probably from there it spread to Mesopotamia toward the close of the third millennium.[20]

At Megiddo, in addition to a direct-entrance gate, there is one with an indirect entrance. At present it is the only one of its kind (Fig. 15). Megiddo's excavators uncovered only one section of the fortification complex that should be attributed to Strata XII–XIIIA. Presumably the gate is part of the city's citadel, whose main entrance was east of the road going up to the gate with an indirect entrance. A part of the entrance pier has been preserved, and of course it is possible that in the eastern fortifications there was a direct-entrance gateway.[21] The gate with the indirect entrance reflects sophistication and a long

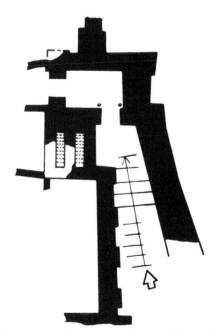

15. City-gate, Megiddo Stratum XIII. *Megiddo* II, Fig. 378.

19. A. Kempinski: Tell Mardikh-Ebla, *Qadmoniot* 12 (1979), p. 110 (Hebrew).
20. Kaplan (above n. 6) as well as a similar gate of the Akkadian period, J. Reade: Tell-Taya, *Iraq* 30 (1968), pp. 247–248.
21. It is hard to estimate the correlation between this gate and the lower city of Megiddo built in Stratum XIII or early XII. And see now A. Kempinski: *Megiddo, A City-State and a Royal Center in North Israel*, Bonn, 1989, pp. 110–111.

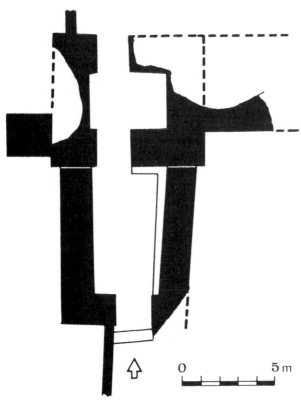

16. City-gate, Tell Akko. *Qadmoniot* 12 (40–47) (1979), p. 56.

building tradition. It is made of mud bricks on a stone foundation; access to the gate itself was from a staircase that led to the first chamber. At that point there was a right-angle turn in order to enter the second chamber; only then did one enter the city. Remains of a staircase were found in a tower to the left of the first entrance.

Contemporary with, or somewhat later than, the Megiddo gate is the sea gate at Akko (Fig. 16),[22] which had two building phases. In the early one a mud-brick gate was built on a low stone foundation that abutted a mud-brick wall. The wall was connected to an early rampart.[23] The gate had a central chamber and two sets of piers. In the second building phase, a long room built entirely of stone was added in the front. Two piers at the entrance to this room deviated slightly from the axis of the entrance of the mud-brick gate. When the stone-built front room was added, the gate had two chambers and three sets of piers. The gate from the late phase was about 15 m. long, and 8 m. wide. There were two living floors in the

gate that have been dated to the MB IIA on the basis of finds. It is not yet clear whether the addition of the stone wall was merely technical or indicates a later chronological phase. Should the latter prove to be the case, it will constitute proof of the development of the three-piered gate from the two-piered gate. The development probably resulted from the desire to update the plan of the small local gate according to the model of the contemporary Syrian gate, which had three piers on each side.

One-chambered gates with two piers on either side have been found at Tell Beit Mirsim, Stratum F; at Shechem — the Eastern Gate (its date is still unclear; it may have been built in the Late Bronze Age or even the Iron Age); at Ashdod and at Tell el-Far'ah (North).[24] This gate, which is the most basic, first appeared in the MB IIA, but continued in use in the MB IIB.

The Three-Piered 'Syrian' Gate. The most common type of gate in the MB II was the three-piered Syrian gate which was flanked by two chambers. In Palestine the gate's various units were about 12–15 m. long and 8–10 m. wide in each wing. The entrance was *ca.* 2.5–3 m., certainly wide enough to admit a chariot (Fig. 17). Remains of stairwells have been found in most of the gate towers. The stairwells were square (Fig. 18), built around a pier or set against the central wall (Fig. 19). At Tell Mardikh the door sockets for the gate were found *in situ* (Fig. 17). This find permits the reconstruction of the way in which the city doors opened and closed: from the front chamber inward (toward the city) and from the rear chamber outward. When the gate was open, the doors leaned toward the central pier, although they were not supported by it.[25]

The excavations at Tel Dan have clarified the nature of the gate's roof.[26] There the gate was found entirely submerged inside the late phase of the city rampart. The opening and the space of the inner chamber were roofed with a mud-brick arch. A gate with an identical arch was also found in the excavations at Mumbaqah in northern Syria.[27]

Presumably then, in Palestine and Syria the gate was fitted with only two doors, despite the fact that this was a weak point in the city's defenses. An MB IIB Hittite text describing the siege of the city

22. M. Dothan: The Sea Gate of Akko, *IEJ* 34 (1984), pp. 189–190.
23. And for restoration see there.

24. Z. Herzog: Das Stadttor in Israel und in den Nachbarländern, Mainz, 1986, pp. 14–15.
25. Op. cit., p. 58.
26. A. Biran (above n. 7), pp. 89–91.
27. For Mumbaqat see H. Kühne: Das Nordost-Tor von Tell Mumbaqat, in: J. Margueron (ed.), Le Moyen Euphrate, Strasbourg, 1979, p. 209.

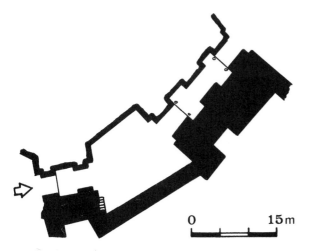

17. City-gate, Ebla (Tell Markikh, Syria). P. Matthiae: *Ebla, an Empire Rediscovered*, London, 1980, Fig. 25.

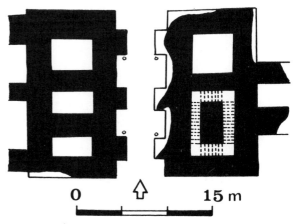

19. City-gate, Tel Yavneh-Yam. *ZDPV* 91 (1975), p. 10, No. 13.

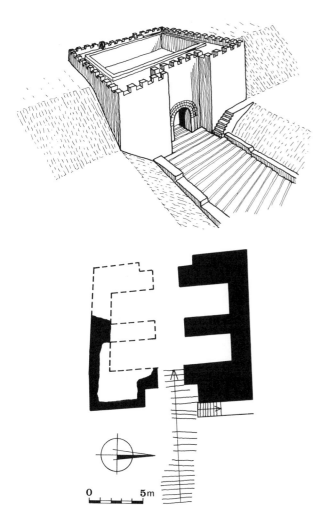

18. City-gate, plan and reconstruction, Tel Dan. *IEJ* 34 (1984), pp. 12–13.

of Urshu in northern Syria shows that, in order to take the city, siege towers and a battering ram were brought up to the gate but proved useless. It is reasonable to assume that several documents from Mari in which a siege tower and battering ram are mentioned deal with the attack, which was concentrated mainly on the gate, rather than on the city-wall or rampart.[28]

Among the distinctly Syrian gates found in Israel are those at Yavneh-Yam (Fig. 19), Tell ẹl-Far'ah (South), Bet Shemesh, Hazor (Fig. 21) and the North Gate at Shechem (Fig. 20). All are identical in their general plan but vary in details — of the staircase or the tower rooms. The almost total similarity between the gates in Palestine and Syria indicates that they are part of a uniform type of fortification. See especially

28. A. Gurney: *The Hittites,* London, 1969, pp. 178–179. Y. Yadin: Hyksos Fortifications and the Battering Ram, *BASOR* 137 (1955), pp. 23–32, suggested that the ramparts appeared as a reaction to the appearance of the battering ram and similar seige apparatus at the end of the Middle Bronze Age. The archaeological data in the Syro-Mesopotamian area do not confirm this suggestion; on the contrary, these weapons were developed because the usual means did not suffice in conquering the cities. This is also clear from the above-mentioned story of Urshu: in northern Syria the Hittites adopted the local tactics of the Hurrians because their methods (seige and famine) were not adequate for this area. At any event, it is clear today that earthen ramparts were known before the archive of Mari, see for example the earthen rampart of Tell Mardikh (above n. 6). Most of the Mari documents, which deal with the battering ram and seige tower, probably refer to attacks on the gate. There is an interesting letter, ARM I, 135, written by Isme-Dagan to Yasmah-Adad, concerning the city of Qir-Hadat, where it is specified that part of the city-wall was destroyed with the help of a battering ram. But this is probably a specific case! Normally those seige apparatus were aimed at the gate.

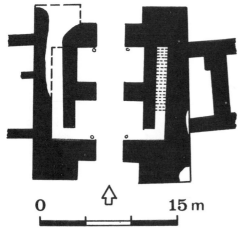

20. City-gate, Tell Balata (Shechem). **Shechem**, Fig. 9.

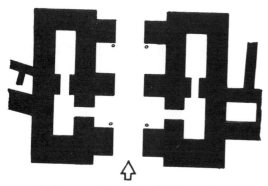

21. City-gate, Hazor, Area K. **Hazor**, Fig. 14.

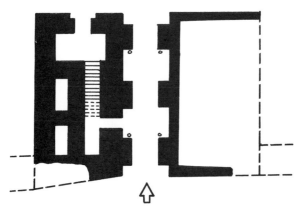

22. City-gate, Alalakh (Turkey). L. Woolley: **Alalakh**, London, 1950, Fig. 55.

the resemblance between the gate at Shechem (Fig. 20) and the gate at Alalakh (Fig. 22).

One problem as yet unsolved is the existence of three-piered gates that seem to lack tower rooms and

stairwells, as at Hazor Area K, Stratum IV, and Gezer's South Gate (Fig. 13).[29] Apparently in these structures the contours of the tower rooms were not preserved (as at Hazor Area K), so that the excavators' reconstruction is misleading. At Gezer the brick debris that covered the two tower rooms was not excavated and the excavators treated them as filled-up blocks.[30]

The Late Bronze Age

The continuity of the material culture in Palestine from the MB II to the Late Bronze Age finds clear expression also in the art of fortification. There is almost no innovation that can be assigned to the Late Bronze Age. In fact, at times there even seems to have been decline and neglect. In several LB cities and forts the fortifications are weak, with thin walls and an absence of ramparts and glacis. In those cities that continued to use their MB fortifications, the residents relied entirely on the work of their forebears; there is no evidence that they renovated or repaired ramparts. Only in the case of Megiddo does the glacis appear to have been repaired on both sides of the gate. This phenomenon is the exact opposite of the prevailing custom in Syria (Alalakh) and Anatolia (the glacis and ramparts of Hattusa), where glacis and ramparts were used without interruption.

The appearance of forts and towers in Palestine is a phenomenon that should be attributed to its Egyptian rulers, as forts are attested in Egypt from the Middle Kingdom onward. The appearance of forts all through the Late Bronze Age, but especially during its final phase, indicates a new concept of defense that was subsequently to become dominant in the Iron Age.

City-Walls. — At most LB sites continuity in the use of the MB city-walls can be discerned. At Hazor (Area K), in the only area where the city-walls and gates have been uncovered thus far, it became clear that during an early stage of the Late Bronze Age the MB casemate wall was still in use. At a later stage, however, in Stratum Ib, a wall *ca.* 3 m. thick abutted the gate, and the casemate wall which had in the meantime fallen into ruins, disappeared.[31]

At Megiddo, in the vicinity of the gateway, a palace was built in Stratum IX; its outer wall served as the wall of the citadel. West of it, in Square K6, part of

29. Herzog (above n.24), p. 53. See *Hazor*, pp. 59–60, where it is reported that only a small part of the gate has been excavated.
30. This was my impression after visiting the site. Cleaning the large masses of the gate's mud brick towers may reveal the gate rooms.
31. *Hazor*, p. 62.

Megiddo. Late Bronze Age city-gate (Strata VIII-VII).

what seems to belong to a casemate wall of the citadel was preserved in Strata IX–VIII.

In Strata VIIA–B, there are no traces of fortifications. Although the outer wall of the palace was decorated with pilasters, they have no defensive function (Fig. 23). The LB fortifications at Megiddo are an example of the seeming discrepancy between the written sources and the archaeological finds: according to the written record, the city withstood a siege of several months before capitulating to the armies of Thutmose III in 1482 B.C. The excavators identified the city that surrendered with that of Stratum IX, only a small part of whose fortifications has been uncovered near the gate.[32] On the whole, the strength of the LB and MB fortifications of the citadel of Megiddo should be correlated with the fortifications of the lower city, which have not yet been excavated,

except for a trench cut in the rampart by a bulldozer.[33]

At Bet Shean (Stratum IX), a mud-brick city-wall was built in the Late Bronze Age that was some 3 m. wide (Fig. 25). The wall abuts a wing of the gate of which only the northern part has been preserved (see below). A city-wall also was built at Tell Abu Hawam, in the second phase of Stratum V (late fifteenth century B.C.?) that was approximately 2 m. wide.[34]

33. Y. Yadin: Megiddo, *IEJ* 22 (1972), pp. 161–163. A. Eitan's soundings at the edge of the bulldozer trench did not solve any problem. The impression during the excavation was that, similar to Tel Dan and Akko, the Middle Bronze Age IIA tombs were cutting into the deposits of the early ramparts which encircled the lower city of Megiddo. As for the Late Bronze Age fortification system in the lower city, only future investigation will show if it ever existed.

34. For Bet Shean, see *EAEHL* I, p. 207. For the city-wall of Tell Abu-Hawam, see L. Gershuni: Stratum V at Tell Abu-Hawam, *ZDPV* 97 (1981), pp. 36–44 as well Tell Abu Hawam, *QDAP* IV (1935), Pl. XI, pp. 11–13.

32. Wilson, in *ANET*, p. 237.

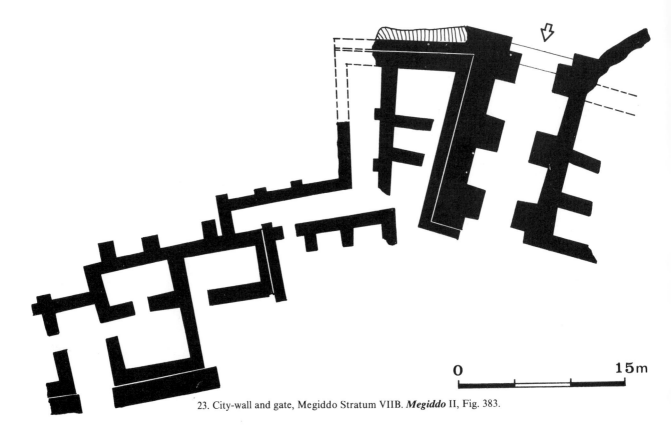

23. City-wall and gate, Megiddo Stratum VIIB. *Megiddo* II, Fig. 383.

At Shechem the excavator noted the continuity into the LB of most of the line of MB fortifications. Wall A was strengthened, while north of the East Gate (Area III) casemates were built on the offset-inset MB wall.[35] At Gezer the situation was probably the same, for the 'inner wall' and its towers continued in use along with the South Gate.[36] At Ashdod part of a wall was discovered that has been identified by its excavator as a casemate; it appears more likely that these are structures built against a weak line of fortification (a mere 1.2 m. thick). Since the excavated section is only in Area G, it is not definite that this was the only fortification surrounding Ashdod in the Late Bronze Age.

At Gaza, which was the capital of the Egyptian government in Palestine all through the Late Bronze Age, the city-wall was discovered in a narrow trench dug by Phythian-Adams. His description leaves no doubt that this wall is part of the city's fortifications. It is possible that the early phases of this fortification system belong to the Late Bronze Age.[37]

35. Wright (above n. 13), pp. 76–79.
36. A. Kempinski: Review of *Gezer II, IEJ* 26 (1976), pp. 212–213.
37. W.J. Phythian-Adams: Reports on Soundings at Gaza, *PEFQSt* 55 (1923), pp. 11–36.

In addition to the archeological evidence, the reliefs of Sethi I and Rameses II and III that depict various Canaanite cities in Palestine should be mentioned.[38] Usually, the representation of the city-wall and citadel is only schematic, so there is no way of knowing how accurate it is (Fig. 24). Unlike the depictions of Iron Age cities in the Assyrian reliefs, the Egyptian artists' engravings of the Canaanite cities were a kind of hieroglyphic ideogram.

Gates. — Most LB gates were those built in the Middle Bronze Age. In several cases they were repaired and orthostats were added to the renovated gate pilasters. By the Middle Bronze Age, orthostats were already the most common architectural detail, principally

38. Y. Yadin: *The Art of Warfare in Biblical Lands*, I, New York, 1963, pp. 96–97. In one case, that of Qedesh in central Syria, there is evidence that the Egyptians gave a precise description of the topography. The relation between the city of Qedesh, the Orontes River and the Sea-of-Homs are correct. But, also here we are unsure whether the description of the city itself is not schematic, for the Egyptian artist may have described the city as a kind of hieroglyphic-ideogram 'Canaanite City' as it appears in other descriptions of cities. Naumann thinks that although the description may be ideogramic, one can learn a great deal from the details of the fortifications. Cf. R. Naumann: *Architektur Kleinasiens*², Tubingen, 1971, p. 312 and Fig. 421.

24. Egyptian relief depicting the conquest of the city of Ashqelon. W. Wieszinski: *Atlas zur altaegyptischen Kulturgeschichte* II, Leipzig, 1923-1932, Taf. 58.

in Syria, for example at Tell Mardikh (Ebla) and Alalakh.[39]

39. An early form of orthostats can be found in the Middle Bronze Age city-gates of Gezer and Shechem. As a decorative element they also appear in the gate of Tell Mardikh.

At Hazor (Fig. 21) no changes were made in the plan of the gate in Area K; in Stratum II (the beginning of the Late Bronze Age), the gates' piers were faced with ashlar stones. At Megiddo (Fig. 23) no changes were made apart from raising the level of the gate

139

AHARON KEMPINSKI

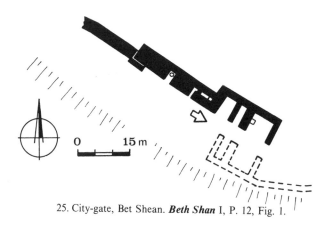

25. City-gate, Bet Shean. **Beth Shan** I, P. 12, Fig. 1.

in the Late Bronze Age. In the Eastern Gate there is clear evidence that the level of the entrance was raised, and several finds in loci near the gate indicate that it was used in the Late Bronze Age.[41]

Forts and Fortresses. — Beginning in the Middle Bronze Age, under Egyptian influence, a form of regional defense based on the fortress or fort, evolved. There are only a few examples from the Middle Bronze Age, but apparently the two compounds fortified with ramparts at Tel Mevorakh and Tel Masos (with areas of 10–15 dunams) were forts protecting the road that ran alongside them.[42]

A greater number of fortresses are found from the

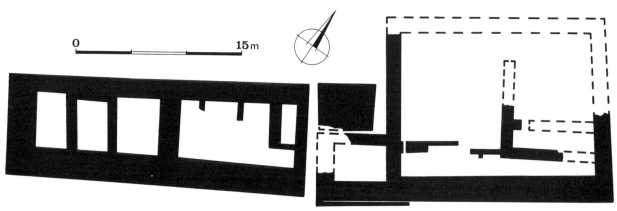

26. Fort, Tell el-'Ajjul. **Ancient Gaza** II, Pl. XLVIII.

and the access to it. The ashlar facing that originally belonged to the gate was ascribed by the excavators to Stratum IX or X (the end of the Middle Bronze Age). The rooms of the tower in Stratum VIII are not the narrow tower rooms used primarily as stairways in the Middle Bronze Age, but rather spacious units that were entered from the inner space of the gate.

At Bet Shean a city-wall was built in Stratum IX, along with a gate of which only the northern wing has survived (see the reconstruction in Fig. 25). The gate has three piers and two chambers. In the inner chamber there is a relief carved on a basalt orthostat that depicts a dog fighting with a lion, a scene that probably has mythological-cultic significance. The practice of decorating gates with carved orthostats originated in northern Syria (and Anatolia?).[40]

The plan of the two gates built in the Middle Bronze Age at Shechem also underwent no changes

Late Bronze Age. The earliest known example, from LB I, is Fort III at Tell el-'Ajjul, which should be attributed to the time of Hatshepshut and Thutmose III (the early fifteenth century B.C.). This structure is a rectangular block 27 m. long and 9 m. wide, built solely of mud bricks. The walls are 2.5–3 m. wide. Another fortified block extends from it on its northeastern side that is partly destroyed and whose plan is unclear (Fig. 26). Other structures at the site with a similar architectural organization, but largely destroyed, are Forts IV and V. Fort IV, which was built on top of Fort III, should be attributed to the fourteenth century. Fort V was built above it; it was probably destroyed at the time of the Egyptian retreat from Canaan in the middle of the twelfth

40. A. Rowe: *The Topography and History of Beth Shean*, Philadelphia, 1930, p. 16 and frontispiece. This one fragment of the decorated city-gate is probably only a remnant of a large number of decorative orthostats which had been robbed from the gate in antiquity.

41. Wright (above, n. 13), p. 76.
42. Egyptian fortresses are known especially toward the Nubian border. The most famous ones are those of Buhen and Mirgisa. On the eastern border there was the famous 'Wall of the Governor', which was a chain of fortresses (known only from historical literature) facing the eastern desert. A small fortress which certainly belonged to the period of the Middle Kingdom, was revealed by E. Stern: Tel Mevorakh II, [*Qedem* 28], Jerusalem, 1984, pp. 49–69.

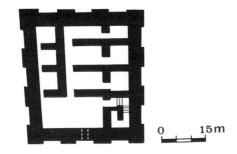

27. Fort, Tel Mor. *EAEHL* Vol. III, p. 888.

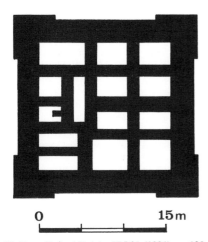

28. Fort, Deir el-Balah. *IEJ* 31 (1981), p. 128.

century.[43] The purpose of the forts at Tell el-'Ajjul was to guard the coastal road joining 'the way of Horus' that ran along the Sinai peninsula and the coast of Palestine, up to Gaza. It may also have been a defensive fort for the anchorage in the estuary at Nahal Besor.

A similar series of forts was discovered at Tel Mor in the estuary of Nahal Lachish. In Strata 7–8 (the Nineteenth Dynasty, thirteenth century B.C.), a fort was built in the Egyptian style (Fig. 27) — constructed entirely of mud bricks without stone foundations. It measures 23 × 23 m., and its walls are *ca.* 3 m. thick. Its outer walls have alternating salients and recesses, and corner towers. The rooms are divided symmetrically in the Egyptian style. A stairwell in the southeastern corner led to the top floor.

Above this fort, in Strata 5–6, was a small fort (11 × 11 m.) with walls *ca.* 4 m. thick. It bears a certain resemblance to the fortified tower at Bet Shean (see

below) from the late thirteenth–early twelfth centuries B.C.[44]

The fort at Tel Mor is very similar to the Egyptian fort uncovered at Deir el-Balah (Fig. 28). Like the one at Haruvit (see below), it is in the chain of Egyptian forts that guarded the military route along the Sinai peninsula.[45] The fort is *ca.* 23 × 23 m., with walls some 2.5 m. thick. It is built entirely of mud bricks without stone foundations. Sand was spread as an insulating embedment. The stairwell is in the centre of the area that served as the living quarters for the commander of the fort.[46] The fort had four corner towers and bordered on a central pool (*birkeh*) that was the water source for the soldiers and caravans. The fort is dated to the thirteenth century B.C.[47]

A building of another type, unquestionably a fort or fortress, was uncovered at Haruvit in northern Sinai (Fig. 29).[48] The building measures 50 × 50

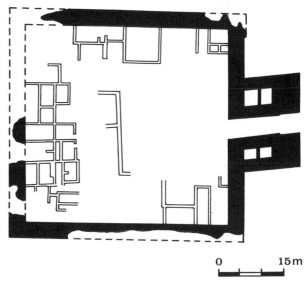

29. Fort, Haruvit (northern Sinai). *Qadmoniot* 13 (49-50) (1980), p. 27.

m. and is also built entirely of mud bricks without stone foundations. The wall is *ca.* 4 m. thick. Rooms used as living quarters and service rooms for the soldiers were built parallel to the inner walls. The

43. A. Kempinski: Tell el-'Ajjul, Beth Aglaim or Sharuhen?, *IEJ* 24 (1974), pp. 148–149, n. 18.

44. M. Dothan, *EAEHL*, pp. 888–890.

45. E. Oren: Egyptian Sites in Western Sinai, *Qadminiot* 13 (1980), pp. 26–33 (Hebrew).

46. Chap. 14, p. 119.

47. T. Dothan: Deir el Balah, IEJ 31 (1981), pp. 127–129.

48. Oren (above n.45).

entrance was flanked by two rectangular watchtowers (or towers) measuring 9 × 13 m., with a space 4 m. wide between them. In the centre of each of the watchtowers are two rooms used as guardrooms. The date of the fortress is indicated by the sherd of a pithos bearing a cartouche of Sethi II (the late thirteenth century). Hence, this fortress, like those of Tel Mor and Haruvit, continued in use up to the beginning, or even the middle, of the twelfth century B.C.

The Fortified Tower. A type of building already mentioned here in connection with Tel Mor is the fortified tower. It is depicted in Egyptian paintings and reliefs. The excavators of Bet Shean thought they had found one — as an inner fortress — in Stratum VII.[49] It was a mud-brick building whose facade was embellished with three decorative pilasters. Its dimensions are 8 × 12 m.; its walls are *ca.* 3 m. wide.

Influenced by these buildings, Canaanite architects also began to build forts, although with local building techniques and in the local style. One example is at Shiqmona, where a segment of a fort, or fortified tower, was discovered. The wall of the fort was of cyclopean construction and *ca.* 2 m. thick. A tower abuts it in the corner that was excavated.[50]

Undoubtedly, the existence of Egyptian forts in Palestine in the Late Bronze Age had an impact on the integration of this military architecture in Canaan. In the twelfth and eleventh centuries B.C. the Philistines adopted it, as did the Israelite tribes in the central hill country and, somewhat later, in the northern and central Negev. The later form of the LB fort was probably the prototype of the Iron Age II Israelite fort.

49. Rowe (above n. 40), p. 21, Fig. 2.

50. It is hard to agree with the explanation of the excavator, J. Algavish: Shikmonah 1977, *IEJ* 28 (1978), pp. 122–123. The fortification wall is not megalithic but cyclopean. These fortification walls which were found near the centre of the tell show that the earliest fort was a kernel for the later development in the Late Bronze Age as well as in the Early Iron Age. And see also there, Fig. D:22, where the corner of the fort with part of a tower are clearly seen.

17

URBANIZATION IN THE LATE BRONZE AGE

Jacob J. Baumgarten

Settlement patterns in Palestine in the Late Bronze Age were similar to those of the Middle Bronze Age. This was particularly true of urban settlements. There was a decrease in the total number of sites,[1]

1. Based on incomplete data from partial surveys in Israel. See M. Kochavi (ed.): *Judaea Samaria and the Golan — Archaeological Survey 1967–1968*, Jerusalem, 1972, pp. 83–84, 146–147, 189–190, 237–238 (Hebrew); for more in-depth surveys of small areas, see N. Tsori: *The Land of Issachar*, Jerusalem, 1972, pp. 152–154 (also on the survey of the Bet Shean Valley) (Hebrew); Z. Gal: *Ramat Issachar*, Jerusalem, 1980 (Hebrew); Y. Porath: Late Bronze (Canaanite) Age, in Y. Porath, S. Dar, S. Applebaum (eds.): *The History and Archaeology of Emek-Hefer*, Tel Aviv, 1985, pp. 51–54 (Hebrew); Y. Portugali: A Field Methodology for Regional Archaeology (The Jezreel Valley Survey), *Tel Aviv* 9 (1982), pp. 170–188; A. Rosen: *Cities of Clay*, Chicago, 1986, pp. 46–52. On some of the subjects discussed here, see G.R.H. Wright: *Ancient Building in South Syria and Palestine*, Leiden, 1985.

The following sites should be considered cities: 1. Tell el-'Ajjul — A. Kempinski: *Syrien und Palastina (Kanaan) in der Letzten phase der Mittelbronze IIb — Zeit*, Weisbaden, 1983; R. Gonen: Tell el-'Ajjul in the Late Bronze Age — City or Cemetery?, *EI* 15 (1981), pp. 69–78 (Hebrew); J.J. Baumgarten: City *Plan and City Planning in the Late Bronze Age Levant*, M.A. Dissertation, Hebrew University, 1978 (Hebrew); K.N. Yassine: City Planning of Tell el-Ajjul — Reconstructed Plan, *ADAJ* 19 (1974), pp. 69–78; many details differ in O. Tufnell's plan: *Studies on Scarab Seals*, II, Warminster, 1984, Fig. 1; 2. Tell el-Far'ah (South); 3. Tel Sera' (E. Oren: Ziglag — A Biblical City on the Edge of the Negev, *BA* 45 [1982], pp. 155–166); 4. Tel Halif (J.D. Seger: Investigations at Tell Halif, Israel 1976–1980, *BASOR* 252 [1983], pp. 1–23); 5. Tell el-Hesi; 6. Ashdod; 7. Kh. Rabud (M. Kochavi: Khirbet Rabud — Ancient Debir, in Y. Aharoni (ed.): *Excavations and Studies*, Tel Aviv, 1973, pp. 49–76); 8. Tell Beth Mirsim; 9. Jericho (P. Bienkowski: *Jericho in the Late Bronze Age*, Warminster, 1986); 10. Lachish (D. Ussishkin: Excavations at Tel Lachish — 1973–1977, Preliminary Report, *Tel Aviv* 5 [1978], Fig. 1; *idem*, Level VII and VI at Tel Lachish and the End of the Late Bronze Age in Canaan, in J.N. Tubb (ed.): *Palestine in the Bronze and Iron Ages*, London, 1985, pp. 213–230); 11. Tel Batash (G.L. Kelm and A. Mazar: Three Seasons of Excavations at Tel Batash — Biblical Timnah, *BASOR* 248 [1982], pp. 1–36); 12. Gezer (W.G. Dever: Late

Bronze Age and Solomonic Defenses at Gezer: New Evidence, *BASOR* 262 [1986], pp. 9–34); 13. Jaffa; 14. Aphek (M. Kochavi: *Aphek-Antipatris, 1972–1973*, Tel Aviv, 1976; *idem*, Canaanite Aphek and Israelite *Even-Ha'ezer*, *Cathedra* 27 [1983], pp. 4–18); 15. Beth El; 16. Shechem (D. Milson: The Design of the Temples and Gates at Shechem, *PEQ* 119 [1987], pp. 97–105); 17. Ta'anakh (A.E. Glock: Texts and Archaeology at Tell Ta'annek, *Berytus* 31 [1983], pp. 57–55); 18. Megiddo (I. Dunayevsky and A. Kempinski: The Megiddo Temples, *ZDPV* 89 [1973], pp. 161–187; R. Gonen: Megiddo in the Late Bronze Age — Another Reassessment, *Levant* 19 [1987], pp. 83–100; A. Kempinski: *Megiddo, A City State and Royal Centre in North Israel*, Bonn, 1989); 19. Tell Abu Huwam (J. Balensi: Revising Tell Abu Huwam, *BASOR* 257 [1985], pp. 65–74); 20. Acco (M. Dothan: Ten Seasons of Excavations at Ancient Acco, *Qadmoniot* 18:1–2 [1985], pp. 2–24 [Hebrew]); 21. Bet Shean (P.E. McGovern: *Ornamental and Amuletic Jewelry Pendants of Late Bronze Age Palestine: An Archaeological Study*, Ann Arbor, 1980, pp. 41–48; Y. Yadin and S. Geva: *Investigations At Beth Shean, The Early Iron Age Strata* [*Qedem* 23], Jerusalem, 1986); 22. Hazor (P. Bienkowski: The Role of Hazor in the Late Bronze Age, *PEQ* 119 [1987], pp. 50–61); (23) Dan.

On the decrease in the number of sites, see Y. Aharoni: *The Archaeology of the Land of Israel from the Prehistoric Beginnings to the End of the First Temple Period*, Philadelphia, 1982, pp. 115–118, and Fig. 28. See also R. Gonen: Urban Canaan in the Late Bronze Period, *BASOR* 253 pp. 61–74. For the picture that emerges from the historical sources, see B. Mazar: The Historical Development, in B. Mazar (ed.): *The World History of the Jewish People*, Tel Aviv, 1974, pp. 3–22; A. Malamat: The Egyptian Decline in Canaan and the Sea-People, in ibid., pp. 23–38; Y. Aharoni: *The Land of the Bible, A Historical Geography*, London, 1974, pp. 138–140; N. Na'aman: *The Political Disposition and Historical Development of Eretz-Israel According to the Amarna Letters*, Ph.D. Dissertation, Tel Aviv University, 1975 (Hebrew); S. Ahituv: *The Egyptian Topographical Lists Relating to the History of Palestine in the Biblical Period*, Ph.D. Dissertation, Hebrew University, Jerusalem, 1979 (Hebrew); and J.M. Weinstein: The Egyptian Empire in Palestine: A Reassessment, *BASOR* 241 (1981), pp. 1–28.

particularly in the number of small sites and satellite settlements outside the main cities. The number of settlements was greater on the coastal plain than in the mountain areas. In the settlements themselves there was a decrease in the density of structures and, not infrequently, even gaps in the continuity of occupation.[2] Only a few new sites were established during the period,[3] and even these were usually at locations that had been settled in earlier periods and then abandoned.[4]

In size, plan, and organization, LB cities display the same tendency toward preserving the achievements of the preceding period. Most cities were confined to the flat, uppermost part of the tell on which they had been founded. No attempt to expand their area was made, in contrast to the custom during the Middle Bronze Age. The towns were usually on the fringe of cultivated areas, in both coastal and mountain regions, along roads or thoroughfares, or at a natural harbour, such as an inlet or the mouth of a stream.

Establishment of Permanent Settlements

Undoubtedly the main factor determining the choice of a permanent settlement site in Palestine was the availability of an abundant and constant water source. The need was especially great for developed cities with a large population[5] because they periodically had to withstand sieges for months, or even years.[6] In such cases the water source would have to be inside the city or very close to it. Towns such as Dan, Hazor, Megiddo, Jerusalem and Aphek had springs just outside the city-walls, and others, such as Tell Abu Huwam and Tell el-'Ajjul, were near streams.[7] Because it was impossible to draw on those external water sources in time of war, extensive use was made of rainwater reservoirs and cisterns

(Hazor, Ta'anakh, and Ashdod).[8] The cisterns were plastered to prevent seepage. In other places wells were dug to reach ground water (Tell Abu Huwam and Bet Shean).[9] It can be concluded that the use of wells was not restricted to the coastal region, although they were more common there because of the higher groundwater level. Water-supply facilities were installed in both private dwellings and public buildings (the temple area at Bet Shean; near the palace at Hazor), but their presence neither affected nor dictated the organization of the built area, nor greatly influenced the general plan of the city.

Types of Settlements

Cities, the main subject of urbanization, are only one of a variety of settlement forms revealed at LB sites. There are also satellite settlements, such as Tel Ma'aravim,[10] which was a satellite of Tel Sera'; villages, such as Tel Kittan;[11] solitary temples as at Tel Mevorakh;[12] copper-mining settlements, as at Timna;[13] and fortresses, such as those at Har'uvit, Bir el-Abed, and Deir el-Balah — all of them on the international road to northern Sinai — and Tel Mor.[14]

In accordance with the political-historical conditions of city-states, the majority of the population concentrated in the metropolises and in their satellite towns. The roadside temple at Tel Mevorakh is in the tradition of roadside temples that

2. Aharoni (above, n. 1), p. 115–77.
3. E.g., Tell Abu Huwam and Tel Sera'.
4. Baumgarten (above, n. 1), pp. 5–14.
5. It is difficult to estimate the size of the population at LB sites. Very roughly, in small towns there would be two hundred inhabitants or more, and in large cities about a thousand — in exceptional cases even several thousands. See Baumgarten (above, n. 1), p. 13, and the bibliography.
6. *ANET*, pp. 234–238.
7. For the water system at Megiddo, see *Hazor*, p. 161; and Baumgarten (above, n. 1), pp. 30–31. It should be noted that at Megiddo the level of the LB settlement in the area of the gate was only 10 m. higher than the opening of the cave of the spring. In Jerusalem the spring of Gihon was probably one of the chief factors determining settlement. For Warren's pier, see Chap. 25 in this volume.

8. The cisterns in the lower city at Hazor were bell-shaped, and the reservoir on the tell was a cloverleaf shape. The reservoir was entered through a diagonal tunnel that was partly hewn in the rock and partly built. The reservoir was plastered. See *Hazor*, pp. 126–128; also *Hazor* I, pp. 82, 107–109, 125. See also P.W. Lapp: The 1968 Excavations at Tell Ta'anek, *BASOR* 195 (1969), pp. 31–33, Figs. 21–22; and M. Dothan: Ashdod, *EAEHL* I, p. 107.
9. R.M. Hamilton: Excavations at Tell Abu Hawam, *QDAP* 4 (1934), section opposite p. 1; N. Tzori: Beth-Shean, *EAEHL* I, p. 209, map no. 5, Level IX.
10. E. Oren and A. Mazar: Tel Maaravim (Notes and News), *IEJ* 24 (1974), pp. 269–270.
11. E. Eisenberg: The Temples at Tell Kittan, *BA* 40 (1977), pp. 78–81.
12. E. Stern: *Excavations at Tel Mevorakh*, (*Qedem* 18) Jerusalem, 1984, pp. 28–39.
13. B. Rothenberg: *Timna*, London, 1972, pp. 63ff.
14. E. Oren: Egyptian New Kingdom Sites in North-Eastern Sinai, *Qadmoniot* 13 (1980), pp. 25–30 (Hebrew); *idem*, An Egyptian Fort on the Military Route to Canaan, *Qadmoniot* 6 (1972), pp. 101–103 (Hebrew); T. Dothan: Deir el-Balah 1979, 1980, *IEJ* 31 (1981), pp. 126–131; *idem*, Lost Outpost of the Egyptian Empire, *National Geographic* 162:6 (1982), pp. 738–769; M. Dothan: Tel Mor, *EAEHL* II, pp. 889–890.

prevailed in the Middle Bronze Age. The Egyptian rulers of Canaan established mining settlements and fortresses to secure a supply of copper and protect the road to and from the province.

The cities were usually fortified;[15] often the fortifications of the previous period were reused after being repaired. Satellite settlements and villages were not fortified, but there were fortresses on the main roads, in particular on the coastal road. Such fortresses have been found in northern Sinai, approaching Canaan, and farther along the road at Tell el-'Ajjul (in the second and third stages of the Late Bronze Age) and at Tel Mor. Fortified structures, or citadels, built inside the cities along the road and designed for their protection also have been found at Jaffa[16] and Bet Shean.[17] Besides safeguarding the roads, these citadels housed the garrisons that both protected and ruled the cities.

There is a large number of cemeteries from this period; not all of them are near settlements. Often their number exceeds the number of towns in their vicinity, which may indicate a nomadic population that left only its burial grounds. This hypothesis has yet to be substantiated.[18]

City Size and Shape

We have only fragmentary knowledge of the size of the sites because at each of them limited and noncontiguous sections have been excavated. It is nonetheless possible to classify the sites into four categories according to size:[19]

1. Small towns (1.5–5 hectares): Tel Sera', Tell Beit Mirsim, Bet Shemesh, Shechem and Tell Abu Huwam.

2. Medium-sized towns (5–10 hectares): Tell el-Far'ah (South), Kh. Rabud, Ta'anakh, and Megiddo.

3. Large cities — metropolises (over 10 hectares): the cities in this category can be divided into subgroups of 10-15 hectares (Tell el-'Ajjul and Gezer) and over 20 hectares (Ashdod).

4. Megalopolises (over 25 hectares): in Palestine only one such city has been found, Hazor (approximately 80 hectares).[20]

The size of satellite settlements and villages is usually between one-tenth to one hectare.[21]

A vertical section of LB cities usually reveals a trapezoid, a consequence of their being located on ancient tells whose height increased and whose slopes became progressively steeper with the destruction of each settlement. In some cases the trapezoidal shape was created 'artificially' by building fortifications — a glacis or an earthen rampart. This practice is what made the cities appear to be 'cities great and fortified to heaven' (Deuteronomy 1:28).

In an aerial view, small and medium-sized towns usually look oval or circular; they followed the natural contour of the tell on which the original settlement had been established. In the same view the larger cities are sometimes rectangular, or between an ellipse and a rectangle — a result of the artificial extension of the tell area, e.g. the lower city at Hazor, which had been established in the Middle Bronze Age.

15. The controversy on the fortifications is rather semantic: was there or was there not a city-wall? It is senseless to have a gate if it is not connected to some kind of fortification. The city should *look* fortified, and that need not be necessarily a solid wall; the outer wall of the line of buildings on the edge of the tell will do. In the Egyptian monuments showing Canaanite cities we can identify windows — in a solid wall there are no windows! More than that, the fortified city was the symbol of Canaan. On gates see Z. Herzog: *The City-Gate in Eretz-Israel and its Neighboring Countries*, Tel Aviv, 1976, pp. 80–81 (Hebrew). On fortifications on Egyptian monuments see Y. Yadin: *The Art of Warfare in Biblical Lands in the Light of Archaeology*, London–Tel Aviv–New York, 1963; and Chap. 00 in this volume.
16. M. Prausnitz: Plain of Accho, *EAEHL* I, p. 24; H. and J. Kaplan: Jaffa, *EAEHL* II, pp. 535–538; Weinstein (above, n. 1), pp. 17–19.
17. P.E. McGovern (above, n. 1), Map 2.
18. For period tombs, see R. Gonen: *Burial Patterns and Cultural Diversity in Late Bronze Age Canaan* [ASOR Dissertation], (forthcoming), and in this volume.
19. Of all the cities mentioned, only Tell el-'Ajjul, Tell el-Far'ah (South), Bet Shemesh, Gezer, and Hazor have been excavated

to an extent that makes it possible to estimate their size with a reasonable degree of certainty. The area of Megiddo given here assumes that it had no lower city, which is not at all certain. Concerning the remaining sites, estimates in the literature often tend to expand their area, or refer to the maximal area of the tell, which was not necessarily its area in the Late Bronze Age. A survey attempting to obtain more exact information on the size of the tells was carried out by Portugali (above, n. 1).
20. Categories 2 and 3 have several traits in common: both consist of masses of buildings encircled by wide streets, forming neighbourhoods. In the more developed cities (in terms of their plan) these streets form a grid pattern. In both categories there are open spaces in front of the temple or palace that were intended for commercial activity and that should be seen as public squares. In both there is also a disjunction between the traditional main temple and the palace of the ruler (which may have a small private temple adjoining it). See Baumgarten (above, n. 1), pp. 125–126, Table XVII.
21. The size of Tel Ma'aravim is approximately 0.1 hectare; the area of Tel Michal is 0.6 hectare.

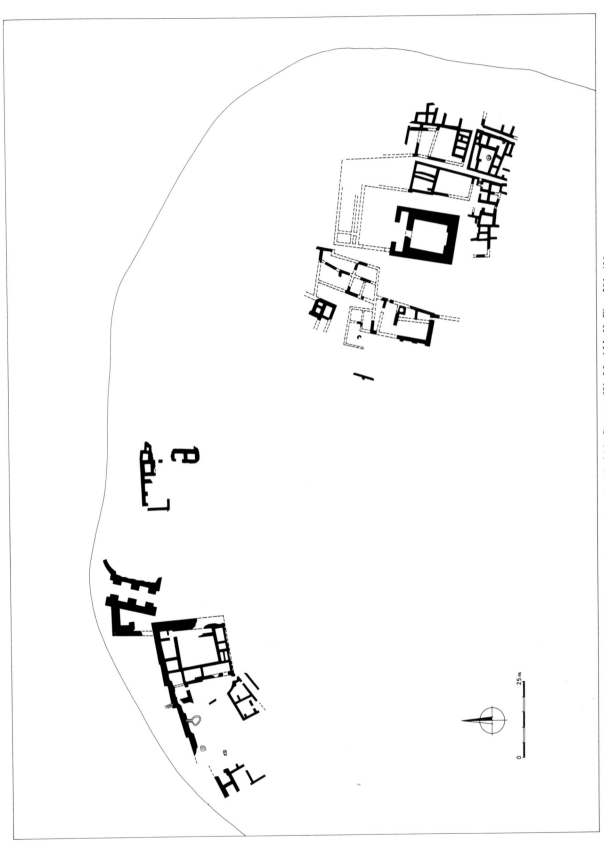

1. City plan (detail), Megiddo Stratum IX. *Megiddo* II, Figs. 381, 401.

City-planning

The town was first and foremost a place of residence. Even farmers and soldiers, whose occupations took them out of town, had their dwellings in the city. That is why most of the structures in the cities were residential (Figs. 1–3).[22] The dwellings formed a ring adjoining the fortifications on the outside and a circular/peripheral street on the inside. The peripheral street ran from the city-gate around the central mass of buildings or settlement nucleus, and back to the gate. This way of organizing the area probably originated in the Middle Bronze Age. It appears at Tell el-'Ajjul, which may be the connecting link to later manifestations of the phenomenon.[23]

In large cities such as Hazor,[24] the buildings forming the ring between the peripheral street and the fortifications were concentrated in large clusters around the palaces and temples in the gate area.[25] The nucleus was divided differently from that of medium-sized towns, such as Megiddo, where the nucleus was divided by streets that separated one residential unit from another. In the larger cities the nucleus held large masses (of structures) each one the size of the entire nucleus at Megiddo (Figs. 1–3). Large cities may have had several nuclei. It is the number of nuclei that distinguishes a large city from a medium-sized one.

The economy of LB cities depended chiefly on agriculture, the occupation of the majority of their inhabitants. The few nonagricultural residents included the king or other local ruler, the priests, artisans, and warriors, although as landowners they were indirectly connected to agriculture.

Commerce in the Late Bronze Age took place in the street. Not all streets were suitable — only the main streets, on both sides of the gate (inside and outside), and the open spaces in front of the palaces and temples were wide enough. Such commercial areas have been found at Megiddo and Shechem;[26] they usually do not exceed 70 sq. m. Other public areas that may have been used for commerce in LB cities have been found at the foot of the road leading to the city-gate,

near the water source, and on the river bank or, in ports, at the harbour.[27]

Centres of ritual, namely the temples, were usually located in the nucleus, as at Megiddo (Fig. 2), Shechem, and Bet Shean.[28] An exception was Lachish, where one of the temples was built at the foot of the tell, outside the city.[29] Temples were scattered throughout the larger cities, in which several gods were worshipped.[30]

Government buildings include palaces or fortresses and governors' residencies. Palaces have been found at Megiddo (near the gate) and at Shechem (between the temple and the rest of the city). The location of the citadel at Bet Shean is near the temple and at Jaffa it is unclear. At Bet Shean the fortress citadel seems to have been located next to the granary, which was probably used to store the grain collected as taxes.

A few structures can be identified as governors' residencies, either based on their plan or on written evidence discovered in them. No such structures have been found in the vicinity of the city-gate.[31] An adjoining temple and palace have been found at Shechem and at Hazor: in both cases they are part of a single complex of structures. This may indicate that the temple was for the private use of the king or governor. It also suggests the extent to which the secular authorities may have influenced the priesthood. The disjunction of the temple, which remained on traditional, sacred ground, and the palace, which was moved to the gate area, may point to an intention in the Late Bronze Age to separate the two authorities.

No specific section for artisans and craftsmen has been found, and therefore it is assumed that they went about their business in some of the structures already mentioned here.

Fortifications. — LB cities were encircled by fortifications — walls in which openings, namely gates, were set. The course of the wall was determined by the contour of the tell and by the requirements of defense in time of war or siege. The technology of fortification in the Late Bronze Age was essentially a

---

22. Baumgarten (above, n. 1), pp. 26–27, n. 96–97. Figures 1–3 are based on the excavation maps. The diagonal projections have been abolished and the data from the different areas combined. In preparing the figures, the maps by I. Dunayevsky (above, n. 1) have been used.
23. Yassine (above, n. 1), Fig. 1.
24. In Area C, see *Hazor* II, Pl. CCVI.
25. A. Harif: Common Architectural Features of Alalakh, Megiddo and Shechem, *Levant* 11 (1979), pp. 162–167.
26. For example, at Megiddo, Level VIII, see *Megiddo* II, Fig. 382. For Shechem, see Harif (above, n. 25), Fig. 6.

27. M. Avnimelech: Remark on the Geological Features of the Surroundings of Tell Abu Hawam and the Cemetery in the Area of the Qishon Mouth, *'Atiqot* 2 (1957–1958), pp. 103–105.
28. Harif (above, n. 25).
29. Ussishkin (above, n. 1), Fig. 1.
30. *Hazor*, pp. 67–105.
31. This holds concerning the end of the period. See E. Oren: 'Governors' Residencies' in Canaan under the New Kingdom: A Case Study of Egyptian Administration, *Journal of the Society for the Study of Egyptian Antiquities* 14:2 (1985), pp. 37–56. Also see Weinstein (above, n. 1).

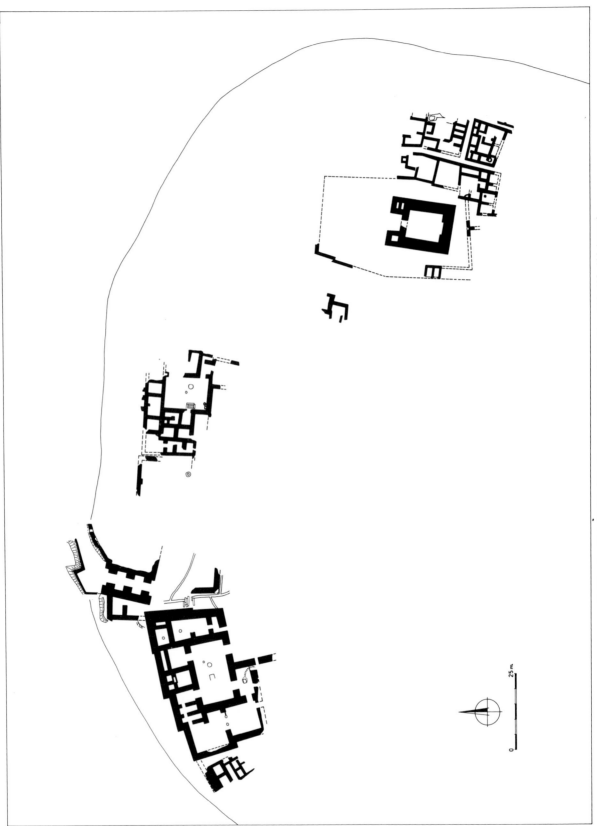

2. City plan (detail), Megiddo Stratum VIII. *Megiddo* II, Figs. 382, 402, 411 (upper).

25 m

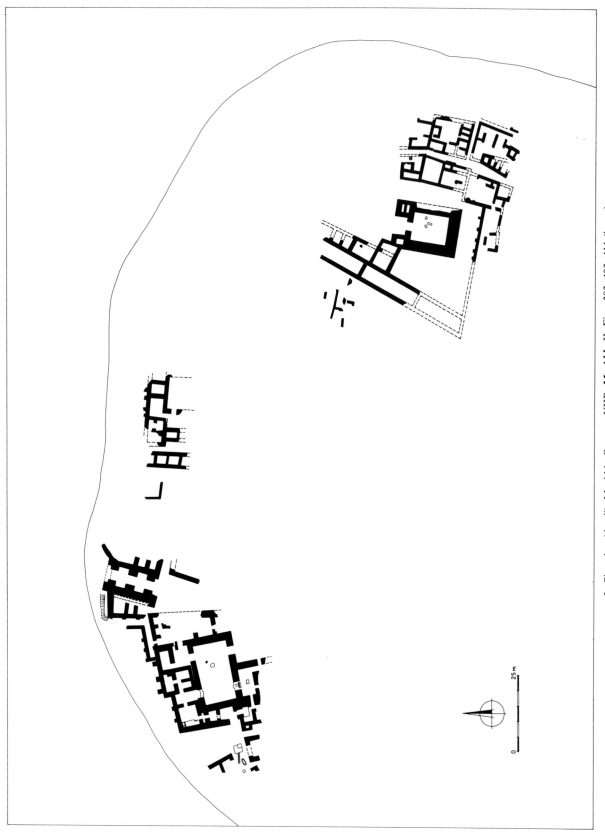

3. City plan (detail), Megiddo Stratum VIIB. *Megiddo* II, Figs. 383, 403, 411 (lower).

25 m

0

continuation of MB technology, without elaboration or development.

Water Facilities. — Water facilities were privately owned, either by the residents of the individual units or the public buildings (the temples, the ruler's palace). Cisterns and underground reservoirs collected rainwater, and wells reached groundwater level. Each unit saw to its water supply independently.

Sewage Systems. — The sewage system was partly public and partly private. The private section was designed to ferry waste from the residential units or palaces to the street or out of the city. The public section passed through the main streets, in particular the peripheral street and in or near the gate, and branched out in a way that indicates that other streets led from the nucleus to the peripheral street and the gate.[32] Because a sewage system requires regular upkeep, it was laid out in accessible locations. It was built on a declivity and had an outlet in the gate area. These factors needed to be considered in planning the peripheral street and the gate (the distance of the sewage system from the fortification line was determined by the size of the residential units. The existence of a sewage system points to a high level of sanitation, and is, in general, an index of the sophistication of urban planning and control.

Public Buildings. — No structures specifically intended for mass events (assemblies, processions, games) have been discovered in LB cities, so it may be that such events took place in the wider streets. Religious activities were carried out at the temples, but they were for a restricted audience of priests and clerics and were not intended for the masses. The activities of government took place in the city's nucleus: judiciary at the governor's house, the ruler's palace, or the city-gate, and tax-collection in the commercial area near the gate, or at the citadel, palace, or temple.

Public Thoroughfares. — The entire constellation of urban activity depended on the street system and on the accessibility of individual elements and the main building complexes of the urban system.

The streets can be classified into three main types, according to size: 1. The main street, or gate street, was the widest (often 5–7 m.) in the town. It carried most of the traffic, including whatever entered and left the city. Occasionally the main street merged with the gate square. 2. The peripheral street and the streets crossing the nucleus were narrower (3–5 m.), and the streets crossing the nucleus were somewhat narrower than the peripheral street. 3. Alleys normally leading

to only one residential unit were narrow dead ends (2 m.).

The available data are insufficient for determining with any certainty which of the streets served vehicle traffic (carriages and freight carts). Such traffic was possible in the gate and peripheral streets (provided, of course, that the vehicles could clear the gate itself) but unlikely on the streets that crossed the nucleus. Steep inclines, steps, and sharp turns would have made it very difficult to maneuvre vehicles. In the larger cities, because of the heavier traffic they had to accommodate, the streets were usually quite wide; the alleys were the same width everywhere. In these cities one finds around each of the neighborhoods, or clusters forming the extended nucleus, streets as wide as the peripheral street of a small town.[33]

In an aerial view the street plan looks like a ring. The more-or-less parallel streets that cross the nucleus branch out from the peripheral street. The distance between them is the width of the residential units. Such was the temenos at the centre of the nucleus at Megiddo: individual units connected by narrow passageways with steps were built between parallel streets. The residential unit had streets on all sides, thereby creating a grid pattern. A similar pattern is evident in the large cities, although here it was not single buildings but groups of buildings that were encircled by streets. This street system was often elaborated on in order to increase the accessibility of important buildings. Creating the shortest possible routes to buildings, even from the outlying parts of the city, totally disregarded the general street plan.

Street plans show a consideration of the uneven topography of the site. The builders refrained from laying streets on the steepest slopes, and we find that neither the main street, the peripheral street, nor the streets crossing the nucleus are ever steep. It is also evident that the planners or builders consciously utilized the slope's natural incline in constructing the sewage system. This principle was not followed in the alleys that connected the streets that crossed the nucleus, however, and the builders were obliged to put in steps.

The urban system, whose constituents and their interrelation have been described here, was the joint product of a tradition that had evolved over generations, and the technological and planning possibilities of the Late Bronze Age. The combination reached its climax in this period and made possible the flourishing of the Canaanite towns, as reflected in the city plans and structures surveyed here.

32. *Megiddo* II, Fig. 381; see also Fig. 402, L. 3010, an installation that may be a cesspool, and Fig. 382.

33. For example Tell el-'Ajjul.

18

STRUCTURAL TOMBS IN THE SECOND MILLENNIUM B.C.

Rivka Gonen

Tomb architecture is known in Israel and other Near Eastern lands from as early as the end of the Chalcolithic period and the Early Bronze Age. The underlying concept common to all the cultures of this region was apparently the necessity of providing a house for the deceased in which he would continue to dwell after his death.

At the start of the second millennium B.C., a distinct tomb architecture began to develop in the Syro-Palestinian region that distinguished it from its neighbours. The prevailing architectural forms were modest in their dimensions and generally consisted of a small internal space, in contrast to the contemporaneous monumental tomb architecture of Egypt and Mycenaean Greece.

The most common form of interment in this period was collective burial outside the settlements, in natural caves or in burial caves that had been cut in earlier periods. A second, less common, form was individual inhumation in simple pits dug in the ground. In the first half of the second millennium pit graves were located for the most part within the settlements, under the floors of houses; in the second half of the millennium, burials inside the city ceased and were replaced by pit graves outside the cities. The natural and man-made caves were used for burial without any alterations or special installations. The pit graves, on the other hand, exhibit several interesting variations and additions, primarily the lining of walls and roofing of the inner space of the pit with stones. These variations, which range from very simple to extremely complex in form, are the subject of this discussion. This survey presents the various forms of structural tombs, their development, and their possible sources of influence.

Cist Graves in Cemeteries Outside the City

The simplest structural tomb is the cist grave. This is a rectangular pit dug in the ground, its sides lined with courses of unhewn stone and its inner space roofed with stone slabs laid transversely. This type of grave had no entrance and it seems likely that it was meant to be used only once. Indeed, in most of these graves only one body was interred, very rarely two or three bodies. Moreover, the graves were generally only large enough to receive one burial. Cist graves of this type were widespread throughout the second millennium. The earliest examples are four MB IIA graves at Aphek.[1]

The use of cist graves increased in the Late Bronze Age. They have been found in five of the seventeen cemeteries of pit graves from this period,[2] usually alongside simple pit graves that were not built.[3] Because the cist graves and the simple pit graves are similar in dimension, in the number of interments they contained, and in their grave goods, they should be considered a single burial type. The cist grave was a development and improvement of the simple pit grave, and therefore no other origin should be sought for it. It can be assumed that wherever and whenever pit burial was practised, cist graves will also be encountered.

1. R. Amiran: *Ancient Pottery of the Holy Land*, Jerusalem-Ramat Gan, 1969; M. Kochavi: A Built Shaft-Tomb of the Middle Bronze Age I at Degania, *Qadmoniot* 6 (1973), pp. 50–53 (Hebrew).
2. R. Gonen: *Burial Patterns and Cultural Diversity in Late Bronze Age Canaan* [ASOR Dissertation] (Forthcoming).
3. E. Anati: Excavations at the Cemetery of Tell Abu Hawam, *'Atiqot* 2 (1959), pp. 89–102.

Cist Graves with a Dromos

This is a more developed version of the cist grave, the innovation being the addition of a passageway, or dromos. The passageway enabled repeated burials to be made in the same grave. Although the addition of a dromos appears to be a significant element in the construction of the grave, reflecting changes in burial customs, it is possible to find a direct line of development from the simple cist grave to the grave with a dromos.

Thus far only eight structural tombs with a dromos have been found, all of them in the Late Bronze Age cemetery at Tell el-'Ajjul.[4] These tombs are bigger than the ordinary cist grave, the number of interred is larger and often several stages of burial are discernible. The burial gifts are richer. This small group of tombs had a long time span. Its earliest appearance was in the middle of the sixteenth century B.C., continuing until the thirteenth century B.C. It is possible to trace a development from tombs that contain only some of the typical elements to those that have them all. The earliest is Tomb 1663 in the Lower Cemetery north of the mound. It has been attributed to this group only because at least three persons were interred in it at various times in the LB I and II. In form, this grave may represent a connecting link between the simple cist graves and those with a dromos, for although it is roofed with stone slabs, its walls are not stone-lined and it has no dromos.

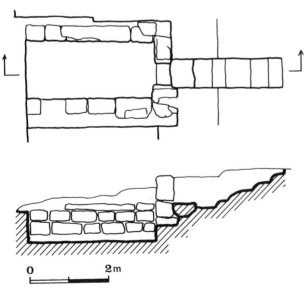

1. Tomb 1969, Tell el-'Ajjul. *Ancient Gaza* IV, Pl. LVIII.

4. W.F. Petrie: *Ancient Gaza* IV, London, 1934, Pl. LXIV.

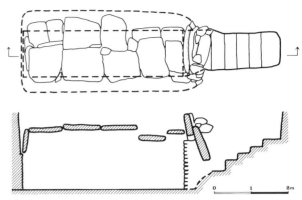

2. "Governor's Grave", Tell el-'Ajjul. *Ancient Gaza* III, Pl. XII.

A more developed example of the dromos type is Tomb 1969 in the Lower Cemetery at Tell el-'Ajjul.[5] It is built of limestone and has a stepped dromos (Fig. 1). The tomb was found looted and without a roof.

The best known tomb in this category is No. 419, the 'Governor's Grave'.[6] It was entered through a stepped dromos, and its walls were lined with *kurkar* stones laid horizontally one above the other. The inner space was covered with a unique gabled roof consisting of five *kurkar* slabs on either side (Fig. 2). Because of the space he detected between the tops of the walls and the roof slabs, the grave's excavator, W. F. Petrie, concluded that the roof had been laid after the final burial took place. It seems likely that the roof was removed during each stage of burial and that the dromos was not in use. This tomb should therefore probably be considered merely a large cist grave, to which a dromos was added to enhance its grandeur. It should be noted that when these, and other tombs at Tell el-'Ajjul were in use, no settlement existed at the site.[7]

Another tomb of this type was uncovered at Sasa in Upper Galilee.[8] It contained a dromos cut in the rock and a burial chamber with a rock-cut front and a built rear. It was roofed with stone slabs. The tomb is unusual because of its location — all the other cist graves, with or without a dromos, are concentrated on the coastal plain — and the period in which it was hewn and used, the MB IIB. No explanation can yet be offered for the origin and significance of this unusual grave.

5. Petrie (above, n. 4), Pl. LVIII.
6. W.F. Petrie: *Ancient Gaza* III, London, 1933, pp. 5ff., Pls. VI-XIII, XLVIII.
7. R. Gonen: Tell el-'Ajjul in the Late Bronze Age — City or Cemetery?, *EI* 15 (1981), pp. 69–78 (Hebrew, English summary p. 80*).
8. D. Davis: Sasa, *Hadashot Arkheologiyot*, p. 9 (Hebrew).

Intra-mural Structural Tombs

In the MB IIB the usual method of disposing of the dead was to bury them in simple pit graves under the floors of houses. In the city of Megiddo it is possible to trace the development of regular pit graves into structural tombs (the term used by the excavator). The earliest of these structural tombs is Tomb 3130 from Stratum XIIIA.[9] Another — Tomb 3095 — belongs to Stratum XII.[10] This type appears the most frequently in Stratum XI: six in Area BB,[11] and another three in Area AA.[12] They decrease in number in Stratum X: only one was found in Area BB[13] and three in Area AA.[14] There were, then, structural tombs at Megiddo in all MB II strata, where their earliest appearance is coeval with the cist graves at Aphek.

The structural tombs within the city limits consist of a hewn pit lined with stone courses and roofed with stone slabs. The ceilings in most of these tombs create a rounded projection on the floor of the room above them, making it difficult to use those rooms.[15] Only one flat ceiling was found; it formed the paved floor of the room above it.[16] It is not clear how the descent to the burial chamber was made, for no vertical or stepped shafts were found leading to a lower level. At tomb level a very small passage occasionally led to a narrow doorway, which in some cases was blocked by a stone slab.[17] In Tomb 3085, on the other hand, the doorway was blocked by storage jars.[18] It thus seems that the tombs were entered from above, and after the burial was performed, the tomb was sealed with roof slabs and never reopened. This assumption is strengthened by the very uniform character of the grave goods contained in the tombs.[19]

Two of the structural tombs exhibit unusual features. In Tomb 3070 the stone slabs of the roof were supported by a central pillar[20]. This tomb also had two burial levels: the first is attributed to Stratum XI

9. *Megiddo* II, Fig. 397.
10. *Ibid.*, Figs. 202–205, 398.
11. *Ibid.*, p. 92, Figs. 214–223, 320, 322, 399, Tombs 2129, 3070, 3075, 3080, 3085, 3110.
12. *Ibid.*, p. 15, Figs. 29–34, 379, Tombs 3175, 4055, 4098.
13. *Ibid.*, Figs. 330, 400, Tomb 3048.
14. *Ibid.*, Figs. 328, 380, Tombs 3139, 4043, 4054. It should be noted that there is no correspondence between strata in Area AA and strata in Area BB, those of Area AA being earlier, see Gonen (above, n.2), pp. 159–160.
15. *Megiddo* II, Figs. 34A, 202, 219.
16. *Ibid.*, Fig. 33A.
17. *Ibid.*, Figs. 32, 218.
18. *Ibid.*, Fig. 221.
19. *Ibid.*, Fig. 205.
20. *Ibid.*, p. 97, Figs. 230–238.

and the second to Stratum X.[21] The narrow entrance to the tomb suggests that the roof was removed for the second stage of burial, and only when the ceiling slabs were restored to their original position was the stone pillar erected to support them. The second tomb — 3085 — consists of two chambers, both of which were used for burial. They occupy different levels and are connected by a well-built doorway.[22] The door jambs, stone lintel, and some of the stones of the walls of the burial chamber were constructed of elongated, dressed stone slabs. The roof of the upper chamber was supported by a one-course corbelled vault[23] (Fig. 3). This tomb represents the transition to the full corbelled-vault tombs.

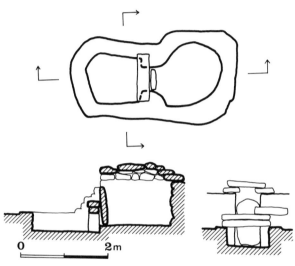

3. Structural tomb 3085, Megiddo. *Megiddo* II, Fig. 218.

Corbelled-vault Tombs

The tombs with corbelled vaults are the most interesting of the structural tombs in Canaan. To form these vaults each course was laid slightly shorter than the course below it; the interior space was thus gradually reduced until an opening was left at the top that could be closed by a stone slab. The line produced by the vault is thus not smooth, but stepped. The main advantage of this construction method is that there is no need for long roof beams, and large spaces can be roofed without supporting pillars. The most

21. Contra Kenyon and Epstein. See K. Kenyon: The Middle and Late Bronze Age Strata at Megiddo, *Levant* 1 (1969), p. 47; C. Epstein: *Palestinian Bichrome Ware*, Leiden, 1966, pp. 95–96; They both dated the tomb of Stratum IX. See also Gonen (above, n. 2), pp. 196–197.
22. *Megiddo* II, Figs. 218–223.
23. *Ibid.*, Fig. 218.

impressive examples of the constructional advantages of this method are the Mycenaean tholos tombs, which represent the largest spaces roofed without the use of pillars in antiquity.[24] A further advantage of the corbelled-vault method is that because each course projects inward only slightly, no scaffolding was needed to support the vault during construction. This is particularly true if all the courses, up to the top of the structure, project inward equally, in which case a conical, and not a domed, shape is achieved. To produce a domed structure, the upper courses would have to project inward to a much greater extent. This was done only in small spaces, and scaffolding may have been required.[25] An additional important advantage of the method is that the corbelled-vault construction is very strong and thus especially well suited to roofing subterranean spaces, which must support an immense weight.

The corbelled vault is especially suitable for enclosing circular spaces; when it is used above square or rectangular areas it presents difficulties for which there are three possible solutions: 1. turning the square into a circle by means of pendentives;[26] 2. building all the walls corbelled and incorporating the corner stones of adjoining walls; 3. constructing the two narrow walls vertically and the long walls in a stepped manner.

Five tombs with corbelled vaults have been found in Israel so far, and, if the corbelled tombs from Ugarit are included, most of the possible methods of constructing vaults were employed here. The only type not encountered in Israel is the conical Mycenaean tholos.

Corbelled-vault Tombs at Megiddo

Three tombs constructed by the corbelled-vault method have been found at Megiddo, all beneath houses inside the city. The three have entrance shafts and could thus be entered to carry out additional interments without removing the roof. In this sense

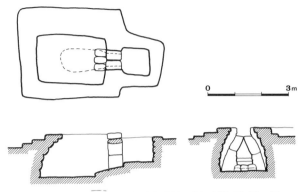

4. Structural tomb 4089, Megiddo. *Megiddo* II, Fig. 29.

they resemble the cist graves with dromos found at Tell el-'Ajjul.

Tomb 4098 in Stratum XI in Area AA[27] is the least elaborate of the group (Fig. 4). It consisted of a rectangular burial chamber, the internal dimensions of which are 1.8 × 2.7 m.; it is thus larger than the simple structural tombs. The entrance was through a small shaft to a doorway 1.3 m. high that opened into the burial chamber. The vaulted doorway was built of stone slabs laid at an angle with their upper ends touching. The other three walls of the burial chamber were corbelled, slanting inward from their bases while reducing the internal space of the tomb. The tomb was preserved to a height of only 1.6 m., and it is not known what was the original height or how the opening at the apex of the vault was closed. Furthermore, the tomb served in later periods as a sump; when it was found it was open and empty.

At the beginning of the twentieth century, G. Schumacher uncovered two vaulted tombs at Megiddo beneath the floors of a building in a section of the town he called 'Mittelburg': the city centre.[28] Tomb 1 was well built.[29] It was entered by means of a vertical shaft; a low opening at the side of the shaft was blocked with stone. A relatively long passage led to the burial chamber, which was 1.8 × 2 m. and 1.8 m. high (Fig. 5). The projection of the vault began at the very bottom of the wall, and the rectangular shape of the building was turned into a circle by means of pendentives. The stones of the vault are flat and were laid on their sides, with their edges facing the interior of the tomb. The opening left at the top of the vault, which was 0.5 m. in diameter, was closed by a large flat stone slab. Between this capstone and the floor of the room above it, there

24. The diameter of the tomb of Clytemnestra is 13.5 m., its height 13 m., length of the dromos 37 m.; the diameter of the tomb of Atreus is 14.5 m., its height 13.5 m. See A.B. Wace: *Mycenae*, Princeton, 1949, Figs. 5, 6; G.E. Mylonas: *Mycenae and the Mycenean Age*, Princeton, 1966, pp. 118–131, Fig. 116.

25. C.L. Woolley: *Ur Excavations*, Vol. II: *The Royal Cemetery*, London, 1934, p. 106.

26. The 'pendentive' is a concave architectural element which joins the square building to the true arch above it. In this case, as we are not dealing with a true arch, 'pendentive' is used for lack of a more exact term, as Woolley (above, n. 25).

27. *Megiddo* II, Figs. 27–31.

28. *Tell el-Mutesellim* I, Taf. IV.

29. *Ibid.*, Taf. V.

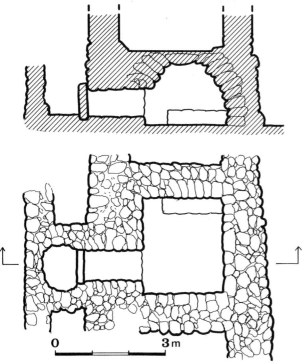

5. Tomb with corbelled-vault, Megiddo. *Tell el-Mutesellim* I (Tafeln), Taf. I, Grabkammer I.

was only a thin fill — the floor, in fact, rested directly on the vault. The tomb and the superstructure were therefore probably constructed as a single unit. A single body was laid on a stone bench built along one side of the chamber. At least five more bodies were laid on the floor. It appears likely that the tomb was reopened from time to time to receive additional burials, and that the entrance shaft and passage were used. Tomb 2 closely resembles Tomb 1 but is of inferior construction.[30]

The two tombs contained a rich collection of grave goods, mainly of the MB IIB.[31] By analogy with the tomb finds in the later, 1920's–1930's excavations, these corbelled tombs should be attributed to Stratum XI.

The origin of the construction method for the Megiddo tombs has been discussed in a single study only, in which it was proposed that they had a Mycenaean origin.[32] This conclusion was based not only on the incorrect dating of the tombs to the thirteenth century B.C., but also on the great impression made by the Mycenaean tholos tombs,

built with similar construction methods. There is now no doubt that the Megiddo tombs are earlier than even the earliest of the Mycenaean tholos tombs and that they differ from them in important constructional details. The inward projecting course of Tomb 3085 discussed above proves that the corbelled vault was a local development, perhaps an attempt to improve the simple cist grave.

Corbelled-vault Tombs at Ugarit

As was already noted, the corbelled-vault tombs at Megiddo are unique in Israel, but in most of their details they resemble the numerous tombs unearthed at Ugarit. In the upper city of Ugarit, in the residential quarters south and east of the palace, magnificent tombs built of ashlar masonry were found under all of the houses. The tombs were dug into the debris of the ruins under the cellars. They had been entered by means of stepped shafts that led down from the first floor. The tombs were uniform in plan - rectangular, sometimes almost square in shape. Unlike the Megiddo tombs, the square was not turned into a circle; the narrow walls of the burial chamber were vertical and the longer sides were built in the corbelled method, thus producing what the excavator called a 'Gothic vault'[33] (Fig. 6). The ashlar blocks were laid in a step-like manner, one above the other, their inner projecting edges dressed and smoothed. These vaulted tombs at Ugarit are unquestionably among the finest examples of Canaanite architecture. According to their excavator, they show clear Mycenaean influence. He has suggested that a Mycenaean colony was located at Ugarit.[34]

Structural tombs, identical in plan and building method, were also uncovered in the northeastern quarter of the city, at the foot of the mound. This quarter was established in the eighteenth and seventeenth centuries B.C. The grave goods found in these tombs were typical MB II pottery vessels,[35] including Tell el-Yahudiya juglets.[36] There is therefore no doubt that the corbelled-vault tombs first appeared at Ugarit in the MB II and continued to be built and used in the LB I and II. These tombs represent an advanced architectural development of a local burial

30. *Ibid.*, Taf. VI.
31. *Tell el-Mutesellim* II, Taf. 1–9.
32. S. Yeivin: *Enc. Miq.* II, p. 200.

33. See for example C.F.A. Schaeffer: *Ugaritica* I, Paris, 1939, Pl. XVII, Figs. 75, 78, 79, 80, 86; idem, *The Cuneiform Texts of Ras Shamra-Ugarit*, London, 1939, p. 18.
34. Schaeffer: *Ugaritica* (above, n. 33), pp. 99–103.
35. *Ibid.*, Figs. 50, 62.
36. *Ibid.*, Fig. 53 G,H.

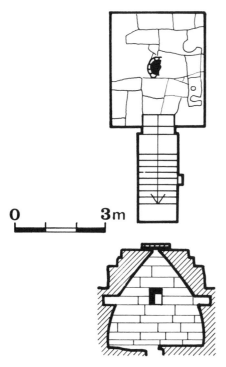

6. Structural tomb, Ugarit (Syria). C.F.A. Schaeffer: *Ugaritica* I, Paris, 1939, pp. 87, Fig. 80.

custom, and no foreign influence should be sought for them.

It is interesting to note that the only tomb in Mycenaean Greece that is similar in plan and building method to the vaulted tombs at Ugarit is Tomb RhO in Grave Circle B at Mycenae.[37] This tomb was originally a simple pit grave, one of the eleven comprising the grave circle. In the fifteenth century B.C. the grave was enlarged and a burial chamber with a corbel-vaulted ceiling and a passage were added. According to the excavator the tomb's plan and building method are unusual in Greece but are common in Ugarit. Unfortunately the tomb had been plundered in antiquity and was found empty.

It is evident here that the influence worked in the opposite direction than that generally assumed. The rectangular tomb with a corbelled vault evolved in Canaan out of simple structural tombs, a development that can be traced at Megiddo, where all the types of structural tombs occur simultaneously. These tombs reached their apogee in the wealthy city of Ugarit, from which they exerted a singular one-time influence on Mycenaean Greece. Nevertheless, it cannot be assumed that vaulted buildings developed only in

37. G.E. Mylonas: *Grave Circle B of Mycenae*, Lund, 1964.

Palestine and that their influence spread from there to other parts of the region.

The 'Mycenaean' Tomb at Tel Dan

A 'Mycenaean' tomb, dating to the LB II, was unearthed in the inner face of the massive rampart erected in the MB II around the site of Tel Dan.[38] To build the tomb a rectangular pit was dug into the rampart; a stone structure with thick walls built of unhewn stones was constructed inside it. Each course of stones projected slightly inward from the one beneath it (Fig. 7), producing sloping walls with a more-or-less uniform incline. There is no indication of a dome; the walls apparently continued with a uniform incline up to an opening at the top that was closed with a capstone. The tomb measures 2.2 × 2.4 m. (internal dimensions). The floor was paved with flat basalt stones. The upper courses of the walls are missing, but the tomb could not have been much higher than its preserved height of 2.4 m. How the tomb was entered is unclear, for no opening was found. If the tomb had a doorway, it must have been in the western wall that was destroyed; because the tomb was dug as a pit in the rampart and no entrance shaft was found nearby, it is also possible that the only entrance was from above.

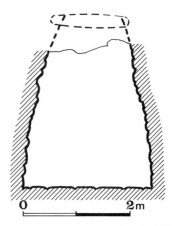

7. The "Mycenaean Tomb", Dan. *Qadmoriot* 4 (13) (1971), p. 5.

In this tomb, called the 'Mycenaean Tomb' by its excavator, many Mycenaean objects were found. It is doubtful, however, that the numerous Mycenaean pottery vessels and other objects can attest to the

38. A. Biran: Laish-Dan — Secrets of a Canaanite City and an Israelite City, *Qadmoniot* 4 (1971), pp. 2–10 (Hebrew).

Tel Dan. Late Bronze Age tomb.

origin of the bodies interred here or to the source of its architecture. Only in very general terms is the tomb reminiscent of the Mycenaean tholos tombs. Their only real similarity is the corbelled-vault construction method, which, as we have noted, is not foreign to Canaanite architecture. Perhaps this tomb belonged to foreigners who were passing through the site of Dan on their way to sell Mycenaean products in Canaan.[39]

The Aphek Tomb

The latest of the tombs built in the corbelled-vault method was uncovered at Tell Aphek.[40] Only the lower part of this tomb has survived, the upper part having been destroyed during the laying of a mosaic floor in the Roman period. It cannot be established whether the tomb was constructed inside a hewn pit or if it was a freestanding structure above ground. It also is not known how the tomb was entered. Eight skeletons and more than sixty funerary offerings from the thirteenth century B.C. were found in the tomb, which represents a continuation of the local tradition of vaulted tombs.

Corbelled Vaults in Early Architecture

The method of roofing by means of corbelled vaults is encountered at various sites and in various periods

39. Near the tomb were found two LB II pottery vessels on a section of floor. These are the only remains of the period, and it is impossible to know the connection between the floor and the tomb. In any case, the grave was not dug into the floor. I would like to thank Prof. Biran and Gila Kook who donated their time to the clarification of questions concerning this tomb.

40. M. Kochavi: Excavations at Aphek-Antipatris. Preliminary Report, *Tel Aviv* 2 (1975), pp. 17–43.

in the ancient Near East, but its appearance is sporadic. As early as the sixth millennium B.C., in a village at the site of Khirokitiya in southern Cyprus,[41] numerous strata of circular houses were found built with corbelled vaults. The stone-built lower courses of the houses were preserved, but the upper courses, which were probably of mud brick, had been washed away. A development from a very inferior building standard in the early strata, to better quality and much more advanced architectural techniques in later phases of the period, can be traced at the site. This village represents a unique phenomenon in Cyprus, for its building method left no mark on the architecture of later periods. The origin of the inhabitants of this village is not clear,[42] so that it is not yet known where their building technique came from, if indeed it was foreign.

Two groups of structures that also use corbelled vaults are known from the fourth millennium B.C. One group is the *nawamis* tombs in the Sinai.[43] These unique and well-built structures are preserved to their full height with their roofs intact. They were built within a relatively short period of time and exerted no influence on the architectural traditions in the region. The builders of the *nawamis* are also of unknown origin, and we have no way of establishing whether their building method came from a foreign source (Fig. 8).

The tholos structures at Arpachiya in northern Mesopotamia, on the banks of the Euphrates, are earlier.[44] Four strata of superimposed tholos structures were uncovered at the site, and in all of them only the lowest stone courses had survived. The upper part — probably of brick — had vanished. The more advanced tholoi of Strata 8 and 7 had a long dromos, and the standard of their construction resembles that of the later Mycenaean tholoi. The purpose of these structures is unknown; neither bones, grave goods, hearths, nor household objects were found in them.

Subterranean tombs with corbelled vaults were built at Ur in the third millennium B.C. One tomb, PG/1054,[45] was constructed wholly of stone rubble

at the bottom of a deep, wide pit. The tomb was rectangular in shape and measured 2.2 × 2.6 m. A court was built in front of the tomb and a corridor around it. The vault started approximately one metre above the floor and rested on projecting stones that formed pendentives. The tomb had a very low entrance, and access to it was possible only by crawling. After a body was buried, the lower part of the deep pit was filled with hard clay and brick debris that completely covered the vaulted tomb. Above this fill additional structures were built, and in and around them numerous levels of burials were made, until the entire pit was filled. Aside from the tholoi at Arpachiya, these tombs at Ur are the only structures with corbel-vaulted roofs known in ancient Mesopotamia down to the first millennium B.C.

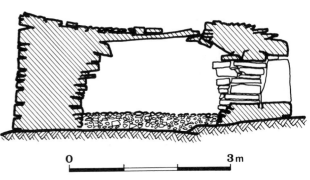

0   3 m

8. Architectural cross section of nawamis, area of ʿEin Ḥudra, Sinai. *IEJ* 27 (1977), p. 68, Fig. 2.

In Egypt in the third millennium B.C., barrel vaulting built in the corbelled-vault method was used to roof large spans in brick buildings — perhaps as early as the end of the First Dynasty and certainly during the course of the Second Dynasty.[46] This method was employed to roof stone buildings, such as the Medum and Dahshur pyramids from the end of the Fourth Dynasty.[47] The best-known example of this method of roofing is the Grand Gallery that led to the burial chamber in Khufu's pyramid at Giza.[48]

One tomb with a corbelled vault was uncovered in Cyprus; it dates to the second millennium B.C. Tomb 21 at Enkomi was built inside a circular, rock-cut

41. P. Dikaios and J.R. Steward: The Stone Age and Early Bronze Age of Cyprus, *Swedish Cyprus Expedition*, Vol. IV, Part 1A, Lund, 1962, pp. 5–14, 58–59, 177–179.

42. H.W. Catling: Cyprus in the Neolithic and Chalcolithic Periods, *Cambridge Ancient History*, Vol. I, Part I, London, 1970, p. 544.

43. A. Goren: The Nawamis of Southern Sinai, in Z. Meshel and I. Finkelstein (eds.): *Ancient Sinai*, Tel Aviv, 1980, pp. 243–264.

44. M.E.L. Mallowan and J.C. Rose: *Prehistoric Assyria, The Excavations at Tell Arpachiya*, London, 1935, pp. 25–34.

45. Woolley (above, n. 25), pp. 97–107, Figs. 16–17.

46. G.A. Reisner: *The Development of the Egyptian Tomb Down to the Accession of Cheops*, Cambridge, 1936, pp. 124–134, 335.

47. *Ibid.*, pp. 197–201.

48. W. Stevenson-Smith: *The Art and Architecture of Ancient Egypt*, Great Britain, 1965, p. 53, Pl. 27A.

'Ein Ḥudra (Sinai). Namus.

pit.[49] Its corbel, which formed a round cone, started at the lowest courses and continued with a gradual incline to a height of 2.43 m. The aperture at the top (1.2 m. in diameter) was closed with a large stone slab. The building is of stone rubble set in irregular courses, but the entrance was well-built of ashlar masonry and was sealed with a stone slab. The entrance to the burial chamber was through a narrow dromos and a *stomion*, which formed a high step. In the centre of the floor of the tomb was a circular depression surrounded by a stone bench. The tomb projected about one metre above the upper edge of the rock-cut pit and was covered with a low tumulus.

The best-known corbelled tombs are the Mycenaean tholos tombs. This type of tomb made its first appearance at the end of the Middle Helladic period and reached its apogee in the thirteenth century B.C.[50] Its origin is unknown, but it is generally agreed today that it was a local development in which the economic and military power of the local dynasty of rulers found expression.[51] The Mycenaean tholoi were royal family tombs of outstanding building standard and immense in size. The tomb of Clytemnestra, for example, is 13.5 m. in diameter and 13 m. high. The dromos is 37 m. long. The tholoi and their dromoi were built in a kind of long, unroofed passage cut into the slope of the mountain. The walls of the passage were lined with ashlar masonry to form the dromos, and the tholoi were at the end of the passage. Only the top of the tomb projected above the surface of the mountain slope, and it was covered with a tumulus. The tholoi were thus also mainly subterranean structures.

Is it possible to find a link among the appearances of the corbelled vault at different sites in the ancient world? G. A. Reisner, in his study of the development of the Egyptian tombs, suggested that the corbelled vault was intended to lighten the great weight of the brick material that covered the wood ceiling of

49. E. Gjerstad *et al*: *Swedish Cyprus Expedition*, Vol. I, Stockholm, 1934, pp. 570–573.
50. Mylonas (above, n. 24), pp. 111, 120.
51. Mylonas (above, n. 24), p. 132.

the burial chambers.[52] This functional explanation may indeed be valid. At every site containing a subterranean structure of this type — the royal tombs at Ur and the tombs beneath the houses at Megiddo and Ugarit — it was necessary to employ a method of construction that would prevent the ceiling from collapsing from the great weight that covered it. The long postern gates beneath the walls of Hattusas, the capital of the Hittite kingdom, were also roofed with corbelled vaults.[53] There too the building method was probably adopted to reduce the immense weight of

the thick stone wall that rose above the postern. It is also possible that the tholos structures covered with tumuli found at Enkomi and in the Mycenaean world employed the method of construction suitable for underground buildings. The tombs at Dan and Aphek may have been built inside a pit and covered with tumuli. We should therefore not seek a common origin for all of these constructions. It seems very likely that the builders at each of these sites arrived independently at the same architectural solution. This functional explanation, however, does not hold for the houses in the village of Khirokitiya, the Sinai *nawamis*, or the Arpachiya tholoi, all of which were built above ground. Their origin is unknown, and there is no evidence of a connection among them.

52. Reisner (above, n. 46), p. 321.
53. E. Akurgal: *The Art of the Hittites*, London, 1962, pp. 97–98, Pl. 73.

19

TEMPLES OF THE MIDDLE AND LATE BRONZE AGES AND THE IRON AGE

Amihai Mazar

Numerous cult sites and temples of the Middle and Late Bronze Ages and the Iron Age have been uncovered in Israel.[1] A number of these structures can be grouped into homogeneous categories displaying common characteristics while others are unique in plan and contemporary parallels cannot be easily pinpointed. In several cases there is no correlation between archaeological periods and the history of the temples: some sanctuaries were established in the Middle Bronze Age and continued to exist in the Late Bronze Age; others were erected in the Late Bronze Age and remained in use or were rebuilt in the Iron Age I.

This discussion will begin with temples of the Intermediate Early Bronze/Middle Bronze Age, proceed to those of the Middle Bronze Age II, then to the Late Bronze Age and Iron Age I temples which will be treated together, and conclude with the meagre material dating to the Iron Age II.

Intermediate Bronze Age

Only scanty remains of this period have been uncovered in Israel and they include practically no temples or shrines. At Megiddo the tradition of the sacred precinct of the Early Bronze Age continued in this period.[2] Temple 4040 was covered with an

artificial fill and in its centre was a one-roomed chapel with a niche at its end (Stratum XIVA).

Middle Bronze Age IIA

Although this period witnessed a gradual renewal of the urban culture of Palestine, cult sites are still scarce and no actual temple dating to the MB IIA has been discovered.[3] The sacred precinct of the Early Bronze Age at Megiddo now became an open cult area surrounded by an enclosure wall.[4] In Stratum XII in the southwestern part of this area was erected a single broad-room sanctuary which was entered from the west. A paved area to its east contained stones set on their narrow sides; these were probably *massevot* (stelae).

To this period also belongs the early phase of the sacred area at Nahariya (Fig. 1).[5] This is a cult site situated on a low hill outside the settlement near the shore. The excavators attributed to this early phase a square room (6 × 6 m.) to which was attached a *bammah* (high place) about 6 m. in diameter, on which were strewn objects of a cultic nature. This sacred area thus resembles the contemporary sacred precinct at Megiddo. A similar conception apparently underlies the construction of the Temple of Obelisks at Byblos dating to the same period. In this temple obelisk-shaped stelae were erected around a central structure in the form of a high place set in the midst of a court enclosed by a kerb wall. Megiddo,

1. For previous general works on this subject see G.R.H. Wright: Pre-Israelite Temples in the Land of Canaan, *PEQ* 103 (1971), pp. 17–732; idem, *Ancient Building in South Syria and Palestine*, Leiden-Koln, 1985, pp. 43–89 (passim), 215–254, Figs. 135–181; Th. Busink: *Der Tempel von Jerusalem*, Leiden, 1970; M. Ottosson: *Temples and High Places in Palestine*, Uppsala, 1980; A. Kuschke: *Biblische Reallexicon* (2nd ed.) (K. Galling), Tubingen, 1977, pp. 333–342.
2. I. Dunayevsky and A. Kempinski: The Megiddo Temples, *ZDPV* 89 (1973), pp. 161–187.

3. A temple at Tell el-Hayyat is reported to have been founded in the MB IIA period (below, n. 21).
4. Dunayevsky and Kempinski (above, n. 2), pp. 175–178.
5. I. Ben-Dor: A Bronze Age Temple at Nahariyah, *QDAP* 14 (1950), pp. 1–41; M. Dothan: The Excavations at Nahariyah, Preliminary Report (Seasons 1954/55), *IEJ* 6 (1956), pp. 14–25; M. Dothan: Nahariya, *EAEHL* II, pp. 908–912.

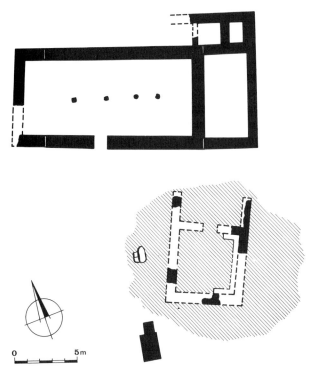

1. Temple and 'high place', Nahariya. *IEJ* 6 (1956), Fig. 1, following p. 16.

Nahariya and Byblos should be considered a group of cult places characteristic of the Middle Bronze IIA.[6]

Middle Bronze Age IIB-C

Open cult places. — At Megiddo the sacred area continued to exist in Stratum XI (seventeenth century B.C.). At Nahariya the sacred area underwent extensive changes: in the second phase, attributed by the excavator to the seventeenth century B.C. (but which in fact may date to the eighteenth century), the square structure of the preceding phase was covered by a stone-built circular platform having a diameter of about 14 m. North of this platform a broad building, 6.2 × 10.7 m., was erected. It was equipped with a row of stone bases of wooden columns set along the central longitudinal axis of the building to support the ceiling. This plan is reminiscent to some extent of the Acropolis Temple at 'Ai and to the 'White Building' at Tel Yarmut, both dating to the EB III. It thus may represent a continuation of the architectural tradition of the Early Bronze Age. Several stages of development can be distinguished in this building. In

6. M. Dothan: The Cult at Nahariyah and Canaanite High Places, in *Western Galilee and the Coast of Galilee*, Jerusalem, 1965, pp. 63–75 (Hebrew).

the second stage the outer walls were rebuilt, a small doorway was opened in the northern wall and two rooms were added on the short sides, the one on the eastern side apparently serving as the kitchen in which the sacred meals were prepared.[7]

The excavators, I. Ben-Dor and M. Dothan, interpreted the building as a temple despite the lack of a holy-of-holies in which the statue of the divinity could be placed. A further difficulty with this identification is the presence of a doorway in the north (rear) wall of the building. Dothan accordingly has recently suggested that this building was not the actual temple but served as an auxiliary structure (see I Samuel 9:22, where the 'chamber' appears as the building in which public ceremonies were performed near the *bammah*, which was undoubtedly an open cult place).[8]

Another open cult place from this period is the stelae field at Gezer, uncovered by R.A.S. Macalister and later studied anew by the Hebrew Union College expedition.[9] It consisted of a row of eleven large stone monoliths standing in a north–south alignment in the centre of a large open area, about 40 × 50 m. All the stelae, apart from one, were found *in situ*. Among them was a rectangular-shaped stone basin which was apparently used in ritual ceremonies. W.F. Albright and S. Yeivin compared the site with the stelae field at Assur in which stone pillars were erected in honour of deceased kings, ministers and high officials[10] (Fig. 2).

2. Row of stelae and basin, Tel Gezer. *Qadmoniot* 3 (10) (1970) p. 62.

7. J. Kaplan has suggested that the side chamber served as a holy-of-holies and that the temple was of a 'bent axis' type, like Sumerian temples. However, this suggestion has no foundations — J. Kaplan: Mesopotamian Elements in the MB II Culture of Palestine, *JNES* 30 (1971), pp. 294–295; also Wright (above, n. 1, 1985), p. 227.

8. M. Dothan: Sanctuaries along the Coast of Canaan in the MB Period: Nahariyah, in A. Biran (ed.): *Temples and High Places in Biblical Times*, Jerusalem, 1981, pp. 74–81.

9. W.G. Dever: The Gezer Fortifications and the 'High Place': Illustration of Stratigraphic Methods and Problems, *PEQ* 10 (1973), pp. 61–70.

10. W.F. Albright: *Archaeology and the Religion of Israel*, (5th ed.), New York, 1969, p. 103.

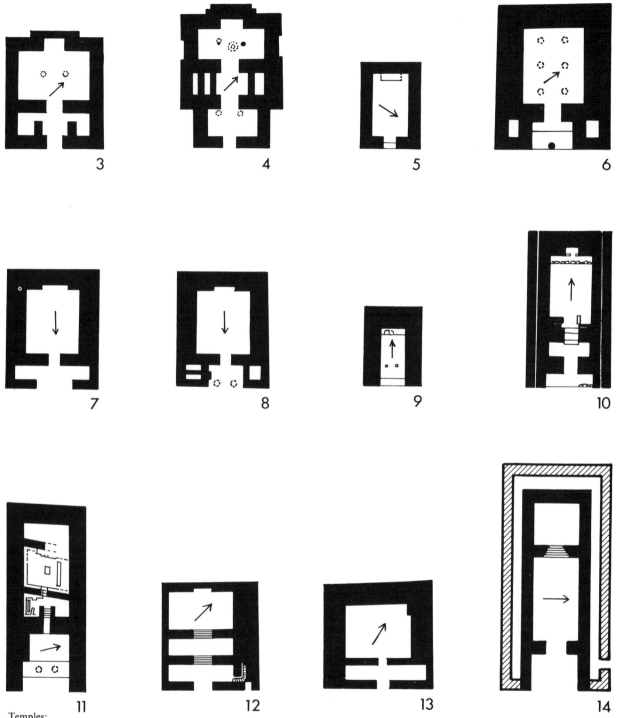

Temples:
3. Hazor Area H, Stratum 3. *Hazor*, Fig. 18.   4. Hazor Area H, Stratum 1B. *Hazor*, Fig. 20.   5. Hazor Area A. *Hazor*, Fig. 26.   6. Tell Balata (Shechem). *Shechem*, Fig. 41.   7. Megiddo, Temple 2048, Stratum X, early phase, reconstruction. *EI* 11 (1971), Figs. 16-17.   8. Megiddo, Temple 2048, Stratum VIII. *Megiddo* II, Fig. 247.   9. Tell Mardikh (Syria). P. Matthiae: *Ebla, An Empire Rediscovered*, London, 1980, Fig. 28.   10. Tell Mardikh (Syria). Matthiae (*ibid.*), Fig. 30.   11. Tell Mumbaqat (Syria). J. Boese and W. Orthmann: *Mumbaqat, eine 5000 Jahre alte Stadt am Euphrat, Saarbruecken*, 1976, p. 4, Fig. 5.   12. Alalakh (Turkey), Temple Stratum VII. L. Woolley: *Alalakh*, London, 1955, Fig. 35.   13. Alalakh (Turkey), Temple Stratum VI. Woolley (*ibid.*), Fig. 30.   14. Solomon's Temple, reconstruction.

Megiddo. Late Bronze Age temple (Strata VIIB-VIIA).

At Shechem the complex of buildings uncovered beneath the Fortress Temple and interpreted by Wright as a 'Courtyard Temple' should probably be interpreted as part of a large public building, perhaps a palace.[11]

Monumental Symmetrical Temples ('The Syrian Temple'). — During the course of the last century of the Middle Bronze Age, a new type of temple made its appearance in the Canaanite cities. The temples of this type consisted of a monumental, freestanding building, which was situated in the centre of a temenos; its plan is symmetrical, with the entrance set along the central axis. There is a well-defined holy-of-holies where the image of the divinity was located. Temples of this type known in Canaan include examples from Megiddo, Shechem and Hazor (Areas H and A). In most cases they continued to be in use in the succeeding period. The temple at Megiddo remained in use for hundreds of years, up to the Iron Age I.

Shechem.[12] The temple building (Fig. 6) was uncovered by E. Sellin and G. Welter in 1926 and was newly investigated by G.E. Wright in the 1960's. The building is situated close to the city-wall, southwest of the northwestern gate, partly above an embankment of an earlier phase of the Middle Bronze Age and partly above a thick artificial fill. The temple, 21.2 × 26.3 m. (i.e., 40 x 50 long Egyptian cubits) has massive walls, 5.1 m. thick (i.e., about 10 long Egyptian cubits). The preserved walls form a broad stone foundation with a levelled top above which was laid a brick superstructure.

It can be assumed that the space inside the massive walls contained several levels of corridors and rooms, though none have been preserved. Two square towers in the eastern facade of the temple flanked an entrance porch (5 × 7 m.) in the centre of which stood a single column with a stone base (*ca.* 0.78 m. in diameter) which supported the lintel of the entrance. The main

11. *Shechem*, pp. 103–122; G.R.H. Wright: Temples at Shechem, *ZAW* 80 (1968), pp. 2–9.

12. *Shechem*, pp. 80–102; pp. 251–252, nn. 1–6; Wright (above, n. 11), pp. 16–26; Busink (above, n. 1), pp. 388–394.

part of the temple (the cella, or *hekhal* according to biblical terminology) was a long-room (11 × 13.5 m.) which was divided longitudinally by two rows of octagonal Egyptian-style limestone columns.[13] The original floor of the cella (Phase 1a) was composed of a thick layer of beaten lime in which two pits had been dug. At least one of these pits had probably held a liquid substance for use in ritual ceremonies. The floor of the second phase (1b) was built on an artificial fill, 0.75 m. above the original floor. Wright attributed it to the MB IIC, but it may in fact represent a rebuilding in the LB I.[14] In this phase the entrance to the building was altered; the original wide symmetrical entrance was narrowed by means of a wall and an indirect approach to the building was created. Two stone bases attached to the temple's outer facade on either side of the entrance had grooves cut into the tops to hold stelae. A square structure built of bricks and measuring 4.2 × 4.2 m., discovered in the court in front of the temple, was interpreted by the excavators as an altar.

Another possible temple at Shechem is Building 7300, located along the fortification line south of the northwestern gate.[15] The size of this building is 12 × 19.5 m.; it has an entrance room, a long main hall with two pillars supporting the roof and a room at the back. The definition of this building as a temple was based on its plan, which Dever interpreted as tripartite recalling the Solomonic temple at Jerusalem, the temple at Tell Ta'yinat, etc. However, the back room in this building has a corner entrance, unlike the other tripartite temples, where the entrance to the back chamber is in line with the central axis of the building. If this building was a temple, the back room should be interpreted as a treasury, rather than as a holy-of-holies. The focal point of cult in this building could be a dais located at the back of the main hall. The building was not freestanding, and perhaps served as a chapel in a larger complex which included the 'tower temple'.

Megiddo.[16] Temple 2048 (Fig. 7) was erected above the sacred precinct of the Early Bronze Age. The building, which was oriented in a south–southwest direction, measured 16.5 × 21.5 m. and its walls were about 4 m. thick. It contains an entrance porch between two square towers whose inner dimensions were 9.6 × 11.5 m. A niche at the end of the main hall served as the holy-of-holies in the first phase of the temple. The plan of the temple has been studied by C. Epstein who concluded that the square towers were later additions. The original structure perhaps had been provided with an entrance porch whose plan could not be established. I. Dunayevsky and A. Kempinski's reconstruction of the entrance porch as a broad-room was inspired by the temple of Stratum VII at Alalakh.

The excavators of Megiddo assigned the initial phase of the temple to Stratum VIII, dating to the fourteenth century B.C. Wright and Epstein suggested that the temple should be dated to the Middle Bronze Age, and Dunayevsky and Kempinski, on the basis of the stratigraphic evidence, assigned it to Stratum X, the latest Middle Bronze Age stratum at Megiddo. According to their reconstruction, the temple in Stratum X stood in the middle of a large courtyard which was bounded on the north by service rooms and on the west by the governor's palace. The proximity of the palace and the temple is reminiscent of the plan of the contemporary city of Alalakh Stratum VII.

Hazor. The temple uncovered at Hazor in Area H (Fig. 3)[17] is a monumental, symmetrical, freestanding structure (exterior dimensions 18 × 20 m.), which was oriented northwest. A spacious courtyard used for cult ceremonies was located at its front. It differs from the two temples described above in details of its plan and mainly in the fact that the main hall — the cella — is a broad-room, while at Megiddo and Shechem it was a long-room. The temple is known primarily in its latest building stages, from the LB II, but the excavators uncovered sufficient evidence to reconstruct its original plan in Stratum XVI (Stratum 3 of the lower city of Hazor), dating to the last phase of the MB II. The building was constructed close to the northern tip of the lower city, partly above the rampart and partly above an artificial fill on the slope. It includes an entrance porch, main hall (cella) and a niche in the back wall. Symmetrical in plan, the corners of the building were constructed at exactly ninety-degree angles and the entrances were along the main central axis. It is possible that the orthostats found in secondary use in the building in Strata XIV–XIII date to this

13. G.R.H. Wright: Fluted Columns in the Bronze Age Temple of Baal-Berith at Shechem, *PEQ* 97 (1965), pp. 66–84; also, *Shechem*, pp. 24–25. Similar columns, though much smaller, were found in the temple of Lachish, Area P (below, p. 176).

14. Y. Yadin: A Note on Dating the Shechem Temple, *BASOR* 150 (1958), p. 34 and G.E. Wright's answer there, pp. 34–35.

15. W.G. Dever: The MB IIC Stratification in the Northwest Gate Area at Shechem, *BASOR* 216 (1974), pp. 40–48.

16. C. Epstein: Interpretation of the Megiddo Sacred Area During Middle Bronze II, *IEJ* 15 (1965), pp. 204–221; *Shechem*, pp. 94–95; Dynayevsky and Kempinski (above, n. 2), pp. 179–186.

17. *Hazor*, pp. 75–79, Fig. 18.

initial phase of the temple. A raised platform, 2.3 m. wide, at the front of the building, was approached from the court by two basalt steps. The entrance was flanked by two square rooms, apparently high towers. The basalt sockets of two doors which opened inward were found in the opening between the entrance porch and the main hall. The hall is 13.5 m. wide and 8.9 m. deep. The ceiling was apparently supported by two columns which were set on the axis widthwise. Two architectural fragments — flat stones with conical projections — were apparently the bases or capitals of these columns. The floor of the temple was of terre pisee. A court paved with a pebble floor extended about 30 m. in front of the building.

In Area A on the high mound of Hazor, another temple of the monumental symmetrical type (Fig. 5) was unearthed.[18] This was a long-building (exterior dimensions, 11.6 × 16.2 m.). The walls, which were 2.35 m. thick, were built of mud brick on a stone foundation. The building consisted of one long hall which terminated in a platform, 1.5 × 4.8 m., built of plastered bricks. The temple was erected in Stratum XVI and continued in use in Stratum XV (LB I). An entranceway built of two basalt orthostats and a sill of four well-dressed basalt slabs was attributed by the excavators to Stratum XV; but since this building technique was widespread in northern Syria in the MB II,[19] it may be suggested that these orthostats were part of the original construction of the temple in Stratum XVI. The walls of the building were plastered and displayed traces of painting, providing a further parallel with northern Syria, where wall paintings have been uncovered at Alalakh Stratum VII. The temple of Area A was situated close to a probable palace of the Middle Bronze Age. This proximity resembles the Middle Bronze temples at Megiddo and Alalakh which also stood near palaces.

Tel Kittan and Tell el-Hayyat. Other temples of this type have been unearthed in Strata V–IV at Tel Kittan in the Jordan Valley (both are dated to the MB II)[20] and at Tell el-Hayyat east of the Jordan, in the same region.[21] The earlier of the Tel Kittan

temples, from Stratum V, and the temple at Tell el-Hayyat are megaron-type buildings. Both had an open portico between antae, and a nearly square cella. Both are small buildings (the temple at Tel Kittan is 5.5 × 6.9 m.). The presence of the portico at the entrance may reflect a continuation of the tradition of the EB III temples at Megiddo. A large court in front of the temple at Tel Kittan contained a row of *massevot* made of large pebbles. In Tel Kittan Stratum IV the earlier temple was replaced by a larger temple. The builders of the new temple took care not to destroy what had survived of the earlier building: the new walls surround the remains of that building without damaging them or the row of *massevot* in the court. The new building, 11.5 × 14.3 m., resembles the temple in Area A at Hazor: it is a rectangular structure containing a single hall with an entrance on the east. The temples at Tel Kittan and Tell el-Hayyat can be interpreted as typical cultic centres of small communities of the Middle Bronze Age and as such they complement the large urban sanctuaries at Shechem, Hazor and Megiddo.

A small shrine of this period was uncovered in the unwalled Middle Bronze Age settlement at Giv'at Sharett near Bet Shemesh.[22] It stood in the upper part of the settlement. It consisted of an elongated rectangular hall entered from the east with benches along its walls. A holy-of-holies with a raised stone platform was separated from the main hall by an *in antis*(?) entrance.

The temples of Megiddo, Shechem and Hazor can be grouped under the general category of 'monumental symmetrical temples'. They share the following features: 1. several are constructed on raised ground high above their surroundings (Shechem, Megiddo and Hazor, Area H); 2. their walls are thick (more than 2 m. wide) and consist of stone foundations and brick superstructures; 3. the entrances are placed along a longitudinal central axis; 4. they contain no more than two architectural units, the main one (the cella) large and either a long-room or broad-room;[23] 5. the holy-of-holies is usually a clearly

18. Above, n. 17, pp. 102–104, Fig. 26.
19. Orthostats are known in Alalakh Stratum VII, in the 'North Palace' at Ugarit and at the palace of Tilmen Huyuk. L. Woolley: *Alalakh*, Oxford, 1955, Pls. XIII:C, XV:B; XXIV, etc; H. de Contenson *et al.*: *Syria* 49 (1972), pp. 15–21; C.F.A. Schaeffer: *ibid.*, pp. 27–33.
20. E. Eisenberg: The Temples at Tell Kitan, BA 40 (1977), p. 80.
21. S.E. Falconer: The Development of Middle Bronze Age Villages in the Jordan Valley: New Perspectives from Tell el-Hayyat, *Abstracts, Society of Biblical Literature, Annual Meeting*, 1986, p. 227.

22. D. Bahat: Excavations at Giv'at Sharett near Beth-Shemesh, *Qadmoniot* 8 (1975), pp. 64–67 (Hebrew).
23. Kuschke (above, n. 1) divides these temples into two groups: (a) long-buildings with antae at the front; (b) long-buildings with towers at the front. But among the 'long-buildings' he includes the temple of Area H at Hazor, which has a broad-room as its main space. Thus a definition of a building as a 'long-building' when based on the outer dimensions of the structure may lead to different conclusions than a definition based on the inner dimensions of the main space. The latter criterion seems to be more significant.

defined element represented by a niche or a raised platform attached to the back wall, directly opposite the entrance; and 6. the facade of the temple is plain but it sometimes has two front towers which rise above the other parts of the building and give access to the roof or the upper parts of the building. The facades of these buildings resemble those of contemporary city-gates; this resemblance might have some religious significance.[24] The two rows of columns placed lengthwise in the hall of the Shechem temple is an anomaly and has no parallels in other buildings of this type.

Various theories have been proposed regarding the origin of this type of temple and the historical significance of its appearance in Palestine. B. Mazar suggested calling them 'Tower (*migdal*) Temples' and identified them with the towers mentioned in the biblical sources, in relation to various Canaanite cities mainly in the period of the Judges. The most well-known of these is *migdal-Shechem*, i.e., 'the house of El-berit', which is identified with the temple of Shechem.[25] In the opinion of Mazar, who was followed by Wright, these temples were introduced into Canaan toward the end of the Middle Bronze Age in the wake of the invasion of new ethnic elements from the north — Hurrian and Indo-European — who acquired control over the local Semitic population. Discoveries in northern Syria in recent years have shed light on the origin of this type of temple. The third-millennium B.C. temples at Tell Chuera in northern Mesopotamia are composed of a main hall in the form of a long-room with antae in the facade.[26] They provide evidence of the early tradition of such buildings in the region and serve as the connecting link between the temples of Tepe Gawra of the fourth millennium

and those of the second millennium. At Ebla (Tell Mardikh) in northern Syria, the Italian expedition uncovered two temples of the Middle Bronze Age (apparently dating to 2000–1800 B.C.), which are the most definitive prototypes of the temples with a main hall in the form of a long-room (Megiddo, Shechem and Hazor, Area A).[27] The temple in Area D is a long-room with porch between two antae, which can be considered the forerunner of the towers in the temples of Shechem and Hazor. Two additional temples at Ebla (Areas B1 and N) have analogies with the temple of Hazor in Area A in that they consist of a single long-room terminating in a raised platform. Another monumental symmetrical temple is the Dagan Temple at Mari.[28] It is symmetrical in plan (18.5 × 35.5 m.) and its walls are massive (up to 6 m.). The entrance is through a porch flanked by antae and leads into a long-room terminating in a raised platform. Following the best Mesopotamian tradition, a ziggurat adjoins the temple at Mari, but the plan of the temple itself points to a northern Syrian and northern Mesopotamian tradition. The Mari temple was in use in the eighteenth century B.C. (though it may have been erected as early as the twentieth-nineteenth centuries B.C.) at which time Mari had strong political, ethnic and cultural ties with Syria and Canaan. The strength of this architectural tradition in Syria can be attested by the discoveries in recent years of similar temples of Late Bronze Age date at Tell Mumbaqat (Fig. 11) and Tell Meskene, along the upper Euphrates. At both of these sites two temples of this type were uncovered; they possess an entranceway set between antae and a cella in the form of a long-room.[29]

The tradition of long temples with a symmetrical plan thus appears to be firmly anchored in the

24. Wright (above, n. 1, 1985), pp. 233–234. Wright defines the temple at Hazor Area H in the German term 'Tor Temple' (= Gate Temple) and suggests seeing in this element a Mesopotamian influence. Dunayevski and Kempinski (above, n. 2) claim that towers were added to such temples only in the Late Bronze Age. But this claim is not sufficiently proven. The temple at Shechem with its two towers is most probably a Middle Bronze temple. On towers in Syrian architecture of the Middle Bronze Age see *Shechem*, p. 25.

25. *Shechem*, pp. 123–138; B. *Mazar: The Early Biblical Period, Historical Studies*, Jerusalem, 1986, pp. 27–29 (first published in *IEJ* 18 [1968]); Wright (above, n. 11), pp. 18–19.

26. A. Moortgat: *Tell Chuera in Nordost-Syrien; vorlaufiger Bericht uber die dritte Grabungskampagne 1960*, Cologne, 1962, Plan I; idem, *Tell Chuera in Nordost-Syrien; Bericht uber die vierte Grabungskampagne 1963*, Cologne, 1965, p. 11, Plans V–VI; idem, *Tell Chuera in Nordost-Syrien; vorlaufiger Bericht uber die funfte Grabungskampagne 1964*, Wiesbaden, 1967, pp. 8–38, Fig. 17.

27. P. Matthiae: *Ebla*, London, 1980, pp. 125–132, 200–203; idem, *Ebla nel periodo delle dinastie amorree a della dinastia di Akkad. Scoperte archeologiche recenti a Tell Mardikh*.

28. A. Parrot: Les fouilles de Mari, Syria 19 (1938), p. 22, Fig. 13; *ibid.*, 20 (1939), Pl. II; also Wright (above, n. 11), p. 30.

29. E. Heinrich *et al.*: Vierter vorlaufiger Bericht uber die von der Deutschen Orient-Gesellschaft mit Mitteln der Stiftung Volkswagenwerk in Habuba Kabira (Hububa Kabira, Herbstkampagnen 1971 und 1972 Sowie Testgrabung Fruhjahr 1973) und in Mumbaqat (Tell Munbaqa, Herbstkampagne 1971) unternommenen archaologischen Unterschungen, erstattet von Mitgliedern der Mission (Fortsetzung), *MDOG* 106 (1974), pp. 11–27, Supp. 2; W. Orthman and H. Kuhne: Mumbaqat 1973, *MDOG* 106 (1974), pp. 77–79, Supp. 6; J. Margueron: Quatre campagnes de fouilles a Emar (1972–1974): un bilan provisoire, *Syria* 52 (1975), pp. 62–63.

Hazor. Late Bronze Age Orthostat Temple (Stratum 1b). Top: general view: bottom: detail.

cultural tradition of northern Syria and northern Mesopotamia and their appearance in Canaan in the Middle Bronze Age is an expression of the cultural links and common traditions in this epoch between the West Semitic states in the various parts of the Levant and of northern Mesopotamia.[30]

The temple at Hazor in Area H (Fig. 3) is similar in its general layout to temples of this group, but it differs from them in that the main hall is a broad-room and the ratio between the internal width and length is nearly 1:1.5. In this aspect the temple is analogous to the contemporaneous temple in Level VII at Alalakh (Fig. 13) and also, to a certain extent, to the Baal and Dagan Temples at Ugarit, both of which were apparently established in the Middle Bronze Age.[31] The origin of such a ratio between the length and width of the main hall can be traced back to the third millennium B.C., as exemplified by the temples of Megiddo (Strata XVII–XV, above, p. 57) and also the temples at Mari from the Pre-Sargonic period.[32]

The tradition of 'broad-room' temples is indigenous to Canaan and probably to central and southern Syria, in contrast to the tradition of long-rooms predominant in northern Syria and northern Mesopotamia.[33] It can be concluded, therefore, that the two forms of monumental symmetrical temples, as defined here, represent the continuation of two architectural traditions which originated in Canaan and Syria in the third millennium B.C.

Two temples uncovered at Tell ed-Daba' (identified with Avaris, capital of the Hyksos) display a close resemblance to the temples in Area H at Hazor and to the temple in Alalakh, Level VII.[34] Since the

Hazor. Late Bronze Age Stelae Temple (Stratum 1b).

material culture of Avaris in the Middle Bronze Age should be regarded as an extension of the Canaanite material culture, these temples should accordingly be considered additional clear examples of Canaanite temples of this period.

The Late Bronze Age and Iron Age I.

Many temples and cult sites of the Late Bronze Age and Iron Age I (1550–1000 B.C.) have been discovered in Israel. The examination of their plans reveals a great diversity making it difficult to establish patterns and clear rules which governed their development in this period. These buildings will be classified into groups sharing common characteristics, while problems associated with the classification will be noted.

Open Cult Places. — The tradition of open cult places did not cease in this period. A good example of an open cult site of the LB II was uncovered in Area F at Hazor (Stratum XIII-XIV).[35] This area consists of a paved piazza ascending to a stone platform on its west side. At the eastern end of the square was found a monolithic stone altar, 2.4 m. long, 0.85 m. wide and 1.2 m. high. The altar is well-dressed and has recesses in the upper surface to drain the blood of the sacrificed animals.

30. For an extensive discussion on the origins of the 'Syrian Temple' and the parallels between the temples of Syria and Palestine see: P. Matthiae: Le Temple dans la Syrien du Bronze Moyen, in *Le Temple et le Culte, Compte Rendu de la Vingtieme Rencontre Assyriologique Internationale*, Leiden, 1975, pp. 43–72.

31. For the temple of Alalakh see Woolley (above, n. 19), pp. 43–59. For Ugarit see C.F.A. Schaeffer: Les fouilles de Minet-el-Beida et de Ras Shamra, *Syria* 12 (1931), p. 9, Fig. 2; *ibid.*, 14 (1933), p. 122; *ibid.*, 16 (1935), pp. 154–156, Pl. XXXVI.

32. A. Parrot: *Mission Archeologique de Mari*, I: *Le Temple d'Ishtar*, Paris, 1956, Pls. V–VIII.

33. Ottosson (above, n. 1), pp. 23, 33–36, 121, n. 12. Ottosson correctly emphasizes the resemblance between the Early Bronze III temples of Megiddo and the Middle Bronze temple at Hazor Area H. The addition of towers at the front of the temple at Hazor was intended in his mind to separate the divinity from the worshippers, while in the Early Bronze period the statue of the divinity was more accessible.

34. M. Bietak: Avaris and Piramese, Archaeological Explorations in the Eastern Nile Delta, *Proceedings of the British Academy* 65 (1979), pp. 247–252, 284–285.

35. *Hazor* II, pp. 127–164; *Hazor*, pp. 100–101.

Open cult places are known also from the Iron Age I. At Hazor, Stratum XI (eleventh century B.C.), a cult site was uncovered with a stone platform located in a paved area surrounded by walls.[36] An open cult place dating to the early twelfth century B.C. was found on a hill in the northern Samarian hills, in the heart of the settlement area of the tribe of Manasseh.[37] A boundary wall built of large stones surrounded a circular area, 21 m. in diameter, in the centre of which was a flat stone set on its side (a *massevah*) with a paved area in front of it. The outstanding find at this site was a bronze figurine of a bull, which doubtless played a central role in the cult. The earliest cult place at Arad (Stratum XII, tenth century B.C.) was also apparently an open site.[38] It contained an altar and high place. These three cult sites may be identified as Israelite. They recall open cult places mentioned in the Bible, especially in stories related to the Patriarchs and the Judges as, for example, the cult places of the Patriarchs near Shechem, Bethel and Beersheba and the altar of Manoah at Ophrah (Genesis 12:8; 28:18–22; Joshua 24:26; Judges 6:11 ff.).[39]

Monumental Symmetrical Temples. — The four temples of this type which were erected in the Middle Bronze Age at Shechem, Megiddo and Hazor (Areas A and H) also continued in use in the Late Bronze Age, and at Megiddo as late as the Iron Age I.

Shechem.[40] The meticulous stratigraphic excavation carried out by Wright in the debris left in the temple of Shechem (Fig. 6) by Sellin and Welter led him to conclude that the monumental temple of the Middle Bronze Age (Temple 1) ceased to exist at the end of that period and a gap in settlement ensued in the LB I. In Wright's opinion, a new temple (Temple 2), 16 m. wide and 12.5 m. long, was established on the same spot in the LB II. He compared this temple with those of Alalakh, Ugarit, Hazor and Bet Shean. The reconstruction of its plan, however, is based solely on two walls and it must therefore be treated with caution. The temple was entered from the east, but its orientation differed somewhat from the previous temple. Sections of a pavement were discovered as

well as evidence of a podium, built at the western extremity on the base of the western wall of Temple 1. Wright also distinguished two phases in the existence of Temple 2: in the earlier phase (Temple 2a), dating to the LB II, a brick altar in the form of a large platform (5.2 × 7 m. and preserved to a height of 0.27 m.) was erected in the court in front of the building and in the second phase (Temple 2b), a new stone altar, measuring 1.65 × 2.2 m., was built above the earlier one. The two stelae in the facade of Temple 1 continued in use in this period. According to Wright, the second phase persisted into the Iron Age I (until 1100 B.C.) and this last temple is to be identified with the *migdal Shechem* or 'the house of El-berit' in which the aristocracy of Shechem (*ba'aley migdal Shechem*) met their death in the war with Abimelech (Judges 9:46–49).[41]

If Wright's version of the development of the temple of Shechem is correct, this is an interesting phenomenon of a return to the tradition in which the main hall (the cella) is a broad-room, following the Middle Bronze Age temple with the cella in the form of a long-room. Since the origin of the broad-room cella is rooted in the local architectural tradition of the third millennium B.C., this phenomenon can be considered a revival of an early local tradition and the abandonment of the northern Syrian architectural tradition which was introduced into Palestine in the Middle Bronze Age.[42]

Megiddo. Temple 2048 at Megiddo seems to have continued in use without interruption throughout the Late Bronze Age and the Iron Age.[43] The building

---

36. *Hazor*, pp. 132–133.

37. A. Mazar: The Bull Site — An Iron Age I Open Cult Place, *BASOR* 247 (1982), pp. 27–42.

38. Y. Aharoni: Nothing Early and Nothing Late: Rewriting Israel's Conquest, *BA* 39 (1976), pp. 60–61.

39. B. Mazar: *Canaan and Israel*, Jerusalem, 1974, pp. 144–151 (Hebrew); M. Haran: *Temples and Temple Service in Ancient Israel*, Oxford, 1978, pp. 48–57; B. Levine: Book Review of above Haran, *JBL* 99 (1980), p. 451.

40. *Shechem*, pp. 95–101.

41. Above, n. 40, pp. 123–138.

42. The identification of 'Temple 2' at Shechem is not certain. Only foundations were found, and they fit the contours of the Iron Age 'Granary Building'. It is thus possible that the foundations related to 'Temple 2' are in fact foundations of the large Iron Age II building which was erected in this place. In this case, the monumental 'Tower Temple' ('Temple 1') could have been in continuous use until the Iron Age I, like Temple 2048 at Megiddo. In this case, the Temple of El-berit at Shechem may be identified with the old, monumental, Middle Bronze structure, which was perhaps in use for many centuries.

43. *Megiddo* II, pp. 104–105 and the references in n. 16 above. The pottery found on the floor of this building was assembled by K. Kenyon: The Middle and Late Bronze Age Strata at Megiddo, *Levant* 1 (1969), p. 54, Fig. 25. She dated this assemblage to the fourteenth century B.C., but it cannot be earlier than the Iron Age I. This pottery should be attributed to Stratum VI at Megiddo, and thus the temple may have been in use until the eleventh century B.C. It should be noted that the plan of Stratum VI does not include any building remains in the area of the temple. The earliest buildings found above the temple are of Stratum IVA (Iron Age II).

underwent substantial changes during the course of the Late Bronze Age and Iron Age I but the exact dates of the changes are difficult to establish. Two towers were erected in the facade flanking a portico with two columns (Fig. 8). The base of one of these columns, made of well-dressed basalt stone and having a diameter of 0.65 m., was preserved *in situ*. The towers were built partly of large ashlars (several of which measure 1.2 × 0.55 × 0.6 m.) laid in the header and stretcher technique, one of the earliest examples of this technique found in Israel. The holy-of-holies of the temple was radically changed: the rear wall was rebuilt and the wide niche of the first phase was replaced by a long, narrow, raised platform extending along the length of the back wall of the cella. The floor was composed of a layer of beaten lime inlaid with basalt slabs which may have served as the bases of cultic installations. The excavators attribute these changes to Stratum VIIB. The temple of this stratum was destroyed and rebuilt along similar lines in the third phase of its use, which is attributed by the excavators to Stratum VIIA. In the opinion of C. Epstein, and following her, Dunayevsky and Kempinski, the ashlar towers are to be assigned to Stratum VIII and the other changes to Strata VIIB–VIIA, as was proposed by the excavators.

Remains of the temenos, which surrounded the temple in the Late Bronze Age, were uncovered to the west of the building. These were assigned by the excavators to Stratum VIIB. The remains included a court bounded on the west by two parallel walls with long halls between them which probably served as offices or storerooms of the temple. No traces of an altar or other installations were encountered in the court.

Hazor. The two temples of Hazor, in Areas H and A, also continued in use in the Late Bronze Age.[44] The temple of Area A (Fig. 5) which, as was noted, was erected in the MB II, was still in existence in the LB I (Stratum XV), at which time, according to Y. Yadin, the orthostat entranceway was added (but see above, p. 165). The temple was razed at the end of this period and the area became a heap of ruins during the LB II. The remains of stelae and cultic installations of the LB II discovered near the facade of the temple, however, indicate that even after the temple ceased to exist, its site was preserved as a sacred area and ritual ceremonies were performed there.

In Area H, the Middle Bronze Age temple of Stratum XVI continued in use in the LB I (Stratum

XV) almost without change.[45] Alterations were made in the cella and the holy-of-holies, however, which point to a change in the cultic practices. The niche of the earlier phase, which apparently held a statue of a god, was now closed with a narrow wall and transformed into a small closed area. West of it, against the western wall of the temple, a podium (1.2 × 1.5 m.) was added. Wide benches, apparently for offerings, were built along the eastern and western walls of the cella.[46] In the opinion of Yadin, the orthostats found in secondary use in the following stratum originated in the temple of this stratum, though they might have belonged to the original structure of the Middle Bronze Age. The temple court of the following period was meticulously designed along a new plan and, together with its various equipment, forms the finest example of a Late Bronze Age temple court. It was composed of two parts: an outer (southern) court and an inner (northern) court which were separated by a *propylaeum* consisting of a gate chamber in the form of a broad-room built exactly on the continuation of the longitudinal axis of the temple.

After a destruction which resulted in a thick accumulation of debris, the temple was rebuilt (Stratum XIV — fourteenth century B.C.). An entrance porch was added at the front (4.8 × 9.8 m.; width of walls, 1.2 m.). The main entrance of the temple was apparently located in the middle of the porch facade, but it has not survived. From the porch a side doorway led to a square hall (5 × 5.8 m.) which was flanked by narrow rectangular spaces which served as stairwells for a second storey, and which apparently rose as towers above the rest of the building. From this room two steps descended to the temple's main room — the cella (8 × 13.3 m.; width of walls, 2.1 m.). In the northern wall of the cella was a niche, 3.75 m. wide and 2.1 m. deep, which

---

44. *Hazor*, pp. 103–104.

45. *Hazor*, pp. 79–95. Yadin claims that the temple of Stratum XVI was rebuilt in Stratum XV without significant change in its plan. But there is no evidence for violent destruction of the temple of Stratum XVI. It appears that there was a peaceful continuation between these two strata, and in fact the temples of both levels are the same building, in which a few alterations and floor raisings were made.

46. Ottosson (above, n. 1), p. 28 claims that the niche, in this phase, served as a closed holy-of-holies, in which the statue of the divinity was hidden. But such an explanation contradicts the basic concept of Canaanite temples, where the statue of the divinity stood opposite the entrance. It is possible that the closed niche served in Stratum XV as the temple's treasury, and that the statue stood on the raised dais which was found in front of the niche.

required that the back wall be widened, which was done by gradations in a stylized manner. The niche could be closed by means of a curtain (as is evidenced by recesses for poles to hold a curtain). A narrow bench, 1.1 m. wide, was built in its inner part. The ceiling of the cella was supported by two columns set on the broad axis of the room. A deep pit, probably to drain liquids, was dug between the columns. The well-dressed basalt orthostats, which lined the inner walls of the cella and some of the walls of the porch, were assigned to this phase, although, as mentioned above, they might have been removed from the ruined temple of the previous period and incorporated into the new building.[47] The same orthostats continued to be used without change in Stratum XIII.[48] Two round holes, 5 cm. in both diameter and depth, were drilled in the upper surface of each orthostat to hold the wooden beams which strengthened the brick superstructure. At the entrance to the temple stood two orthostats carved in the form of crouching lions, the heads sculptured in the round and the bodies carved in relief.

The temple is thus composed of three elements: a porch, a middle area, and an inner area with a niche. Yadin designated the main hall of this temple the 'holy-of-holies' (debir), in analogy with Solomon's Temple in Jerusalem. This, however, would make the small area between the stairwells in the Hazor temple analogous to the hekhal of Solomon's Temple. This is not logical, however, since the hekhal in Solomon's Temple represented the main hall of the building while the debir was the inner area which contained the Holy Ark. From the standpoint of function, the comparison of Solomon's Temple with the Hazor temple requires that the main hall of the Hazor temple be designated hekhal, the niche at its northern end be comparable to the debir (holy-of-holies), and the central area, between the two stairwell towers, be considered the hall ('ulam). If this is correct, then in its internal arrangement the temple in its original form (Strata XVI–XV) recalls Solomon's Temple, while the porch added in Stratum XIV (1b) has no parallel in the Jerusalem temple. It is not unlikely that Busink and Ottosson are correct in their assumption that the porch was not roofed.[49]

In the following stratum (XIII 1a), the temple was rebuilt after its destruction on a similar plan to that of the previous temple. In front of the opening leading from the porch to the central hall two column bases were found which have no structural function. They were apparently erected in the previous stratum and continued into this stratum. Yadin assumed that their function was cultic and he compared them with the Jachin and Boaz pillars in Solomon's Temple.

The temple court also underwent changes in Strata XIV–XIII. In Stratum XIV it was divided by a wall into an inner court and an outer court. The inner court was entered through two corner entrances, in one of which stood a cultic installation (for libations?). An obelisk-shaped object which stood in the court probably served as a small altar. Further repairs and changes were carried out in the court in Stratum XIII, when it was again separated from the rest of the city by a series of walls.

Close parallels can be noted between the development of the temples at Hazor and those at Alalakh.[50] The similarity between the earliest temple of Hazor (Stratum XVI) and that of Level VII at Alalakh has been mentioned above. The temple of Level IV at Alalakh (Fig. 12) still closely resembles that of Level VII, and accordingly also the Stratum XV temple at Hazor, though at Alalakh a porch was apparently added (mostly reconstructed). The lion orthostats found in secondary use in the later levels probably originated in this temple, again paralleling the situation at Hazor. The temples of Levels III and II at Alalakh were built on different plans but those of Levels 1A and 1B, from the end of the Late Bronze Age, display a return to a central main axis, as in the temples at Hazor. An especially striking resemblance can be noted between the latest temple, that of Level 1B, and the temples of Strata XIV–XIII at Hazor. The open forecourt, which is bounded by solid walls, can be compared with the porch added to the temples at Hazor in these strata, which may have served as an unroofed forecourt.

Another structure which can be associated with this group of temples is Building 50 at Tell Abu Hawam.[51]

47. Above, p. 165.
48. *Hazor*, p. 20, n. 5; Ottosson (above, n. 1), pp. 35–36.
49. Busink (above, n. 1), p. 400; Ottosson (above, n. 1), p. 30. According to their suggestions, the square installation in the entrance porch (*Hazor* III-IV, Pl. 128:1) was a sacrificial altar and the entire entrance porch was an unroofed courtyard. The two pillars in the inner part of this space, close to the entrance of the building proper, could have been freestanding in an unroofed space, like Jachin and Boaz in the temple of Solomon. Ottosson suggests that these two pillars are a degenerated remnant of the two pillars *in antis* which stood at the entrance to the Early Bronze III temples at Megiddo.
50. Woolley (above, n. 19), pp. 71–90; *Hazor*, pp. 86–87; Ottosson (above, n. 1), pp. 34–37.
51. R.W. Hamilton: Excavations at Tell Abu-Hawam, *QDAP* 4 (1935), p. 12, Pl. XI; Busink (above, n. 1), pp. 404–405.

It measures 7.5 × 11 m. and consists of a single main hall with a small unit at its eastern end which may have served as a porch.

The examination of the buildings from Shechem, Megiddo and Hazor indicates that the monumental buildings of the Middle Bronze Age continued in use with changes and repairs which were made to conform with the cultic practices of the Late Bronze Age. If Wright's analysis of the finds at Shechem is accepted, then the temple of Megiddo is the only one from this period which preserved the tradition of a true *langhaus* (long-house). In all the other temples the main hall was a broad-room. (From the standpoint of a typological classification, the temple at Hazor is an interesting combination in which the exterior proportions of the building correspond to a *langhaus* and the interior proportions of the cella correspond to a broad-room.) It must be stressed that in this period no new monumental temples were erected.

Temples with Raised Holy-of-Holies: Bet Shean and Lachish. — The temples uncovered in Strata VII–VI at Bet Shean and in Stratum VI at Lachish, exhibit many common characteristics and thus form a separate category. These points of resemblance include the internal division of the building; the dimensions and proportions of the main hall, the elevated holy-of-holies which was approached by a staircase and set in a separate architectural niche (*adyton*) and the Egyptian architectural elements incorporated in the buildings, especially the stone column capitals.

The temple uncovered in Stratum VII at Bet Shean was erected in the sacred enclosure of the city which was the site of the temenos in Stratum IX (see below).[52] The external dimensions of its main part (excluding the entrance rooms) are: length, 14.85 m.; width, 14.2 m.; the brick walls are 1.2 m. wide. The approach to the temple was an indirect one, through an entrance hall in which the visitor had to turn at a right angle to enter the main hall. The latter was a broad-room whose proportions were similar to those of the Hazor temple of Area H (8.4 m. deep and 11.7 m. wide). Two columns stood on the main broad axis of this hall, 4.42 m. apart. Benches were built along the walls. The holy-of-holies was elevated 1.23 m. above the floor of the hall, and was reached by seven steps. Its assymmetrical placement was the result of the assymmetrical division of the inner space into an eastern part (6.75 m. wide; 2.75 m. deep) — occupied

by the holy-of-holies itself — and a western part, which apparently served as the treasure room of the temple. A raised brick installation at the foot of the stairs was probably an incense altar.

Based on a comparison with Egyptian funerary chapels at el-Amarna (see below), Rowe concluded that the entrance hall, the room east of it, and the southern part of the main hall, were all unroofed. This, however, cannot be confirmed and all other scholars who have examined this temple have reconstructed it as a roofed structure.[53] An additional room east of the entrance hall contained remains of an oven and a mould for baking. The sacred bread for the ritual meals may have been prepared here. Whereas the main hall and the holy-of-holies are built with straight angles and their walls have a uniform thickness, the walls of the entrance hall and the room east of it are thinner and their axis is not aligned with the rest of the building and therefore may have been added at a later stage to the building, which probably consisted in its original form only of the main hall, holy-of-holies and adjacent storeroom.

In his isometric reconstruction Rowe depicted Egyptian lintels in the doorways and Egyptian-style capitals on the columns; such stones were discovered north of the temple of Stratum VI; their use in Stratum VII remains a possibility. Little is known of the court surrounding the temple. Remains of an altar for burnt offerings were found north of the temple, i.e., behind and not in front of the temple as was customary with altars of this type. The altar, 1 × 1.4 × 1.25 m., was identified both by its form and by the remains of animal bones and ashes found in its vicinity.

Rowe assigned the temple to the reign of Amenhotep III on the basis of the foundation deposit which contained two cartouches of this pharaoh.[54] However, these objects should be considered as giving a *terminus post quem* for the construction. The temple may have been founded during either the fourteenth or thirteenth centuries B.C. The objects found on its floor date to the thirteenth century B.C.[55]

This temple at Bet Shean appears to have been a purely Canaanite sanctuary. The Egyptian architectural elements attest to a strong Egyptian influence, probably due to the special status of Bet Shean as a centre of Egyptian rule, but Rowe does

52. *Beth Shan* I, p. 19, Pl. 24:1; *Beth Shan* II, pp. 6–10, Pls. VI–VII; Ottosson (above, n. 1), p. 44.

53. Busink (above, n. 1), p. 414; Ottosson (above, n. 1), p. 44.
54. A. Kempinski: Beth-Shean, *EAEHL* I, pp. 213–215.
55. B. Mazar: The Chronology of the Temples at Beth-Shean, *BIES* 16 (1952), pp. 14–19 (Hebrew).

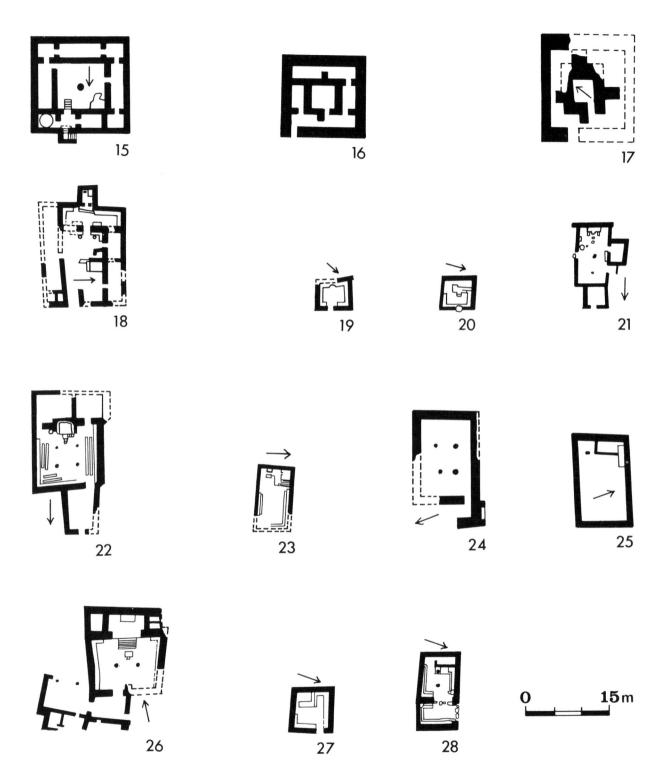

15. Mt. Gerisim. **BA** 32 (1969), p. 83, Fig. 2; p. 108, Fig. 20.   16. Amman. **PEQ** 98 (1966), p. 158, Fig. 2.   17. Hazor, Area F. **Hazor**, Fig. 24.   18. Arad, Israelite temple. **BASOR** 254 (1984), p. 10, Fig. 10.   19. Hazor, Area C. **Hazor**, Figs. 15–16.   20. Tell Qasile Stratum XII. **Qedem** 12 (1980), Fig. 13.   21. Lachish, Fosse Temple, Phase II. **Lachish** II, Pl. LXVI.   22. Lachish, Fosse Temple, Phase III. **Lachish** II, Pl. LXVIII.   23. Tel Mevorakh. **Qedem** 18 (1984), Fig. 25.   24. Bet Shean Stratum V. **Beth Shan** II, Pl. XII.   25. Tell Abu Hawam Stratum IV. **QDAP** IV (1935), Pl. IV, Locus 30.   26. Bet Shean Stratum VI. **Beth Shan** II, Pl. VIII.   27. Tell Qasile Stratum XI. **Qedem** 12 (1980), Fig. 13.   28. Tell Qasile Stratum X. **Qedem** 12 (1980), Fig. 13.

Tell Qasile. Iron Age I temple (Strata XI-X). Below: detail.

not seem to have been correct in his suggestion that the temple was built on an Egyptian plan.[56]

The temple of Stratum VI (Fig. 26) is merely a reconstruction of the temple of the previous stratum during the twelfth century B.C.[57] The entrance was now through a new antechamber or forecourt. In its facade were two column bases of unequal diameters; they apparently came from earlier strata. From this court one entered the porch and the cella, which adhered to the basic plan of the previous temple. Two column bases stood on the broad axis of the hall, 2.92 m. apart. The bases, made of limestone, are cylindrical in shape; they are 0.8 m. in diameter and 0.51 m. high. Two lotus-shaped limestone capitals in Egyptian style (see above, p. 11, Fig. 15) were found north of the temple. These are large capitals (0.75 m. high with a maximum diameter of 1.73 m.) made in two sections. Depressions in the upper

and lower surfaces enabled them to be attached to wooden pillars and wall constructions. Near these capitals were found fragments of cornices carved in typical Egyptian style. As in the previous temple, benches extended along the walls of the cella. The holy-of-holies was now 6 m. wide, 4 m. deep, with a 5 m. wide opening and approached by a broad staircase.

56. R. Giveon: *Footsteps of Pharaoh in Canaan,* Tel Aviv, 1984 (Hebrew), pp. 101–105.
57. F.W. James: *The Iron Age at Beth Shan*, Philadelphia, 1966, pp. 14–17; *Beth Shan* II, pp. 14–20.

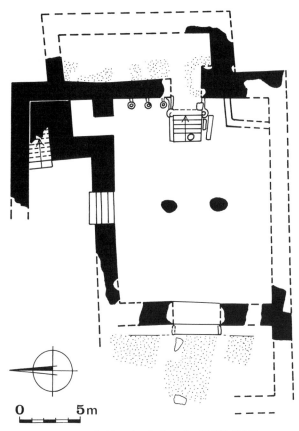

29. Lachish, Acropolis Temple. *Qadmoniot* 10 (40) (1978), p. 108.

Its floor was 0.89 m. above the floor of the cella and was painted light blue. Small chambers on either side of the holy-of-holies were perhaps treasure rooms of the temple. An incense altar similar to the one in the previous temple stood in the cella at the foot of the steps leading to the holy-of-holies.

Rowe attributed this temple to the reign of Seti I (end of the fourteenth century B.C.), but the pottery found in Stratum VI, as well as the lintel bearing the cartouche of Ramses III found in the government building adjoining the temple, indicate that it should be assigned to the Twentieth Dynasty, when Egyptian rule still held sway in the country. The period of Ramses III seems to be the most appropriate time for the construction of this temple.[58]

The temple of Stratum VI at Lachish[59] (Fig. 29) was uncovered in a poor state of preservation, which

made it difficult to clarify several basic features of its plan, in particular the entrance. In the opinion of the excavators, a square broad-room in the western part of the building served as the entrance hall. It was about 1.3 m. lower than the level of the main hall, which can be explained by the fact that the entire temple was built on a slope rising to the east. The excavators reconstruct a wide opening with a monumental staircase leading from this entrance room to the main hall. If this reconstruction is correct, then all the doorways are located on the longitudinal axis of the building, in contrast to the Bet Shean temples, where the entrance was an indirect one.[60] The main hall (cella) was 16.5 m. long and 13.2 m. wide. On the broad axis of the temple stood two round bases (0.85 m. in diameter), as in the Bet Shean temples. According to D. Ussishkin, the column shafts were of stone, as is evidenced by the discovery of a fragment of a cylindrical-shaped stone shaft carved on the top in typical Egyptian style with five horizontal bands. The columns carried papyrus-shaped stone capitals, similar to the capitals found at Bet Shean but somewhat larger (estimated diameter, 1.5 m.). Remains of ten cedar beams which had spanned the width of the building were revealed in this temple. Near the western wall of the cella stood three round stone column bases. Each of these bases was attached to the wall by means of a plastered brick partition wall. The bases had well-hewn projecting circles made to fit into octagonal columns which were crowned with square capitals. The excavators reconstruct these columns as rising to a height of about 1.7 m. and supporting a horizontal cornice. They had no structural function, but were purely ornamental. Two of the bases bore four incised lines in the exact direction of the cardinal points of the compass, a practice used in Egyptian construction to mark the position of the columns during building. The octagonal columns resemble column fragments found in the Middle Bronze Age temple at Shechem.[61] A well-plastered square installation found in the southeastern corner of the cella probably held liquids used in the ritual ceremonies. A monumental staircase (see above, p. 16., Fig. 22) led from the cella to the holy-of-holies. It consists of seven steps (identical to the staircase in the Stratum VI temple at Bet Shean!), made of wide stone slabs, of which only four have

58. B. Mazar (above, n. 55). In contrast, Kempinski (above, n. 54) claims that the temple was founded during the time of Ramesses II, on the basis of foundation deposits which include the names of Ramesses I and II.

59. D. Ussishkin: Excavations at Tel Lachish — 1973–1977, Preliminary Report, *Tel Aviv* 5 (1978), pp. 10–25.

60. Against this interpretation see A. Kempinski: On the Architectural Characterization of the Canaanite Temple at Lachish, *Qadmoniot* 11 (1978), pp. 95–96 (Hebrew).

61. *Shechem*, pp. 66–84 and G.R.H. Wright (above, n. 13).

survived. Two of the steps had been hewn out of a single stone block. On the floor of the cella, alongside the fifth step, were two round column bases which bore wooden pillars, perhaps to support a canopy over the steps. Flanking the four lower steps was a well-made stone parapet which rested against the wooden pillars. The staircase, which was oriented due east, did not stand exactly on the central long axis of the temple.

Fragments of plaster painted black, white, red, yellow and light blue (compare the light blue in the Bet Shean temple) attest that the walls of the temple had been decorated on the inside. The holy-of-holies had been almost totally destroyed, but it can be reconstructed as a broad-room, about 2.5 m. deep and 12 (?) m. wide. There were two side rooms north of the cella. The western room, which was almost completely in ruins, was connected to the temple through an ornate entrance which contained a threshold composed of three well-hewn limestone slabs and a wooden plank inserted between two of them. On either side of the plank stood round wooden posts. All the wooden components were of cedar of Lebanon. Rectangular depressions in the door jambs indicate that the door frames were also of wood.[62] The eastern side room contained cultic vessels. North of this room was a solid base, perhaps belonging to a staircase leading to a second storey or to the roof of the temple.

The position of the Lachish temple in the development of the Canaanite temples in Palestine depends largely on the manner in which its entrances are reconstructed and the interpretation of the plan and function of the western part of the building. If Ussishkin's interpretation of the building is correct, then his view should be accepted that this building forms a connecting link between the temples of Alalakh and Hazor and Solomon's Temple in Jerusalem: it is symmetrical and composed of three units terminating in a holy-of-holies which is defined as a single architectural space, and all the entrances are placed on a single axis. However, if Kempinski is correct in challenging the reconstruction of the entrance from the west, then the building more closely resembles the temples in Strata VII–VI at Bet Shean: it has an indirect entrance, a large cella divided by a pair of columns and a raised holy-of-holies. In the writer's opinion, the excavator's reconstruction of the building should be accepted.

Both the Egyptian architectural elements found in the Lachish temple, as well as its plan, link it to the Bet Shean temples. These temples should therefore be considered as a single group, characteristic of the period of Egyptian rule in Canaan during the Nineteenth and Twentieth Dynasties. Whereas the temples at Bet Shean were founded in a centre of Egyptian government and were most certainly used by Egyptian soldiers, officials and mercenaries in the Egyptian army, the temple at Lachish was erected on the acropolis of a royal Canaanite city and should be regarded as a reflection of Egyptian influence on Canaanite architecture.[63]

Temples with Indirect Entrances and Irregular Plans. — An important group of Late Bronze and Early Iron Age temples in Israel is characterized by an indirect entrance and a plan which lacks all attempt at symmetry and clear architectural rules and principles. This group comprises the Fosse Temples of Lachish, the temple at Tel Mevorakh, the Bet Shean temples of Strata IX and V (the temples of Strata VII–VI at Bet Shean were discussed above in the preceding section, even though they have more in common with the present group and their detachment from it is to a great extent artificial), the Tell Qasile temples of Strata XI–X, and several buildings whose identification as temples is not certain: Building 30 at Tell Abu Hawam and the 'Lion Temple' at Jaffa.

In the chart below are presented the dimensions of the above temples and details of their plans.

Despite the differences in their plans and their diversity, it can be seen from the chart that these buildings exhibit many common characteristics. A brief description of the temples included in this group is presented below.

Late Bronze Age. Bet Shean, Stratum IX.[64] The excavator, A. Rowe, assigned a complex cluster of buildings of this stratum to the reign of Thutmose III, but scholars are generally agreed that they should be dated to the fourteenth century B.C. The interpretation of these structures is fraught with difficulties due to the fact that they were not fully excavated, their complex nature and Rowe's frequent flights of fancy with regard to their interpretation. The complex consisted of a central court surrounded by various structures, of which the main ones include

62. Kempinski (above, n. 60) interprets this room as the entrance room of the temple.

63. Kempinski (above, n. 60) and Ottosson (above, n. 1), pp. 79–80 see in this temple a royal temple, attached to the palace. But no remains of the Late Bronze II palace of Lachish were found nearby.

64. *Beth Shan* I, pp. 10–14; Ottosson (above, n. 1), pp. 81–82.

The Dimensions and Construction Details of the Irregular Temples of the Late Bronze Age and the Iron Age I
(measurements in metres)

Temple	Exterior Dimensions	Dimensions of Cella	Width of Walls	Entrance Hall	Corner Entrance	Entrance Chamber	Columns in Cella	Raised Platform	Storage Capacity
Lachish I	10 × 15.5	5 × 9.8	0.7	–	–	×	×	×	×
Lachish II	13 × 25	10.2 × 10.6	0.7	×	×	×	×	×	×
Lachish III	13 × 25	10.2 × 10.6	0.7	×	×	×	×	×	×
Tel Mevorakh	6.4 × 11.4	ca. 5 × 10	0.7	–	×?	×	–	×	–
Bet Shean VII	14 × 19	8.4 × 11	1.4	×	–	×	×	×	×
Bet Shean VI	14 × 19	–	1.1	×	–	×	×	×	×
Bet Shean (South) V	18.4 × 24	7.9 × 21.8	1.0	×	×	–	×	?	–
Beth Shean (North) V	11.9 × 19.5	8.2 × 12.5	1.5(?)	fragmentary	×	–	×	?	–
Tell Abu Hawam Building 30	8.2 × 14	6.5 × 9.5	ca. 1.0	–	?	–	×	–	×
Tell Qasile Temple 200	7.75 × 8.5	5.9 × 6.4	0.9	–	×	×	–	×?	×
Tell Qasile Temple 131	8 × 14.5	5.65 × 7.4	1.2	×	×	×	×	×	×
Ashdod, Area D* Stratum VIII	6.5 × 7.4	–	0.75	×	×	×	–	×	×

* Part of a larger building.

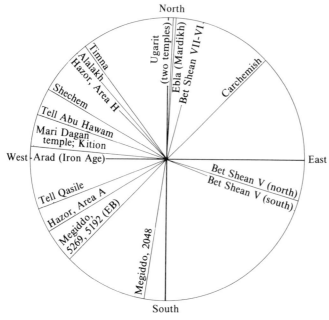

The Orientation of Temples to Directions of the Compass

a long corridor south of the court, a brick platform beside it on which stood a basalt *massevah*(?), a raised dais north of the court which was defined as an altar, a wide staircase leading up to this altar, and a stepped entrance behind it which connected the corridor with the court. Beside this entrance was a room with benches extending along its walls. Square installations in the court probably served as sacrificial altars. Two important buildings stood east of the court. The northern one was a long-room, 5.5 × 7.5 m., and the space in its rear was occupied by a broad-room, 1.5 m. deep, which was separated from the main hall by a pair of wide piers. The entrance to the hall, 1.5 m. wide, was located in the corner of the western wall. In the opinion of Ottosson, this was the only temple in the entire complex but Rowe regarded it as only one unit of a larger ritual complex. There is no doubt that this was a unique temenos with at least one or two cellae situated on the eastern side of a large court. A stele of the god Mekal, a relief depicting a struggle between a lion and a dog (or a lion and a lioness) and other important objects found in this enclosure attest to its function, despite the difficulties in defining its architectural form.

The Fosse Temples at Lachish.[65] The Fosse Temple was erected during the LB I in the western fosse of the Middle Bronze Age. The temple in fact stood outside the city and was very likely not the main temple of the city (which was probably the temple uncovered in Area P, see above).

Temple I (Fig. 21) consisted of a rectangular cella which was entered through two doorways in the long walls and which obliged the worshipper to turn at a ninety-degree angle to face the cultic focal point. The ceiling of the cella was supported by two wooden columns set on stone bases along the long axis of the building. The holy-of-holies consisted of a raised platform of brick, 3 m. long, 0.6 m. wide and 0.3 m. high, with three front projections. Alongside the platform was a small storage compartment. A bench for offerings extended along the western wall. Small subsidiary rooms were located to the west and north of the cella.

Temple II was constructed during the reign of Amenhotep III or later (a scarab of this king was uncovered in its foundations) and it thus dates to the fourteenth century B.C. For its construction the preceding temple was enlarged and altered, but the north-south direction of the ritual was retained, as was the location of the holy-of-holies. The main hall was doubled in width and four columns arranged in a square supported its roof. The room north of the cella was utilized as an entrance hall. The cella was entered through a doorway in the corner of the short northern wall of the temple. Benches extended in two and three tiers along the walls of the cella. The holy-of-holies, situated in the innermost part of the cella, consisted of a raised platform of stone, 3.5 m. long, 0.65 m. deep and 0.25 m. high, and had one front projection. In front of the platform were a hearth and a raised installation on which offerings of food were probably placed. There was a doorway on either side of the platform, one leading outside the building (an unusual feature for a temple, which generally did not have an outer doorway in the area of the holy-of-holies; it is also possible that this was

a stratigraphic error made by the excavator, and this doorway in fact belonged to Temple III where it led to a back room). A second doorway led to a back room which may have been the treasure room of the temple.

Temple III (Fig. 22), which was in existence in the thirteenth century B.C., was better preserved than its predecessors and its walls were still standing to a height of 3 m. This temple was a rebuilding of the destroyed previous temple. The floor was raised 0.6 m. but the ground plan of the temple remained virtually unchanged. Even the four columns in the cella and the benches along its walls were rebuilt in almost the identical positions as in the preceding temple. In the eastern wall of the building three niches were preserved, 1.1 m. above floor level. A second back room was now added to the temple. Changes were made in the holy-of-holies during this period. In its original state it had consisted of a niche (2.5 m. wide and 2 m. deep) recessed in the south wall of the cella, which held a platform 0.85 m. higher than the floor of the cella. A narrow, raised bench extended along the back of the platform. In the second stage the sides of the platform were raised by means of a brick railing and it was equipped with a square front projection (1 × 1 m.) about one metre higher than the floor of the cella. This projection was ascended by means of three brick steps. A low installation in front of it contained two round depressions (hearths?). Evidence was found of a spacious open area around the temple containing subsidiary buildings and *favissae*.

Tel Mevorakh.[66] The temple (Fig. 23) erected at this site in the LB I was apparently a 'road sanctuary'. Tel Mevorakh was a small site, whose total area did not exceed one dunam (a quarter of an acre), located on the main highway leading to the Carmel coast. The temple was oriented to the west and consisted of a single hall with the entrance probably in the southeastern corner. In the northwestern corner of the building was a raised brick platform coated with white plaster which was approached by five broad steps. A double tier of plastered benches was built along the walls. Two depressions in the floor apparently held wooden pillars which supported the ceiling, as did a large stone which was found standing in the centre of the building (though the latter may have served as an offering table). A drainage channel ran along the southern wall. This feature is absent in

---

65. *Lachish* II, pp. 19–45; Busink (above, n. 1), pp. 405–412; Ottosson (above, n. 1), pp. 86–92. The latter denies the identification of the 'Fosse Temples' as temples and interprets them as pottery workshops. This extraordinary interpretation is baseless, as the Fosse Temples include all the attributes of temples.

66. E. Stern: *Tel Mevorakh*, II [*Qedem* 18], Jerusalem, 1984, pp. 4–39.

other temples and it seems to indicate that sacrifices were performed within the temple itself.[67]

In the second phase of the temple, the platform was rebuilt and somewhat enlarged. Evidence was found that later temples were built above this temple in the LB II, but their plans could not be established.

Tell el-Far'ah (North). Building 487-491 at Tell el-Far'ah was interpreted as a temple by R. de Vaux but in the final excavation report this designation was no longer accepted and the building was defined as an Iron Age I dwelling.[68]

Iron Age I. Tell Abu Hawam. Building 30 (Fig. 25) in Stratum IV is a reconstruction of Building 50 of the Late Bronze Age (see above).[69] The entrance appears to have been in a corner of the building. The structure consists of a rectangular hall with a small chamber in the northwestern corner. In the space formed south of this corner room stood a monolithic column topped with a square capital (incense altar?). Some of the column bases attributed by the excavators to Building 50 may have belonged to this temple. It is also likely that the cultic vessels found inside this building above the western wall of the destroyed Building 50 should be attributed to this structure. Building 30 was apparently erected in an early phase of Stratum IV, at the beginning of the Iron Age.

Jaffa — The Lion Temple.[70] This building, which stood adjacent to a fort from the end of the Late Bronze Age or beginning of the Iron Age, consisted of a rectangular hall with two column bases placed along the longitudinal axis of the building. Its entrance was not preserved but in the opinion of the excavators it was located in the short northern wall. The excavators interpreted the building as a temple on the basis of its plan and the discovery of a lion's head in a corner of the building. This interpretation, however, is doubtful.

Bet Shean, Stratum V.[71] The pair of temples in Stratum V at Bet Shean were built above the ruins of

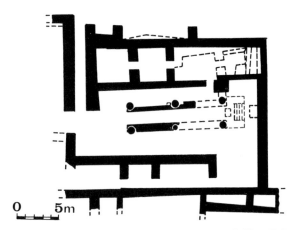

30. Bet Shean Stratum V (Southern Temple). ***Beth Shan*** II, Pl. X.

the temple and the temple court of Stratum VI. There was a complete change of plan and a ninety-degree shift in orientation so that the cultic focus was now on the eastern side. The southern temple (Fig. 30) consists of a large long-room — the cella — which was divided by two rows of three columns into a narrow central area and two aisles. Partition walls filled the spaces between the columns. The cella was flanked by a row of rooms on two of its sides. The entrance was through a wide doorway in the centre of the western facade of the cella. West of the cellá was a spacious area whose function is unknown — it may have been an open court or a roofed porch. A narrow corridor connected the entrance to this building with a passage which led to the northern temple. In the eastern part of the building — which should have been the site of the holy-of-holies — the building widens, indicating the existence of a broad-room separate from the cella, but nothing has survived of the interior of this holy-of-holies. The plan is unusual and bears no resemblance to any known temple. The identification of this building as a temple is based mainly on the numerous cult objects uncovered in its rooms, especially in the small rooms north of the main hall.[72]

The northern temple (Fig. 24) consists of a single hall with walls 1.5 m. thick. The entrance was through a corner doorway.[73] The ceiling was supported by four

67. Compare a similar practice in the temple of Enkomi in Cyprus: J.C. Courtois: Sanctuaire du dieu au l'ingot d'Enlomi-Alasia, *Mission Archeologique d'Alasia*, Alasia, I, Paris, 1971, pp. 151-362.

68. A. Chambon: *Tell el Far'ah* I, *L'Age due Fer*, Paris, 1984, pp. 19-21.

69. Hamilton, (above, n. 51), p. 10, Pl. XI. See also *ibid., QDAP* 3 (1934), pp. 76-77, Pls. XIX-XX.

70. J. Kaplan: The Archaeology and History of Tel Aviv-Jaffa, *BA* 35 (1972), pp. 83-84; idem, Jaffa, 1972-1973 (Notes and News), *IEJ* 24 (1974), pp. 135-137, Pl. 22D.

71. *Beth Shan* II, pp. 22-35, Pls. X-XIII; *Beth Shan* I, pp. 31-38; F.W. James: *The Iron Age at Beth-Shan*, Philadelphia, 1966, pp. 140-144.

72. James (above, n. 71) claimed that the pillars are not part of the original building, but were added in a secondary use, when the building was used as a store house. Ottosson (above, n. 1), pp. 63-76 claims that the building should be defined as a palace, and the cult objects found in it should be attributed to the previous building of Stratum VI.

73. S. Yeivin: Was there a High Portal in the First Temple, *VT* 14 (1968), p. 339, Fig. 4, where a special entrance room is reconstructed for this building.

columns whose bases had apparently been removed from earlier buildings since they all differed in form. None of the interior installations of the building has survived. The building underwent a fundamental change in the last phase of Stratum V, at which time a new floor was laid and covered the four column bases, which now went out of use. An Egyptian stela dedicated to the goddess Anat was found in the temple, as were fragments of another stela, a statue and various broken cult objects (all of them on the floor of the early phase of Stratum V). In a large court in front of the temple stood various Egyptian monuments which had originated in earlier strata. These included a statue of Ramses III and stelae of Ramses II and Seti I, which had been placed in niches made especially for this purpose. The earlier phase of Stratum V is assigned to the eleventh century B.C. In the later phase of this stratum, which is dated to the tenth century B.C., the northern temple underwent a complete change and may have served at this time as a secular building.[74]

Tell Qasile, temples of Strata XI–X.[75] The two temples of Strata XI–X at Tell Qasile, which were erected above the temple of Stratum XII (which will be discused below), have irregular plans and indirect entrances. The temples were erected in the temenos of the Philistine town which was established in the middle of the twelfth century B.C. The temple of Stratum XI (Fig. 27) was founded *ca.* 1100 B.C. The walls, of sandstone, are about 1.1 m. thick. The temple consists of a single hall with a corner entrance in the eastern wall. Benches lined the walls, and a small compartment at the southwestern corner of the hall served as a treasury. The holy-of-holies was probably located directly opposite the entrance within a recess formed by the partition walls.[76] A spacious court in front of the temple contained two rectangular subsidiary rooms.

A tiny shrine was built of mud bricks against the western wall of the main temple. It consists of a single room (2.2 × 4.18 m.) and an entrance area. Its entrance was an indirect one through an opening at the end of the northern wall. Benches extended along the walls, and a stepped, raised platform was located in the southwest corner. Three plastered brick projections on the floor of the shrine most likely served as bases for ritual stands.

Stratum X, which was founded in the middle of the eleventh century B.C. and was destroyed in a fierce conflagration at the beginning of the tenth century B.C., exhibits changes both in the plan of the temple and in the court to its east (Fig. 28). The previous temple was enlarged to the east by the addition of an antechamber which was entered through a wide opening on the northern side. In this way an indirect corner entrance was created. A stepped bench extended along all walls of the antechamber and of the cella. The ceiling of the cella was supported by two pillars of cedar wood, 0.3 m. in diameter, which were set on cylindrical stone bases along its long axis. The doorway of the cella and the raised platform opposite it were situated somewhat to the north of the central axis of the building so that the pillars would not interfere with the approach to the platform. The latter was built of brick (1.12 × 1.3 m.; height, 0.9 m.) and had plastered steps on the northern and southern sides. The platform was built against an inner brick partition wall. A rectangular chamber behind this wall served as a treasure room. The temple court of Stratum X, about 100 sq. m. in area, was entered from a street on the northern side and was enclosed by a stone wall. A square base of a stone sacrificial altar (1.3 × 1.5 m.) was located in the court north of the temple. Another court led to the miniature shrine of the previous stratum which continued in use in this stratum.

The sacred enclosure continued in use also after Stratum X was destroyed and burnt at the beginning of the tenth century B.C. In the next two phases (Strata IX–VIII), the floor of the spacious court surrounding the temple was rebuilt and the temple itself was partially reconstructed.

This group of temples of the Late Bronze Age and the Iron Age I, which has been designated as temples with irregular plans, is a diversified group which is difficult to treat as a homogeneous unit with distinct characteristics. At the same time, these buildings share a number of common features: their size; in several cases they are not freestanding buildings; they have a corner or indirect entrance which does not allow the holy-of-holies to be seen from the doorway; benches are built along the walls; the ceiling is supported by columns; the holy-of-holies is in the form of a raised platform; and the temples contain back rooms which

---

74. James (above, n. 71), p. 140 claimed that the building was not a temple at all, but an administrative building. The original identification of the building as a temple seems more probable in light of the fact that it contains one major space, and that cult objects were found in it.

75. A. Mazar: *Excavations at Tell Qasile*, Part One: *The Philistine Sanctuary: Architecture and Cult Objects* [*Qedem* 12], Jerusalem, 1980, pp. 21–49.

76. Another possibility which was raised is that the mud-brick partition wall at the back of the building was not an actual wall, but served as a raised platform.

served as treasure rooms or storerooms for offerings. This type of temple can be considered a Canaanite temple which developed in Canaan in the Late Bronze Age and continued in use in the Iron Age I, at which time it was also adopted by the Sea Peoples. There is a possible analogy between these buildings and a group of temples of the thirteenth-tenth centuries B.C. in the Aegean world and in Cyprus. These include the small temple at Mycenae (thirteenth century B.C.), the temple at Phylakopi and the temples at Kition in Cyprus.[77] Though none of these temples is exactly identical in plan with the temples discussed here, they display many similar features which indicate a possible link between them. It is very likely that this temple architecture originated in Israel, yet this subject needs further clarification.[78]

Small Temples with Direct Access. — A small number of temples of the Late Bronze Age cannot be assigned to any of the above groups. These include the temple in Area C at Hazor, the temple in Stratum XII at Tell Qasile and perhaps also the temple at Timna. The small temple at Hazor in Area C (Fig. 19), of the fourteenth-thirteenth centuries B.C., consists of a single room built on the slope of the city's western rampart.[79] It measured 4.5 × 5.8 m. in Stratum XIV (1b) and 5.2 × 5.8 m. in Stratum XIII (1a). Benches line the interior of its walls and the focus of the cult was a raised niche in the centre of the western wall, opposite the entrance, where a row of eleven basalt stelae, a statuette of a seated male figure and the statuette of a crouching lion ('the protector of the temple') were found. In front of the temple was an open sloping area which bordered on a residential quarter whose inhabitants apparently used this temple.

The earliest temple at Tell Qasile (Stratum XII) (Fig. 20) resembles the temple in Area C at Hazor in plan and orientation, though it differs from it in its interior layout.[80] The temple consists of a single room (6.4 × 6.6 m.). The entrance was located in the middle of the eastern wall, and a raised plastered brick platform with a central projection stood opposite the entrance. A spacious court in front of the small building was bounded on the south by houses. On the northern side of the court was a long rectangular auxiliary room. The building was erected in the middle of the twelfth century B.C. and went out of use toward the end of that century, when it was replaced by the stone building of Stratum XI.

The temple at Timna was erected in the thirteenth century B.C. as part of the Egyptian copper-mine complex.[81] It consists of a broad-room (an open court according to the excavator), whose exterior measurements are *ca.* 8 × 10 m. The entrance was located in the middle of the eastern wall and opposite it was the holy-of-holies in the form of a raised platform. The plan, as well as the building's dimensions and orientation, recall the above two temples and there may be a link between them, especially since no close parallel for the Timna temple can be found in Egyptian architecture. In a later phase, which is dated to the reign of Ramses III, the room was enlarged to 10 × 10 m. A bench was added along the interior of the eastern wall and the holy-of-holies was rebuilt as a raised platform with an Egyptian architectural facade. Among the installations found in the building were three 'basins' and a row of stone stelae, on one of which was carved the figure of the goddess Hathor.

These three temples, with the common features of a broad-room with an entrance on the eastern side and the holy-of-holies on the western side, may be considered a sub-type of the group of symmetrical temples with a direct approach to the statue of the divinity.

'Square Temples'. — Three square buildings uncovered at Amman, Mt. Gerizim (Tananir) and in Area F at Hazor have been interpreted by several

77. For discussion and references see Mazar (above, n. 75), pp. 66–68 and Fig. 15.

78. The phenomenon of grouping temples in clusters is found in Cyprus and the Aegean, as well as at Tell Qasile XI-X, but is unknown in Canaanite temples. This feature at Tell Qasile might represent Aegean traditions which were brought by the Philistines (especially interesting is the combination of main temple and a subsidiary shrine with bent-axis approach at both Tell Qasile and Phylakopi). The alliance of the 'irregular temples' to the main stream of Canaanite temples led to the suggestion (Mazar above, n. 75, pp. 62–68) that they might belong to foreigners. Indirect entrance was common in the Sumerian temples, but almost disappeared during the second millennium B.C., except in a few cases, like the temples of Nuzi, which retained this feature until the Late Bronze Age. Is it possible that these irregular temples in Canaan were constructed by foreigners, such as Hurrian immigrants? It should be noted that the Fosse Temple at Lachish was constructed outside the city proper, and that the temple at Tel Mevorakh is located in a small isolated site.

79. *Hazor* I, pp. 83–93; *Hazor*, pp. 67–74; W.F. Albright, *The High Place in Ancient Palestine* [Vetus Testamentum Supplementum 4], 1957, pp. 242–258; K. Galling, Erwagungen zum Stelenheiligtum von Hazor, *ZDPV* 75 (1959), pp. 1–13; Ottosson (above, n. 1), pp. 39–41.

80. Mazar (above, n. 75), pp. 13–20.

81. B. Rothenberg: *Timna*, London, 1972, pp. 19–37. A detailed description of the temple appeared in B. Rothenberg: The Timna Mining Sanctuary, *Israel — People and Land* [Museum Haaretz Year Book I], Tel Aviv (1983–1984), pp. 85–122 (Hebrew).

scholars as temples. The building on Mt. Gerizim (Fig. 15) is the earliest of this group and dates to the MB IIC.[82] The building (exterior measurements, 18 × 18 m.) consists of a large central space (9 × 9 m.) surrounded on all sides by rooms. The entrance to the court is an indirect one, through a special antechamber. A round base, 0.67 m. in diameter, found in the centre of the court, was interpreted by the excavators (E. Sellin, G. Welter as well as E.F. Campbell and G.E. Wright) as the base of a *massevah*. Others, however, regard it as the base of a column which supported the roof of the central space.[83] The finds uncovered in this building have not been published but Welter and Sellin describe objects which were possibly ritual vessels. W.F. Albright rejects the identification of the building as a temple,[84] but Wright, Campbell and R. Boling, who made soundings in the building, accept the identification, mainly on the basis of its comparison with the building at Amman.[85] However, it is extremely doubtful that this building was a temple.

The building at Amman (Fig. 16), whose external measurements are 15 × 15 m., consists of six rooms surrounding a main area, 6.5 × 6.5 m.[86] A round pillar, made of two superimposed stones, was located in the centre of the central space, and in the opinion of B. Hennessy, served as an altar; Wright and Campbell consider it the base of a *massevah* and Ottosson maintains that it was the base of a column which supported the roof of the main hall. The entrance to the building was an indirect one. It is a symmetrically planned, strongly-built structure which attests to an advanced building tradition. In excavations carried out in the building and its environs by L. Herr, many burnt bones of adults and children were uncovered.[87] In Herr's opinion, the building was used as a crematorium, a practice related, in his view, with an Indo-European population which settled in the area. This conclusion is difficult to prove, however, since there are no parallels for the existence of special cremation buildings in the ancient Near East.

The building in Hazor Area F, Stratum XV (Fig. 17), of the LB I, in the opinion of Y. Yadin, was a square temple which was erected above the ruins of the 'double temple' of the Middle Bronze Age (see above).[88] The building was only partially preserved. Its estimated dimensions are 18 × 18 m. and it contained a square central space (about 4 × 4 m.) surrounded by rooms. It seems clear, however, that this building was not a temple but represents the rebuilding of the Middle Bronze Age palace.

To summarize, the existence of a group of 'square temples' in Canaan cannot be accepted. Each of the three buildings may be interpreted in a different way: the Mount Gerizim building and the building at Hazor were most probably secular buildings; the Amman structure remains enigmatic.

Iron Age II Temples

Whereas finds from the Late Bronze Age are abundant, only a small number of sacred structures from the Iron Age II (tenth-sixth centuries B.C.) have been uncovered in Israel. These buildings are diversified in form and each of them is problematic.

Solomon's Temple. Known only from the literary sources of the Bible (I Kings 6:1-7; II Chronicles 3:1-10; Ezekiel 40-43), this temple (Fig. 14) has been the frequent subject of discussion. Only the major problems connected with the origin of the plan of the temple will be mentioned here.[89]

The Solomonic temple was apparently erected on the sacred site of the Jebusite city. It was a rectangular, long-room building, with the entrance on the eastern side. It was extremely large in comparison with other temples in the Land of Israel, measuring 50 x 100 cubits (exterior dimensions, equivalent to approximately 25 × 50 m.). The walls were 2.5-6 m. thick. The entrance was through a broad-room porch (*'ulam*), 10 × 20 cubits. Two ornamented pillars, called Jachin and Boaz, stood in the facade of the porch; they probably had no architectural function.[90] The main

82. R. Boling: Excavations at Tananir [*BASOR*, Supplementary Studies 21], Cambridge, Mass., 1975, pp. 25-85.
83. Ottosson (above, n. 1), p. 104.
84. W.F. Albright: *The Archaeology of Palestine*, Harmondsworth, 1960, p. 92.
85. E.F. Campbell and G.E. Wright: Tribal League Shrines in V. Fritz: Amman and Shechem, *BA* 32 (1969), pp. 104-116; *ZDPV* 87 (1971), pp. 140-152.
86. G.R.H. Wright and B. Hennessy: *PEQ* 108 (1966), pp. 155-162; G.R.H. Wright: The Development of Canaanite Temples, *ZAW* 78 (1966), pp. 351-357; Ottosson (above, n. 1), pp. 101-104.
87. L. Herr: The Amman Airport Structure and the Geopolitics of Ancient Transjordan, *BA* 46 (1983), pp. 223-229.

88. *Hazor*, pp. 98-100.
89. Busink (above, n. 1) is the most complete work on this subject, with full previous bibliography; Wright (above, n. 1), pp. 254-267; see also Ottosson (above, n. 1), pp. 111-113 and p. 135, n. 27; V. Fritz: What Can Archaeology Tell Us About Solomon's Temple?, *BAR* 13:4, pp. 38-49.
90. Most scholars interpreted these pillars as lacking any structural function. Fritz (above, n. 89) locates them at the entrance to the building, as supports of the porch lintel.

hall (*hekhal*), a vast long-room measuring 20 × 40 cubits (interior measurements) terminated in the holy-of-holies (*debir*), a cube, 20 × 20 × 20 cubits. One of the central problems of this temple is whether the holy-of-holies was separated from the main hall by an actual wall or just a thin partition wall made of perishable material, since the dimensions given in the Bible make no allowance for such a wall. Those scholars who maintain that a wall separated the *hekhal* from the *debir*, compare Solomon's Temple with the temple at Tell Ta'yinat of the eighth century B.C., which exhibits a similar division of porch, main hall and a holy-of-holies. A three-fold division may be seen in several second-millennium B.C. temples. Those scholars who do not accept the existence of this wall suggest that the origin of the plan should be sought in the long-room monumental temples of Syria and Palestine of the second millennium, such as the temples at Shechem (Fig. 6) and Megiddo (Fig. 8).[91]

Apart from its vast size, another unique feature of the Jerusalem Temple is the side chambers (*'azarot*) surrounding it. The close proximity of the temple to the royal palace of Jerusalem has analogies in various cities in the second and first millennia B.C. (Megiddo and Alalakh, Level VII in the Middle Bronze Age; Hazor Area A, in the Late Bronze Age I; Tell Ta'yinat in the Iron Age II and others). According to the Bible, Phoenician craftsmen were employed in the construction of the Temple. These architects and artisans were probably responsible for the importation of the Canaanite-Phoenician building tradition to Jerusalem, a tradition that is reflected both in the design of the building and in the details of its ornamentation. The plan of the Temple of Solomon can also contribute to the understanding of the development of the Greek temple, but this subject is outside the scope of this article.

Tel Dan. Of the royal temples from the period of the Monarchy, archaeological evidence has been uncovered at only one site — the royal temple erected by Jeroboam at Dan.[92] The plan of the early phase

91. Busink (above, n. 1), pp. 616–617 and reconstruction of the plan p. 165; Ottosson (above, n. 1), p. 113; Matthiae (above, n. 27); Kuschke (above, n. 1); Fritz (above, n. 89).
92. A. Biran: Tel Dan, *BA* 37 (1974), pp. 40–43; idem, Tell Dan Five Years Later, *BA* 43 (1980), pp. 175–176; idem, Tel Dan, 1977 (Notes and News), *IEJ* 27 (1977), p. 244; idem, *Temples and High Places in Biblical Times*, Jerusalem, 1981, pp. 142–148; idem, The Temenos at Dan, *EI* 16 (1982), pp. 15–43; idem, The Dancer from Dan, the Empty Tomb and the Altar Room, *IEJ* 36 (1986), pp. 168–187.

(Stratum IV, tenth-ninth centuries B.C.) has not yet been clarified in all its details, but it apparently consists of a podium built of large ashlar blocks (1.5 m. long, 0.8 m. wide and 0.6 m. high) with marginal drafts. The podium was more than 8 m. wide; its length is unknown. A temple, of which no trace has been preserved, apparently stood on this podium. To its south was a spacious court which contained various cultic installations, the most outstanding of which was a square foundation, 4.5 × 5.5 m., built of ashlar stones, which was very likely the base of a great sacrificial altar.

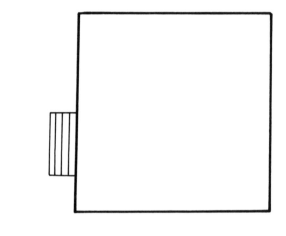

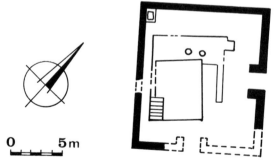

31. The 'Podium', Tel Dan. *EI* 16 (1982), p. 19, Fig. 4.

In the next phase (Stratum III, ninth-eighth centuries B.C.) the podium was enlarged and now measured 19 × 19 m. (Fig. 31). It was constructed of ashlar stones laid in headers and stretchers in the finest Israelite royal building tradition. The southern facade of the podium, which was preserved to a height of three courses, was especially well-constructed. Layers of undressed basalt stones were laid between the faces of the outer walls of the podium and created a strong

Tel Dan. The Iron Age II Cultic Platform.

fill. The podium rose to a height of at least 3 m. above its surroundings and on it, apparently, stood a temple which was approached from the south by a staircase.[93] On the southern, western and eastern sides, the podium was surrounded by a floor of yellowish *huwar*. A square enclosure (12.5 × 14 m.) was situated about 8 m. south of the podium. It had entrances on the eastern and southern sides and surrounded the ashlar foundation of the early phase, which was apparently the base of an altar. The latter was enlarged to the north; in the new part were found two depressions, 0.8 m. apart, perhaps for wooden columns which could have served as sacred pillars (*asherim*?). In the southwestern corner of the ashlar

foundation was a row of five ashlar steps, 1.5 m. wide and 0.25 m. high. In the opinion of the excavator, these steps led to an altar for burnt offerings. And indeed a stone horn of an ashlar horned-altar was found in the vicinity.

The temenos at Dan was enclosed on the west by a series of auxiliary rooms (defined by A. Biran by the biblical term *lishkah*) arranged in a well-planned row. One of these was an elongated rectangular hall with a raised platform in its short end. It appears to be an assembly hall or a subsidiary temple. South of it there were two shorter rooms; in one of them a square foundation was found, most probably an altar. This western wing shows that the temenos was an elaborate, monumental architectural complex with various parts and auxiliary structures.

According to the excavator, the early phase (Stratum IV) was erected during the reign of Jeroboam I; the later phase (Stratum III) dates to Ahab; it was enlarged and repaired during the period of the Monarchy. The temenos at Dan is the most complete

93. Y. Shiloh: Iron Age Sanctuaries and Cult Elements in Palestine, in F.M. Cross (ed.): *Symposia Celebrating the 75th Anniversary of the Founding of the American Schools of Oriental Research*, Cambridge, Mass., 1979, pp. 147–157. (This paper includes a survey of most of the structures dealt with in this section). Biran himself recently also admitted the possibility that the podium supported a real temple structure.

royal cult centre known so far from the First Temple period.

Arad. The temple unearthed in the royal citadel at Arad (Fig. 18) is the only known Israelite temple discovered in Judah.[94] It consists of an open court (9 × 10 m.) with the entrance on the east side, divided into an eastern part which contained an altar for burnt offerings, and a western part. A broad-room (interior measurements in the first phase: 2.7 × 9 m.) was entered from the court. This was the cella of the temple. In the middle of its western wall was a niche (1.5 × 1.5 m.) which served as the holy-of-holies. The walls of the cella were lined with benches. Three steps led up to the holy-of-holies and in its entrance stood two stone altars. Inside the holy-of-holies were two *massevot*, one of them very well hewn and painted red. These apparently represented the symbols of divinity at the site. Several phases, in which the position of the entrance to the court was shifted, could be distinguished in the temple. Its area on the north was reduced by the construction of long-rooms (these were apparently auxiliary rooms that were used in the temple ritual) and the cella was lengthened (from 9 to 11 m.); in consequence the holy-of-holies was no longer in the centre of the building. The altar for burnt offerings in the court was built of stone rubble and earth in accordance with the biblical precept (Exodus 20:24-26) and even its dimensions (2.5 × 2.5 m.) correspond with biblical law (5 × 5 cubits).

In the opinion of B. Mazar, the temple was erected on a sacred site connected with the settlement of Hobab the Kenite at Arad (Judges 1:15).[95] Y. Aharoni considered this temple and others, such as the ones at Dan and Bethel, as 'border temples' which were built on the fringe of the Israelite and Judean Kingdoms, and he attributed its destruction to the religious reforms instituted by Josiah. He also attempted to find a relationship between the plan of the temple at Arad and that of the Tabernacle. The fact that the Tabernacle was described as a long-building, he maintained, was merely the influence of the Temple in Jerusalem, whereas the temple at Arad actually reflects the early Israelite tradition of 'broad-house' temple construction, perhaps rooted in the form of a tent.[96]

An exceptional late Iron Age sanctuary was found at Horvat Qitmit, on a remote hill, southwest of Arad.[97] It included a structure consisting of three elongated rooms, most probably a triple holy-of-holies, facing south. In front of the structure was a fenced courtyard containing cultic installations. Exceptional cult objects, pottery and inscriptions led the excavator, I. Beit Arieh, to suggest that this was an Edomite shrine, erected in Judah. This sanctuary is unique in its plan and design, and should be seen as a foreign intrusive sanctuary.

In addition to the buildings described above, various other cult installations and cult rooms have been discovered at Israelite sites. Since they are not included in the category of temple buildings, they will not be discussed here.[98]

Knowledge of temples outside the borders of the kingdoms of Israel and Judah is currently very limited. Only at Ashdod was a building discovered which was defined as a temple, but it is in fact a cult room which was part of a larger architectural complex.[99] In it was found a plastered podium (1.15 × 1.35 m.) with a low bench behind it which apparently stood in a rear storage compartment, recalling those in the Tell Qasile temple.

The Orientation of Temples

Discussions of temple architecture have focused considerable attention on the question of the direction of the buildings. Scholars have attempted to draw

The C.H. Gordon Festschrift, Neukirchen-Vluyn, 1973, pp. 1–8; V. Fritz: *Tempel und Zelt*, Mainz, 1977. The resemblance between the temple at Arad and the so-called 'Sun Temple' at Lachish led Aharoni to identify the latter as a Jewish sanctuary of the late Persian or Hellenistic period. *Lachish* V, pp. 3–11, 42–43; Ottosson (above, n. 1), p. 110; Z. Herzog: Israelite Sanctuaries at Arad and Beer-Sheba, in A. Biran (ed.) (above, n. 8), pp. 120–122. Yeivin suggested that the Arad temple served foreign mercenaries and thus should not be identified as an Israelite shrine; see S. Yeivin: *Proceedings of the American Academy of Jewish Research* 35 (1968), pp. 152–154. Haran (above, n. 39), pp. 37–38 has reservations as to the definition of the structure at Arad as a temple.

97. I. Beit-Arieh: *Edomite Shrine — Discoveries from Qitmit in the Negev* [Israel Museum Catalogue No. 277], Jerusalem, 1987.

98. See the surveys of Shiloh (above, n. 93), pp. 147–152; Ottosson (above, n. 1), pp. 97–99. On the cult room at Lachish see *Lachish* V, pp. 26–32, Figs. 5–7. On the altar from Beersheba see Y. Aharoni: The Horned Altar of Beer-sheba, *BA* 37 (1974), pp. 2–6; idem, Excavations at Tel Beer-sheba, *Tel Aviv* 2 (1975), pp. 154–156.

99. M. Dothan and D.N. Freedman, *Ashdod*, I ['Atiqot 7], Jerusalem, 1967, pp. 132–139.

94. Y. Aharoni: Arad, Its Inscriptions and Temple, *BA* 31 (1968), pp. 18–32; P. Welten, Kulthohe und Jahwetempel, *ZDPV* 88 (1972), pp. 19–37. For additional literature see Ottosson (above, n. 1), p. 135, n. 7; Shiloh (above, n. 93), pp. 153–156.

95. B. Mazar: The Sanctuary of Arad, *JNES* 24 (1965), pp. 297–303.

96. Y. Aharoni: The Solomonic Temple, the Tabernacle and the Arad Sanctuary in H.A. Hoffner (ed.): *Orient and Occident*,

various conclusions from the orientation of temples in Israel and the Levant in general.[100] The diagram on p. 178 summarizes the data on this subject.

The diagram indicates that the orientation of the temples in Israel follows no consistent pattern. The majority of the temples (with the exception of Lachish Area P and Bet Shean) point to the western part of the compass rose, but within this general direction there are extreme variations for which no set rule can be established. A general orientation to the west (between northwest and southwest) appears to be common in the second millennium B.C. and becomes widespread in the Iron Age II, as is evidenced by the Temple of Solomon and the Arad temple. Several of the monumental symmetrical temples (Hazor, Areas H and A; Temples 5269 and 5192 at Megiddo; the temples at Shechem and Alalakh) were constructed so that their corners were oriented to the four points of the compass — like the Mesopotamian temples — but other temples of the same category, both in Israel and Syria, do not follow this rule.

Summary

It is possible to distinguish two parallel lines of development in temple architecture of Israel. The main group consists of temples with a symmetrical plan and a direct approach to the statue of the god. This is a diversified group in which a continuous course of development can be traced from the Chalcolithic period to the Persian-Hellenistic periods. Most of the buildings in this series are monumental freestanding structures which were situated in a sacred enclosure (temenos) and served as the principal sanctuaries of the cities. These temples were frequently built adjacent to royal palaces, and in such cases there was surely a link between the temple and the palace as is also indicated by the biblical reference to 'the king's sanctuary and royal house' (Amos 7:13). The identity of the gods worshipped in these temples is difficult to determine as only rarely is there precise information on this subject. Thus it was proposed that the temple in Area H at Hazor was dedicated to the cult of the storm god Hadad (Baal) and Ishtar was worshipped in the temple of Alalakh.[101] Most of

the temples of this type were probably dedicated to the cult of the chief Canaanite god, the storm god, known as Baal. This group of temples also served as the inspiration for the Temple of the God of Israel in Jerusalem. The group of small temples with direct access to the statue of the divinity (Hazor Area C, Timna, Tell Qasile XII, Arad) is a sub-type of this main category. As for the identification of the god worshipped in these temples, it is known that the goddess Hathor was worshipped in the Timna temple, the Hazor temple was probably dedicated to the cult of the lunar god, and in the Arad temple the God of Israel was apparently worshipped.

As noted above, the temples of the Late Bronze Age and the Iron Age I, despite their variety, reveal a considerable number of common characteristics. At the same time, their diversity, the differences in their plans and in their size may possibly attest, if only to a small extent, to the diversity in the composition of the population of Palestine. It is very likely that the new ethnic elements — Hurrians, Indo-Europeans and Sea Peoples — which penetrated into the country, brought with them a variety of conceptions regarding temple construction.[102]

The temples uncovered in Israel are for the most part isolated structures; only rarely are a pair of temples found (Bet Shean, Stratum V; Tell Qasile, Strata XI–X). It is possible that this phenomenon is also the result of outside influences, for the concentration of a number of temples in one temenos is typical, for example, of the temples at Kition in Cyprus, of Phylakopi in the Cyclades, etc. It is therefore suggested that the symmetrical monumental temples represent the main tradition of temple architecture in the West Semitic world during the course of the Bronze and Iron Ages, whereas the other temples reflect atypical varieties and traditions which may express a particular ethnic and cultural phase characteristic of the period of its appearance.

Various elements in the temple architecture of the Late Bronze Age exhibit foreign influences: the orthostats in the Hazor temples point to a tradition which developed in northern Syria in the Middle Bronze Age. Egyptian architectural features, on the other hand, appear in the Bet Shean, Lachish and Timna temples. This intermingling of Syrian and Egyptian elements clearly illustrates the position of Palestine and of the Canaanite culture in this period.

100. *Hazor*, p. 104, n. 4; S. Yeivin: Mycenaean Temples and their Possible Influence on the Countries of the Eastern Littoral of the Mediterranean, *Atti e Memorie del 1 Congresso Internazionale di Micenologia 1967*, Rome, 1968, pp. 1130–1148.

101. N. Na'aman: The Ishtar Temple at Alalakh, *JNES* 39 (1980), pp. 209–214; *Hazor*, p. 95.

102. See above, n. 78.

THE IRON AGE

20 THE IRON AGE: INTRODUCTION

Aharon Kempinski and Ronny Reich

The characteristic cultural features of the Iron Age in the Land of Israel began to crystallize in the middle of the twelfth century B.C. when Israel attained complete liberation from what was left of Egyptian domination of the inland coastal area and the valleys. Each of the three peoples that then occupied the land — the Canaanites, Israelites, and Philistines — possessed its own architectural traditions. During the course of the eleventh century B.C. those traditions underwent a process of synthesis and the ensuing culture of the tenth century can be seen as the direct outcome of this fusion.

The Canaanites, whose area of influence in the twelfth and eleventh centuries was restricted to urban enclaves on the coastal plain and to city-states in the interior (Shechem, Megiddo, and Jerusalem), made significant contributions to this architectural synthesis: city planning, construction in dressed stone (smooth ashlar masonry), and the variety of public and private buildings (palaces, temples, gatehouses, and courtyard houses) that were in widespread use in Late Bronze city-states.

The Philistine contribution to architecture, on the other hand, was meagre. This people may have been the cultural intermediary between the Canaanite coastal cities and the areas of Israelite settlement in the interior hill country. It is likely that they introduced gatehouses, fortifications, and probably even fortresses into the areas of Israelite occupation.

The main contribution of Israelite material culture, which crystallized in the central hill country during the thirteenth and twelfth centuries B.C., was the three- or four-room farmhouse. From the eleventh century onward, this building was the prototype for private houses in rural and urban settlements in most of the country. It also influenced the development of other types of buildings, such as the storehouse/stable

that became an increasingly prominent feature in Iron Age II cities.

In the eleventh century, during the Israelite-Philistine struggle for hegemony over the land, Israelite elements penetrated into exclusively Philistine areas in the wake of population migrations and deportations. Evidence of such incursions are the four-room dwellings at Tell Qasile and Ashdod. At the same time architectural elements characteristic of the coastal plain penetrated into the Israelite settlements in the interior; one example of this is probably the fort at Tel Masos in the northern Negev.

The beginning of the tenth century is considered the period of transition to Iron Age II, in which all the above-mentioned cultural features were fused within the Kingdoms of David and Solomon (1005 –925 B.C.). The creation of a United Monarchy with dominion over the entire Land of Israel brought about the termination of the Canaanite city-state as a political entity, and from the middle of the tenth century a radical change can be seen, especially in urban planning. Alongside the capital cities, which were turned into centres with a wide variety of functions, other cities were established that possessed a single main function: administrative centers, chariot cities, store cities, and cities containing a regional or national cult.

Information about the architecture of this period and onward, is available from archaeological remains and supplemented to a large extent by documentary evidence, mainly the Old Testament. Our knowledge of the grandiose building operations carried out by the kings of Israel and Judah, especially those undertaken in Jerusalem, comes not from archaeology but primarily from the Bible. In recent years archaeological research has shed new light on the true dimensions of Jerusalem, which, by virtue of its city planning, diverse types of public building, and successful and ingenious method of solving the water-supply problem, is one of the most progressive urban centres in the ancient world. However, despite this progress, many gaps still exist in our understanding of the architecture of Jerusalem, that can be filled only by further archaeological research.

The diverse international relations that characterized the United Monarchy, especially during Solomon's reign in the second half of the tenth century, and of the Kingdom of Israel in the first half of the ninth century, led to the adoption of architectural elements — design, technical details, and ornamentation — from Phoenicia and the Neo-Hittite kingdom in northern Syria. These elements can be observed first and foremost in the public buildings. Although there were differences in various aspects of the material cultures of Israel and Judah, one architectural element, namely the private house, is encountered in its new form in both kingdoms, from Hazor in the north to the Beersheba Valley and the Negev in the south. At the same time, other architectural features were the direct result of the geographic character and perhaps even the political status of specific regions. For example, the exact nature of the Negev fortresses is still in dispute, but not the fact that they appear only in the Negev.

With the development of military conflict due to the resurgent and expanding Assyrian Empire, and especially with the phased conquest of the land by the Assyrians beginning in the last third of the eighth century B.C., the penetration of foreign elements into the Land of Israel can again be observed. The Assyrians required buildings for their army and for the administration of the lands they conquered therefore their influence was restricted to public buildings. The local inhabitants continued building according to their own architectural conventions, although the plans of cities may have followed much stricter frameworks as a result of the conquest, as is attested by the plan of Stratum III at Megiddo. There is no evidence so far that the foreign ethnic elements who were exiled by the Assyrians into the Land of Israel from the north, introduced new architectural features into the country.

Although the Babylonians concluded the conquest that the Assyrians began, and determined the fate of the Judean Kingdom at the beginning of the sixth century B.C., they made no impact on the country's architecture. The reason for this may have been twofold: the scope of their operations in the country was much more limited than that of the Assyrians and they were in the country for a relatively short time.

21 DOMESTIC ARCHITECTURE IN THE IRON AGE[1]

Ehud Netzer

A new type of house established itself at the end of the Late Bronze Age and the beginning of Iron I in Palestine, Transjordan, and parts of Syria and Lebanon. Within a short time it replaced the traditional courtyard house of the Middle and Late Bronze Ages, although in some areas they existed side by side.

Iron Age dwellings have been excavated in all areas of Israel — from Hazor in the north to Tel Masos and Atar Ha-Ro'ah in the south. At some sites, such as Tell el-Far'ah (North), Tell en-Nasbeh, Tell Beit Mirsim, and Tel Beersheba, relatively well-preserved residential quarters have been uncovered. Thus, it is now possible to study in detail the place of domestic architecture in the urban fabric.

The Three- or Four-Room House

The characteristic features of the three- or four-room house, and its attribution to the new population that settled in Palestine at the beginning of the Iron Age, have already been described by S. Yeivin and Y. Shiloh. Yeivin identified this house with the Israelite population and termed it the 'Israelite House'.[2] Shiloh published an almost complete list of three- and four-room houses and defined their characteristic architectural features: the oblong, or infrequently square, overall plan;[3] the broad-room at the back, which is the main space; the three front spaces (in the four-room house) built at right angles to the back room; the solid walls enclosing the back

room; and the row of pillars separating the lateral front spaces from the central space (a courtyard?). These pillars are one of the important characteristics of the four-room house. Shiloh considered the central space, built at right angles to the back space, to be the internal service courtyard of the house, providing light and air for the rooms around it.[4] Together with the main house type, Shiloh distinguished a secondary type with three spaces, as well as a two-room house that seemed to be an early prototype. However, lack of evidence prevented Shiloh from tracing the development from the two-room house to the three- and four-room house.

A full catalogue of the architectural evidence, updated to 1982, was published by F. Braemer, who attributed the origin of the house type to architectural elements he considered to have been present in the Late Bronze Age.[5]

Recent excavations at Tel Masos, Giloh, and Izbet Sartah[6] make it possible to trace the internal development of domestic architecture beginning with the seminomadic population that began to settle in permanent villages toward the end of the thirteenth century B.C. It may well be that the house type under discussion goes back to a broad-room with an enclosed courtyard in front. However, from the beginning these broad-room units tended to be clustered and to use stone pillars and stone beams as structural elements integrated into the walls or the courtyards. The three-room house, with a corner courtyard and adjacent

1. The author wishes to thank Annabel Zarzetski for her help in preparing this chapter.
2. S. Yeivin and M. Avi-Yonah: *The Antiquities of Israel*, Tel Aviv, 1955, p. 90 (Hebrew).
3. Y. Shiloh: The Four-Room House — The Israelite Type-House?, *EI* 11 (1973), pp. 277–285 (Hebrew).

4. *Ibid.*, p. 278.
5. F. Braemer: *L'architecture domestique du Levant a l'age du fer.* Paris, 1982, pp. 102–105. However, this writer does not agree with Braemer's typology.
6. *Tel Masos*, pp. 31–34; A. Mazar: Giloh, *IEJ* 31 (1981), pp. 8–11; I. Finkelstein: *The Excavations at Izbet Sartah and the Settlement of the Israelite Tribes in the Hillcountry*, Ph.D. Dissertation, Tel Aviv University, 1983, Pl. 4 (Hebrew).

1. Dwelling, Giloh, House No. 22. *IEJ* 31 (1981), p. 7, Fig. 3.

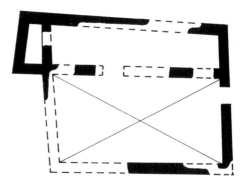

2. Dwelling, Tel Masos, House No. 34. *Tel Masos* I, p. 32, Fig. 5, (Plan 9).

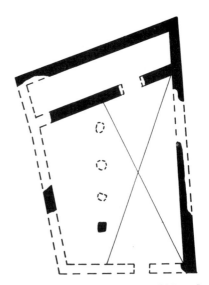

3. Dwelling, Tel Masos, House No. 74. *Tel Masos* I, p. 32, Fig. 5 (Plan 9).

long compartment, both attached to the broad-room at the end of the building, already appears at an early stage. Houses with two broad-room units fronted by a courtyard continued to exist alongside this type. In the last stage of development it was realized that the most convenient form was oblong, with the entrance in the short side opposite the main room. In most cases the entrance was situated in the centre of the wall in the central space.

The earliest building types that have been preserved are the house at Giloh (late thirteenth century B.C.), two houses at Tel Masos, and several fragmentary structures at Izbet Sartah.

House 22 at Giloh. — The Giloh house (Fig. 1) appears to consist of a nuclear unit that corresponds to the definition of the primary structure at the beginning of the Iron Age: a broad-room measuring 2.5 × 7.7 m., with a row of pillars on the west side facing a rectangular courtyard (4.3 × 7.7 m.). The courtyard floor was not uniform and the natural rock, bearing some installations, protruded from the southwestern corner. The courtyard entrance was in the south, opposite the row of pillars. West of this nuclear unit was an additional space, between the wall of the house and the fence that enclosed the unit and its precinct. There was probably an opening between the courtyard and this space. Remains of only two pillars are preserved, but it is likely that the two monoliths found in the courtyard belong to the other pillars or to the lintels carried by them as at Tel Masos. North of the nuclear unit (House 22),

there had been another room, but its connection to the unit is unclear.

House 34 at Tel Masos. — The house at Tel Masos (Fig. 2) closely resembles House 22 at Giloh. It has identical elements: basically, it is a broad-room (2.5 × 10 m.) faced by an enclosed courtyard (4.5 × 10 m.). Here too the entrance to the house is through the courtyard, opposite the broad-room wall (no pillars were uncovered because the house was badly ruined). A small storeroom was attached to the main room.

House 74 at Tel Masos. — House 74 (Fig. 3) shows the continued development of the house type: the courtyard becomes rectangular, and its long axis is perpendicular to the main broad-room — a feature that will continue to appear in the later four-room house. At a later stage a row of pillars was erected along one side of the courtyard, thus creating a three-

Tel Masos. Iron Age I private dwelling.

room house. The entrance to this house is placed in the short side of the courtyard, opposite the doorway into the main room, a common feature in the later buildings.

House 1016 at Izbet Sartah. — Although the remains of House 1016 at Izbet Sartah (Fig. 4) were fragmentary, they could be seen to contain some of the elements found in Houses 34 and 74 at Tel Masos. However, it could not be established whether pillars had been used, as they had been in the houses at Tel Masos and Giloh.

Despite a range of geographic locations — the northern Negev, the Judean hill country, and the Sharon — the four examples discussed here present a uniform picture: the three- and four-room house grew out of a nuclear unit consisting of a broad room and a courtyard.[7] In this early stage, pillars were already

7. Although this theory is supported by several scholars, this writer hesitates to accept it and finds more convincing the assumption that the three- or four-room house developed independently. For the possibility that this unit developed from the nomadic tent or booth, see *Tel Masos* (above, n. 6), p. 34.

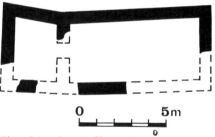

0   5m

4. Dwelling, Izbet Sartah, House No. 116. I. Finkelstein: *The Excavations of Izbet Sartah and the Israelite Settlement in the Hill Country*, (Ph.D. dissertation), Tel Aviv University, 1983, Pl. 3.

used at a number of sites where the houses were dated to the late thirteenth and early twelfth centuries B.C.

The development of the late three- or four-room house resulted in a dwelling with a distinctive plan. One of the main problems to be discussed here concerns the function of the space in the centre of the house: was it indeed an open-air courtyard, as has been generally accepted? Or, was it a covered space of which the roof served as the floor of a second-storey open-air courtyard? In many cases there is evidence that it indeed was an enclosed space and that the open courtyard was on the second storey.

The central of the three parallel spaces in the four-room house, and one of the two parallel spaces in the three- room house, is generally considered to be an open courtyard. This space, which will be called 'the central space', is usually wider than the structure's other spaces. The entrance into the house was in most cases at the short end of the central space, opposite the broad-room. The central space was usually paved with beaten earth and the lateral adjacent spaces with stone, especially when a row of pillars separated them from the central space (for instance, Buildings 436 (Fig. 5), 440, and 443 in Stratum III at Tell el-Far'ah (North).[8] Various installations, such as cooking pits and ovens, have been uncovered in the central space, in greater concentrations than in other areas.

with flat ceilings, based on the wooden beams used in the roofing technique common in the Land of Israel in the Iron Age.[10] Roofing the central space was a function of the layout of the rooms in the upper storey.

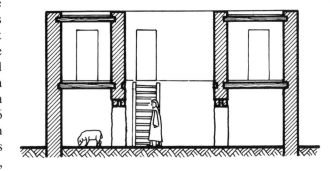

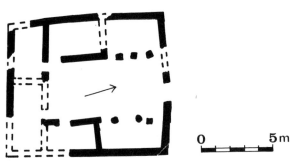

5. Dwelling, Tell el-Far'ah (N), Building 436. **RB** 62 (1955), Pl. VI, following p. 552.

There are considerable difficulties in defining the central space in this group of buildings as an open-air courtyard, even though that is the considered opinion of most archaeologists. The difficulty arises when these spaces are long, narrow rectangles, in some houses no more than 2 m. wide (for instance, House A 11 NW 33 at Tell Beit Mirsim).[9] While an oblong space is convenient for storage and can be used to lodge people or animals, it offers no advantages as a courtyard. An open courtyard does not have to be rectangular. The main consideration, which could have resulted in such oblong central spaces with a fixed width (especially in houses with such a well-defined plan) was the wish to cover these spaces

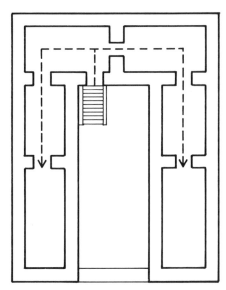

6. Schematic reconstruction of a dwelling with unroofed central courtyard on lower floor.

Various scholars have discussed the possibility that some of these buildings had a second storey, at least over part of the ground floor.[11] It appears that these houses, with their well-defined plans, not only had a second storey, but one that covered the entire building. Indeed, the careful planning of the ground floor, as mentioned above, derived from the planning of the storey above it. In fact, it would have been

8. R. de Vaux: Les fouilles de Tell el Far'ah pres de Naplouse, *RB* 62 (1955), Pl. VI.
9. *Tell Beit Mirsim* III, Pl. 7.

10. Chap. 2 in this book.
11. *Tell Beit Mirsim* III, pp. 22-51; *Shechem*, p. 161, Fig. 79; *Hazor*, pp. 183–184.

difficult to organize the lay-out of the second storey without a floor covering the central space below (as would have been the case if this space were an open courtyard). From a planning point of view, the passage from room to room, especially when the rooms are as narrow as these lateral rooms often

air penetrated into the lower level through the outer doorway (usually located at the end of this space), through the opening in the ceiling that gave access to the upper level (Fig. 7),[13] and perhaps also through the intervals left intentionally between the wooden beams (or branches) that constituted the floor of

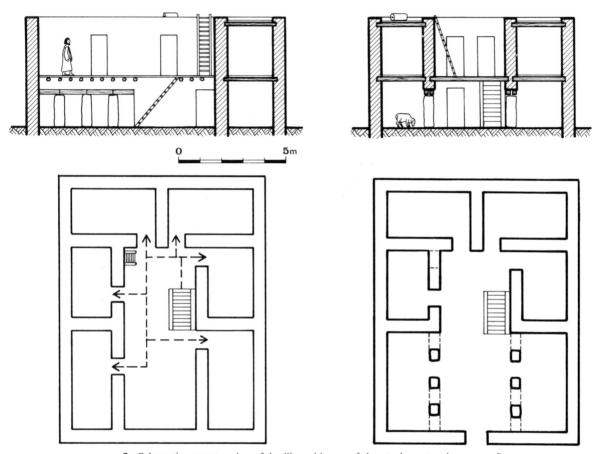

0   5m

7. Schematic reconstruction of dwelling with unroofed central courtyard on upper floor.

are (1.5–2.0 m.), would not have been logical (Fig. 6).

The central space of these houses can be reconstructed, therefore, on two levels. Most of the lower level was roofed, and this roof functioned as the floor of the open-air courtyard of the upper level. A wooden ladder or a steep flight of stairs would have connected the two levels.[12] The lower level served as an entrance and communication area, where various domestic activities were also carried out. Light and

the upper level. The upper level of the central space served both as communication between the rooms on that storey and as an important source of light and air for the entire building. It was also a place where domestic activities could be carried out and where the family group could gather. Thus, the upper level took the place of the open courtyard that characterizes the Mediterranean region.

Some of the 'long-spaced' houses, a description more suitable than three- or four-room houses, have

12. It is possible that stone steps were also used, or that there were stone steps below, continued above by wooden steps.

13. The possibility cannot be ruled out that the opening between the two levels was larger than that required for the steep stairs.

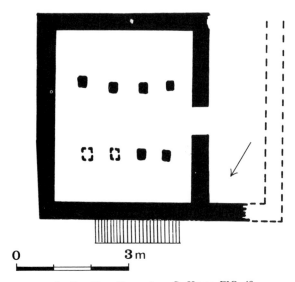

8. Dwelling, Hazor Area G. *Hazor*, FIG. 49.

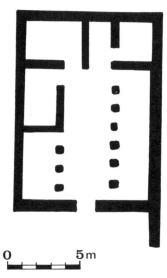

9. Dwelling, Tell en-Nasbeh, House M.379. *Tell Nasbeh* I, p. 208, Fig. 51.

stone steps on the outside (for example, Building 10370 in Stratum VI in Area G at Hazor; Fig. 8).[14] These steps gave direct access to the upper storey, without going through the ground floor. The outside steps, which probably were used in addition to internal wooden ones, furnish additional evidence for the existence of an upper storey.[15] Moreover, the rows of relatively closely spaced pillars on the ground floor encourage this assumption. Surely only the need for a strong substructure to support the walls of an upper storey would call for such pillars. Otherwise fairly narrow wooden posts spaced at greater intervals would have sufficed. Both the similarities and the differences in the houses discussed here (especially the houses with two rows of pillars, such as the Hazor house and Building M 379 at Tell en-Nasbeh [Fig. 9],[16]) and the outstanding group of pillared buildings discussed in Chap. 23 (the stables or storerooms)[17]

deserve attention. The common elements in these two groups of buildings are the oblong compartments (one next to the other), the rows of pillars between them, and the stone pavements in the lateral compartments. Presumably, such stone pavements were used where animals were to be housed. Although there are differences of opinion concerning the function of the paved lateral compartments in the pillared buildings (stables or storerooms) many archaeologists assume that in the three- or four-room houses such pavements do indicate the housing of animals.[18] In any case, it is very probable that the lateral spaces had ceilings much lower than the pillared stables/storerooms. The rooms on the ground floor were often very low indeed,[19] and the combined height of both storeys was usually no more than 4–5 m.

14. *Hazor*, pp. 183–184, Fig. 49.
15. The theoretical possibility that the buildings had only one storey and that the masonry steps served as access to the roof seems unlikely. Yadin stated that at Hazor this building certainly had a second storey; *Hazor*, pp. 183–184.
16. *Tell Nasbeh*, p. 208, Fig. 51.
17. Chap. 23, p. 223. In this writer's opinion, most of the pillared buildings were stables, not storehouses. The area available for storage, according to Herzog, would have been small and out of proportion to the building's total area. Unless the installations (tables?) between the pillars were troughs, they would have been a nuisance. On the other hand, unloading need not have been done inside the storehouse, but could have taken place outside or at the entrance, if the buildings were storehouses. The use of some of these buildings for storage before they were abandoned (for example at Beersheba) does

not preclude their having been built as stables. For this and other reasons, this writer believes that the pillared building uncovered in Area A at Hazor was intended as a stable.

As for the possible reconstruction of the pillared buildings, in this writer's opinion, they, whether stables or storehouses, should be reconstructed with a 2 to 3 m. high wall resting on the pillars, interrupted by clerestory windows, and not as Herzog suggests (Chap. 23). Such a wall would make the height of the various spaces to be built independent of the height of the pillars, which surely did not exceed 2 m. In addition, it would also create a suitable difference of height between the roofs of the lateral spaces and the roof of the central space.

18. *Tell Nasbeh*, p. 213; G. E. Wright: A Characteristic North Israelite House, in R. Moorey and P. Parr (eds.): *Archaeology in the Levant, Essays for Kathleen M. Kenyon*, Warminster, 1978, p. 151.
19. For instance, the reconstruction of House 167 at Tel Masos. See Tel Masos: 1972, 1974, 1975, *EI* 15 (1981), p. 162, Pl. 27:2.

According to Shiloh, the back room in the three-or four-room house was the main room, or living quarter.[20] Although the room may have been used for that purpose, the main living area must have been on the second floor, around the upper courtyard, which was airy, had plenty of light, and was isolated from the inhabitants of the ground floor — the chickens, sheep, goats and cattle quartered there.[21] The construction of the house on two levels made possible the convenient functional division between the storage, livestock, and workshop accommodations on the ground floor and the family living quarters on the upper floor. Here it must be said that the commonly held view that the natural location of cooking stoves and baking ovens (tabuns) is in an open courtyard is not necessarily correct, as such courtyards were open to rain and wind. Indeed, at some sites, cooking facilities have been uncovered in closed rooms (although most were near doors leading outside). This was, for example, the case in the Zealots' living quarters in the casemate wall at Masada.[22] Although this example dates from a later period, no known significant changes had occurred in cooking and baking facilities. All the installations set up in the lower, roofed part of the central space enjoyed, as already mentioned, reasonable amounts of light and air.

The fact that the long-spaced house continued to be built throughout most of the Iron Age, and that its dispersal roughly corresponds to the areas settled by the Israelite tribes or by related tribes in Transjordan, as Shiloh has noted,[23] raises the question whether the distinctive layout of this house, as well as its frequent occurrence, is a result of the Israelite tribes' way of life. This is a subject worthy of attention and further study.[24]

It appears that the house with long spaces, in its distinctive layout (either as a three- or a four-room

house), became common mainly under conditions of dense urban building, when houses were contiguous and there was no possibility of enlarging a building horizontally. The division of functions between the two storeys made it possible to crowd the houses. On the other hand, if the supposition that the division of functions (between the two levels) had special significance for the Israelite tribes is correct, then, it explains its existence in sites that were not particularly densely built up (for instance, Tel Masos).

The size of the buildings discussed here — their height, the narrowness of the spaces, and their relatively thin walls — ensured that building costs would be low. The choice between a three-room and a four-room house was almost certainly determined by the size, needs, and wealth of the family and by conditions in the urban complex. From an architectural point of view, the four-room house is the optimal type among these 'long-spaced' houses.

Courtyard Houses

'Long-spaced' houses constitute the majority among the houses built according to a well-defined plan in the Israelite period. The few buildings with a characteristic plan that do not belong to this large group are located mainly in the large royal cities (Hazor, Samaria, and

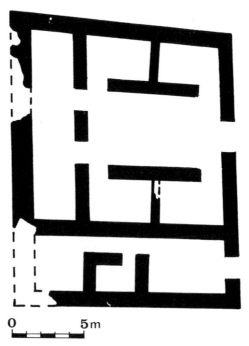

10. Dwelling, Tell Beit Mirsim, the 'western tower'. *Tell Beit Mirsim* III, Pls. 6, 8.

20. Shiloh (above, n. 3), p. 280.
21. Evidence for this has been found, *inter alia*, at sites such as Atar Ha-Ro'ah and Tel Masos, where lintels were preserved between the pillars. The pillars are so low, however, they could have supported the lintels at a height suitable only for animals.
22. Y. Yadin: *Masada: Herod's Fortress and the Zealot's Last Stand*, London, 1966, pp. 154–156 and photograph on pp. 158–159. This writer was one of the architects on the expedition, so that these opinions are based on first hand acquaintance with the site.
23. Shiloh (above, n. 3), pp. 280–282.
24. In a general discussion of this subject with Prof. M. Weinfeld of the Hebrew University, one of the subjects tentatively explored was the issue of the separation between purity and impurity — such as the avoidance of a woman during menstruation. This writer wishes to thank Prof. Weinfeld for his insights.

EHUD NETZER

Megiddo), buildings which Herzog has defined as scribes' offices (Chap. 23), or are of an administrative nature (like the western tower at Tell Beit Mirsim, Fig. 10).[25] In fact, there is a typological connection between them. They can be described as rectangular houses, with rectangular courtyards surrounded on two or three sides by rows of rooms; for convenience we have designated them as 'courtyard houses'.[26] Although there is a close resemblance between some courtyard houses and some houses with long spaces, the courtyard houses, however, are characterized by a clearer and more uniform division of the rooms around the central space. Here there are no long spaces divided into rooms or compartments, but definite rooms built one next to the other. The evidence for this is the larger size, the more careful planning of these rooms, and the attention expended on their doorways. The courtyard houses are generally larger and better built than the houses with long spaces; they have wider courtyards and rooms, thicker walls, and more generous measurements. Generally speaking, courtyard houses do not have rows of pillars.

The size of the courtyards (usually 4 m. or more in width) and of the rooms, as well as their organization, suggests that the open-air courtyard in these houses was on the ground floor. However, it is probable that in some cases there was a second storey (as in Houses 3100, 3601, and 3208 in Stratum VIII at Hazor, Area B).[27] If so, there must have been some means of connection among the rooms on the upper floor. Although the rooms are wider than the lateral spaces in the houses with long spaces, the absence in the courtyard houses of an internal space on the upper floor to give access to the rooms is similarly problematic (see above). Perhaps access to the rooms was by means of narrow wooden balconies that ran around the courtyard walls at the upper floor level.[28] Although no evidence of such wooden balconies has been found, it seems that such an arrangement could have, tentatively, provided the access to and between the rooms. Such an arrangement would have been impractical in courtyards less than 4 m. wide, but

25. *Tell Beit Mirsim* III, pp. 46–47, Pl. 6.
26. Because there are only a few of these buildings, they are not regarded as a definite typological group, in contrast to houses with long spaces.
27. This is especially so because these buildings were integrated into the city-wall and in fact replaced it, requiring a height of at least two storeys. *Hazor*, Fig. 45.
28. These balconies, if they indeed existed, must have rested on beams that protruded from the wall and probably were a continuation of the ones covering the rooms on the ground floor.

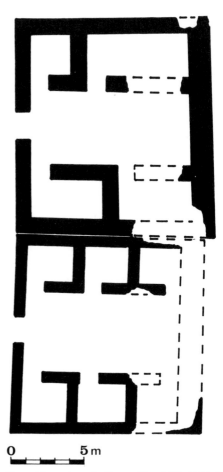

11. Dwellings, Hazor Area B, Houses Nos. 3100, 3067. *Hazor* II, Pls, CCV, CCIV.

in cases of courtyards wider than 4 m. the balconies (which could be as narrow as 0.7–0.8 m.) could have been built along two side walls rather than along only one of the longitudinal ones. In the absence of a built staircase, access to the upper floor was most probably by means of a ladder or steep wooden stairs. The following buildings belong to this limited group of courtyard houses.

Courtyard Buildings with Rows of Rooms on Two Sides. — Buildings 3100, 3067, and 3208 in Stratum VIII, Area B at Hazor (Fig. 11 and see above); Buildings 409, 424, and 406–408 at Samaria;[29] and the northern and central units in Building 1482, Stratum IVB at Megiddo[30] have rows of rooms on two sides. At Samaria and Megiddo, the buildings are not freestanding structures, but units incorporated into larger complexes. At those two sites they were

29. C.S. Fisher, D.G. Lyon, and G.A. Reisner: *Harvard Excavations at Samaria 1908–1910*, Cambridge, Mass., 1)924, pp. 114–17, Fig. 41.
30. *Megiddo* I, pp. 24–27, Fig. 12.

Hazor. A Four-Room Building, Iron Age II.

probably one-storey buildings, but at Hazor two storeys almost certainly existed.

Courtyard Buildings with Rows of Rooms on Three Sides. — Building 14, Stratum A at Tell Beit Mirsim (the western tower)[31]; the house uncovered in the northeastern quarter at Tell el-Hesi;[32] and the Stratum VIII citadel in Area B at Hazor[33] are courtyard houses with rows of rooms on three sides. The remains clearly indicate two storeys for the first two; the thickness of the walls shows that the citadel at Hazor could have had three or four storeys. The courtyard here was located on the second floor and access to the rooms on the tentative third and fourth floors may have been by means of wooden balconies around the courtyard walls. Typologically this large building should be defined as a courtyard house rather than a four-room house, as Shiloh has suggested.[34]

A few buildings are difficult to classify as either courtyard houses or houses with long spaces. House 2a in Stratum VI, Area A at Hazor, is a case in point.[35]

The location of most, if not all, the courtyard houses indicates that they were primarily intended as administrative offices or as dwellings for functionaries. However, it may be that some of the houses with long spaces also were living quarters for officials (for instance, Houses 3148 and 3169 in Stratum VA, Area B at Hazor;[36] the four-room house near the water supply system in Area L at Hazor;[37] and the four-room houses Nos. 23, 226, and 379 at Tell en-Nasbeh).[38]

It could be argued that the courtyard house developed from a type of LB house built around a courtyard (Chap. 13). However, the clear and characteristic features of the courtyard house attest to meticulous central planning — also evident in the fortifications, water-supply systems, stables, and/or storehouses of the period — that assigns it to the Iron Age.

31. *Tell Beit Mirsim* III, pp. 46–47, Pl. 6.
32. F. Bliss: *A Mound of Many Cities*, London, 1898, p. 72.
33. *Hazor*, pp. 169–71, Fig. 45.
34. Shiloh (above, n. 3), p. 277.
35. See House 29 at Hazor (*Hazor*, pp. 179–180). Although on the eastern side there is a row of pillars characteristic of houses with long spaces, and in spite of the size and organization of the rooms on the north and the west, the building is best classified, in this writer's opinion, as a courtyard house.
36. *Hazor*, pp. 174, 177, Fig. 46.
37. *Ibid.*
38. *Tell Nasbeh*, pp. 206–212, Figs. 51, 52A, 52B.

22 PALACES AND RESIDENCIES IN THE IRON AGE

Ronny Reich

Palaces are defined as buildings which served as royal residences of the monarch, members of his family and his household staff, and also functioned as centres of administration due to the offices of the ruler and the court officials located in them. Also defined as palaces are official buildings which served as residences and offices of high officials, local rulers, governors of districts and towns, etc.

On the basis of the archaeological remains, no distinction can be made between the two types of palaces. Although the royal palace was situated in the capital city (Jerusalem, Tirzah, Samaria), additional palaces were also maintained in other cities, such as Jezre'el (I Kings 21:1) and Lachish (II Chronicles 25:27), so that without the aid of epigraphic material, it is impossible to determine the identity of the owners of these buildings. Consequently, all the buildings of this type will be treated here as a single category and designated as palaces (*armon*).[1]

There is little difficulty in distinguishing between palaces and ordinary private houses. This is easily done on the basis of architectural differences, such as the size of the building and its location in the most desirable area of the city, the limited number of palaces in a city in comparison with ordinary houses, the extensive use of rare and costly building materials in palaces, and the types of small finds recovered from the buildings which attest to the owner's superior rank. The palace also generally contained an audience or throne room in which the monarch received his subjects and functionaries. Special annexes — treasure houses, archives, etc. — were sometimes also included in the palaces.

Palaces of the United Monarchy Period.

No palaces of the Late Bronze Age have been discovered so far which were re-used, for the same purpose, by the Israelites in the period of their settlement. The Israelites, at this early stage, belonged to a seminomadic society whose social structure and system of government differed from that which prevailed in the country before their arrival, and their way of life would hardly have required special government buildings. In fact, no building of this type has been uncovered which was constructed by the Israelites prior to the tenth century B.C.

Only scanty details of the earliest palaces of the Iron Age can be gleaned from the Bible. King Saul apparently continued to dwell in his own house in Giv'at Shaul (I Samuel 10:26; 11:4; 15:34; 20:25). The first palace (*bet ha-melekh*) was built by David for his own use (II Samuel 5:11; 7:2; I Chronicles 17:1; II Chronicles 2:2) and the Bible emphasizes that this structure was also erected on the initiative of the Phoenicians and under their influence. Features distinguishing it from an ordinary house are already present: the building materials employed in its construction — cedar wood and dressed building stones (*even kir*) were not in widespread use. Unfortunately, the Bible provides no details of the building nor have any of its remains been recovered in excavations.

The technical knowledge, construction materials and architectural plans imported into the Land of Israel in the tenth century B.C. from Phoenicia and northern Syria for the construction of Solomon's Temple were also employed in the royal palaces and their annexes. K. Galling[2] and C. Watzinger[3] were the

---

1. The terms *hekhal* and *bet melekh* also designate a royal palace, see: *Enc. Miqr.*, s.v. *armon, beniyah* [b]; K. Galling (ed.): *Biblisches Reallexicon*, Tubingen, 1977.

2. *Idem*, Archaologisches Jahresbericht, *ZDPV* 55 (1932), p. 243.
3. C. Watzinger: *Denkmaler Palastinas*, I, 1933, p. 96.

first to note a possible connection between Solomon's Palace (I Kings 7:1–12) and the building type known as *bit hilani*, excavated at Zinjirli (Sham'al) and Tell Halaf (Gozan).[4] Galling went still further and interpreted the biblical account as a reference to three separate buildings of this type adjoining one another. He thus sought to draw a parallel with the northern Syrian method of adding a building when necessary instead of expanding the original structure.[5] In a further development of Galling's theory that the biblical account of Solomon's Palace parallels that of the northern Syrian palaces, D. Ussishkin maintained that the reference in the Bible is to only *one* building unit erected in the 'large courtyard' (excluding 'the house of the forest of Lebanon' which was apparently a separate structure).[6] Ussishkin pointed out that the order of the parts of the building in the biblical account corresponds to the order of the units of the northern Syrian palace, namely, the entrance was through the 'porch of pillars' which led into the 'porch for the throne' and 'another court' which was an interior court inside the building. A passage in this court led to 'his house' (Solomon's) and to 'a house for Pharaoh's daughter' which composed the private living quarters in the interior of the building (see below, the Megiddo palaces).

As noted above, 'the house of the forest of Lebanon'[7] was not incorporated within Solomon's Palace but adjoined it. Its distinctive feature, according to the Bible (I Kings 7:2–6), was three or four rows of cedar columns set in the central hall. Rows of columns as a construction element appear neither in northern Syrian architecture, which served as the prototype for the adjacent royal palace, nor in Canaanite buildings. Architectural parallels for this building should most likely be sought in the Phoenician coastal region where, unfortunately, very few early Phoenician remains have survived. The closest parallel, it would seem, is the first Phoenician temple of the ninth century B.C. uncovered at Kition (Cyprus) (Fig. 1).[8] In this building, which was approximately 22

4. R. Koldeway: Die Architektur von Sendschirli, in *Ausgrabungen von Sendschirli*, II, Berlin, 1898, pp. 183–191; F. von Luschan: *Ausgrabungen in Sendschirli*, IV, Berlin, 1911, pp. 246–262, 272–301; *Tell Halaf* II, pp. 23–86.
5. Cf. Galling (above, n. 1), p. 11.
6. D. Ussishkin: King Solomon's Palace and Building 1723 in Megiddo, *IEJ* 16 (1966), pp. 174–186; *idem*, King Solomon's Palaces, *BA* 36 (1973), pp. 78–105.
7. *Enc. Miqr.*, s.v. *beyt ya'ar haLebanon*; M.J. Mulder: Einige Bemerkungen zur Beschreibung des Libanon-waldhaus in Reg. 7, 2f, *ZAW* 88 (1976), pp. 99–105.
8. V. Karageorghis: *Kition*, London, 1976, Fig. 18.

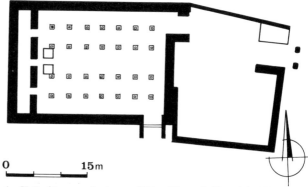

1. Hall with rows of columns, Kition (Cyprus), Phoenician Temple. V. Karagheorghis: *Kition*, London, 1976, Fig. 18.

× 35 m., four rows of stone bases, seven bases to a row, were preserved. Judging from the indentation (0.04 × 0.06 m.) at the top of each base, wooden columns had been attached to them. In Ussishkin's opinion, a close parallel for the building — despite its great geographical distance — is the palace of the eighth–seventh centuries B.C. at Altintepe in Urartu. This palace is a rectangular building, approximately 32 × 50 m., with stone foundations and three-metre thick walls. In its hall stood three rows of six pillars each ('the house of the forest Lebanon' had three or four rows of 15 pillars). It is therefore possible that 'the house of the forest of Lebanon' originated in the Phoenician or Cyprian coast, whence it was adopted by Israelite architecture and was carried further by the Phoenicians to Urartu in eastern Anatolia.[9]

In Jerusalem 'the house of the forest of Lebanon' could not have been a temple and it probably served either as a reception hall or for official ceremonies.

Palaces in the Kingdoms of Israel and Judah

Megiddo. — No remains of Solomon's Palace in Jerusalem have been found so far. Archaeological evidence of northern Syrian and Phoenician influence on palace construction in the tenth century B.C. can be observed in Buildings 1723 (Fig. 2) and 6000 (Fig. 3) excavated at Megiddo.[10] In plan they resemble palaces of the *bit hilani* type known from Zinjirli (Fig. 4), Tell Ta'yinat, etc. Their similarity can also help in reconstructing the character and pian of Solomon's Palace.

9. D. Ussishkin (above, n. 6), pp. 92–94, Fig. 8; T. Ozguc: *Altintepe*, I, Ankara, 1966, pp. 44–46, Pls. V-VI, XVII-XIX.
10. *Megiddo* I, pp. 17–24; *Hazor*, pp. 150–158.

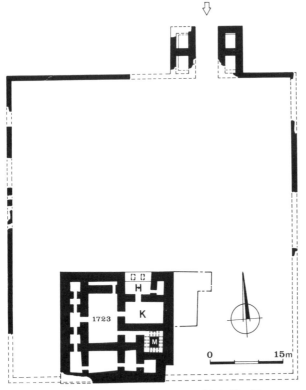

2. Megiddo, Building 1723. *Megiddo* I, Fig. 12.

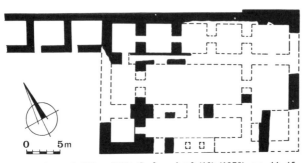

3. Megiddo, Building 6000. *Qadmoniot* 3 (10) (1970), pp. 44–45.

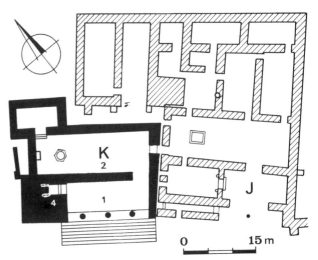

4. Zinjirli (Syria), Bit Hilani K (marked in black) and J (marked with lines). R. Naumann: *Architektur Kleinasiens* (2. Auflage), Tuebingen, 1971, Plan 549.

The discovery of the Zinjirli palaces and their identification as *bit hilani* type buildings, which are palaces (or parts of palaces) called by this name and described in Neo-Assyrian documents (which are later than the Zinjirli palaces), posed a number of questions for scholars, namely:

What is the semantic origin of the term? I. Singer, in a recent treatment of this question and a summary of the history of the research of the problem, assigned the term, following others, to a Hittite source.[11]

Does the term indicate the complete building (as maintained by H. Frankfort) or does it designate only the facade, in which the pillared entrance at the top of the staircase occupies a central position, as is attested by the philological analysis of the Hittite term?

What is the architectural origin of the building? This question has been studied at length by Frankfort,[12] who described it as a palace composed of two elongated halls with the longitudinal axis parallel to the facade. The first hall, in the outer doorway of which stood from one to three columns, constitutes a portico (*hilammar*). A stairway leads up to this entrance. Another, inner staircase leading to a second floor, is situated to the side of the portico. The long inner hall served as the throne room. Frankfort observed that the earliest architectural features of this type appeared in the palaces of Yarimlin and Niqmepa' at Alalakh (Strata VII, IV) in northern Syria and he considered them the antecedents of the *bit hilani*.[13]

These questions are, however, of only secondary importance for this discussion. There is no doubt that Israelite architecture of the tenth century B.C. was influenced by northern Syria, as is attested by the two buildings at Megiddo, and it is therefore suggested that it would be preferable to designate this type of building a 'northern Syrian palace'.

In both of these buildings at Megiddo, only the foundations of the walls have survived, projecting

11. I. Singer: Hittite *hilammar* and Hieroglyphic Luwian ʿhilana, *ZA* 65 (1975), pp. 69–103.

12. H. Frankfort: The Origin of the Bit Hilani, *Iraq* 14 (1952), pp. 120–131.

13. L. Woolley: *Alalakh*, Oxford, 1955, pp. 91–131.

Megiddo. Iron Age II Palace 1723.

one or two courses above ground. The foundations were built of carefully-laid ashlar stones with marginal dressing. The superstructure consisted of sun-dried bricks which were found collapsed in the ruins (Building 6000). The foundation course also served as the threshold of the doorways, although since nothing of the superstructure was preserved, the exact location of the openings between the rooms cannot be determined. The doorways of Palace 6000 should probably be reconstructed according to Ussishkin's proposed reconstruction of Building 1723.[14] In the chart, the details of the palaces at Megiddo are compared with a number of northern Syrian palaces, and the following features should be emphasized: the 'northern Syrian palace' is a very condensed structure, limited in size and in the number of its rooms. It consists of a public wing comprising the

14. D. Ussishkin: On the Original Position of Two Proto-Ionic Capitals at Megiddo, *IEJ* 20 (1970), pp. 213–215.

above-mentioned entrance hall and throne room, and a private wing with only a few rooms. There were probably living quarters on the second floor. The palace was small-scale in comparison with the vast area and multitude of rooms of the Hittite and Egyptian palaces and even of the Canaanite palaces of the Late Bronze Age.

V. Fritz[15] does not accept the identification of Buildings 1723 and 6000 as palaces that follow the *hilani* type, since they include an inner courtyard. An inner courtyard is an architectural element absent in northern Syrian *hilani* palaces. However, Megiddo's palaces should not be evaluated according to the strict northern Syrian building formulae. It might be that these buildings (or at least Building 1723) were in a way an architectural hybrid in which northern Syrian and Canaanite architectural concepts and elements were mingled together, as is the case with buildings during the Assyrian occupation (see below).

Adjoining the palace proper was an extensive court bounded by a wall. In Palace 1723 the entire line of the wall has survived.[16] The court, 56.8 × 58 m., was entered from the city through a gatehouse. It is thus probable that the 'Western casemates' excavated by Y. Yadin near Building 6000 are the ruins of adjacent buildings which faced a similar court south of the palace[17].

The recent discovery at Lachish (see below) of a spacious court bounded by a wall to which were attached not only the palace but additional buildings, provides evidence that in the Iron Age the royal palace in the principal Israelite cities was an extensive architectural complex which differed from both the earlier Canaanite and the later Assyrian palaces. The main difference between them was the limited size of the Israelite palace and the fact that it formed only a single component in a huge building complex which was grouped around a broad court. In the Canaanite and Assyrian palaces, on the other hand, the court and surrounding service rooms were incorporated into the palace proper.

In general, the Israelite palace, with its courts and annexes, occupied a large proportion of the area of the city, as is attested by the remains of Megiddo VA-IVB, Lachish IV-III and Samaria (Chap. 21).

Samaria. — On the summit of the hill on which stood Samaria, capital of the Israelite kingdom, were uncovered what are considered to be the most

magnificent and unsurpassed remains of buildings belonging to the First Temple period in the Land of Israel. Samaria also contains the only known example of a royal palace in a capital city from this period[18]. The remains include:

A. *Fortification walls and a retaining wall enclosing the palace complex.* Scattered around the site were the remains of two fortified enclosures dating to the ninth century B.C., the later one being an extension of the earlier one. The earlier enclosure, which was surrounded by a retaining wall about 1.6 m. thick, covered an area of 89 × 178 m. (*ca.* 15 dunams). This wall was replaced by a casemate wall which expanded the enclosure northward and eastward and enlarged it to an area of 106 × 208 m. (*ca.* 22 dunams). The immense size of these areas exceeded the dimensions of entire cities in the Iron Age (Beersheba, for example, was 10 dunams in area). Nevertheless, the fortified complex situated on the summit of the hill should be defined as a palace and not a city or 'inner city', as proposed by Z. Herzog (below, p. 250). Evidence supporting the 'palace' definition has been uncovered recently at Lachish where the Israelite palace complex measured 13.5 dunams (see below).

B. *Building remains.* Unfortunately, very scanty remnants of buildings have been preserved. These include:

1. Several walls, whose complete plan cannot be established, were uncovered in the centre of the enclosure to the north. This was the spot in which the famous Samaria ivories, which attest to the ornateness of the decoration of the building and especially of its furniture, and which also provide additional confirmation of the royal character of the remains, were discovered. The ivory hoard also indicates that Ahab's 'ivory house' (I Kings 22:39), which was the official and ceremonial wing of his palace, was built nearby.[19]

2. Remains abutting the early enclosure wall in the south. Here were found foundations of walls belonging to a complex of rooms arranged around a central hall (inner court?), 8.5 × 9 m., with two rectangular-shaped rooms on its eastern side. With great difficulty these remains could perhaps be identified as belonging to a structure built on the plan of the northern Syrian

15. F. Fritz: Die Syrische Bauform des Hilani und die Frage seiner Verbreitung, *Damaszener Mitteilungen* 1 (1983), pp. 43–58.

16. *Megiddo* I, pp. 11–17, Fig. 12.

17. *Hazor*, pp. 156–158, Fig. 40, Loci 6001–6003.

18. *Samaria-Sebaste* I, pp. 5–20, 94–117, Pls. I, II, VIII; N. Avigad: Samaria, *EAEHL* IV, *passim* (bibliography).

19. N. Avigad: The Ivory House which Ahab Built, in *Eretz-Shomron*, The Thirtieth Archaeological Convention, The Israel Exploration Society, 1973, pp. 75–85 (Hebrew).

palaces (*bit hilani*). The building is quite small (outer dimensions approximately 28 × 45 m.) and somewhat resembles in plan Buildings 1723 and 6000 at Megiddo.

3. A building complex on the western side of the enclosure, between the early enclosure wall and the casemate wall. The Samaria ostraca were discovered at this spot. The administrative nature of the contents of these ostraca indicates clearly that this wing contained the offices and storerooms (Chap. 23, pp. 229).

4. Remains of a square tower (?) and several rooms (18.8 × 34.4 m.) attached to the southwestern corner of the casemate wall. These remains may represent a further expansion of the palace.

5 Remains of a large pool (5.2 × 10.2 m.) in the northwestern corner of the enclosure.

6. Large areas in the fortified enclosure may have originally been open spaces, and probably served as broad courts, similar to the court in the palace at Lachish.

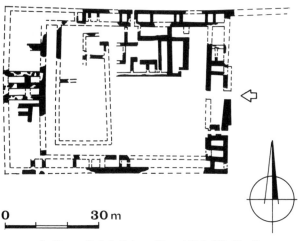

0   30 m

5. Ramat Rahel, Palace. **Ramat Rahel** II, Fig. 6.

Ramat Rahel. — On a hill about 4 km. south of Jerusalem were unearthed the remains of an elaborate and complex building (Fig. 5) which was defined as a palace by Y. Aharoni.[20] The stratigraphic details of the building are a subject of controversy, as is the exact date of its construction. Most of the building was composed of dressed limestone blocks of an extremely high building standard, almost equal to the quality of the ashlar masonry in the palace at Samaria. This fact may be the underlying cause of the problem for, due to their excellent quality, the stones

20. *Ramat Rahel* II, pp. 23–28, 49–60, Fig. 6.

were looted in later periods. Some light can be shed on the ground plan of the building by the surviving walls and the foundation trenches cut into the rock.

The structure, measuring 56 × 72 m., consisted basically of a series of rooms, somewhat like a casemate wall, surrounding a central court (*ca.* 24 × 30 m.). These casemates apparently served as storage rooms or as various service rooms. North of the court was a series of rooms grouped around a small court, probably the living quarters of the owner. The rooms west of the central court were interpreted by the excavator as a casemate wall containing a double row of rooms (similar to the northern wall at Samaria), but this was, in fact, another wing of rooms, 14 m. wide. From its meagre remains it appears that this wing was divided in a more complex fashion. A pair of elongated rooms, both partitioned identically into short and longer areas, situated in the western wall, should be noted.

Hazor. — The remains of the Israelite period at Hazor are centred on the high mound. From the tenth–ninth centuries B.C. (Strata X–IX, the beginning of which is assigned to the time of Solomon) evidence of government construction is provided by the fortification system and it can be assumed, by analogy with Megiddo, that the city also contained an official building for the use of the ruler in this period, but none has so far been uncovered.

A building at the edge of the mound (Area B) (Fig. 6) was dated to the period between the middle of the

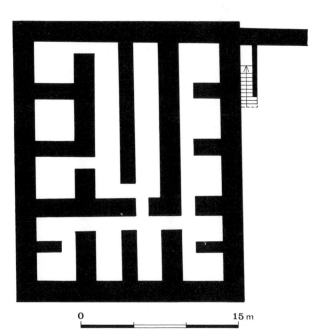

0   15 m

6. Hazor, Area B, the 'citadel'. **Hazor** II, Pl. CCV.

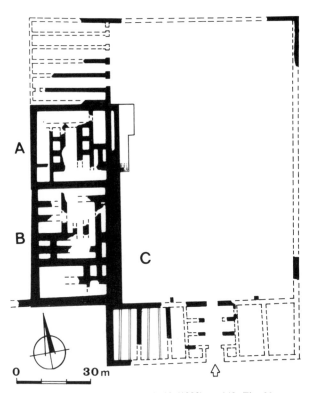

7. Lachish, Palace. *Tel Aviv* 10 (1983), p. 148, Fig. 23.

ninth century and the Assyrian conquest in 732 B.C. (Strata VIII–V).[21] Since up to that time the city had successfully withstood the Assyrian military threat, the building had not been enclosed by a wall (Stratum V), its defense based only on the strength of its walls (which were *ca.* 2 m. thick) and its location at the edge of the mound. It was therefore designated a 'citadel'.

The building does not differ from Buildings 1723 and 6000 at Megiddo in its external measurements (21.5 × 25 m.) but rather in the appearance it presented to one approaching. In the Megiddo buildings the emphasis was placed on an impressive entrance, which was also achieved by the huge open area before it, so that the structures were worthy of the designation 'palaces'. At Hazor, on the other hand, the building's location at the side of the mound, the concealment of the lower storey among ordinary houses, the modest entrance in the corner of the building at the top of a side stairway, all indicate that greater importance was laid on the building's functional rather than official aspect. It is almost impossible to reconstruct an ornamental entrance to the court (which is also long and narrow and lacks grandeur) with proto-Aeolic capitals in front of the building. It is also likely that another building at Hazor was used as a 'palace' in this period.

The plan of the building is extremely simple, consisting of two elongated rooms surrounded by rooms on three sides. On the basis of its massive walls and the side stairway, the excavators identified these remains as the foundations which supported the main storey built of sun-dried mud bricks. The upper storey was apparently identical in plan with that of the foundation level, except for the centre of the building which contained a broad-room, 6 × 14 m., (unroofed?), in place of the two adjoining halls in the lower level.

The Lachish Palace. — The Israelite palace uncovered at Tel Lachish (Fig. 7) is the largest fully preserved palace of its kind known in Israel. Due to the lack of architectural data concerning the palaces and official buildings situated in Jerusalem, the Lachish palace can serve as a model for the royal residences which may have existed in the Judean capital and will be described in detail.

Location. The palace was situated at the heart of the mound of Lachish, though not in its actual centre.[22] Assuming that a structure of at least two to three storeys rose above the high podium, which was preserved to its full height, it would have been possible from there to view at a single glance the entire city inside the inner wall, and to see far to the east, north and west and a small way to the south. The site of the palace was not selected by chance but seems to have been the optimal choice, continuing the tradition of the Canaanite acropolis, whose public buildings have been revealed beneath its foundations.

The Podium. The palace was erected above a large podium which has been preserved in its entirety (external dimensions, 36 × 76 m., i.e. *ca.* 2.7 dunams). The podium is not a single unit but is composed of three sections of varied size, which represent three different stages of construction (the original stage and two additional ones). These construction stages are considered to correspond to the three Iron Age strata of settlement on the mound (V, IV, III). This fact indicates that, like houses, the palaces also underwent changes during their existence (although, unlike houses, these changes were carefully planned). According to Ussishkin, the later stages of construction consisted of the addition of new wings to the existing palace and did not represent the renovation and expansion of a building in ruins.

21. *Hazor* II, pp. 51–54, Pl. CCV; *Hazor* III-IV, Pls. XXXI–XXXII; *Hazor*, pp. 187–190.
22. D. Ussishkin: Excavations at Tell Lachish 1973–1977, *Tel Aviv* 5 (1978), pp. 27–42, Figs. 1 (no. 5), 7–8.

Lachish. Iron Age II palace.

The purpose of the podium was to elevate the palace well above the summit of the mound. It was of very strong construction to bear the weight of a building of several storeys and also provide the palace with maximum protection. The foundations were thus massive walls (2–3.5 m.) built of fieldstones laid in the header and stretcher method and sunk to a great depth. The spaces between these stones were filled with debris from the mound. This building method resembles that of the podiums of the Mesopotamian palaces (*tamlu*) but due to the use of stone, it is even stronger. The walls of the superstructure were apparently made of mud brick and for the most part followed the ground plan of the foundations.

In its earliest phase (Palace A), the building was square in plan (32.1 × 31.45 m., equivalent to one dunam). The builders of the palace did not make use of the Canaanite building remains nor did they remove them, but laid the walls of the podium above them. The podium was sunk to a depth of three to seven metres, depending on the height of the ground. Judging from the foundations, there seems to have been a long

rectangular area (4.8 × 13.2 m.) in the centre of Palace A which was flanked by two rows of small square-shaped rooms. Surrounding the building were rectangular-shaped rooms. In Ussishkin's opinion, the entrance hall was in the eastern side.

In the second phase (Palace B), a large wing was added on the southern side and together with the original structure formed a rectangular-shaped podium measuring about 32 × 76 m. Its foundations were similarly built of thick stone walls sunk deep into the ground (in the southwestern corner they reached a depth of 12 m.).

In the third phase (Palace C), an area about 3.4 m. wide was built on the eastern side along the full length of the building. With this addition the palace reached its greatest extent (36 × 76 m., i.e. 2.7 dunams). This area in itself did not greatly extend the built-up area of the palace and its purpose may have been merely the strengthening of the foundations on the eastern side. It is also possible that they wished to create (after Palace B was already constructed) a kind of porch along the facade of the palace overlooking the large court. This porch would also have enabled the direct passage from the great staircase in the northeastern corner of the palace not only to Wing A, but also to Wing B without the necessity of crossing Wing A.

The palace at Lachish was at the heart of a large complex of buildings which provided numerous and varied services for the court, including maintenance, administrative affairs, the local guard, etc.

A large court (*ca.* 70 × 106 m.) east of the palace was enclosed by various buildings. To the south were remains of buildings whose inner space was divided into three elongated areas (of the type known as 'stables' or 'storerooms', Chap. 23). Abutting the palace on the north was a building containing six long narrow rooms (each *ca.* 12 × 22.8 m.) with doorways only in the narrow side facing the court. These rooms have been identified as storerooms. The total dimensions of the enclosure-royal complex were approximately 106 × 130 m., or 13.5 dunams.

In a large court of the type found at Lachish, various ceremonies could be conducted; people waiting to be received by the king could assemble; horsemen and grooms could perform their duties; and everyday household tasks of the palace could be carried out. It should be recalled that Israelite cities contained very little open space, most of the city area being occupied by houses, so that a court of this type was of considerable value.

An interesting construction feature, encountered so far only at Lachish,[23] is the massive wall (*ca.* 4 m. thick) connecting the palace to the city-wall near the gate. This wall may have delimited an area of the city belonging to the palace and at the same time it could have served as a viaduct leading to the wall.

An inclined earthen ramp, coated with plaster, was built against the base of the podium of the palace. The ramp added considerably to the thickness of the podium and prevented access to it. These features point to the stringent measures taken to protect the palace inside the city precincts.

Jerusalem. — The foundations of an extremely broad structure (at least 30 × 50 m.) and an adjacent city-gate were revealed on the northeast side of the City of David[24] near the top of the slope descending to the Kidron Valley. It was built of very thick walls (*ca.* 1.6 m.) laid directly on bedrock. Due to the absence of *in situ* finds in the building, it only can be assumed that this was a public building, one of the royal

palaces or administrative buildings which was in use in the period of the First Temple.

Official Buildings in the Provincial Towns

The greater the distance from the capital cities — Jerusalem in Judah and Samaria in Israel — and from the other major cities (such as Hazor, Megiddo, Lachish and Gezer), the smaller is the architectural difference between the residence of the local governor and the house of the average town dweller. Though the house of the governor is still larger in area than the private house, the use of uncommon building materials, ornamental features and plans of foreign origin decrease until in fact in the provincial towns the residence of the ruler resembles an ordinary private house, perhaps a little larger than the average. Since there was generally only one building of this type (or, at the most, a limited number) in the town, in partially excavated sites it cannot be certain that this particular building was indeed uncovered.

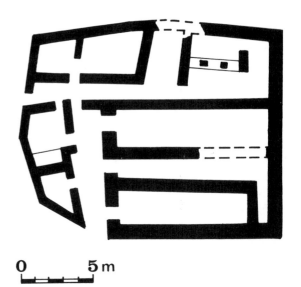

8. Beersheba, Governor's Residency. Aharoni: *Archaeology of the Holy Land*, Jerusalem, 1978, Plan 70.

Beersheba (Strata II–III, 9th–8th centuries B.C.). — The excavator, Y. Aharoni,[25] identified the governor's residence as the building uncovered near the city-gate (Fig. 8), which measures about 10 × 18 m. (external dimensions). The average house in the city, in contrast, was 5 × 9 m. Small rooms on the western and southern

23. D. Ussishkin (above, n. 22), pp. 46–53; 'enclosure wall'.

24. E. Mazar: Jerusalem — The Ophel — 1986, *ESI* 5 (1986), pp. 56–58.

25. Y. Aharoni: *The Archaeology of the Land of Israel*, London, 1982, Fig. 70.

sides served as living quarters and service rooms, whereas the ceremonial area was apparently located in the long halls found on the eastern side on the second floor. Only in this part of the building was ashlar masonry employed, the rest of the building being constructed in the usual method of mud bricks on fieldstone foundations. From this spot there was also a direct view of the city-gate.

Israelite Ashlar Masonry

From the tenth century B.C. onward, along with the appearance of large-scale royal structures (temples, palaces, public buildings, citadels), the ashlar masonry method of stone dressing and its incorporation in buildings is encountered (Chap. 1, Fig. 7; Chap. 27, Fig. 1).[26] In this method the stones were dressed into long rectangular blocks and laid side by side in courses with no space between them, to form a strong, stable structure. This method is totally different from the one in which stone rubble gathered in the field was integrated into structures with no further dressing and was usually part of the foundations.

Characteristic features of ashlar masonry include:

1. *Nari*, of all the types of stone found in Israel, was the stone preferred by the masons because it was relatively easy to dress, as was pointed out by Y. Shiloh and A. Horowitz.[27]

2. The stones were dressed into elongated rectangular blocks. Shiloh[28] distinguished several grades in the quality of the stone dressing. When fully dressed the stone was rectangular and smooth on all sides, or rectangular with at least the outer face having a smooth finish, as can be seen in the buildings of Samaria and Ramat Rahel. Dressing of this quality attested to a degree of ostentation not often encountered, and certainly not in fortifications or in the foundations of structures which were set partly below ground level. Dressing the sides of the stones into right angles was the absolute minimum for bonding the stones together. In this way 'marginal drafting' was created in which the angles were somewhat widened to form smooth margins while the rest of the face was left undressed and projecting. Such 'margins' were smoothed near one or more of the edges of the stone's faces.

3. Ashlar stones were laid in courses in such a manner that the long side of some of the stones was laid parallel to the line of the wall (stretcher) and others perpendicular to the wall (header) (Chap. 27, Fig. 1). Headers and stretchers were combined in various patterns. R. Frankel[29] has shown that a connection exists between walls built of dressed stone of a certain size and the method in which they were laid (as is indicated by the biblical term 'measures of hewn stones' (I Kings 7:9). This method of construction created strong points along the length and width of the walls.

Hazor. Detail of ashlar construction, Iron Age II.

It should be noted that no precedents have been found for this method in Israelite settlements of the 12th–11th centuries B.C. Its details, however, appear in a very highly developed state in buildings uncovered in strata of the tenth century B.C. (as, for example, in Buildings 1723 and 6000 at Megiddo). Many scholars are convinced that the biblical account of the construction of Solomon's Temple and palaces in Jerusalem by Phoenician craftsmen, expert in the tradition of building in stone and wood, reveals the true source of influence of the remains in the Land of Israel. Unfortunately, only scanty remains of the tenth century B.C. or earlier have been uncovered on

26. Y. Shiloh: *The Proto-Aeolic Capital and Israelite Ashlar Masonry* [*Qedem* 11], Jerusalem, 1979.

27. Y. Shiloh and A. Horowitz: Ashlar Quarries of the Iron Age in Palestine in the Hill Country of Israel, *BASOR* 217 (1975), pp. 37–48.

28. Y. Shiloh (above, n. 26), pp. 66–67, 79.

29. R. Frankel: The Measure of Hewn Stones, *Tel Aviv* 3 (1976), pp. 74–78.

the Phoenician coast and therefore cannot confirm this view. Shiloh,[30] on the other hand, maintained that Israelite ashlar masonry differs in its essential features and also in its details from the buildings found on the Phoenician coast and in Cyprus and concluded that it should be considered to have originated in the Land of Israel. In his opinion, ashlar masonry in the neighbouring lands was used mainly in buildings with orthostats for facing or as a base for fieldstone or mud-brick walls, whereas the Israelite ashlar masonry usually extended the full height and width of the wall, which explains the substantial difference in the structural strength of the wall and the building as a whole.

Shiloh also interpreted the biblical text literally and understood it as mainly recording the skills of the craftsmen from Tyre, Sidon and Byblos in cutting timber, shipping it to building sites and processing it, whereas stone cutting, dressing and building are less clearly attributable to them.

At the same time, it should not be forgotten that aside from Phoenicia, there were other regions with a well-developed tradition of building in dressed stone. Among these are the northern Syrian cities (Zinjirli, Tell Halaf, Alalakh, Tell Ta'yinat),[31] from which the ground plans of buildings were probably borrowed (Chap. 19 on the plan of Solomon's Temple; and above on the Megiddo palaces) as well as structural details (for example, the round column bases of the dais of the throne in the gate at Tel Dan). Some stone dressing, however, must also have been borrowed from them.

Though this type of masonry was indeed characteristic of Israelite public architecture, not all buildings of this type employed this technique. Some walls of this type rose to a considerable height (as at Samaria) but in most of the buildings ashlar masonry appeared as the foundation for plastered mud-brick superstructures. Another technique found is a combination of ashlar masonry constructed with a stone rubble fill between the ashlar wall segments (Chap. 27, Fig. 2).

Most of these building techniques continued in use in the Persian period (Chap. 27).

Proto-Aeolic Capitals

Capitals of columns, dressed and carved from large stone blocks, appear alongside ashlar masonry

9. Proto-aeolic capitals. *Qedem* 11 (1979), Pl. 11:1.

construction in the Iron Age, from the tenth century B.C. onward (Fig. 9). In the past these capitals were designated proto-Aeolic on the assump-tion that they were the antecedents of the Aeolic and Ionian capitals of Greek architecture. Shiloh[32] recently proposed changing this name since no actual connection could be distinguished between this capital and the classical ones. In his opinion, they depict stylized palm trees and he therefore suggested calling them 'timora capitals' (based on I Kings 6:29, 32, 35; 7:36, Ezekiel 40:22, 26, 31, 34, 37; 41:18–20, 25, 26; II Chronicles 3:5) or 'Israelite capitals'. Shiloh published a corpus of all 34 (or 33) capitals found thus far in Israel.

Capitals of this type are known from Hazor, Dan, Megiddo, Samaria, Ramat Rahel, Jerusalem and Medeibiyeh in Transjordan. Though none were found *in situ* at these sites, all of them were uncovered near administrative buildings and palaces. Shiloh classified the capitals into five typological categories, according to the buildings they belonged to and their decorative elements, and these are divided into a northern, Israelite group and a southern, Judean group.

A survey of these capitals reveals that they were carved out of rectangular stone blocks averaging 0.5 × 0.5 × 1 m. in size. Several of the Megiddo capitals were exceptionally long, about 2.40 m., (but not broader or taller).

From the architectural standpoint the most important factor is the original position of the capital in a building, since none was found *in situ*. A number of capitals were carved on both faces and should be restored as crowning a column with a square cross-section of the same size as the base of the capital (about 0.4 × 0.5 m.). This column must have been freestanding and placed in the centre of a wide opening to support the lintel.

30. Y. Shiloh (above, n. 26), pp. 79–81.
31. R. Naumann: *Architektur Kleinasiens*, Tubingen, 1971, pp. 38–43, 68–86.

32. Y. Shiloh (above, n. 26), pp. 1–49, esp. pp. 88–91. The capital found at Tel Dan should be added to Shiloh's corpus. A. Biran: Tel Dan 1984 (Notes and News), *IEJ* 35 (1985), pp. 186–189, Pl. 24:D.

Most of the capitals are carved on one face only and it can be assumed that the rear part was set into the wall and that it crowned an engaged column. It can further be assumed that capitals of this type were placed on the two jambs (which are in fact engaged columns) of a large opening.

As for the two long capitals from Megiddo, Ussishkin proposed restoring them in the doorway of the facade of Palace 1723.[33] Shiloh, however, because of the extreme length of their bases (*ca.* 1.40 m.), did not accept this proposal and agrees with the excavators that they probably belonged to a larger, more massive structure, perhaps the gatehouse (1567) leading to the court of this palace.[34]

It can be assumed that the other capitals ornamented door jambs in entrances of various ashlar buildings, such as Buildings 1723, 6000 and 338.

The excavators of Hazor suggested that the capitals found there originally stood in the entrance to the long passageway (room?) connecting the northern corner of the citadel in Area B to the staircase leading to the second floor.[35] However, this cannot be correct since one of the capitals is bifacially decorated and the entrance, only 4 m. wide, is too narrow to have had a freestanding column (with a bifacial capital) in its centre. This would have left two openings of only 1–1.1 m. wide each (Fig. 10).

According to the excavators of Samaria,[36] the capitals found there crowned a row of engaged columns attached to an elaborate building. It should be noted that this type of structure would require numerous capitals identical in size and walls strengthened with pilasters along its length. The absence of such remains at the site casts doubt on the proposed restoration.

Other structural elements characteristic of ashlar masonry, such as ornamental parapets of windows, crenellated walls and openings with recesses are discussed below in Chap. 27.

The Integration of Wooden Beams in Stone Construction

Aside from the ordinary usage of wooden beams in roofing for rooms and halls, a typical feature of

10. Proto-aeolic capitals, reconstructed in gate.

public buildings in the Iron Age was the construction of walls of wooden beams laid horizontally between courses of ashlar masonry.[37] The Bible records that the king's palace was built of 'three rows of hewn stone, and a row of cedar beams' (I Kings 6:36; 7:12). In the subsequent Persian period, the temple of the returnees from the Babylonian exile was built in a similar fashion (Ezra 6:4). These descriptions seem to conform with the archaeological evidence. At Hazor, Megiddo and Samaria small horizontal gaps were found between the ashlar courses, which are apparently evidence of the presence of wooden beams that had totally disintegrated. But there is still no complete explanation for these gaps in the local masonry. Did the wooden planks have a structural purpose, for instance, to create some measure of flexibility or stability, or were they solely decorative? The integration of wooden beams along the length and width of walls of stone and brick construction has a long and well-developed history in Anatolia and northern Syria,[38] especially in buildings in which orthostats are employed as wall panels. A wooden beam was generally placed above a row of orthostats in these buildings. It is possible that a technique that was more suitable for orthostat-and-brick construction was adopted into ashlar masonry construction without any particular need.

33. D. Ussishkin (above, n. 14).
34. Y. Shiloh (above, n. 26), pp. 21–25.
35. Y. Shiloh (above, n. 26), p. 24; Y. Yadin: *Hazor, The Discovery of a Great Citadel of the Bible*, Jerusalem, 1974, reconstruction on p. 168.
36. *Samaria-Sebaste* I, pp. 14–15, Figs. 6–7.

37. Y. Shiloh (above, n. 26), p. 61.

RONNY REICH

Wooden planks were also used in public buildings as panelling in some of the rooms. Though no archaeological remains of this usage have survived, the Bible provides evidence in its description of cedar wood lining walls (I Kings 6:15; 7:7, etc.), and of cypress planks lining the floors of the temples and various administrative buildings (*ibid.*, 6:15). The ultimate aim was apparently a complete wooden surface: 'all was cedar; there was no stone seen' (*ibid.*, 6:18). Another verse records that the wooden panelling sometimes appeared in alternating recesses and projections: 'And he covered in the house with planks of cedar over beams' (*ibid.*, 6:9). Evidence of this can perhaps also be provided by the exterior of the monumental (royal?) tombs in northern Jerusalem which may imitate the outer walls of public buildings.[39]

Carved designs may have decorated wooden panelling of this type and ivory inlays of the kind found at Samaria and probably belonging to Ahab's 'ivory house', could have been inserted into it.

Assyrian Royal Buildings in the Land of Israel

The Neo-Assyrian Empire, which enjoyed a resurgence of power from the ninth century B.C. onward, also reached the Land of Israel after a series of wars and conquests. With the conquest of the northern part of the Israelite kingdom by Tiglath Pileser III (II Kings 15:29) in 733/732 B.C., a substantial part of the kingdom was turned into Assyrian provinces.[40] The Assyrian practice of erecting centres of civil administration and military rule in subjugated lands was carried out in the Land of Israel and consequently a number of Assyrian architectural concepts are encountered.

Royal Assyrian architecture is distinguished by a series of architectural conventions, uniform ground plans and characteristic building materials and architectural elements. These features have been studied by G. Loud and G. Turner in a survey of

Assyrian architecture in the Assyrian imperial centre and its provinces in northern Syria.[41]

With the discovery of Buildings 1369 and 1052 at Megiddo and the Residency at Lachish, the excavators of these sites noted for the first time a resemblance between these buildings and the Assyrian structures in Mesopotamia and northern Syria.[42]

Following the discovery of Building 3002 in Area B (Stratum III) at Hazor, R. Amiran and I. Dunayevsky published a study of similar structures in which they distinguished two main types of buildings in which a large court occupied the central part of the building, which they designated the 'open-court building'.[43] In the first type, comprised of buildings built in the Assyrian and Neo-Babylonian periods in Israel, the court was surrounded by rooms on all sides and access to the building was through an indirect, side entrance. In the second type, attributed to the Persian period, the court was enclosed by rooms on three sides only and the fourth side contained the main entrance that led directly into the building. An examination of this division indicates that this classification by Amiran and Dunayevsky was too general and not entirely accurate.[44]

The degree to which a building is Assyrian in character should be judged on the basis of the architectural concepts established by Loud and Turner. A survey reveals the existence of buildings in Israel that were constructed according to a strict Assyrian formula (layout, building material, etc.) and it can be assumed that these structures were

41. G. Loud: An Architectural Formula for Assyrian Planning Based on Results of Excavations at Khorsabad, *Revue d'Assyriologie* 33 (1936), pp. 153–160; *Khorsabad* II, pp. 10–13; G. Turner: The State Apartments of Late Assyrian Palaces, *Iraq* 32 (1970), pp. 177–213; R. Reich: Dur-Sharrukin (Khorsabad), *Qadmoniot* 12 (1979), pp. 2–11 (Hebrew); E. Heinrich: Neuassyrische Palaste, Palaste in Spatbabylonischen Reich, in E. Heinrich: *Die Palaste in Alten Mesopotamien* [Denkmaler Antiken Architektur 15], Berlin, 1984, pp. 98–197, 198–231.

42. *Megiddo* I, p. 72; *Lachish* III, pp. 133–135.

43. Ruth B.K. Amiran and I. Dunayevsky: The Assyrian Open-Court Building and its Palestinian Derivatives, *BASOR* (1958), pp. 25–32.

44. It seems strange that Amiran and Dunayevsky were not acquainted with G. Loud's study (above, n. 41) on Assyrian architecture, although they quoted the volume in which it appears. Presenting Assyrian architecture as characterized only by a courtyard surrounded by a series of rooms is an understatement. In addition, their thesis is not valid in all the examples they quoted. For example, the Persian Residency from Lachish is totally surrounded by rooms and is provided with an indirect entrance.

40. Much has been written on the historical and military background to these campaigns. See for example: A. Malamat: The Wars of Israel and Assyria, in J. Liver (ed.): *The Military History of the Land of Israel in Biblical Times*, Tel Aviv, 1965, pp. 241–260 (Hebrew); H. Tadmor: The Assyrian Campaigns to Philistia, *ibid.*, pp. 261–285 (Hebrew); A. Malamat: The Last Wars of the Kingdom of Judah, pp. 296–314 (Hebrew); N. Na'aman: Sennacherib's Campaign to Judah and the Date of the *lmlk* Stamps, *VT* (1979), pp. 61–86.

38. R. Naumann (above, n. 31), pp. 86–89, 91–108.

39. G. Barkay and A. Kloner: Jerusalem Tombs from the Days of the First Temple, *BAR* 12 (1986), p. 27.

designed by an Assyrian architect brought especially for this purpose. On the other hand, there are also buildings which exhibit Assyrian characteristics but are not exact replicas of Assyrian buildings, and these may perhaps indicate Assyrian influence only, or the experience acquired by a local architect in Assyria. In Israel, Assyrian building features have been identified with certainty only at a few sites and in a few buildings. These will now be discussed separately.

Hazor. — Stratum V at Hazor, which was destroyed by Tiglath-Pileser III, was replaced by

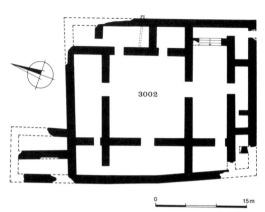

12. Hazor Area B, Building No. 3002. *Hazor* I, Pl. CLXXVII.

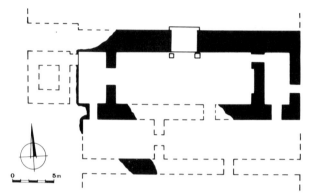

11. Assyrian palace, Ayyelet Ha-Shahar. *IEJ* 25 (1975), p. 234, Fig. 1.

an Assyrian administrative centre which contained a large residence. The Assyrian architect preferred to abandon the settlement on the small mound (small in Assyrian terms)[45] for the plain northeast of the mound (the site of the present Kibbutz Ayyelet Ha-Shahar), where P.L.O. Guy uncovered a monumental building (Fig. 11).[46] This building, in all its aspects, was constructed according to strict Assyrian conventions, a fact which enabled it to be easily identified despite its re-use in the Persian period. The series of rooms uncovered belong to the reception wing of the building and contain the main audience hall in its centre (this was the largest room in the building — a kind of throne room for the local governor). It is identical in design to buildings known from the heart of the

Assyrian Empire and from sites within the area of Assyrian rule in northern Syria, such as Arslan Tash, Til Barsip and Zinjirli.[47]

Other features such as the ante-room of the audience hall (and especially the pair of door sockets which held the heavy double doors), the use of shallow niches, the thick plaster floor, the drainage system consisting of sections of terra-cotta pipes, and the thick walls of terre pisee — are all unmistakable characteristics of royal Assyrian architecture.

On the mound of Hazor itself, a tiny settlement was left after the Assyrian conquest, to which belong the meagre remains of Stratum IV. This settlement existed at the same time as the Assyrian residence northeast of the mound.

The citadel in Area B (Building 3002) (Fig. 12), attributed by the excavators to the Assyrians (Stratum III), should be assigned to a later date, to the end of the seventh or beginning of the sixth century B.C.[48] This building was also re-used in the Persian period and no datable pottery from its original phase of use has survived. A comparison of the citadel with a number of buildings in other areas under Assyrian rule reveals close parallels, especially with the upper building on the acropolis of Buseirah and the Assyrian building at Tell Halaf,[49] both of which were constructed on

45. On the enormous dimensions of the Assyrian cities, as well as the magnitude of the palaces within them, see Reich (above, n. 41), p. 4 (bottom) — a comparative plan with schematic plans represented in a uniform scale, of plans of cities in the Assyrian mainland, and in provinces in Syria and the Land of Israel.

46. P.L.O. Guy: Ayyelet Hashahar, *Bulletin of the Department of Antiquities of the State of Israel*, 5–6 (1957), pp. 19–20 (Hebrew); R. Reich: The Persian Building at Ayyelet Ha-Shahar: The Assyrian Palace of Hazor?, *IEJ* 25 (1975), pp. 233–237.

47. F. Thureau-Dangin *et al.*: *Arslan-Tash*, texte et atlas, Paris, 1931; G. Turner: The Palace and Batiment aux Ivoires at Arslan-Tash: A Reapprisal, *Iraq* 30 (1968), pp. 62–68; F. Thureau-Dangin and M. Dunand: *Til Barsip*, texte et album, Paris, 1936; F. von Luschan: *Ausgrabungen in Sendschirli*, I, Berlin, 1893, Tab. 22 (Upper Palace); R.C. Haines: *Excavations in the Plain of Antioch*, II [*OIP* 95], Chicago, 1969, pp. 61–63, Pl. 109.

48. *Hazor* I, pp. 45–54, Pls. XII, CLXXVII; *Hazor*, pp. 191–194.

49. C.M. Bennett: Excavations at Buseirah, Southern Jordan, 1974, Fourth Preliminary Report, *Levant* 9 (1977), pp. 1–4, Fig. 2; *Tell Halaf* II, pp. 203–221.

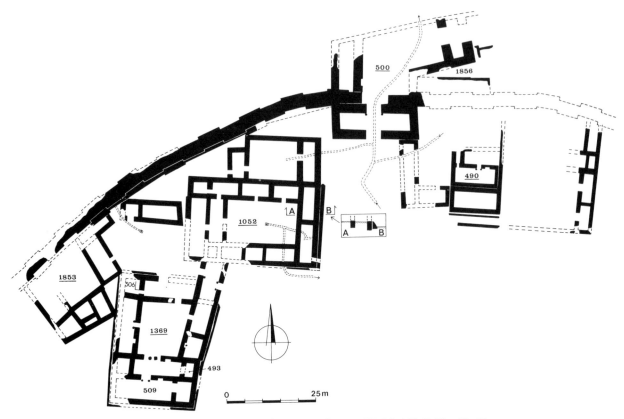

13. Megiddo, Assyrian palaces, Stratum III. *Megiddo* I, Figs. 71, 89.

the ruins of Assyrian structures. Building 3002 at Hazor is also very similar in plan to the houses in the Neo-Babylonian strata at Babylon (Merkes) and Ur.[50] Though the similarity in design between the buildings at Babylon and Ur and Building 3002 at Hazor enables us to lower the date of construction of the Hazor building to the sixth century B.C., archaeological data is lacking to determine whether this citadel was still in use by the Assyrians or whether it already belonged to the Babylonians. This question can be resolved only through an evaluation of the historical evidence.

Megiddo. — The remains of the buildings uncovered from Strata III-II[51] display a strong Assyrian influence

and were probably constructed following the conquest of the city by Tiglath-Pileser III. Two types of buildings can be distinguished here: private dwellings in the city built above the debris of the 'city of the stables' (Stratum IVA and see Chap. 24, Fig. 17); and a number of public buildings situated in the northern part of the city in the vicinity of the city-gate (Fig. 13). Unfortunately, no data are available to enable a comparison with the internal layout of the Assyrian city in Mesopotamia and Syria, and especially the organization of the houses, since practically no private dwellings from this period have been excavated there (these excavations concentrated primarily on palaces, temples and fortifications). Stratum III at Megiddo was planned and laid out according to the 'Hippodamian plan', i.e., the town was divided into blocks (insulae) by a system of streets running north-south and east-west. This geometric layout was apparently intended to enlarge the area available for private housing for a population which was larger than in the previous period.[52] Formerly,

50. O. Reuther: *Die Innenstadt von Babylon (Merkes)*, Leipzig, 1926, pp. 77–122, Tables 17, 19, 20, 22; L. Woolley: *Ur Excavations*, XI: *The Neo-Babylonian and Persian Periods*, London, 1962, pp. 41–48, Pls. 70, 71; and see also V. Fritz: Die Palaste Wahrend der Assyrischen, Babylonischen und Persischen Varherrschaft in Palastina, *MDOG* 111 (1979), pp. 63–74; *idem*, Palaste Wahrend der Brenze — und Eisenzeit in Palastina, *ZDPV* 99 (1983), pp. 1–42, especially pp. 20–42.

51. *Megiddo* I, pp. 62–69, Figs. 71–73, 89.

52. See Chap. 24.

Megiddo. Western area of site, Iron Age II. Shaft to water system on left; Assyrian planned town (Stratum III) with palaces, at top.

50% of the city area at most had been allocated for private housing, this was now increased to *ca.* 75%. No Assyrian influence can be distinguished in the plans of the private houses and it seems that the local population had built them within an urban plan that was dictated by the authorities.

The public buildings uncovered near the city-gate include Buildings 1052, 1369 and 1853 south of the gate[53] and Building 490 and the 'Nordburg' (from G. Schumacher's excavation)[54] east of the gate.

53. *Megiddo* I, pp. 69–74, Fig. 89.
54. *Tell el-Mutesellim* I, pp. 132–138; *Tell el-Mutesellim* II, Table XLIII.

Building 1369 consisted of a series of rooms around a large court. South of the court was the reception wing (Room 509 and the room north of it). The building was erected on a raised platform (podium)[55] 2 m. above its surroundings supported by a retaining wall. Podiums such as this were widespread in Assyria where they were known as *tamlu* (=*millo*, 'fill').[56] Although the remains of the walls that were uncovered were made of stones (incorporating some stones of the previous period in secondary use), there probably had been a mud-brick superstructure, as suggested by the excavators.

The reception wing in the south, as was noted above, followed an Assyrian design, with the exception of two stone slabs placed in the entrance on which stood columns to support the lintel. Columns in entrances are extremely rare in Assyrian architecture and here they probably represent a local solution (perhaps through the influence of northern Syrian architecture) to the problem of roofing the wide entranceway (*ca.* 4.4 m.). In Assyria and Babylonia a large brick arch would have been employed instead.

Additional Assyrian elements in the building include: narrow niches in the reception rooms (see also Room 490 in the adjoining building); a bathroom with a drainage system, with the drain hole set in a niche[57] (the room north of Room 493); thresholds with the doorpost sockets in a deep cavity covered with horseshoe-shaped stones[58] with moulded profile; a stairwell, the base of which was apparently uncovered in Room 506; a trapezoidal appearance to the building due to the angles not being entirely straight.

Building 1052 resembles Building 1369 in that it too contains a court surrounded on all sides by a row of rooms, with a double row on the western side in which the audience halls were situated. Despite this resemblance, Building 1052 seems to have been of a later date (at least its construction) than Building 1369 (unfortunately no study of the finds or further examination of the site can be made since the building was dismantled and removed in its entirety by the excavators). Details of this building have parallels in

Building 3002 at Hazor and in the upper building on the acropolis at Buseirah, and it is therefore possible that it was an addition to Building 1369 erected during the course of the seventh century B.C.

Several rooms were cleared in Building 490. This structure stood adjacent to the city-wall, near the gate. It, too, was constructed on an elevated platform which apparently continued about 5–7 m. beyond the line of the wall on the north side, reaching the road ascending to the city-gate, and was supported at this point by several retaining walls (uncovered in Locus 1856 and vicinity). No remains of the building have survived in the area of the wall or outside it. The estimated dimensions of the building are *ca.* 50 × 55 m.

This building, of which very meagre remains have been preserved, has the same location in the city as Assyrian buildings, though it is smaller in scale. Assyrian public buildings that were built on artificial platforms were also attached to the city-wall and in many instances part of the podium, and one wing of the palace standing on it, projected beyond the city outline (as, for example, Sargon's palace, Palace F at Khorsabad, Fort Shalmaneser at Nimrud, etc.). It seems that Building 490 in Megiddo follows this principle although on a smaller scale.

Several walls of this building may have been unearthed by Schumacher in the building known as the 'Nordburg', while its eastern extremity was excavated by the American expedition (Rooms 452–458).

Y. Aharoni compared Building 1369 at Megiddo with the upper palace at Zinjirli and the Residency at Lachish,[59] and considered this evidence of the Assyrian character of the latter, which in his opinion served as the residence of the Assyrian governor after the conquest of that city by Sennacherib.

The similarity between the Lachish Residency and the other two buildings is superficial, and a fundamental difference does in fact exist between their plans. The reception halls at Megiddo (Room 509 and the room north of it) and at Zinjirli were based on the early Assyrian plan:[60] the entrance is in one of the long walls, as in a broad-room, although the room functioned as a long-room, as in the building at Ayyelet Ha-Shahar. The reception hall of the Lachish Residency, on the other hand, belongs to the later

55. Building 1369 is elevated by means of a podium similar to Building 1052, *Megiddo* I, pp. 70–77, Figs. 81, 89, Section A-B; as is the case of the Assyrian citadel of Sheikh Zuweid (below, n. 68).

56. It seems that the building technique as well as the term were adopted here.

57. See the examples presented by Turner (above, n. 41), pp. 190–194.

58. Megiddo I, Fig. 84:1.

59. Y. Aharoni: *The Residency*, in *idem* (ed.), Investigations at Lachish (Lachish V), Tel Aviv, 1975, pp. 33–40.

60. G. Turner (above, n. 41), especially Type A (which serves in the palaces as a throne room) and Types B-E, of other state apartments.

type of plan[61] (which appears for the first time at the end of the Neo-Assyrian period [end of the seventh century B.C.] and is in frequent use in the Babylonian and Persian periods), in which both the entrance and the use of the hall are as in a broad-room, and the focus of the building is not in the large hall but in a small inner room, opposite the main entrance.

Samaria. — In the city of Samaria, which was conquered by Sargon, King of Assyria, and turned into the capital of the province of Samaria, no remains of Assyrian public buildings have been discovered. One possible explanation for their absence is that the ornate Israelite palaces were put to secondary use by the Assyrians, but it is also possible that the Assyrian architects established the military and civil centre in the plain beyond the mound, as at Hazor (the Assyrian residence found northeast of the tell at Ayyelet Ha-Shahar) and these buildings should be sought in that area.

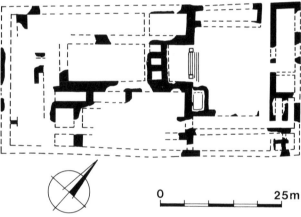

14. Buseireh (Transjordan) Area A (lower building). *Levant* IX (1977), p. 5, Fig. 3.

Gezer.[62] — Evidence for the existence of an Assyrian administrative building at this site from the second half of the seventh century B.C. is contained in two legal documents written in Akkadian. Architectural confirmation is provided by the remains of the

doorway of a building of which nothing else remains. On either side of the doorway is a horseshoe-shaped stone with moulded profile which covered cavities in the ground containing the stone door sockets. The discovery of these coverstones — a typical Assyrian element — close to the two cuneiform tablets, is conclusive evidence of the existence of an administrative Assyrian building.

Buseireh. — A number of public buildings were uncovered at this Transjordanian site (identified with the Edomite capital, Bosrah) which exhibit Assyrian architectural elements.[63] On the acropolis (Area A) two buildings were excavated, one above the ruins of the other. The lower one (Fig. 14) was a large-scale structure (38 × 77 m.) consisting of two suites of rooms disposed about two large courts. Room V-7 (5.3 × 9 m.), situated in a row of rooms between the courts, served as a temple as is attested by the following details: a wide staircase the full width of the room ascending to the floor which was raised above the court; two stone bases at the sides of the staircase which had originally held statues or cult objects (and not columns, as maintained by the excavators); the plan of the entrance being identical with that of Assyrian temples in the imperial centres (for example, at Khorsabad),[64] in the provinces under Assyrian rule (e.g. Tell Halaf)[65] and in the temple at Sheikh Zuweid (see below).

The building in the upper stratum (Fig. 15) is smaller (39 × 48 m.). It consists of a row of rooms around a single court and thus resembles the plan of Building 3002 in Area B at Hazor. Unfortunately, very few datable finds were discovered in the buildings at Buseirah, but the fact that the upper building was erected above a building containing Assyrian elements attests that the former should be assigned to the end of the seventh or the sixth century B.C.

Another building of a public character was discovered in Area C (dimensions *ca.* 67 × 105 m.), but only a small part of it has been excavated so far. The remains uncovered belong to a large hall, about 6.5 m. wide and about 14 m. long. An interesting

61. This type, as well, was discussed by Turner (above, n. 41), Type F, but Turner did not elaborate on the idea of the development of this type and its continuous use through the Neo-Babylonian and Persian periods. On this, see M. Roaf: The Diffusion of the 'Salle a Quatre Saillants', *Iraq* 35 (1973), pp. 83–93; P. Amiet: 'Quelques Observations sur le Palais de Darius a Suse', *Syria* 51 (1974), pp. 65–73; R. Ghirschman: L'architecture elamite et ses traditions, *Iranica Antiqua* 5 (1965), pp. 93–102.
62. R. Reich and B. Brandl: Gezer under Assyrian Rule, *PEQ* 117 (1985), pp. 41–54.

63. C.M. Bennett: Excavations at Buseirah, Southern Jordan, *Levant* 5 (1973), pp. 1–11; 6 (1974), pp. 1–24; 7 (1975), pp. 1–19; 9 (1977), pp. 1–10; *idem*, Some Reflections on Neo-Assyrian Influence in Transjordan, in R. Moorey and P. Parr (eds.): *Archaeology in the Levant, Essays for K.M. Kenyon*, Warminster, 1978, pp. 164–171.
64. *Khorsabad* I, Figs. 98, 119, 121, 123, pp. 114–122; *Khorsabad* II, pp. 56–64, Pls. 79, Rooms: 12, 14, 21, 23; 84.
65. R. Naumann (above, n. 49), pp. 349–357.

Comparison between buildings of the *Bit Hilani* type in Megiddo and Zinjirli (Northern Syria)

	Megiddo, Building 1723 Stratum IVB–VA	Megiddo, Building 6000 Stratum IVB–VA	Zinjirli Hilani III	Zinjirli Building K
Date	10th century BC	10th century BC	end of 8th century BC *Barrakub* period	end of 8th century BC *Barrakub* Palace
Outer measurements	22×23 m (excluding the outer platform)	21×28 m	28.5×32.5 m	25×26 m (excluding the staircase)
Number of columns in Portico	(2?)	(2?)	2	3
Entrance hall and its measurements	H, 2.75×5 m	3.5×14.25 m	A, 6×13.5 m	K-1, 6.2×16.8 m
Throne room and its measurements	K, 4.25×8 m	6×14.25 m	D, 8×20 m	K-2, 8.25×23.5 m
Tower and staircase	M, found	found	B, found	K-4, found
Number of Rooms	10–11	8	7	2 (additional rooms in the adjacent building)
Location in relation to the City's fortifications	Abbuting the southern city wall	Abutting the northern city wall	Abutting the acropolis wall on the west	In close proximity to the acropolis wall on the north
Courtyard	on the front	on the front (?) and on the west (?)	on the front	on the front, in common use with Building

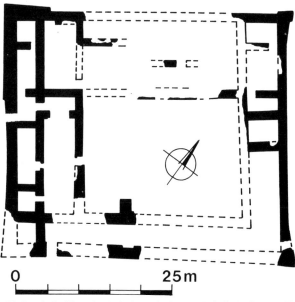

0   25m

15. Buseireh (Transjordan) Area A (upper building). Levant IX (1977), P. 4, Fig. 2.

feature linking this building to the Assyrian world is the broad shallow niche (0.5 × 2.5 m.). It lacked the layer of thick plaster covering the floor of the hall which indicates that it had originally held a stone

slab (later removed), so common in Assyrian audience halls.

These two buildings — the lower one in Area A and the partially excavated one in Area C — represent the two large public buildings erected at Buseirah after its conquest by the Assyrians, one serving as a residence, the other as a temple.

Building remains of a royal Assyrian character have also been unearthed in several sites in the northern Negev and in the northern part of Sinai. These include: *Tell Jemmeh.* — In excavations carried out by G. van Beek,[66] part of a building containing a number of adjoining rooms was uncovered (Fig. 16). Although a clear plan pointing to an Assyrian origin cannot yet be deduced from these remains, the building technique and the small finds (which include Assyrian 'Palace Ware') do attest to the source of influence. The building was constructed in its entirety — walls, floors and roof — of rectangular mud bricks, which were laid in headers and stretchers in the walls. The brick vaults were laid in the pitched brick technique, in which the vault was in fact composed of arches

66. G.W. Van Beek: Digging up Tell Jemmeh, *Archaeology* 36 (1983), pp. 12–19; *idem*, Arches and Vaults in the Ancient Near East, *Scientific American*. July 1987, pp. 78–85, 98.

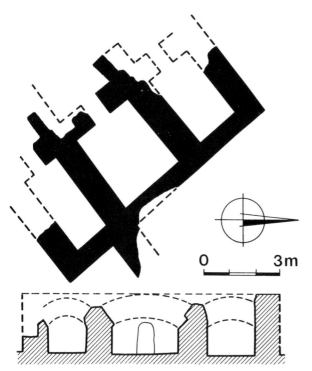

16. Assyrian building (section in which mud-brick arches are preserved), plan and cross section, Tell Jemmeh. *Qadmoniot* 6 (21) (1973), p. 25.

mities of the mound (Areas A and D, respectively) in Stratum VI which is attributed by the excavators to the seventh–sixth centuries B.C. These remains belong to a mud-brick structure consisting of thick walls (1–4.5 m.) with long narrow spaces between them. Its location at the edge of the mound indicates that it also had a defensive function. Finds (bronze, weapons and pottery) of Mesopotamian origin (Assyrian, Babylonian) were uncovered in the spaces between the walls and it is therefore possible that it served, in part, the Assyrian or Babylonian military administration. *Sheikh Zuweid.* — The fortress excavated by Flinders Petrie at Tell Abu Salima near Sheikh Zuweid (Fig. 17) was apparently built by the Assyrians as a defense against the Egyptians.[68] It consists of a series of rooms around a central court and was protected by an offset-inset wall with a stepped base in the outer face. The wall also supported an earth fill which raised the fortress above the terrain, as was common in Assyrian buildings. The construction material was sun-dried mud brick.

of square bricks (except for the keystone which is trapezoidal. The first arch is slightly inclined and rests on the back wall, and so with the other arches. The bricks were bonded with mud mortar and the joint strengthened by means of grooves made in the lower surface of the bricks. Since brick vaults are an extremely rare find due to poor preservation, parallels for this roof are difficult to find, but it can be assumed that many Assyrian buildings employed brick vaults for roofing the halls and some of the rooms. At Ayyelet Hashahar, for example, the long walls of the building are considerably thicker than the other walls and probably carried vaults of mud brick which have not survived.

At Tell Jemmeh a very low space was left beneath the vaults (about 1.40 m. in the centre of the vault) therefore the rooms in this level were probably not used for dwelling but for storage, and the vaults raised the level of the houses about 2.25 m. above the surface.

Tel Sera'.[67] — Massive building remains were uncovered here in the southern and northern extre-

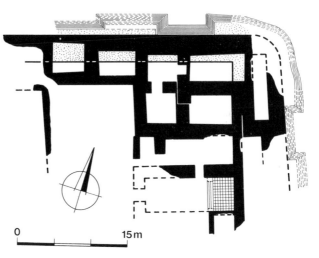

17. Fortress and Assyrian temple, Sheikh Zuweid (northern Sinai). *EI* XX (1989), p. 284, Fig. 2.

The identification of the site as Assyrian was based on the existence of a small temple (with a cella, 2.89 × 4.42 m.) which was erected for the use of the local Assyrian administration and army. The most distinctive Assyrian element here was the floor of

67. E. Oren: Esh-Shari'a, Tell, *EAEHL* IV, pp. 1060–1062, Figs. on p. 1068.

68. F. Petrie and J.C. Ellis: *Anthedon, Sinai*, London, 1937, pp. 6–7, Pls. II:7, X, XI, XXXI. On the identification of the site and the reconstruction of the plan of the citadel and Assyrian temple in it, see R. Reich: The Identification of the 'Sealed *Karu* of Egypt', *IEJ* 34 (1984), pp. 32–38.

RONNY REICH

the cella which was paved with square fired bricks (measuring 10.1 × 36.8 × 36.8 cm.). The steps leading to the cella were similarly paved. Two pedestals stood on either side of the steps, another widespread feature in Assyrian temples.[69]

69. See for example *Khorsabad* I: Pl. 76, Rooms 165, 166, 169, 142–143, 146–147, 173, 177, 192; *Khorsabad* II, Pl. 26:E, 18:A-C; *Tell Halaf* II, pp. 349–357, Fig. 165, Tables 66:1, 67:2.

Floors paved with fired bricks were a common element in Assyrian architecture, but so far this is the only example which has been uncovered from this period in Israel. As precise chronological data is lacking, perhaps these bricks can be used for dating purposes. They appear to be larger than the average-sized bricks employed in the Neo-Babylonian period and smaller than those from the ninth century B.C. In size, they seem to be closest to the bricks used in Mesopotamia in the eighth–seventh centuries B.C.

23 ADMINISTRATIVE STRUCTURES IN THE IRON AGE

Zeev Herzog

Within the urban system of Iron Age Israel, the most widespread structure used for administrative purposes was unquestionably the pillared building. Among the buildings found alongside it are long structures without pillars, public silos and structures which will be referred to here as scribes' chambers.

Pillared Buildings

Pillared buildings are a well-defined architectural group in the framework of Iron Age construction. They are rectangular and their space is divided longitudinally by pillars into three narrow halls. The flanking halls are generally paved with flagstones, and the floor in the central hall is beaten earth. Shallow troughs, made of a single stone with a depression on the top or of unhewn stones, are set in the spaces between the pillars. The entrance to the pillared building was generally in the short side, making its plan that of a longhouse. At several sites complexes of several adjoining pillared buildings have been uncovered, whereas at others there was only a single structure. To judge from their plan, these structures must have served some public function, other than that of dwellings. To date, pillared building have been found at the following eight Iron Age settlements.

Hazor[1]. A single pillared building was discovered at Hazor in Strata VIII–VII. It is 14 × 21 m. and is divided longitudinally into three halls by two rows of columns. The two flanking halls and the central hall are 2.4–2.6 m. and 3.6 m. wide, respectively. The columns are made of dressed stone and reach 2 m. in height. They are incorporated into a low wall of unhewn stone. Portions of stone flooring were found only in the flanking halls; the floor of the central

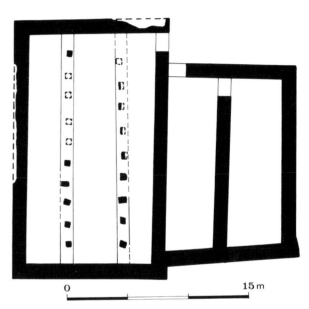

1. Hazor, Area A, Building 71a. *Hazor* II, Pl. CC, CCI.

hall was beaten earth. The finds in the building were meagre, sherds from a few vessels. The entrance to the building was in its narrow side, in the northwestern corner, so that upon entering the halls, one faced left. Abutting this pillared building on the north is another structure with rectangular rooms and stone floors, but there are no internal pillars. The uniformity of the orientation and thickness of the walls of the two structures shows that they were erected as part of a comprehensive plan (for their purpose, see below). The building was constructed in the eighth century B.C. (Fig. 1).

Tell Abu Hawam[2]. Building 33–35 in Stratum IVB at Tell Abu Hawam has three long halls, each one

1. *Hazor*, II, pp. 5–8, Pls. CC, CCI (Hebrew).

2. R. W. Hamilton: Excavations at Tell Abu Hawam, *QDAP* 4 (1935), pp. 8–10, Pls. IV, VII:1, 2.

9 × 11 m. The entrance to the building was in the middle of its narrow side, but it was blocked in a later phase. The two inner walls consist of a socle of unhewn stones surmounted by segmented stone columns that were preserved to a height of 1.5 m. The building was destroyed by a violent conflagration. On its floors several clay vessels were found, including a storage jar, jugs, cooking pots, and sherds from a bowl. The stratum is largely from the end of the eleventh century.

Megiddo[3]. In the original phase of Stratum IV at Megiddo (designated IVB by this writer, see Chap. 24, p. 254, Fig. 16 below), seventeen units of pillared buildings were uncovered in four groups. The northern block includes two parallel units, with five pillared building in each (407 and 364) and an eastern unit of only two buildings (403–404). The southern block also has five pillared building (1576) with a large square adjacent courtyard. The dimensions of the pillared buildings are not uniform, the length of the units varying from 22 to 26.5 m., and their width varying from 11 to 12.5 m. The quality of the construction of the pillared buildings and the installations between them at Megiddo is the highest among the examples cited here. Each pillar was made from a single block, square in section, as are the installations between them; the latter are 1.2 m. long and have a rectangular depression 0.12–0.15 m. deep on the top. At Megiddo, as at the other sites, both the pillars and the troughs were constructed above foundations of unhewn stone. In some of the pillars holes had been drilled diagonally through the corners, usually on the side facing the central hall.

In each unit of the pillared buildings there is only one opening which led to the central hall. Passage from that hall to the flanking halls was effected only in the space between the first column and the outer wall. The buildings at Megiddo were empty but for some individual objects.[4]

Tell Qasile[5]. A pillared building, 9 × 14 m., was uncovered at Tell Qasile, Stratum X, in the southern part of the mound. The building was only partially preserved, but it may be included in this category. Although the entrance was not found, the building is located at the corner of two streets, therefore entrance was probably through the long northern wall or the short western wall. Stratum X was occupied by the Philistines in the latter half of the eleventh century.

Bet Shemesh[6]. At Bet Shemesh a structure that can be reconstructed as a pillared building was uncovered in Stratum IIA. It is 13 × 18 m. and is divided by two rows of pillars set on unhewn stone bases. The width of the flanking halls and the central hall are 2.4 m. and 3 m., respectively. The entrance was not located, but it can be reconstructed in the northwestern corner. The stratum is dated to the first half of the tenth century.

Tell el-Hesi[7]. A complex of three adjoining pillared buildings was discovered in City V, in the northern part of the mound of Tell el-Hesi. Rectangular monoliths 0.4 × 0.8 m. divided each building into three halls. The width of the halls is not uniform, except in the middle building where they are 2.2 to 2.5 m. The overall dimensions of this house are 12.5 × 16 m. Owing to the proximity of the structure to the edge of the mound, the entrance could only have been in the southern wall, which was the shortest. The date of City V is the tenth or early ninth century.[8]

Beersheba. An almost complete complex of three pillared buildings was uncovered at Beersheba in Stratum II (see Chap. 24, Fig. 19). It was first built in Stratum III, during the ninth century. The complex is adjacent to the city-gate, and the facade of each building faces the street, as does the doorway of each halls were sunk *ca.* 0.4 m. below the level of the street divided the buildings into three halls, with a separate doorway for each hall. The width of the central hall and the flanking halls were about 2 m. and 2.5 m. respectively. The cobblestone floors in the flanking halls were sunk ca. 0.4 m. below the level of the street and below the floor of the central hall, which was beaten earth. Stratum II was destroyed by a violent conflagration that completely buried the building. Most of the finds were in the paved flanking halls, although some were also scattered in the central hall of each building. The finds include many clay and stone household vessels, figurines, mallets, metal tools (knives, an axe, and arrowheads), bone tools, a stone altar, and two ostraca[9] (Fig. 2).

3. *Megiddo*, I, pp. 32–47.
4. For the register of finds in the pillared buildings at Megiddo, see V. Fritz: Bestimmung und Herkunft des Pfeilerhaus in Israel, *ZDPV* 93 (1977), pp. 38–39.
5. B. Mazar: Tell Qasile, *EAEHL* IV, pp. 971–974.
6. *'Ain Shems* II-III, Plan of the Iron Age (II-III), *'Ain Shems* I-II, p. 15.
7. F. D. Bliss: *A Mound of Many Cities*, London, 1894, pp. 90–98.
8. R. Amiran: Tell Hesi, *EAEHL* II, p. 517.
9. The finds from the storehouse were studied by L. Singer of the Institute of Archaeology, Tel Aviv University, and published in *Beer-Sheba* II.

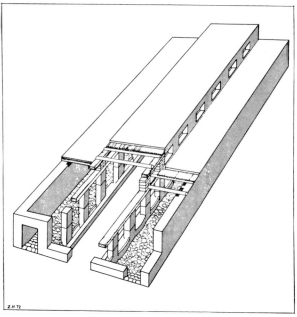

2. Storehouse. ***Beer-Sheba*** I, p. 27, Fig. 2.

Tel Malhata[10] *and Tel Masos*[11]. Two structures uncovered at the neighbouring sites of Tel Malhata and Tel Masos include a variant of the pillared building, whose most salient feature is the narrowness of the central space (only 0.9–1 m.). In Structure 1039 at Tel Masos (Stratum II, from the twelfth-eleventh centuries), the row of pillars does not extend along the entire length of the building, but abuts a wall at its southern end. The pillared building at Tel Malhata is part of a larger structure that has not been completely excavated. However, it is possible to discern, in addition to the pillared building, a long hall with a cobblestone floor and four small rooms. The structure belongs to Stratum II (tenth century).[12]

The Superstructure of the Pillared Building. — In reconstructing the superstructure of the pillared building, the main problems are whether the central space was roofed and, accordingly, the purpose of the rows of pillars. The excavators of Megiddo decided that the central space had a roof supported by pillars that was higher than the roofs of the flanking spaces. This allowed light and air to enter the long halls through windows along the raised walls — the clerestory principle in Egyptian architecture. This author has proposed the same reconstruction for the pillared building at Beersheba. V. Fritz recently suggested a second possibility: that the central space was an unroofed court.[13] He believes that this was the only way in which the flanking rooms could have been lighted and ventilated. Fritz also claims that the pillars could not have supported real walls. The first proposal is more plausible because the exposure of the central space to sun, wind, and rain would have rendered the flanking halls useless. In this way the pillared building differs from the four-room house: in the latter, the room that is separated from the court by the row of pillars was a work and storage area; it was the living area. The assertion that the pillars could not have supported walls is not necessarily valid, and at any rate, there are no walls. Rather, the pillars were raised to the height of the ceiling of the central hall, and the spaces between them acted as windows to admit light and air into the flanking spaces. (For a different reconstruction, see Chap. 21, p. 198, n. 17).

The Function of the Pillared Building. — There are various scholarly opinions about the function of pillared buildings: that they were stables, storehouses, or barracks — in other words, it was a basic type of building that could be adapted to various purposes. However, it seems more likely that the plan of the buildings limited their function. Assuming that the structure's plan was a response to specific problems that faced the planner, rather than its having been modelled after other structures, it remains to discover the function most suited to its design and to what extent the excavated finds fit the attributed purpose.

The long narrow shape of the building suggests that it was an administrative rather than a residential unit.[14] The tripartite division of the halls by two rows of pillars and the different paving materials (earth in the central space and stone in the two flanking halls) indicate their different uses. The excavators of Megiddo, who hypothesized that the buildings were stables, suggested that chariots were kept in the central space. However, the buildings should be identified as storehouses, with the central space used for loading and unloading the goods and products stored there.

10. M. Kochavi: The First Season of Excavations at Tell Malhata, *Qadmoniot* 3 (1970), pp. 22–24 (Hebrew).

11. A. Kempinski *et al.*: The Excavations at Tel Masos: A Summary of Three Seasons of Excavations (1972, 1974, 1975), *EI* 15 (1981), p. 159 (Building 1039) (Hebrew).

12. *Ibid.*, p. 177.

13. Fritz (above, n. 4), p. 41. The excavators of Megiddo note that they found remains of a roof over the central hall (Room 1483). See *Megiddo* I, p. 39.

14. The existence of an architectural group distinct from the four-room house was first dealt with by Y. Shiloh: The Four-Room House, its Situation and Function in the Israelite City, *IEJ* 20 (1970), pp. 182–183.

Megiddo. Iron Age II, Southern Administrative Complex ('Stables' No. 1576 with central courtyard, and Building 1482 at bottom).

It is obvious that the flanking halls were the building's main areas — that is, stables or storehouses. The idea that they were stables is based largely on the troughs or mangers between the pillars and on the tethering holes in the pillars, even though the plan of the halls seems to militate against the hypothesis. First, there is the problem of how the horses exited the building. The narrowness of the hall would have prevented easy passage, and in the event of an urgent need to take care of the last horse, all the animals between that horse and the entrance would have had to have been led out.[15] Furthermore, at Megiddo there are no doorways leading directly from the outside to

15. The excavators of Megiddo have already dealt with this problem. See *Megiddo* I, p. 37.

226

the flanking halls; hence the horses would have had to manoeuvre at the end of the hall and make two right-angle turns in very close quarters. This would clearly have been·a strange arrangement for a stable, especially as it was feasible to have separate doorways leading directly outside.[16] (Such openings have only found been at Beersheba.)

Another feature that makes it difficult to accept the hypothesis that the pillared buildings were stables is the lack of drainage in the flanking halls. The presence of fifteen horses in a single hall, as proposed by the excavators of Megiddo, would have meant the accumulation of large quantities of urine and droppings that, without proper drainage, would have endangered the health of the animals. None of the pillared buildings surveyed had drainage channels for the flanking halls, and at Beersheba the floors of those halls were some 0.5 m below street level. Additional flaws in the stable theory are the danger of slipping and the possibility that such a structure would make the horses uneasy.[17]

By contrast, the plan of these structures would have suited storehouses, the biblical *bet ha-miskenot*. The division of the flanking halls from the central hall would have facilitated the separation of tasks for those responsible for the warehouse and those who received the goods. The spaces between the pillars could have been used as counters for receiving or delivering goods and, at the same time, served to admit light and air from the clerestory windows. The paving in the flanking halls would have insulated the floor from the damp ground, while the long, narrow shape of the rooms permitted the orderly storage of products along the walls.

The mangers and tethering holes in the pillars were the pivotal evidence in favor of the theory that the pillared buildings at Megiddo were stables. However, the argument can be made that these installations also belong in storehouses; since goods were usually transported on beasts of burden (donkeys and mules),

it can be assumed that caravans of laden animals were taken inside the central hall. During unloading and reloading, the animals would have been tethered to the pillars and fed or watered after their long journey.[18] The few droppings that would have accumulated could have been removed as soon as the caravan departed.[19] It is possible that the spacious courts inside the pillared buildings, like the court discovered at Megiddo, were a loading place for the caravans or army units that took on supplies there.

Finally, the interpretation of the use of the buildings must be correlated with the finds discovered in them. It is instructive that not one of the buildings uncovered so far has yielded a single object that would suggest its identification as a stable. By contrast, the many potsherds found in them, especially in the pillared buildings at Beersheba, as already noted, clearly indicate that the buildings were used for storage and not as stables.

The abundant finds at Beersheba are another important source for understanding the use and operation of Iron Age storehouses. From the varied ceramic assemblage found in the pillared buildings (which are distinctly different from the assemblages found in the dwellings),[20] it is clear that various foodstuffs were stored in each of the halls, together with implements for grinding flour, various clay vessels, and stone and bone tools. These were part of the goods in the storehouses and were meant for distribution to government officials or for sale. In light of the finds from Beersheba, the storehouse was a vital and versatile institution meant to meet the

16. It should be noted that the existence of the side door in the pillared building at Hazor was one of the arguments (in addition to the finds of the structure) against its identification as a stable, despite the architectural resemblance to the pillared buildings at Megiddo. See *Hazor* II, p. 8. However, such a doorway might have saved one turn and therefore could have been more convenient for the horses if indeed this were a stable.

17. The observations on the lack of drainage, the danger of slipping, and upsetting the horses if the pillared buildings were, in fact, stables, were made by Mrs. M. Littauer, an expert in the military uses of horses in the ancient Near East, in a letter to Prof. A. Rainey dated October 4, 1975. The writer thanks Mrs. Littauer for her permission to quote her remarks here.

18. Z. Herzog: The Storehouses, in *Beer-Sheba* I, p. 29. In a critique of the identification of the Megiddo structures as stables, J.B. Pritchard stressed the architectural problems but did not propose a convincing solution for the mangers and the holes in the pillars. See J. B. Pritchard: The Megiddo Stables: A Reassessment, in J.A. Sanders (ed.): *Near Eastern Archaeology in the Twentieth Century, Essays in Honor of Nelson Glueck*, New York, 1970, pp. 268–276.

19. In considering this interpretation, the late Y. Yadin maintained that the animal droppings were the main difficulty. See Y. Yadin: The Megiddo Stables, *EI* 12 (1975), p. 62 (Hebrew). Because Yadin proposed to explain the broad steps in the water system at Hazor as accommodating beasts of burden transporting water, the question has to be asked whether the droppings in the storeroom at Beersheba from the brief time the caravan stopped there, could have been more noxious than the droppings in Hazor's water system. See Y. Yadin: *Hazor the Head of All Those Kingdoms*, Tel Aviv, 1975, p. 247 (Hebrew).

20. The contrast is obvious in the comparative research on these assemblages in *Beer-Sheba* II.

complex needs of the administrative units located in the city or to hold the supplies they required.[21]

Public Silos

In addition to structures for storing and distributing foodstuffs, special installations were required to store large quantities of grain. For this purpose large public silos were built, some of which have been uncovered in several Iron Age cities. The silos are round, which probably facilitated filling and emptying them efficiently (there were no corners to catch the grain). The silos were dug into the ground and could be emptied only from above. As a result it was not possible to ensure the use of the oldest grain first. Silos in granaries built above ground were filled from above and emptied through an opening below.

The largest silo was discovered at Megiddo, in Stratum II, assigned to the period of Assyrian rule.[22] It is lined with unhewn stones, and its diameter narrows towards the bottom; its upper diameter is 11 m., its lower diameter is 7 m., and its depth is 7 m., making its total volume about 450 cu. m. Two staircases were installed along its sides. The excavators hypothesized that there were two staircases to avoid collision; some workers could descend while others ascended. This explanation is implausible because the workers descending into the silo would have had to cross the middle of the silo when it was full of grain. It therefore makes better sense to assume that by using two staircases the grain could be emptied rapidly when necessary. It is possible, for example, that large quantities of grain were needed by the Assyrian army in its campaigns to Philistia and Egypt (see Chap. 22 above).

A smaller silo was uncovered at Bet Shemesh, Stratum II.[23] It is oval with upper diameters of 7.5 m. and 6.5 m. Its depth and volume are about 4 m. and 150 cu. m., respectively. Two silos, each with a diameter of 3 m., were uncovered near the northern complex of the storehouses at Megiddo in Stratum IVB (Nos. 414 and 415) that were undoubtedly meant for grains in bulk.[24]

At Tell en-Nasbeh, at the end of the tenth century B.C., a different storage method was used. Scores of small silos, ranging in diameter from 1.2–2 m., were dug in an extension of the city created by the erection of a solid wall. The concentration of silos in this extended area is evidence that they also served the needs of the royal administration (see Chap. 24 below).

'Treasuries'

In the Bible, in addition to 'storehouses', or *miskenot*, the term *osarot*, 'treasuries' is found. Unlike storehouses which are 'for the yield of grain, wine, and oil' (II Chronicles 32:28), treasuries are meant for storing weapons and precious metals: 'he made for himself treasuries for silver, for gold, for precious stones, for spices, for shields, and for all kinds of costly vessels' (II Chronicles 32:27). It seems reasonable to identify the treasuries with another type of administrative building — different from the pillared building but also used for storage — namely, the long, narrow structures without rows of pillars that have been uncovered in several Iron Age cities. The structural difference between the two types of buildings is readily accounted for by their different uses. Whereas the pillared buildings were for storage and perhaps also for the preparation of foodstuffs (which made ventilation and lighting essential), mostly metal objects, such as weapons, would have been stored in the treasuries, as they required neither ventilation nor lighting. Although there is no archaeological evidence to support the hypothesis, metal objects would have been kept in sealed rooms and removed from the treasuries only in an emergency or by an enemy plundering the city.

Examples of this type of hall were uncovered in the area of the acropolis at Lachish, north of the palace. They were assigned to Stratum IV (the reign of Rehoboam). In the northwestern corner of the area there were apparently six halls (only three of which have been excavated), about 30 m. long and 4 m. wide (see Chap. 22 above, Fig. 7). Pillarless halls were also uncovered alongside the pillared buildings at Hazor,[25] in Strata VIII–VII. The fact that both

21. On the basis of the varied finds, Yadin *EI* 12 (above, n. 19) and Fritz (above, n. 4) proposed that the 'storehouse' at Beersheba was an 'army barracks'. This theory apparently arose from the mistaken assumption that storehouses must contain nothing but storage vessels. On the other hand, after studying the quantity of vessels found in the storehouses, and especially their total number after they were restored from sherds, it is inconceivable that there would have been enough room in the building to billet regular army units as well. At most they could have housed the officials responsible for guarding the goods in the storehouses.

22. *Megiddo* I, pp. 66–68, Fig. 72, 77.

23. *'Ain Shems* V, pp. 70–71.

24. *Megiddo* I, p. 47, Fig. 49.

25. Hazor, II, p. 6, Pls. CL–CCI.

units share a wall is evidence that they were planned at the same time. The inner dimensions of the halls at Hazor are 4 × 14 m.

The long, narrow rooms in the so-called Ostraca House at Samaria should also be interpreted as treasuries, as should the long-room in Building 1482 at Megiddo VA. In Stratum IVB, the long-rooms in Building 401 (which is not divided by rows of pillars), near Palace 338, must have served the same purpose.[26] If these interpretations are correct, it can be said that treasuries are always in close association with an official palace in the capital city (Samaria) or in the main administrative centres (Lachish, Hazor, and Megiddo).

'Scribes' Chambers'

Following S. Yeivin, the term 'scribes' chambers' is used in this discussion to refer to a special type of administrative building that has been uncovered at Samaria, Megiddo, and Hazor in the vicinity of the royal palaces.[27] Their administrative character is apparent not only from their location, but also from their symmetrical plan and the difference between them and typical Iron Age dwellings.[28] Some evidence of their use comes from the excavations at Samaria, where scores of administrative documents were found in the building consequently dubbed the 'Ostraca House'.[29] This find is sufficient evidence that the building was used by official scribes and should be identified with the biblical 'scribes' chamber' (Jeremiah 36:10, 12, 20, 21).

The plan of the scribes' chamber is a basic unit that could be doubled or tripled. Each unit included a long, narrow corridor (or inner court), on the long sides of which were doorways to two or three square, or nearly square, rooms (Fig. 3).

The earliest of these chambers is Building 1482 at Megiddo.[30] It was first built to full scale in Stratum VA (Fig. 4) (according to the terminology adopted by this writer, Chap. 24 below), and continued in use

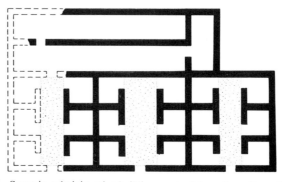

3. Samaria, administrative buildings west of the palace. *Samaria-Sebaste* I, Pl. II.

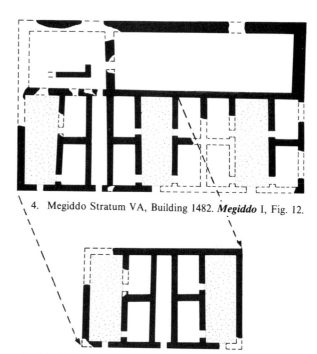

4. Megiddo Stratum VA, Building 1482. *Megiddo* I, Fig. 12.

5. Megiddo Stratum IVB, Building 1482. *Megiddo* I, Fig. 34.

on a smaller scale in Stratum IVB (Fig. 5). In the first phase its overall outer dimensions were about 19 × 35 m. This included two spaces on the western side (which may have been treasuries) and three units of chambers on the eastern side. The two reconstructed northern chambers included a central court and a pair of rooms on each side, while the southern chamber comprised a court and only two rooms. It is possible that the narrow space, 1482, served as a corridor-passageway to the western rooms. In Stratum IVB, near the southern complex of pillared buildings and Structure 1482, the scribes' chamber was reduced in size; it continued to serve its original purpose, but without the western wing. The treasury rooms were probably moved to Building 401 in the northeastern

26. The dimensions of the rooms are about 3.5 × 14 m. See *Megiddo I*, p. 47, Fig. 49.

27. M. Avi-Yonah and S. Yeivin: *Antiquities of Israel*, Tel Aviv, 1955, p. 18 (Hebrew).

28. Unlike residential buildings, these structures have no rear living space. In addition, the division of the spaces on the sides of the courtyard into symmetrical chambers is not common in residential buildings.

29. G. A. Reisner, C. S. Fisher, and D. G. Lyon: *Harvard Excavations at Samaria 1908–1910*, Cambridge, Mass., 1924, pp. 114–117, Fig. 42.

30. *Megiddo*, I, pp. 24–27, Figs. 12, 34.

Beersheba. Iron Age II storehouse.

part of the city when the governor's palace (Building 338) was moved. The dimensions of the building in this phase were 11 × 19 m.; it included only two units, each of which comprised a court and a pair of rooms alongside it. The two phases at Megiddo date to the tenth century B.C. The example at Samaria is from the ninth century (Fig. 3).[31] The Ostraca House at Samaria had three units (although there, as at

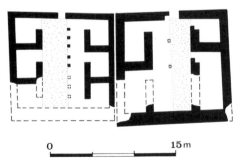

6. Hazor Area B, Buildings 3067, 3100. *Hazor* II, Pl. CCIV.

Megiddo, the northern unit is reconstructed). Each unit comprised a court and three square rooms on each side. East of these chambers were long, narrow rooms that may have been treasuries. The external dimensions of each building are 11.3 × 31.8 m.; each room is about 2.5 × 3 m.

Two scribes' chambers were uncovered at Hazor (Fig. 6), in Stratum VB, from the eighth century.[32] From their plan it is clear that they were built separately and that there are differences in their outer measurements, in the thickness of their walls, and in the number and size of their flanking rooms. Nonetheless, their basic plan is similar: each unit has a broad court divided in two by a row of stone pillars, with a row of rooms on each side. The western building measures 13 × 13.7 m and has two rectangular rooms on each side; the eastern building measures 12.4 × 12.6 m. and has three rooms on each side. The row of pillars in the courts is evidence that part of the court was covered and probably used as a shaded work area.

31. Above, n. 29.

32. *Hazor* II, pp. 40–42, 50, Pl. CCIV.

24

SETTLEMENT AND FORTIFICATION PLANNING IN THE IRON AGE

Zeev Herzog

The study of settlement planning in the Land of Israel is subject to a number of limitations.[1] First, the

1. Among the earlier studies which have dealt with settlement planning should be mentioned Lampl's comprehensive but not exhaustive book which confines itself to presenting settlement plans without analysing them. See P. Lampl: *Cities and Planning in the Ancient Near East*, New York, 1968. The first analysis of the Iron Age city was made by Y. Shiloh who defined the characteristics and principles of the Israelite city in 1970 — Y. Shiloh: The Four-Room House, its Situation and Function in the Israelite City, *IEJ* 20 (1970), pp. 180–190. Later Shiloh characterized several phases in the development of the Israelite city — *idem*, Elements in the Development of Town Planning in the Israelite City, *IEJ* 28 (1978), pp. 36–51. Mention should also be made of Shiloh's discussion of estimates of population density in Iron Age cities and his attempts to determine the average number of persons per dwelling unit and per dunam — *idem*, The Population of Iron Age Palestine in the Light of a Sample Analysis of Urban Plans, Areas and Population Density, *BASOR* 239 (1980), pp. 25–35. The author has made a study of the planning principles at Beersheba in Stratum II as an example of a planned Israelite city, and used it as the basis for an attempt to distinguish between groups of cities and settlements reflecting various degrees of planning — Z. Herzog: Israelite City Planning Seen in the Light of Beer-Sheba and Arad Excavations, *Expedition* 20 (1978), pp. 38–43. The problem regarding the existence of fortifications in the Iron Age I was recently discused by A. Mazar in connection with his excavations at Giloh — A. Mazar: Giloh, an Early Iron Settlement Site Near Jerusalem, *IEJ* 31 (1981), pp. 1–36. On Iron Age II fortifications, first and foremost the comprehensive studies of Y. Yadin and E. and S. Yeivin must be cited — Y. Yadin: *The Art of Warfare in the Biblical Lands in the Light of Archaeological Study, Jerusalem and Ramat-Gan, 1963 (Hebrew); E. and S. Yeivin: The Ancient Fortifications in the Land of Israel, in Y. Liver (ed.): The Military History of the Land of Israel in Biblical Times*, Jerusalem, 1964, pp. 362–399 (Hebrew). The fortifications of the city-gate were briefly summarized by E. Stern: The Fortified City Gate and the Struggle for it under the Monarchy, *ibid.*, pp. 400–409 (Hebrew) and summarized at length by Z. Herzog: *Das Stadttor in Israel und in den Nachbarlandern*, Mainz-am-Rhine, 1986.

excavated area at many sites is too small to permit the study of planning principles in the settlement. Second, there are difficulties in analysing sites at which the stratigraphy has not been properly discerned, for example, at Tell en-Nasbeh. Third, for many of the sites, no overall plan has been prepared or published, or the excavation plans were published according to different scales as at 'Ai and Bet Shemesh (Iron Age I) and Megiddo. This chapter emphasizes the general principles of planning by integrating excerpts of separately published plans into a single plan with a uniform scale and topographical features. In addition, an attempt will be made to reconstruct areas not yet excavated, or since destroyed.[*]

The following discussion distinguishes between the Iron Age I (twelfth–eleventh centuries B.C.) and the Iron Age II (tenth–sixth centuries B.C.) which represent two different conceptions of settlement planning. The Iron Age I is characterized by a low level of planning and an absence of public buildings and fortifications, as expected of a society in the process of settlement. The Iron Age II is notable for the planning of its fortifications and public buildings alongside residential buildings, appropriate to a stratified urban society with economic, military, and religious institutions. The settlement models from each of these phases of the Iron Age will be classified by types in an attempt to broaden the discussion beyond the above-mentioned, commonly accepted generalizations.

The Iron Age I (Twelfth–Eleventh Centuries B.C.

The number of settlements from this period which have been completely exposed is quite small. A study

* The plans in this article were prepared by Mrs. Yehudit Dekel.

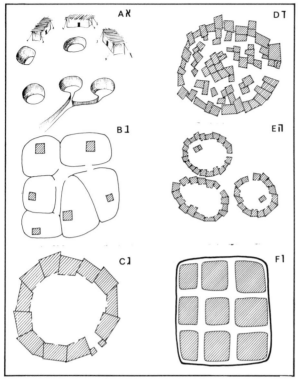

1. Schematic Iron Age I settlement models.

of the various sites reveals considerable architectural differences between settlements during the same period, although occasionally the concentration of one settlement model in a specific geographical area indicates the existence of a particular ethnic group in that area. The appearance of settlements composed of huts and pits (see below) in many areas of the Land of Israel indicates that this settlement type was, from the very beginning, part of the settlement process. Single-period sites such as 'Ai, Tel Masos and Giloh will also aid in developing this study.

The settlement models of the Iron Age I may be classified into seven types: 1. settlements of huts and pits; 2. clusters of pens; 3. enclosed settlements; 4. Israelite settlement villages; 5. clusters of enclosures; 6. planned cities; 7. Canaanite cities and Egyptian administrative centres.

Settlements of Huts and Pits

The geographic distribution of these settlements extends over the northern valleys, the hill country, the Sharon Plain and the Negev. In these settlements, of which some were built on top of ruined Canaanite settlements and others on mounds unoccupied in

the Late Bronze Age, there were strata which were devoid of building remains except for pits. These pits contained finds which indicated that they served a population which resided on the site. In the vicinity of some of the pits there are various installations, particularly cooking ovens. It is commonly accepted that huts or tents, remains of which have not been preserved, were the dwellings while the pits served as silos (Fig. 1A).

In Stratum IX at Tel Beersheba, seven pits were exposed; they reached a depth of over 3 m.[2] In at least one pit (No. 1321) there was clear evidence that it was used as a dwelling. In Stratum VI at Tel Dan, twenty-five silos were found,[3] one of which was full of pottery, mostly storage jars. At Hazor[4] many pits were found in Stratum XII, some of which were originally lined with stone, and next to which were found remains of huts. Pits and depressions for hut poles were uncovered at Tell Deir 'Alla in an early phase of the Iron Age.[5] Pits were also uncovered at Tel Zeror[6] and Tel Burgeta,[7] both in the Sharon Plain, at Tell Beit Mirsim (Stratum 1B)[8] and Tel Masos.[9] The wide distribution of hut settlements leads to the conclusion that this model of settlement was used by a population in the transition stage from nomadism to permanent settlement.

Clusters of Pens

It is possible that the long walls uncovered at Giloh,[10] south of Jerusalem, were the walls of sheep pens inside which were also dwellings, although the excavator has interpreted some of the segments of the exposed walls as remains of a city-wall. It seems that the settlement at Giloh comprised five pens which served as dwellings for five families and their herds (Fig. 1B). It may be surmised that similar pens also existed at other sites

2. The pits were hewn in the conglomerate bedrock, *Beer-Sheba* II.
3. A. Biran: Tell Dan, Five Years Later, *BA* 43 (1980), pp. 173–177.
4. *Hazor*, pp. 120–130.
5. H.J. Franken: *The Excavations at Tell Deir 'Alla*, I, Leiden, 1969, pp. 33–43.
6. K. Ohata: *Tel Zeror*, Tokyo, 1967, pp. 16–19, Pl. V.
7. R. Gofna: *Notes on the Archaeological Survey of Emek Hefer*, Emek Hefer, 1970, p. 12 (Hebrew).
8. *Tell Beit Mirsim* I, pp. 53–61.
9. A. Kempinski *et al.*: The Excavations at Tel Masos, 1972, 1974, 1975, *EI* 15 (1981), p. 158 (Hebrew).
10. See Mazar (above, n. 1). A good parallel for this model, cited by A. Shmueli, is a Beduin settlement east of Bethlehem (which is also located close to Giloh) — A. Shmueli: *Nomadism about to Cease*, Tel Aviv, 1980, Picture 3 on p. 81 (Hebrew).

in the hill country. The relative paucity of dwellings at Giloh may be evidence that the settlement on the site was in the earliest stages of permanent settlement.

Enclosed Settlements

This type of settlement is characterized by dwellings encircling a central court. This layout affords the settlement protection even without a freestanding system of fortifications.[11] A good example of an enclosed settlement is found in Stratum VII at Tel Beersheba (Fig. 2).[12] The main characteristics are: 1. the contours of the settlement fit the conditions of the location, preferably on a slope, probably for protection against high winds; 2. the dwellings are adjacent to one another;[13] 3. the centre of the settlement served as a court, probably for penning

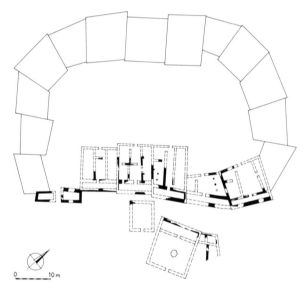

2. Beersheba Stratum VII. *Beer-Sheba* II, Figs. 2, 6.

the herds of the residents at night. The houses are of uniform size with no public buildings among them. The entrance was placed in a space intentionally left between two houses and was sometimes guarded by two rooms that made the passage narrower. Similar settlements which are characteristic of the Negev and Judah and the wilderness of Beersheba were discovered at Hatira, Refed, and Rahba.[14] A larger settlement was discovered at Tel Esdar.[15] Settlements of this type have been discovered in other areas as well: Izbet Sartah, in western Samaria,[16] and Horvat 'Avot in the Upper Galilee.[17] Apparently in all these areas the settlements were built in this way essentially for defense, a need which grew out of the expansion and consolidation of Israelite settlement in the eleventh century B.C.[18]

The prototype of these settlements is probably to be found in the Canaanite settlements which were built in a similar fashion,[19] for example, Megiddo Strata VIIB and VIIA in which the governor's palace and the adjoining buildings served as a defensive belt (Fig. 3). It does not seem reasonable to identify the prototype of this model as a nomadic settlement surrounded by a ring of tents.[20]

Israelite Settlement Villages

Unlike the enclosed settlements, the Israelite settlement villages are characterized by the fact that every area of the settlement is covered with dwellings which have no central court. It may be surmised, therefore, that these settlements evolved as a result of the transition to permanent settlement, increasing the utilization of the land for cultivation while decreasing the extent of sheep and cattle herding.[21] Settlements of this type were discovered at 'Ai and Bet Shemesh.

11. Z. Herzog: Enclosed Settlements in the Negeb of Judah and the Wilderness of Beer-sheba, *BASOR* 250 (1983), pp. 41–49.
12. For a full report see *Beer-Sheba* II.
13. For a detailed discussion of this problem see Herzog (above, n. 11). In Beersheba and elsewhere dwellings are of the four-room house type or one of its subtypes, though the fact that the back rooms of these houses are broad-rooms may mislead us into thinking that this is a casemate wall. For this reason some of the settlements in the Negev have been erroneously termed 'fortresses'. However, a detailed examination of the plans shows that the dwellings were built as freestanding units without any continuation of the facade line or of the inner wall. It should also be recalled that for the early settlers, the casemates were houses in every sense.

14. Herzog (above, n. 11).
15. M. Kochavi: The Excavations at Tel Asdar, *'Atiqot* (Hebrew Series) 5 (1969), pp. 14–48.
16. M. Kochavi and I. Finkelstein: Isbet Sartah, 1976–1978 (Notes and News) *IEJ* 28 (1978), pp. 267–268.
17. Nabratein-1980, *Hadashot Arkheologiyot* 74–75 (1981), p. 4 (Hebrew).
18. Herzog (above, n. 11).
19. Herzog (above, n. 1), p. 80; and R. Gonen: *Burial in Canaan of the Late Bronze Age as a Basis for the Study of Population and Settlement*, Ph.D. Dissertation, Hebrew University, Jerusalem, 1979, pp. 228–229 (Hebrew); and see below, p. 242.
20. Kempinski *et al.*, (above, n. 9), p. 176.
21. I. Finkelstein proposed this idea which is developed at length in his doctoral dissertation, *The Izbet Sartah Excavations* BAR (Inter. Series) No.

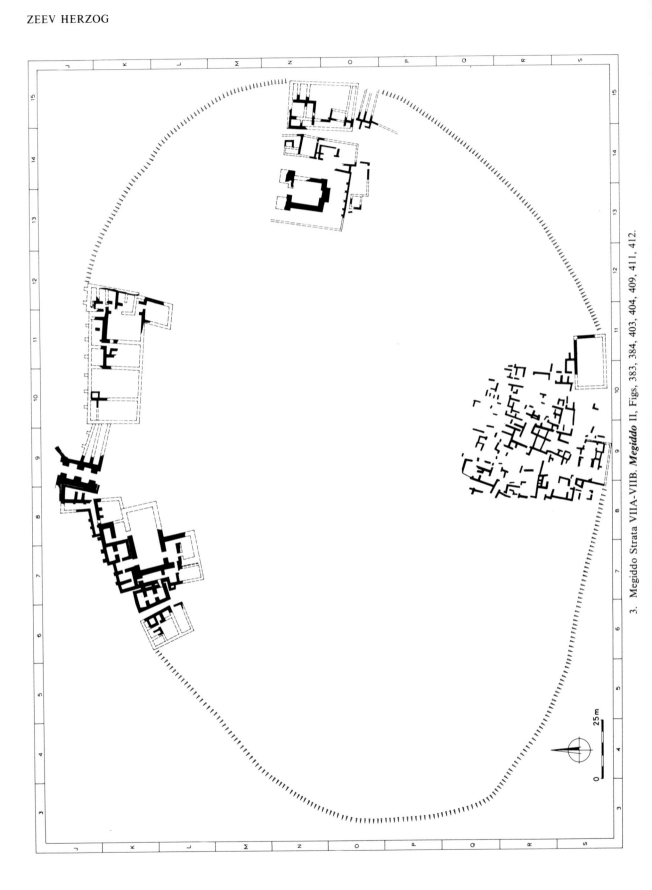

3. Megiddo Strata VIIA-VIIB. *Megiddo* II, Figs. 383, 384, 403, 404, 409, 411, 412.

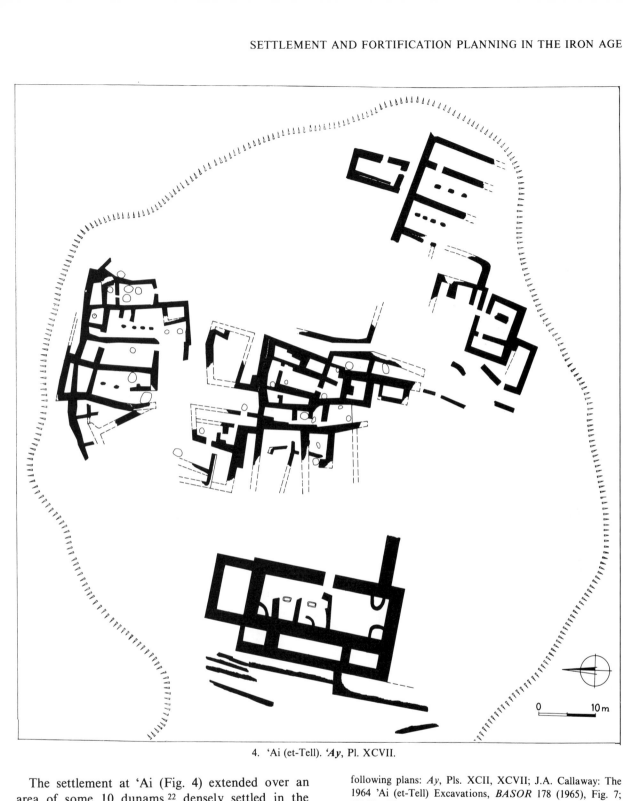

4. 'Ai (et-Tell). *'Ay*, Pl. XCVII.

The settlement at 'Ai (Fig. 4) extended over an area of some 10 dunams,[22] densely settled in the

22. Close to half the area of the mound has been exposed in the excavations. An attempt was made to overcome the handicap of the partial publication of both Marquet-Krause and Callaway's excavations by processing and integrating the partial plans which were published with the overall plan of the site (Fig. 4). The plan is based on an integration of the

following plans: *Ay*, Pls. XCII, XCVII; J.A. Callaway: The 1964 'Ai (et-Tell) Excavations, *BASOR* 178 (1965), Fig. 7; (1965), Fig. 7; *idem*, The 1966 'Ai (et-Tell) Excavations, *BASOR* 196 (1969), Figs. 3–4 and photographs (in the absence of any plan of the eastern area); *idem*, The 1968–1969 'Ai (et-Tell) Excavations, *BASOR* 198 (1970), Figs. 3, 5, 6. For the general contour, the excellent aerial photograph (although part of the excavated areas were recovered with soil) which was published in *idem*, Excavation 'Ai (et-Tell): 1964–1972, *BA* 39 (1976), pp. 22–23 was of great help.

235

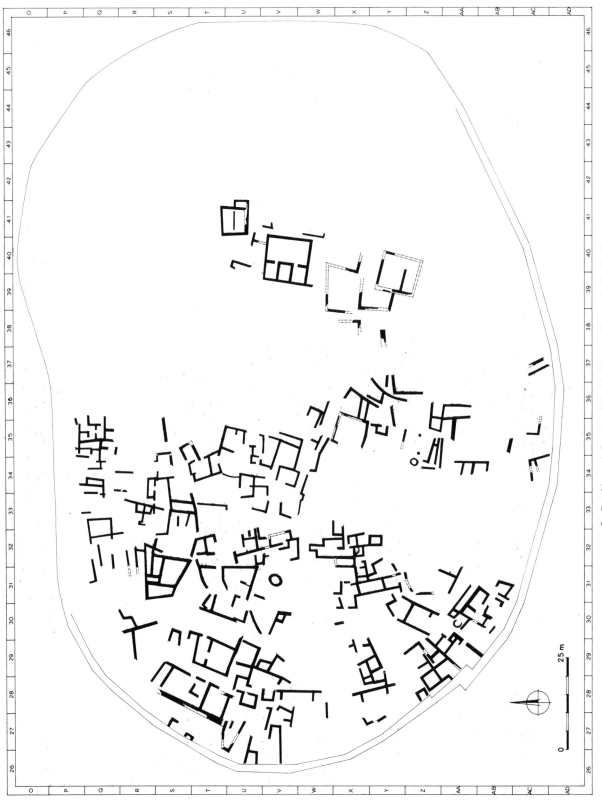

5. Bet Shemesh Stratum III. *Ain Shems*, plans at back of volume.

northern part, without a peripheral belt of buildings. Apparently the settlement here arose gradually, in an unplanned fashion, until it was entirely filled with buildings. This settlement is in fact an example of agglutinative growth in which a settlement that begins with sporadic houses comes to be filled up during its entire existence.[23] Remains of the sanctuary ('palace') from the Early Bronze Age in the western part of the settlement were also incorporated into the new settlement by dividing the building into small dwelling units. The rock-hewn cisterns for storing rainwater inside the settlement show that care was taken to insure a steady supply of water. The spaces between the buildings served as passages (alleys) although some of them were blocked in the second phase of the settlement by silos.[24]

The settlement from the Iron Age I at Bet Shemesh (Stratum III) (Fig. 5) was larger and extended over most of the mound's surface (*ca.* 26 dunams). Unfortunately, it is difficult to analyse the site due to the excavators' problems in distinguishing the phases of the Iron Age.[25] Apparently it is impossible to discern a circumvallation of the settlement in Stratum III by a fortification wall, although perhaps sections of the Bronze Age city-wall which were still standing were incorporated into the dwellings.

Despite its considerable size, Bet Shemesh Stratum III is not an urban settlement, but a village similar to 'Ai. The distribution of the buildings and the random orientation of the houses and walls indicate that the residents had no experience in construction. There is no evidence of streets or alleys. Since the silos are located inside the houses, it is possible to discern in the open areas between the buildings cooking ovens, wine presses, furnaces, and kilns for the metal and pottery industries. Many of the rock-hewn cisterns which were exposed on the site belong to this stratum, although most of them were also in use in later periods.

The population of the settlement can be estimated by analysing the finds from the 1933 season in which fifteen dwelling units were exposed in an area of 1,200 sq. m. Accordingly, in an area of 26 dunams there were approximately 137 units serving as dwellings for around 1,500 persons (based on an average of eight persons per unit); in other words, a density of 57 persons per dunam. This population density, though slightly higher than the average,[26] is evidence of the poverty of the village.

As at 'Ai, at Bet Shemesh there are no prominent buildings, although possibly the well, uncovered in the southern part of the mound, was first dug in this stratum, as was the Iron Age I well at Beersheba. Perhaps the main building in Stratum II[27] (in Squares X-W/30-28) was first erected in this stratum.

In summary, it seems that the settlement of Stratum III at Bet Shemesh was a village of settlers which developed according to the agglutinative principle and whose economy was based, in addition to agriculture, on various crafts such as metal working, pottery production and wine making. The settlement is dated on the basis of the ceramic finds (including Philistine ware) to the twelfth–eleventh centuries B.C.[28]

Other settlements like those at 'Ai and Bet Shemesh apparently existed in the hill country[29] and the coastal plain. At Tell Beit Mirsim there was a find from the period in question, but it is difficult to separate the

23. For a detailed analysis of this principle in Syria and Mesopotamia see J. Schmidt: *Die agglutinierende Bauweise im Zweistromland und in Syrien*, Ing. D. Diss., Berlin, 1963. For this reason Y. Shiloh's reconstruction as representing the plan of the entire settlement cannot be considered, Y. Shiloh (above, n. 1, 1978), pp. 45–46 and Fig. 8. See Callaway (above, n. 22, 1976) p. 30.
24. Callaway sees this as evidence of the penetration of a new population into the area, a population lacking any experience of village life. However, it may simply have been the result of population growth or an increase in agricultural production.
25. The absence of an overall plan of the building remains and the lack of a unified grid in the plans from the various seasons of excavations were a severe handicap. An attempt was made to overcome these handicaps by matching sections of the plans and attaching them to a single map which includes all the building remains which can be ascribed to Stratum III. It should be mentioned that not every structure can be ascribed with certainty to Stratum III, but the plan can serve as a basis for analysing the general characteristics of the settlement. The map is made up of the following plans: excavations from the 1928–1930 seasons, *'Ain Shems* I, Pls. IV-V; excavations of the 1931 season, *'Ain Shems* II, Pl. XXV; excavations from the 1933 season, *'Ain Shems* III, Map II; the 1911–1912 excavations, D. Mackenzie: Excavations at Ain Shems, *APEF* 2 (1912–1913), Pls. II-III. The combination of the plans was made possible by the map of the areas which was published in *'Ain Shems* III, Fig. 1.
26. Shiloh (above, n. 1, 1980). The datum which leads Shiloh to the area of Bet Shemesh (40 dunams) does not fit the area of the Iron Age settlement.
27. E. Grant: *Beth Shemesh, A Report of the Excavations Made in 1928*, Haverford, 1929, p. 221. Its use as a sanctuary during this phase may be indicated by the magnificent three-tiered incense-burner which was discovered there (*ibid.*, p. 103).
28. T. Dothan: *The Philistines and their Material Culture*, Jerusalem, 1982, pp. 50–51.
29. *Tell Nasbeh* I, Survey Map. It is doubtful whether the section of the plan which Shiloh adduces (above, n. 1, 1978), Fig. 3, really represents the earliest phase of the history of the settlement.

buildings belonging to it from the other buildings. It would seem that a similar type of village existed at Khirbet Raddanah where buildings of the 'four-room-house' type were found with rock-hewn cisterns underneath.[30]

Clusters of Enclosures

In the opinion of the author, contrary to that of the excavators,[31] the settlement at Tel Masos (Fig. 6), which extended over a rather large area of at least 50 dunams (five times larger than any other settlement from this period), was not built with a peripheral belt of dwellings surrounding the entire settlement for protection, but rather was created from a group of separate enclosures. The main problem with the excavators' proposal stems from the fact that in Area A (where the most extensive excavations on the site were carried out) all the doorways of the houses face outward rather than toward the inside of the settlement. This would mean that the settlement had no peripheral defense.[32] For this reason, the remains at Tel Masos are interpreted here as a cluster of enclosed settlements built next to each other. The main drawback of an enclosed settlement is that it cannot be enlarged. The large number of enclosures was probably meant to solve the problem of population growth in a settlement of this type. Possibly the enclosure in Area C, close by the well and containing a public building, Building 480,[33] was

the first enclosure built on the site; it may have served some administrative purpose.

Planned Cities

An interesting example of a planned city is to be found in Stratum X at Tell Qasile (Fig. 7) which boasts an orthogonal network of streets[34] which divides the settlement into insulae, and creates a functional division of the insulae themselves. In the earlier strata, XII and XI, only limited areas were exposed. On the other hand, in Stratum X, 2.5 out of 10 dunams of the settlement's area were uncovered. However, it is still not clear whether the 5-metre-thick wall, uncovered in the northwestern part of the mound, belongs to a building or was part of the city-wall.

The author accepts the basic street system proposed by the excavator (two streets running north–south and four streets running east–west), but suggests that the city's area more closely corresponded to the topography of the hill, resulting in a clearer geometrical link between the street system and the outer framework, which, in the opinion of the author, was rectangular.[35]

Inside the city area were twelve blocks of buildings of unequal size. Nonetheless, it is possible to estimate that the average block comprised six units. The entire settlement consisted of approximately 72 houses with a population of some 550 persons. Apparently, whole families engaged in the same occupation resided in some of the blocks. Area A, for example, was probably for crafts and storage. In another block, the sanctuary and the buildings annexed to it are prominent. Inside the blocks the location of the buildings is not very precise and the house facades do not form a uniform line with respect to the street.

In disagreement with the excavator, who considers the continuation of the sanctuary from Strata XII and XI as evidence of the organic development of the city, it is proposed that the orthogonal planning of Stratum X indicates a new plan which took into account only the location of the sanctuary, since the quarter in Stratum X in which the sanctuary was located does not symmetrically fit the orientation of the streets in

30. The plan of the remains which were exposed has still not been published. For the preliminary report see J.A. Callaway and R.E. Cooley: A Salvage Excavation at Raddanah, in Bireh, *BASOR* 201 (1971), pp. 9–19.

31. Kempinski *et al.* (above, n. 9), Figs. 3, 12. In the excavators' opinion, this hypothesis cannot be valid since the belt of houses abutting the wall follows the topographical boundaries of the settlement. Sections of this belt were also found in Area B. See the final report, *Tel Masos*, pp. 34–35.

32. In the writer's opinion, the solution lies in the interpretation of the belt of houses in Area A as the outer part of the compound which continues northwestward rather than southward. Hence the doorways of the dwellings would face the center of the compound while the rear of the houses would face its outer periphery. The remains of the houses in the southern areas would belong to separate compounds. This interpretation is based on two facts: first, the topographical conditions in Area A do not tell anything about the perimeter of the hill, but only about a clear continuation to the north (see the 3 m. and 4 m. lines of elevation in the plan); second, the dwellings ('House 1000' on the overall map *ibid.*, Fig. 2) to the northeast, outside the conjectured outer area of the settlement, certainly prove that the belt of structures in Area A does not mark the perimeter of the settlement.

33. *Ibid.*, p. 180, n. 74.

34. A. Mazar: *Excavations at Tell Qasile*, I: *The Philistine Sanctuary: Architecture and Cult Objects* [*Qedem* 12], Jerusalem, 1980, pp. 76–77, Fig. 17.

35. An additional correction in A. Mazar's original suggestion regards the western road which runs south to north. For no apparent reason, the road deviates from its course and bears northwestward. According to this writer's reconstruction, the road continues northward symmetrically in a straight line.

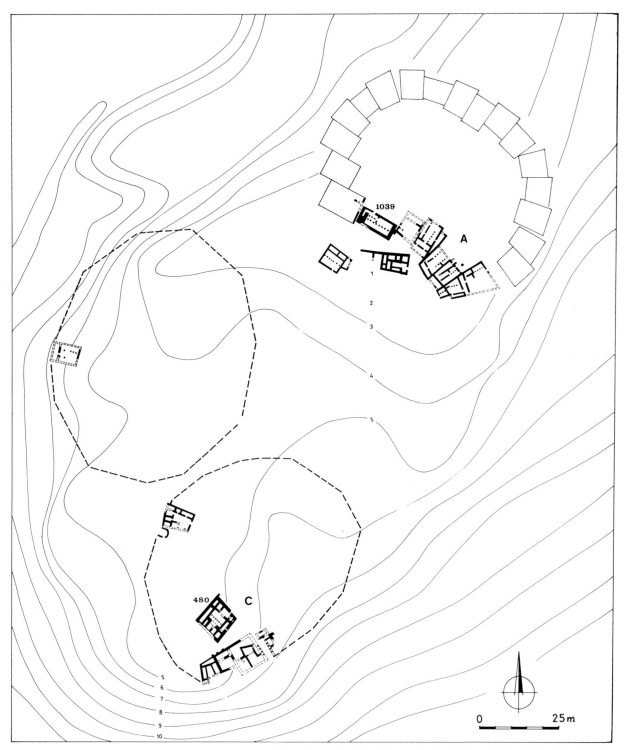

6. Tel Masos Stratum II a reconstruction, after *Tel Masos* III, Plan. 2.

Tel Masos. Iron Age I (Stratum 2), aerial view.

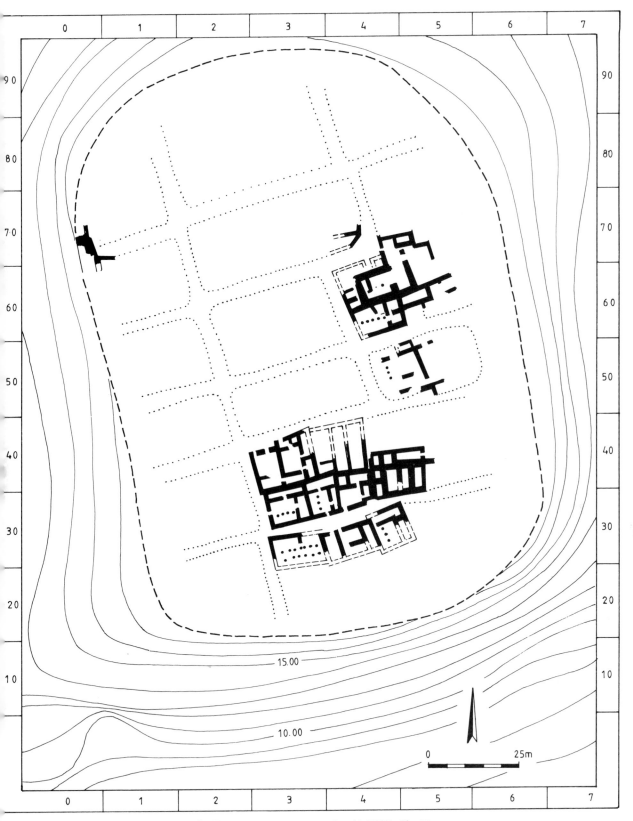

7. Tell Qasile Stratum X. *Qedem* 12 (1980), Fig. 17.

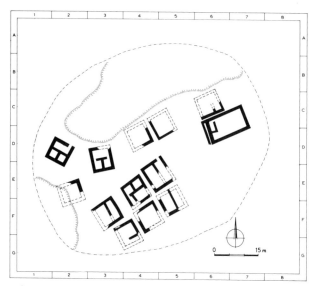

8. Tell Abu Hawam Stratum IVA. *QDAP* IV (1935), Pl. IV.

this stratum. The conclusion that the city of Stratum X was planned at one time is based also on the fact that the extensive areas in the south of the mound contained no buildings in Strata XII–XI. The origin of the orthogonal plan, in the excavator's opinion, is Cyprus (perhaps Enkomi), a conclusion based on the absence of parallels in the Land of Israel from the Late Bronze and Iron Ages, and on the ties between the Philistines and this island.[36]

The settlement in Stratum IVA at Tell Abu Hawam (Fig. 8) should be attributed to the Sea Peoples. Although this settlement has no overall planning principle, the repeated use of square buildings (measurements: *ca.* 7.5 m. × 9.5 m.), which indicates the possible origin of the inhabitants from among the Sea Peoples,[37] is notable. Two similar buildings were also found at Tel Aphek in Stratum X, where there also seems to have been an earlier occupational wave of Sea Peoples. At Aphek, in the same stratum, a sparse residential quarter was discovered in which the

finds indicate that the residents engaged in fishing.[38] The areas exposed thus far in the Philistine strata at Ashdod and Tel Gerisa are too small to enable us to determine whether these settlements were built according to a crystallized plan.

Canaanite Cities and Egyptian Administrative Centres

Unlike the settlement models examined thus far, which are characteristic of new settlements, these are cities which continued to exist from the Bronze Age. Such settlements are found mainly in the valleys, but can also be seen in other areas such as Lachish in the coastal plain and Shechem in the hill country. Bet Shean and Megiddo provide extensive information for the following discussion.

Bet Shean was one of the Egyptian administrative centres in Canaan. A considerable portion of its acropolis has been excavated (approximately 8 dunams) and a large number of dated monuments of pharaohs were found, more than at any other site in Palestine. Strata VI and V are assigned to the Iron Age.[39] A comparison of the overall plan of these strata[40] indicates the continuity in the location of the temple area, but a change in the overall planning conception.

In Stratum VI the acropolis was divided into two blocks with an open area, probably a courtyard, between them. The area in the north of the acropolis was built around Building 1500 which served as a citadel or palace for the Egyptian governor. The southern area was built around Temple 1032 and most likely was used for cultic purposes. This division also reflects the division of the population: the local Canaanite inhabitants lived in the vicinity of the

36. Mazar (above, n. 34), p. 77. If this be the case, the absence of ashlar construction, so common in Kition but lacking in Tell Qasile, is quite surprising. On ashlar construction in Cyprus, see N.K. Sanders: *The Sea Peoples, Warriors of the Ancient Mediterranean 1250–1150 B.C.,* London, 1978, pp. 144–153.

37. R.W. Hamilton: Excavations at Tell Abu Hawam, *QDAP* 4 (1934), pp. 8–11, Pl. IV and Y. Aharoni: *The Archaeology of the Land of Israel,* Philadelphia, 1982, pp. 184–185. For the date of the stratum and a somewhat different proposed reconstruction see L. Gershuny: Stratum V at Tell Abu Hawam, *ZDPV* 97 (1981), pp. 36–44, Fig. 3. It is interesting to note that one structure of this type (Building 61) exists already in Stratum V. See Hamilton, *ibid.,* Pl. V.

38. M. Kochavi: The History and Archaeology of Aphek-Antipatris, *BA* 44 (1981), pp. 80–81.

39. There are differences of opinion among scholars as to the dating of the strata and the sanctuaries. Strata VI and V belong to the Iron Age although in the opinion of several scholars the beginning of Stratum VI dates to the time of Rameses II, that is, towards the end of the Late Bronze Age. In this summary the dating of F. James with which T. Dothan concurs, and according to which the beginning of Stratum VI dates to the time of Rameses III, is accepted. Stratum V is divided into two phases, the earlier of which (Stratum V lower phase) is from the eleventh century B.C. For a summary of the various opinions see F. James and A. Kempinski: Beth Shean, *EAEHL* I, pp. 214–215; Dothan (above, n. 28), pp. 81–82.

40. F.W. James: *The Iron Age at Beth Shan,* Philadelphia, 1966, Figs. 74–77.

9. Bet Shean Stratum VI. F. James: *The Iron Age at Beth-Shan*, Philadelphia, 1966, Figs. 76–77.

temple, while the Egyptians resided in the vicinity of the palace. Perhaps, with some reservations, these blocks can be seen as being divided by a network of orthogonally laid out streets. If this reconstruction is correct it is evidence of Egyptian influence, since this type of plan is well known in Egypt[41] (Fig. 9).

41. A. Badawy: Orthogonal and Axial Town Planning in Egypt, *Zeitschrift fur Agyptische Sprache und Altertumskunde* 85 (1960), pp. 1–12. From here it is only a small step to raise

In the early phase of Stratum V the plan was different. Temple 1024 (Fig. 10) served to divide the blocks and the open area. Division into residential quarters cannot be discerned and there are almost no regularly laid out streets (except for 1524). The

the possibility that the orthogonal plan of Tell Qasile is also a product of Egyptian influence on the Philistines (or the Sea People in general) arising from the cooperation in the government of Canaan during the twelfth century B.C.

243

10. Bet Shean Stratum V. James (*ibid.*), Figs. 74-75.

uniformity of the plan (single orientation, right angles, parallel walls and a tendency to small rooms) indicates that in this stratum the acropolis was a military and administrative centre resembling a citadel. There is no information about the extent of the acropolis, but the city-wall seems to have been built in conformity with this complex. The difference between Strata VI and V stems most probably from the transfer of control from the Egyptians to the Philistines. The military character of Stratum V reflects the Philistines' struggles with the Israelites which reached their height in the time of Saul at the end of the eleventh century B.C.[42]

42. S. Yeivin considered the change in the plan of the sanctuaries in Stratum V as a result of the Philistine conquest. See M.

At Megiddo three different Iron Age I strata were uncovered. Stratum VIIA (twelfth century) continues the building characteristics of Stratum VIIB (thirteenth century). In this stratum some 20% of the area of the tell was exposed, most of which consisted of public buildings that covered an estimated 40%

Avi-Yonah and S. Yeivin: *The Antiquities of Israel*, Tel Aviv, 1955, p. 181 and n. 60 (Hebrew). It is interesting to note that in the upper phase of Stratum V, from the tenth century, there were no significant changes in the plan. Perhaps the new settlers simply conquered the fortress and made changes only in the vicinity of the entrance where they built a gate and storehouse — James (above, n. 40), Fig. 73.

of the area of the city (Fig. 3).[43] The location of the palace in the west, and the sanctuary in the east continues the tradition of the Late Bronze Age. In the vicinity of the sanctuary a new building was constructed which may have served as a residence for the priests of the sanctuary. In addition to the western palace there was a second palace (in Area DD and in Square K 10) of comparable size,[44] which was first built in Stratum VIII.[45] This building, which has not yet been entirely exposed, comprises a central court ringed by rooms. The courtyard between the two palaces may have served as a plaza. The city itself was not surrounded by a wall in Stratum VII, but by a ring of peripheral structures. The gate built in Stratum X was still in use. The pillars uncovered near the western palace, which in the author's opinion may have resembled the pillars near the eastern palace, may also have supported a balcony from which it was possible to shoot down at attackers. The absence of fortifications is widespread in the Late Bronze Age.[46]

In the residential area in the south of the mound (Area CC), where the excavators had difficulties distinguishing between Stratum VIII and Stratum VII, it is difficult to discern the organization of the streets or alleys. The quality of the construction was quite poor and the quarter seems to have expanded according to the agglutinative principle. A comparison of this quarter with the public buildings in the north and the quarter in the south of the mound shows a pronounced polarization of socioeconomic classes.

The transition between Stratum VIIA and Stratum VIB is extremely sharp at Megiddo. The contrast is particularly noticeable in the palace area where poor dwellings lacking any uniform plan were built on top of the palaces. The settlement, which resembles the Iron Age villages at 'Ai and Bet Shemesh (see above), may not have extended over the entire surface of the mound; Areas BB and CC lack remains from this stratum.

In Stratum VIA the city again covers the entire surface of the hill. In the north a planned palace (2072) was built, which together with the buildings west of it creates a peripheral belt (Fig. 11). This required the construction of a new gate with one chamber on each side.[47] Perhaps the late phase of Sanctuary 2048 can be assigned to this stratum.[48] East of the gate a well-planned quarter was built in which Building 5000 stands out. In Areas BB and CC, on the other hand, there seems to have been an unplanned residential quarter which housed a poorer population.

It is worth noting the similarity between Strata VIIA and VIA and the difference between these two strata and Stratum VIB between them. Stratum VIB in fact fits the definition of a typical Israelite settlement village and its inhabitants were probably Israelites,[49] while Stratum VIA was most likely inhabited by a Canaanite population (Philistine?) which returned to the city after a brief time and rebuilt it according to the city model of Stratum VIIA,[50] making secondary

43. The plan was made up from the following sources: *Megiddo* II, Figs. 384, 404, 409, and 412 which were superimposed on the topographical map, Fig. 377. For a similar processing of the plans of Late Bronze Age Megiddo see I. Baumgarten: *The City Plan and City Planning in the Late Bronze Age in the Levant*, M.A. Dissertation, Hebrew University, Jerusalem, 1978, Pls. III–V (Hebrew), and Chap. 17 in the present volume.

44. Baumgarten (above, n. 43), pp. 32–33, proposes to interpret this building as a sanctuary. In light of the reconstruction proposed here, it is difficult to accept his theory. For parallels of the plan of the palace in Megiddo Stratum VII and Hazor Area F see I. Dunayevsky and A. Kempinski: The Megiddo Temples, *ZDPV* 89 (1973), pp. 161–187. Unfortunately, large portions of the plans of all these buildings have been reconstructed.

45. This is the earliest stratum which the excavators reached in Area DD aside from several sections of walls on its western side (*Megiddo* II, Fig. 411), which are assigned to Stratum IX and may indicate continuity in this phase. It would seem possible to hypothesize that between Stratum VIIB (Fig. 411) and Stratum VIIA (Fig. 412) there was a real change in the plan. However, since the entire eastern wing of the building in Stratum VIIA comprises precisely the same walls as in Stratum VIII, it is obvious that it must have been in use also in the transitional Stratum VIIB, and for some as yet unknown reason it was omitted from the plan of this stratum.

46. It would seem that the absence of fortifications in the Late Bronze Age cities in Canaan is a widespread phenomenon resulting most probably from the policy of the Egyptian rulers of discouraging rebellion amongst the local kings. A peripheral system of defense of this type does not preclude the need for an entrance gate to the city, and indeed the gate, which most probably originated in Stratum X, was in use until Stratum VIIA.

47. Herzog (above, n. 11), pp. 103–118. The plan of Stratum VIA (Fig. 12) is based on *Megiddo* II, Figs. 386, 405, 410, and 413.

48. A. Mazar: *The Sanctuaries at Tell Qasile*, Ph.D. Dissertation, Hebrew University, Jerusalem, 1977, p. 340 and n. 1137.

49. Aharoni (above, n. 37), pp. 179–180; B. Mazar: An 'Orpheus' Jar from Megiddo, *Canaan and Israel, Historical Essays*, Jerusalem, 1974, pp. 174–175 (Hebrew). On the attribution of Stratum VIB to Israelite settlers see A. Kempinski in A. Kempinski and M. Avi-Yonah: *Syria Palestine*, II, Geneva, 1978, p. 76.

50. It must be born in mind that most of the Philistine pottery was found in Stratum VIIA, a few vessels were found in Stratum VIA, and only a few single sherds in Stratum VIB. See Dothan (above, n. 28), pp. 70–80. Aharoni's claim as to the Israelite nature of Stratum 'VI' (above, n. 37) may be appropriate only to Stratum VIB, but not to Stratum VIA. On the other hand, this explanation obviates the need for Dothan's attempts to assign Philistine pottery found in Stratum VIA to loci from VIB, *ibid.*, pp. 76–80.

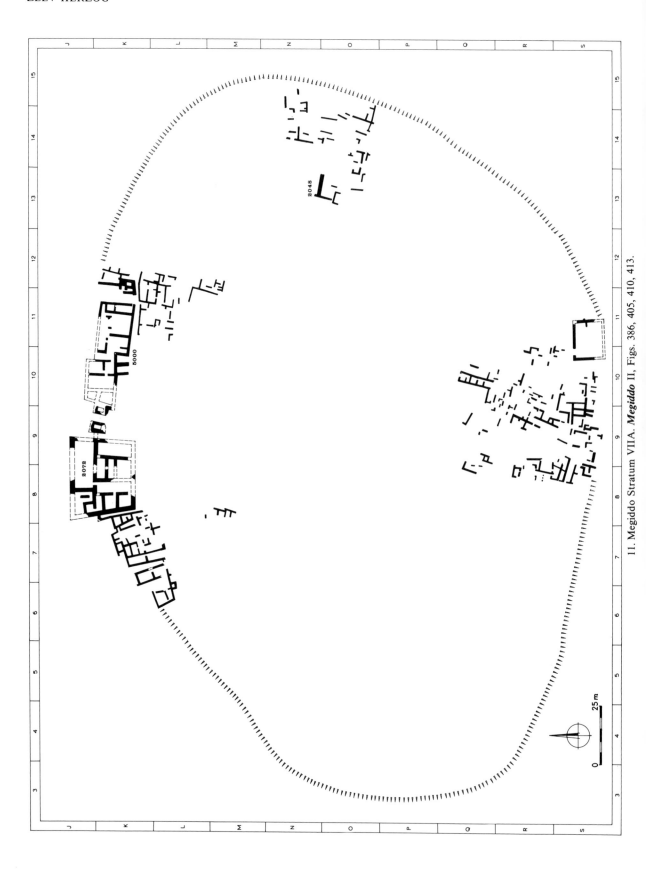

11. Megiddo Stratum VIIA. *Megiddo* II, Figs. 386, 405, 410, 413.

use of partially burnt bricks which were removed from the ruins of the city.

Summary of the Iron Age I

The settlement models which were surveyed from the Iron Age I clearly show the multiplicity of plans typical of this period in the history of the Land of Israel. Apparently the settlements of the Iron Age I defy the simple distinctions which are usually made in the classification of settlements, for example, as cities or villages. Furthermore, the usual variables in the analysis of urbanization, such as the existence of a city-wall as a criterion of an urban settlement or the area of the settlement, do not suit an analysis of the settlement models in question. For example, Tel Masos Stratum II, which covers an area of approximately 50 dunams, is not defined as a city, whereas Tell Qasile with its 16 dunams is considered a planned city. On the other hand, Megiddo of Strata VIIA and VIA, although unwalled, is indubitably an urban settlement.

Another difference between most of the Iron Age settlement models and the Canaanite city in Megiddo VIIA (and to a lesser extent in Bet Shean VI, Megiddo VIA and Tel Masos II) is the existence of sharp socioeconomic distinctions revealed by the existence of splendid palaces alongside poor dwellings. In the settlements typical of populations in a settlement process, whether in enclosed settlements or in villages attributed to the Israelites or even in Philistine Tell Qasile, there is an obvious uniformity in the size and plan of the dwellings which undoubtedly represents a high degree of economic equality.

Iron Age II (Tenth-Sixth Centuries B.C.)

Planning Principles in the Cities

Iron Age II remains have been exposed in scores of settlements, but due to reduction in the extent of excavations, the settlement and fortification plans from only a few sites can be discussed. It is possible, however, to discern planning to some extent in all the settlements of this period. In order to determine the degree of planning, a number of criteria will be proposed which will serve as a basis for comparison and will then be used to create a typology. Three aspects of settlement planning will be considered.

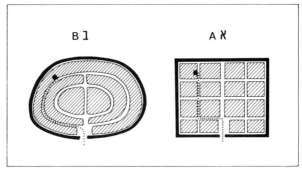

12. A) orthogonal city plan. B) peripheral city plan.

Orthogonal Planning, Peripheral and Radial Plans.[51]
— The outer contour of the settlement is an important criterion of planning. The orthogonal contour based on the square may be distinguished from the oval contour which fits the natural surface conditions of the site (Fig. 12). The oval settlements, it seems, may be divided into two types. The first is the peripheral settlement in which the line of the city-wall is planned in accordance with the topography of the mound but the houses are built without any uniform plan, as in the settlement in Tell Beit Mirsim A. The second type, which may be defined as radial, is planned with the help of radii emanating from central points, as in Beersheba II.

Orthogonal planning does not conform to the natural contours of the hill or mound on which the settlement is built; hence the settlement stands out from its surroundings, lending it a monumental character. This plan was preferred at settlements of social, political or military importance as on the acropolis of a capital city or main administrative city, as well as in fortresses. The orthogonal plan also made it easier to integrate square building units into the settlement and to divide it into quarters. Orthogonal planning required great engineering work (levelling and quarrying) and prevented the maximal utilization of the area possible in an oval settlement. The well-planned construction also demands more skillful building. The number of orthogonal Iron Age II settlements is small, apparently due to the numerous difficulties inherent in this plan. It is notable that in these few cities there is also greater use of monumental building techniques (ashlars, proto-Aeolic capitals, carved window balustrades, etc.).

51. For the application of these terms to the Late Bronze Age see Chap. 17 in this volume.

The peripherally organized settlement represents the simplest city plan and refers in fact only to the lines of the city-wall which were built at government initiative. It is possible that in several of the peripherally planned cities the radial plan was used, as can be discerned in Beersheba (see below). The main question regarding these settlements is whether the diagonal lines are the result of strict planning and the use of foci from which lines were drawn toward the sections of the circumference, as seems more likely, or the result of pure chance, the buildings erected according to an oval circumference.

The orthogonal plan is, as mentioned above, the most difficult and costly to apply.[52] Hence, in many cases the planners of the Israelite city compromised by combining official orthogonal building units within a peripherally contoured city, as in Lachish Stratum III.

The quantitative relationship between public structures and private dwellings (Fig. 13). — This relationship may shed light on the importance of the city in the administrative hierarchy.[53] In this case, the category of public structures should also include the city-walls, the city-gates, the storehouses, water systems, the palaces and their courtyards, etc. It is assumed that the more important the city in the eyes of the royal planners, the greater the area of the settlement devoted to such structures, while the greater the area devoted to private dwellings, the less important the city and hence less planning went into it. It is possible that the residential units may also have served the representatives of the Monarchy, and not only private citizens. For example, the residential buildings in the citadel at Arad are unquestionably 'public structures' which served the representatives of the administration. For this reason the relationship between the two types of structures should not be

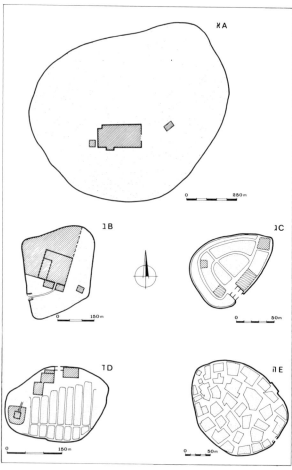

13. Schematic plans of land use in Iron Age II cities.

considered independently or definitively, but only by comparison with the other criteria of planning. Generally speaking, this relationship will be examined by considering whole blocks of buildings within the settlement whose overall character is unequivocally public or private.

Streets and open areas in the urban system. — The system of streets and open areas between the buildings of the settlement is an excellent criterion of the degree of planning. There is a broad spectrum of systems ranging from settlements without any streets, with open, irregularly shaped areas connecting the various parts, and settlements with a high level of planning, with streets of uniform width, uninterrupted by buildings. In general, a planned settlement utilizes its area more efficiently, particularly the open areas, but there are also areas which were planned as open spaces, for example in Megiddo and Lachish. These courtyards must have been for the encampment of

52. A comparison of the three models presented above shows that the orthogonal plan is the most difficult and costly, as is immediately evident from a simple calculation of the length of the city-wall. In an orthogonally laid out settlement, covering an area of 10 dunams, the length of the city-wall would be 400 m., while in a radially or peripherally planned settlement it would be 350 m. long. In other words, the cost of building materials and man-hours would be 12.5% higher in an orthogonal settlement. In fact, in orthogonal settlements or compounds wide use of costly building materials such as ashlars, proto-Aeolic capitals, carved window balustrades, etc., used only for monumental construction, is found.

53. The importance of public structures for defining the type of urban plan has been treated extensively by Y. Shiloh (above, n. 1, 1978), pp. 46–50 and Z. Herzog (above, n. 1, 1978), p. 43.

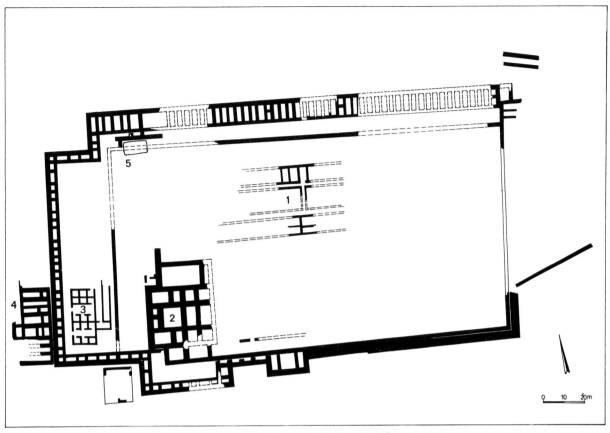

14. Samaria, plan of the acropolis. *Samaria-Sebaste* I, Pl. II.

army units or the setting for market places or for other commercial activity.

The ease of transportation in cities with a peripheral (or radial) plan, where some of the streets lead directly to the gate thereby permitting the free flow of traffic, should be noted. By contrast, procession through cities with an orthogonal plan requires many turns and a longer course.

Capital Cities

To this category belong primarily the capital cities of Jerusalem and Samaria. Of the royal acropolis of Jerusalem nothing seems to have survived. However, many parts of the upper city of Samaria, the capital of the Kingdom of Israel, have been exposed, making it possible to discover the principle of its plan. While the area of the acropolis (Fig. 14), which was uncovered under the enormous structures from the Hellenistic and Roman periods, is known, only single remains were found on the lower terraces of the mound. Apparently, however, the lower city extended over hundreds of dunams.

The acropolis was built in two phases. The first (Stratum 1), from the first half of the ninth century B.C., most probably from the time of Omri,[54] extended over an area of approximately 17 dunams and was surrounded by a wall 1.6 m. thick. In the southeastern corner of this enclosure a large building, doubtless the royal palace, was erected. The area east of the palace served as a large court. On the northern side remains of dwellings were exposed. In the small area which was uncovered, an intersection of streets was found among the remains of the houses. This shows that most likely the residential quarter was divided by a network of streets.

In the second phase (Stratum II), also from the first half of the ninth century B.C., most probably from the reign of Ahab, the acropolis was enlarged and surrounded by a casemate wall on at least three sides (see below). The acropolis now covered an area of approximately 26 dunams. In another area to the west was erected a structure symmetrically divided

54. For a summary of the opinions on the date of the two phases see N. Avigad: Samaria, *EAEHL* IV, pp. 1041–1043.

into rooms on both sides of central corridors. This is clearly an administrative structure. Most of the Samaria letters discovered to date strengthen this interpretation. At a later phase, a large building, perhaps another palace or an extension of the citadel, was added to the western part of the acropolis.

The construction at Samaria is remarkably precise, and undoubtedly the planners' intention was to erect a rectangular building with true right angles. Upon closer examination, however, discrepancies of up to three degrees from a right angle are detectable.

Even though the acropolis has not been entirely excavated, it is unquestionably of a royal, monumental character which is manifested in the orthogonal plan, the devotion of a large area to public structures, and perhaps also the regularly laid out streets. All this, along with the high quality of construction, perfectly fits the role of the acropolis of the capital of the Kingdom of Israel. The structure of the acropolis, at any rate, clearly indicates that the planners made certain to separate completely the royal enclosure and the civilian residential quarters. It may be supposed that this model also applied to the acropolis of Jerusalem, capital of the United Monarchy and the Kingdom of Judah.

Major Administrative Cities

Major administrative centres are cities in which the public complexes occupy the largest part of the settlement plan. These complexes are orthogonal units within the framework of the peripheral settlement plan. Included in this model are the cities which were uncovered in Megiddo Strata VA (VA–IVB according to Yadin and others), VIB (according to Yadin), and IVA, and in Lachish Strata IV and III. Probably other cities such as Hazor Strata X–IV, Gezer and Tel Dan in the strata from the tenth century on, were similarly planned, but the archaeological data are insufficient.

Megiddo. — The excavations in Iron Age Megiddo are very extensive, but the stratigraphy and chronology of various strata are unclear.[55] Various excavators

55. The terminological confusion stems from the fact that the stratum under the offset-and-inset city-wall was called IVB in the first volume of the report, and VA in the second volume. Since there was no doubt that in both volumes it was the same stratum which was referred to, scholars accepted Albright's suggestion that the stratum be called VA-IVB. However, this did not solve the problem because two phases were also attributed to the period of the existence of the offset-and-inset

have tried to clear up the difficulties centering mainly around Stratum VA (or VA-IVB according to Albright's suggestion) through the early phases of Stratum III. Their various approaches are summarized in Table I which refers to strata, chronology, 'Solomon's Gate', the offset-and-inset wall, and the possible existence of a casemate wall from the time of Solomon, a possibility which Aharoni and the author reject. The following discussion is based on the stratigraphic division proposed below.

city-wall which was generally attributed to Stratum IVA. The earlier phase had the six-chambered gate while the later had a four-chambered gate. Y. Yadin proposed that the earlier phase be called IVA1, and the later IVA. See Y. Yadin: The Megiddo of the Kings of Israel, *Qadmoniot* 3 (1970), pp. 38–56 (Hebrew). The author favors Aharoni's suggestion that the designation VA be retained for the stratum beneath the offset-and-inset wall, and he calls the phase of the construction of the city-wall IVB. See Y. Aharoni: The Stratification of Israelite Megiddo, *JNES* 31 (1972), pp. 302–311. The second phase of use of the city-wall (with the four-chambered gate) should be called (following Yadin) IVA. A more difficult problem is that of the stratigraphic attribution of several structures to the various strata. Opinions differ most sharply over the possibility of the existence of an early phase of use of 'Solomon's Gate'. In Yadin's and Shiloh's opinion, such a phase does exist and it was during this phase that Megiddo was surrounded by a casemate wall. See Yadin, *ibid.*; Y. Shiloh: Solomon's Gate at Megiddo as Recorded by its Excavator, R. Lamon, Chicago, *Levant* 12 (1980), pp. 67–76. In the opinion of Aharoni, Herzog, and Ussishkin, there is no stratigraphic possibility of the existence of such a phase. See Aharoni, *ibid.*; Herzog, the city-gate (above, n. 1), pp. 102–118; D. Ussishkin: Was the 'Solomonic' City Gate of Megiddo built by King Solomon?, *BASOR* 239 (1980), pp. 1–18. Ussishkin accepts Aharoni's and Herzog's stratigraphic conclusions but proposes to date the settlement level under the offset-and-inset city-wall to the time of Solomon, and the city-wall and Solomon's Gate to a later period. There is also disagreement over the dating of the strata in question and their link to the period of the kings of the United Monarchy and the Kingdom of Israel. The excavators of Megiddo ascribed Stratum VA to the time of David; Aharoni and Herzog concur in this date. Yadin, on the other hand, ascribes this stratum (which he calls VA-IVB) to which he adds 'the early phase' of the six-chambered gate, to the time of Solomon, while Ussishkin ascribes it to the time of Solomon but without including the gate. Yadin ascribes the new city of Stratum IVB (which he calls IVA1) to the time of Jeroboam I. Aharoni ascribes it to the time of Solomon, and Ussishkin to one of the kings of Israel after the time of Solomon. In Stratum IVA of the city a few changes were made, the most conspicuous being the replacement of the six-chambered city gate by a four-chambered gate. There is unanimous agreement that this change was made in the ninth century, probably in the time of Ahab.

The urban plan of Megiddo in the strata which we call VA and IVB (see table) maintains certain common characteristics, but nonetheless there is a significant difference between them. The resemblance lies in the contour of the periphery and the inner structure. In both phases large public structures were erected alongside residences. The differences are in the type of fortifications and the extent (or strength) of the public structures.

Table 1. Megiddo: The Stratification According to Various Excavators

Megiddo I	Megiddo II	Y. Yadin	Y. Aharoni	Z. Herzog
1939	1948	1970	1971	1976
IIIB	—	IVA	IIIB	IVA
Main phase of IV	IV	IVA1	IVB	IVB
IVB	VA	VA-IVB	VA	VA
V	VB	VB	VB	VB

The plan of Megiddo Stratum VA[56] (VA–IVB according to Albright, Yadin, and others). Only some 15 out of 53 dunams have been exposed, of which *ca.* 10 dunams are devoted to public buildings (Palaces 6000, 1723), and the rest to private houses (Fig. 15). It can be assumed that most of the public buildings have been uncovered, and that houses covered the remaining 75% of the city area.

The plan of the settlement consists of a belt of houses around the periphery of the mound. This is a continuation of a local tradition from the Late Bronze Age.[57] At least two enclosures were incorporated into the peripheral plan, Palace 1723 in the south and Palace 6000 in the north. In front of Palace 1723 there was a walled plaza with an entrance gate, thus confirming the administrative character of the building. No similar compound was exposed in front of Building 6000, however there is a possibility that its remains were uncovered between the palace and the city-gate.

The early phase of Structure 1482, whose plan indicates its administrative character,[58] also belongs to this stratum. The city-gate is beneath the foundations of 'Solomon's Gate'[59] and to it led Access Road 2160 onto which a cultic structure may have abutted.[60] Parts of the residential quarter which were exposed indicate irregularly planned peripheral buildings. The houses lack a uniform plan or orientation as they do in Strata VIB and VB. At any rate, the very noticeable contrast between the residential quarters and the public enclosures indicates the difference in standards of living and most probably reflects the contrast between the agricultural population and the representatives of the royal administration.

The plan of Megiddo Stratum IVB[61] (IVA according to Albright and others). A new planning concept is evident in this stratum of which much was exposed (37 dunams). First and foremost is the defensive military trend which is embodied in a massive offset-and-inset wall (3.6 m. thick) which comprises a large inner six-chambered gate with a facade of two towers separated from an outer gate by an inner courtyard (Fig. 16).

The public buildings cover a larger area. West of the enclosure of Palace 1723 (the palace itself was destroyed but the enclosure is still standing) was built a large complex of pillared buildings which served as stables for horses, in the opinion of some scholars, or as storehouses, in the opinion of others, including the author (and see p. 224). The southern complex, together with a large court, covers *ca.* 10 dunams. A second, trapezoidal, complex of stables (or storehouses) was built abutting the city-wall in the north. The governor's palace was erected at this time south of this complex and was defended by

56. Fig. 15 was made from a combination of the following plans: *Megiddo* I, Figs. 6, 12, 388, 406, and 414; Yadin (above, n. 55), Fig. on p. 44.

57. These residential quarters were omitted in the plans of Megiddo published by Yadin. Their appearance proves that there is no trace of a casemate wall in Stratum VA in the areas which the excavators of Megiddo exposed — Yadin (above, n. 55), p. 41.

58. The plan of this building resembles that of the 'Ostraca House' which was discovered at Samaria, and it may have served a similar administrative purpose (Chap 23 in this volume).

59. Yadin does not mention this gate in his discussion of the relationship between 'Solomon's Gate' and Stratum VIA (above, n. 55), pp. 50–51, and therefore he is inclined to ascribe the drainage channel of Stratum VA to Stratum VIA (above, n. 55, Fig. on p. 51), despite the fact that the channel is incorporated into the outer wall of the access road of Stratum VA (*Megiddo* II, Figs. 91, 338).

60. The cultic objects which were found concentrated in a corner of Courtyard 2081 in this stratum (*Megiddo* II, Figs. 100–102) may well have originated in the gate sanctuary and been hastily taken inside the city in times of war.

61. The sources for Fig. 16 are *Megiddo* I, Figs. 3, 49; *Megiddo* II, Figs. 389, 414; R.S. Lamon, *The Megiddo Water System*, Chicago, 1935, Fig. 2.

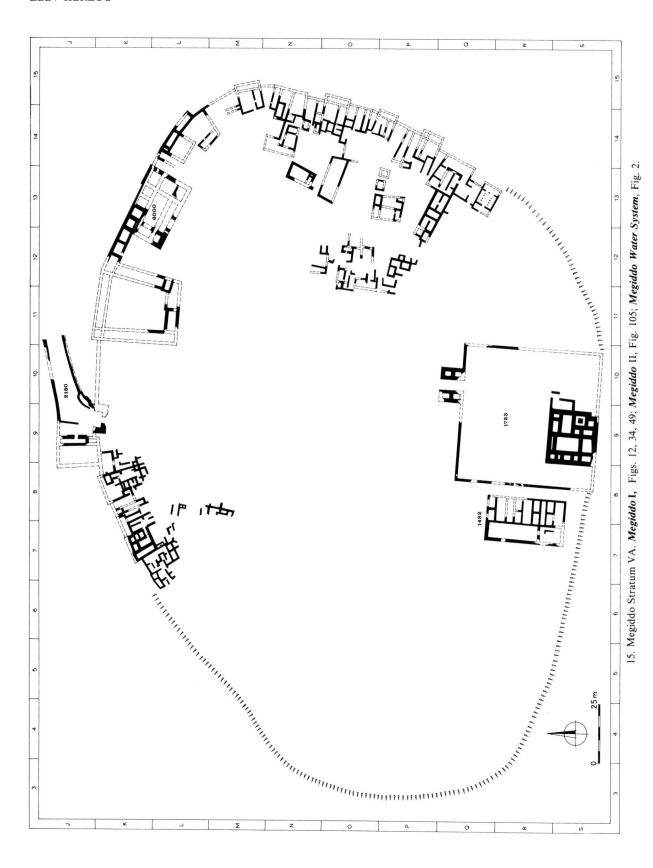

15. Megiddo Stratum VA. *Megiddo* I, Figs. 12, 34, 49; *Megiddo* II, Fig. 105; *Megiddo Water System*, Fig. 2.

a freestanding gatehouse.[62] Administrative Building 1482 (an archive?) was reduced in size and nearby there may have been à secondary city-gate at the point where the city-wall deviates from its course. Most probably the first phase of the water system also belongs to this stratum.

The residential buildings were exposed in only one area, west of the city-gate. The houses, unlike those in the earlier stratum, are not located on the perimeter but were built separately from the city-wall with a rather uniform orientation.

An analysis of the lines of the urban plan in the stratum in question reveals the sharp contrast between the peripheral line of fortifications and the orthogonal units within. These complexes were built parallel to the line of the adjacent city-wall with only partial coordination between the units. The spaces between the units are irregular and are not properly utilized.

In contrast with 75% in the earlier stratum, private houses covered only *ca.* 18% of the city area (5 dunams for a population of approximately 500). The rest of the area was for stables (or alternatively, for the storage of agricultural and other products) and some of the courtyards were most probably used for encampments of army units or passing caravans.

Megiddo as an Assyrian Administrative Centre (Stratum III). Although the entire city area in Strata III–II has been excavated, stratigraphic problems prevented the excavators from publishing the plan of Stratum III separately from that of Stratum II in the southern area, and from publishing the plan of the central area of the mound. With the aid of the published aerial photographs it was possible to provide at least a partial reconstruction of the missing parts (Fig. 17).

Megiddo of Stratum III, aside from the offset-and-inset wall which continued in use, was replanned according to new principles and is a fine example of an Assyrian administrative centre in the Land of Israel.[64] Innovations include the concentration of all the administrative buildings close to the city-gate (in the north) and the distribution of the residential

structures, which covered the rest of the city, into parallel bands of buildings comprising dwellings which were divided by straight streets. In addition to the main streets running north to south, there were also streets crossing from east to west. Unlike the main streets, the bisecting streets do not continue uninterrupted, and the spaces between them are not uniform.

The city-gate was replaced at this time by a new two-chambered gate. On the western side two palaces (1052 and 1369) were exposed while another palace (490) was uncovered east of the gate.[65] Each of the three palaces has a large central court and sophisticated drainage system. Erected in the northeastern corner of the city were several enclosures not used for residences. Perhaps they were open courtyards for encampments of army units. Within the residential area was a large public silo (11 m. in diameter and 7 m. deep with a total volume of *ca.* 450 cu. m.).

The bands of houses were built with great precision. Each band is 20–23 m. wide; the width of the streets is 2.5–3 m. An examination of the measurements shows that the planning was based on the Assyrian cubit.[66]

In this stratum, the residential structures covered *ca.* 35 dunams, some two-thirds of the city's area. Their excellent planning and the existence of the public silo within the residential area may indicate that this quarter was meant for royal officials. Stratum III is dated by most scholars to the time of Assyrian rule when Megiddo was the provincial capital. In

---

62. Shiloh was the first to propose that the structure be reconstructed as a gate — Y. Shiloh: *The Proto-Aeolic Capital and Israelite Ashlar Masonry* [*Qedem* 11], Jerusalem, 1979, Fig. 73.

63. The sources for Fig. 17 are Lamon (above, n. 61), Fig. 2 and *Megiddo* I, Figs. 17, 27, 89, 115–118.

64. K.M. Kenyon, *Archaeology in the Holy Land*, London, 1960, p. 286; Y. Aharoni: *Archaeology in the Holy Land* (Review), *IEJ* 11 (1961), p. 90.

65. R. Amiran and I. Dunayevsky defined the western palaces as Assyrian open-court buildings, but they did not propose a plan for the eastern palace — Ruth B.K. Amiran and I. Dunayevsky: The Assyrian Open-Court Building and its Palestinian Derivatives, *BASOR* 149 (1958), pp. 25–32. On the other hand, the *Nordburg* of Schumacher's excavations, which they considered another example of an Assyrian palace, cannot be from Stratum III since it was 'cut by one of the storehouses of Stratum IVB'. The excavators in the American expedition ascribed this building to the Middle Bronze Age (Strata XII, XI) — *Megiddo* II, Fig. 415.

66. The length of the Assyrian cubit is 49.5 cm. — R.B.Y. Scott: 'The Hebrew Cubit', *JBL* 77 (1958), p. 297. It may be surmised that the width of the blocks of buildings between the streets was set at 42 cubits (or 7 reeds) which is approximately 21 m. The width of the streets was certainly 6 cubits (one reed) or *ca.* 3 m. When the width of the entire area is calculated, a length of 157.5 m. is yielded which comprises 7 blocks of buildings (i.e. 294 cubits or 145.5 m.) and 6 streets (36 cubits or 17.8 m.) and their planned length must have been 163.5 m. The deviation from the plan was thus 5.8 m., an error of only 3.6%. When it is considered that the lines of the streets are parallel, it can be seen that this error is quite small, showing great engineering capability.

16. Megiddo Stratum IVB

Megiddo. Northeastern section of Iron Age II town: city-wall 325, northern complex of 'stables' 407.

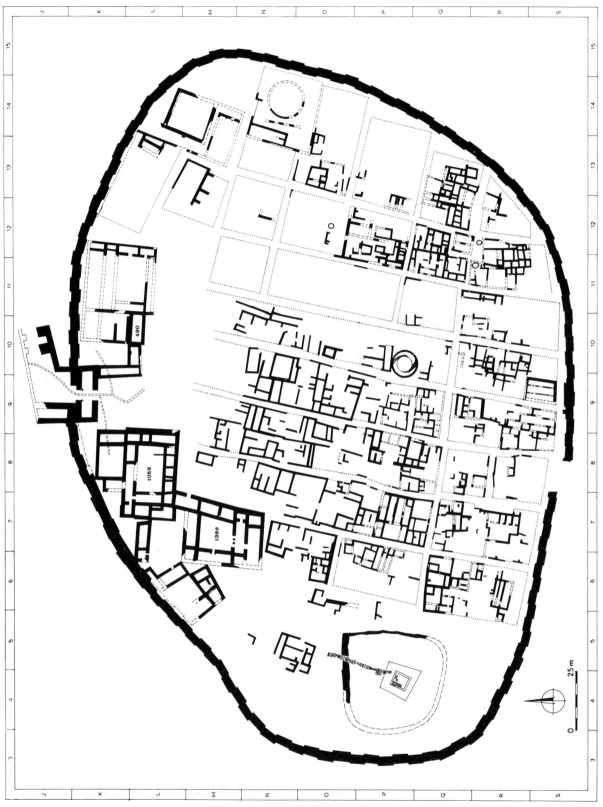

17. Megiddo Strata III–II. *Megiddo* I, Figs. 71-73, 89.

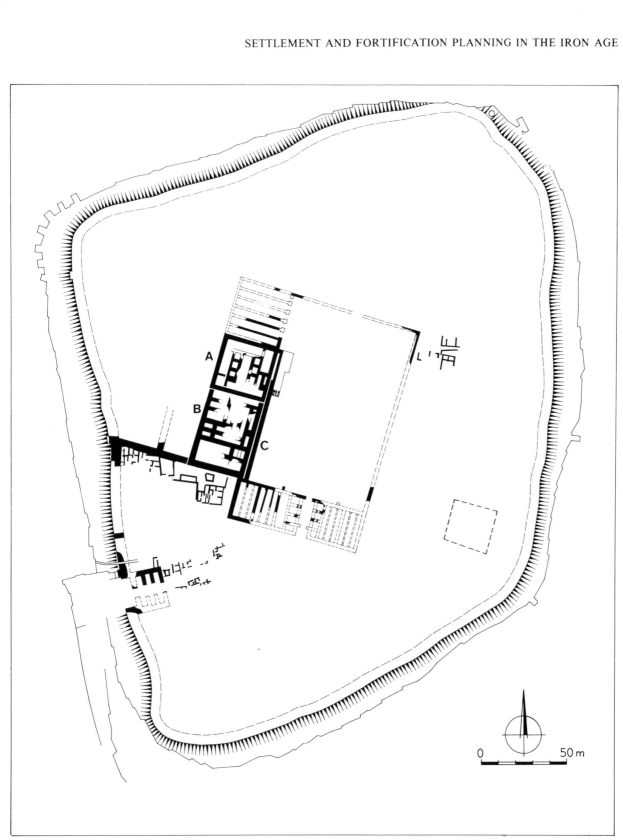

18. Lachish Strata V-III.

Stratum II (reign of Josiah)[67] part of the residential area continued in use while on the eastern part of the settlement a fortress was built.

Lachish Stratum III. — Most available data from the Iron Age at Lachish (Fig. 18) is derived from Stratum III.[68] The most prominent element of the plan in this stratum is the spacious enclosure which occupies the major part of the settlement's interior — a square enclosure measuring 106 × 106 m. (200 × 200 cubits?) to which was annexed a wing of storehouses in the south. The total area is *ca.* 13 dunams. The enclosure comprised a raised palace, a court, royal storehouses, and an additional group of structures south of the court which may have been warehouses or stables. The central court was probably used to accommodate passing caravans and army units. There may have been another public area north of the thick revetment which is a continuation westward of the palace's southern side. Another public area consists of a large pit, perhaps an unfinished quarry or water system, uncovered southeast of the city. The entire public area, along with the city-gate, covers *ca.* 15 dunams.

The residential quarters uncovered at Lachish lie east of the gate, unlike at Beersheba or Gezer, where there is no inner plaza. Several shops open onto the street leading to the gate from the east. The residential quarters were not built in accordance with any clear, well-defined plan, or for the maximal utilization of the area for building purposes. It is not clear whether all the residential quarters have been uncovered, but there are indications that the residential structures covered only a small area of the city, perhaps only 15% of its 70 dunams, in which a population of 500 persons resided.

The contrast between the monumental planning of the public part of Lachish and the poor residential quarters, indicates a predominantly administrative function which accounts for the presence of the fortifications, palace, court, storehouses, and perhaps also the stables.

An analysis of the city plans of Megiddo Stratum IVB and Lachish Stratum III indicates the obvious predominance of the well-planned public-administrative units over the poor, irregularly-planned private residential quarters. This may indicate the existence of two groups of residents, the representatives of the Monarchy who lived in sumptuous buildings, and the private residents who built their houses themselves.

Secondary Administrative Centres

Tel Beersheba is the only city which may be categorized as a secondary administrative centre, although typologically there are points of resemblance between Beersheba and the royal fortresses which have been uncovered in Judah.[69]

The area of the city was approximately 11.5 dunams, *ca.* 60% of which has been excavated in the latest Iron Age city (Stratum II) from the eighth century (Fig. 19).[70] Of the earlier cities only very small portions have been exposed, but apparently there was continuity in the city plan beginning with Stratum V, the first royal city from the time of the United Monarchy. The continuity is embodied in the continuous existence of the peripheral road (beginning in Stratum V) and in the western residential quarter (beginning at least from Stratum III).[71]

Unlike Megiddo Strata VA and IVB and Lachish Stratum III, Beersheba seems to have been planned all at one time when the areas for public building and the areas for dwellings were incorporated into a single harmonious system. This is evident in the street system. The outer peripheral road is parallel to the city-wall and separated from it by a row of buildings. The inner peripheral road is parallel to the outer one; the distance between them is twice the distance between the outer road and the city-wall. In addition, the settlement is divided down the middle by a street emerging from the city-gate. The street layout enables efficient internal transportation as well as drainage of runoff water through the gate. The streets are of quite uniform width (*ca.* 2.5 m.). The house facades are generally straight; the curve required by the oval contour of the city was achieved by varying the angles between the houses.

---

67. For a discussion of the historical considerations in favour of viewing Stratum II as the result of Israelite or Egyptian initiative see A. Malamat: Josiah's Bid for Armageddon, *JANES* 5 (1973), pp. 267–279.

68. The plan is based upon the following sources: *Lachish* III, Pl. 114 and *Lachish* V, Pl. 58 and plans from Ussishkin's excavations which were copied with his kind permission. D. Ussishkin: Lachish in the Days of the Kingdom of Judah — The Recent Archaeological Excavations, *Qadmoniot* 15 (1982), p. 42 (Hebrew).

69. On the functional parallel between Beersheba and Arad see Herzog (above, n. 1).

70. The plan of the settlement in this stratum and the proposed reconstruction of the blocks of buildings and streets and parts of the city which were not excavated, were processed and prepared anew by the author.

71. I. Beit-Arieh: The Western Quarter, in *Beer-Sheba* I, pp. 31–37.

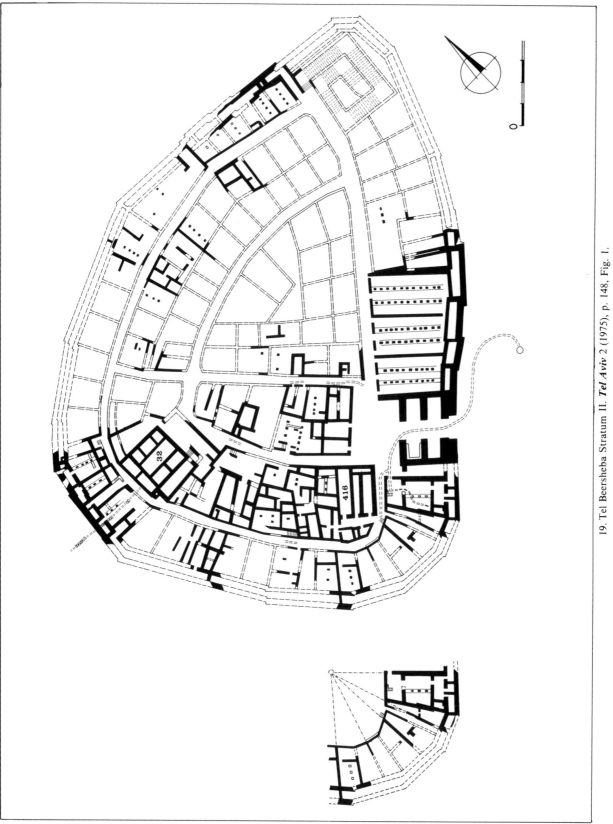

19. Tel Beersheba Stratum II. *Tel Aviv* 2 (1975), p. 148, Fig. 1.

259

Beersheba. Iron Age II (Stratum II), aerial view.

A characteristic phenomenon at Beersheba is the incorporation of the houses into the casemate wall, unlike the casemate wall at Hazor (Strata X–V) for example, which is separated from the city by a road.[72] The public buildings at Beersheba included the city-gate, the forecourt of the gate, three units of storehouses covering an area of *ca.* 600 sq. m.), and a water system most probably built in Stratum V. Of the rest of the city buildings which served as dwellings, Building 416 is noteworthy. It may have been the residence of the governor of the city, while Building 32 (the 'cellar house') may have been erected

to replace the destroyed sanctuary.[73] Common in the residential area is a structure consisting of a pair of long halls separated by a row of pillars, with a long space behind them. In some of these structures there is another hall in the front, sometimes with stairs leading up to the roof.

According to this analysis, Beersheba exhibits a radial city plan. This conclusion is based on the fact that the main construction lines in all the exposed dwelling blocks converge at a single point within the city's area (Fig. 19).[74] Therefore, it may be inferred that the planners used cords anchored with a tent

72. *Hazor* II, Pls. CXCIX–CCIII. It should be noted that the example from Hazor as well as the city plans of Megiddo, Gezer, and Tell el-Far'ah (North) indicate that the conception of the existence of a ring road within the peripheral belt of houses does not appear universally in the planning of Israelite cities as one might suppose from the discussion in Shiloh (above, n. 1, 1978).

73. Z. Herzog, A.F. Rainey and S. Moshkovits: The Stratigraphy at Beer-sheba and the Location of the Sanctuary, *BASOR* 225 (1977), pp. 49–58. For another suggested location for the horned altar at Beersheba see Y. Yadin: Beer-sheba: The High Place Destroyed by King Josiah, *BASOR* 222 (1976), pp. 5–7.

74. This idea was suggested by the architect Shlomo Lavi during a class on city planning which was given at Tel Aviv University in 1981.

peg at several pivotal points which can be located. Apparently, the length of the cord was equal to the radius of the outer line of the city-wall. The relation between the various angles of the house walls may be due to chance (in keeping with the curves of the settlement as a whole), but this seems unlikely. Rather, the plan was determined by the pivotal points used when planning with the cord.[75] In the first phase of the building process, the city-wall was built in accordance with the shape of the hill, but in straight sections, and projections were created in the angles between these sections. In the second phase the blocks of dwellings were built leaning against the city-wall with the aid of the pivotal points, and only afterward was the inner part of the city planned. The public buildings (the gate, storehouses, water system, and governor's residence) were planned in the third phase, using the orthogonal method, with slight deviations deriving from the adaptation of the structure to the street lines.

The harmony of the plan of Beersheba, by contrast with those of Megiddo and Lachish (see below), may result from the fact that public needs were limited, and the population consisted of administrative officials whose houses were part of the public-administrative system. This fits a small city the size of Beersheba which served as an administrative centre for a geographical area of secondary importance. The dwellings take up 9 out of 11.5 dunams (approximately 78%). Some 600 persons inhabited 75 residential units, an average of approximately 52 persons per dunam.

Provincial Towns

Several settlements may be defined as provincial towns. The main examples discussed here are Tell Beit Mirsim and Tell en-Nasbeh.

Tell Beit Mirsim.[76] — The city's area is *ca.* 30 dunams, of which approximately seven have been exposed in two separate quarters. The city-wall is ascribed to Stratum B3 (first half of the fifteenth century B.C.), but most of the city excavated belongs to Stratum A2, which is contemporary to Beersheba Stratum II.[77]

The clearest architectural unit in the city is the city-wall which was built according to the topography and the peripheral plan. The excavated part of the city has no public buildings. Even the city-gate with its two

phases is not a gatehouse but only a simple entrance guarded by towers. The layout of the houses shows that few were built according to a plan,[78] in contrast with the high degree of planning at Beersheba. The streets are not of uniform width and are, in fact, little more than open areas between the houses. Access to some of the houses is through winding alleys. Unlike in Beersheba, in Tell Beit Mirsim there is no uniform row of houses parallel to the city-wall. In a few of the dwellings, the residents could not use the rooms of the city-wall. Unlike in Beersheba, where all the houses have a common wall, in Tell Beit Mirsim there are many instances of double walls which may indicate that the dwellings were the property of the residents. Moreover, the erection of the dwellings in the centre of the city indicates a lack of any planning in their orientation, as can be seen in several of the areas of settlement. Apparently here, too, there was a process of agglutinative growth. The land was not utilized efficiently — *ca.* 53% of the area as opposed to *ca.* 92% in Beersheba. The number of inhabitants of Tell Beit Mirsim, based on Shiloh's estimate of 164 dwellings, was approximately 1300 persons (eight persons per family) and the population density was around 44 persons per dunam.[79] This waste of space in Tell Beit Mirsim can be considered as further proof of lack of planning.

With the exception of the city-wall, no public buildings were discovered in the excavated areas. The western tower does not belong to the original plan, while the public building (citadel?), only partially exposed near the city-gate, was probably built at a later phase[80] (both are most likely from the seventh century B.C.). In light of all these facts, it seems quite certain that Tell Beit Mirsim was not a planned city, and was, therefore, entirely different from the administrative cities discussed above. Thus, it should be considered a provincial town, differing from a village mainly in size and fortifications.

Tell en-Nasbeh. — Despite stratigraphic problems, it is apparent that a great part of the remains uncovered thus far belong to the late phases of the city from the Iron Age II (Fig. 20). Of the city, whose area is *ca.* 30 dunams (like Tell Beit Mirsim), some 70% has been excavated. The city comprises four elements: 1. the massive city wall; 2. densely packed dwellings;

75. It is a fact that other settlements with peripheral houses do not seem to exhibit this trait.
76. For plans see *Tell Beit Mirsim* III, Pls. 3–7.
77. *Beer-Sheba* I, p. 6.
78. Kenyon was the first to note this fact which Aharoni stressed, contrary to Shiloh — Kenyon (above, n. 64), p. 273; *Beersheba* I, p. 17 and n. 9; Shiloh (above, n. 1, 1970), p. 185.
79. Shiloh (above, n. 1, 1978), pp. 28–29. Shiloh estimated the empty and the public areas at only 25% of the total area.
80. Above, n. 77.

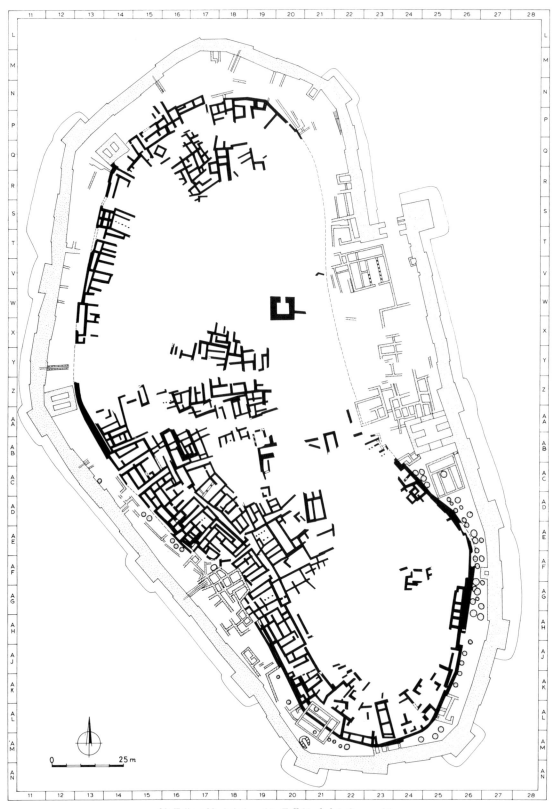

20. Tell en-Nasbeh (north). *Tell Nasbeh* I, Survey Map.

3. three four-room houses; 4. tens of silos located between the houses and the city-wall.

The city-wall was built at the beginning of the ninth century B.C. The area of the settlement which preceded it (in the eleventh–tenth centuries B.C.) was smaller, only 15 dunams in all. Of the 15 additional dunams, the city-wall, its towers and the glacis occupied some 6 dunams, while the area of the city, enlarged by the city-wall, reached ca. 9 dunams.

It is difficult to determine the plan of the early settlement. In disagreement with Shiloh, this should not be considered as a planned settlement with a casemate wall and peripheral road,[81] but as a provincial settlement partly surrounded by a peripheral belt of houses and partly by a city-wall 1–2 m. thick (indicated in solid lines in the figure).

The plan of the enlarged city (indicated with dotted lines in the figure), is clearer. In addition to a massive city-wall and towers, three four-room houses were erected in the new area and several buildings were annexed to them, especially in the area south of the city-gate. The setting of the structures and their regular plan indicate that they were built for the officials of the Monarchy who were in command of the city when it became a fortress-city.[82] In addition to these structures, the new area contained 40 stone-lined silos. The concentration of the silos in this area shows that they belonged to the Monarchy, but supplied the needs of the public, that is, the storage and supply of grain. In those cities which were originally built as administrative centres, special storehouses were built for this purpose, but at Tell en-Nasbeh, where the existing provincial town was not destroyed, the planners found an original solution to the problem of storage.

A similar solution was also adopted to solve the water supply problem. In the early settlement, water was collected in rock-cut cisterns inside the houses of the settlement. When the massive city-wall was built, at least six additional cisterns were hewn beneath the planned course of the city-wall and the wall was built over them. The rain which fell on the enlarged city area collected in drainage channels leading to the cisterns and went to fill the city's reserves, increasing its capacity to withstand a siege.

These data from Tell en-Nasbeh present a unique model of an Israelite city which began as a provincial town and which, with its conversion to an administrative city, was not re-planned: the royal administrative units — fortifications, storehouses, and water supply system — were located in the belt of buildings which was added by enlarging the area of the city.

The enlargement had almost no effect on the size of the population. If it is assumed that 750 persons inhabited the original area of 15 dunams, then the new structures added at most 50 persons when the area of the city was doubled. Therefore, the population density in the enlarged city would have been only 26.7 persons per dunam.

In addition to Tell Beit Mirsim and the early city of Tell en-Nasbeh, a provincial town was also uncovered in Bet Shemesh Stratum IIA, but a plan of this city cannot be published due to imprecision in the stratigraphic data. In its essential characteristics, this city is a continuation of the Iron Age village from Stratum III, except that in several places a casemate wall was added in the fifth century B.C.

Conclusion: Urban Settlement Models in the Iron Age II

In his study of the Israelite city, Y. Shiloh proposed a model with the following essential characteristics: a city-wall with a peripheral belt of houses abutting it, and parallel to it a peripheral road; the nucleus of the settlement lay within the area bounded by this road.[83] An analysis of the city plans surveyed above shows that there are a number of different models of Iron Age II cities whose architectural characteristics indicate their differing functions within the framework of the royal administration. The models of the Iron Age II urban settlement are:

Capital City. — The only example is the royal acropolis at Samaria with its orthogonal plan both

---

81. Shiloh (above, no. 1, 1978), pp. 38–40, Fig. 3. Yadin's attempt to reconstruct 'an early casemate wall' in the area south of the northern gate is not plausible. The two sections of walls which were uncovered in this place are not parallel or connected to each other. Furthermore, the walls are located on a stone terrace which is 10 m. lower than the houses of the city to the west of them and stratigraphically they cannot serve as fortifications. See Y. Yadin: The Archaeological Sources for the Period of the Monarchy, in A. Malamat (ed.): *The World History of the Jewish People, The Age of the Monarchies: Culture and Society*, Jerusalem, 1979, pp. 131–168 (Hebrew).

82. Branigan emphasized the uniqueness of the four-room houses and proposed that they be viewed as the residence of the army officers in command of the sections of the city-wall. In the writer's opinion, their administrative functions also included the food and water supplies as shall be stressed below. See K. Branigan: The Four-Room Buildings of Tell en-Nasbeh, *IEJ* 16 (1966), pp. 206–208.

83. Shiloh (above, no. 1, 1978).

ZEEV HERZOG

in the outer contour and its internal layout. The royal
enclosure at Samaria covered an area of 26 dunams,
which is nearly the same as the area of Tell en-Nasbeh
or Bet Shemesh, and more than double the area of
Beersheba. In terms of area, fortifications, and closed
plan, Samaria constitutes an organic administrative-
military unit totally separate from the lower city
around it. It can be surmised that a similar royal
enclosure was also built in Jerusalem on the hill north
of the City of David.

Major Administrative City. — In contrast with the
acropolis at Samaria, the contour of the administrative
cities is oval and built according to the peripheral
principle. The distinction between the parts of the city
which served the royal administration and the areas
devoted to the dwellings of the civilian population
is clear and highlighted by the differences in the
planning principles: the structures serving the needs
of the administration were erected according to
the orthogonal principle, whether in separate units
distributed over the area of the city (Megiddo
Stratum IVB) or concentrated in a single enclosure
(Lachish Stratum III). On the other hand, the civilian
dwellings were built according to the peripheral
principle but were extremely poor in comparison. The
predominantly royal function of the city is reflected
in the layout of the areas within it. The limited
area designated for private dwellings indicates that
the population of the chief administrative cities was
only 500–750 persons. The great majority (82–84%)
of the area of these cities was devoted to public
structures such as storehouses or stables, palaces, large
courtyards, water systems, etc. Hence the population
density in these cities was only 10 persons per
dunam, a mere one-fifth of the generally accepted
estimate! The concentration of royal structures in the
administrative city is evident in the city of Megiddo
Stratum VA in which *ca.* 25% of the area was devoted
to official functions, and whose population numbered
approximately 1700 persons, that is, 32 persons per
dunam. The difference between Megiddo Strata VA
and IVB exemplifies the depletion of the civilian
population from the administrative cities as their
importance within the royal administration grew.

In addition to Megiddo and Lachish, most probably
the cities which existed in the Iron Age II at Hazor,
Gezer, and Tel Dan belong to this model, but the
architectural data are too meagre to confirm this
supposition.

Secondary Administrative City. — A clear example
of this model is Beersheba Stratum II. Its plan
exhibits a striking absence of any distinction between

administrative areas and private residential quarters,
while the overall radial arrangement of the city is
pronounced. Presumably in small administrative cities
in secondary areas, the whole city was erected at the
behest of the Monarchy for the exclusive needs of the
officials of the administration. From this standpoint
Beersheba is a 'public city' in every sense and played
a role similar to that of the royal fortresses uncovered
in Judah and the Negev.[84] Excellent planning enabled
maximum utilization (92%) of the area for building.
The population of the city numbered approximately
600 persons, with a population density of 52 persons
per dunam.

Provincial Town. — By contrast with the
administrative cities, the provincial towns have no
or few public structures. Most of the city's area is
occupied by private dwellings which are not planned
but rather emerged within the city according to the
agglutinative principle. The influence of the central
government is discernible in these towns in the
construction of the city-wall around the settlement.
The secondary role of the provincial town meant that
the city-wall was generally an economical casemate
wall (Tell Beit Mirsim) whose rooms partly served
the residents of the adjacent houses. In a number
of cases the provincial town was protected by a belt
of peripheral houses, and partly by sections of a
city-wall (as in the early city at Tell en-Nasbeh and
Bet Shemesh Stratum IIA). The lack of planning in
the provincial town is also reflected in the inefficient
utilization of the urban area for building: nearly 40%
of the area of Tell Beit Mirsim was empty as opposed
to a mere 8% of the area devoted to streets and the
enlargement of the gate at Beersheba.

Tell en-Nasbeh is a good example of the conversion
of a provincial town into an administrative city in
which the administrative area surrounded the early
provincial town which remained intact. This change in
the function of Tell en-Nasbeh may be understood in
light of its identification with biblical Mizpah/Mizpeh
which, with the division of the Monarchy, became a
border town in the north of the Kingdom of Judah.

Y. Ikeda has studied the terms *al sarruti* — 'royal
city' and *al dannuti* — 'fortified city' in the Neo-
Assyrian sources referring to the kingdoms of the
house of Adan and Hammat in northern Syria. He
noticed that in the area of one kingdom there was
more than one royal city and hence the capital was

84. Chap. 26 in this volume.

not the only city so designated.[85] According to the city models which have been discerned in the Land of Israel, the capital cities and main administrative cities fit the Assyrian definition of a 'royal city', whereas the secondary administrative cities, fortresses, and provincial towns fit the Assyrian term 'fortified city'.

The city in Megiddo Stratum III is an outstanding example of an Assyrian administrative city in the Land of Israel. It is characterized by overall planning and regularly laid-out streets which have no parallel in the Iron Age II.

Fortifications in the Iron Age II

Typological Classifications

In the early 1960's Y. Yadin proposed a schematic development for the fortifications in the Land of Israel whose main features were as follows: until the time of Solomon the fortified cities were protected by casemate walls, whereas beginning in the ninth century, the walls were of the offset-and-inset type. 'The reason for this was, most likely, that during this period the armies of Assyria began to make use of mighty battering rams which casemate walls could not withstand ... hand in hand with the change in the style of city walls there also began a change in the plans of city gates. Instead of the six-chambered gates, in the beginning of the ninth century they started to build four-chambered gates. The reduction in the size of both storeys of the gate made it sturdier, less apt to be toppled by the battering ram. This process was gradually improved until finally a small, two-chambered but not massive, gate came into use'.[86] Yadin never modified this scheme[87] but his starting point, which exclusively links changes in type of city-walls and gates with the appearance of the Assyrian battering ram, may be attacked on four major grounds:

Chronology. — The battering ram appeared in Assyria several decades later than the appearance of massive walls in the Land of Israel, even according to Yadin's own estimates. The earliest battering rams are depicted

in Assyrian reliefs from the time of Assurnasirpal II (883–859 B.C.), but these battering rams are still rather crude, clumsy and difficult to transport long distances. Tiglath-pileser III, in the eighth century B.C., was the first to introduce light, manoeuverable battering rams into his army, and he owed the conquest of many strong fortified cities to this invention.[88] On the other hand, Yadin himself assigns the offset-and-inset wall at Megiddo to the time of Jeroboam I, that is, the last quarter of the tenth century — decades before the appearance of the early battering ram and 175 years before the light, transportable battering ram came into use.

Methodology. — No one factor can be cited as the sole determining factor for the types of fortifications. Even if chronologically it were possible to weigh the impact of the appearance of the battering ram, the urban planners still had to take into account additional factors before they decided what type of fortifications best suited each city. First and foremost among these factors was the role of the city within the Monarchy. Whether capital city, major or secondary administrative city, or provincial town, it would affect the position of the city within the overall strategic system of the Monarchy. For example, in the provincial town of Tell en-Nasbeh, a massive city-wall was built because the city stood on the northern border of the kingdom of Judah, while in Tell Beit Mirsim, which is not near any border, a casemate wall was preferred. A third functional factor was certainly the economic consideration. Undoubtedly in those areas in which economizing was important, the casemate wall was preferred because of its obvious advantages: it requires less building materials and fewer man-hours than a massive wall, and more efficiently utilizes the area of the city.

The Archaeological Finds. — An analysis of the archaeological finds, both from Megiddo, on which Yadin based his scheme, and from many other sites excavated in the last 20 years, does not substantiate his scheme. A stratigraphic analysis of the Israelite strata at Megiddo[89] shows that the settlement of Stratum VA (Fig. 15) was surrounded by a belt of houses without any freestanding wall, whereas the offset-and-inset wall and the six-chambered gate were first built in Stratum IVB (see Fig. 16). The excavators of Megiddo considered the possibility that this gate had two phases of use, the earlier being adjacent to

85. Y. Ikeda: Royal Cities and Fortified Cities, Iraq 41 (1979), pp. 75–87. The author would like to thank Israel Ephat for drawing his attention to this article.
86. Y. Yadin: Hazor, Gezer, and Megiddo in Solomon's Times, in A. Malamat (ed.): *The Kingdoms of Israel and Judah*, Jerusalem, 1962, pp. 107–108 (Hebrew).
87. Yadin (above, n. 81).
88. Y. Yadin: *The Art of Warfare in Biblical Lands in the Light of Archaeological Study*, Jerusalem, 1963, pp. 313–316.
89. Herzog (above, n. 1), pp. 109–118.

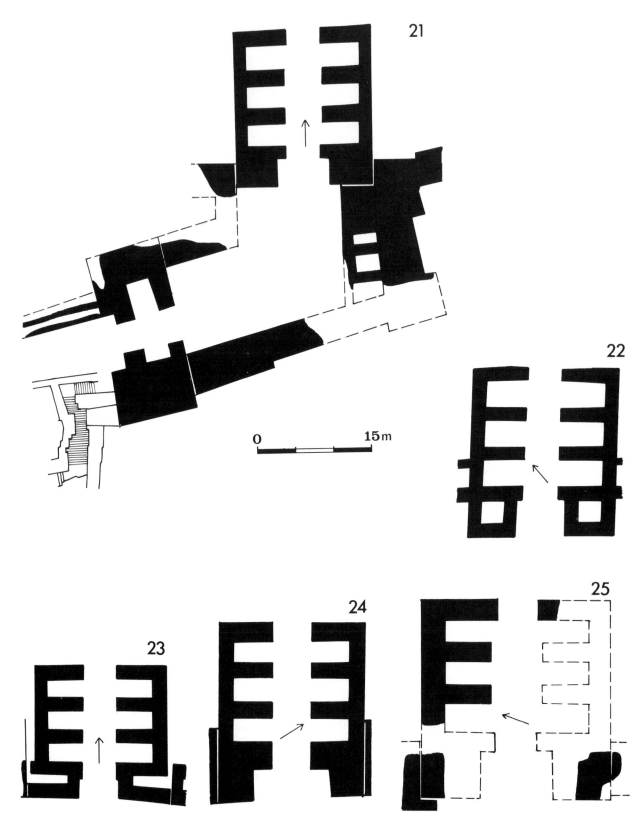

21. Megiddo. Z. Herzog: Das Stadttor in Israel und in den Nachbarländern. Fig. 83.   22. Hazor. *Ibid.*, Fig. 81.   23. Gezer. *Ibid.*,
Fig. 82.   24. Ashdod. *Ibid.*, Fig. 80.   25. Lachish. *Ibid.*, Fig. 84.

the access road of Stratum VA, as became apparent from an examination of the diary of excavations kept by Y. Shiloh.[90] However, the fact that the excavators were aware of such a possibility yet decided to reject it, and even omitted it from the final publication of the excavations, proves that they possessed clear stratigraphic data militating against it. In fact, these data are also clear in their tentative plan: the walls of Access Road 2150 do not touch the offset-and-inset wall or the gate, but are clearly 'cut' by them, and the drainage channel built into the northern wall of the road passes under the base of the southeastern pilaster of the gate. Thus the six-chambered gate at Megiddo was built at the same time as the offset-and-inset wall and both of them preceded by several decades the introduction of the battering ram into the Assyrian army.

Nor does an examination of the types of gates confirm Yadin's scheme. First of all, there is no basis for his assumption that the four-chambered gate is stronger than the six-chambered. The Iron Age II city-gates, which measure *ca.* 20 m. × 20 m., were massive fortifications so solid that they could not be knocked down as a complete unit. Only the outer walls were for defensive purposes, and these did not change at all at Megiddo when the six-chambered gate was replaced by the four-chambered. Apparently, in choosing the city-gates, the planners were moved by consideration of the many and varied uses (civil and military) of the gate chambers, which would influence the appearance of various types of structures during that period.

Unequivocal archaeological-stratigraphic proof of the incorrectness of the schematic approach comes from the latest excavations at Ashdod. Here two gates were discovered. The earlier one, from the end of the eleventh century B.C., has four chambers while the later gate, from the tenth century, has six chambers (Fig. 24).[91] In other words, the order of development was just the reverse of that postulated by Yadin. Yet another example comes from Beersheba (see Fig. 19) where two four-chambered gates were found, the earlier from the tenth century and the later from the ninth century.[92]

Function. — In any examination of Iron Age II fortification methods, due emphasis must be placed

upon the highly impressive water systems in such cities as Hazor, Megiddo, Gezer, Jerusalem, Beersheba, and Gibeon (see Chap. 25), for these, too, must be studied in light of methods of warfare during this period. The tremendous engineering and technical efforts invested in these systems clearly show that the planners of the fortifications sought a solution to the problem of prolonged siege and that this problem was even more pressing than that of frontal assault upon the city with battering rams. In this connection it is instructive to note that some of the cities in which elaborate water systems were constructed, such as Gezer and Beersheba, were protected by casemate walls against frontal assault. From this it can be concluded that frontal assault with the aid of battering rams was not the overriding consideration in planning defenses for the Israelite cities.

The appearance of the glacis, another feature of Iron Age II fortifications, which was meant to protect the city-walls from without, is not consistent with the assumption that the fortifications of this period were determined by the introduction of the battering ram. The obvious function of the ramparts was to protect the foundations of the city-wall from erosion and to impede the attacker's efforts to penetrate into the city by digging down under the wall. On the other hand, if the attackers intended to use a battering ram to breach the city-wall, the first thing they would do, obviously, would be to heap up a ramp of dirt and rocks on top of which they would move the heavy battering rams close to the wall. In that case, the sloping glacis would have made a solid base for the attacker's ramp. Once again we see that the threat of the battering ram was not the overriding factor in the choice of defense systems for the Israelite city. Sloping dirt glacis have been uncovered in many Iron Age II sites such as Beersheba, Lachish, and Tel Malhata, while stepped (or sloping) glacis built of stone have been found at Tell en-Nasbeh and Gezer.

It may be surmised, then, that most of the city-walls were strengthened with outside glacis, even if the area outside the city-wall has not been excavated. At any rate, in all examples cited above, the glacis, which would actually have facilitated the use of the battering ram, abuts the massive city-wall whose main purpose was, presumably, to make this more difficult.

On the basis of the above chronological, methodological, stratigraphic, and functional considerations, a different approach is proposed for the analysis of the methods of fortification in the Iron Age II. Instead of a rigid scheme based on a single functional factor, the variety of fortification methods which

---

90. Shiloh (above, n. 55), Fig. 3.
91. *Ashdod* IV, pp. 52–56.
92. Y. Aharoni: The Building Activities of David and Solomon, *IEJ* 24 (1974), pp. 13–16; Herzog (above, n. 1), pp. 132–139; and *Enc. Miqr.* VIII, s.v. 240–243 (Hebrew).

Table 2: Characteristics of Six-Chambered Gates
(measurements in metres)

Site	Overall Measurements		Width of Passage	Thickness of Walls		Dimensions of Chambers		Forecourt of Gate		Type of Wall	Date of Construction
	Facade	Depth		Length	Width	Width	Depth	Width	Depth		
Megiddo IVB	17.50	19.75	4.25	1.47	2.10	2.80	4.80	6.50	3.50	Massive	Mid-10th Cent.
Hazor X	18.20	20.50	4.20	1.60	1.60	3.00	5.00	6.10	4.50	Casemate	Mid-10th Cent.
Gezer	17.00	17.00	4.10	1.60	1.60	2.20	4.50	5.00	3.00	Casemate	Mid-10th Cent.
Lachish IV	24.50	25.00	5.20	2.80	2.20	*2.80	6.00	17.00	*6.50	Massive	End-10th Cent.
Ashdod	18.40	20.90	4.90	1.70	1.95	*3.30	5.00	10.00	3.70	Massive	End-10th Cent.
Tel 'Ira ?		18.00	?	1.60	1.60	*2.50	?	?	?	Casemate	8th Cent.

* Average measurement.

Table 3: Characteristics of Four-Chambered Gates
(measurements in metres)

Site	Overall Measurements		Width of Passage	Thickness of Walls		Thickness of Towers on Facade	Dimensions of Chambers		Date of Construction
	Facade	Depth		Length	Width	Width	Depth	Width	
Megiddo IVA	25.00	15.50	4.20	2.30	2.20	5.00	*3.00	8.20	End–10th Cent.
Beersheba V	20.80	12.60	4.20	2.00	2.00	3.00	3.00	6.00	Beg.–10th Cent.
Beersheba III	16.60	13.60	3.60	1.00	2.00	3.80	3.00	5.00	9th Cent.
Tel Dan	29.50	17.80	3.70	3.60	2.20	5.00	*4.50	9.00	10th Cent.
Ashdod 10	16.50	13.75	4.20	1.00	1.20	4.80/6.10	2.40	3.80	End–11th Cent.
Tell en-Nasbeh (Early)	15.00	12.00	4.00	1.50	2.10	6.60	1.80	*4.40	End-10th Cent.

* Maximum measurement

Table 4: Characteristics of Two-Chambered Gates
(measurements in metres)

Site	Overall Measurements		Width of Passage	Thickness of Walls		Dimensions of Chambers		Former type of Defense	Date
	Facade	Depth		Length	Width	Width	Depth		
Megiddo IVa	13.00	7.00	3.00	1.80	1.80	3.00	3.00	Indirect approach	End of 11th Cent.
Megiddo VA	11.50	6.00	3.00	2.00	2.00	2.50	2.50	Indirect approach	Beg. of 11th Cent.
Tell Beit Mirsim B3	13.50	6.00	4.00	1.50	1.50	2.00	3.00	Towers	Beg. of 11th Cent.
Tell Beit Mirsim A2	13.50	6.00	2.00	1.50	2.00	2.00	3.00	Indirect entry	8th Cent.
Megiddo III	24.50	12.50	4.20	2.20	2.60	4.60	8.00	Front gate	8th Cent.

existed side by side at various times during this period, chosen as a result of various functional considerations, should be emphasized. One such consideration was the function of the city within the monarchical administration, its location and strategic importance, and the adaptation of the fortifications to the expected form of attack upon the city.

In order to demonstrate how varied were the methods of fortification, the various components of the fortifications will be presented and summarized, in a chronological-typological table (Table 5).

A Peripheral Belt of Houses

This form of defense, which is clearly a continuation of the tradition of Iron Age I enclosed settlements (see above), existed in several cities in the Iron Age II, particularly in the first part of the tenth century.

A distinctive example of this can be seen in Megiddo Stratum VA (Fig 15), which continues the local tradition of Late Bronze Age Megiddo. The settlement was defended by the walls of the peripheral houses and palaces, from the roofs of which the defenders could observe and fire down upon the attackers. For this reason, the palaces were built around the perimeter rather than in the center of the settlement. In the excavations at Gezer, Macalister uncovered large portions of the city from Stratum VI. In the northern part of the city continuous parts of dwellings creating a peripheral defense system are discernible. If the six-chambered gate (Fig. 23) and the fortress abutting it in the west, are added to these remains, it may be hypothesized that Gezer, like Megiddo Stratum VA, was protected by a belt of houses along its perimeter into which an administrative unit was incorporated and which was the only part of the city protected by a casemate wall.[93] This principle of defense was also adopted at Tell en-Nasbeh, in the early settlement which continued to exist in the tenth century, and most probably in Lachish Stratum V where the dwellings extended all the way to the edge of the mound.[94]

Examples from Megiddo, Gezer, Tell en-Nasbeh, and Lachish show that in the period of the United Monarchy there was still no need in the hinterland to fortify provincial towns (Tell en-Nasbeh and Lachish Stratum V) or administrative centres in the early stages of crystallization (Megiddo and Gezer). In all four of those cities massive city-walls were erected in the early period of the Kingdoms of Israel and Judah, almost certainly as a result of the destruction wrought by Shishak's campaign, the creation of the new border between the two kingdoms, and the conversion of these cities into important administrative centres.

Casemate Walls

Casemate city-walls are characteristic of Iron Age fortifications in the Land of Israel from the tenth century to the end of the eighth century B.C. Three subtypes of casemate walls may be distinguished which differ from each other in their dimensions and their relation to the houses of the city.

Freestanding Casemate Walls. — This type of casemate wall is separated from structures within the city by a road onto which the entrances to the rooms of the wall opened. A good example of this type is the casemate wall in Hazor Stratum X from the tenth century, assigned to the time of Solomon.[95]

As noted above, the casemate wall at Gezer does not surround all of the city, but is confined to a fortress in the gate area; thus it is not bordered by a road. The casemate wall at 'En Gev Stratum IV (second half of the tenth century) is possibly of this type.[96]

Integrated Casemate Wall. — This type of wall is integrated into the dwellings inside the city. The best and most complete example is found in Stratum III at Beersheba (ninth century) and continued to exist until it was destroyed in the late eighth century (Stratum II). Due to a lower level of planning at Tell Beit Mirsim, the residents of the adjacent houses made use of the rooms of the casemate wall even though they were not always integrated into them. Albright assigned the construction of the casemate wall at Tell Beit Mirsim to the time of David, in the first half of the tenth century.[97]

Filled Casemate Wall. — In this type, the rooms of the wall were not meant for daily use, but most probably served as a framework to be filled with earth. This method created a structure far more stable by comparison with the empty casemate wall, which could be built to a much greater height. On the other hand, this type of wall is no more resistant to the battering ram than the empty casemate wall, for in both types the outer wall served as the defensive link in the fortifications. When a battering ram breached

93. *Gezer* III, Pls. IV–VI; *Gezer* I, 1970, Plan I.
94. Ussishkin, (above, n. 68), p. 44.

95. *Hazor* II, pp. 1–2, Pl. CXCIX (Hebrew).
96. B. Mazar *et al.*: Ein Gev Excavations in 1961, *IEJ* 14 (1964), pp. 1–13, Fig. 2.
97. *Tell Beit Mirsim* III.

Table 5: Typological-Chronological Summary of Details of Fortifications

Type of Fortifications	End of 11th cent.	First half of 10th cent.	Second half of 10th cent.	9th cent.	8th cent.	7th cent.
Peripheral belt of houses	Megiddo VIA,VB Bet Shemesh III Tell en-Nasbeh	Megiddo VA Bet Shemesh IIa Tell en-Nasbeh	Gezer 6 Lachish V			
Casemate wall separate from the settlement	— —	— —	Hazor X 'En Gev IV			
Casemate wall incorporated into the settlement	—	Tell Beit Mirsim B3 —		Beersheba III		
Filled casemate	— —	— —	— —	Samaria II Hazor VIII		
Offset-and inset wall	—	—	Megiddo IVB			
Massive wall with towers	— —	— —	Lachish IV Gezer-outer wall	Tell en-Nasbeh	Hazor VA	
Regular massive wall	Ashdod 10 — — —	Ashdod 9 Beersheba V 'En Gev V Dan (?)	Tel Malhata — — Dan (?)	— — —	Jerusalem Tell Batash III Ashdod-Yam	Lachish II
6-Chambered Gate	— — —	Ashdod 9 — —	Hazor X Gezer 6 Megiddo IVB Lachish IV	—	Tel 'Ira	
4-Chambered Gate	Asdod —	— Dan (?) Beersheba V	Megiddo IVA Dan (?) —	Tell en-Nasbeh —(early) Beersheba III		
2-Chambered Gate	Megiddo VIA —	Megiddo VA — Tell Beit Mirsim B3 —	— —	Tell en-Nasbeh —(late) —	Megiddo III (Assyrian) Tell Beit Mirsim A2	
Gate without Chambers	—	—	—	—		Lachish II

the outer wall, the dirt fill in the casemates spilled out or could easily be scooped out so that the inner wall could be demolished. Therefore the filling in of the casemate wall at Hazor (Stratum X) by the builders of Stratum VIII (ninth century) did not make the wall better able to withstand the Assyrian battering ram as Yadin thought[98], but simply enabled it to be built higher (probably because of the rise in the level of the floors inside the city). The most typical example of a filled casemate wall is in Samaria and it, too, is from the ninth century (the time of Ahab). It must be emphasized that the fortifications of the upper city of the capital of Israel combined a section of a massive wall (in the southeast of the acropolis) with a casemate wall. This shows how local considerations — not a rigid scheme — might influence the choice of fortifications.

Massive Walls

The massive walls from this period are not constructed according to any uniform technique, but consist of several subtypes.

Offset-and-Inset Wall. — A typical wall of this type is the city-wall of Megiddo Stratum IVB from the middle of the tenth century (Fig. 16). The wall is built of sections *ca.* 6 m. long which alternately project and recede. The degree of projection, 0.5–0.6 m., is not sufficient to enable enfilade as the balustrade protecting the defenders on top of the wall prevented

98. Yadin (above, n. 86), pp. 69–70. That the fill in the casemate wall was not added in response to the threat of the battering ram is proven also by the construction of regular dwellings in the continuation of the line of the filled wall, in the northwestern corner of the city. *Hazor*, pp. 169–170, Fig. 45.

them from obtaining the right line of sight. On the other hand, the great advantages of the offset-and-inset wall were that they probably lent greater stability to the wall, and the insets which faced outward could be used for building balconies with holes below them for shooting straight down. In this way it was possible to compensate for the 'dead area' at the foot of the wall. It must be stressed that the offset-and-inset wall at Megiddo is the only one of its kind, so far, to be discovered in Israel.

Wall with Towers. — In this type of massive wall, towers are built into the wall which project quite far (*ca.* 3 m.) and so it is clear that they served as bases for enfilade. The towers must certainly have risen to a much greater height than the other sections of the wall. Inside the towers were rooms, as seen in the Assyrian reliefs showing fortifications in the Land of Israel during the eighth and seventh centuries.[99] A massive wall with towers was uncovered at Tell en-Nasbeh (Fig. 20) from the beginning of the ninth century, at Gezer from the end of the tenth century,[100] and probably at Lachish from the same period.[101] A section of the wall built in Stratum VA at Hazor is also of this type.[102]

Regular Massive Wall. — This group comprises simple massive walls. To be sure, even here there are differences in building techniques, especially in the thickness, but they all lack offsets and insets. Chronologically, the massive wall appeared in the Land of Israel already at the end of the eleventh century, in Stratum 10 at Ashdod. The mud-brick city-wall, 4.5 m. thick, was replaced during the tenth century (Stratum 9) by a thicker wall, 5.6 m. wide, which thickens to 8.9 m. in the vicinity of the gate.[103] The massive wall from Stratum V at Beersheba[104] in the 'sawtooth' style[105] is attributed to the first half of the tenth century. Sections of the wall deviate at intervals in the same direction some 0.3–0.5 m., like the teeth on the blade of a saw, rather than alternately projecting and receding as in the offset-and-inset wall. This technique also appears in the casemate wall

of Strata III–II at Beersheba (see Fig. 19), as well as in the massive wall at Arad in Stratum X. In addition to stability, the projections were possibly meant to break up the smooth expanse of the wall by creating a vertical shadow which would make the wall appear higher, and therefore more formidable, to anyone outside.[106] A narrow section of a massive wall, 1.85 m. thick, was uncovered at 'En Gev in Stratum V from the first half of the tenth century (beneath the casemate wall of Stratum IV).[107] The end of the tenth century was also the period of the massive wall uncovered at Tel Dan, although Aharoni dates it even earlier, to the beginning of that century.[108] The massive wall at Tel Malhata is also dated to the tenth century.[109]

The construction of the mighty seven-meter-thick wall on the western hill of Jerusalem,[110] the four-meter-thick city-wall of Tel Batash in Stratum III,[111] and the city-wall integrated into the dirt rampart at Ashdod-Yam[112] are assigned to the eighth century.

The City-Gate

The approximately 20 Iron Age II city-gates discovered in Israel provide information for understanding the functions of the gate, the various types of gates, and the phases of their use. The functional uniqueness of the city-gates of this period stands out by comparison with the gates of the Middle Bronze II. To be sure, in both periods the passageway of the gate is flanked by two large towers, but whereas in the Bronze Age the rooms of the towers are closed and separate from the passage, and only narrow pilasters projected into it, in the Iron Age II the chambers of the gate open onto the passage all along their width. Their openness, the considerable size of the gate chambers, and the fact that some of them contain benches and stone basins indicate that by contrast with the purely defensive military character of the Bronze Age gates, in the Iron Age the structure of the gate was also suited to daily

99. Yadin (above, n. 88), pp. 360–365.
100. I. Finkelstein: The Date of Gezer's Outer Wall, *Tel Aviv* 8 (1981), pp. 136–145.
101. Ussishkin (above, n. 68), Fig. on p. 45.
102. *Hazor*, pp. 187–189, Fig. 52.
103. Above, n. 91.
104. Aharoni (above, n. 92).
105. *Beer-Sheba* I, Pl. 87.
106. Z. Herzog *et al.*: The Israelite Fortress at Arad, *BASOR* 254 (1984), p. 9.
107. B. Mazar et al. (above, n. 96).
108. Aharoni (above, n. 92).
109. M. Kochavi: The First Season of Excavations at Tel Malhata, *Qadmoniot* 3 (1970), p. 23 (Hebrew).
110. N. Avigad: *The Upper City of Jerusalem*, Jerusalem, 1980, pp. 46–60 (Hebrew).
111. A. Mazar and G.L. Kelm: Canaanites, Philistines and Israelites at Timna/Tel Batash, *Qadmoniot* 13 (1980), pp. 89–137 (Hebrew).
112. J. Kaplan: The Stronghold of Yamani at Ashdod Yam, *EI* 9 (1969), pp. 130–137 (Hebrew).

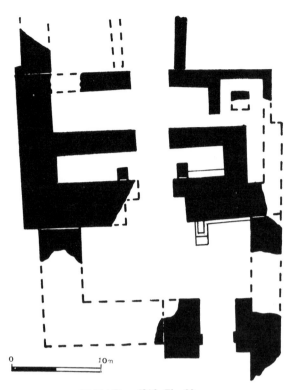

26. Tel Dan. *Ibid.*, Fig. 88.

peacetime civilian needs. The gate chambers, together with the adjacent open places ('the square at the gate of the city', II Chronicles 32:6), were used for drawing up agreements before witnesses and for concluding business deals, as a seat for the elders, the judges, and the prophets, and sometimes, in an emergency, as a seat for the king himself. In several of the gates, such as at Megiddo Stratum VA and Tel Dan, there is evidence of cultic rituals at the 'high places of the gates' (II Kings 23:8). The archaeological and literary evidence present a vivid picture of the Iron Age city-gate which became the social, economic, and military centre of the city.

As stressed above, the archaeological finds are not rich enough to confirm Yadin's hypothesis that there was a gradual decline in the number of gate chambers in the Land of Israel, similar to the change in types in Strata IVB–III at Megiddo. In addition to the contradictory examples cited from Ashdod and Beersheba, the six-chambered gate recently uncovered at Tel 'Ira, a large city founded in the eighth century,[113] should be presented.

113. I. Beit-Arieh: Tel 'Ira — 1980, *Hadashot Arkheologiot* 74–75 (1981), pp. 31–33 (Hebrew). The author would like to thank I. Beit-Arieh for permission to study the plan of the remains from Tel 'Ira and to publish the dimensions of the gate (Table 2).

What was the reason for the change in the number of chambers? It was obviously not connected with forms of warfare, since for that purpose it would have been sufficient to change or strengthen the outer wall of the gate. It must be explained in terms of the daily civilian uses as well as military functions. The pair of chambers closest to the opening of the gate was the area into which the doors turned when opened, and according to the evidence (for example Tel Dan) (Fig. 26), special blocking stones the open doors at right angles to the gate facade. Hence the open doors blocked the greater part of the opening to the first pair of chambers. From this it can be concluded that in two-chambered gates, the gate had the primarily military function of sheltering the guard at the gate (when the gates were locked) and containing the open doors during the day. On the other hand, in the four-chambered gates, an additional pair of chambers was left open and available for civilian activities. A good example of the difference between the two pairs of chambers is in Stratum II at Beersheba where plastered benches were found only in the rear chamber closest to the square.

In terms of the emphasis on the civilian functions of the city-gate, the six-chambered gate may be viewed as the culmination of a process. Even though the two front chambers were largely blocked by the doors, there were still four chambers available for various peacetime activities. The rooms were serving as shops in the marketplace. In the evening the merchants gathered their wares, the doors were closed, and the gate then assumed its military function of transforming the city into a fortress.

Six-Chambered Gates (Table 2). — To date, six gates of this type have been discovered in Megiddo (Fig. 21), Hazor (Fig. 22), Gezer (Fig. 23), Ashdod (Fig. 24), Lachish (Fig. 25), and Tel 'Ira. Despite typological similarity, they differ from each other in external dimensions and in many constructional details. They also differ in the type of city-wall to which they are attached. In Megiddo, Lachish, and Ashdod the gates abut a massive wall; in Hazor and Tel 'Ira they abut a casemate wall, while in Gezer the gate chambers abut a casemate wall which most probably surrounded only an inner citadel. The towers in the facades of the gates also differ. At Hazor the towers are hollow and project beyond the line of the city-wall. At Megiddo they are filled and form a continuation of the line of the city-wall, and only here is there also a sophisticated front gate. At Tel 'Ira the towers are hollow but do not project beyond the line of fortifications.

Tel Dan. Iron Age II city-gate.

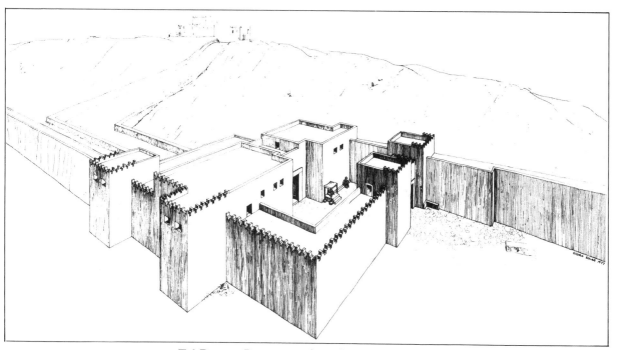

Tel Dan — Reconstruction of Iron Age II city-gate

The gate at Lachish (Fig. 25) is the largest gate excavated so far (*ca.* 25 m. × 25 m.). The gate at Gezer, excluding the outer walls of the casemates, is the smallest. The differences in the thickness of the walls and the dimensions of the chambers show that the gates were not built according to a single fixed plan. There is a certain similarity between the gates at Megiddo and Hazor, but even here the details vary so greatly that they cannot be attributed solely to errors in measurement. This fact, in addition to the other reasons mentioned above, must serve as additional evidence of the absence of schematization in the planning of fortifications, even of a single type of gate. The gates of this type appear from the tenth to the end of the eighth centuries.

Four-Chambered Gates (Table 3).[114] — As in the preceding type, the main similarity among them is the number of chambers, but beyond this, the differences are great. At Tel Dan, Beersheba Stratum V and Megiddo Stratum IVA, the gates are connected to a front gate; in the other gates there is no such structure and so the towers in the facade of the gate are even more prominent. In Beersheba Stratum II (see Fig. 19) the gate abuts a casemate wall, whereas in all the other examples it abuts a massive wall.

Gates of this type appear all through the Iron Age II. A four-chambered gate from the end of the eleventh century has been uncovered at Ashdod. The gates in Beersheba Stratum V and perhaps also at Tel Dan have been assigned to the time of David, in the tenth century. At Megiddo the gate was most probably built after Shishak's campaign at the close of the tenth century, and in that same period a similar gate was built at Tell en-Nasbeh, but was removed from use by the decision to extend the territory of the city toward the north.

Two-Chambered Gates (Table 4).[115] — This type, the simplest of all Iron Age gates, is essentially a framework for the doors. Most of the gates in this group are small gates of cities of only secondary importance. Noteworthy for its unique character and large dimensions is the gate of the Assyrian city in Stratum III at Megiddo (Fig. 27). This fact, too, is sufficient to warn against viewing Megiddo as a schematic model for the changes in the structure of gates. Gates of this type were in use all through the Iron Age II, from the end of the eleventh century in Megiddo Stratum IVA to the eighth-century gate in

Stratum A2 at Tell Beit Mirsim. These gates, except for that of Megiddo Stratum III, are quite small (an average of 6 × 12.5 m.). To this group belongs the late gate at Tell en-Nasbeh which was built between two large towers (see Fig. 20).

27. Megiddo. *Ibid.*, Fig. 96.

Inner Gates of Fortified Palaces. — In several administrative cities the entrance to the royal enclosure was guarded by a gate within the city limits, intended to protect the administrative officials from the civilian population. These gates generally project outward from the enclosure wall and form a type of watch tower and freestanding lookout. Inner gates are found in Megiddo Stratum VA dating to the tenth century (Fig. 15), at the entrance to the enclosure of Palace 1723, in Megiddo Stratum IVB (Fig. 16) at the entrance to Palace 338, and most probably this was also the purpose of the acropolis gate in Bet Shean Stratum V (upper phase).[116] Recently, it was proposed that a freestanding gatehouse be reconstructed in the entry to the acropolis of Lachish (Strata IV–III) (see Fig. 18).

Summary of Types of Fortifications in the Iron Age II

The great variety of fortifications is evidence of the complex of functional considerations facing the planners. This range of military, economic, social, and religious considerations reflects the social institutions which operated within the Israelite city and shaped its character.

The types of fortifications and their chronological distribution are summarized in Table 5 above. The table emphasizes those phases in which the features of the fortifications were first built in the various cities.

114. Z. Herzog (above, n. 1), Figs. 85, 86, 88, 90, 100; *Ashdod* IV, Plans 5–10.
115. Z. Herzog (above, n. 1), Figs. 93–96, 101.

116. *Beth-Shan* I, pp. 1–2, Fig. 2.

25 UNDERGROUND WATER SYSTEMS IN THE LAND OF ISRAEL IN THE IRON AGE

Yigal Shiloh

The regular supply of water, whether in times of peace or war, has always presented a primary challenge to the planners and builders of royal centres in the Near East. The efficient exploitation of water sources, encatchment, storage and distribution, has determined the standard of living of the populace in this mostly semi-arid region. As water resources are better utilized, agriculture is more productive, commerce and the economy in general gain in strength, and the population increases. Developed water systems were especially essential for strengthening settlements, and particularly royal centres, in preparation for war and siege. In a survey of the utilization of water sources in Israel, clear evidence was found that an active approach typifies flourishing periods: the Iron Age, the Early Roman period, the Byzantine period and recent times. In other periods, when there was a decided drop in settlement and central authority, there was also a passive attitude toward the development of water resources and no major engineering projects were undertaken, with a corresponding total reliance upon available sources.

One of the most important factors dictating the location of large settlements in Israel, from the beginning of urbanization in the third millennium B.C., was the proximity of a water source. During the course of the Bronze Age, we find evidence of the construction of reservoirs (some subterranean) and pools for rainwater within the fortified areas of towns, as at Arad,[1] 'Ai,[2] Hazor and Ta'anakh.[3] These

water systems were a more efficient development of the method of storing water in cisterns, common in the Land of Israel, a subject outside the scope of our present discussion. The underground water systems discovered in the royal centres and settlements of the Iron Age II in the Land of Israel, are the earliest examples of engineering activity within the framework of overall urban planning, of which they comprised an essential component.

In the Bible there is considerable evidence of the practical knowledge amassed by the inhabitants of the Land of Israel concerning the various types of water source and their utilization: for instance, the basic difference between a regular supply — flowing streams, such as those in Mesopotamia (Isaiah 8:7), or seasonal flooding of the Nile in Egypt (Exodus 7:19, 24; Isaiah 19:5–9) — and dependence upon irregular sources, such as the quantity of rainfall (Leviticus 26:5; Deuteronomy 11:10–11, 14, 17; I Kings 8:35; Isaiah 30:23), streams (Deuteronomy 8:7), floods (II Kings 3:17) and pools (gbym; II Kings 3:16), dew (Genesis 27:28), springs (Deuteronomy 8:7), wells (Genesis 21:25), cisterns (Deuteronomy 6:11; II Samuel 2:13; II Kings 18:31; I Kings 22:38; Isaiah 22:9, 11). Several artificial, underground water systems are also mentioned in the Bible, particularly those in Jerusalem (II Kings 20:20; II Chronicles 32:30; Isaiah

---

1. Cf. *Arad*, pp. 13–14; R. Amiran: Arad, *Hadashot Arkheologiyot* 74–75 (1980), p. 34.
2. J.A. Callaway: The 1968–69 Ai Excavations, *BASOR* 198 (1970), pp. 7–31.
3. An extensive network of tunnels and drainage channels of the Middle Bronze Age II has been revealed in the lower city of Hazor, mainly in Area F, as well as in the fields to the

east, near the local museum. Cf. *Hazor*, pp. 43–44, 65–66. A large subterranean cistern was also found, hewn into bedrock beneath the Late Bronze Age II palace in Area A (*Hazor*, pp. 126–128). This latter resembles a similar system discovered at Taanakh, of the Late Bronze Age I; cf. P. Lapp: *BASOR* 195 (1969), pp. 31–33. The large depression at the southeastern corner of the enclosure at Hazor served, in our opinion, as a large reservoir for rainwater (*Hazor* I, Pls. I–II; Yadin: The Fifth Season of Excavations at Hazor 1968–1969, *BA* 32 (1969), pp. 50–71.

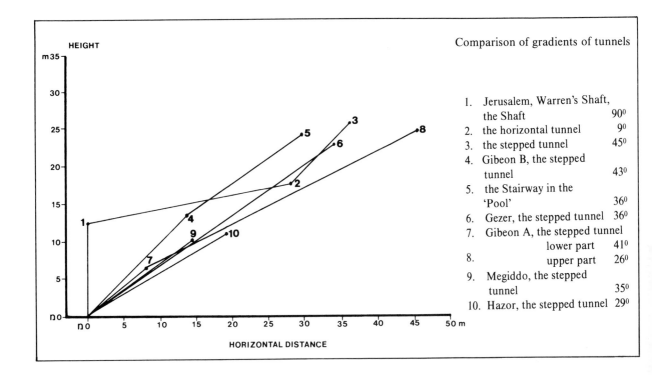

Comparison of gradients of tunnels

1. Jerusalem, Warren's Shaft,
   the Shaft   90⁰
2. the horizontal tunnel   9⁰
3. the stepped tunnel   45⁰
4. Gibeon B, the stepped
   tunnel   43⁰
5. the Stairway in the
   'Pool'   36⁰
6. Gezer, the stepped tunnel   36⁰
7. Gibeon A, the stepped tunnel
                     lower part 41⁰
8.   upper part 26⁰
9. Megiddo, the stepped
   tunnel   35⁰
10. Hazor, the stepped tunnel   29⁰

22:9, 11). These man-made water systems, much in evidence amongst the archaeological discoveries, are the subject of our present discussion.

Though these water systems are quite impressive in their planning and execution, till now they have been the subject of very few comprehensive reviews. The water systems themselves have been treated by the excavators of the various sites — Megiddo, Hazor, Gezer, Ible'am, Gibeon, Beersheba and Jerusalem. The summary by Ruth Amiran[4] was the first to treat the group as a whole, and it has only recently been superseded by the work of the present author[5] and that of D. Cole.[6]

REVIEW OF THE REMAINS

MEGIDDO (Fig. 1)

There are two springs adjacent to Megiddo: the northern spring, 'Ain el-Qubi and the spring at the southwestern corner of the mound, to which the city's water system was connected (Locus 925). The

investigation of another water installation (Locus 2153), adjacent to the city-gate, began in 1967.[7]

The Water System (Locus 925). — The principal water system of Megiddo was investigated by the Chicago Oriental Institute expedition[8] and by the Hebrew University expedition in 1960–1970.[9] These investigators noted several stages in its development:

a. The spring at the base of the mound served in the ordinary manner as a source of water beyond the fortified area.

b. The earliest water system, Gallery 629, was constructed of fine ashlar masonry,[10] and was integrated into the city fortifications of Strata VA–IVB. From the passage through the defences, a stairway continued down to the spring. This system was unsatisfactory for securing the water source in time of war.

c. The major change in the planning of the water system of Megiddo came about in Stratum IVA. Gallery 629 was blocked by the construction of the inset-and-offset wall (325), and a shaft, protected by

4. R. Amiran: Water Supply Tunnels, *EI* 1 (1951), pp. 35–38 (Hebrew).
5. Y. Shiloh: The Ancient Water Systems in Eretz-Israel, Their Date and Typological Classification, *2nd Archaeological Congress*, Jerusalem, 1972 (Unpublished).
6. D. Cole: How Water Tunnels Worked, *BAR* 6 (1980), pp. 8–29.

7. *Hazor*, p. 164.
8. R.S. Lamon: *The Megiddo Water System*, Chicago, 1935.
9. *Hazor*, pp. 161–164.
10. Lamon (above n. 8), pp. 10–12 and Fig. 8.

TABLE 1. MEASUREMENT SPECIFICATIONS OF WATER SYSTEM COMPONENTS

Site	Water System	General gradient		Shaft			Steps			Stepped Tunnel					Horizontal Tunnel				Water Chamber		
		L	D	L	W	D	W	L	%	L	W	H	D	%	L	W	H	D	L	W	H
Megiddo	Gallery 629	49	34												15	1.3	2	1			
	Water System	127	36	6.5	5.0	16	1.2	28	57	(14.5) 18	?	2-3.5	10	69	50	2	3	1	4	4	7
	Northern Water System 2153	22+								(15) 22+	1.5-2.6		11	50							
Hazor	Water System	80	36	16	13	19	2-6	44	43	(19) 22	4	4.5	11	58					5	5	5
Gezer	Water System	29	52							(34) 41	3-3.5	4.5-7	23	67					32	3-8	5+
	Reservoir(?)	73?	18	17/14		18		73?													
Gibeon A	Tunnel	48	24.6							(45) 48	1.2	2-5	24.6	55					7	5	3
Gibeon B	The 'Pool'	38	24.4	10.3/12.3		10.8	1.5	(15.5) 19	70	(14) 19	1	2-9	13.6	97					6.8	3.4	2.5
Ible'am	Tunnel	30+								30	3+	4.2+									
Jerusalem	Warren's Shaft	69	32							(8) 13	2	2.8-3.8	8?	100					4.8	1.8	1.2 / 2.5-5.8
	Siloam Channel	400?													28	2-2.3	2-6	5?			
	Hezekiah's (Siloam) Tunnel	553																			
Tell es-Sa'adiyeh	Stepped ascent																				
Lachish	The 'Great Shaft'	40-50?	25.2	22	25																
Beersheba	Shaft			35+	17+	17?	3.3														
Arad	Cistern																				
Kadesh Barnea	Cistern																				

L = lenght; D = depth; H = height; elevation difference % = gradient percentage; measurements in brackets () = horizont All measurements in metres.

YIGAL SHILOH

Megiddo. Iron Age II, Gallery 629.

supporting walls, was driven down through earlier strata and then hewn to a total depth of some 36 m. below the level of the mound's surface. Steps were hewn around the walls of the shaft, leading to the opening of a stepped tunnel, in turn giving access to a horizontal tunnel running about 50 m. to the spring. The natural, external opening to the spring was then blocked by a massive wall.

d. At this stage, the water system was further improved: the level of the tunnel at its inner end was lowered to the level of the spring and the stepped section was removed up to the base of the shaft — so that now the water could flow freely from the spring inward to the very base of the shaft, where it could be drawn up directly rather than hauled through the long tunnel, as in stage c.

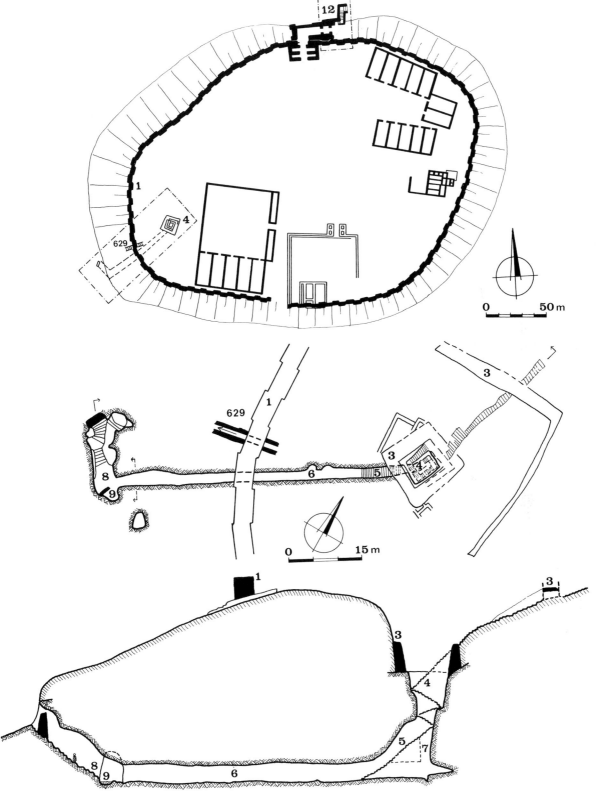

1. The water systems of Megiddo, map of location, plan and section. R.S. Lamon: *The Megiddo Water System*, Chicago 1935, Figs. 2–3.

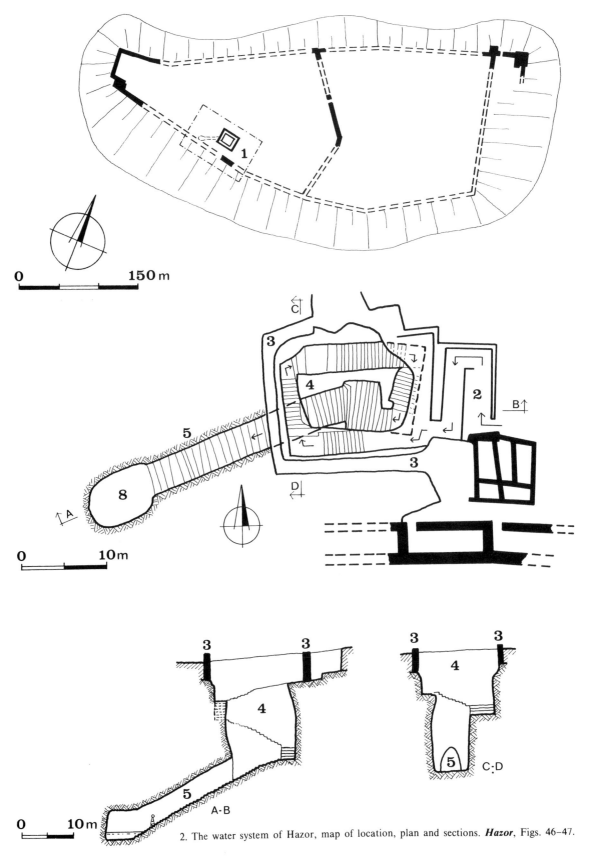

2. The water system of Hazor, map of location, plan and sections. *Hazor*, Figs. 46–47.

e. For reasons unclear to us, in this stage the builders reverted to the method of stage c. Steps were built down to the base of the shaft, on a new fill.

f. It can be assumed that the water system served the royal Israelite center at Megiddo up to the destruction of the Northern Kingdom by the Assyrians in the eighth century B.C. The large depression formed on its site after it fell into neglect and became partially filled with debris, served as a reservoir for runoff, providing water for the city in its final stages.[11]

HAZOR (Fig. 2)

The water system of Hazor was uncovered in 1968 by the Hebrew University expedition under Y. Yadin and the present author.[12] The water source is visible south of the upper mound, in Nahal Hazor. During clearance of the water system, special attention was paid to planning details and the stratigraphic relationship between its various components and the surrounding town, in an attempt to determine its precise date. The water system in Area L was hewn alongside the wall of the Upper City, above the region of the springs. Four components could be distinguished: 1. an entrance structure; 2. a rock-hewn shaft; 3. a stepped tunnel; 4. a water chamber.

The builders of this water system initially dug through the accumulation of earlier strata, from Stratum X down to bedrock. The entrance structure, made up of two elongated spaces, connected the occupation level of the Israelite city with the beginning of the stairway descending around the rock-hewn shaft to the stepped tunnel. This tunnel, some 22 m. long, was hewn in the soft conglomerate bedrock and is of impressive dimensions: about 4 m. wide and 4.5 m. high. It descended to the water chamber 36 m. beneath the surface of the mound, the floor of which was at the level of the water table. This level rises or falls according to the season and the quantity of rain in a given year. This water system was destroyed along with Stratum V. The tunnel and the shaft became filled to the upper supporting walls as a result of neglect. Later, the deep depression formed on the surface served as a reservoir for rainwater.

GEZER (Fig. 3)

The Water System. — The water system was excavated by Macalister,[13] adjacent to the line of fortifications on the eastern edge of the mound.[14] The water system has three components: 1. an entrance area; 2. a stepped tunnel; 3. a water chamber. The builders dug through earlier strata, which they apparently shored up with supporting walls, till bedrock was reached. Here they hewed obliquely into the rock, without a vertical shaft, and continued this stepped tunnel for 41 m., reaching a depth of 43 m. beneath the surface of the bedrock, where they encountered the water table. The water chamber was not entirely cleared by Macalister; its dimensions (some 32 m. long!) indicate that it was originally a natural cavern.

Macalister made several suggestions concerning the role of this underground water system ('subterranean temple'; sewage system; secret tunnel). He found it difficult to assume that this rock-hewn tunnel was pre-planned as a means of assuring a steady supply of water for the city directly from the water table. In his opinion, 'The discovery of the spring was a happy accident — made in the course of quarrying the tunnel for some entirely different purpose — most probably to serve as an exit from the city in time of siege'.

Dating. The extant data are insufficient to determine the precise date of the Gezer water system. In our perusal of the various finds from the fills in the tunnel, we have come to the conclusion that they are unreliable as indicators for dating (this includes, e.g., the Mycenean cup).[15] Macalister assigned it to his 'Second Semitic period', now ascribed to the Middle Bronze Age II. Other scholars have ascribed the water system to the Late Bronze Age.[16]

Yadin's opinion seems most acceptable to us, which notes the typological-architectural-hydro-geological similarities[17] between the water systems at Hazor and Gezer, and thus ascribes it to the Iron Age II. It would then have served as part of the new urban system of Gezer, beginning in the tenth century B.C., details of which have been clarified in the recent excavations of the Hebrew Union College.

The Reservoir. — A further water installation was uncovered by Macalister north of the Israelite city-gate.[18] This was an oval pool 14–17 m. in diameter, hewn into the bedrock to a depth of some 18 m. A

11. The excavators hesitated in their chronological and stratigraphical ascriptions for the later part of the water system, such as the later stairway (L. 951); cf. Lamon (above, n. 8), pp. 31, 37 and Fig. 29.
12. *Hazor*, p. 164; idem, *EI* 11 (1973), pp. 139–143.
13. *Excavations of Gezer* I, pp. 256–265.
14. W.G. Dever: The Water System at Hazor and Gezer, *BA* 32 (1969).
15. Amiran (above, n. 4), p. 36.
16. Dever (above, n. 14).
17. Y. Yadin: The 1968–69 Seasons of Excavations at Hazor, *EI* 11 (1973), p. 143.
18. *Gezer* I, pp. 265–268.

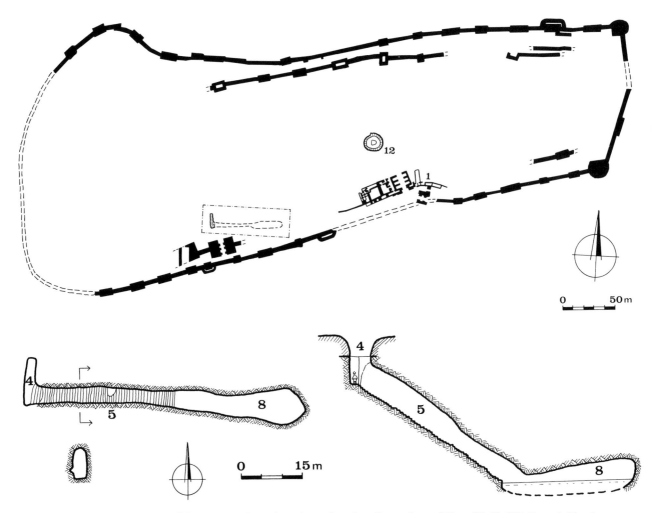

3. The water system of Gezer, map of location, plan and section. *Excavations of Gezer* III, Pl. LII; *Gezer* I, Plan 1.

stairway descends around the wall to the floor. The walls were crudely plastered. We possess insufficient data to enable a dating of this installation or to understand its precise function, whether it was a huge reservoir or possibly the initial stage of a projected water system, like the round shaft at Gibeon.[19]

GIBEON (Fig. 4)

During Pritchard's excavations in 1956–1957, two water systems were discovered — the tunnel and the 'pool' at the top of the eastern slope of the mound, above 'Ain el-Balad — adjacent to one another and fed by the same spring and the water table, and still serving the inhabitants of el-Jib village.[20]

Gibeon A — The Tunnel. — The components of this water system are clear: 1. entrance structure; 2. stepped tunnel; 3. water chamber; 4. feed channel. Above the spring, alongside the line of Iron Age fortifications, a small entrance chamber was built, leading to an oblique, stepped tunnel hewn into the bedrock. The tunnel, around 48 m. long, descends to a depth of about 24 m. down to a water chamber. A part of the ceiling of the tunnel, in the upper part, was open and roofed with stone slabs. In the lower part the tunnel was entirely rock hewn. The water was collected in the water chamber by means of a feeder conduit leading from the spring proper and hewn alongside the aquifer feeding it.[21]

19. J.B. Pritchard: *The Water System of Gibeon*, Philadelphia 1961, pp. 12–13.
20. Pritchard: *Gibeon*, 1962, pp. 53–78.

21. In the opinion of the geologist Dan Gil, the feeder conduit of irregular form, is an artificial expansion of a natural tunnel formed by dissolution of the limestone bedrock, utilized by the builders of the Gibeon water system.

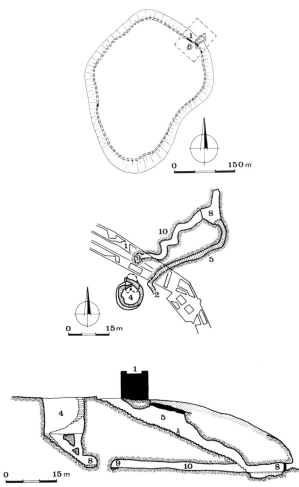

4. The water systems of Gibeon, map of location, plan and section. J.B. Pritchard: *The Water System of Gibeon*, Philadelphia, 1961, Figs. 2–4.

proposed that the 'pool' at Gibeon was initially a round reservoir which was subsequently expanded into a more sophisticated system reaching down to the water table. Pritchard proposed two other alternatives.[23]

IBLE'AM (Fig. 5)

The water system at Tell Bal'amah was surveyed by Schumacher[24]. There is a source of water at 'Ain Sinjil, on the eastern flank of the mound. It is possible

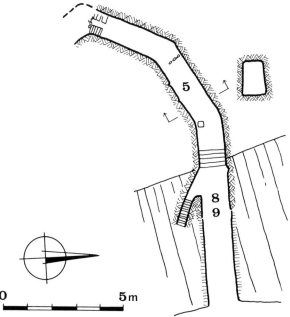

5. The water system of Tell Bal'amah (Ible'am). *PEFQSt* (1910), Pl. II, facing p. 107.

Gibeon B — The 'Pool'. — In contrast to the tunnel, the 'pool' includes: 1. a round shaft; 2. a stepped tunnel; 3. a water chamber. The hewing of the shaft, some 11 m. in diameter, began very close to the surface. A stairway with a railing was hewn around the walls, descending to the floor of the shaft, which was 11.8 m. deep. At the bottom, a stepped tunnel led down to a water chamber at a depth of 24 m. beneath the surface, and two small vertical shafts provided air and light. The water chamber is at the same level as the water chamber of 'Gibeon A', and only about 5 m. away from the spring at the head of the feeder conduit. Thus, the two systems are fed by one and the same source.

Location, Function and Dating. — Cole[22] has

to penetrate into a stepped tunnel at its lower end and ascend for some 30 m. The tunnel's dimensions are impressive: about 3 m. wide with a vaulted ceiling 4.2 m. high. There are numerous traces of secondary use since the tunnel was originally hewn (as noted already by Schumacher and recently confirmed by Z. Yeivin in trial excavations near the lower end of the stepped tunnel).

Dating. This water system can be ascribed to the Iron Age II on the basis of circumstantial evidence, foremost typological and architectural: the manner of planning and hewing, and its function well match the water systems datable to the Iron Age, as noted

22. Cole (above, n. 6), pp. 28–29.

23. Pritchard (above, n. 19, 1961), p. 10.

24. G. Schumacher: The Great Water Passage of Khirbet Bel'ameh, *PEFQSt* 43 (1910), pp. 107–112.

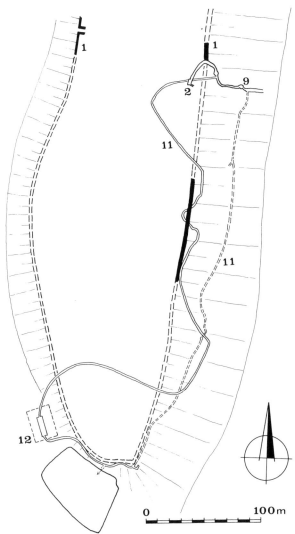

6. The water systems of the 'City of David', Jerusalem, topographical plan with location of systems. **Qedem** 19 (1984), pp. 66–67, Fig. 30.

already by Schumacher. Secondly, on geographical-historical grounds, Ible'am was one of the urban centres on the border of Samaria and the Jezreel Valley. It is logical to assume that its town-plan in the Iron Age included a subterranean system to assure a regular supply of water.

JERUSALEM (Fig. 6)[25]

The Gihon Spring, at the base of the eastern slope of the City of David, has served the inhabitants of

Jerusalem since its foundation at the beginning of the Early Bronze Age. The water systems stemming from this spring include: 'Warren's Shaft', the 'Siloam Channel' and 'Hezekiah's (or the 'Siloam') Tunnel'. The City of David expedition, directed by the author on behalf of the Hebrew University, began the re-investigation of these systems in 1978.

Warren's Shaft (Fig. 7). — This system was discovered by Charles Warren in 1867.[26] It was examined in detail by the Parker expedition, the results of which were published by Vincent.[27] Since 1979, archaeological excavations have been conducted here by the City of David expedition[28] and a hydro-geological survey was carried out by Dan Gil. The system contains several components: 1. an entrance area; 2. a stepped tunnel; 3. a horizontal tunnel; 4. a vertical shaft; 5. a connecting tunnel; 6. the spring.

The entrance is hewn into the rock at the head of the stepped tunnel, which descends to a depth of about 8 m. to the beginning of the horizontal tunnel. (Several parts of the water system have not yet been examined fully, and thus there may still be changes in the dimensions given here.) The latter, some 28 m. long, is slightly oblique, descending to the head of the vertical shaft. This shaft, oval in section, descends 12.3 m. down to the level at which water is met, coming from the spring some 22 m. away through the connecting tunnel.

Other secondary features include the following: in the upper entrance area, a later building phase is evident — the 'vaulted chamber' protecting the entrance from silting and debris from the eastern slope. An entry tunnel was built within it, connecting this later phase with the surface. The additional shaft — the 'trial shaft' and the blocked entrance to the cave at the lower end of the horizontal tunnel — can now be understood in the light of the hydro-geological survey: it transpires that the additional shaft, the cave and the vertical shaft, as well as the lower part of the horizontal tunnel, are all natural karst clefts and shafts, utilized and integrated into the water system. This fact serves to explain the anomaly and irregularity of the plan and dimensions of some of these components.

25. R. Amiran (above, n. 4); *idem*, The Water Supply of Israelite Jerusalem, in Y. Yadin (ed.): *Jerusalem Revealed,* Jerusalem, 1975, pp. 75–78; J. Simons: *Jerusalem in the Old Testament,* Leiden, 1952, pp. 157–194; L.H. Vincent: *Jerusalem de l'ancient Testament,* Paris, 1954, pp. 260–297.

26. C. Wilson and Ch. Warren: The Recovery of Jerusalem, London, 1871, pp. 248–255.

27. L.H. Vincent: *Underground Jerusalem,* London, 1911.

28. Y. Shiloh: Jerusalem's Water Supply During Siege, *BAR* 7 (1981), pp. 24–39; as well as D. Gil and Y. Shiloh: Subterranean Water Supply System of the City of David: Utilization of a Natural Karstic System, in *Annual Meeting 1982, Elat and Eastern Sinai,* Elat *Israel Geological Society* (1982), pp. 32–34.

Jerusalem. Iron Age II, 'Warren's Shaft' stepped channel.

Location and Function. The water flowed from the spring through the connecting tunnel to the base of the vertical shaft, whence it could be drawn, as in a well, by anyone having come down the upper tunnels to the head of the shaft. Here we see a unique exploitation of a series of natural tunnels and shafts, which were integrated to form a continuous water system.

The discovery of the line of the city-wall by Kenyon and Shiloh[29] indicates that the entrance area known to us today was indeed within the fortifications at a spot apparently adjacent to the 'Water Gate'.

The Siloam Channel. — Segments of this water system have been investigated by various scholars.[30] The City of David expedition has uncovered three segments, totalling a length of some 120 m. (out of an overall length of about 400 m.). It differs basically from the other water systems reviewed here in that it carried water partly in a rock-hewn and stone-covered channel and partly in a rock-hewn tunnel. Its use

was threefold: 1. for conducting the waters of the Gihon spring along the Kedron Valley to the region of reservoirs at the lower end of the 'Central Valley', at the southwestern tip of the City of David; 2. in the eastern wall of the channel, facing the valley, there are window-like openings through which the flow of water could be diverted for irrigation of agricultural plots in the valley; 3. the upper openings along the channel could be utilized for gathering the runoff from the rock surface outside the city-walls on the slope above, thus diverting them to the above-noted reservoirs. The major disadvantage of this system was its vulnerability, its entire course being outside the fortified area of the city. Thus, it was necessarily a peace-time system.

The inauguration of Hezekiah's Tunnel (see below) superseded the Siloam Channel in its first function, but the southern end of the channel was integrated into the new system, as an overflow channel to the Siloam Pool. By lowering the level of its bottom, the direction of flow in this part of the channel was reversed, and the water now ran from west to east.

Hezekiah's Tunnel. — Hezekiah's Tunnel has occupied the attention of various scholars since the beginning of modern archaeological research in Jerusalem.[31] This water system solved the special problems of water supply in the City of David in a sophisticated though simple manner. Its components are 1. the spring; 2. the tunnel; 3. the Siloam Pool; 4. an overflow channel.

From the spring, the tunnel continues some 533 m. under the spur of the City of David till it reaches the Siloam Pool. The survey of the current archaeological expedition revealed that — in contrast to all that has previously been published — the difference in height between the beginning of the channel at the spring and the end of the tunnel is only about 30 cm. (a gradient of only 0.06%). The average height of the tunnel is around 2 m. At its southern end the height reaches 5 m. The remains of the reservoirs and parts of the fortifications which were uncovered at the bottom of the Central Valley by Guthe, Bliss, Weill and Shiloh are no earlier than Second Temple times (cf. the references cited above, n. 31). The reservoirs of First Temple times should, most probably, be restored on the same site, originally fed by the Siloam Channel. We should also restore here the beginning of the new line of defences from the days of Hezekiah,

29. K. Kenyon: *Digging up Jerusalem*, New York, 1974, pp. 144–151;

30. Y. Shiloh: The City of David Archaeological Project: The Third Season — 1980, *BA* 44 (1980), pp. 161–170.

31. Vincent (above, n. 27), pp. 33–35; Y. Shiloh: *Qadmoniot* 14 (1981), pp. 85–95 (Hebrew).

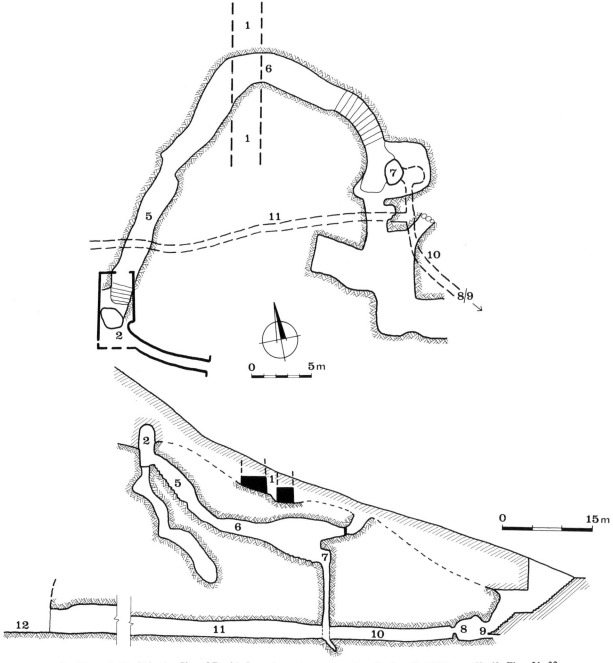

7. 'Warren's Shaft' in the City of David, Jerusalem, plan and section. *Qedem* 19 (1984), pp. 68–69, Figs. 31–32.

ascending westward and encompassing the Western Hill.[32] According to this view, the site of the main reservoir is not to be sought beyond the line of

the dam to the east, in the Kedron Valley.[33] The overflow channel of the Siloam Pool, which utilized

32. H. Geva: The Western Boundary of Jerusalem at the End of the Monarchy, *IEJ* 25 (1979), pp. 84–91.

33. For various opinions, see K. Kenyon (above, n. 29), pp. 152–159; D. Ussishkin: The Original Length of the Siloam Tunnel in Jerusalem, *Levant* 8 (1976), pp. 82–95; J. Wilkinson: The Pool of Siloam, *Levant* 10 (1978), pp. 116–125; D. Adan: The 'Fountain of Siloam' and 'Solomon's Pool' in the First Century C.E. Jerusalem, *IEJ* 29 (1979), pp. 92–100.

the southern-most part of the Siloam Channel, led the surplus water into the Kedron streambed in a controlled manner. Here, too, the water could be gathered in additional reservoirs, though these could be of value only in times of peace, their location being far outside the line of fortifications. The overflow channel was blocked up by a stone wall in Second Temple times.[34]

Function and Dating of the Three Jerusalem Water Systems. — There is general agreement amongst scholars as to the relative chronology of these three water systems: Warren's Shaft is certainly the oldest; the Siloam Channel is contemporaneous with it or slightly later, while Hezekiah's Tunnel is the latest of the three, built at the end of the eighth century B.C.

The ascription of the hewing of Hezekiah's Tunnel to the reign of that king, late in the eighth century B.C., is based on specific evidence in the Bible (II Kings 20:20; II Chronicles 32:30) and the Apocrypha (Sira 48:17), as well as on palaeographic analysis of the Siloam Inscription, discovered near the southern terminus of the tunnel in 1880. At its upper end, Hezekiah's Tunnel utilizes the connecting tunnel running between the spring and the bottom of Warren's Shaft. The southern end of the Siloam Channel was utilized as an overflow channel for the Hezekiah's Tunnel water system, which also included the replanned Siloam Pool. Hence, the date of the Siloam Channel (generally identified with the 'waters of Shiloah that flow gently' of Isaiah 8:6) and of Warren's Shaft must be prior to the late eighth century B.C., i.e. the period of Hezekiah's Tunnel. In other words, these two earlier systems are from the tenth–ninth centuries B.C.

Warren's Shaft was built according to the usual formula for underground water systems at royal centers in the tenth–ninth centuries B.C. It connected the northern part of the City of David (and perhaps even its citadel) with the water source. In the late eighth–sixth centuries B.C., the three systems could have functioned simultaneously, all fed from the single source, and the flow of water through them could have been controlled. Hezekiah's Tunnel has continuously conveyed water to the Siloam Pool ever since. Water could also reach the base of Warren's Shaft, from whence it could be drawn for use in the city directly above.

The late phase in the entrance chamber of Warren's Shaft — the vault and the entrance tunnel — indicate

that in the first century B.C. this installation was still being maintained, either as a water system *per se* or for some other use of the extensive subterranean chambers in its upper parts. The Siloam Channel went out of use as the main conduit of water at the time of the construction of Hezekiah's Tunnel, which cut the channel off from direct contact with the spring. The channel could have continued in use, however, till the end of the First Temple period, as a regular means of distributing irrigation water in the Upper Kedron Valley, and for feeding various reservoirs there.

We still lack all data on the supply of water to the uppermost and most important parts of Jerusalem in this period — the Temple Mount and the adjacent palace complex.

LACHISH

The 'Great Shaft' at Lachish, investigated by Starkey in 1935–1937, remains one of the enigmas of this site.[35] It was hewn adjacent to the line of fortifications at the southeastern corner of the settlement. Starkey examined it by tunnelling along its walls, and found that it measures 22 × 25 m. and is about 25 m. deep. Since no tunnel was found at its bottom, the excavator assumed that it was never completed.[36] It can be assumed that the hewers intended the shaft to reach down to the level of the water table, some 40–50 m. below the present surface (this level was known on the basis of the level of the ground water in the well mentioned immediately below).

The well uncovered at the northeastern corner of the mound is one of the few examples of a deep well found in an Israelite city.[37] In concept, it resembles the other water systems: it was hewn to a depth of some 44 m. at the lowest point on the mound's surface, but still within the line of fortifications, which slightly deviates here to accomodate it.[38]

BEERSHEBA

The plan of Stratum II at Beersheba[39] shows one of the most complete examples of town-planning in this period, with all the requisite components. At the northeastern corner of the mound, the top of a flight of stairs came to light, along with supporting walls built around the top of a shaft. The excavator quite reasonably assumed that these elements belonged

---

34. Y. Shiloh: City of David Excavations — 1978, *BA* 42 (19??), pp. 165–171.

35. *Lachish* III, pp. 158–163.
36. *Lachish* III, p. 162, Fig. 14.
37. *Lachish* III, pp. 92–93.
38. *Lachish* III, p.161.
39. *Beer-Sheba* I, pp. 9–18.

to a water system, which as yet remains to be cleared. Aharoni thought that the shaft led to a series of subterranean cisterns hewn beneath; the water — floodwaters from the adjacent Nahal Beersheba — would somehow have been diverted into them. If this were indeed the case, it would be an interesting integration of the engineering methods noted in the northern parts of the country and the specific conditions of water supply in the semi-arid Negev (and see below on the water systems of Arad and Kadesh Barnea). On the basis of this reconstruction, we would expect the shaft and the cisterns to be located closer to the stream-bed, at the southeastern corner of the city. Another reconstruction can, however, be made for the functioning of this water system: the level of the water table was surely well-known to the local populace, on the basis of the ancient deep well situated outside the city-gate. The hewing of the above-noted shaft, at the northern corner of the city, was a planned effort to reach this level, in the manner seen at other royal centres in the north. Stratum II has been ascribed to the eighth century B.C.

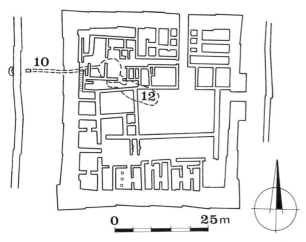

8. The water system of the Arad fortress. *EAEHL* Vol. I, p. 83.

ARAD (Fig. 8)

The inhabitants of Arad in the Iron Age utilized the ancient well located at the base of the citadel, at the centre of the depression within the walled area of the Early Bronze Age II city.[40] A large underground reservoir was hewn into the soft limestone bedrock beneath the center of the citadel, as an integral component of its initial plan, in Stratum X.[41] This

40. *Arad*, pp. 13–14.
41. Y. Aharoni: Arad: Its Inscriptions and Temple, *BA* 31 (1968), pp. 6–7, Fig. 5.

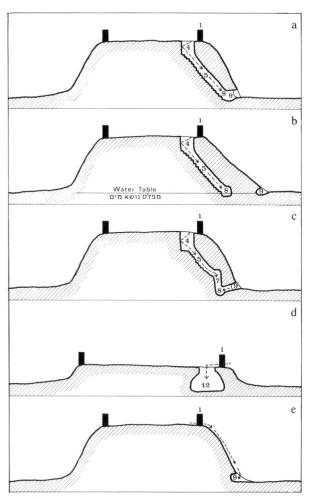

9. Schematic tell indicating the various types of water systems.

cistern was fed by a rock-hewn channel entering the citadel from the west. At the point of entry the walls of the channel were integrated into and covered by the solid structure of the wall of Stratum X. (Besides the engineering feat of building an outer feeder channel to the inner cistern, this arrangement precluded the need for bringing beasts and their drivers, bearing water containers, into the densely built fortress.) The 32 m. long channel was covered over by stone slabs. The channel was fed with water brought in containers from some outside source which flowed into the cistern beneath the citadel. When the cistern was filled, the water supply for the garrison was assured for a given period. This freed it from dependency upon the well and other outside sources of water in time of war, and improved the standard of living in time of peace. The water system served the Arad citadel in Strata X–VI, in the ninth–sixth centuries B.C.

KADESH BARNEA

In R. Cohen's 1981–1982 excavations at Kadesh Barnea, a water system was uncovered resembling that at Arad.[42] The Israelite fortress here was built adjacent to a streambed fed regularly by the waters of 'Ain Qudeis. These waters had been diverted into a well-constructed channel leading through the southern wall of the fortress into a large cistern within. In the excavated section, a broad stairway was revealed descending into the cistern. The excavator ascribed the use of this cistern to the Iron Age II, like that at Arad, with which it is typologically identical.

TELL ES-SA'IDIYEH

In 1964, while seeking a connecting path between the fortified settlement at the top of Tell es-Sa'idiyeh and the spring at the base of its northern slope, Pritchard discovered a built ascent, defined by him as a 'secret tunnel',[43] made up of 98 steps, each being 2 m. wide. During its construction, a channel was dug and its walls lined with stone. The ascent was divided down its length by a central wall; in the excavator's opinion, it had been roofed and covered over with earth, to conceal it from the view of an enemy (though in our opinion the invulnerability of such a water system is doubtful).

At the top of the mound, a well-planned settlement was revealed, with a street system and structures of the four-room type. The settlement has been ascribed to the tenth century B.C. Its identification as the biblical Zarethan — a centre of bronze manufacture where some of the vessels for Solomon's Temple were made — would point to its importance (cf. I Kings 7:45–46). Pritchard ascribed the water system to 1200–900 B.C.; we assume that it should be ascribed to the principal occupational phase of the planned settlement on the site, i.e. the tenth century B.C.

Typological Classification of the Water Systems

A. *Shaft and Tunnel Leading to a Source Outside the City* (Fig. 9a). — Examples: Megiddo — third and fifth phases; Gibeon A — the tunnel; Ible'am.
b. *Shaft and Tunnel Leading to the Water Table at the Base of the Mound* (Fig. 9b). — Examples: Hazor; Gezer; Gibeon B — the pool; Lachish — the shaft(?).
c. *Shaft and Tunnel Leading from an External Source to the Base of a Vertical Shaft* (Fig. 9c). — Examples: Jerusalem — Warren's Shaft; Megiddo — fourth phase.
d. *Tunnels and Feed Channels Supplying Large Reservoirs* (Fig. 9d). — Examples: Jerusalem — Siloam Channel, Hezekiah's Tunnel and Siloam Pool; Megiddo — northern water system(?); Arad; Kadesh Barnea; Beersheba(?); Gezer — the reservoir(?)
e. *External Approaches to Sources at the Base of the Mound* (Fig. 9e). — Examples: Megiddo — Gallery 629; Tell es-Sa'idiyeh.

The Hydro-Geological Structure and the Functioning of the Water Systems

In light of the data accumulated in recent years concerning hydro-geology, it transpires that the planners of the water systems utilized the abundant practical knowledge at hand on the nature of bedrock, location of water sources, water table levels and efficient modes of exploiting them.[44] For lack of data, we have not discussed the matter of rate of flow of the sources. The utilization of an ordinary spring as a source of water was the simplest type of water system (Megiddo, Ible'am, Gibeon A). This was improved upon by means of feeder conduits, a method which also served in the development of the water supplies near various springs in the Judean Hills.[45] Type B, as at Hazor, Gezer and Gibeon B, was more sophisticated; here, the planners — on the basis of their practical knowledge — were able to pre-determine their route toward the water table deep within the bowels of the mound. The theories of 'accidental' arrival at the water level at Gezer or Gibeon B,[46] or the possibility that Gibeon B evolved in two phases,[47] are contrary to the very concept, and thus to be rejected.

The water source unique to Jerusalem, the Gihon (literally, a 'gushing' spring), dictated particular conditions, for its waters gush forth regularly every few hours. If its waters were not gathered and diverted

42. R. Cohen: *Kadesh Barnea* (Catalogue, Israel Museum), Jerusalem, 1983, p. XI and Fig. 13.
43. J. Pritchard: Two Tombs and a Tunnel in the Jordan Valley, *Expedition* 6 (1964), pp. 3–9.
44. Gil and Shiloh (above, n. 28).
45. A. Issar: The Evolution of the Ancient Water Supply System in the Region of Jerusalem, *IEJ* 26 (1976), p. 136.
46. Cole (above, n. 6), pp. 27, 29.
47. This is in contrast to Cole (above, n. 6), who suggests that Gibeon B was a prototype which influenced the development of Type B and C at other sites.

TABLE 2. IRON AGE WATER SYSTEMS: TYPOLOGY AND CHRONOLOGY

		A	B	C	D	E
		Shaft/tunnel to exterior spring	Shaft/tunnel to water table	Water conducted to bottom of shaft/tunnel	Feeding tunnel and channels to reservoirs	Exterior approach to water source
Megiddo	Gallery 629					*
	Water system phase A	*				
	phase B		*			
	phase C	*				
	Northern water system				*	
Hazor	Water system		*			
Gezer	Water system		*			
	Reservoir				*	
Gibeon A	Tunnel	*				
Gibeon B	The 'Pool'		*			
Ible'am	Tunnel	*				
Jerusalem	Warren's Shaft			*		
	Siloam Channel				*	
	Hezekiah's (Siloam) Tunnel				*	
Tell es-Sa'adiyeh	Stepped ascent					*
Lachish	The "Great Shaft"		* (?)			
Beersheba	Shaft	* (?)			* (?)	
Arad	Cistern				*	
Kadesh Barnea	Cistern				*	

to a reservoir, they would continue to flow into the Kedron Brook. The moment a system for gathering its waters in large reservoirs was evolved, the local inhabitants were freed from their dependence upon the gushes of the spring. Drawing of water from the reservoirs could be controlled, according to need. We have found that the planners of Warren's Shaft utilized a series of karst tunnels and dolines as parts of their water system. The vertical shaft enabled access to the water at its base, but precluded penetration into the city. Most of the waters of the Gihon still flowed into the Kedron Brook. The Siloam Channel answered a functional, engineering problem — the conveying of the water to reservoirs. In this phase, still, the entire system was outside the fortified city.

Hezekiah's Tunnel was the sophisticated remedy for this fault: it gathered the entire yield of the spring and conveyed it in an entirely secluded manner to the region of the Siloam Pool which, in the period of the hewing of the tunnel, was already included within the fortified area.

In general plan, Warren's Shaft serves as an intermediate type between Types A and B, specifically in its successful integration of a vertical shaft of natural form. The plan of this water system — in Jerusalem, the capital — may well have served as the prototype for the first modification of the water system at Megiddo (transition from the third phase to the fourth phase), and for the even more sophisticated development finding expression in the systems of Type B.

THE DATING OF THE WATER SYSTEMS

The dating of the water systems, like that of any archaeological find, must be based upon the entire body of evidence stemming from several factors: the stratigraphic relationship of its architectural components with the series of strata encompassing it, and with the general town-plan; typological comparison; the nature of the small finds discovered within it; and historical documentation.

The dating of these water systems has undergone various metamorphoses, largely because of only partial utilization of the available data, or because of ignorance of the data. R. Amiran, in her pioneer study published in 1951, ascribed five (out of six) of the water systems then known, to the end of the Late Bronze Age.[48] Various scholars often relied on sparse pottery evidence from one part or another of a water system in order to date it.[49] Our experience in clearing the water systems at Hazor and Jerusalem has shown that, as a rule, such finds are not to be relied upon solely, for they may well have been deposited at the find spots in various manners and at various times, and that in the main they actually stem from the debris and structures surrounding the water systems. At most, they can comprise auxiliary, supporting evidence for the dating of the destruction or abandonment of the installations. Thus, for instance, a large quantity of finds from the Early Bronze Age till the end of the Iron Age came to light in the fill of the shaft at Hazor; they clearly found their way there from the buildings adjacent to the edge of the shaft, after its destruction.

Despite the difficulty of relating the components of the water systems to the surrounding stratigraphic series, this relationship indeed holds the major key to accurate dating. At Hazor, this was the basis for ascribing the water system to Stratum VIII, of the ninth century B.C. Gallery 629 at Megiddo served Strata VA–IVB, of the tenth century B.C., and the two major water systems at Gibeon also began in the tenth century B.C. (see above, p. 282). Those at Beersheba, Kadesh Barnea, Arad, Tell es-Sa'idiyeh and Lachish (?) can be broadly ascribed to the Iron Age II. In Jerusalem, chronology is based on the definite historical date of Hezekiah's Tunnel, i.e. the late eighth century B.C. We have proposed above a dating for the Siloam Channel, which is earlier than

48. Amiran (above, n. 4), pp. 36–37; this ascription was based on stratigraphic chronological data which were later corrected for most of the sites concerned.
49. Amiran (above, n. 4); Lamon (above, n. 8), pp. 8–10; K. M. Kenyon: *Archaeology in the Holy Land*, London, 1979 (4th ed.), pp. 269–272.

the tunnel, and for Warren's Shaft, in the tenth–ninth centuries B.C. (see above, p. 284).

The picture emerging from analysis of the body of chronological evidence (Table 2) reveals that underground water systems in the Land of Israel first made their appearance in the tenth century B.C., as one of the components in the building complexes of the United Monarchy. We can also see considerable efforts to improve upon them in the ninth century B.C., apparently as part of the overall program to develop royal centres in Judah and, especially, in the northern kingdom of Israel in the days of Ahab. In most instances, these systems continued in use down to the destruction of the two kingdoms. In Jerusalem, we have found that Warren's Shaft was maintained throughout Second Temple times and, of course, Hezekiah's Tunnel is still in active use today.

The process of destruction of the water systems is identical at most sites: quantities of debris fell into them, blocking the tunnels and shafts. The depressions remaining at the head of the blocked shafts continued to be utilized - at Megiddo, Hazor and Lachish, even after the destruction of these royal centres, and as long as they were occupied — as convenient spots for storing rainwater and floodwater atop the mounds, just as there are pools adjacent to most Arab villages today.

DATING AND TYPOLOGY OF THE WATER SYSTEMS

The chronological data are still insufficient to determine whether there is a correspondence between the chronological data and the typological development of the water systems. Even if outwardly Type C appears to be a development of Type A, and Type B the final, developed form, it is still difficult to prove this due to lack of precise chronological data for the tenth–ninth centuries B.C. It should be emphasized that the water systems themselves were planned and adapted to suit local natural conditions and the existing urban plan on the respective sites. Thus, in each instance, a similar overall concept can be seen — in both planning and execution — as well as an identical functioning of the respective components, though each is suited to its respective local system. Moreover, we should note that general analysis reveals the extent of practical knowledge available to the planners concerning the location of underground water sources and the modes of exploiting them. At both Hazor and Gibeon, the entire systems were planned so that the end of the respective tunnels would precisely reach the aquifer, lying immediately over an impermeable layer. Its location could have been determined through studying the flows of external springs connected with the same aquifer at the base of the slope of the hill. Water systems of this type, of known date, are no earlier than the tenth century B.C. On the basis of comparative typological study, we can thus compare the systems at Hazor and Gibeon B (both of known date) and that at Gezer.[50] By the same means, we can determine that the Middle Bronze Age II date of the Ible'am water system, as given by Schumacher, is far too early, and should be assigned to the Iron Age II. Warren's Shaft has also been dated by the same manner (analogous with the fourth phase of the system at Megiddo), and by its relative position amongst the other water systems in the City of David, to the tenth–ninth centuries B.C., despite the popular appeal of ascribing it to the tradition of the conquest of Jebus in the days of David.

WATER SYSTEMS IN NEIGHBOURING CULTURES

Earlier studies have raised the question of the origin of this method of water system: was it developed in Iron Age Israel, or did it stem from engineering concepts of some neighbouring culture?[51] Our present discussion allows for only a brief treatment, although this is a subject worthy of a study in itself. *A priori*, we can eliminate urban water systems in both Mesopotamia and Egypt, which were fed, in most instances, by the major rivers.[52] Illuminating examples of constructed or hewn tunnels, serving as subterranean passageways, secret passages (postern gates), reservoirs and water systems, are known from the second millennium B.C. onward in Syria, Anatolia, Persia, and Mycenean fortresses.

The major problem in discussing the examples in Syria, Anatolia and Persia is that no detailed information is available concerning their date and function, though some of them certainly served as water systems.[53] The picture clarifies somewhat concerning water installations in Anatolia toward the end of the Iron Age, especially in Phrygia, where several interesting examples have been described.

Haspels[54] holds that they are no earlier than the Phrygian period, i.e. the end of the eighth century B.C., possibly even of the Lydian period, the golden age of monumental architecture in the sixth century B.C.

Better examples for comparison are to be found in the Aegean sphere, where they served the fortresses of the Mycenean III period, mainly of the thirteenth and early twelfth centuries B.C.[55] At Mycene, a built and hewn tunnel was discovered beneath the foundations of the city-wall, leading to a small reservoir at the bottom of the slope. The water was conveyed to the reservoir from a far-off spring by means of a segmented pottery pipe.[56] A similar installation, with two parallel tunnels, was discovered integrated into the fortifications of Tiryns.[57] At the Acropolis in Athens, a built passage was integrated into the fortifications of the thirteenth century B.C., utilizing a geological cleft in the rock, descending acutely to a natural, hidden cave. This cave is located some 34 m. lower down, at the bottom of the northern slope of the hill.[58]

There is certainly a similarity between the water systems of Mycenean Greece and those of Iron Age Israel. In both instances, they were intended to assure the regular supply of water to cities in time of war as in peace. Would it be correct to suggest that the water systems in the Land of Israel were inspired by those existing in the Mycenean sphere? If so, we would have to prove a typological, chronological and cultural tie, a contemporaneous link, between the two cultures. The water systems in the Land of Israel, mainly those of Types B and C, are much more developed typologically than the Mycenean examples. In addition, the Aegean water systems are not rock hewn in the form of shafts and tunnels leading to ground water. If it could be proved that there did exist such subterranean water systems in Late Bronze Age Palestine — as seemed to be the picture when R. Amiran wrote her review of this subject[59] — there would be good reason to seek actual contacts between the two groups. However, there is

50. Y. Yadin: The Fifth Season of Excavations at Hazor, 1968–69, *BA* 32 (1969), p. 70.

51. Amiran (above, no. 4), pp. 37–38; as well as Pritchard (above, n. 19), p. 14.

52. Senaclienb's Aqduct at Jerwan, Chicago 1935.

53. M.M. van Loon: *Urartian Art*, Istanbul, 1966, pp. 38–41; as well as R. Naumann: *Architektur Kleinasiens*, Tübingen, 1971, pp. 190–197.

54. Especially C.H.E. Haspels: *The Highlands of Phrigia*, I, Princeton, 1971, pp. 36–40, 144.

55. N.C. Scoufopoulos: *Mycenean Citadels*, (SMA 22), Goteborg, 1971, passim.

56. G. Karo: Die Perseia von Mykenai, *AJA* 38 (1934), pp. 123–127; A.J.B. Wace: *Mycenae*, Princeton, 1948, pp. 99–100.

57. G.E. Mylonas: *Myceane and the Mycenean Age*, Princeton, 1966, pp. 14–15.

58. J. Travelos: *Pictorial Dictionary of Ancient Athens*, London, 1971, pp. 52, 72.

59. Amiran (above, n. 1), pp. 37–38.

a decided geographical-cultural division between the two cultural spheres, finding expression in all realms of archaeological finds. The Phrygian water systems, in contrast, are some two hundred years later than the group under consideration here. This fact leads us, at least for the time, to doubt possible influences from the West upon the planners of the water systems in the royal centres of Judah and Israel.

SUMMARY

The water systems discussed in the present study served as organic components within the town-plans of the important centres in the Kingdoms of Judah and Israel.[60] From the beginning of the development of these centres, in the days of Solomon in the tenth century B.C., and with renewed vigor on a broader scale in the days of Ahab, in the ninth century B.C., the planners turned their attention to the matter of water supply. It was one of the important factors in the Israelite city, from both the military and civil engineering aspects, which also took into account the convenience of the citizens. The protected access to water sources, the efficient exploitation of the various sources by means of installations for feeding the principal source, the gathering of water in central reservoirs which could be controlled, and proper maintenance of the various facilities, assured a regular supply of water in times of peace as well as war. To this end, considerable areas within the fortified cities were allotted to these water systems, as can be seen at Hazor, Megiddo, Beersheba and the City of David. There was much variety in the type of water systems and in their modes of functioning, varying

according to the local needs, local conditions and type of water source — as can be learned from the models of Jerusalem and Gibeon.

The Bible informs us mainly of reservoirs (at Jerusalem, Hebron, Samaria, Gibeon and Heshbon). Only in connection with the building activities of King Hezekiah do we learn from a first-hand source of Hezekiah's Tunnel. The mention of the hewing of an 'asuah in the Mesha Stele apparently refers to the execution of a similar type of water system in Moab by King Mesha in the ninth century B.C. (as suggested by Yadin). Could the technical knowledge for this project in Moab have come from Judah and Israel?[61]

The various types of subterranean water systems are further evidence of the broad architectural initiative which finds expression in the development of the Israelite town-plan, with all its components — fortifications, public and religious structures, residential quarters and various urban installations (such as water systems). They are a further example of the outstanding cultural differences between the Bronze Age cultures and those of the Iron Age: the inhabitants of the Bronze Age cities were passive in their reliance upon existing water sources and the storage of rain- and floodwaters. The approach of the Iron Age town-planners was much more active: seeking out and locating water sources, improving water yields and storing in a controlled manner. After the destruction of these urban centres, at the end of the First Temple period, the installations were neglected. The next phase in the development of water systems for major urban centres in Israel would come only at the end of the Hellenistic period and during the Early Roman period.

60. Shiloh: The Proto-Aeolic Capital and Israelite Ashlar Masonry, *Qedem* 11, Jerusalem, 1979, pp. 84–86; *Hazor*, pp. 135–178.

61. H.O. Thompson and F. Zaydin: The Tell Sirhan Inscription, *BASOR* 212 (1973), pp. 5–11.

26 THE ARCHITECTURE OF THE ISRAELITE FORTRESSES IN THE NEGEV

Zeev Meshel

Introduction

A series of casemate structures, generally thought to have been Israelite fortresses, has been uncovered and investigated in the Negev. However, despite recent studies,[1] major questions remain: the identity of their builders, the date of their construction, and their intended purpose. The answers to these questions involve the general concept of settling the desert: whether the 'flowering of the desert' in antiquity was the result of an external royal initiative or the enterprise of its nomadic inhabitants.

A close examination of the architectural features of the Negev fortresses will shed light on these questions. The elements treated include the plans of the fortresses and their component architectural features such as casemate rooms and gates, as well as structural details (types of stone, thickness of walls, etc.).

The General Plan of the Fortresses

The Negev fortresses are characterized by a common general ground plan: rows of casemate rooms surrounding a central courtyard. The term 'casemate rooms' is used to differentiate them from casemate walls, of which the defensive aim is not in doubt. It should be stressed that these casemate rooms were built as a complete architectural unit and therefore have no resemblance to sites which were encircled by a series of separate structures attached, more-or-less, to each other, as in Stratum VII at Beersheba and Stratum III at Izbet Sarta.[2]

Y. Aharoni used the criteria of size and shape to classify the fortresses.[3] R. Cohen suggested a different method of classification, based only on the shape, or ground plan, of the fortresses: 1. roughly oval, 2. rectangular, 3. square, and 4. with towers (which are later in date then the others). Recently, he combined 2. and 3. into one class: 'rectangular'.[4]

The search for an essential rather than a merely technical criterion for classification derives from the assumption that the plan of the fortresses reveals a common purpose. An examination of the shape of the fortresses is required to discern whether it was pre-planned or created by other factors. It is the thesis of this article that the ground plan of most of the roughly oval and rectangular fortresses was primarily a response to topographical conditions, whereas the shape of fortresses with towers was determined by an overall plan.

As the size of the fortresses was not fortuitous — on any given summit the structure did not have to encompass the entire surface — size is the initial criterion for classification. The second criterion should be the conformity or nonconformity of the plan to the natural contours (see table).[5]

Several conclusions can be derived from an analysis of the data included in the table.

1. The most recent studies, including bibliographies, are R. Cohen: *The Settlements in the Highlands in the 4th–1st Millennia B.C.* Ph.D. Dissertation, Hebrew University, Jerusalem, 1986 (Hebrew with English abstract); I. Finkelstein: The Iron Age 'Fortresses' of the Negev Highlands: Sendentarization of the Nomads, *Tel-Aviv* 11(1984), pp. 189–209.

2. In contrast with the opinions of Z. Herzog: Enclosed Settlements in the Negev and the Wilderness of Beer-Sheba, *BASOR* 250 (1983), pp. 41–47; and Finkelstein (above, n. 1)

3. Y. Aharoni: Fortresses of the Limes: Iron Age Fortressess in the Negev, *IEJ* 17 (1967), pp. 1–17.

4. Cohen (above, n. 1), pp. 329–330.

5. For full details and references see Cohen (above, n. 1), pp. 330–331 and Finkelstein (above, n. 1), p. 191.

Israelite Fortresses in the Negev

Fortress	Figure	Shape	Size (in metres)
1. Fortresses with towers			
Arad		Square	50 x 50
Uza		Rectangular	42 x 51
Kadesh Barnea	11	Rectangular	34 x 52
2. Large Fortresses			
a) *Shape conforms to topography*			
Rahba		Oval	50 x 75
Yotvata		Trapezoid	40 x 64
Hatira	7	Rectangular	32 x 78
Refed		Rectangular	42 x 57
'Ein Qadeis	3	Oval	31 x 42
Quseima 'Aharoni' fortress		Oval	30 x 80
b) *Pre-planned shape*			
Tell el-Kheleifeh		Square	45 x 45
Ha-Ro'ah	1		42 x 50
Kadesh Barnea (the earliest)		Oval	26 x 28
Horvat Tov		Square	30 x 40
3. Small fortresses			
a) *Shape conforms to topography*			
Ketef Shivta	4	Oval	25 x 35
Nahal Horsha		Oval	21 x 34
Esbo'a (Ramat Boqer)	8	Triangular	33, 31, 28
Har Boqer	6	Rectangular	18 x 27
Qaṣr Ruḥeiba		Square	19.5 x 21.5
Har 'Arqov		Rectangular	18 x 24
Beer Hafir		Square	20 x 20
Har Sa'ad			17 x 21
Site 108			
(at foot of Har Horsha)		Oval	13 x 27
La'ana	5	Oval	12 x 23
Nahal Loz		Oval	15 x 19
Qatun		Oval	9 x 14
Quseima		Rectangular	16 x 30
b) *Pre-planned shape*			
Haluqim	2	Round	Diam. 23
Ritma		Square	21 x 21
Har Raviv	9		19 x 22
Mesora	10	Square	20 x 20
Hanazir		Square	20 x 20
Shluhat Kadesh Barnea			17 x 22
Mishor Ha-Ruah			16 x 19
Nahal Boqer			

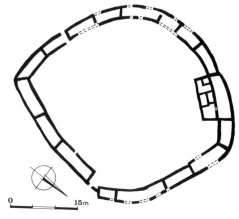

1. Fortress at Ha-Ro'ah.
Qadmoniot 12 (46–47) (1979), p. 41:2.

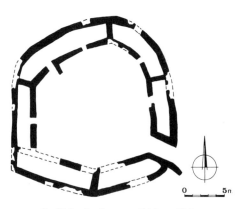

2. Haluqim fortress. *Ibid.*, p. 41:3.

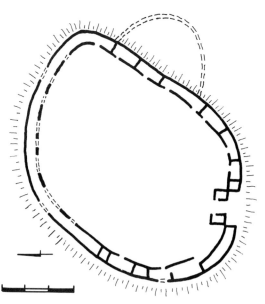

3. 'Ein Qadeis fortress. *Ibid.*, p. 41:1.

The oval plan is primarily the result of the desire to conform to topographical conditions, rather than of tendentious planning. Only the fortresses at Ha-Ro'ah (Fig. 1), Haluqim (Fig. 2), and possibly the early stage of Kadesh Barnea, were located on even ground. The builders were therefore free of topographical restraints, and the shape was probably pre-planned. The first two fortresses differ greatly in size but are located very close to each other. Their similarities suggest that they had the same builder.[6] On the other hand, no conclusions about the planning intentions can be drawn from the similarity between the Ha-Ro'ah fortress and the fortress near 'Ein Qadeis (Fig. 3), because the latter is in full conformity with the natural contours of the hill.

The appearance of a 'rectangular' plan is always the result of the desire to conform to topographical conditions. Thus, comparing the ground plans of rectangular fortresses will illustrate their variety; to classify them as a preplanned group is artificial.

Among the small fortresses there is a large group of nearly square fortresses (*ca.* 20 × 20 m.). Although the majority are not precisely square, and their sizes differ slightly, a uniform master plan may be postulated. The variations may have been the result of topographical constraints or the builders' decision that it was not important to strictly adhere to the exact details of the master plan.[7]

The ground plan of all the fortresses with towers are similar and certainly reflect pre-planning.[8] Nonetheless, differences in size and detail exist. The masons presumably retained the prerogative to make changes in the master plan at each site.

Architectural Elements

The major features of the fortresses, including casemates, gates, towers, internal structures, and animal pens, are compared here. Their ground plans are a basis for assessing the degree of conformity and disparity among them.

Casemates. — A feature common to almost all the Negev fortresses is the line of rooms formed by two parallel walls intersected by transverse walls. Several exceptions to this basic concept exist. The

fortresses at Mishor Ha-Ruah[9] and that above Kadesh Barnea[10] lack casemates along one side, having instead a solid outer wall. The fortress near Quseima (the 'Aharoni' fortress)[11] has irregularly-placed casemates, and only the outer wall extends continuously around the structure. At the Hatira fortress (Fig. 7)[12] there is more than one row of casemates along a single side.

The casemates are not uniform in length or width, even within a single fortress. Therefore, their dimensions cannot serve as a basis for comparison. This variation is noteworthy in itself. The interior width of the casemates ranges from 1.5 to 2.5 m. Generally, ingress to the casemates is from the central courtyard, in a few cases access is from adjacent rooms. Although the entrances are not uniform, they are usually located approximately in the centre of the long wall, as at Har Boqer (Fig. 6), Raviv (Fig. 9), Haluqim (Fig. 2), and Ha-Ro'ah (Fig. 1). At 'Ein Qadeis (Fig. 3) no underlying principle could be discovered.

Gates. — Complete details of the gates are available from only a few of the fortresses surveyed and excavated. Two main types can be distinguished: simple gates created by the space left between two casemate rooms, and planned gates. For example, simple gates have been uncovered in the fortresses at Raviv (Fig. 9), Nahal Sirpad, Har Sa'ad, Mishor Ha-Ruah, Ketef Shivta (Fig. 4), Haluqim (Fig. 2), Har Boqer (Fig. 6), Esbo'a (Fig. 8), Yeter, Horsha, Zen'a, and above Kadesh Barnea. With the exception of the occasional addition of short walls that narrow the passageway (and which resemble pilasters), these gates are unsophisticated. Perhaps the designation 'gate' is inappropriate, because it is unlikely that they had doors or other means of blocking the entrance.

Only three examples of planned gates are known: at the 'Ein Qadeis fortress (Fig. 3), the Hatira fortress (Fig. 7), and the fortress near Quseima (the 'Aharoni'). At 'Ein Qadeis the gate was created when a small room (3 × 3 m.) was added to each of the two interior corners of a space left in the line of casemates. This created an outer gate area in front of the passageway between the

---

6. No proof has been discovered yet of Herzog's idea (above, n. 1) that the large fortresses are earlier than the small ones.
7. Three of the small square fortresses were found to belong to the Persian period (Nahal Ha-Ro'ah, Ritma and Mesora) — Cohen (above, n. 1), p. 329.
8. Aharoni (above, n. 3). It should be stressed that this group of fortresses is more than 200 years later than the others.

9. Y. Aharoni *et al.*: The Ancient Desert Agriculture of the Negev, *IEJ* 10 (1960), p. 100.
10. B. Rothenberg: *Discoveries in Sinai*, Tel-Aviv, 1958, p. 140, Fig. 9 (Hebrew). During a visit to the site, this writer found a section of inner wall on the eastern side as well; therefore, there may have been casemates on all sides.
11. This fortress, named in memory of Yohanan Aharoni, was excavated in 1981. The report is forthcoming.
12. Z. Meshel and R. Cohen: Refed and Hatira: Two Iron Age Fortresses in the Northern Negev, *Tel-Aviv* 7 (1980), pp. 70–81.

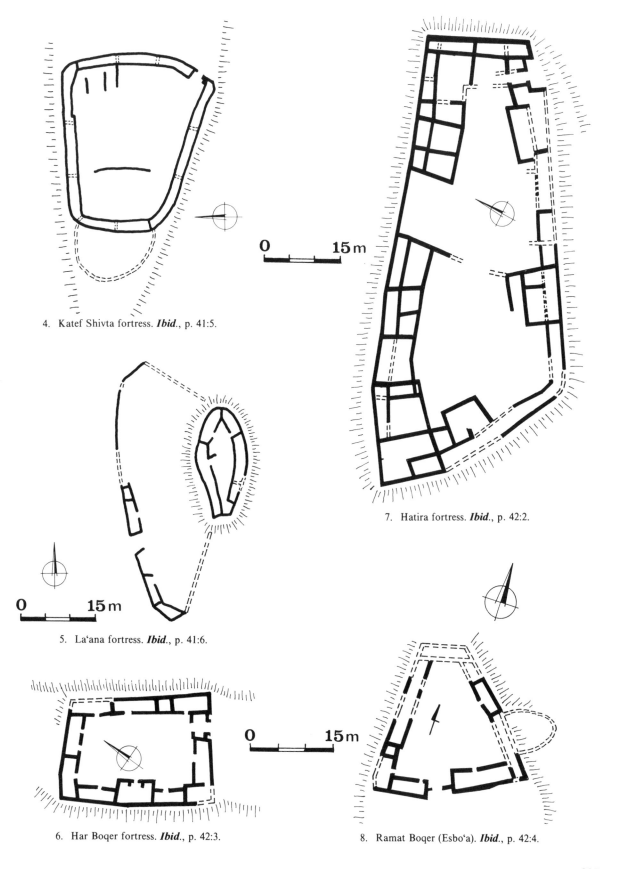

4. Katef Shivta fortress. *Ibid.*, p. 41:5.

5. La'ana fortress. *Ibid.*, p. 41:6.

6. Har Boqer fortress. *Ibid.*, p. 42:3.

7. Hatira fortress. *Ibid.*, p. 42:2.

8. Ramat Boqer (Esbo'a). *Ibid.*, p. 42:4.

0   15 m

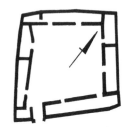

9. Har Raviv fortress. *Ibid.*, p. 43:1.

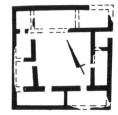

10. Mesora fortress. *Ibid.*, p. 43:3.

rooms. The gate at the Hatira fortress resembles the one at 'Ein Qadeis; here also an outer space in front of a passageway was created in the line of casemates. The passage is located between a room joined to the casemates on the east and an addition to the casemate on the west. The entrance narrows slightly and jambs are created for the doors that almost certainly hung between them. The structural quality of the features of this gate exceeds that of the parallel structures at 'Ein Qadeis, further indicating some degree of pre-planning. The gate at the fortress near Quseima is a fine, albeit simple, example of an indirect gate, undoubtedly the result of thoughtful planning. The walls of this well-built gate are preserved to a height of approximately 2 m. A socket for a hinge was found in the interior threshold, the sole example uncovered ᴉ date in the gates of the Negev fortresses.

Unfortunately, no clear data exist for gates of the fortresses with towers. No gate was discovered at the Kadesh Barnea fortress (Fig. 11), excavated in its entire perimeter, despite the well-preserved state of the walls and towers. Perhaps a dirt ramp, unnoticed during the course of the excavations, or wooden stairs, led to an unpreserved opening in the wall itself. The gate of the tower-fortress at Arad is largely reconstructed; its exact construction cannot be established with certainty.

Towers. — It is generally held, despite the lack of conclusive evidence, that sections projecting from the fortress wall also extended above it. There is, however, no proof that such projections were sections of towers. In fact, towers existed definitely only in the structures

designated herein as 'fortresses with towers'. The lack of uniformity in the ground plans of 'fortresses with towers' applies also to the towers themselves. Even within the same fortress, differences exist in their shape and details.

Internal Structures. — The interior space of fortresses with towers contains many structures; in most of the other types of fortresses the inner courtyards were empty, although there are exceptions. At the Yeter fortress a square structure (10 × 10 m.) composed of rooms around a courtyard was erected in the centre of the main courtyard. Although the interior structure is not parallel to the fortress walls, pottery finds in both structures are similar. A square structure (8.4 × 8.4 m.) also stands in the centre of the courtyard at the Sirpad II fortress located between the tributaries of Nahal Sirpad. It, however, resembles a four-room house. Its central space is about 4 m. wide, and its side rooms are about 2 m. wide.

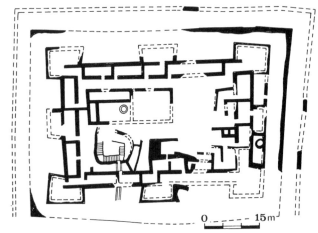

11. Kadesh Barnea. *Qadmoniot* 27 (61) (1979), p. 10.

A structure with similar dimensions consisting of rooms around a central courtyard was uncovered in the fortress at Har 'Arqov. There are comparable structures at the Ha-Ro'ah fortress (Building II, 8 × 12 m.) (Fig. 1), and at the Mesora fortress (11 × 17 m.), (Fig. 10) although these were some distance from the fortress, connected to it by rows of casemate rooms.[13] In this context Building A at Ritma (9×9.5m). should also be mentioned. Although it is not attached to the fortress, it is in close proximity to it.[14]

13. For plans and details of all these, see Cohen (above, n. 1). He places them together in a group of 'forts'.
14. Z. Meshel: Horvat Ritma — An Iron Age Fortress in the Negev Highlands, *Tel Aviv* 4 (1977), p. 114.

Kadesh Barnea. Iron Age II fortress, general view.

It is likely that the preceding structures filled similar administrative or official functions, serving as a sort of commander's house, and were located either within the fortress or nearby. The structure incorporated into the western row of casemates at the Har Boqer fortress (Fig. 6) may have had a similar function. It has three rooms divided by rows of pillars.

In some fortresses an inner wall divides the central courtyard. At the Hatira fortress (Fig. 7), at Quseima (the 'Aharoni'), and perhaps at Ketef Shivta (Fig. 4), it is a single wall; at the Refed fortress, a row of rooms, similar to casemates, crosses the courtyard.

Remains of structures have also been found in the inner courtyards of the Rahba and Ha-Ro'ah fortresses, but they appear to have been small. In contrast, the fortresses with towers at Kadesh Barnea (Fig. 11), 'Uza and Arad contained many structures

in their courtyards, almost equalling the density of the buildings in Byzantine monasteries.

Animal Pens. — This discussion is restricted to the central structure — the 'fortress' — and its associated or adjacent elements, and does not include dwellings, water catchment systems, or agricultural installations connected with it. Worthy of mention, however, are stone fences whose rubble indicates unstable construction that are identified as animal pens. It is not always clear whether the pens are contemporaneous with or postdate the period of the fortresses, but several were in concurrent use.[15] If the pens attached to the fortresses of Ketef Shivta (Fig. 4), Raviv (Fig. 9), Ramat Boqer and the smaller

15. Cohen ignores their existence, omitting them in his description and plans.

pens at 'Ein Qadeis (Fig. 3), Horsha, Har Sa'ad, and Sirpad II were indeed used concurrently, their close proximity to the fortresses is a clue to the occupation of some of the fortresses' inhabitants.

Structural Details

Structural details are a yardstick for measuring the skill and building traditions of masons, and indicate the degree to which foreign influences were adopted. Some structural details in the Negev fortresses are discussed here.

Floors. — Most of the Negev fortresses were built on bedrock, whose surface tends to be grooved, inclined, and even stepped. Thus the builders had to create a horizontal surface for each room; to that aim they chose a beaten-earth floor. A dirt fill covered the bedrock. At present, there are no known plaster floors in the Negev fortresses.

Masonry. — In all of the fortresses discussed here, locally available stone was the building material. Weathering and natural cracks determined the size and shape of the stones. For example, the Ha-Ro'ah fortress was erected on a flint bed, and its masonry is composed entirely of that material. The nearby Haluqim site is located in a limestone area, so its fortress is built of limestone. The stones at the Ha-Ro'ah fortress are larger than those at Haluqim because flint tends to break into larger pieces than limestone. Small, irregular stones were used at the Ketef Shivta fortress because it was erected on the geological Nezer formation. The Raviv and Zen'a fortresses are built on Eocene limestone, which breaks into larger blocks (their dimensions reach 0.5 × 1 m.) than the Turonian limestone used for the Mishor Ha-Ruah fortress. The tendency of both Eocene and Turonian limestone to break into almost rectangular blocks explains the prevalence of this shape for masonry in limestone areas.

Building blocks were undoubtedly detached from the bedrock by widening already existing cracks, although no traces of the wooden wedges or chisels that may have been used have survived. Nor are there dressed stones or signs of the use of quarrying tools in any of the Negev fortresses.[16]

Walls. — Walls of the Negev fortresses are generally one or two stones wide. When the stones are large, the wall is generally one stone wide and ranges from 0.4 to 0.6 m. in width (as at the Ha-Ro'ah, La'ana,

---

16. The only exceptions are the ashlars at the Arad fortress, whose date is the subject of debate.

(Fig. 5) Mishor Ha-Ruah, Ketef Shivta, Hatira, Yeter, and 'Ein Qadeis fortresses). Walls that are two stones wide vary in width from 0.7 to 1 m. (as at the Haluqim, Ritma, Mesora, Ramat Boqer, Har Boqer, and Horsha fortresses). In some fortresses the outer walls of the casemates are two stones wide, whereas the inner walls are only one stone wide, regardless of the type of stone used (Refed, Rahba, Beer Hafir, Har Boqer, and Horsha).

The difference in width between the inner and outer walls of the casemates generally varies from 0.2 to 0.4 m., but occasionally reaches 1 m. (as at the Horsha fortress). These variations in the width of walls indicate differences in the height and strength of the fortresses.

A third method of construction, utilizing a core of small stones between two rows of masonry, is known at only three sites: at the fortress near Quseima (the 'Aharoni'), in the northern wall (1.4 m. thick), at the fortress at Mishor Ha-Ruah, where the width of the only wall built by this method reaches approximately 1.5 m., and at Shluhat Kadesh Barnea.

Stone Pillars. — Monolithic stone pillars, occasionally reaching a length of 1 m., were widely used in the Negev fortress sites and are a typical feature. However, closer scrutiny reveals that the monoliths were more commonly used in the dwellings than in the forts themselves. Sectional (drum) pillars were found at Har Boqer and Sirpad. Apparently these findings have functional rather than chronological significance.

Jambs, Lintels, and Corners. — Jambs, corners, and especially lintels are characterized by the use of relatively large stones. At the Raviv and 'Ein Qadeis fortresses stone slabs about 1.75 m. in length were found. At these fortresses, as well as the Ha-Ro'ah, Zen'a, and Refed fortresses, for example, rather large stones were also used for the door jambs and corners. If large stones were unavailable, the door jambs were occasionally strengthened by using the system of headers and stretchers, as at the Ramat Boqer and Har Boqer fortresses.

Conclusions

The sites known as Israelite fortresses in the Negev are characterized to a large degree by lack of uniformity. Ground plans of most of the forts were modified in accord with natural conditions. The shape of most of the fortresses is the direct result of the topography of their location. Analysis by shape is therefore irrelevant. The criteria for classification should be

1. the degree of accommodation to the topography and 2. size.

An analysis of the ground plans of the Negev fortresses which are free of topographical constraints reveals two basic models: 1. square, relatively small, fortresses (20 × 20 m.) and 2. fortresses with towers. The archaeological data indicate that the two kinds were not contemporaneous. In addition, the builders did not feel constrained to adhere exactly to a master plan and exercised freedom with regard to the size and details of the fortresses.

Casemate rooms are a fixed feature of all the Negev fortresses. It is difficult to ascertain whether this indicates adherence to tradition, sophisticated building methods or skill. Gates are usually a simple break in the outer wall in front of a space left in the line of the casemates. Only at three fortresses can special gate features be discerned, apparently based on tradition or architectural ideas. The same also appears to be true regarding some of the central structures found at several fortresses that may have functioned as the 'commander's house'.

The Israelite fortresses in the Negev demonstrate a low degree of planning and building traditions with a large measure of improvisation, accommodation to environment, and enterprise. Unfortunately, these observations do not tell us whether the Negev fortresses were the result of royal or local initiative. It can only be concluded from the architectural data, in conjunction with the archaeological findings, that external (royal) and local (nomad) initiative coexisted.[17]

17. Figs. 1, 2, 3, 4, 8, 10 and 11 are according to Cohen (above, n. 1). The additions of topographical details and animal pens are the writer's.

THE PHOENICIAN ARCHITECTURAL ELEMENTS IN PALESTINE DURING THE LATE IRON AGE AND THE PERSIAN PERIOD

Ephraim Stern

A number of features characteristic of Israelite construction in the tenth through ninth centuries B.C. are referred to as 'Phoenician': marginal drafts on ashlars; headers and stretchers; ashlars, piers, and fieldstone fills for walls; proto-Aeolic capitals; recessed openings; decorated balustrades; 'three-step' crenellations; and a unique technique for filling square areas of pavement.

Recent finds from all over Israel, as well as from Jordan and the Phoenician coast, show that these architectural elements appear without interruption from the end of the Iron Age through the Persian period, and down to the beginning of the Hellenistic period.

Smooth and Marginally-drafted Ashlar Blocks in Header and Stretcher Construction

The use of headers and stretchers was widespread in the royal cities of Israel and Judah in the tenth-ninth centuries B.C. (Chap. 22). Of significance to the discussion is whether this ashlar construction is also found outside the Land of Israel in the Iron Age — that is, along the Phoenician coast — and whether it is continued into later periods in the areas of Phoenician settlement. In excavations at Tyre, walls were discovered that were assigned to Stratum V (760–740 B.C.). They were built with headers and stretchers and most probably had typically dressed margins. The excavator also noted that the entire area of excavation was covered with a layer of stone chips, indicating that the stones had been dressed at the site.[1] At Sarepta there was construction with headers and stretchers, built of ashlars with marginal

1. P.M. Bikai: *The Pottery of Tyre*, Warminster, 1978, p. 12, Pl. LXXXIX, Walls No. 2, 28.

1. Casemate wall, built with a combination of dressed stones and fieldstones, Tel Mevorakh. ***BASOR*** 225 (1977), p. 19, Fig. 5.

drafts, that was assigned to Stratum D, dating to the end of the Iron Age. The excavator compared this building technique with that found at Samaria.[2] At Tel Mevorakh and Tel Dor, Persian-period casemates were uncovered bounding a large structure (Fig. 1). The outer wall of the casemate at Tel Mevorakh is built entirely of headers and stretchers, but the ashlars are of smooth local sandstone without marginal drafts. At Tel Dor, ashlar piers built in the header and stretcher system with marginally-drafted stones, also appear

2. J.B. Pritchard: *Recovering Sarepta, A Phoenician City*, Princeton, 1978, pp. 93–94, Fig. 92; see also I. Sharon: Phoenician and Greek Ashlar Construction Techniques at Tel Dor, Israel, *BASOR* 267 (1987), pp. 30–31, for additional examples along the Phoenician–Israeli coast.

regularly in walls in which ashlars and fieldstones alternate.[3]

Walls with Ashlar Piers and Fieldstone Fills

The construction of walls with ashlar piers and fieldstone fills is a feature of monumental architecture from the beginning of Iron Age II, as for example, at Megiddo (Strata VA–IVB, IVA) (Fig. 2) and at Hazor (Stratum VIII). Y. Shiloh, in his comprehensive treatment of this type of construction, correctly points out that its appearance as early as the tenth century proves that it was not a degeneration in ashlar building but, rather, was one of several techniques used alongside the more splendid examples of ashlar construction.[4]

An examination of the finds from the coasts of Phoenicia and Palestine makes it clear that this element, which began in Phoenicia in a period roughly parallel to its appearance in Palestine, continued without interruption until the Hellenistic period. Walls of this type have been discovered at a large number of sites. At Tell Sukas, structures assigned to Period E of the Hellenistic period were found scattered all over the surface of the mound;[5] at Tell Kazel, a city-wall and opening were dated to the Persian period;[6] at Tabaat el-Hammam a Hellenistic wall was uncovered;[7] at Tyre a wall in this style was assigned to Stratum IX (850–800 B.C.);[8] at Sarepta a residential building was uncovered that should be assigned to the upper Iron Age stratum (D);[9] and at Akko, walls of this type were discovered in the north and south of the mound in Strata IV–III, from the Late Persian and Hellenistic

2. Walls constructed of fieldstones and dressed stones, Megiddo. *Megiddo* I, p. 11, Fig. 13.

periods.[10] Construction of this type found at Akhziv has not yet been published, but M. Prausnitz assigns it to strata from the end of the Iron Age to the Hellenistic period. At Tell Abu Hawam, this type of construction was typical[11] only in the upper phase, Stratum II, of the fourth century B.C.[12] At Tel Mevorakh a casemate wall of this type encircled a large structure from the Late Persian period, and many others such walls were uncovered recently at Tel Dor, dating from the Iron Age to the Hellenistic period.[13]

South of this area, at Tell esh-Shuni (Tell Kudadi), a section of a Persian period wall was discovered;[14] and at Jaffa the most beautiful example of this technique was uncovered in Level II, dating from the middle of the fifth century B.C. to the Macedonian conquest.[15] Mention should also be made of the remains found at Tel Mikhal (Makhmish) and Mikhmoret.[16] A summary of the chronological data emerging from this survey shows almost unbroken continuity.

The controversy over the architectural significance of this method of construction — that is, whether

3. E. Stern: Excavations at Tel Mevorakh and the Late Phoenician Elements in the Architecture of Palestine, *BASOR* 225 (1977), p. 19, Figs. 5, 8–9; and I. Sharon (above, n. 2).

4. Y. Shiloh: *The Proto-Aeolic Capital and Israelite Ashlar Masonry* [*Qedem* 11], Jerusalem 1979, p. 63; cf. bibliography therein.

5. P.J. Riis: L'activite de la mission archeologique phenicienne en 1960, *AAAS* 11–12 (1961–2), p. 120, Figs. 9–10; *idem, Sukas I: The North-East Sanctuary and the First Settling of Greeks in Syria and Palestine*, Copenhagen, 1970, pp. 107–108, n. 390, Figs. 38–39.

6. M. Dunand, A. Bauni and N. Saliby: Fouilles de Tell Kazel, Rapport preliminaire, *AAAS* 14 (1964), p. 8, Pl. IV.

7. R.B. Braidwood: Report on Two Sondages on the Coast of Syria South of Tartous, *Syria* 21 (1940), p. 196, Pl. 21:1.

8. Bikai (above, n. 1), pp. 10–11, Pl. LXXXIX:5–6.

9. J.B. Pritchard: The Phoenicians in their Homeland, *Expedition* 14 (1971), pp. 19–20; *idem* (above, n. 2), pp. 93–94, Fig. 91.

10. M. Dothan: Accho (Notes and News), *IEJ* 23 (1973), p. 258; *idem*, Akko: Interim Excavation Report, First Season, 1973/4, *ASOR* 224 (1976), pp. 27, 30, 41, Figs. 29, 43, 44.

11. E. Stern: The Dating of Stratum II at Tell Abu Hawam, *IEJ* 18 (1968), pp. 213–214.

12. R.W. Hamilton: Excavations at Tell Abu Hawam, *QDAP* 3 (1933), pp. 78–79, Pls. 20, 21:2; *ibid.*, 4 (1935), pp. 2–5, Pls. 1, 2:1.

13. Stern (above, n. 3), p. 18, Figs. 5–7 and also *idem, Excavations at Tel Mevorakh (1973–1976)*, Part I: *From the Iron Age to the Roman Period* [*Qedem* 9], Jerusalem, 1978, pp. 73–75, Fig. VIII; on the recent finds of Tel Dor, see Sharon (above, n. 2) and bibliography therein.

14. E.L. Sukenik: Tell esh-Shuni (Tell el-Kudadi), *QDAP* 8 (1938), pp. 167–168 (no photograph has been published).

15. J. Kaplan: Jaffa, *EAEHL* II, p. 539; H. Ritter-Kaplan: The Ties Between Sidonian Jaffa and Greece in the Light of Excavations, *Qadmoniot* 15 (1982), pp. 64–66 (Hebrew).

16. N. Avigad: Excavations at Makhmish, 1958, *IEJ* 10 (1960), Pl. 9; The Mikhmoret walls have not been published yet and I am grateful to J. Porath of the Israel Antiquities Authority for this information.

Tel Dor. Persian period city-wall.

it was used for aesthetic reasons, as J.B. Pritchard thinks,[17] or for structural reinforcement, as others surmise — will not be discussed here.[18] Of interest is that these scholars all conclude a definite similarity between this and the style of ninth-century structures.

All the excavators agree on the Phoenician origin of this method of construction. M. Dothan designates the find at Akko as Phoenician or Punic;[19] Kaplan calls it Sidonian construction;[20] and Pritchard mentions that a similar building technique is known from the Punic colonies in the western Mediterranean — Carthage, Motya, and Nora,[21] where it is known as *a-telaio*.[22]

There is, thus, ample reason to view its appearance in the west as a continuation of a construction technique that had been developed on the Phoenician-Palestinian coast in the tenth-ninth centuries B.C.

Proto-Aeolic Capitals

The corpus of Palestinian proto-Aeolic capitals published by Shiloh[23] comprises thirty-four capitals (Chap. 22, Figs. 9, 10), to which should be added one from Tel Dan and two designs of capitals on ivory carvings from 'Aro'er[24] and Samaria.[25] The capitals from Israelite royal cities (Dan, Hazor, Megiddo, and

17. Pritchard (above, n. 9), pp. 19–20.
18. K.M. Kenyon: *Royal Cities of the Old Testament*, London 1971, pp. 95–105; Hamilton (above, n. 12, 1933), p. 79; Shiloh (above, n. 4), p. 63.
19. Dothan (above, n. 10, 1973), p. 258.
20. J. Kaplan (above, n. 15), p. 539.
21. Pritchard (above, n. 9), pp. 19–20; *idem* (above, n. 2), pp. 93–94; D. Harden: *The Phoenicians*, London, 1963, p. 303, Pl. 13; G. and O. Van Beek: Canaanite-Phoenician Architecture: The Development and Distribution of Two Styles, *EI* 15 (1981), pp. 70*–77*; J. Elayi: Remarques sur un type de mur

Phenicien, *Revista di Studii Fenici* 8 (1980), pp. 165–180; Sharon (above, n. 2).
22. Shiloh (above, n. 4), pp. 74, 84; Sharon (above, n. 2), p. 35 for additional finds. To our surprise this technique has been found also at Tel Dor in Area D1 (not yet published), for the first time in the eastern Mediterranean coast.
23. Y. Shiloh: New Proto-Aeolic Capitals found in Israel, *BASOR* 222 (1976), pp. 67–77; *idem* (above, n. 4). Since then only one more has been found at Tel Dan.
24. A. Biran: 'Aro'er, *Hadashot Arkheologiyot* 74–75 (1980), p. 31, and Fig. on cover.
25. *Samaria-Sebaste* II, Pl. XXII:1

Samaria) as well as that depicted on the ivory from Samaria, which date from the tenth-eighth centuries B.C., differ in design from the capitals from Judean cities (Jerusalem and Ramat Rahel), as well as from the capitals from Medeibia in Edom and the ivory carving from 'Aro'er. These differences undoubtedly represent local variations and, perhaps, chronological differences. The find from 'Aro'er is from the seventh century B.C., which supports Y. Aharoni's suggestion that this is the date of the Ramat Rahel capitals,[26] and refutes the theory of Y. Yadin[27] and Shiloh[28] that they belong to the ninth century B.C.

No other proto-Aeolic capitals appear in the Land of Israel between the end of the Iron Age and the Hellenistic period, although there are scores of them from Phoenician settlements in Cyprus.[29] Some of these capitals are in the style common in the Land of Israel; the rest are in what Shiloh has termed the 'Cypriot' style, with its additional motif of the Phoenician palmette. These capitals are dated to the seventh century and onward.

Proto-Aeolic capitals have been discovered at Punic sites, but they are later than the Cypriot capitals — continuing up to the second century B.C.[30] In addition, this capital is depicted on Punic stelae.[31] At Oumm el-'Amed near Tyre, in a late Phoenician settlement (end of the Persian/beginning of the Hellenistic period), a capital was discovered on a stone orthostat that had been worked on both sides. This is the latest example from the Phoenician coast, and it demonstrates the preservation of this decorative tradition there up to the Hellenistic period.[32]

The distribution of the proto-Aeolic capital can also be traced in the clay temple models discovered in Israel, Jordan, and Cyprus.[33] The model from Tell el-Far'ah (North) (Fig. 3) has been dated to the tenth century B.C. The models from Tel Rekhesh, Akhziv and Jordan have been dated to the end of the Iron Age. A similar date has been assigned to the models from

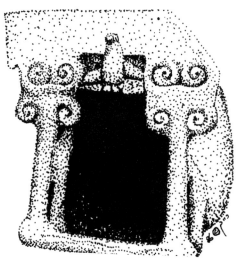

3. Clay model of a temple, Tell el-Far'ah (N). *QDAP* XI (1945), Pl. XXI.

Cyprus. The appearance of the capitals on models, and their geographical distribution, have led most scholars (Iliffe, Weinberg, and Betancourt) to identify them as a Phoenician invention. The distribution of the proto-Aeolic capitals clearly overlaps that of the other capitals in Israel, Jordan, the Phoenician coast, later in Cyprus; and in another form (on stone stelae) in the western Mediterranean Punic colonies.

Hathor Capitals

Another type of capital that probably should be included in the monumental Phoenician style of construction is a representation of the head of the goddess Hathor. This decoration, which was borrowed from Egyptian architecture, is known at present only from Cyprus. Two limestone capitals, each with two faces, are known from Larnaka (probably having originated in Kition).[34] They are engraved on both sides. They should be dated to the seventh or sixth century B.C. A capital from Vouni, on Cyprus, from a Persian period palace, is the same type.[35] Above the head of the goddess is a model of the facade of a temple with a recessed opening flanked by pillars (Fig. 4). Although capitals of precisely this type have not yet been found on the Phoenician or Palestinian coast, they should not for this reason be disassociated from the assemblage of Iron Age-Phoenician monumental architectural decorations. It

26. *Ramat Rahel* I, pp. 14–15; *Ramat Rahel* II, pp. 28–29.
27. Y. Yadin: The City of Beit Ba'al, in J. Aviram (ed.): *The Land of Shomron*, Jerusalem, 1973, pp. 52–56 (Hebrew).
28. Shiloh (above, n. 4), p. 10.
29. Shiloh (above, n. 4), pp. 36–39, counts 29 finds from Golgoi, Idalion, Koukliah, Salamis, Thamasos, Kition and Trapeza.
30. J.M. Blazquez: *Tantessos y los Origines de la Colonizacion Fenicia en Occidente*, II, Salamanca, 1975, Pl. LXIII.
31. Harden (above, n. 21), Pl. 34; Shiloh (above, n. 4), pp. 39–41.
32. M. Dunand and R. Duru: *Oumm el-'Amed*, Paris, 1952, Pl. XXVIII:2.
33. S.S. Weinberg: A Moabite Shrinegroup, *Muse* 12 (1978), pp. 30–48, and see bibliography therein.

34. M. Ohnefalsch-Richter: Kypros, *The Bible and Homer*, Leiden, 1893, pp. 477–479, Pl. CC:113.
35. *SCE* IV, 2, p. 24.

4. Stone capital depicting a temple facade. Byblos. **BASOR** 225 (1977), Fig. 16.

5. Ivory relief with 'woman-in-window' motif. D. Harden: *The Phoenicians*, London, 1971, Pl. 62.

Recessed Openings

A recessed opening is one whose frame (lintel and jambs) has from two to five 'steps', each of which is recessed farther back from the opening than the one before it. Variations of this type are known primarily from the group of Phoenician ivories that depict the 'woman-at-the-window' motif from Samaria, Arslan Tash, Nimrud and Khorsabad, dating to the ninth-eighth centuries B.C. [36] It appears that this type of opening, of two or more steps, is a common type of entrance and not confined to windows.

From random finds it is clear that this opening continued in use from the end of the Iron Age through the Persian and Hellenistic periods. Two examples are known from the Phoenician coast. One is carved on a tiny stone votive stele from Persian period Akhziv, depicted on the facade of a temple.[37] The other is a monumental stone lintel discovered in the 'temple est' at Oumm el-'Amed from the end of the Persian period and the Hellenistic period.[38] Most finds, however, are from Cyprus. There are two outstanding examples: a limestone capital from Larnaka (Kition), mentioned above,[39] and a stone grille, engraved on both sides to look like a complete window, which was found at Kaloriziki near Kourion[40] and has affinities with the monumental architecture of the Phoenician tombs in Cyprus. This type of opening was also discovered on the monumental tomb at Tamassos in Cyprus, ornamented on both sides with proto-Aeolic capitals.[41] The finds from Cyprus are from the seventh century and later, but most are from the Persian period. Similar openings have also been discovered on Punic stone stelae at various sites in the western Mediterranean.

Decorated Balustrades

Another element of Phoenician monumental architecture from Iron Age II is the decorated balustrade in windows or perhaps on balconies. This

would seem that these capitals should be viewed as a continuation of the Phoenician monumental style of construction on the Phoenician coast and on Cyprus at the end of the Iron Age and the Persian period based on the following data: the depiction of the 'Phoenician palmette' carved on two sides of the temple model; the recessed openings; and the covered head of the woman resembling the 'woman-at-the-window' on Phoenician ivories and in the actual figurines that ornament windows of this type (Fig. 5).

36. C. Decamps de Mertzenfeld: *Inventaire commente des ivoires pheniciens et apparentes decouverts dans le Proche-Orient*, Paris, 1954, Pls. LXXVI–LXXVII, XLIX, C, CI.
37. Stern (above, n. 3), Fig. 16.
38. Dunand and Duru (above, n. 32), Pls. LXIII:1–3, LXIV:1–3.
39. Stern (above, n. 3), Fig. 16.
40. V. Karageorghis: Chronique des fouilles a Chypre en 1969, *Bulletin de Correspondance Hellenique* 44 (1970), pp. 226–231, Fig. 80 (and see bibliography therein); Shiloh (above, n. 4), Pl. 19.
41. Shiloh (above, n.4), Pl. 18.

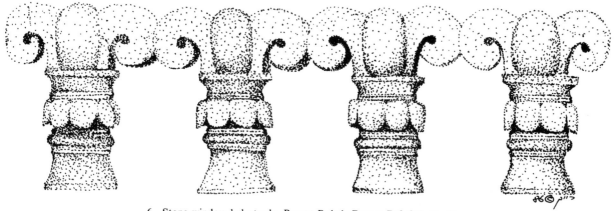

6. Stone window balustrade, Ramat Rahel. *Ramat Rahel* II, Pl. 48.

element is known largely from the 'woman-at-the-window' motif on the ivories, where it is generally depicted as a row of small columns with capitals that end in a double volute, like that of the proto-Aeolic capital, under which there is a ring of 'drooping leaves'. Moreover, windows with such grilles (but without the woman's head), known as 'Phoenician windows', are found on various reliefs and Assyrian depictions,[42] but it was not clear whether the columns on the balustrade were sculpted in the round or only in relief on a stone orthostat until the remains of two balustrades from Ramat Rahel were found (Fig. 6) which demonstrate that both techniques were used. One example is a stone orthostat 6 cm. thick that was carved on both sides with a row of columns;[43] the other consists of fragments of small columns that were sculpted in the round.[44] These finds were not discovered *in situ*. Aharoni dated them to the seventh century B.C.[45]

Evidence of the continuity of this element in Late Phoenician architecture in the eastern Mediterranean is found in the limestone model of a window from the seventh-sixth centuries B.C. from Kourion on Cyprus,[46] depicting two columns nearly identical to those from Ramat Rahel.

Another example is the fragment of a real balustrade discovered at Oumm el-'Amad near Tyre in the temple of Milk 'Ashrt, dating to the beginning of the Hellenistic period.[47] Finally, there is the recent discovery at Rabbat Ammon of four sculpted two-faced (Janus) female heads (not found *in situ*). The sculptures are limestone and most closely resemble the women's heads on the 'woman-at-the-window' ivories. In the excavator's opinion, they were taken from a monumental building (Stratum V, Phase 1) dating to the end of the seventh century B.C. There are shallow indentations on the head and base of the statue into which metal was cast in order to fasten the head to the lintel of the window above it and to the carved balustrade below it.[48] A stylistic and functional analysis of the heads led the excavator to conclude (and this writer concurs) that these were not capitals but rather part of the window's architectural decoration. Hence the 'woman-at-the-window' ivories actually depict the entire construction of these openings, consisting of two separate elements: a balustrade of columns and a woman's head. This discovery allows us to conclude: 1. the distribution of this style of monumental construction even reached the royal palaces at Rabbat Ammon; and 2. this type of construction lasted through the end of the seventh century B.C.

Crenellation

Another type of architectural decoration that is typical of Phoenician, Israelite, and Judean monumental

42. N. Avigad: The Ivory House that Ahab Built, in J. Aviram (ed.): *Eretz-Shomron*, Jerusalem, 1973, p. 28 (Hebrew).
43. M. Stekelis: A Jewish Tomb from Ramat Rahel, in N. Slouschz (ed.): *The Mazia Festschrift*, Jerusalem, 1934, pp. 27–28, Pl. 3; M. Cohn: On the Stone Capitals from Ramat Rahel, *BIES* 13 (1947), pp. 83–86 (Hebrew); Stern (above, n. 3), Fig. 17.
44. *Ramat Rahel* II, pp. 56–58, Fig. 38, Pls. 44–48.
45. *Ramat Rahel* II, p. 58; wood and stone carvings have also been uncovered at the excavations of the City of David, also dating to the seventh-sixth centuries B.C.
46. Shiloh (above, n. 4), Pl. 19.
47. Dunand and Duru (above, n. 32), Pl. XXXVII.
48. F. Zayadine: Recent Excavations on the Citadel of Amman, *ADAJ* 18 (1973), pp. 17–35, Pls. XVIII:1, I, XXII.

Tel Dor. Persian period dwellings.

architecture in the early period of the monarchy is crenellation, which appears on the upper part of important structures. All the crenellated upper walls from this period discovered to date have three 'steps': in the governor's palace at Megiddo (Fig. 7),[49] in the palace of the kings of Israel at Samaria,[50] in the palace of the kings of Judah at Ramat Rahel,[51] and most recently at Tel Mevorakh in a tenth-century building.[52]

There is now evidence that this type of crenellation with three steps continued in the coastal region even in the Persian period. In a temple from that period excavated in the area of the southern port of Tell Sukas, two such crenellation stones were discovered, of limestone.[53] It would seem that in this late period

the uniformity of this type was not always maintained, as the two latest examples already have four steps, in imitation of the design common in Mesopotamia.[54]

Paving Square Areas

Sometimes the continuity of the Phoenician tradition of construction (from the early period of the United Monarchy to the Persian and Hellenistic periods) finds expression in secondary details of construction. An interesting example is the technique used to pave square areas with ashlars. At Tel Mevorakh, in Stratum III dating to the Hellenistic period, a one-metre-square stone-paved area was discovered. This area is paved with eight elongated, beautifully dressed ashlars uniquely laid: four widthwise and four lengthwise. This turned out to be the same technique used for the so-called stairwell in Palace 1723 from Strata VA-IVB at Megiddo (tenth century B.C.), mentioned here in connection with other architectural elements that persisted into the Persian and Hellenistic periods.[55]

49. *Megiddo* I, pp. 28–29, Fig. 36.
50. *Samaria-Sebaste* I, p. 65, Pl. 60:1.
51. *Ramat Rahel* II, pp. 55–56.
52. Stern (above, n. 3), p. 19, Figs. 2–3; *idem* (above, n. 13), pp. 48, 71, Fig. VII, Pl. 19:2–3.
53. P.J. Riis: *Sukas*, VI, Copenhagen, 1979, pp. 47–48, Figs. 149–153; M. Dunand and N. Saliby: Le sanctuaire d'Amrit, rapport preliminaire, *AAAS* 11/12 (1961/1962), pp. 3–12, Pls. 1:1–2; 2:1–2, 3:4; G. Contenau: *La civilization Phenicien*, Paris, 1934, p. 120

54. Stern (above, n. 13), Fig. VII:5–6.
55. Stern (above, n. 3), p. 18, Figs. 10–11.

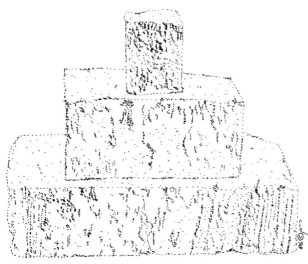

7. Crenellated wall, Ramat Rahel. *Ramat Rahel* II, Pl. 44:1.

Conclusions

The finds mentioned here, although few and widely scattered, are evidence that the various elements of monumental architecture in use at the beginning of the Iron Age did not disappear in the late eighth century B.C. but continued into the Persian and Hellenistic periods. Only in the third century B.C. were they partly supplanted by Greek building traditions. Two phenomena are apparent: 1. at the end of the Iron Age,

Phoenician construction traditions spread to areas off the Phoenician coast and the western Land of Israel. Remains have been found not only within the borders of the kingdom of Judah, but also in the kingdoms east of the Jordan River: Ammon, Moab, and Edom — until they were destroyed by the Babylonians. 2. Even after the Babylonian destruction, this type of architecture existed, although it disappeared from the hill country and was concentrated on the Phoenician coast and in northern coastal sites of Israel, from Tell Sukas to Jaffa. It is well known from the historical sources that these areas were then settled almost entirely by the Phoenicians.[56] This shift from the hinterland to the coastal areas was generally accompanied by changes in the building materials — from the limestone typical of the hill country to local sandstone.

It is now possible to demonstrate the recently contested Phoenician origin of this monumental architecture — beyond the traditional biblical sources — with two new pieces of evidence: its appearance at Tyre in the ninth century B.C. and its continuation on the Phoenician coastal strip down to the third century B.C.

56. E. Stern: *The Material Culture of the Land of the Bible in the Persian Period 538–332 B.C.*, Warminster, 1982, pp. 15–18, 241–243; K. Galling: Die Syrisch-Palastinische Kuste nach der Beschreibung bei Pseudo-Skylax, *ZDPV* 61 (1938), pp. 66–69.

GLOSSARY OF ARCHITECTURAL TERMS

Ronny Reich and Hannah Katzenstein

The glossary deals with architectural terms related to the architecture of the Ancient Near East in the pre-classical era (preceeding the Greek culture). However, archaeologists and art historians make use of terms adopted from Greek terminology (e.g.: stylobate, temenos, dromos, etc.).

For a number of architectural phenomena there are in use several synonymous terms, usually originating in different languages, for example: naos, debir, cella, holy-of-holies, adyton. Such terms are cross-referenced.

Abutment	A solid structure (wall, pilaster etc.) which receives the thrust of an arch or vault (s.v.).
Acropolis	(Greek: ἄκρος = high, edge; πόλις = city). The highest and most fortified part of a city, the inner citadel of a city.
Adyton	(Greek: ἄδυτον = not to be entered). The innermost sacred part of a temple into which entrance is restricted to priests. Also called: holy-of-holies, *debir*, naos, cella (s.v.).
Alley	A narrow street or passage between buildings.
Anta, antae	(Latin). Pilaster-like door jambs. Thickening of the end of a wall. Antae are occasionally provided with a base and a capital. A porch or portico, in which columns are located between the antae, is called *in antis*.
Antechamber	Room leading into a more important chamber such as an antechamber into a throne room in a palace (s.v.), or into the naos in a temple.
Apse	Part of a structure with a rounded wall, or a semicircular niche or recess in a wall. See also: Apsidal building.
Apsidal building	Building with one semicircular wall.
Apsis	(Greek: ἀψίς = outer circle of wheel, vault). See: Apse.
Aqueduct	Water channel which carries water by gravity; usually covered. See also: Water channel.
Arch	Built series of stones or bricks, placed one next to the other to form a curved construction (usually a semicircle) in such a way that each member of this series supports the other as well as the heavy burden resting upon them and being diverted sideways and downwards.
Architrave	Beam of wood or stone resting upon columns.

Archaeological cross-section	Graphical presentation of building details and the various adjacent layers of debris, floors, pits etc. as they appear on the sides of the excavation trench.
Architectural cross-section	Graphical presentation of all architectural elements of a building as they appear along a certain line (axis) within the building. The elements on this line are given in section, whereas those seen from that line — in elevation (side view). Serves to describe the dimension of height of the building.
Ashlar	A cut and dressed stone, worked by means of a chisel to the desired shape (usually rectangular).
Bamah	(Hebrew, from Greek: βῆμα = a raised podium or pulpit for a speaker). A raised platform used for cultic purposes; high-place.
Barrel vault	A vault (s.v.) with a semicircular cross-section.
Basalt	Black stone of volcanic origin. Covering large areas in the eastern Galilee, the Golan and the Bashan.
Base, column base	The lower part of a column (or pilaster, anta). Usually somewhat broader than the column itself. Where there is no stylobate, the base prevents the column from sinking into the ground. See: Stylobate.
Basement	Any structure built on or below ground level. See also: Cellar.
Bastion	Part of fortification standing out from the general line of fortification (e.g. the L- shaped retaining wall supporting and defending the ramp which leads upward and turns sharply into the city-gate).
Battlement(s)	Projecting constructions, with gaps in between, built on top of the parapet of a city-wall, tower or gate; constructed to give protection to defenders fighting from the top of the fortification.
Beam	Long, thick piece of timber or an elongated block of stone used to support a ceiling or roof.
Bench	Low construction made of stone, mud brick or the like, sometimes plastered; usually built against and along a wall to be used for sitting (in private houses) or for display of offerings (as in certain temples).
Block	Basic urban unit of buildings grouped together. Usually bounded by streets or alleys on all sides. See also: *insula*.
Breithaus	(German). Building whose main room (e.g. throne room, cella) is a *Breitraum* (s.v.).
Breitraum	(German = broad-room). Room whose entrance is located in one of its long walls, on its width-wise axis.
Brick	Unit of building material made of clay mixed with other materials (e.g. straw, crushed pottery, sand). See also: Burnt, baked brick; Plano-convex brick; Mud brick.
Broad-room	See: *Breitraum*.
Burial chamber	Built or rock-cut room which contains burial places (loculi, troughs etc.).

Burnt, baked brick	Brick made of clay and additives which was fired in a kiln, similarly to the production of pottery vessels.
Buttress	Projection built to support a wall or city-wall and to minimize lateral thrust. Sometimes a buttress is used as a mere decoration.
Cairn	See: Tumulus.
Capital	The uppermost element of a column, usually decorated. It receives the thrust of a lintel, architrave, arch, roof, etc.
Casemate wall	Defensive wall constructed of two parallel walls, which are usually thinner than a solid city-wall; the space between these is divided by short partitions into rooms (casemates).
Catacomb	(Latin: *catacumbas* — district near ancient Rome where one of the earliest Christian cemeteries was located). Subterranean rock-cut burial complex.
Cella	The innermost and holiest room within a temple. Also called: holy-of-holies, *debir*, naos, adyton (s.v.).
Cellar	Room located below ground level of a building. Used for storing provisions or as a vault for the safekeeping of valuable goods.
Cement	Substance applied to building materials to bind them together; it sets hard when mixed with water. Before the invention of Portland cement in modern times, lime or clay were usually used as cement, with different aggregates to create plaster (s.v.).
Cistern	Space cut in bedrock or in the earth and faced with masonry, for the collection and storage of water. To prevent the water from seeping out of the cistern, it was usually coated with hydraulic plaster (s.v.).
Citadel	Fortified complex of buildings within a town, usually providing extra protection for palace or temple. See also: Fort, Fortress, Acropolis.
City-gate	Main opening in the line of fortifications of a city for in- and outgoing traffic. Usually provided with large doors or other movable barriers. Often located within a large and elaborate building — the gatehouse (s.v.).
City-wall	A thick wall built around a city in order to protect it from enemy attacks. The city-wall incorporated other means of fortification, such as city-gates, towers, etc. (s.v.).
Clay	Fine-grained earth, often accumulated in wadi beds. After proper preparation (such as mixing with other materials like straw, crushed pottery, sand, stone grits, etc.), it is used for the production of bricks and pottery vessels.
Colonnade	Series of columns with entablature.
Column	A tall architectural element (with a height much larger than its width), made of solid material (stone, wood); it usually serves to support roofs, lintels, arches, etc. See also: Engaged column.
Column base	See: Base, column base.
Column drum	The architectural element which forms part of a column shaft (s.v.).

	In earlier times drums were made of large shapeless fieldstones. From the Persian period onwards, drums, made of cylindrical dressed stones, were adequately fitted to each other.
Column shaft	Central, main part of column resting upon the base and supporting the capital. It may be made of one piece (monolith; s.v.) or of several blocks (drums).
Continuous foundation	Elongated foundation built continuously under a wall and any openings in that wall.
Corbelled vault, dome	Vault or dome (s.v.) built on the principle of the false arch (s.v.).
Course	Continuous horizontal layer of stones or bricks in a wall.
Court, courtyard	Unroofed space, surrounded by buildings, walls, fences or porticos. See: Open-court house.
Cyclopean masonry	(Named after the Cyclops — one-eyed giants known from Greek mythology to be master masons). Type of masonry which makes use of large irregular boulders fitted well to each other as building stones.
Dado	Lower part of wall faced with wood panels or stone orthostats or painted.
Debir	See: Cella.
Dolmen	(Celtic: *tol* = table; *men* = stone; or from Cornish: doll = hole). Megalithic (s.v.) structure composed of several upright stones which create a compartment, roofed by an additional large stone. Often used for burial.
Dome	Spherical roofing, usually covering circular spaces. Seldom in use before the Roman period, and then only as corbelled dome (s.v.).
Door axis	See: Pivot.
Door jamb	See: Jamb.
Door socket	A stone with a cavity on its upper side in which the door pivot (s.v.) or axis turns. Sometimes a cavity in the threshold serves the same purpose.
Dressed stone	See: Ashlar; Stone dressing.
Dromos	(Greek: δρόμος = course, lane). A corridor-shaped approach to a tomb or catacomb.
Drum	See: Column drum.
Enclosure wall	Fence. A built partition, usually not part of a building, demarcating a large open space, e.g. courtyard.
Engaged column, pilaster	Column or pilaster partially incorporated in a wall, protruding about half its thickness. Its constructive contribution to the building is limited, and it is used mainly for decorative purposes. See also: Buttress, Anta, Pilaster.
False arch	A curved construction resembling an arch but differing from it in principle. Created by stones protruding from both sides of the wall's

courses into the opening until they meet in the uppermost course. All the joints of this arch are vertical, as opposed to the joints of a true arch which radiate.

Fence	See: Enclosure wall.
Fieldstone	See: Rubble.
Flagstone	Flat stone used for paving halls, courtyards, streets, etc.
Flat roof	Simple type of roofing in which a series of wooden beams (rarely stone beams) bridge the gap between the room's walls, with or without the support of columns.
Floor	The bottom of a room, courtyard or any other space made for people or animals to stand upon. Made of beaten earth or from rigid materials (stone, wooden planks, etc.). See also: Pavement, paving.
Fort, fortress	Fortified building within a city or erected on crossroads, frontiers or at strategic points to guard and protect them.
Fortification(s)	Complex of buildings and earthworks erected for the protection of a settlement. Fortifications may include: city-walls, towers, city-gates, postern gates, fosse and ramparts, forts and citadels (s.v.).
Fosse	Trench excavated around outer perimeter of a city-wall, to prevent the enemy from easily approaching the city-wall. Moat.
Foundation	Lower part of building upon which rests its upper structure (walls, columns, stairs etc.); its purpose is to render stability. Usually laid in a subterranean foundation trench, its masonry is more massive and wider than the walls which it supports.
Foundation trench	Trench cut in bedrock or earth to receive the foundations of a wall.
'Four-room' house	Domestic building typical of the Iron Age. Its basic plan comprises four oblong rooms or spaces. Of these the central space is usually identified as an inner courtyard, with the other three arranged on three of its sides and the main entrance on the fourth.
Framework	Series of wooden beams and struts which form the skeleton of a building, especially of a gabled roof (s.v.).
Gable	Triangular-shaped front of a roof sloping to two sides.
Gabled roof	Roof of wooden beams with supporting struts constructed to form a framework; or simply made by leaning large stone plates one against the other, to form a triangular-shaped, double sloping roof.
Gallery	1. Long, narrow space which is partly open behind a portico (colonnade). 2. Long, narrow room or corridor. 3. Raised floor within a room or hall, usually supported on columns or extending from the wall.
Gate	See : City-gate, Postern, Gatehouse, Gateway.
Gatehouse	Elaborate gate either incorporated into the city-wall, or a separate building, with both an outer and inner opening.

Gateway	Path, usually paved, which crosses the gate or the gatehouse.
Glacis	Outer facing of earthen rampart which serves as fortification of the lower slope of a mound (tell), or the lower outer-sloping part of the city-wall. Constructed of different materials such as: beaten earth, lime plaster, bricks, stones, etc.
Hall, *'Ulam*	1. A large, spacious room. 2. The room which occupies the forepart of a temple, from which one passes into the holy-of- holies. See: *Hekhal.*
Header(s)	Ashlar or brick incorporated into a wall with its long axis perpendicular to the line of the wall. See also: Stretcher(s).
Header(s) and stretcher(s)	Method of wall construction in which the ashlars or bricks are laid alternately as headers (s.v.) and stretchers (s.v.).
Hekhal	(Hebrew) 1. Temple; 2. Palace; 3. One of the halls in the temple. In a two-spaced temple it is identical with the 'hall' (*'ulam*); in a three-spaced temple it is the central space, located between the *'ulam* and the holy-of-holies (*debir*).
Hewn stone	Fieldstone or rubble which is roughly worked to a desired shape (usually rectangular) by several blows of a hammer.
Hippodamic layout	Orthogonal layout in town-planning; named after Hippodamus of Miletus, the fifth-century B.C. Greek architect.
Holy-of-holies	See: Cella.
Hydraulic plaster	Watertight plaster used to coat cisterns, pools, water channels, etc. See: Plaster.
Insula	(Latin: *insula* = island). Basic urban unit of buildings which occupy one block (s.v.).
Intercolumniation	Placing of columns at intervals; also such intervals.
Intercolumnar space	The distance between any two adjacent columns of a colonnade (s.v.). Usually measured at the base or bottom of the column shafts.
Jamb, door jamb	Each of the two side posts of an entrance, upon which the lintel rests.
Joint	Area of contact between two adjacent building components: ashlars, bricks, etc.
Keystone	Central stone (usually dressed) at the top of an arch.
Kurkar	Type of sandstone found in the coastal plain of Israel. It is easily cut and frequently used as building stone.
Langhaus	(German). Building whose main room (e.g. throne room, cella) is a *Langraum* (s.v.).
Langraum	(German = long-room). Room whose main entrance is located in one of its short walls, on its longitudinal axis (s.v.).
Lime	Common building material with adhering qualities. Produced from limestone burnt in a kiln and then mixed with water.
Lime plaster	Plaster in which the adhering component is burnt lime which solidifies when mixed with water.

Lintel	Upper part, of an entrance usually consisting of a single stone or wooden beam resting on the door jambs. Sometimes constructed as an arch (s.v.).
Loculus, loculi	(Latin: casket). Long, narrow rock-cut cavity in a burial chamber designed to receive a body. (Hebrew: *kokh*).
Longitudinal axis	Imaginary line drawn lengthwise through a building, usually through its centre.
Long-room	See: *Langraum*.
Lotus capital	Capital in the shape of a lotus. Typical of ancient Egyptian architecture.
Marginal dressing	Method of dressing ashlars in which a frame is cut along the four edges of the stone (sometimes only along part of the edges), leaving the central part of the stone's face protruding.
Mason's mark	Sign incised on dressed stones to direct the mason in the correct placing of building components (e.g. column drums in the correct order); also sign used by mason as his personal mark.
Mausoleum	Large, magnificently decorated tomb (named after the tomb of Mausolus, king of Caria, considered one of the world's seven wonders)
Megalithic	(Greek: μέγας = big; λίθος = stone). Constructed of very large boulders, e.g. dolmen (s.v.).
Megaron	(Greek: μέγαρον = Shrine etc. or a temple). Temple, usually built as a long-room, with side walls projecting from the façade as two antae, with two columns in between (*in antis*) (s.v.).
Moat	See: Fosse.
Model	Small scale design of a building used as a construction guide.
Monolith	(Greek: μονόλιθος; μόνος = single; λίθος = stone). Made of a single stone.
Monolithic column	Column of which the shaft is made of a single block of stone; as opposed to a column made of drums or segments.
Mortar	1. Mixture of earth or clay to which other components are added, such as straw, sand, potsherds, gravel, etc. In its plastic state this mixture is used for producing bricks (mud bricks, s.v.) and for plastering walls (see: Plaster). Sometimes this mortar was cast in a large mould made of wooden planks (*terre-pisée*). 2. Plastic mixture with a high percentage of clay or other adhering components. Used as binding material between building stones or bricks.
Mud brick	Brick (s.v.) made of mud mortar (s.v.) and dried in the sun. Early mud bricks were shaped by hand. Since the Early Bronze Age II bricks were cast in moulds as rectangular blocks.
Naos	(Greek: ναός). 1. Temple; 2. the holy-of-holies, innermost part of a temple. See: Adyton, Cella, Pronaos.
Niche	Recess in a wall or rock-cut face designed for a definite purpose such as storage or the placing of a statue.
Obelisk	(Greek: ὀβελός = spit, a pointed pillar). Tall tapering stone shaft, usually

monolithic, square or rectangular in cross-section, set up as a monument. Often covered with inscriptions and decorations. The obelisks of Egypt were made of immense blocks of stone, which required special effort and know-how to be quarried, transported and erected.

Offset/inset wall	City-wall whose outer face is not straight but built with sections projecting and receding from the general line of the wall.
Open-court house	House with a central courtyard (s.v.), surrounded on all sides by rooms. The courtyard occupies a significant part of the house's area.
Opening	An unbuilt open space in a wall, which serves for entrance and exit. Closed by a door. See also: Gate, Postern gate, City-gate.
Orientation	(Latin: *oriens* = east, the main direction of the compass, towards which maps were directed in antiquity, similar to modern-day north). The point of the compass to which a building's plan is directed (its façade, corners, or main axis, etc.). Orientation is particularly significant in temple planning.
Orthogonal layout	Urban plan and layout in which the streets intersect at right angles thus forming square- or rectangular-shaped insulae. Also called: Hippodamic layout (s.v.).
Orthostat	(Greek: ὀρθοστάτης = upright shaft; pillar; ὀρθός = straight; στατός = standing). 1. A large stone slab, sometimes carved in the shape of an animal (lion, hybrid animal, etc.), often flanking the entrance into a temple or palace. 2. One of a series of large flat stones, usually worked, forming the lower part of a wall.
Outer gate	Gate located in the outer wall of city fortifications. Sometimes connected to the main (i.e. inner) gate by short wall segments so that a small inner space is created between the gates.
Outer wall	An additional wall to the city's fortifications, intended to prevent the enemy from easily approaching the main wall.
Oval, circular building	Building which has an oval or circular plan, different from the usual orthogonal plan. See also: Apsidal building.
Pavement, paving	A solid covering which creates a hard floor. Made of stone (pebbles, slabs, tiles, tesserae, etc.), burnt bricks, plaster or wooden planks.
Palace	Building, usually large, spacious and elaborate, serving as the residence of a sovereign, high official, local governor etc., including his household and administration.
Panel	Broad wooden plank, usually square or rectangular, used as wall facing.
Parapet	Narrow wall on edge of city-wall, tower or gate serving to protect the defenders fighting from behind it.
Partition wall	Wall which does not reach the full height of a room, designed to divide it into separate spaces. Usually built on the floor without foundation.
Pilaster	Column with rectangular cross-section, built of stones, bricks or drums, in contrast to a column which is made of a single block (monolith). See also: Engaged pilaster.

Pivot	Projection at the lower corner of a door (and sometimes also at the upper corner) placed in a socket, upon which the door revolves.
Plan	Graphical representation of the architectural elements and components of a building (wall system, rooms, courts, openings, stairs, columns, etc.).
Plano-convex brick	Mud brick with one flat side and the opposite side rounded (convex).
Plaster	Mixture of materials (including lime, sand, etc.) used to coat walls to make them smooth or watertight. See also: Hydraulic plaster.
Podium	Raised platform, constructed of retaining walls, fills of debris and loose stones. Used for raising a building of special status (e.g. palace, temple) above its surroundings.
Polygonal masonry	(Greek: πολύς = many; γωνία = corner, angle). Masonry style which employs polygonal stones fitted to each other as closely as possible. No courses can be distinguished in this style.
Pool	Natural, rock-cut or constructed space, used to collect and store large quantities of water (runoff, or diverted into it by an aqueduct). Usually not covered.
Portico	Part of the façade of a building, consisting of a row of 2-3 columns standing in front of the building or within its opening.
Postern	Secret passage, usually a narrow tunnel, which traverses the fortifications of a city or citadel.
Post hole	Small, narrow pit in which a post or column was erected. Usually marked by small stones put into it in order to steady the post.
Pronaos	(Greek: πρό = in front of; ναός = the holy- of-holies). The hall in the forepart of a temple. The pronaos sometimes has only the shape of a portico.
Propylaea	Elaborate entrance or gatehouse in public buildings (temple, palace) incorporating columns.
Proto-aeolic capital	Capital usually made of a single rectangular limestone block of which one or both elongated faces are adorned in relief with a motif comprising a central triangle and two volutes. This type of capital is characteristic of the Iron Age.
Public building	A building which functions, in whole or in part, to serve the public, or is open to the public, such as: temples, fortifications, city's stores, and that part of the sovereign's palace to which the public has access.
Quarry	Site where stone is cut from the ground, in an open pit or in a mine, for constructional purposes.
Ramp	Sloping causeway, designed to enable easier approach to a city-gate, an altar, etc. Usually composed of debris and loose stones beaten to a compact surface. See also: Siege ramp.
Rampart	Earthen mound piled up around a city as a fortification or part of it. It is typical of the Middle Bronze Age II.
Relieving arch	Arch (s.v.) built over a lintel (s.v.). It is intended to divert the weight of the wall resting upon the lintel to the door jambs. An arch of this

319

type may be constructed within the solid masonry of a wall and not necessarily over an opening.

Repository	Niche or depression in the bottom or the side of a burial chamber, into which the loose bones of the dead were collected and deposited for secondary burial.
Residency	Palace of a high official.
Retaining wall	Wall built to support a fill of debris and loose stones piled up on one of its sides. See also: Podium, Terrace wall.
Rise of step	Vertical part of a step which connects two treads of a staircase.
Robber's trench	Foundation trench out of which the building stones of a ruined wall and its foundation were extracted for reuse somewhere else, the open trench then left to be filled with debris. It indicates the existence of a wall in antiquity.
Roof, roofing	The upper part of a building, covering its rooms and walls. Can be constructed in different ways and materials. See also: Flat roof, Gabled roof, Vault, Dome.
Room	The basic unit of a house, a space surrounded by walls, a floor and ceiling.
Rubble	Stones collected in the field (fieldstones), or fragments of stones from old buildings, incorporated in a wall, without any dressing.
Sanctuary	See: Temple.
Seam	Line along which two segments of walls or two buildings, meet. In the seam, the vertical joints form a straight continuous line.
Secondary use	The reuse of building materials (ashlars, columns, flagstones, etc.) which have been extracted from old ruined buildings.
Shaft	Long, narrow vertical or inclined tunnel giving access to a subterranean structure, cut in bedrock or in the earth.
Shrine	See: Temple
Siege ramp	Ramp (s.v.) piled up against a besieged city's fortifications to facilitate the ascent of a battering ram or other siege machinery.
Silo	Structure for the storage of provisions. Usually built without openings in its sides as protection against rodents.
Socket	See: Door socket.
Socle	Plain, low rectangular block serving as support for pedestal, vase, statue, etc.
Staircase	Flight of steps, within a stairwell (s.v.), or free-standing, which enables access from floor to floor, or up to a higher construction (such as: podium, altar, etc.).
Stairwell	Space in building which houses the staircase.
Stele	Upright slab of stone, worked or unworked, erected for memorial or cultic purposes. Sometimes inscribed or decorated.

Step	A built or rock-cut flat and narrow surface with which one climbs from a lower to a higher level. Usually grouped in a staircase.
Stoa	(Greek: στοά). Building with one or more sides consisting of a colonnade.
Stone dressing	The art of shaping fieldstones (with chisel and mallet).
Stonework	Masonry, the part of a building made of stone, with or without mortar.
Street, alley, path	An elongated space between houses of a settlement, created for communication. It may be comprised of beaten earth or paved with rigid materials such as pebbles, crushed limestone, flagstones, etc.
Stretcher(s)	Ashlar or brick incorporated in a wall with its long axis parallel to the line of the wall. See also: Header(s); Header(s) and stretcher(s).
Structure	1. Building; 2. The way a building, or part of it, is constructed in terms of selection of building materials, architectural elements and method of assemblage.
Stylobate	(Greek: στῦλος = column; βάσις = base, foot). Foundation upon which columns are placed to prevent them from sinking into the ground due to their weight. Usually a subterranean construction, sometimes protruding from the ground. See: Base; Column base.
Temenos	(Greek: τέμενος). Holy precinct within a city or close by, separated by a wall from the secular parts of the city.
Temple, sanctuary, shrine	The dwelling of the god. A public building to house the god, in which the god's statue was erected and his cult and rites performed.
Terrace wall	Wall built on a slope to retain fills of earth and stones, thus creating patches of level ground suitable for agriculture. Usually only the exterior side has a neatly constructed face.
Terre-pisée	See: Mortar.
Tholos	(Greek: θόλος). Circular building, usually roofed by a dome.
Threshold	Part of doorway, usually made of stone; on one or both sides are the sockets in which the door pivot turns.
Throne room	Most important ceremonial room in a palace, in which the throne stands and the ruler gives audience. Usually one of the largest and most richly decorated and equipped rooms in the building.
Tower	Building constructed for defensive purposes, permitting a good view and firing position. A tower may be an isolated construction, or part of the city's fortifications, projecting outwards from the city-wall's line, or built as part of the gatehouse.
Tread of step	The horizontal part of the step, upon which the foot is placed. Designates the horizontal depth of the step. See also: Rise of step.
Tumulus	(Latin: mound of earth, tomb). Heap of stones and earth, usually round in outline, which covers one or several tombs. Cairn.
Tunnel	Long, narrow subterranean passage, usually horizontally cut in bedrock or earth.
Twofold door	Door with two wings, designed to close a large opening (in the city's

321

	gate, palace, temple). Its axes turn in two sockets located on either side of the threshold (s.v.).
'Ulam	See: Hall, *Hekhal*
Undressed stone	Stone gathered on the ground, of different sizes: boulder, rubble (s.v.), pebble, etc., and used in construction without being worked. See: Ashlar.
Upper structure	The main part of a building which is above ground level, as opposed to the foundations and cellar.
Urbanization	(Latin: *urbs* = city). A sociological and architectural process of establishing cities; the process in which a rural settlement turns gradually into a city.
Vault	Arched roof made of stones or bricks in the shape of a half cylinder.
Voussoir	Each of several wedge-shaped stones or bricks forming an arch or vault.
Wall	A vertical, continuous construction of stones, bricks, wood, etc. which forms any of the sides of a room, courtyard. The basic construction unit. See also: Fence, Partition.
Water channel	A long artificial waterway, cut in bedrock or constructed, to conduct spring water, runoff, sewage, etc. See also: Aqueduct.
Water system	Complex of natural cavities and rock-cut shafts and tunnels, used for easy and safe access to the water source (spring or water table) of a settlement during a siege.
Well	Shaft cut in the earth or bedrock down to water level. A well cut in the earth is usually lined by masonry or bricks.
Window	Opening in the wall, usually located at a high level, made to let air and light into a room. Seldom found in archaeological excavations, as the upper part of walls, in which the window was located, is rarely preserved.
Yard	See: Court, courtyard.

ABBREVIATIONS

AAAS	*Annales archeologiques arabes syriennes*
AASOR	*Annual of the American Schools of Oriental Research*
ADAJ	*Annual of the Department of Antiquities of Jordan*
ADPV	*Abhandlungen des Deutschen Palästina-Vereins.|Wiesbaden.*
'Ai(et-Tell)	J.A. Callaway: *The Early Bronze Age Sanctuary at 'Ai (et-Tell)*, I, London, 1972
Ain Shems I	E. Grant: *Ain Shems Excavations*, I, Haverford, 1931
Ain Shems II	E. Grant: *Ain Shems Excavations*, II, Haverford, 1932
Ain Shems III	E. Grant: *Rumeileh, Being Ain Shems Excavations*, III, Haverford, 1934
Ain Shems IV, V	E. Grant and G.E. Wright: *Ain Shems Excavations*, IV (Plates), Haverford, 1938; V (Text), Haverford, 1939
AJA	*American Journal of Archaeology*
AJSL	*American Journal of Semitic Languages and Literature*
Ancient Gaza V, I–IV	F. Petrie: *Ancient Gaza*, I–IV, London, 1931-1934
ANEP	J.B. Pritchard: *The Ancient Near East in Pictures Relating to the Old Testament*, Princeton, 1954
ANET	J.B. Pritchard (ed.): *Ancient Near Eastern Texts Relating to the Old Testament*, Princeton, 1950
AnSt	*Anatolian Studies*
APEF	*Annual of the Palestine Exploration Fund*
Arad	Ruth Amiran *et al.*: *Early Arad*, I, Jerusalem, 1978
Archaeology	Archaeological Institute of America, Boston.
ARM	*Archives royales de Mari*
Ashdod I	M. Dothan and D.N. Freedman: Ashdod I. *'Atiqot* 7, 1967
Ashdod IV	M. Dothan, Y. Porath: Ashdod IV. *'Atiqot* 15, 1982
'Atiqot	Journal of the Israel Department of Antiquities and Museums
'Ay	J. Marquet-Krause: *Les fouilles de 'Ay (et-Tell), 1933–1935*, Paris, 1949
BA	*Biblical Archaeologist*
BAR	*British Archaeological Reports*, International Series
BASOR	*Bulletin of the American Schools of Oriental Research*
Beer-Sheba I	Y. Aharoni (ed.): *Beer-Sheba* I: *Excavations at Tel Beer-Sheba, 1969–1971*, Tel Aviv, 1973

Beer-Sheba II	Z. Herzog: *Beer-Sheba* II, Tel Aviv, 1984
Beth Pelet I, II	W.M. Flinders Petrie *et al.*: *Beth-Pelet*, I–II, London, 1930, 1932
Beth Shan I	A. Rowe: *The Four Canaanite Temples of Beth-Shan*, Philadelphia, 1940
Beth Shan II	G.M. Fitzgerald: *The Four Canaanite Temples of Beth-Shan*, 2, *The Pottery*. Philadelphia, 1930
Byblos	M. Dunand: *Fouilles de Byblos* I–V, Paris, 1939–1973
EAEHL	M. Avi-Yonah and E. Stern (eds.): *Encyclopedia of Archaeological Excavations in the Holy Land*, I–IV, Jerusalem, 1975-1978
EI	*Eretz-Israel: Archaeological, Historical and Geographical Studies*
Enc. Miqr.	Encyclopaedia Miqra'it (Biblical Encyclopaedia), Jerusalem, 1950-, (Hebrew)
ESI	*Excavations and Surveys in Israel*
Excavations of Gezer I-III	R.A.S. Macalister: *The Excavations of Gezer, 1902–1905 and 1907–1909*, I–III, London, 1912
Expedition	The University Museum, University of Pennsylvania, Philadelphia
Gerar	W.F. Petrie: *Gerar*, London, 1928
Gezer I	W.G. Dever *et al.*: *Gezer*, I: *Preliminary Report of the 1964–1966 Seasons*, Jerusalem, 1970
Gezer II	W.G. Dever *et al.*: *Gezer*, II: *Preliminary Report of the 1967–1970 Seasons*, Jerusalem, 1974
Ghassul I	A. Mallon *et al.*: *Teleilat Ghassul*, I, Rome, 1934
Ghassul II	R. Koeppel *et al.*: *Teleilat Ghassul*, II, Rome, 1940
Ghassul 1960	R. North: *Ghassul 1960, Excavation Report, Rome*, 1961
Hazor	Y. Yadin: *Hazor*, The Schweich Lectures of the British Academy 1970, London, 1972
Hazor I	Y. Yadin *et al.*: *Hazor I*, Jerusalem, 1958
Hazor II	Y. Yadin *et al.*: *Hazor II*, Jerusalem, 1960
Hazor III, IV	Y. Yadin *et al.*: *Hazor III-IV*, Jerusalem, 1989
HA	*Hadashot Arkheologiyot* (Archaeological Newsletter)
IAWA Bulletin	*International Association of Wood Anatomists Bulletin*, Netherlands
IEJ	*Israel Exploration Journal*
JAOS	*Journal of the American Oriental Society*
JBL	*Journal of Biblical Literature*
Jericho I-III	K.M. Kenyon *et al.*, *Excavations at Jericho*, I–III, London, 1960, 1965, 1981

Jericho IV	K.M. Kenyon *et al.*: *Excavations at Jericho*, IV, London, 1982
JNES	*Journal of Near Eastern Studies*
JPOS	*Journal of the Palestine Oriental Society*
Khorsabad I	G. Loud: *Khorsabad*, I: *Excavations in the Palace and at a City Gate* (OIP 38), Chicago, 1936
Khorsabad II	G. Loud and Ch.B. Altmann: *Khorsabad*, II: *The City and the Town* (OIP 40), Chicago, 1938
Lachish II	Olga Tufnell *et al.*: *Lachish*, II: *The Fosse Temple*, London, 1940
Lachish III	Olga Tufnell: *Lachish*, III: *The Iron Age*, London, 1953
Lachish IV	Olga Tufnell *et al.*: *Lachish*, IV: *The Bronze Age*, London, 1958
Lachish V	Y. Aharoni: *Investigations at Lachish: The Sanctuary and the Residency*, Tel Aviv, 1975
Levant	Journal of the British School of Archaeology in Jerusalem and the British Institute of Amman for Archaeology and History, London
MDOG	*Mitteilungen der Deutschen Orient Gesellschaft*
Megiddo I	R.S. Lamon and G.M. Shipton: *Megiddo*, I, Chicago, 1939
Megiddo II	G. Loud *et al.*: *Megiddo*, II, Chicago, 1948
Megiddo Cult	H.G. May: *Material Remains of the Megiddo Cult*, Chicago, 1935
Or. Antiq.	*Orientalia Antiqua*
PEFQSt	*Palestine Exploration Fund, Quarterly Statement*
PEQ	*Palestine Exploration Quarterly*
PPS	*Proceedings of the Prehistoric Society*
QDAP	*Quarterly of the Department of Antiquities in Palestine*
Qedem	Monographs of the Institute of Archaeology, the Hebrew University of Jerusalem, Jerusalem
Ramat Rahel I	Y. Aharoni *et al.*: *Excavations at Ramat Rahel*, I: *Seasons 1959 and 1960*, Rome, 1962
Ramat Rahel II	Y. Aharoni *et al.*: *Excavations at Ramat Rahel*, II: *Seasons 1961 and 1962*, Rome, 1964
RB	*Revue biblique*
Samaria-Sebaste I	J.W. Crowfoot *et al.*: *Samaria-Sebaste*, I: *The Buildings at Samaria*, London, 1942
Samaria-Sebaste II	J.W. Crowfoot *et al.*: *Samaria-Sebaste*, II: *Early Ivories of Samaria*, London, 1938

SCE IV	E. Gjerstad *et al.*: *The Swedish Cyprus Expedition*, Stockholm, 1961
Shechem	G.E. Wright: *Shechem, the Biography of a Biblical City*, New York, 1965
Tel Aviv	Journal of the Institute of Archaeology, Tel Aviv University, Tel Aviv
Tell Beit Mirsim I	W.F. Albright: *The Excavation of Tell Beit Mirsim in Palestine*, I: *The Pottery of the First Three Campaigns* (AASOR 12), 1932
Tell Beit Mirsim IA	W.F. Albright: *The Excavation of Tell Beit Mirsim*, IA: *The Bronze Age Pottery of the Fourth Campaign* (AASOR 13), 1933
Tell Beit Mirsim II	W.F. Albright: *The Excavation of Tell Beit Mirsim*, II: *The Bronze Age* (AASOR 17), 1938
Tell Beit Mirsim III	W.F. Albright *et al.*: *The Excavation of Tell Beit Mirsim*, III: *The Iron Age* (AASOR 21-22), 1943
Tell Halaf II	R. Nauman *et al.*: *Tell Halaf*, II: *Die Bauwerke*, Berlin, 1950
Tel Masos	V. Fritz and A. Kempinski: *Ergebnisse der Ausgrabungen auf der Hirbet al-Msas (Tel Masos) 1972–1975*, Wiesbaden, 1983
Tell el-Mutesellim I	G. Schumacher: *Tell el-Mutesellim*, I, Leipzig, 1908
Tell el-Mutesellim II	C. Watzinger: *Tell el-Mutesellim*, II (*The Objects*), Leipzig, 1929
Tell Nasbeh	C.C. McCown: *Tell en-Nasbeh*, I, Berkeley and New Haven, 1947
VT	*Vetus Testamentum*
ZAW	*Zeitschrift für die alttestamentliche Wissenschaft*
ZDPV	*Zeitschrift des deutschen Palästina-Vereins*

List of Photographs

Photo Credits
CNRS — Centre National de Recherches Scientifiques
HUJ — Hebrew University of Jerusalem
IAA — Israel Antiquities Authority
IES — Israel Exploration Society
OI — Oriental Institute, University of Chicago
TAU — Tel Aviv University

Index of Names of Sites and Geographical Regions

The site names and those of. geographical regions are arranged in alphabetical order. The following words or their abbreviations: Ḥurvah (Ḥ.), Arabic Khirbeh (Kh.); Tel, Arabic Tell are given after the site name (e.g. Dor, Tel) and were not taken into account in the alphabetical order. The same applies to the Arabic article: el-, er-, esh-, etc. (e.g. Ram, er-), except where the article forms part of the name (e.g. El-Wad).

Where a site is shown in an illustration, the relevant page number is printed in italics (e.g. *23*), whether the site concerned is also mentioned in the text on the same page or not.

With reference to three site names mentioned repeatedly in the text (Hazor, Lachish, Megiddo), only the pages on which there is an illustration of the site in question were entered in the Index.

The United Library
Garrett-Evangelical/Seabury-Western Seminaries
2121 Sheridan Road
Evanston, IL 60201